# Tactics & Techniques of
# COMMUNITY
## INTERVENTION
### FOURTH EDITION

# Tactics & Techniques of
# COMMUNITY
# INTERVENTION

## FOURTH EDITION

**EDITORS**

### John E. Tropman
UNIVERSITY OF MICHIGAN

### John L. Erlich
CALIFORNIA STATE UNIVERSITY,
SACRAMENTO

### Jack Rothman
UNIVERSITY OF CALIFORNIA,
LOS ANGELES

F.E. PEACOCK PUBLISHERS, INC.
ITASCA, ILLINOIS

Copyright © 2001 by F.E. Peacock Publishers, Inc.
All rights reserved
Library of Congress Catalog Card No. 00 134168
ISBN 0-87581-435-2
Printed in the United States of America
10  9  8  7  6  5  4  3  2  1
04  03  02  01  00

# Contents

## THANKS TO THE FOLLOWING AUTHORS
## AND PUBLISHERS

"The Shelter in Limbo" by Michael Betzold. Reprinted by permission of the author from the *Ann Arbor Observer,* December 1998, p. 29. Copyright © 1998 by Michael Betzold.

"The Great Flood of 1993: Response and Recovery in Five Communities" by Margaret Sherrard Sherraden and Ellen Fox from *The Journal of Community Practice,* Vol. 4(3), pages 23–45. Reprinted with permission of The Journal of Community Practice, 301 Pittsboro Street, CB#3550, Chapel Hill, NC 27599-3550; E-mail: akj3po.cwru.edu or telephone for subscription information: (440) 338-4856.

"Perspectives on Neighborhood and Community: A Review of the Literature" by Robert J. Chaskin from *Social Service Review,* Vol, 71(4), December 1997, pages 521–547. Reprinted with permission of the author and The University of Chicago Press. Copyright © 1997 by The University of Chicago Press.

"The Revitalization of Community Practice: Characteristics, Competencies, and Curricula for Community-Based Services" by Alice K. Johnson from *The Journal of Community Practice,* Vol. 5(3), pages 37–62. Reprinted with permission of The Journal of Community Practice, 301 Pittsboro Street, CB#3550, Chapel Hill, NC 27499-3550; E-mail: akj3po.cwru.edu or telephone for subscription information: (440) 338-4856.

"Experiences of Women Activists: Implications for Community Organizing Theory and Practice" by Cheryl Hyde from *Journal of Sociology and Social Welfare,* Vol. 23(3), pages 545–562. Reprinted with the permission of the School of Social Work at Western Michigan University from the JOURNAL OF SOCIOLOGY AND

"The Effective Meeting: How to Achieve High-Quality Decisions" by John E. Tropman and Gersh Morningstar. Reprinted with the permission of the authors and F.E. Peacock Publishers, Inc., from TACTICS AND TECHNIQUES OF COMMUNITY INTERVENTION (Third Edition). Copyright © 1995 by F.E. Peacock Publishers, Inc.

"Women, Community, and Organizing" by Marie Weil. Reprinted with the permission of NASW Press from FEMINIST VISIONS FOR SOCIAL WORK. Copyright © 1986, National Association of Social Workers, Inc., Feminist Visions for Social Work.

"For a Democratic Revolution: The Grass-Roots Perspective" by Warren C. Haggstrom. Reprinted with the permission of F.E. Peacock Publishers, Inc., from TACTICS AND TECHNIQUES OF COMMUNITY INTERVENTION (Third Edition). Copyright © 1995 by F.E. Peacock Publishers, Inc.

"An Investigation of Religious Support of Public and Private Agencies in One Community in an Era of Retrenchment" by Robert J. Wineburg from *The Journal of Community Practice,* Vol. 3(2), pages 35–55. Reprinted with permission of The Journal of Community Practice, 301 Pittsboro Street, CB#3550, Chapel Hill, NC 27599-3550; E-mail: akj3po.cwru.edu or telephone for subscription information: (440) 338-4856.

"Social Planning: A Child Welfare Exemplar" by Geoffrey Pawson and Terry Russell from "The Practice of Community Work in Child Welfare." Republished with permission of Columbia University Press from THEORY AND PRACTICE OF COMMUNITY SOCIAL WORK, edited by Samuel H. Taylor and Robert W. Roberts, copyright © 1985 Columbia University Press, New York. Permission conveyed through Copyright Clearance Center, Inc.

"Organizing with People of Color: A Perspective" by Felix G. Rivera and John L. Erlich. Reprinted with the permission of the authors from COMMUNITY ORGANIZING A DIVERSE SOCIETY, edited by Felix G. Rivera and John L. Erlich, Allyn & Bacon, 1992.

"Alternative Frameworks for Program Evaluation" by Robert O. Washington. Reprinted with the permission of the author.

"The Nitty Gritty of Program Evaluation: A Practical Guide" by William C. Birdsall and Roger W. Manela. Reprinted with the permission of the authors.

"The Politics of Program Evaluation" by Eleanor Chelimsky from *Society,* Vol. 25(l), pages 24–32. Reprinted with the permission of Transaction. Copyright © 1987 by Transaction.

"Promoting Research on Community Practice: Using Single-System Designs" by Bruce A. Thyer. Reprinted with the permission of The Haworth Press, Inc., 10 Alice Street, Binghamton, N.Y. 13904 from *Research Strategies for Community Practice,* edited by MacNair, pages 47–61. Copyright © 1998 by The Haworth Press, Inc.

"How to Use and Present Community Data" by Richard L. Douglass. Reprinted with the permission of the author and F.E. Peacock Publishers, Inc., from TACTICS AND TECHNIQUES OF COMMUNITY INTERVENTION (Third Edition). Copyright © 1995 by F.E. Peacock Publishers, Inc.

"Troubleshooting Guide for Research and Evaluation" by John Gottman and Robert Clasen from TACTICS AND TECHNIQUES OF COMMUNITY INTERVENTION (Third Edition). Reprinted by permission of F.E. Peacock Publishers, Inc. Copyright © 1984, 1995 by F.E. Peacock Publishers, Inc.

"Index of Dissimilarity and the Professional Unit Method of Analysis" by John E. Tropman and Elmer J. Tropman. Reprinted with the permission of the authors and F.E. Peacock Publishers, Inc., from TACTICS AND TECHNIQUES OF COMMU-NITY INTERVENTION (Third Edition). Copyright © 1995 by F.E. Peacock Publishers, Inc.

"Core Concepts for Community Change" by Barry Checkoway from *The Journal of Community Practice,* Vol. 4(l), pages 11–29. Reprinted with the permission of The Journal of Community Practice, 301 Pittsboro Street, CB#3550, Chapel Hill, NC 27599-3550; E-mail: akj3po.cwru.edu or telephone for subscription information: (440) 338-4856.

"On-Site Analysis: A Practical Approach to Organizational Change" by Robert J. Myers, Peter Ufford, and Mary-Scot Magill. Reprinted with the permission of the authors and OSCA Publishing from INTRODUCTION TO ON-SITE ANALYSIS. Copyright © 1989 by OSCA Publishing.

"Use of the Internet for Community Practice: A Delphi Study" by Matthew Nartz and Dick Schoech from *The Journal of Community Practice* (forthcoming). Reprinted with permission of The Journal of Community Practice, 301 Pittsboro Street, CB#3550, Chapel Hill, NC 27599-3550; E-mail: akj3po.cwru.edu or tele-phone for subscription information: (440) 338-4856.

"The Human Service Executive" by David M. Austin from *Administration in Social Work,* Vol. 13(3/4), pages 13–36. Reprinted with the permission of The Haworth Press, Inc., 10 Alice Street, Binghamton, N.Y. 13904. Copyright © 1989 by The Haworth Press, Inc.

"Policy Management in the Social Agency" by John E. Tropman. Reprinted with permission of the author and F.E. Peacock Publishers, Inc., from TACTICS AND

# Preface to the Fourth Edition

This edition of *Tactics* involves changes over the third one, in both organization and content. The basic goal remains, however, to provide a "hands-on," more "recipe-oriented" book for community practitioners, specifically, and for macro practitioners, generally. The aim continues to be to offer some "how to do it" pieces that professionals can use as they get into the practicalities of social change implementation.

We are continuing with the title—new to the third edition—*Tactics and Techniques of Community Intervention,* which was designed to be a companion title to *Strategies of Community Intervention,* as is this version. Over time, the definition of community organization has changed a bit, and we are seeking to take that into account.

In its early days, the term community organization was broadly inclusive, involving policy interests, administrative interests, and a broad range of styles of community intervention. Over the years, the phrases "community organization" and "community practice" have come to evoke more neighborhood-based kinds of community activities. And while "community organization" was becoming more focused, training programs in universities were becoming broader. Developments in nonprofit management, policy analysis, fund-raising, and public policy all represent parts of what once was "community organization." Thus, the title, *Tactics and Techniques of Community Intervention,* is designed to appeal to the broadest possible range of practitioners in a community setting, including administrators, policy makers, nurses, teachers, clinicians, and so on. Similarly, community has a broad definition, referring as it does to communities defined by geography (urban, suburban, and rural, as well as neighborhoods), identification (the African-American community, the community of scholars, the Jewish community, etc.) and loci of activity—the university community (all people who work for a particular university), the manufacturing community, the shipping community, and so on. Based upon the word itself, "community" means bonds (unity) that are generated by things people have in common. This commonality suggests another problem with the "C.O." formula. To have a practice of "community organization" implies that communities are, actually, *dis*-organized. That perspective we believe to be fundamentally untrue, for one thing, and misleading, for another. It is a kind of "problem" perspective, or "weakness" perspective. We prefer the "strengths" perspective. Communities have organization, and this book focuses on providing specific tools for assisting practitioners who are trying to build community, and change community, whether that community is one of workplace, geography, or common identification (race, gender, or membership).

What does "build or change" mean in this context? At least four steps are involved: One is community-creating, which involves developing an awareness of the unity—from commonality that is present, but not, perhaps, recognized; a second step is the development of community capacity, which here refers to the ability of the community to take action on its own behalf; third is the development of capability, meaning movement to the actuality of community activity (just having the capacity does not mean one does anything with it); and step number four involves community competence, which means not only taking steps (capability) but also doing them well (being competent at those steps). This volume provides practitioners with tools to assist communities in each of these areas.

Community is, perhaps, the greatest challenge facing developed countries today. While there are encouraging signs of long-standing enmities and differences falling away, new ones seem to be developing almost on a daily basis. Practitioners need to work within communities to assist them in formulating and moving toward their goals while at the same time working between communities to try to ensure that "my goal achievement" does not come at "your expense." Good intentions are not enough. Larger strategies have to be bonded with specific tactics. Community organization professionals need to do more than "good"—they need to do it right, and do it well. This volume assists materially in that direction.

I would like to thank my colleague editors, John Erlich and Jack Rothman, for their constant support and encouragement throughout this process. To our colleague and former editor Fred Cox, now retired, we express thanks and appreciation for his outstanding contributions in laying such a successful foundation. Finally, I would like to express a special note of recognition of and fondness for my father, the late Elmer J. Tropman. His work has appeared in a previous edition of *Tactics,* and he was excited to be working on another contribution. Though he was ill, we collaborated on one of the articles, but he died before he could see its fruition. His influence suffuses all of my contributions.

—John E. Tropman

# PART ONE
# OVERVIEW OF TACTICS

# Introduction

This fourth edition of *Tactics and Techniques of Community Intervention* is a "row of books" comprised of six parts. It begins with an overview—one bookend. In the middle are sections on assessment, generating and deciding upon what work needs to be done, doing the work, evaluating the results, changing, and starting all over again. Part six—the other bookend—deals with issues of the community practice organization and the vital elements of administration and management.

In this overview are a series of articles that highlight tactical issues and concerns for community practitioners. *Tactics* are the day-to-day decisions that practitioners make and which, they hope, will steer them toward the accomplishment of their goal—more inclusiveness, a safer street and neighborhood, a clean corner lot, better cared for homes, more inclusiveness in city decision making by neighborhood influentials, a better community for one and all. For the community practitioner, knowledge of tactics is an important tool; skill in executing the tactic is, of course, yet another.

## THINKING ABOUT TACTICS IN COMMUNITY PRACTICE

In this first section, the reader and student is presented with a range of pieces that both present the kinds of problems community practitioners face and suggest some of the tools and tactics that community practitioners might wish to employ. But what *are* tactics, really? If *strategy* is the general plan for goal accomplishment that extends over time, then *tactics* are the day-to-day actions that make strategy a reality. If one's *strategy* for health includes working out and daily exercise, then *tactics* involve the specific steps of getting one to that point. If *strategy* involves finding an appropriate shelter for the homeless, then *tactics* involve the steps of working with the community of stakeholders to find an appropriate facility.

There are, of course, more specific answers as well. Community Practice involves building solutions to three kinds of community problems broadly conceived. One is the **problem of cohesion,** in which the community is not, as yet, a community in the connected sense. Here a community development strategy is appropriate, and community development tactics of engagement, involvement, and participation are invoked. Development tactics also involve the accomplishment of tasks (paintup/fixup is a popular one), but the "task"—while important—really has a "process" goal in mind. As members of the community-in-development experience working with each other, they become a community-in-creation.

A second is the **problem of capability.** Capability flows from cohesion, and implies—indeed requires—at least a beginning amount of cohesion to be present. Capability involves strategies of social action and tactics of social action as well. Capability involves *doing* things as a community. Here, though, the goal is actually the accomplishment of the task. Process gains will be present, but they are a by-product. Community members need to *mobilize and act* around particular goals of interest. For example, in a community, some cohesion has developed through a paintup/fixup campaign. The community looks better because of the work, of course, but the real goal was to give people the experience of working together. Next, the community decides to press city hall for better health inspections. Here we move into a capability phase, where the "task" goal of better inspections is a "real" goal, and joins "process" gains (and there will be some, regardless of success or failure of the effort). Community practitioners here have twin goals: task and process.

As capability increases, the **problem of competence** emerges. Just doing things is not enough. One has to do them right and do them well. In other words, as time goes on, the community has to become *good* at acting on its behalf. Here is where social planning enters the picture. Strategies of planning and tactics of planning are involved. Planning is associated with competence, because planning works ahead of the problems in a proactive way, rather than responding to problems in a reactive way. To continue our example, the community involved in paintup/fixup could not act at all because it did not have its "stuff" together. Development becomes the first step. As community oneness begins to emerge, the issue of capability—through action—surfaces. We have moved from no action to re-action. Planning deals, then, with the issue of competence and moves from re-action to pro-action. Planning—working ahead of the problems—is successful because of the principle of leverage: It works ahead of the problem where small interventions can have larger results. Task goals are predominant, and process gains (and there will be some here, too) are a welcome by-product.

Given the three major approaches and their focal problems and sequences, this volume looks at tactics in particular. In spite of the differences in the problems of cohesion, capability, and competence, there are also common elements. In this first section, a number of common, overarching, issues are considered.

Tactics—the actual activities of day-to-day intervention—follows a common sequence. In the first phase, there are issues of assessment. What is the problem, and how do we know it? Part two deals with these issues.

In the next phase, the generation of options for intervention and picking one—decision making—become key. Assessment and the generation of options might be thought of as the "fuzzy front end" of the community practice problem. Part three considers these issues.

In the next phase three approaches—development, mobilization and action, and planning—become centrally relevant. Frequently, of course, there is not a neat progression, but rather simultaneous as well as back-and-forth work. Part four addresses these elements.

In Part Five evaluation and change complete the cycle, which began with "assessment." In this phase, interventions draw to a close and practitioners and community members alike look to see what was accomplished, what was not accomplished, what went right, what went wrong, and how the next cycle can be improved. This "next cycle" idea means that—like the snake eating its tail—each cycle connects to the next one, each "evaluation" connects back, through change, to assessment. And we start all over again. That connection is why evaluation and change are linked together here.

For community practice to "work," there has to be a community practice "organization—a planning body, a community center, a neighborhood council, or some particular "entity" where the community practitioner works, and, of course, from which the community practitioner draws her or his pay. An important part of the success of any community practice enterprise rests on how well these organizations are administered and managed. Part Six considers issues of administration and management, as the second bookend on our shelf of tactics.

## THE ARTICLES

*Conflicting Expectations in Community.* Selection and execution of tactics are frequently entangled in the mesh of conflicting expectations, demands, and wishes of community stakeholders. We begin with a newspaper account of a conflict over the location of a shelter: "Everyone wants to do something about the homeless problem so that it will go away. . . . There is no easy solution." This is an example of the central kind of problem that community practitioners think through on a community-wide, country-wide basis—how to convert good community intentions into good community programs. Balancing competing values (discussed in selection 11, "Value Conflicts and Decision Making") is a constant tactical concern for community practitioners in situations of this kind. Moreover, issues of American ambivalence toward the disadvantaged continually surface.[1]

*Differential Response to Community Stress.* The discussion in the previous article of the homeless shelter occurred in Ann Arbor—a college town. Community practitioners may properly think that communities, like people, differ. In "The Great Flood of 1993: Response and Recovery in Five Communities," Margaret Sherraden and Ellen Fox address the element of differential community response.[2] Community practitioners need to "start where the community is" in terms of tactical considerations.

---

[1] See John E. Tropman, *Does America Hate the Poor?* (Westport, CT: Praeger, 1998).

[2] For another treatment of differential responses to floods, along with an outstanding discussion of the problem of competing values in such a framework, see Kai Erikson, *Everything in Its Path: Destruction of Community in the Buffalo Creek Flood* (New York: Simon and Schuster, 1972). This discussion is more than 25 years old, yet has a totally contemporary feel.

This particular point requires community practitioners to know where the community is, skills for which are presented in Part Two on assessment.

*The "Experienced" Community and Neighborhood.* This aspect of differential community responses is extended as Robert Chaskin talks about "Perspectives on Neighborhood and Community." He points out that people in neighborhoods and communities experience them differently, an important point in thinking about "community" response. Neighborhoods, a physical element in community, can become a unit of identification and community work. Community workers should keep in mind that a "neighborhood" can exist within an organization too.

*Key Dimensions of Community Work.* As community workers serve in communities and neighborhoods, what kinds of "work themes" should they bear in mind? Alice Johnson, in "The Revitalization of Community Practice," argues that new community-based services need to be characterized by the following elements: They should be neighborhood-based and family-focused, strengths- and empowerment-oriented, culturally sensitive and multiculturally competent, and comprehensive; they should involve access to integrated services and supports, as well as teamwork and leadership. These are goals that community practitioners can both employ themselves and encourage in others. Even though one starts where the community is, and empowers communities to configure *their* solutions, having a preference template is always helpful.

*Women in Community Practice.* We have spoken of the "worker" or the "community practitioner" in a somewhat disembodied way. Workers are both women and men, among other identifications, and women community activists have special issues and concerns, which Cheryl Hyde addresses. In "Experiences of Women Activists," she directly confronts considerations of gender and "women's issues" in a helpful and tactical manner.

*Selecting Appropriate Tactics.* In the last article in this section, Ellen Netting, Peter Kettner, and Steve McMurty deal with the issue of "Selecting Appropriate Tactics." When to take what out of your toolkit is always an issue. And what kinds of tools you might find helpful to bring along is an issue even before *that!* These writers are helpful in both departments, providing community organization practitioners with a set of tools, and suggestions for the conditions under which they might apply.

—John E. Tropman

*After years of drift, the county and a dozen nonprofit groups want to create a state-of-the-art program for the homeless. But neighbors and advocates question plans for a new shelter on Ellsworth, and time may be running out.*

*It was a stifling August night when Barbara Penrod first walked inside the other world. She saw cockroaches skittering beneath cramped bunks where men lay sweating. The room's only two fans were broken. Flies buzzed through unscreened windows. In another building a few blocks away, twenty women were crammed into a small basement, vying for two rusty showers in a furnace room.*

*"I was stunned," said Penrod, an administrator at St. Joseph Mercy Health System. "It was shocking to me as a resident of Ann Arbor that a community with our resources and the kind of caring people we have—that we would allow any human being to stay in these facilities."*

*At thirty-eight, Steve Darty says he's trying to get his entertainment agency off the ground, and that he's just served two years as a Democratic precinct delegate. But his mind is too troubled to work sometimes. Evicted for not paying rent, he has landed in Ann Arbor's homeless shelter for the second time in five years. The worst things, he says, are the lack of privacy and the mad dash in the early morning for one of the four showers or three sinks. But it's better than sleeping outside, as some of his friends do.*

## 1.

### Michael Betzold

### THE SHELTER IN LIMBO

What's daunting about homelessness, says Ellen Schulmeister, the tireless director of Ann Arbor's Shelter Association, is there's no easy fix. The reasons why people end up homeless are complicated. No remedy works for everybody. Tackling the issue requires patient, creative attention from lots of caring, efficient people.

If any place could get a handle on homelessness, it ought to be Ann Arbor. Yet efforts over the past fifteen years have been piecemeal. Stalwart volunteers have cob-

bled together a patchwork of services. Six dozen men sleep most nights in a former church on West Huron Street. Two dozen women, a few with children, bunk in the basement at Felch and North Main. Downtown churches serve breakfasts and dinners. Food Gatherers provides lunch in a shabby day shelter on Ashley, where there's a free health clinic and a small staff who provide referrals to service agencies. The threadbare, dilapidated shelters are run by the Shelter Association, a nonprofit group chronically short on funds. The system requires the homeless to walk miles each day in and around downtown to get fed and sheltered.

---

Michael Betzold is a writer for the Ann Arbor Observer, Ann Arbor, Mich.

Homeless families stay, week to week, at twenty area churches and temples that participate in the Interfaith Hospitality Network. SAFE House harbors fifty women and children who are domestic violence victims. Ozone House has emergency shelter for five teenagers. Other families stay at the Salvation Army's Arbor Haven or the SOS Crisis Center's Prospect Place in Ypsilanti.

The network is frayed and bulging at the seams, scrapping for funds and struggling for respect. "We should be ashamed of the existing conditions," says Carole McCabe, director of Avalon Housing and a longtime advocate for the homeless. Through fifteen years of mounting needs and dwindling government programs, the Shelter Association has often been reduced to panhandling from city and county government just to keep the doors of its inadequate facilities open.

In 1996, a dozen nonprofit agencies that serve the homeless sought to end turf battles and look for a permanent, coordinated, comprehensive solution. At the same time, county and city leaders decided it was crazy to keep feeding emergency funds to an unhealthy bastard of good intentions and poor management.

Two years later, there is hope and dismay. The city and county have set aside $3.1 million to build and upgrade shelter facilities. St. Joe's [St. Joseph, Michigan, Health System] is leading a coalition of providers who plan a far-reaching program to attack the causes and treat the symptoms of homelessness. But there is no assurance that this new public-private partnership will succeed. Like the people they intend to serve, the grand plans remain homeless and unsettled. What has happened is a story of competing philosophies, delicate unions, politics, and prejudices. It's a lesson in how hard it is for even the most resourceful,

well-intentioned community to get a handle on homelessness.

Ann Arbor has always dealt with the homeless problem on a crisis basis. The community's response "never was designed in an effective way from the beginning," says Jean Barney, an early shelter board member. "No one ever stopped to ask how a shelter should be run or how programs should be organized."

People have always lived on the margins in Ann Arbor. Sleeping on streets or in parks, they used to be called hoboes or bums. Their plight was largely considered their own fault until the recession of the early 1980s, when layoffs plunged many once-independent people into homelessness. St. Andrew's Episcopal Church opened its doors to them in 1983.

Church members figured it was a charitable response for a temporary need. But soon, so many cold and hungry people came knocking that the church leased a nearby house to handle the overflow. Neighbors squawked and got the place shut—and NIMBY has shadowed the homeless shelter ever since.

In 1984, the Shelter Association was incorporated and used $76,000 in government funds to buy the 1921-vintage First Free Methodist Church building at 420 West Huron. The shelter opened that November. For its first six years, the director was Carol Zick, a charismatic Catholic who approached the shelter with missionary fervor but little political savvy. Zick built a large donor base, but as shelter use soared, staffers were not well paid, and debt mounted.

Even as Michigan's economy recovered, the number of people seeking shelter grew. The reasons, says Avalon's McCabe, included disappearing federal housing programs, continued "deinstitutionalization" of the mentally ill, and the economy's shift toward poorly paid service jobs.

In 1990, Zick was succeeded by Jean Summerfield. A zealous advocate and political strategist, Summerfield aggressively sought services for the shelter's troubled clients. She also spun off Avalon, a nonprofit corporation that now rents 138 low-income apartments to former shelter users. But Avalon took many of the shelter's strongest staffers and volunteers. After Summerfield left in 1993, the shelter cycled through four directors in as many years, each unable to curb growing debt and management problems.

Meanwhile, welfare cutbacks threw even more people onto the street. "There was never enough money," Barney says. "We tried so many times to reorganize and put it on a firm footing, but it didn't work."

A long-standing theoretical debate among homeless advocates became an open battle in 1995, when director Lisa O'Rear-Lassen began enforcing a sixty-day limit for shelter stays. The policy exposed two camps: "tough love" adherents who argued that clients needed to do more to help themselves, and "homeless advocates" who blamed the system for its lack of services and affordable housing. That winter, the City Council funded a warming center for people evicted from the shelter, either for exceeding the sixty-day limit or for misconduct.

The "homeless advocates" included many of the nonprofit service agencies that had sprung up to deal with housing-related issues. In 1992, the Interfaith Hospitality Network started coordinating congregations that housed homeless families on a rotating basis. With Ypsilanti's SOS Crisis Center, SAFE House, and other groups, IHN formed the Family Support Network in 1995 to coordinate services to area homeless families. The leaders of those agencies and others, including Avalon's Carole McCabe, met in the summer of 1996 to ward off another winter of discontent. They decided that an effective long-term solution required a communitywide approach that included government and business leaders. "The only way you can realistically solve problems that are so deeply and structurally embedded as homelessness and housing is when you bring all the players to the table," observes Chuck Kieffer, director of SOS.

For years, the county and city had supported the Shelter Association with annual allotments and frequent emergency allocations. In 1996, the county and the city provided almost 40 percent of the association's $721,000 budget. As the winter of 1996–97 approached, the shelter wasn't paying its bills and could afford only one staff member to supervise seventy people all night. Some volunteers saw the situation as so dangerous that they stopped coming.

"Every November they would come to us asking for $75,000 to keep them open," says Washtenaw County Administrator Bob Guenzel. "The commissioners had questions about where the money was going." Guenzel says the Shelter Association had "significant problems—organizational, monetary, programmatic" that could all be traced to underfunding.

The nonprofits say they asked Guenzel to take the lead in convening a task force. When pressed, Guenzel acknowledges that invitation, but otherwise portrays the county as taking the initiative: "We said to the shelter, 'We'll bail you out.' But we told the Shelter Association, 'You have to get your act together.'" On November 20, 1996, at Guenzel's urging, the County Commission approved giving $40,000 to the shelter and creating a task force on homelessness, on the condition that the shelter accept county oversight.

Ann Arbor City Administrator Neal Berlin, who headed the task force with Guenzel and Ypsilanti City Manager Ed Koryzno, takes credit for the new effort. "It certainly didn't come to head because the community was saying we have to do something," Berlin insists. "Bob and I said we're not going through this every year. Bob and I discussing it is what brought it to a head." City Council signed on quickly—for weeks, they'd been battling disruptive protesters who demanded they turn the former National Guard armory into a new homeless shelter.

Everyone came to the table with a different view of the problem. To Guenzel, Berlin, and some other officials, the issue was primarily inadequate facilities and mismanagement. "My initial goal was to fix up the problem and find a new location for the shelter," Guenzel recalls. In comments he made at the time, Guenzel called the shelter board "dysfunctional."

Ann Arbor Mayor Ingrid Sheldon saw too much attention to long-term solutions. "The emphasis on permanent housing was shortchanging the emergency shelter provision," she says. She applauds the agencies' willingness to get involved. "Prior to that, most people acted like it was the government's responsibility to take care of the homeless," she complains. Sheldon says she hoped that the task force "would finally depoliticize the homelessness issue, because such a broadly based group had been assembled."

Republicans on the Board of Commissioners see the county's involvement with the homeless issue as a purely political, and big-government program rammed through by the board's ten-to-five Democratic majority. There's other ways to deal with these social issues than to continue to throw government money at them all the time," protests Commissioner Joe Yekulis of Chelsea.

Downtown merchants, meanwhile, continue to see ragged people on Main Street, and imagine their customers fleeing to the malls. "The image of homelessness has been the problem, the perception that they seem to

be everywhere," says Woody Holman, president of the Ann Arbor Chamber of Commerce. "If there are people on the streets pushing their shopping carts, while that may be an isolated phenomenon, they call attention to themselves. I hear a lot about it from the retail community."

Most shelter users have drug or alcohol addictions, mental health problems, or both. But "the biggest surprise for most people is that about sixty percent of our people work," says James Bryant, manager of the day shelter. Most are employed full time, Bryant says, typically for $5 to $7 an hour, but some for as much as $10. "If somebody's working every day and can't afford a place to live, that's a community issue," he says.

Bryant acknowledges that someone earning $10 an hour can afford to rent an efficiency apartment, even in Ann Arbor. But, he points out, "budgeting is a big problem [even] for so-called normal people."

Believers in "tough love" see the problem primarily in terms of individuals overcoming addictions. In their view, a system that feeds and houses people without requiring their recovery from self-destructive behavior becomes a "codependent," enabling them to indulge their habits. The tough-love faction would refuse services to clients who don't make progress in overcoming their problems within a certain time period, regardless of the obstacles they face.

The "advocates," meanwhile, see homelessness as a systemic problem. "You can achieve all the independence you want, but if you can't afford to pay for housing, it doesn't do any good," says shelter director Schulmeister. If you're just scraping by on a minimum-wage job, she says, "any medical emergency will sink you. You can't pay rent, you get evicted, you get a bad credit rating, and it's harder to get another place.

If you don't address the problem of affordable housing, you end up with more and more people being at the shelter."

With so many competing perceptions, it's no wonder the task force participants have had trouble getting on the same track. And no one is sure how many homeless people there are in Washtenaw County. Count the number taking up shelter spaces each night, and you get to about 200. But there is no way of knowing how many "make the rounds" from place to place—at least until the county sets up its planned computerized data base.

Despite the lingering questions, much has changed since the task force set to work. In the past two years, plans have been developed for an all-new shelter south of town, and an alliance of social service groups has been retained to run it. This proposed new system of care would complete a transformation in which the growing numbers of homeless have gone from scarcely noticed "bums" to an object of focused charity, and finally to a major government and social-service priority.

If, that is, the plans ever get off the ground.

Though there is disagreement on whose ball was brought to the game, there is little doubt that Bob Guenzel took it and ran with it. Even in a brief conversation, it's clear that patience isn't Guenzel's long suit. He can't wait to get to his next point.

Guenzel's vision of the problem drove the process. From the start, the nonprofits wanted to address issues related to all homeless people, including families. Instead, Guenzel set up a task force to study how to shelter single adults. Overruling a preliminary task force report that called for building a new shelter with fifty beds, Guenzel proposed in March 1997 that county-owned property in Pittsfield Township, on the southeast corner of Ellsworth and Stone School road, be used to build a 200-bed shelter.

Guenzel had no approval from commissioners before making his plan public. He hadn't talked to area residents or officials from Pittsfield Township. They all read about the plan in that afternoon's *Ann Arbor News*.

Among Guenzel's selling points: The site already housed the county's human service agencies building and the state's Family Independence Agency (formerly the Department of Social Services); it wouldn't cost anything to acquire; it was centrally located in the county. "I thought that among the advantages of Ellsworth were that it was closer to Ypsilanti, and it was next to a pig farm, so there were no neighbors," Guenzel explains.

"The positives are that it's available—and land is not cheap—and that there is bus service," says Woody Holman. "And it looked like this would reduce the impact of homelessness on the downtown area." Ingrid Sheldon says she, too, found Ellsworth "attractive" because "it is not located in downtown Ann Arbor, and another municipality would be sharing the responsibility for caring for the population."

Many homeless advocates, however, felt blindsided by Guenzel's blitz. "Almost all the service agencies were pretty much against it because of the whole idea of warehousing two hundred people in one place," recalls Doug Smith, director of the Interfaith Hospitality Network. "It was an obscene thought to everyone. And moving them out of the downtown area, that was buying into the business community's prejudice against homeless people."

Advocates point out that many homeless people work downtown and that many of the churches, clinics, and other institutions that serve them are there. Yet despite these and other objections, the task force approved Guenzel's recommendation.

"Nobody who had been involved in sheltering felt that was the way to do it," explains Barney. "But they felt that the only way to move ahead in a politically effective way was to go along with it, but figure out how to work with it. Leaders of agencies can't afford to alienate a source of their support." Smith recalls, "We had a choice. Do we condemn the process or participate?"

"Ellsworth became a very emotional and philosophical argument," Guenzel acknowledges. "Some people went so far as to say, "We need the homeless to be in our face every day, and you want to hide them away out in the country."" Guenzel contends the location doesn't matter to him. "I never had a disagreement with downtown," Guenzel insists. "My issue was 'I have a site. Does anybody else?' And nobody did. Even to this day, they don't."

How hard city and county officials searched for another site remains a bone of contention. The facilities siting subcommittee, which included Schulmeister, favored four smaller shelters. But, she says, "We trusted the experts in the [city and county] planning departments, who said there was nothing else available."

Berlin says he asked his staff and the City Council for a suitable site early in 1997. "There wasn't an appropriate site that could be identified anywhere else," he says. "And as we moved down the road, we could see: What site wouldn't have problems? It [Ellsworth] became the site sort of by default."

Guenzel explains his eagerness to name a site as an important step in moving the process forward. "I've been criticized as being too pushy and not involving anybody," he says. "But I thought it was important to get the task force off the dime." He also needed to get funds for the shelter into the county's building budget, and the deadline for adopting that was approaching. "That was driving the process," says Schulmeister. "We just weren't aware of it at the time."

Guenzel worked out a plan to include $3.1 million for the shelter in the county plan; Berlin agreed the city would repay one-third of the total. City Council members didn't like giving the county control of the project, and some fretted about the site and the lack of an operating plan. In the end, council approved the joint venture over the objections of three Democrats: Jean Carlberg; Heidi Cowing Herell, whose constituents are the nearest neighbors to the Ellsworth site; and Tobi Hannah-Davies.

The five Republican county commissioners also opposed the plan, though for different reasons. Chelsea's Joe Yekulis says that his constituents don't support using tax dollars for a shelter. "The church community has provided a tremendous service in taking care of the homeless,' says Yekulis, "And that's where it needs to remain, within the private sector."

Under Michigan law, a two-thirds supermajority of county commissioners must approve any plan to site county buildings and finance them with bonds. But with the ten-to-five Democratic edge, Guenzel felt he could count on passage.

After a brief defection by Vivienne Armentrout, who was concerned about the Democratic City Council members' objections, the only question mark was Leah Gunn. Gunn had just been elected in 1996 to represent the Twelfth District, which includes the proposed shelter site on Ellsworth.

Under pressure from constituents to scotch the plan, Gunn cast the deciding vote to approve it. Gunn says she liked the Ellsworth site "because it's free, we own it, and we won't be taking land off the tax rolls."

Claudia Myske is manager of the Forest Hills Co-op Apartments, one of three federally subsidized townhouse complexes in south-east Ann Arbor. She says the neighborhood is one of the few places in the city that actually have the diversity to which so many Ann Arborites give lip service. We have all types of folks living here—doctors, lawyers, engineers, people on assistance," Myske says. "It's a good cosmopolitan mix of people."

To area residents, Guenzel's announcement that a huge homeless shelter was going to be their new neighbor came with a sickeningly familiar thud. 'For years, the neighborhood had lived in the shadow of the city landfill and had wrestled with the city to get a local park. As Myske puts it, "The feeling of the people here was 'Here we go again.'" We were again being looked at as an area where anything could be done—'low income' being synonymous with 'Who cares?'"

Myske says she filed several requests under the Freedom of Information Act for lists of suitable parcels owned by the city and county. She says that officials provided only "helter-skelter types of lists that you couldn't decipher" and that Guenzel and Berlin were not helpful in meetings called to clear up the issue. "There was not any time spent looking for alternative sites," Myske charges.

But when angry southeast area residents tried to recall Gunn, they had trouble getting their petition language approved, and the drive fizzled. In last month's election, Gunn was challenged by Ken Dignan, who made the shelter the key issue in the campaign. She won easily.

At public meetings, officials promised that no shelter would be built unless neighborhood concerns about services and transportation were satisfied. Neighborhood representatives joined the task force, which downsized the plan to 125 beds and recommended keeping emergency sheltering downtown. Providers also convinced offi-

cials to convene a second task force to study families and more comprehensive, long-term solutions to homelessness.

So far, the Ellsworth site has survived challenges from service agencies, from Republicans on the county board, and from southeast area neighbors. But now it faces what may be the biggest obstacle of all: Pittsfield Township has filed a lawsuit demanding that the county comply with its zoning restrictions, which specify industrial uses for the site.

"I didn't expect Pittsfield's negative reaction," Guenzel admits. "After all, it's a neighborhood that doesn't have any Pittsfield residents."

"We're trying to protect future residents in advance," replies Pittsfield Township Supervisor Doug Woolley. He says he's concerned that if the social services coalition that will operate the shelter falls apart, or if member agencies lose their funding, the building might be abandoned and turned over to the state for a halfway house. Guenzel says he offered to provide written assurances against that, but Woolley wasn't impressed.

Woolley says it's unfair for township fire and police to bear the burden and costs of security for the proposed shelter. Neal Berlin says that could be avoided if the city annexed the site. However, that, too, is unacceptable to Woolley: "We have an agreement that they will not ask for any more annexation."

The township and the city and county are also fighting over plans to build a vehicle garage at the landfill. Woolley says the city promised a park there; Berlin disagrees. Guenzel says a different shelter site might "make the township feel a little better about the fleet garage." He adds, "We floated a trial balloon on that, but we got no response."

With no give in Pittsfield's position, the lawsuit will almost certainly go to trial.

Woolley says, flatly, "They're not going to be able to offer us anything that will change our mind."

Poor people know the drill. It's called hurry up and wait. Since Guenzel's opening rush, the homeless-shelter game seems to have bogged down in an endless series of committee meetings and political squabbles. But some major decisions have been made in the past eighteen months.

The service providers have used the time to advance their vision of a broadly based attack on homelessness. "We had to move them off the idea of constructing just an emergency network," says Doug Smith. "It's been an education of our political leaders." In January 1998, the Joint Steering Committee on Homelessness, composed primarily of city and county officials, issued a report that emphasized affordable housing and recommended downsizing Ellsworth further, to a 90-to-120-bed facility, and keeping a strong downtown component.

More important, in a head-to-head battle over who would run the shelter, the progressive wing of the service providers roundly defeated the more conservative adherents of a "tough love" approach. The dozen liberal-minded nonprofits strengthened their credibility by creating a new Washtenaw Housing Alliance and approaching the St. Joseph Mercy Health System to be its lead agency. "We felt it was very much in sync with our mission," says Barbara Penrod, who is the system's director of "healthy communities."

In April 1998, the alliance submitted a proposal to the county to operate the shelter. The ambitious plan called for a comprehensive approach to sheltering, combing and coordinating existing services and implementing new ones. The budget looked enormous—$8.3 million a year—but almost all of it was money already being spent by alliance member agencies for existing services. The city and county would chip in their customary annual sheltering allocation, about $100,00 to $200,00 apiece.

The other proposal came from the Salvation Army. Founded to minister on skid row, the church has vast experience dealing with the homeless and strong ideas about what approach is right for them. Since 1981, it has operated Arbor Haven, a homeless shelter on Henry Street, off South Industrial. Initially a one-night drop-in shelter, Arbor Haven is now a twenty-four-hour-a-day program with seventeen spaces. Individuals are admitted only if they agree to "work a program" to resolve issues that led to their homelessness. There's a ninety-day limit on stays.

The Salvation Army pledged $1.1 million to operate the shelter programs and vowed to kick in another $1 million to start an endowment fund. "In four years the county wouldn't have to give us a dime" to operate the shelter, says Captain Gary Felton.

The committee asked the two groups to try to merge their proposals. But after hours of meetings, the effort failed. The Army insisted on independent fund-raising and refused to bend on its stricture against cohabitation of unmarried couples in the shelter. The alliance insisted on handling shelter admissions, effectively barring the Army from implementing its policy of accepting only people willing to work on their problems.

At the steering committee's August meeting, the Army announced that it could not take responsibility for running the shelter under those conditions. Only Sheldon and [the Chamber of Commerce's Woody] Holman backed the Army, and the alliance won control of the shelter.

As the joint proposal collapsed, it appeared that the Ellsworth site, under discussion for a year and a half, might be abandoned as suddenly as it had been taken up. Guenzel and the joint steering committee confirmed that they were considering an alternative site on North Main.

The property, known as University Park, is a four-acre complex of five buildings. Officials had known about the site for a while. When the owners dropped the price from more than $2 million to $1.5 million, Guenzel jumped. The steering committee toured the site and engaged an architect to see whether renovating the buildings was feasible. The site borders a Girl Scout camp and a nursing home. At a public meeting, a Girl Scout leader spoke out against it, as did nearby residents, a local property, and Sheldon, who objected to having Ann Arbor bear the entire sheltering burden for the county. "I suggested that if we were going to be the host community, then maybe the county would like to pick up the entire bill," she says.

Other officials found the site appealing. "North Main would have been better [than Ellsworth] in that it was closer to the central business district," says Berlin. Guenzel says he liked the site because "it was downtown but not really downtown." Also, he adds, the neighborhood reception was "not as hostile" as at Ellsworth.

One neighbor was not only hostile but well financed. Even before an estimate for renovation costs could be made, the property was snatched up by Farmington Hills developer Steven Schafer. He plans to build an upscale 158-unit condominium project along Main Street just south of University Park, and says the shelter would have jeopardized his $45 million investment.

The collapse of the North Man option put the shelter plans into limbo. The Washtenaw Housing Alliance has drafted an overall plan for operating the shelter system, but details are hard to settle while the site is up in the air. The steering committee is moving toward approval of a contract with the alliance, but that too will be difficult while so many questions remain open. All participants say they are willing to consider another site, but in the absence of any other, they remain committed to—or stuck with—Ellsworth.

While the future is uncertain, things are improving at the shelter. Last year, the county created a thirteen-member Management Oversight Committee (MOC) to bring a firm hand to the Shelter Association's internal organizational problems. The MOC decided to close two auxiliary sites, a transitional house at 411 Ashley and a men's transitional house in Ypsilanti.

The MOC hired Schulmeister, a former business manager at St. Andrew's, after an executive search failed to find anyone else willing to take the job for under $50,000. From October 1997 to February 1998, the MOC board had tried to run the shelter itself, leaving Schulmeister with an administrative mess. A computer crash, which destroyed donor and volunteer records, didn't help. The shelter has about 800 donors, most of whom pay the minimum $10 a year to be members. One of Schulmeister's goals is to centralize and improve volunteer operations, which are now handled at each of the three shelter sites.

Schulmeister gets high marks from all parties. The first shelter director with a business background, she shows a compassionate yet sensible understanding of the challenges of dealing with the homeless. She still enforces the sixty-day rule, but not rigidly. And she says she never liked the everyone-to-Ellsworth option: "It's unrealistic. You're not going to round up people and send them out to Ellsworth and maintain them there as if it's a prison."

The Chamber of Commerce's Woody Holman says even most downtown merchants are now open to keeping some sheltering downtown, "particularly if we are doing a better job of serving the homeless and controlling their actions." But if sheltering is to continue downtown, the present battered facilities will need to be upgraded or replaced.

Schulmeister longs for improvements at the old church building on West Huron—more bathrooms, a new ceiling, more partitions to divide sleeping areas. "We don't expect it to be the Hilton, but it would be nice to have a little more space, a little more privacy," she says.

Unfortunately, the building is in the Allen Creek floodplain. Under federal flood insurance program rules, the city may not permit any new residential construction there, and renovations may not exceed 50 percent of a building's assessed value. Fortunately, that limit doesn't include work needed to comply with building code requirements. Architect Lori Sipes of Architects Four estimates that doing deferred maintenance and meeting code requirements alone will cost more than $180,000. For another $100,000, the shelter could create separate sleeping and lounge areas for men and women, add more storage space, install air-conditioning, and put in a more secure front door.

The Huron shelter is actually the best of the three existing facilities. Under the current thinking, the Felch Street women's shelter would not be maintained because it is too cramped. If Huron Street can be adequately renovated, single women could move back there. Failing that, another site will have to be found for the women.

There is also the question of a new day shelter. Everyone agrees that Ashley Place is too dilapidated to be used. If another site

were found for a men's overnight shelter, the church on Huron could be turned into a day shelter—though once again, floodplain restrictions would limit the renovations. If not, then another day shelter site would have to be found.

Meanwhile, the alliance has formulated a multiprogram model for Ellsworth, with separate "pods" for families, single men, single women, and other services. But it is hard to move forward while so much is undecided. "It is critical to know what the physical space will be," says Penrod. Jane Barney notes, "An awful lot of time and energy was spent designing a plan that would include Ellsworth, and now that might not even happen."

Much hinges on the disposition of the Pittsfield Township suit. The case is assigned to Washtenaw County Circuit Court Judge David Swartz. Both sides have agreed to move for a summary judgment, and are scheduled to file briefs on December 15.

Under Michigan law, local zoning ordinances ordinarily prevail, but exceptions have been recognized. The county is relying on a state law that gives county commissioners the power to erect county buildings. "It seems to us that preempts the township's right to enforce zoning laws," county corporation counsel Curtis Hedger says. But Pittsfield's Woolley says recent court decisions elsewhere strengthen the township's position.

A related question is whether the county's building bonds could be used to finance work at another site. Hedger says, "We can move to a different site because of the lawsuit no matter what the disposition is, because the lawsuit has delayed the project at the Ellsworth site." Asked if the bonds could still be used if the county wins the lawsuit but the alliance and the steering committee opt for another site anyway,

Hedger replies, "I don't know. It would be a fact-sensitive situation." Sheldon says, "I hope the county gave themselves some wiggle room."

The question is relevant because, within the alliance, dissatisfaction with the Ellsworth site runs deep. And now that the alliance has won the battle to operate the shelter, it has gained considerable power in steering the process. In fact, Penrod says she is actively launching a search for a new site. She says she has ordered the real estate division of St. Joe's to begin looking at possible alternative locations for a new shelter, including the hospital's main campus and other health system holdings as well as properties controlled by other agencies in the alliance.

Guenzel concedes that his homelessness initiative has "taken a lot longer than we ever thought it would." But he adds, "The significant thing that's a positive now is that we are talking about a more systematic approach that has the potential to have very long-term positive effects on the issue."

The administrator says he's open to another site, as long as the renewed search doesn't cost the project its momentum. "I don't want to spend another two years look-ing at another site, dealing with the concerns of the neighbors, doing feasibility studies," Guenzel warns. "If we don't do it soon, I'm afraid it will never get done."

Any contract with the new alliance and operating budget for a new sheltering system must still be approved by the City Council and the county commissioners. And even if the county wins the Pittsfield suit, a new legal challenge from the neighborhood is still possible.

Meanwhile, Joe Yekulis worries that the budget will rise and taxpayers will get socked again. As Guenzel himself admits, "Three million might not be enough to build the physical plant." He says the city and county won't commit more funds, but he adds, "We may ask St. Joe's to help us raise the rest."

After two years, Guenzel's patience is wearing thin. "I hope we can get something," he says. "In the end, it may not happen, but at least I know we brought the community together."

"Everyone wants to do something about the homeless problem so that it will go away," Schulmeister says. "But it's not something that you can say, 'this is what we're going to do and it'll be solved.' There is no easy solution."

**2.**

Margaret Sherrard Sherraden and Ellen Fox

# THE GREAT FLOOD OF 1993:
# RESPONSE AND RECOVERY IN FIVE COMMUNITIES

## INTRODUCTION

A month after the 1993 flood peaked, 22 undergraduate social work students undertook a study of five flood communities. The purpose of the study was to introduce students to thinking about community-level factors that affect disaster victims and how social work practice might incorporate community-level interventions. Students' experiences and findings in the field were used as the basis of classroom instruction. The striking differences among the five communities prompted us to continue the study and present the findings to a larger audience.

## BACKGROUND

In 1993, the Midwest endured a "one-hundred year flood." Flood waters covered 15,000 square miles. More than 55,000 homes were damaged or destroyed, 47 people died, and there was $20 billion in damage (Andrews and McMeel, 1993). A year after the onslaught of high water, many

Margaret Sherrard Sherraden is Assistant Professor, Department of Social Work, and Research Associate, Public Policy Research Centers, University of Missouri-Saint Louis.

Ellen Fox is affiliated with the Department of Social Work, University Missouri-Saint Louis.

families were still displaced from their homes. This created feelings of helplessness and frustration for flood victims, and strained social services.

At the same time, the flood brought large numbers of people together to help each other. During the summer of the flood, volunteers came from surrounding neighborhoods and from all over the country to sandbag, cook, distribute supplies, and clean up damaged homes. Relief poured in through the Federal Emergency Management Agency (FEMA), the Salvation Army, the Red Cross, church groups, and international aid agencies.

However, some communities were much less successful than others in obtaining resources for recovery. There were concerns that poor, elderly, and minorities were not given priority in recovery assistance (Ahmad, 1993; De Simone, 1993). There were accusations that some local authorities failed to pursue flood assistance when it would have benefited poor populations (Tighe and Mannies, 1993a).

This study examines differential rates of recovery in five flooded communities. Results may help in developing community-based strategies that respond to the needs of vulnerable groups in the aftermath of disasters.

Our analysis examines two stages of the disaster, the immediate response to the flood and longer-term recovery from the flood. The *response phase* includes the period during and immediately after the disaster. The primary needs and activities of the response phase are evacuation; moving possessions; and obtaining shelter, medical care, food, transportation, supplies, security, and other basic needs. Once the emergency phase ends, the more difficult *recovery phase* begins. During this lengthy process, communities cope with the longer-term implications of disasters.

The recovery phase is costly and includes locating and paying for permanent housing for flood victims, replacing destroyed dwellings and possessions, getting businesses back into operation, and repairing community infrastructure. All of this creates great financial burdens on communities. Much of the cost of the flood is deferred to the recovery phase, when communities compete for finite resources. It is not surprising that criticism and conflict—largely absent in disaster response—tends to emerge in later stages (Quarantelli, 1984; Drabek, 1986).

## PRIOR RESFARCH

While a great deal of research addresses individual or family problems resulting from disasters, less attention has focused on the dynamics of conununity recovery. Of the limited research available, most has been inconclusive (Drabek, 1986). Nonetheless, researchers have suggested several factors that may contribute to recovery. First, the circumstances of the disaster itself—including early waming, less intensity, and low death rates—can make recovery easier (Golec, 1983; Rossi, Wright, Weber-Burdin and Pereira, 1983). Second, communities with prior flood experience may be more effective in responding to crises, especially through greater flood insurance coverage and preparedness (Luloff and Wilkinson,

1979; Gillespie and Banerjee, 1993; Banerjee and Gillespie, 1994). Third, recovery is facilitated in communities with substantial socioeconomic resources (Rossi et al., 1983; Drabek, 1986). Greater financial resources contribute to recovery because disasters are just too large for communities or individuals to rely on basic resources (Quarantelli, 1984). Rubin and Barbee (1985) also note that wealthy communities have assets to protect and, as a result, fare better in recovery. Fourth, the presence of local organizations that are flexibie enough to adapt to contingencies, may help communities recover more quickly (Quarantelli, 1984). Research indicates that impromptu grassroots organizations sometimes emerge in response to inadequacy of official response to promote recovery (Wolensky and Miller, 1981; Walsh, 1981; Rubin and Barbee, 1985). For example, human services initially tend to lack coordination, are duplicated, and do not meet the needs of disaster victims (Mileti, 1975; Birnbaum, Coplon and Scharff, 1973; Taylor, Ross and Quarantelli, 1976). But, over time, service agencies may respond more effectively (Tierney and Baisden, 1979). Fifth, recovery depends on leadership abilities, political awareness, and local government contacts (Mileti, Drabek and Haas 1975; Rubin and Barbee, 1985). Nolan (1979) finds that communities with greater control and decision-making capacity are more successful in recovery.

## RESEARCH QUESTIONS AND METHODOLOGY

This study provides an opportunity to build on our understanding of how community factors affect disaster recovery. The study examines (a) response and recovery experiences, and (b) how the factors discussed above explain differential rates of recovery in five contrasting communities.

The principal data source was extensive interviews with residents and community leaders. In addition, community observations were conducted soon after the disaster, about six months later, and again at one year. Observational data, census statistics, community histories, and other information provide contextual information.

We conducted lengthy interviews with 58 resident informants in the five communities. Half were done by students in the class and half were done by the authors. Interviews provided views of the flood's effects and the recovery process from the perspectives of people who lived through it (Bernard, 1988; Miles and Huberman, 1994). We made a concerted effort to sample key sectors of each community's population, including residents from different social classes, of different ages, renters and homeowners, and so forth (Johnson, 1990). For example, a split in recovery experiences in one community (assistance appeared to have been allocated differentially to different groups) called for interviewing residents from each group. Flood assistance teams from the Salvation Army facilitated recruitment of about two-thirds of the residents. We recruited the remainder of residents through other relief workers and snowball sampling. We talked to many more people informally, including shopkeepers, passers-by, government personnel, and relief workers.

After we completed resident interviews, each student conducted a leader interview. Later, we conducted 10 additional community leader interviews, including one high-level public official (e.g., mayor, city manager, or local politician) and one leader in the voluntary or private sectors who had assumed an important role in flood recovery (e.g., church, business, non-profit agency, or grassroots organization) in each community. Leader interviews offer a window into decision-making throughout the response and recovery phases.

## RESPONSE AND RECOVERY IN THE FIVE COMMUNITIES

Table 2.1 presents a socio-demographic profile of each of the five communities. It is noteworthy that despite great diversity among the communities, there was less diversity among flooded areas only. For example, the range in housing values in the areas where most of the flooding occurred ($32,000 to $48,000) was not as wide as the range in housing values overall ($32,000 to $173,000). The range of median household income in flooded areas ($17,000 to $34,000) was not as wide as the range in median household income in the larger jurisdiction ($19,000 to $67,000).

### Community A

Community A is an upper-middle class suburban community with a significant commercial and light industrial economic base. The population is the largest, wealthiest, and most highly educated of the five communities. This area encompasses considerable numbers of large businesses and public infrastructure projects.

Of the five communities, this was one of the most severely affected by the flood and the one with the least prior disaster experience (Table 2.2 compares factors related to recovery in each of the five communities). However, it is also the community that recovered the fastest and where residents assessed the recovery most favorably (Table 2.3 compares the recovery process, as reported by residents in the five communities).

Initial response in Community A got off to a rocky start because the flooding took the community by surprise—the levee protecting the area was not expected to break. Only a few hours before the levee broke did officials realize that flooding was imminent. There was barely enough time for residents and businesses to evacuate the area; considerable confusion ensued and some residents and business owners narrowly escaped injury.

Response after those first few days improved considerably. Local groups mobilized, including city government, churches, and businesses. These groups collected names of people who could provide services and resources; conducted needs assessments; initiated contacts with other levels of government; organized planning and education sessions; and trained community leaders and volunteers.

What followed was a well-coordinated flow of resources into the area from federal, state, regional, and local government; voluntary disaster and service agencies; business associations; and volunteers. One resident observed that "everyone pulled together," a feeling shared by most respondents. While most other conununities received volunteer muscle for sandbagging, food, clothing, and other necessities, Community A benefited as well from technical contributions such as a communications command center, a computer database to track volunteers, people to provide and operate heavy equipment, and medical personnel to give vaccinations. A year later, most homes and businesses were repaired, many to a higher standard than prior to the flood (Table 2.2). According to one leader, "many residents looked upon the disaster as an opportunity and expanded or totally renovated their homes."

Although individuals in all five communities made considerable contributions to the recovery, individuals in Community A were

TABLE 2.1
Social Demographic Profiles of the Five Communities[1]

|  | Community A | Community B | Community C | Community D | Community E |
|---|---|---|---|---|---|
| Population | 38,000 | 500 | 19,000 | 3,700 | 6,900 |
| Percent age 65 and over | 9.0 | 14.0 | 9.0 | 14.0 | 15.0 |
| Average household size | 2.8 | 2.7 | 2.8 | 2.3 | . 2.7 |
| Decade most structures built | 1970s | 1950s | 1960s | pre-1940 | pre-1940 |
| Percent with 2-year Assoc. Degree or more (age 25+) | 59.0 | 5.0 | 14.0 | 8.0 | 10.0 |
| Percent persons below poverty | 2.0 | 13.0 | 5.0 | 21.0 | 8.0 |
| Median household income | $67,000 | $23,000 | $34,000 | $17,000 | $26,000 |
| Flooded area only[2] | $26,000 | $23,000 | $34,000 | $17,000 | $22,000 |
| Median home value (owned) | $173,000 | $54,000 | $66,000 | $37,000 | $42,000 |
| Flooded area only[2] | $48,000 | $54,000 | $65,000 | $31,000 | $35,000 |

[1]Figures are rounded to protect communities' anonymity. Data represent municipalities in Communities A, B, and C and census tracts in D and E. These areas include flooded and non-flooded areas.

[2]These figures are based on the census block group(s) that most closely approximates the geographical area that was flooded.

SOURCE: U.S. Census, 1990

TABLE 2.2
Factors Related to Recovery from the Flood

| | Community A (n = 11) | Community B (n = 13) | Community C (n = 13) | Community D (n = 10) | Community E (n = 11) |
|---|---|---|---|---|---|
| Flood severity[1] | High | High | Moderate | Low | High |
| Est. number of damaged structures | 286 | 226 | 191 | 85 | 121 |
| Portion of community impacted | Partial | All | Partial | Partial | Partial |
| Prior experience[2] | Very Low | High | High | Low | Moderate |
| Community preparedness[3] | Low | High | High | Moderate | Moderate |
| Socioeconomic resources[4] | High | Moderate | Moderate | Low | Low |
| Community organization resources[5] | High | Moderate | High | Moderate | Low |
| Leadership resources[6] | High | Moderate | Moderate | Moderate | Low |
| Self governance[7] | High | Moderate | High | Low | Low |
| Consensus/cooperation[8] | High | Moderate | Moderate/Low | Low | Low |
| Response | High/Moderate | High | High | High | Moderate |
| Recovery[9] | High | Moderate | Moderate/Low | Low | LOW |
| Homes | 70% | 60% | a few | 20% | 3% |
| Businesses | 60% | 30% | none | 15% | 0% |
| Public Buildings | 100% | 85% | a few | N.A. | N.A. |

[1]Severity is a subjective and comparative assessment, including impact, length of time water remained, and relative damage to buildings.

[2]Prior experience refers to flooding in the past 20 years.

[3]Preparedness refers to the level of disaster preparedness of local government and/or other local agencies.

[4]Socioeconomic resources refer to level of individual and community economic resources.

[5]Community organization resources refers to strength of local organizations that assumed a sustained role in coordinating some aspect of disaster recovery.

[6]Leadership refers to resident assessment of leadership capacity to help in response and recovery to the flood.

[7]Self governance refers to existence and capacity of local government to advocate for flooded residents.

[8]Consensus refers to extent of agreement about recovery goals between residents and leaders.

[9]Recovery is estimate of percent of homes, businesses, and public buildings that were either rehabilitated and inhabited or razed after one year, compiled from public officials estimates in each community and news reports.

able to provide more resources and professional expertise. For example, one community resident coordinated the construction of a temporary levee across the previous breach to protect against a second flooding. In another instance, volunteers with equipment filled the basement of a family's house with rock to bring the house into compliance with regulations requiring buildings to be elevated above a certain level.

Residents and leaders had considerable assets to be protected, including sizable commercial establishments that employed several thousand people, and key infrastructure projects. They also had linkages to external sources for funds. On the basis of the swift and generous response by the State of Missouri, a leader in Community A believed that it was treated the best by state government.

TABLE 2.3
Recovery Process in the Five Communities as reported by Residents (percent)

| | Community A (n = 11) | Community B (n = 13) | Community C (n = 13) | Community D (n = 10) | Community E (n = 11) |
|---|---|---|---|---|---|
| **Assessment of overall recovery** | | | | | |
| Poor | 0 | 23 | 39 | 20 | 55 |
| Fair | 36 | 31 | 31 | 40 | 36 |
| Good | 64 | 46 | 31 | 40 | 9 |
| **Level of community cooperation** | | | | | |
| Low | 9 | 46 | 15 | 40 | 36 |
| High | 91 | 54 | 77 | 60 | 54 |
| **What went well?[1]** | | | | | |
| Volunteer support | 55 | 31 | 23 | 40 | 27 |
| Agencies support | 27 | 38 | 54 | 40 | 9 |
| Family support | 9 | 31 | 8 | 10 | 18 |
| Other[2] | 9 | 0 | 15 | 10 | 46 |
| **What went badly?[1]** | | | | | |
| Financial assistance[3] | 18 | 15 | 46 | 50 | 45 |
| Leadership | 18 | 31 | 23 | 40 | 46 |
| Clean-up | 18 | 46 | 31 | 10 | 0 |
| Permits | 36 | 8 | 0 | 0 | 9 |
| Other | 9 | 0 | 0 | 0 | 0 |

[1]These were open-ended questions. Answers clustered in the categories listed.

[2]In Community E many said that nothing went well. These were classified as "other."

[3]Mostly transactions with Federal Emergency Management Agency (FEMA).

When the flood occurred, the community also had a well-established network of organizations, including local government, business associations, and churches. Early on, a disaster recovery task force—a grassroots effort—was formed by local government officials, church leaders, business leaders, and residents (Table 2.2). This local community organization made a tremendous difference:

Everything that came in was needed but unlike the large charities that have their administrative bookkeeping which needs to be done, we are able to get things done. We are able to manage at the local level and be responsive to the needs. And needs change...it is not a static process. Without our task force this community would still be a disaster.

This organization in cooperation with parishioners and members of other associations helped rebuild homes, provide funding, and locate resources (Table 2.3). One resident expressed a common sentiment:

The community seemed to know our needs before we did. . . . Churches would just find us in our homes working and give [assistance] to us....It was amazing, just when you thought you couldn't go on, someone knocked at the door and had something else for you. This emotionally lifted your spirits.

Political and other community leaders played key roles in flood recovery at all levels. Local officials and business leaders stayed in close contact with federal, state, and local authorities, and facilitated a speedy recovery. For example, local leaders mobilized immediately to educate themselves about the disaster relief process. They helped to organize and support the grassroots recovery organization (Table

2.2). City officials made regulations as flexible and comprehensible as possible to help residents cope with clean-up and construction regulations. Most important, the community made the system work for residents by adopting a home valuation (based on replacement value) that favored rebuilding and rehabilitation over buyout. The higher the valuation of the home, the greater the possibility of rebuilding because homes with more than 50 percent damage had to be razed or elevated above flood stage (Tighe and Mannies, 1993b). (Even with this assistance, obtaining building permits was considered the most problematic in Community A. see Table 2.3.)

Finally, there was a very high level of consensus at all levels about the goals of recovery (Table 2.2). This is also illustrated in Table 2.3 by the high level of cooperation and the low level of conflict. There was no question among community leaders, business owners, and residents that the goal was to rebuild and get everyone back into their homes and places of business as soon as possible. One leader advised residents that they were "setting on a valuable piece of land" and to "keep title" even if they had to demolish their houses. Regional and state leaders also agreed on the desirability to rebuild the levee and community structures. In contrast to other communities where flood plain buyouts were being debated, there was little contemplation of such a policy in Community A. Rebuilding the community was facilitated and encouraged at all levels.

In sum, Community A's successful recovery from the flood was associated with (a) substantial socioeconomic resources and community assets, (b) a high level of prior organization and emergence of a strong grassroots disaster recovery organization, (c) effective leadership, and (d) community consensus and commitment to quick and full recovery (Table 2.2).

## Community B

Community B is a small and modest town, surrounded by farms. The town is incorporated, but local government tends to be informal and officials operate largely out of their homes, due in large part to the rural context and relatively large number of elderly residents (Table 2.1). Although fertile farmland and key infrastructure projects are in the area, Community B is not wealthy. Income levels are modest, education levels are low, and most families' assets are in their homes and land (Table 2.1). Organizational and leadership resources in Community B are fairly informal. The town's political business has been traditionally conducted over the kitchen table. There are no government buildings or offices in the community and some official positions are occupied informally. For example, the director of emergency services assumed his position based on experience, expressed interest, and willingness to do the job.

Community B was seriously flooded. Many previous floods had created problems but damage occurred in lower farm and recreational areas, leaving the more densely populated parts of town relatively unaffected. In 1993, water damaged almost every residence in some way. Although flood waters receded in about a week, repeat flooding later made a quick recovery impossible.

Media attention brought a great deal of help to the community, including food, supplies, volunteers, and money. Residents were safely evacuated by the National Guard, which maintained a lengthy presence. Nonprofit disaster agencies helped residents and businesses. Volunteers from a sister community in another state provided donations, helped with clean-up, and offered professional consultation regarding rehabilitation and refurbishment of the water system and other infrastructure damage.

Recovery was slower and less effective than in Community A. Clean-up took longer and negotiations with federal disaster assistance agencies were slower. The town's small budget was more than drained by the clean-up and repair costs, although donations continued to pour in long after the flood, eventually covering the costs.

At the time of the flood, local officials had little experience dealing with authorities outside the local community. This lack of experience was noted by one official who observed that "now that [the flood] is over, we see a lot of things we missed." There were few formal organizations and even those tended to be voluntary, such as Boy Scouts. Church leaders did not play an extensive role in community affairs. In fact, when flooding began, the largest church closed and its leader left town, causing resentment among some residents.

Despite a lack of formal organizations, a group coalesced quickly to coordinate relief efforts. Leaders attributed their relative success to the resourcefulness and community spirit of residents. Self-reliance, pride, and determination to rebuild were considered the community's most important assets. As one resident put it: "We're a hard-headed group of people. We are out here by ourselves, we're a unique town."

Incorporation as a separate unit of government also helped in recovery. Even though they were only partially successful, elected officials had authority to act (Table 2.2). For example, local officials could influence the housing condemnation process. On the other hand, the community "was left out in the cold" regarding decisions made outside the community. Lack of political influence kept them out of the first round of buyouts (funds went elsewhere), although a later attempt in collaboration with the County for Community Development Block Grant (CDBG) funds appeared to be more successful.

Prior experience with flooding helped leaders come together quickly and also accounted for the relatively high percentage of residents insured through the federal flood insurance program. This sped up recovery because families "knew the ropes" and dealt effectively with FEMA, the Small Business Administration (SBA), and assistance organizations. However, prior policies in the community and the county had not discouraged building on the flood plain and therefore the number of people affected by the flood was somewhat higher.

Some residents said the community's commitment and resources were not made available to everyone. For example, one resident commented that "you have to drink beer with the mayor" for your home to pass inspection. Several complained that food and supplies were hoarded by those in charge (the "movers and the shakers") and were handed out only to friends and relatives. Dumpsters were placed in the community for clean-up, but some residents said that the dumpsters were removed before those in low-lying areas could return to clean up their homes. Some residents believed that damage assessments were too subjective and based on whether leaders in the community wanted the resident to return to the community after the flood. They felt that help was not extended equally to all community residents. These comments reflect the high proportion of residents who said that community cooperation was low and leadership was a problem (Table 2.3).

Overall, a cohesive leadership group, legal authority (incorporation), community consensus about re-building, and prior experience with flooding facilitated recovery in community B. But lack of formal organizations and lack of resources slowed recovery. Moreover, conflict led to lack of comprehensive recovery, as poorer segments of the community were left to fend for themselves (Table 2.2).

## Community C

Community C is a middle-income commuter community with an economy based on services and some light industry (Table 2.1). Lacking a traditional central business district, it is largely a collection of housing subdivisions and service centers.

Damage assessments in Community C were lower than in many other communities because the high water did not strike with the same impact and did not stay as long (Table 2.2). Flooding affected low- to moderate-income family housing but left businesses and infrastructure mostly untouched.

Response and recovery were mixed. Although accustomed to flooding, officials and inhabitants were taken by surprise and had little time to implement the community's disaster plan. After the initial onslaught, emergency relief was more organized and prior experience and planning helped the city in recovery. Prior flood plain management minimized damage because some residential areas in the flood plain had already been cleared. Resources and reimbursement to the city were available quickly because a disaster management plan had been developed in the past and city officials knew how to deal with federal and state bureaucracies in applying for disaster resources (Table 2.2).

However, prior experience with flood management had little positive effect on the city's response to residents' concerns—especially early in recovery—which was reflected in the disappointment in leadership and clean-up expressed by residents (Table

2.3). One resident said that the "city turned its back on people and didn't help until it absolutely had to." Another said that in the beginning it was very difficult to reach city officials or to get a straight answer from them. One resident reported that the city was not very helpful, and at times personnel in city hall seemed to lack compassion. The city "hasn't done anything except haul sandbags away," and then only after volunteers had dragged them to the street.

However, a local church stepped in and played a key organizational role in recovery (Table 2.2). The pastor also brought in external funds from the church's national organization and, with the help of parishioners, provided direct assistance to residents. The church played an intermediary role between city officials and residents, responding to resident concerns and then obtaining resources and assistance. According to one resident, the church was the only organization that did not make residents "feel bad" about seeking assistance.

Thus, the organizational base and leadership resources (especially church leaders and local public officials), and to some extent, moderate socioeconomic resources, appear to have contributed to recovery. But lack of consensus among leaders and residents about the goals in recovery contributed to dissension, confusion about procedures, and slower progress than in Community A (Table 2.2).

## Community D

Community D is an urban neighborhood. It has the lowest incomes and the fewest economic resources of all five communities, and the oldest housing stock (Table 2.1). Unlike the other communities, it has a substantial number of renters.

Response to the flood in this urban neighborhood was fairly effective. National

Guard, Coast Guard, fire and police departments, and non-profit disaster relief agencies (Salvation Army, Red Cross, and others) worked with local officials, organizations, and residents to evacuate and provide for immediate needs. Temporary housing was organized quickly.

However, recovery was more difficult. After the worst of the debris was cleared, efforts to clean up uninhabited structures and assure permanent housing were much slower. Several uninhabited buildings were still not gutted more than a year later, creating a health hazard for the public and financial hardship for the owners.

Residents and leaders in the Community D attributed the lack of official recovery assistance to lack of official responsiveness at the city level, lack of effective advocacy on the part of community officials, and lack of disaster experience (Table 2.2). While grateful for the initial assistance, many residents said that public disaster agencies seemed disorganized and unhelpful, and municipal government did not facilitate recovery efforts.

Contributing to the lack of official support, most residents in the area hit by high water had few resources of their own. Residents struggled to replace even basic items, such as clothing. As one resident put it, "you spend so much" to replace even the "small items." Loans were required to replace higher cost items such as house siding, furniture, and large appliances. One resident's loss of tools and equipment meant that the odd jobs that had brought in extra income were no longer possible. Renters in Community D, especially those with large families, had difficulty finding housing due to the high demand for habitable rental units (Gallagher, 1993). One renter we interviewed had to move into another jurisdiction, creating problems over residency and affecting the public assis-

tance she received from the Division of Family Services.

Nonetheless, an active community organization affiliated with the church pressured the municipal government for assistance. The organization had substantial prior experience in delivering housing and social services. Its efforts to work with local government were largely unsuccessful, but the organization helped residents to repair houses, procure resources, and negotiate rules and regulations.

In sum, lack of resources, a lack of responsiveness by the city, and lack of experience in flood response slowed recovery efforts in Community D. But a community organization took up the role of recovery and helped many residents begin recovery (Table 2.2). Ironically, the large number of renters made "official" recovery swifter because renting families did not have to deal with lengthy insurance and buyout negotiations. However, our interviews indicated that many former residents want to move back to Community D and are unable to find affordable housing there.

**Community E**

Community E is also old and is located in an unincorporated area of a suburban county. Median household income, education levels, and home values are fairly low (Table 2.1). This community was heavily hit by the flood (Table 2.2). Water covered a residential and business area for more than 30 days. All but three of the flooded homes were beyond repair.

Residents' assessment of the emergency response was not as positive as in other communities. Residents told of being awakened in the middle of the night and given 15 to 20 minutes to leave their homes, with little assistance from local authorities or volunteers. Many people had moved belongings out of the basement to the first floor, assuming that the water would not reach that high. But the flood waters rose rapidly. Pets were left behind and prized possessions were lost.

A poor response was followed by a painfully long recovery process. Residents of Community E waited for more than a year for a decision on a buyout, all the while many were unable to make permanent housing arrangements. Some continued to pay their mortgages and insurance, while also paying expenses on another residence. Remaining community residents waited more than a year for demolition of unsafe structures to begin.

Once the buyout began, it used a valuation scheme that was based on tax assessments from years before that were below current market value and much below replacement costs. This meant that residents could not afford to buy similar houses elsewhere. Despite heavy damage, many long-term and elderly residents were unhappy about leaving because they wanted to return to their homes, community, and neighbors (Kilijanik and Drabek, 1979), and also because relatively small amounts of money had been offered in the buyout.

Eventually, the extent of damage to the community convinced government officials that the area should be cleared. Some officials may have hoped to clear the land for development. Residents were not permitted to return to their homes. This was the only community (of the five discussed here) where residents were not permitted to return and rebuild.

What explains the powerless position of Community E? First, the community lacked an effective local voice (Table 2.2). Although there was elected representation, the town was not incorporated and did not have the political autonomy for a more effective platform. If the community was a municipality, one leader declared, "I guarantee that the buyout would be underway right now and there would be bulldozers down there now." Two grassroots organizations emerged after the flood. One was a "coordinating" group that formed in response to a perceived need to keep in touch with each other and to generate political influence (see Stallings and Quarantelli, 1985). Residents said this group organized meetings and put people in touch with each other throughout the first months after the flood, but was not able to help in the longer term. It slowly disappeared as residents were scattered geographically and the organization was unable to influence decisions about the buyout. Another group-focusing on "operations"—carried out fundraising and provided needed assistance, but fell inactive after helping families with basic needs in the early stages of recovery (see Stallings and Quarantelli, 1985). These emergent groups were ad hoc and had no prior organizational base. After they disbanded, residents were left to represent themselves (Table 2.2).

Community E had relatively few resources and little power that might have convinced larger governmental and business entities to re-build or to resettle displaced families in the community (Table 2.2). On the contrary, conflicting goals between residents (who wanted to return) and policy makers (who reportedly wanted to clear the land), contributed to slow recovery. According to one resident, the county did not contribute enough taxes or jobs to be a priority of the state. This was reflected, according to several observers, in the stringent terms of the buyout and its slow pace (Tables 2.2 and 2.3). Thus, lack of socioeconomic resources, lack of local leadership and government, and lack of an organizational base left Community E without an effective voice in the recovery period.

## OVERALL RESPONSE AND RECOVERY

Similar to other disasters, the response phase of the flood of 1993 was marked by high levels of cooperation, voluntarism, and solidarity, and low levels of conflict (Mileti, Drabek and Haas, 1975; Quarantelli, 1984). Time and time again, residents and leaders talked about the extraordinary volunteer response, characterizing it as one of the best features of U.S. society (Table 2.3). Volunteers came from near and far to fight the rising water and help residents evacuate. Businesses donated services and supplies, from free pizzas to bottled water. Financial assistance poured in. Agency experience and readiness and advance notice of flooding facilitated high levels of cooperation, voluntarism, and organization; organizations and agencies were then able to communicate, plan, and coordinate services ahead of time (Banerjee and Gillespie, 1994). Residents and others affected by the flood gave high marks to the National Guard, the Salvation Army, the Red Cross, other service agencies, and churches. Preparedness among regional disaster agencies clearly paid off. Residents in four of the five communities ranked volunteer and agency responsiveness (the disaster agencies coordinated volunteer work) as two factors that went well in the aftermath of the flood (Table 2.3). Social workers' involvement in disaster recovery was primarily through the disaster agencies, as staff or volunteers, although most residents did not identify professional affiliations.

However, recovery was more difficult, involving many more complex tasks. One political official recalled: "I lived, breathed, and ate the flood. I didn't sleep, I didn't eat

because I was [determined] to 'part the waters.' After a month I found out I couldn't part the waters." Communities confronted old problems in addition to new problems caused by the flood. Most critically, lack of income and assets in some communities before the flood meant fewer resources to work with after the flood. A delay in receiving a support check (a very common occurrence) often threatened the security of lower income families, who had little or nothing to fall back on.

The largest obstacle to recovery in all five communities was locating permanent housing for residents. Most homeowners were unable to move back into heavily damaged homes, and at the same time were unable to arrange other permanent housing because their assets were tied up. Problems with the buyout process, in particular, were echoed in all communities except Community A. As one informal leader said: "resolution of buyouts is desperately needed to get people back to where they know where their lives are going to be," and another said, "you can't put your life back in order" without it. Residents yearned for "a place to come home to."

According to many residents, the procedures for federal assistance were protracted; the rules for assistance, buyouts, permits, and loans were constantly changing; and various officials and agency personnel imparted different and sometimes contradictory information (Kilborn, 1993). Reflecting a widespread dilemma, one resident noted that the "response of help is just too slow, and you have to make decisions based on inaccurate information." "Never knowing what your situation is" added to the stresses that everyone already felt.

Problems with housing placed a heavy burden on flood victims, especially the elderly (Tighe, 1994). One elderly resident said she felt guilty needing help when others had lost their homes completely, but she was "too tired and too old" to do everything herself. Another, whose small business was a total loss, lamented that she "never wanted to be rich but didn't want to live on Social Security alone." As another older resident observed: "It's harder for the elderly to rebuild. Younger people still have their health." Among renters, who tended to have lower incomes, the largest obstacles were finding a place to rent in or near their community and replacing damaged possessions, especially expensive large appliances (Gallagher, 1993). Even among renters, there were long-term problems associated with flood recovery, such as the young couple who had to spend all the money they had saved towards a down payment on a first home.

**LESSONS FOR COMMUNITY PRACTICE**

In social work practice, crisis intervention and counseling have traditionally been the primary responses to disasters (Birnbaum, Coplon and Scharf, 1973; Hiratsuka, 1993). This emphasis is not unwarranted. We found that residents wanted to talk to real people, not voice mailboxes and faceless bureaucrats on the other end of the line (Kilborn, 1993). Moreover, 71 percent of our respondents said they or family members experienced emotional difficulties (Tighe and Shirk, 1993). Although relatively few residents (21 percent) actually received counseling, most told stories of disruption, sadness at having to move away from friends and family, financial ruin, confusion, and children struggling to adjust to new communities and new schools without old friends and familiar possessions. Some needed a listening ear as they sorted out what had happened, and what they would do next (Wilkerson, 1993; Murphy, 1984).

"It's hard to explain," said a resident of Community D, "what it does to you to see all that you own destroyed."

But not all issues were mere adjustments to loss. We found that much of the stress experienced in the aftermath of the flood was due to people being economically desperate, trapped by circumstances, subject to bureaucratic procedures and problems that they neither understood nor had time to handle, and made to feel that their predicament was their fault for being "river rats" living on the flood plain (in fact, many residents had never been flooded before, including many who had not been informed that they were living on a flood plain) (Fitzmaurice, 1994). People in these situations certainly appreciate a listening ear and a helping hand, but they also require resources, and the assistance of facilitators, educators, and advocates.

What can be learned from this study of five flooded communities about the potential role for community practitioners in disaster recovery? We found that four factors had the greatest influence on effective recovery. First, community consensus about recovery goals encouraged whole communities to work together. Second, local leaders and existing community organizations that took on responsibility for dealing with the disaster were critical to attracting resources and organizing for recovery. Third, effective local governance gave communities a political "voice" that enabled them to build consensus, to advocate more successfully for the community, and to garner external resources. Fourth, socioeconomic resources, where present, met a broad range of individual and community needs in the aftermath of flooding and gave local communities status and power in the rebuilding process.

It is noteworthy that these key factors are social, political, and economic, rather than physical. Somewhat surprisingly, among the communities studied, recovery was not associated with the flood's severity (Table 2.2). The community that experienced the quickest and most complete recovery (Community A) was also among the most severely affected by flooding.

Prior experience and preparedness for flooding had mixed effects. On one hand, Community A had no prior experience and no flood plain management, but recovered the fastest (Table 2.2). On the other hand, Community C's prior experience with flooding led to flood plain management that minimized damage. In Communities B and C, prior experience with disaster bureaucracies made it easier to bring resources into the community, but this did not ensure that local officials always would be responsive to the "here and now" concerns of residents. These results suggest that flood plain policies have an important prevention effect, and prior experience helps residents "learn the ropes" about disaster assistance, but these alone do not assure an effective recovery.

No single factor explains the differences in recovery among the five communities. Rather it is the combination of the above four factors that makes a difference. For example, community organizations contribute especially to the day-to-day recovery activities such as getting damage estimates, arranging for contractors, and meeting everyday needs of residents. But they need an organizational base as they had in Communities A (government and church, among others), C (church), and D (church). If they do not have an organizational base (emergent organizations in Community E), it is difficult to sustain its activities. If they are not joined in their efforts and supported by local government—as happened in Communities D and E—it is difficult for community organiza-

tions to be effective. Similarly, if there are very few resources to distribute—as in Community D—local organizations have more difficulty addressing concrete needs of residents.

Community practitioners in social work, with their understanding of community processes, are in a unique position to facilitate recovery after natural disasters. Many problems encountered are shared by entire communities and can be effectively addressed at the community level. Using their practice skills and the knowledge gained from this and other studies, community practitioners can address the factors discussed above. For example, they can bring leaders and residents together to articulate common goals and build consensus and cooperation (Gillespie, 1991). They can identify local leaders and provide sustained support to them in their efforts to organize. They can assist residents and leaders in strengthening existing organizations or creating new organizations to articulate demands and bring services and resources into the community. Especially when communities lack an autonomous political voice, community practitioners can assist local leaders in presenting their cases to federal agencies and other key decision makers. Finally, although community practitioners typically are not in a position to provide direct economic support, they can assist in writing grants and soliciting funds for the community.

Community practitioners can play an especially important role in helping communities with large vulnerable populations (e.g., the poor and elderly). As reported in this study, communities that take the longest to recover are also the poorest. In addition, there is inequitable treatment, with poorer segments of one community left out of full recovery assistance. In such instances, social workers can assume advocacy roles and help organize, inform, and empower groups to advocate for themselves.

In addition to general skills in organizing and advocacy, community practitioners should develop a working knowledge of guidelines and procedures for government assistance during disasters. Helping residents with recovery involves understanding federal and state policies for household and community assistance (e.g., FEMA, SBA, CDBG), tax assessment and zoning issues, and so forth. At the community level, understanding taxation issues, community revenues and expenditures, housing and business valuation, and infrastructure costs is also vital. Social workers must become deeply familiar with policy issues if they are to assist residents and leaders in disaster recovery.

In addition, community practitioners should appreciate the role of both income and assets in family and community well-being. Many people lose income and assets during natural disasters. Loss of income can be incurred by the interruption of employment, loss of work tools, and death or injury of employed household members. Loss of income has obvious repercussions in daily living. Loss of assets may include loss of a vehicle, a home, or a business. Asset losses are likely to have immediate impact on income level, and also may affect a family's sense of identity, security, and control over the future (Sherraden, 1991). The destruction of many homes in a community results in massive socioeconomic loss for households, and severe disruptions in neighborhood and community identity as well. No community response can be effective unless it seeks to restore to every possible extent, the losses of both income and assets that occur in disasters. If social workers are to be relevant in these situations, their agenda and expertise must include these basic economic issues.

Finally, it is important to note that this research was initiated in an undergraduate social work course on community practice. Students gained first-hand experience in designing and implementing a research project. They collected and analyzed data using observations, secondary data sources, in-depth interviews, and historical records. In the process of conducting the studies, students gained greater awareness and understanding of community processes. Moreover, students (four of whom worked in flood relief upon graduation) developed proposals for improved service delivery to communities in the aftermath of a natural disaster. Their hard work and insights inspired this comparative study.

## REFERENCES

Ahmad, I.L. (August 26–September 1, 1993). Crystal City Blacks face condemnation. *St. Louis American,* p. IA.

Andrews and McMeel. (1993). High and mighty: The flood of '93. St. Louis, MO: *St. Louis Post-Dispatch.*

Banerjee, M.M., & Gillespie, D.F. (1994). Linking disaster preparedness and organizational response effectiveness. *Journal of Community Practice 1*(3), 129–142.

Bernard, H.R. (1988). *Research methods in cultural anthropology.* Newbury Park, CA: Sage.

Birnbaum, F., Coplon, J., & Scharff, I. (1973). Crisis intervention after a natural disaster *Social Casework 54,* 545–551.

De Simone, P. (October 14, 1993). Getting flood victims back to normal. *St. Louis Post-Dispatch,* p. 7B.

Drabek, T.E. (1986). *Human system responses to disaster: An inventory of sociological findings.* New York: Springer-Verlag.

Fitzmaurice, L. (September 12, 1994). Post-flood snags keep "River Rats" out of homes. *St. Louis Post-Dispatch,* 3W.

Gallagher, J. (October 10, 1993), Unhappy hunting: Apartment seekers face tight market. *St. Louis Post-Dispatch,* 1E.

Gillespie, D.F. (1991). Coordinating community resources. In T.E. Drabek and G.J. Hoetmer (Eds.), *Emergency Management: Principles and Practice for Local Government.* Washington, DC: International City Management Association, Municipal Management Series.

Gillespie, D.F., & Banerjee, M.M. (1993). Prevention planning and disaster preparedness in social work administration. *Journal of Applied Social Sciences, 17*(2), 237–253.

Golec, J.A. (1983). A contextual approach to the social psychological study of disaster recovery. *International Journal of Mass Emergencies and Disasters 1,* 255–276.

Hiratsuka, J. (October 1993). Facing the aftermath of the flood. *NASW News,* p. 3.

Johnson, J.C. (1990). *Selecting ethnographic informants.* Newbury Park, CA:Sage.

Kilbom, P.T. (August 9, 1993). Flood victims find tortuous path to U.S. Relief agency money. *New York Times, A7.*

Kilijanek, T.S., & Drabek, T.E. (1979). Assessing long-term impacts of a natural disaster—focus on the elderly. *The Gerontologist 19*(December), 555–566.

Luloff, A.E. & Wilkinson, K.P. (1979). Participation in the National Flood Insurance Program: A study of Community activeness. *Rural Sociology 44,* 137–152.

Miles, M.B, & Huberman, A.M. (1994). *Qualitative data analysis.* Thousand Oaks, CA: Sage.

Mileti, D.S, (1975), *Disaster relief and rehabilitation in the United States: A research assessment.* Boulder, CO: Institute of Behavioral Science, The University of Colorado.

Mileti, D.S., Drabek, T.E., & Haas, J.E. (1975). *Human systems in extreme environments.* Boulder, CO: Institute of Behavioral Science, The University of Colorado.

Murphy, S.A. (1984). After Mount St. Helens: Disaster stress research, *Journal of Psychosocial Nursing 22*(7), 9–18.

Nolan, M.L. (1979). Impact of Paricutin in five communities. In P.D. Sheets & D.K. Grayson (Eds.), *Volcanic activity and human ecology* (pp. 293–338). New York: Academic Press.

Quarantelli, E.L. (1984). *Organizational behavior in disasters and implications for disaster planning.* Emmitsburg, MD: National Emergency Training Center, Federal Emergency Management Agency, Monograph Series Vol. 1, No. 2.

Rossi, P.H., Wright, J.D., Weber-Burdin, E., & Pereira, J. (1983). *Victims of the Environment: Loss from natural hazards in the United States, 1970*–1980. New York: Plenum Press.

Rubin, C.B. & Barbee, D.G. (1985). Disaster recovery and hazard mitigation: Bridging the intergovernmental gap. *Public Administration Review 45,* 57–63.

Sherraden, M. (1991). *Assets and the poor: A new American welfare policy.* Armonk, NY & London: ME Sharpe.

Stallings, R.A., & Quarantelli, E.L. (1985). Emergent citizen groups and emergency management. *Public Administration Review 45,* 93–100.

Taylor, V., Alexander Ross, G., & Quarantelli, E.L. (1976). Delivery of mental health services in disasters: The Xenia tornado and some implications, Disaster Research Center Book and Monograph Series No. 11. Columbus, OH: Disaster Research Center, The Ohio State University.

Tierney, K.J., & Baisden, B. (1979). *Crises intervention programs for disaster victims: A sourcebook and manual for smaller communities.* Rockville, MD: National Institute of Mental Health.

Tighe, T. (April 18, 1994). For older flood victims, recovery is hard. *St. Louis Post-Dispatch,* p. 1, 4A.

Tighe, T. & Mannies, J. (August 27, 1993a). Homeowners angry over flood rules. *St. Louis Post-Dispatch,* p. 1, 8A.

Tighe, T. & Mannies, J. (September 20, 1993b). Federal rescue could be slow, meager. *St. Louis Post-Dispatch,* p. IA.

Tighe, T, & Shirk, M. (November 7, 1993). Stress-induced misery from flood takes toll. *St. Louis Post-Dispatch,* p. 1, 10A.

Walsh, E.J. (1981). Resource mobilization and citizen protest in communities around Three Mile Island. *Social Problems 29*(1), 1–21.

Wilkerson, I. (September 28, 1993). Anxiety for the Midwest as terrible as the floods. *New York Times,* p. 1A.

Wolensky, R.P., & Miller, E.J. (1981). The everyday versus the disaster role of local officials—citizen and official definitions. *Urban Affairs Quarterly 16*(4), 483–504.

**3.**

Robert J. Chaskin

## PERSPECTIVES ON NEIGHBORHOOD AND COMMUNITY:
## A REVIEW OF THE LITERATURE

A movement has been developing among funders and policy makers toward geographically targeted community-based or neighborhood-based interventions. Its rationale derives, in part, from the conviction that the interrelated needs and circumstances of individuals and families are grounded in a specific context of relationships, opportunities, and constraints, which, to a large degree, are spatially defined or delimited. Many of the interventions within this movement are concerned with issues of scope in linking programmatic efforts ("comprehensive" or "holistic" approaches), issues of citizenship and capacity building (including a concern with "empowerment" and "collaborative decision making"), and issues of social organization and the sustainability of efforts through attempts to rebuild the "fabric of community." All of these issues rest on a premise that neighborhoods are central and viable units of analysis and action, that they can be defined and mobilized, and that they can act and be acted on.

This article provides a historical-theoretical review of perspectives on neighborhood and community. After briefly exploring some basic definitional difficulties, I examine the concept of neighborhood as a social unit, tracing a progression of thought from human ecology through the

"decline-of-community" thesis and several responses to it. I also explore the neighborhood as a spatial unit, focusing in particular on problems of boundary definition. I review empirical findings on the different experiences of neighborhood by different populations in different contexts. Finally, I summarize the implications of these three perspectives on understanding neighborhood, including its component elements, scope, and uses.

## NEIGHBORHOOD AND COMMUNITY: SOME DEFINITIONS

Although there is strong agreement among many that neighborhoods or communities are viable units of action, the operational definitions of these units vary greatly.[1] The two terms themselves are the cause of some confusion, and the distinction between them is often unclear.

On the one hand, "community" implies connection: some combination of shared beliefs, circumstances, priorities, relationships, or concerns. The networks of connection that bind individuals of a given group to one another as a community may or may not be rooted in place. Ethnic and religious communities are bound by culture and systems of belief; professional communities and other "communities of interest" are connected by common interests, circumstances, or priorities. In either case, the community defined may be more or less

Robert Chaskin is a Research Program Director at Chapin Hall at the University of Chicago.

formalized through such local institutions as churches or social clubs or such member organizations as professional societies and associations.

Although local communities are place based, they are not seen as simply geographically bounded subdivisions of land. They are units in which some set of connections is concentrated, either social connections (as in kin, friend, and acquaintance networks), functional connections (as in the production, consumption, and transfer of goods and services), cultural connections (as in religion, tradition, or ethnic identity), or circumstantial connections (as in economic status or lifestyle). In both the local community and the community of interest, it is the existence of some form of communal connection among individuals— whether or not such connection is locality based—that provides for the possibility of group identity and collective action.

"Neighborhood," on the other hand, is clearly a spatial construction denoting a geographical unit in which residents share proximity and the circumstances that come with it. The neighborhood is a subunit of a larger area and is usually seen as primarily, if not exclusively, residential. Howard Hallman suggests a minimal definition: "A neighborhood is a limited territory within a larger urban area where people inhabit dwellings and interact socially."[2] Although this definition does not specify the nature or extent of social interaction, the notion of neighborhood is rarely free of the connotations of connection that inhere in the term community. Indeed, one classic definition of neighborhood provides a grab bag of possible elements that might distinguish individual neighborhoods in the broader metropolitan landscape—the same set of elements (social, functional, cultural, and circumstantial) suggested above as possible elements of connection in the local community. In this formulation, neighborhoods are described as "distinctive areas into which larger spatial units may be subdivided. . . . The distinctiveness of these areas stems from . . . geographical boundaries, ethnic or cultural characteristics of the inhabitants, psychological unity among people who feel that they belong together, or concentrated use of an area's facilities for shopping, leisure, and learning."[3] In the urban context, in fact, the neighborhood is often considered the more primary unit of actual and potential solidarity and social cohesion.[4] There is thus a conflation of community-like expectations for solidarity and connection within the geographical construction of neighborhood and a range of possible expectations, at varying levels of intensity, for the neighborhood and the local community as units of identity, use, and action.

These overlapping definitions have led, in some cases, to new and more clearly defined terms. Harvey Choldin, for example, suggests that the term "subcommunity" is preferable to either community or neighborhood, as it is "connotatively neutral," describing residential areas that are "completely dependent upon other parts of the community for subsistence" and are "less than communities because they do not have governments."[5] Others have suggested that the conflation of neighborhood and community may go beyond a lack of definitional clarity to indicate a more fundamental confusion of principles. Network analysts, for example, have suggested that expectations for community-like solidarity in neighborhoods assume the "a priori organizing power of space" and may "give undue importance to spatial characteristics as causal variables."[6]

There is, however, power in the *idea* of the neighborhood, power that comes not from its precision as a sociological construction but from its nuanced complexity as a vernacular term. Neighborhood is known, if not understood, and in any given case, there is likely to be wide agreement on its existence, if not its parameters. Unfortunately, this generalized notion of neighborhood is not very useful in informing policy or planning for social change. Engaging neighborhoods usefully as units of planning and action would benefit from a better understanding of their nature, dimensions, use, and value.

## THE NEIGHBORHOOD AS A SOCIAL UNIT

There is an ongoing tension in the literature between notions of the existence and nature of community and connection at the local level and the pull away from such connection by the forces of modernization, urbanization, migration, communication, and technological advances.[7] This tension, described by Barry Wellman as the "community question," speaks to one of the core assumptions behind neighborhood-based programming: that neighborhoods are viable units of identity and action.[8] There are several aspects of the community question that may help to develop an operational definition of neighborhood for the purposes of programmatic planning.

### The Ecological Perspective: The "Natural Area," or Urban Village

Before the middle of the nineteenth century, the city was seen as a commercial center of "individuals and institutions gathered together under conditions of relative abundance for the pursuit of commerce and civilization."[9] The notion of the American city as an aggregate of smaller social and functional units called neighborhoods was essentially nonexistent. By the end of the century, however, the city came to be seen as a dif-

ferentiated, organic entity whose various parts—neighborhoods, zones, sectors—existed in interdependence and symbiosis.[10]

The city, in this ecological model, was seen as the product of natural processes of selection and competition. Competition between social groups for scarce resources, especially land, led to domination by the best-adapted groups, to increased division of labor, and to functional specialization by different sections of the city.[11] These processes drove the reconfiguration of the urban landscape and the shifting relationships of its many parts.

Several models were proposed to predict the form and outcome of urban growth on the various parts of the city. One such model described the growth of cities as following a pattern of "concentric zones" emanating from the center.[12] The "central business district," dominated by office buildings, department stores, hotels, banks, theaters, and the like, is surrounded by a "zone in transition," in which manufacturing and wholesale industries gradually invade the older residential areas. These residential sections, in turn, are transformed into centers of poverty or slums. Beyond this zone are three residential zones. The first is dominated by middle-income residences, primarily inhabited by industrial, working-class residents. The second contains higher-income, primarily single-family residences. The third zone is composed of upper-income, suburban residences.

Another model presented the growth of cities as sectoral, following directional trends from the center (again, dominated by financial, retail, and administrative activity) outward along major lines of transportation and toward places with such geographical amenities as high ground, open space, and waterfront access.[13] As in the concentric zone model, the principal direction of this growth is outward from the center, but here it is seen to produce a pattern of settlement in which the directional expansion and movement of banks, office buildings, and retail establishments draw with it the establishment of high-rent residential districts, thus forming concentrated sectors of affluence and activity radiating out from the center.

A third model of urban growth stresses the development of several hubs of commercial and administrative activities within the City.[14] Again, the principal trajectories of growth follow major transportation arteries out of the central business district, but in this model, secondary centers of activity develop at strategic intersections, creating a "polynucleated city."[15]

Within these broad patterns of expansion and change, the organization and development of distinct subareas—neighborhoods—grew. Again, the process of neighborhood differentiation was seen as an organic one in which an efficient and evolving social organization, driven by natural processes of selection, competition, invasion, and succession, produced distinct residential subsystems. A system of "natural areas" was formed by physical forces of industrial development and land use as well as by the distinguishing forces of cultural attraction and identity and by the development and reproduction of locally based sentiments and symbols.[16]

A prototypical example of the urban neighborhood as a natural area is the ethnic enclave, formed by the clustering of immigrants into local communities around particular kinds of available work. Immigrant workers congregated within walking distance of the industry in which they tended to specialize and were further propelled to establish their neighborhoods as communities based on ethnic solidarity and identification through the "social imperatives of their cultural systems."[17] Existing networks of early immigrants embraced new arrivals

from home and offered a sense of identity, security, and belonging. The arrival of different ethnic groups and the development of coexisting sets of networks along these lines within the same geographic area often created some initial conflict until a new balance was worked out.[18] The urban landscape that emerged from this growth was composed of sets of homogeneous neighborhoods within a heterogeneous field, a "mosaic of little social worlds which touch but do not interpenetrate," in Robert Ezra Park's famous phrase.[19]

The ethnic enclave as a natural formation—a transplant of the original close-knit village—is seen as the modern equivalent of the primordial "folk community," in which relations among individuals were based on primary ties of kinship and friendship and were rooted in a common identity with local life. It was based on this view, and the belief in the viability of maintaining and promoting community within distinct, naturally formed neighborhoods, that the earliest neighborhood organization movements, such as the settlement houses, the community center movement, and the social unit experiments, began.[20]

## The Decline of Community

This notion of neighborhood as natural community formed the foundation for theories of its decline. The perception of the decline of community grew out of theories explaining the effect of broad societal changes. The principal argument centered around the effects of urbanization (accompanied by greater specialization and division of labor and the increased size, density, and heterogeneity of settlement) on social action and organization. One effect often cited was the weakening connections among individuals, at the local level and in general, as mobility and the concentration of heterogeneous populations in urban centers increased. Urbanization, in this view, has led to "the substitution of secondary for primary contacts, the weakening of bonds of kinship, and the declining social significance of the family, the disappearance of the neighborhood, and the undermining of the traditional basis of social solidarity."[21] Separation of the workplace from the residential neighborhood and technological advances, particularly in the fields of communication and transportation, were seen to have propelled such disconnection at the local level, as they "freed urbanites from traditional spatial constraints and expanded their range of social choices."[22]

Another argument for the decline of community is found in theories about the rise of an "underclass" in urban neighborhoods of high poverty. [23] In this thesis, the decline is due to neither the increased mobility of the inhabitants nor the increased heterogeneity but, in fact, to just the opposite. This group is often less mobile and more isolated than the rest of the urban population, and because pockets of concentrated poverty in the urban setting are disproportionally African American, they are by definition relatively homogeneous with regard to income and class. Unlike the solidarity that is often fostered among homogeneous populations who live together by choice, the homogeneity of poor minority populations forced to live together does not create solidarity and territorial identity.[24]

Many forces have contributed to the concentration of poverty in contemporary urban centers. These include broad structural changes in the economic base of cities (e.g., the transition from a manufacturing to a service economy, in which wages for low and unskilled workers dropped substantially), the immigration of large numbers of mostly unskilled African-American laborers from the South, and the eventual emigration of many middle-class black families from inner-city neighborhoods.[25] This emigration eliminated, according to some, access to middle-class "role models."[26] It also led to an exodus of capital, making it "extremely difficult for most small, black-owned stores and shops that served ghetto residents to survive" and weakening what had been a generally strong neighborhood-based economy in which "black earnings [were) being expended primarily in black-owned establishments."[27] In addition, the concentration of urban poverty among minority, and particularly black, Americans has been strongly influenced by the forces of racial segregation and policies that support it.[28] The impact of racism and the structural condition of racial segregation, particularly in large, ill-designed public-housing compounds, as well as the timing of the largest migration of blacks from the rural South to the urban North, have created very different circumstances for African Americans than for the primarily European and Asian immigrant groups who preceded them to these urban neighborhoods.[29]

Others have argued against overdrawing the assumption of social disorganization in these neighborhoods. The poor in poor neighborhoods are often more active than the poor in other neighborhoods, and a "sense of community" was found to be a powerful predictor of political participation at the neighborhood level.[30] Further, blacks in poor neighborhoods develop informal neighboring relationships and local self-help networks that are both instrumental and affective, and they continue to use their neighborhoods for both instrumental and social purposes.[31]

There have been several responses to the decline-of-community argument. I will examine three: the "community of limited liability," the model of community as a "social system," and the "community without propinquity." Each, in some way, acknowledges the connection among individuals and groups while simultaneously recognizing a shift in expectations of the role and functions of the local community. In some sense, each of these models suggests that the proponents of the decline-of-community thesis have been looking for community in the wrong place.

## The Community of Limited Liability

The notion that the local community was vanishing was, in Gerald Suttles's words, "wrong on two counts. First it assumed that there was some golden age during which the local community had achieved almost total consensus on its membership and a personal identification on the part of its residents. Second, it assumed that the local community needed the allegiance or recognition of all or most of its members to continue as an influential social unit."[32]

Rather than considering the "natural area," or "urban village," as the primary unit in which local ties reside and on which community identity and action is based, proponents of the community of limited liability envision a different unit. The community of limited liability is a larger area, geographically defined but composed of several neighborhoods, and has an "official" identity—that is, it is recognized internally by residents and organizations and externally by municipal government and other extralocal institutions. Attachment to this unit is contingent, voluntary, and based on instrumental values tied to investment, function, and use as opposed to the affective ties and interpersonal neighbor relations that characterize the natural area, or urban village.[33] Further, individuals attach different degrees of importance and are differently engaged in their local community, and these relationships themselves may shift. "In a highly mobile society people may participate extensively in local institutions and develop community attachments yet be prepared to leave these communities if local conditions fail to satisfy their immediate needs or aspirations."[34]

The nature of residents' membership in the community of limited liability is understood to be partial; this concept of community recognizes the multitude of associations and relationships, within and beyond the local community, that compose the social life of individuals. It does not, however, necessarily replace the natural area, or urban village, as *the* contemporary local community in the urban environment. They are different forms of organization and different fields of activity, and both may still be recognized by urban dwellers. The community of limited liability is more likely than the neighborhood to be defined in terms of the physical territory it encompasses than in terms of relationships with nearby people, but both may inspire a "sense of community." This sense of community in the urban village is based on primarily informal interpersonal ties and in the community of limited liability, on instrumental values—"the protection of status or family needs." The latter is thus more likely to act collectively to protect existing investments or advocate for change through formal channels.[35]

Contrary to the assumptions of the decline-of-community thesis, in communities of limited liability, the extent to which residents identify an area as a neighborhood or community has either remained the same or increased over time.[36] This has been the case even where use of neighborhood services and facilities has declined.[37]

## Social System and Political Economies

Another model, related to the community of limited liability but retaining some elements of the urban village, posits the local community as a social system. Here, the local community is seen as a functional unit in which goods and services are provided and consumed, interpersonal relationships are created and maintained, participation in activities is shared, and the circumstances of local life are held in common.[38] Roland Warren defines five major functions of this local community: (1) "production-distribution-consumption" of religious, educational, and social goods and services as well as conventional commercial and economic activities; (2) socialization, especially through families and schools; (3) social control, both formally through such government agents as police and such other institutions as churches and schools and informally through family and friends; (4) social participation through such formal channels as voluntary organizations and informally through kin and friendship networks; and (5) mutual support, again through both formal institutions and informal networks. The local community is thus defined as "that combination of social units and systems" that provides "the organization of social activities to afford people daily local access to those broad areas of activity that are necessary in day-to-day living."[39]

Similarly, John McKnight speaks of community in terms of functional associations: "the social place used by family, friends, neighbors, neighborhood associations, clubs, civic groups, local enterprises, churches, ethnic associations, temples, local unions, local government, and local media.[40] The local community in this social system model encompasses interpersonal networks, voluntary associations, formal organizations, commercial and economic activities, and involvement in institutions whose fields of activity extend beyond that of the neighborhood itself.

The social system model also stresses the neighborhood's relationship to other units of interaction. The neighborhood or local community is located within a "system of systems"; it contains within it smaller systems not necessarily rationally related to one another and exists as part of larger systems, not in isolation.[41] As in the community of limited liability, membership is seen as variously constructed and not exclusive of membership in other systems. Members of the community are connected to one another as individuals and through association with and membership in informal groups (family, peer groups, patrons, clients), formal groups, and institutions (school, work, religious congregations). These connections in turn link individuals to other and larger systems of activity and identification.

There are thus two levels of integration at work: internal or "horizontal" links among a community's social units and subsystems and external or "vertical" links between these subsystems and systems outside the community.[42] Rather than the "mosaic of little social worlds which touch but do not interpenetrate" that Park envisioned, the social system perspective sees an interconnected and expanding system of social worlds, linked and interpenetrating at numerous points through particular structures and nodes of activity.

The notion that such local units of action should be seen in the context of a political economy provides a backdrop for the community-as-social-system paradigm. Unlike the ecological notion that urban growth and neighborhood differentiation are products of "natural" processes—selection and competition, migratory patterns and market forces—the political economy paradigm sees such processes as mechanical and manipulable, "the result of investments in economic activities and housing, conditioned by government action."[43]

In this perspective, neighborhoods are seen as dynamic, and neighborhood change is subject to the broad external forces brought to bear by virtue of the neighborhoods' "dual nature" as residential areas and units of development.[44] "Land-based elites" compete to develop the land and resources of given neighborhoods. These elites operate with the assistance of governmental authorities to promote growth at the expense of other localities. According to Harvey Molotch, this is a major force behind the "territorial bond among humans"; it is "socially organized and sustained, at least in part, by those who have a use for it. . . . The growth-machine coalition mobilizes what is there, legitimizes and sustains it, and channels it as a political force into particular kinds of policy decisions."[45] In the context of political economy, therefore, community connection among individuals at the local level may exist in many ways and for many reasons but should be seen as subject to the influence of competing interests and external manipulation.

## Network Analysis and the Community without Propinquity

Another response to the decline-of-community thesis arises from the examination of relationships among individuals without regard to group or spatial boundaries, or "network analyses."[46] The community-without-propinquity argument "affirms the prevalence and importance of primary ties, but maintains that most ties are not now organized into densely knit, tightly bounded solidarities."[47] In other words, rather than identifying the nature and extent of community geographically, this argu-

ment looks for community in the aggregation of networks of interpersonal relations. The model places the individual, rather than the place, at its center.

The findings of network analysis suggest that the structure of interpersonal networks in contemporary urban society is multiplex. "Urbanism," says Claude Fischer, "does not seem to weaken community, but it does seem to help sustain a plurality of communities."[48] As the decline-of-community thesis suggests, the proportion of people known by residents—the "density of acquaintanceship"—may be declining, and the number of intimate ties maintained may be relatively low.[49] However, neighbors continue to maintain numerous instrumental ties with one another, exchanging information, favors, and support as well as acting as "gatekeepers" to systems beyond the neighborhood.[50]

Several variables will influence the scope and intensity of individuals' local networks. Most important is residential stability, which influences the formation of locality-based friendships and participation in local activities, which in turn increases residential attachment and social cohesion.[51] The degree of population diversity and the segregation of subsets of the population will also affect the density of acquaintance, decreasing residential attachment and social cohesion.[52] However, the diversity that comes with concentration of heterogeneous populations in urban centers may foster sets of subcultures or subcommunities.[53] The degree to which such subcultures become spatially differentiated by choosing to congregate in neighborhood pockets may in turn increase the density of localized interpersonal networks and the degree of neighborhood attachment. Neighborhoods in which many individuals share a particular lifestyle, for example, or are engaged in particular kinds of local investment, such as home renovation, may foster such attachment, either informally or through formal local organization.[54]

Thus, while some kinds of interpersonal ties extend beyond the neighborhood for most urban dwellers, other such ties continue to thrive at the neighborhood level. The neighborhood or local community may be a less central construct for the concentration of "intimate" ties or networks of "sociability," but it continues to provide a forum for relationships through which information, aid, services, and connection to broader networks and systems are shared.[55]

## THE NEIGHBORHOOD AS A SPATIAL UNIT

Like the natural community and the community of limited liability, the social system and political economy perspectives imply the existence of boundaries that differentiate the neighborhood or local community, and the associations that define it, from its surroundings. Although network analysis does not take such boundaries as given (and individuals may not be likely to think of their kin, friend, and support networks in terms of neighborhood space), sets of interpersonal networks may still be looked at within the confines of a bounded unit such as a neighborhood. Some of these ties will be more important at the neighborhood level than others, but combined with the use of various formal and informal associations, facilities, services, and activities, the neighborhood may still be defined spatially as a viable unit of reference and action.

The geographical boundaries of a set of associations, however, can be hard to fix; individuals may belong to various subsets of the associations and may live at various distances from the loci of associational

activity. Similarly, the boundaries by which formal organizations define their fields of operation are unlikely to coincide perfectly. Although the greatest concentration of relationships and associations will presumably exist within the borders of the unit defined and is likely to "attenuate at its boundaries" without ending there, the act of drawing these boundaries is ongoing and happens at many different levels.[56]

## Mental Maps and Resident Definitions

One way in which neighborhood boundaries are drawn is by individuals as they conceptualize and negotiate their movement through and relationship with their surroundings. Every day, people observe and interpret their surroundings and construct mental maps that guide their relationship to space, their choices of movement, and their approaches to social interaction.[57]

There are several influences at play in constructing these maps. Physical elements of the city are one: the constructed "paths" of movement (streets, bus routes, walkways), the division of the city into subareas defined by physical barriers or "edges" (walls, viaducts, rivers), and the existence of generally recognized landmarks.[58] Social and functional elements also play a role. These include the demographics of an area, the presence of major institutions, the perception of safety or danger, and the relative location and functional opportunities presented by different parts of the city.[59] All of these factors inform individuals' interpretation of space and the delineation of boundaries that order the physical world of the city and help guide their action within it.

The construction of such boundaries is based in part on the degree of emphasis an individual places on the defining characteristics of neighborhood. Four dimensions are particularly important: (1) the neighborhood primarily as a place or unit of space within which various activities occur; (2) the neighborhood as a set of social relationships; (3) the neighborhood as defined by its relationship with one or more institutions; and (4) the neighborhood as a "symbolic" unit with a name and recognized identity.[60]

How an individual defines neighborhood in terms of these dimensions will to a large extent determine his or her view of the physical scope of the neighborhood. Thus, those who define the neighborhood in terms of social relationships are more likely to describe a smaller unit than those defining the neighborhood in terms of institutions. Although residents may stress one dimension over others, their perception of neighborhood rarely focuses on only one. The dimensions of physical space and social interaction, in particular, are nearly always intertwined, and the use of the institutional definition among residents is not particularly prevalent.[61]

How residents define their neighborhood is, in part, a product of who they are—their "social and physical position within urban society."[62] This is true of the dimensions of the neighborhood they are likely to stress, their general perspective of the size and scope of their neighborhood, and the way they construct and interpret particular boundaries. It also extends to the construction of mental maps for the larger metropolitan area.

African-American respondents in one study, for example, were more likely to stress the social dimension of neighborhood than whites (and therefore, presumably, to delimit a smaller area as their neighborhood). They were also less likely to draw on the other three dimensions. The same was true for older people, the unemployed, the unmarried, and long-term residents.[63] In contrast, those "types of residents we might anticipate to lead lives that extend beyond the neighborhood—young persons, whites, the well-educated and employed—define it in primarily territorial (and, secondarily, structural) ways."[64] Similarly, another study showed that those most involved in neighborhood activities, such as socializing with neighbors and participating in club membership, are most likely to provide a social definition of neighborhood.[65]

Regarding size, one study showed that residents of urban neighborhoods tend to define significantly smaller areas as their neighborhood than do suburban residents, although both groups gave equally detailed descriptions, "suggesting that as individuals they seemed to have equally clear images of their neighborhoods."[66] Women, long-term residents, and residents with small children also tend to define a smaller neighborhood area.[67] Still others think not in terms of neighborhood at all, but tend to speak more generally of "where they live" as, for example, the "west side" or the "south side."[68]

The ways in which specific boundaries are drawn are also influenced by an individual's place in and relationship to the larger community. Elijah Anderson, for example, describes the clarity with which a particular street is assigned the status of formal boundary between two neighborhoods. In this case, the street is a clear marker of separation between a neighborhood in transition—racially and economically mixed but becoming increasingly white and affluent—and a poor and primarily African-American neighborhood. The lines between these two neighborhoods are "defined and maintained in different ways by each community."[69]

The meaning and relevance of such socially constructed boundaries may be different for different individuals. One study demonstrated how the difference between maps drawn by black youths in

Boston relate to their different experience and connection with the larger community. For example, although the maps of two children defined a street separating their neighborhood from a primarily white housing project as a major boundary and included detail only from "their" side of the dividing line, the map of one black youth, who attended the Boston Latin School a few blocks away, incorporated with equal detail a larger portion of the area on the other side of the line.[70]

Similarly, a study comparing the mental maps of residents of five neighborhoods in Los Angeles (each neighborhood differing along several demographic dimensions) revealed distinctive perceptions of the city as a whole among these groups. The most restricted representation of the city (providing detail for only those blocks immediately surrounding the respondents' homes) was provided by residents of the primarily Spanish-speaking neighborhood of Boyle Heights. Maps drawn by the predominantly African-American sample from a neighborhood near Watts were also restricted. In contrast, primarily "nonethnic" upper-class respondents provided much more detailed maps of the entire Los Angeles basin.[71]

Given that such mental maps are developed by individuals in response to various social and physical aspects of their environments and that their individual experiences in that environment will inform their perceptions, the degree of consensus that can be reached about any particular set of boundaries is questionable. Some degree of consensus is built through social interaction; thus, some informal boundaries (the border between a neighborhood in transition and a perceived high-crime area, the declared boundaries of a gang's turf) may be acknowledged through informal sharing of information, perceptions, and observations or through active (sometimes violent) campaigns of boundary maintenance. At the same time, boundaries may be drawn by a number of corporate actors—real estate developers, service providers, city planning departments—that differentiate neighborhoods from one another in more formal ways.

### Exogenous Influence and the Role of Organizations

In addition to the ongoing informal processes of mental mapping on the part of individual urban dwellers, several organized groups mark boundaries to differentiate parts of the city from the areas that surround it. These groups may be internal to the neighborhood, as in neighborhood-based or "grassroots" organizations that seek to define (or make clear what is understood as already defined) the boundaries of the neighborhood. The task of boundary definition helps to clarify their constituency and is seen as useful not only for gaining legitimacy within the neighborhood but also for connecting the organization to broader resources in the city.[72] In some cases, neighborhood organizations may push for redrawing boundaries to separate one neighborhood from another, for example, to focus resources on their particular area of concern. They may also mark boundaries with banners proclaiming the name and identifying the blocks included within their purview.[73]

Groups drawing neighborhood boundaries may also be external, such as banks and real estate developers seeking to define new markets or governmental agencies and private service providers seeking to manage the distribution of goods and services to various parts of the city. In some cases, establishing local organizations as representatives of a given neighborhood may be fostered or stimulated by outside organizations (such as government and corporations) in need of information, support, or legitimacy.[74] Researchers also play a role by attempting to aggregate perceptions of individual residents and those of agency heads and leaders of community organizations into composite maps reflecting some collective understanding of neighborhood or community areas.

The specific boundaries defined by these various groups rarely agree precisely with one another and even more rarely agree completely with the perceptions of neighborhood residents. However, there still may be strong agreement between organizationally defined boundaries and resident perceptions of the central blocks within a given neighborhood, with consensus falling off at the outer edges.[75] There may also be reasonable agreement on the name of a neighborhood and the general area it comprises, although several names may be accepted for the same area or portions thereof. Such consensus is often related to clear variations in the physical environment (proximity to parks, the design of streets, the existence of landmarks) and to the income and status levels of the neighborhood.[76]

## Multiple Boundaries and Nesting Neighborhoods

Geographically, the units in which the circumstances and activities of daily life inhere can be "nested," where each member of a community is simultaneously a member of others. Suttles describes one way of looking at such a hierarchical grouping by identifying four levels within a "pyramid of progressively more inclusive groupings."[77] The first is the local network (or "faceblock"), which is constructed individually and has no residential identification. It is composed of a loose network of face-to-face relationships ranging from simple recognition (from using the same facilities, traveling the same paths, and so forth) to various levels of acquaintance.

The second level is the "defended neighborhood" conceived of as a small subsection of the city (which might range in scope from a building in a housing project to several city blocks) that constitutes a "safe haven" for its members. The defended neighborhood possesses a "corporate identity" known to both its members and outsiders and, in some cases, may resemble an urban village.

The third level is the "community of limited liability" discussed above, which has an official identity and a set of officially recognized boundaries. These boundaries are often codified by city planning departments and may, like the defended neighborhood, have symbolic relevance but may or may not have any status as an administrative unit.[78]

The fourth level is the "expanded community of limited liability." These units are variously constructed and vaguely bounded subdivisions of a city, for example, the "east side."[79] Terms for these large areas are little used by most residents; however, they are used in describing parts of a city with known subdistrict (or neighborhood or community area) names.[80]

The boundaries of "nesting neighborhoods" (as units of identity and action) are not easily contained within one another; they overlap on many levels. Boundaries defining the various neighborhood constructions outlined above are further incorporated into and divided by geographically defined administrative units, political boundaries, and service catchment areas. These include school, park, and library districts; police precincts; community-development planning districts; electoral wards; catchment areas for social service providers, community development corporations, citizens' district councils, and other local organizations; church parishes; and so on. For the most part, such constructions cross-cut or subsume rather than coincide with those units recognized by residents as neighborhoods. For certain programmatic ends, however, they do offer some advantages as units of action, such as the existence of clear administrative boundaries and the presence of some administrative mechanisms through which to manage development or provide services.

## EXPERIENCING NEIGHBORHOOD: RELATIONSHIP AND USE

Neighborhood may be recognized, identified, and delineated differently by different individuals, and neighborhoods provide very different contexts for the individuals who reside there. The search for a universal definition of neighborhood may be, as Peter Rossi suggests, a kind of search for the Holy Grail.[81] In addition to the tension between local cohesion and diffusion (the relative importance of individuals' connections locally and beyond the local sphere in contemporary urban society—the tension between "horizontal" and "vertical" links, in Roland Warren's terms), and the multiple ways in which boundaries may be defined, there is the issue of different experiences regarding neighborhood activity and connection among different populations and contexts.[82] In defining the boundaries and elements that compose the urban neighborhood, the questions necessarily arise: Neighborhood for whom? Neighborhood for what?

### Interpersonal Networks and Neighboring Behavior

Just as how individuals perceive and construct the size and boundaries of their neighborhoods depends, in part, on their status in and relationship to the larger society, approaches to neighboring and local interpersonal networks differ for different populations in different contexts. Thus, an individual's neighbor networks and neighboring behavior may vary by gender, age, ethnicity, family circumstances, and socioeconomic status. Such networks are also affected by the neighborhood context in which they develop.

Regarding individual characteristics, the size, density, and nature of such networks depend in large part on the degree to which an individual is socially integrated into the larger society. Individuals most highly integrated (women, married people, people of middle age, people with higher incomes and education) tend to have larger neighbor networks; however, the relationships that characterize these links are generally not particularly intense or likely to involve frequent contact. They are also more casual. In contrast, those less integrated into the larger society (singles, children and the elderly, those with lower income and less education) are likely to have smaller, more intense, and more frequently engaged relationships in the neighborhood. They are more instrumental and substantive.[83] Race seems to play a role similar to socioeconomic status: African Americans tend to have neighbor networks that are both more "spatially proximate" and stronger in that they are more intimate, have endured longer, and are characterized by more frequent contact.[84] In addition to these variables, an individual's length of residence in a neighborhood increases both the size and intensity of neighbor relations.[85]

Neighbor networks and behavior are also affected by contextual circumstances. Just as individuals' length of residence increases the number and intensity of their relationships with neighbors, residential stability of the neighborhood as a whole has a collective effect on the density of interpersonal networks and the extent of residents' social participation.[86] In addition, the built and social environment play a role. One study found that owners of single-family homes could call on a greater number of neighbors for assistance.[87] Another suggests that the density and heterogeneity of settlement in public housing provides "push and pull forces," either presenting greater opportunity and facilitating desire for localized interaction or propelling residents to form networks beyond the development.[88] A third study found that the degree of perceived danger affects neighbor networks in particularly disadvantaged settings by promoting family coping strategies. These strategies seek to increase links outside the neighborhood or residence rather than to develop broad local networks.[89]

## Neighborhood Use and Neighborhood Participation

Just as neighbor networks and relationships are different for different people, the kinds of activities generally supported by different neighborhoods and the extent to which neighborhood services and facilities are used by residents differ among populations. Children, for example, and families with young children (particularly the primary caretakers within the family) are generally less mobile and more likely to concentrate activities within the local neighborhood.[90] The elderly may be equally constrained geographically but may be less likely to make use of neighborhood facilities and services because of more extreme limitations on physical mobility, fear of victimization, reliance on informal personal (especially family) networks, general diminution of social activity, or lack of available or desired services or facilities at the neighborhood level.[91]

The extent to which such differences apply across contexts and population groups defined in other ways is, however, not entirely clear. At the neighborhood level, for example, one study suggests that "only a particular combination of negative characteristics, such as geographic isolation, poverty, and social homogeneity, made for significant concentrated use of local areas."[92] As noted previously, however, in particularly depleted areas (in this case a housing project), a resident may choose to cope by segregating himself or herself from the immediate neighborhood and nurturing links to opportunities outside the neighborhood.[93]

In another example, a recent study of two Chicago neighborhoods shows neighborhood differences in the use of particular kinds of services. In one neighborhood, 75 percent of residents went to church and 81 percent did their banking in the neighborhood, while only 12 percent ate out locally compared with 48 percent, 39 percent, and 14 percent, respectively, in the other neighborhood.[94] These differences may speak to both income and homogeneity. The first neighborhood is almost entirely white, with a mean household income of about $31,000; the second is ethnically mixed (with large African-American and Hispanic populations) with a mean household income of just under $20,000.

At the individual level, another study suggests that higher-income residents, whites, long-term residents, and members of larger households tend to make greater use of neighborhood facilities.[95] The relationship to income here is likely to be an artifact of availability; more affluent neighborhoods generally have available a greater range of facilities and services, and more affluent residents tend to be more aware of and have greater access to such facilities and services.

Residents' involvement in organizational activities may also differ by neighborhood context and individual characteristics. Neighborhoods that are well defined as units, more homogeneous, and of higher socioeconomic status seem to be more inclined to address neighborhood issues through organized means such as community clubs.[96] At the individual level, adults between the ages of 35 years and retirement are more likely to belong to neighborhood organizations and volunteer associations, as are more affluent residents, married couples, and families with children.[97]

Thus, in addition to the variety of ways in which neighborhoods may be identified, recognized, and bounded, different neighborhoods (however defined) provide very different contexts for individuals. Individuals experience their neighborhoods based both on their position in the life course (by virtue of age, marital status, and family composition) and their position in the larger society (by virtue of income, education, employment, and ethnicity).

## CONCLUSION

The preceding review highlights three essential dimensions of neighborhood—the social, the physical, and the experiential—and provides some clarity about the nature of neighborhoods and the elements of their definition. The particular findings that can be distilled concern four aspects of neighborhood: (1) the problems of neighborhood delineation; (2) the nature of neighborhoods as open systems; (3) the relationship between neighborhoods and interpersonal networks; and (4) the ways in which neighborhoods are experienced and used differently by different populations.

First, regarding the problems of neighborhood delineation, it is clear that despite the definitional difficulties involved, differentiated subareas of the city are recognized and recognizable. They have developed and been defined through historical processes and continue to be influenced by circumstance, individual behavior, and the activities of business, government, social service and development agencies, and other corporate actors. However, the delineation of boundaries is a negotiated process; it is a product of individual cognition, collective perceptions, and organized attempts to codify boundaries to serve political or instrumental aims. The attempt to define neighborhood boundaries for any given program or initiative is thus often a highly political process.

Second, neighborhoods are best seen as open systems, connected with and subject to the influence of other systems. Individuals are members of several of these systems at once, and the perceived importance of each affiliation is likely to be situational and changing. Even limiting affiliation to geographically based collectivities, individuals may claim and value membership in more than one at a time. The local community may thus be seen as a set of (imperfectly) nested neighborhoods—a hierarchy of locality constructions—and individuals often recognize such localities by name and are comfortable with more than one name to describe local areas differently constructed.

Third, although relational networks (and particularly "intimate" ties) among individuals are often dispersed beyond the neighborhood, instrumental relationships among neighbors remain common, providing mechanisms through which information and support may be exchanged and links to systems beyond the neighborhood may be fostered. The recognition of a neighborhood identity and the presence of a sense of community seems to have clear value for supporting residents' acknowledgment of collective circumstances and providing a basis and motivation for collective action. In addition, residential stability fosters the development of interpersonal networks among neighbors and, through them, neighborhood attachment and social participation.

Finally, neighborhoods are experienced and used differently by different populations. Regarding experience, those most integrated into the larger society (e.g., women, married people, people of middle age, people with higher incomes and education) tend to have larger, more dispersed, more casual neighbor networks; those less integrated into the larger society (e.g., singles, children and the elderly, those with lower income and less education) tend to have smaller, more intense, and more frequently engaged relationships in the neighborhood. Such organization may also differ across cultures, and the relationship may be curvilinear, with people living in particularly depleted neighborhoods again having fewer intense, frequently engaged relationships within the neighborhood. Regarding use, neighborhoods that are reasonably homogeneous, low-income, and have a fairly high percentage of young people may be the most likely areas for concentrated local use, if the necessary facilities, services, and institutions are available. Again, the relationship may be curvilinear, with populations at both the very high and the very low ends of the socioeconomic spectrum less likely to concentrate their activities within their neighborhoods.

Despite some increased clarity on the nature and dimensions of neighborhoods provided by this review, a central question remains for policy makers and practitioners concerned with using the neighborhood as an effective unit of organization and action. Given the broad range of possibilities for conceptualizing, defining, and acting in (and with) neighborhoods, how might one best define local areas as units

of action for neighborhood-based programs and interventions?

Clearly, there is no universal way of delineating the neighborhood as a unit. Rather, neighborhoods must be identified and defined heuristically, guided by specific programmatic aims, informed by a theoretical understanding of neighborhood and a recognition of its complications on the ground, and based on a particular understanding of the meaning and use of neighborhood (as defined by residents, local organizations, government officials, and actors in the private sector) in the particular context in which a program or intervention is to be based. Such an approach would balance considerations of scale and intended impact with the identification of those elements most critical for supporting a particular change strategy and a knowledge of the social, political, and economic dynamics that provide the context of local life. By providing a synthesis of the literature and distilling its implications for understanding the neighborhood as a social, spatial, and experiential unit, this article attempts to provide the foundation for developing a heuristic framework for considering neighborhoods that might be applied in specific programmatic circumstances.[98]

## NOTES

Research on which this article is based was funded by the Annie E. Casey Foundation.

1. There are several perspectives on the possibilities for and essential elements of promoting collective action at the local level. John Davis suggests that local communities may act "on the basis of interests and solidarities that are endemic to the locality itself," such as to improve services or protect property values. John E. Davis, *Contested Ground: Collective Action and the Urban Neighborhood* (Ithaca, N.Y.: Cornell University Press, 1991), p. 5. David Chavis and Abraham Wandersman suggest that the existence

of a "sense of community" can be a catalyst and can be both cause and effect of local action. David M. Chavis and Abraham Wandersman, "Sense of Community in the Urban Environment: A Catalyst for Participation and Community Development," *American Journal of Community Psychology* 18, no. 1 (1990): 55–81. Charles Tilly stresses that criteria governing other forms of collective action apply to communities as well and that such criteria are more likely to apply in homogeneous communities where conditions favor circumscribed communication and where "control over land. . . is valuable but unstable." Charles Tilly, "Do Communities Act?" in *The Community: Approaches and Applications,* ed. M. P. Effrat (New York: Free Press, 1974), pp. 209–40, quote on p. 213.

2. Howard W. Hallman, *Neighborhoods: Their Place in Urban Life* (Beverly Hills, Calif.: Sage, 1984), p. 13.

3. S. Keller, *The Urban Neighborhood: A Sociological Perspective* (New York: Random House, 1968), p. 87.

4. One exception identifies immigrant communities as embedded within neighborhoods that house several different immigrant groups. Although each community shares a common locality, they form separate units, each defined through networks of affiliation by common heritage, religion, and language. C. Golab, "The Geography of Neighborhood," in *Neighborhoods in Urban America,* ed. R. Bayor (Port Washington, N.Y.: Kennikat, 1982), pp. 70–85. Here, it is affective attributes of community, rather than organizational ones, that drive the distinction.

5. H. M. Choldin, *Sociological Human Ecology: Contemporary Issues and Applications* (Boulder, Colo.: Westview, 1984), p. 243.

6. B. Wellman and B. Leighton, "Networks, Neighborhoods, and Communities: Approaches to the Study of the Community Question," *Urban Affairs Quarterly* 14, no. 3 (1979): 363–90, quote on 366.

7. See, e.g., L. Wirth, "Urbanism as a Way of Life," *American Journal of Sociology* 44 (July 1938): 3–24; G. D. Suttles, *The Social Order of the Slum: Ethnicity and Territory in the Inner City* (Chicago: University of Chicago Press, 1968); W. R. Freudenberg, "The Density of Acquaintanceship: An Overlooked Variable in Community Research?" *American Journal of Sociology* 92, no. 1 (1986): 27–63; C. S. Fischer, "Toward a Subcultural Theory of Urbanism," *American Journal of Sociology* 80, no. 6 (1975); 1319–41; C. S. Fischer, *To Dwell among Friends: Personal Networks in Town and City* (Chicago: University of Chicago Press, 1982); W. J. Wilson, *The Truly Disadvantaged* (Chicago: University of Chicago Press, 1987); R. J. Sampson, "Local Friendship Ties and Community Attachment in Mass Society: A Multilevel Systemic Model," *American Sociological Review* 53 (October 1988): 766–79; and E. Anderson, *Streetwise: Race, Class, and Change in an Urban Community* (Chicago: University of Chicago Press, 1990).

8. B. Wellman, "The Community Question: The Intimate Networks of East Yonkers," *American Journal of Sociology* 84, no. 5 (1979): 1201–31.

9. Z. L. Miller, "The Role and Concept of Neighborhood in American Cities," in *Community Organization for the Urban Social Change: A Historical Perspective,* ed. R. Fisher and P. Romanofsky (Westport, Conn.: Greenwood, 1981), pp. 3–32, quote on p. 5.

10. That the city came to be understood through an organic analogy is consistent with the dominant sociological paradigm of the day, perhaps best exemplified by the works of Herbert Spencer and the translation of Darwinian theories of competition and selection to the dynamics of human society. This worldview reflected the social, political, and economic circumstances present in the decades surrounding the turn of the century, "where the dynamics of privatism and laissez-faire enterprise prevailed." W. P. Frisbie and J. D. Kasarda, "Spatial Processes," in *Handbook of Sociology,* ed. Neil J. Smelser (Newbury Park, Calif.: Sage, 1988), pp. 629–66, quote on p. 632. It was within this epistemological framework that the study of urban ecology developed.

11. R. McKenzie, "The Scope of Human Ecology" (1926), and R. E. Park, "Human Ecology" (1936), both in *Urban Patterns: Studies in Human Ecology,* ed. G. A. Theodorson (University Park: Pennsylvania State University, 1982), pp. 28–34, 20–27.

12. E. W. Burgess, "The Growth of the City" (1925), in Theodorson, ed. (n. 11 above), pp. 35–41.

13. H. Hoyt, "The Pattern of Movement of Residential Rental Neighborhoods" (1939), in Theodorson, ed. (n. 11 above), pp. 42–49.

14. A. H. Hawley, "Human Ecology, Space, Time, and Urbanization" (1971), in Theodorson, ed. (n. 11 above), pp. 111–14; M. J. White,

*American Neighborhoods and Residential Differentiation* (New York: Russell Sage Foudnation, 1987).

15. These three models share some central characteristics and are not entirely incompatible. In his study of American neighborhoods, which is based on census data from 1980, Michael White suggests an integrated model, acknowledging that patterns of urban residential change may differ depending on the issue in question (White [n. 14 above]). Residential distribution by socioeconomic status, e.g., tends to adhere to the sectoral pattern, while distribution by race and ethnicity is clustered.

16. Park, "Human Ecology" (n. 11 above); H. Zorbough, "The Natural Areas of the City" (1926), and W. Firey, "Sentiment and Symbolism as Ecological Variables" (1945), both in Theodorson, ed. (n. 11 above), pp. 50–54, 129–36.

17. Golab (n. 4 above), p. 77; see also D. S. Massey, "Ethnic Residential Segregation: A Theoretical Synthesis and Empirical Review," *Sociology and Social Research* 69, no. 3 (1985): 315–50; and A. Portes and R. D. Manning, "The Immigrant Enclave: Theory and Empirical Examples," in *Competitive Ethnic Relations,* ed. S. Olzak and J. Nagel (New York: Academic Press, 1986), pp. 47–68.

18. Golab (n. 4 above), p. 80.

19. R. E. Park, *Human Communities: The City and Human Ecology* (New York: Free Press, 1952).

20. Miller (n. 9 above); R. Fisher, "From Grass-Roots Organizing to Community Service: Community Organization Practice in the Community Center Movement, 1907–1930," and P. M. Melvin, "'A Cluster of Interlacing Communities': The Cincinnati Social Unit Plan and Neighborhood Organization, 1900–1920," both in Fisher and Romanfosky, eds. (n. 9 above), pp. 33–58, 59–87; and P. M. Melvin, *The Organic City: Urban Definition and Community Organization, 1880–1920* (Lexington: University Press of Kentucky, 1987).

21. Wirth (n. 7 above), pp. 20–21.

22. B. A. Lee, R. S. Oropesa, B. J. Metch, and A. M. Guest, "Testing the Decline-of-Community Thesis: Neighborhood Organizations in Seattle, 1929 and 1979," *American Journal of Sociology* 89, no. 5 (1984): 1161–88, quote on 1163.

23. Wilson, *The Truly Disadvantaged* (n. 7 above); D. S. Massey, "American Apartheid: Segregation and the Making of the Underclass,"

*American Journal of Sociology* 96, no. 2 (1990): 329–57; and P. A. Jargowsky and M. J. Bane, "Ghetto Poverty in the United States, 1970–1980," in *The Urban Underclass*, ed. C. Jencks and P. E. Peterson (Washington, D.C.: Brookings, 1991), pp. 235–73.

24. R. P. Taub, D. G. Taylor, and J. D. Dunham, *Safe and Secure Neighborhoods: Territoriality, Solidarity and the Reduction of Crime* (Chicago: National Opinion Research Center, 1982).

25. Wilson, *The Truly Disadvantaged* (n. 7 above); J. D. Kasarda, "Urban Change and Minority Opportunities," in *The New Urban Reality,* ed. P. E. Peterson (Washington, D.C.: Brookings, 1985), pp. 33–68; and S. Lieberson, *A Piece of the Pie: Blacks and White Immigrants since 1880* (Berkeley: University of California Press, 1980).

26. Wilson, *The Truly Disadvantaged* (n. 7 above).

27. J. D. Kasarda, "City Jobs and Residents on a Collision Course: The Urban Underclass Dilemma," *Economic Development Quarterly* 4, no. 4 (1990): 313–19, quote on 315.

28. Massey, "American Apartheid" (n. 23 above); and D S. Massey and M. L Eggars, "The Ecology of Inequality: Minorities and the Concentration of Poverty, 1970–1980," *American Journal of Sociology* 95, no. 5 (1990): 1153–88.

29. Lieberson (n. 25 above).

30. J. M. Berry, K. E. Portney, and K. Thomson, "The Political Behavior of Poor People," in Jencks and Peterson, ed. (n. 23 above), pp. 357–72.

31. C. B. Stack, *All Our Kin: Strategies for Survival in a Black Community* (New York: Harper & Row, 1974); B. A. Lee, K. E. Campbell, and O. Miller, "Racial Differences in Urban Neighboring", *Sociological Forum* 6, no. 3 (1991): 525–50; B. A. Lee and K. E. Campbell, "Neighbor Networks of Blacks and Whites" (1993, mimeographed); N. M. Bradburn, S. Sudman, and G. L. Gockel, *Racial Integration in American Neighborhoods* (Chicago: National Opinion Research Center, 1970); and A. Lyons, *Tenants in Community: Relationships between People Living in Subsidized Housing and Their Surrounding Communities* (Evanston, Ill.: Northwestern University, Center for Urban Affairs and Policy Research, 1990).

32. G. D. Suttles, *The Social Construction of Communities* (Chicago: University of Chicago Press, 1972), pp. 8–9.

33. Ibid.; Miller (n. 9 above); and A. M. Guest and B. A. Lee, "The Social Organization of

Local Areas," *Urban Affairs Quarterly* 19, no. 2 (December 1983): 217–40.

34. J. D. Kasarda and M. Janowitz, "Community Attachment in Mass Society," *American Sociological Review* 39 (1974): 328–39, quote on 329.

35. Guest and Lee, "The Social Organization of Local Areas" (n. 33 above), quote on p. 23.

36. A. M. Guest, B. A. Lee, and L. Staeheli, "Changing Locality Identification in the Metropolis: Seattle, 1920–1978," *American Sociological Review* 47 (1982): 543–49; A. Hunter, "The Loss of Community: An Empirical Test through Replication," *American Sociological Review* 40 (1975): 537–52; and A. Hunter, *Symbolic Communities: The Persistence and Changes of Chicago's Local Communities* (Chicago: University of Chicago Press, 1974).

37. Hunter, *Symbolic Communities* (n. 36 above).

38. C. P. Loomis, *Social Systems* (Princeton, N. J.: Van Nostrand, 1960): R. J. Warren, *The Community in America* (Chicago: Rand McNally, 1978); and A. D. Edwards and D. G. Jones, *Community and Community Development* (The Hague: Mouton, 1976).

39. Warren (n. 38 above), p. 9.

40. J. L. McKnight, "Regenerating Community," *Social Policy* (Winter 1987): 54–58, quote on 56.

41. E. O. Moe, "Consulting with a Community System: A Case Study," *Journal of Social Issues* 15, no. 2 (1959): 28–35.

42. Warren (n. 38 above), pp. 163–64.

43. D. Bartelt, D. Elesh, I. Goldstein, G. Leon, and W. Yancey, "Islands in the Stream: Neighborhoods and the Political Economy of the City," in *Neighborhood and Community Environments,* ed. I. Altman and A. Wandersman, *Human Behavior and Environment: Advances in Theory and Research,* vol. 9 (New York: Plenum, 1987), pp. 163–89, quote on p. 165.

44. A. Downs, *Neighborhood and Urban Development* (Washington, D.C.: Brookings, 1981).

45. H. Molotch, "The City as a Growth Machine: Toward a Political Economy of Place," *American Journal of Sociology* 82, no. 2 (1976): 309–32.

46. Network analysis provides methods by which the form, nature, intensity, and extent of relationships among individuals and institutions can be formally modeled and quantified. The social network approach focuses on the types of links that define social actors' relationships to one another rather than on the individual attributes of these actors (as does survey research) or on presumably bounded groups (as does institutional analysis). The network approach thus "allows us to dispense with the *assumption* of institutional integration" (J. C. Mitchell, "The Concept and Use of Social Networks," in *Social Networks in Urban Situations,* ed. J. Clyde Mitchell [Manchester: University of Manchester Press, 1969], pp. 1–50, quote on p. 47). This, in Wellman's terms, enables us "to study both ties that do not form discrete groups and networks that are, in fact, sufficiently bounded and densely knit to be termed 'groups'" (B. Wellman, "Structural Analysis: From Metaphor to Theory and Substance," in *Social Structures: A Network Approach,* ed. B. Wellman and S. D. Berkowitz [Cambridge: Cambridge University Press, 1988], pp. 19–61, quote on p. 37).

47. Wellman, "The Community Question" (n. 8 above), p. 1206.

48. Fischer, *To Dwell among Friends* (n. 7 above), p. 264.

49. Freudenburg (n. 7 above); and Wellman, "The Community Question" (n. 8 above).

50. R. S. Ahlbrandt, *Neighborhoods, People and Community* (New York: Plenum, 1984); Lee and Campbell, "Neighbor Networks" (n. 31 above); Stack (n. 31 above); D. I. Warren, "The Helping Roles of Neighbors: Some Empirical Patterns," in *Urban Neighborhoods: Research and Policy,* ed. R. Taylor (New York: Praeger, 1986), pp. 310–30; Wellman, "The Community Question" (n. 8 above); and B. Wellman and S. Wortley, "Different Strokes from Different Folks: Community Ties and Social Support," *American Journal of Sociology* 96, no. 3 (1990): 558–88.

51. R. J. Sampson, "Linking the Micro- and Macrolevel Dimensions of Community Social Organization," *Social Forces* 70 (1991): 43–64; Sampson, "Local Friendship Ties" (n. 7 above); and Kasarda and Janowitz (n. 34 above).

52. Freudenburg (n. 7 above); and Fischer, *To Dwell among Friends* (n. 7 above).

53. Fischer, *To Dwell among Friends* (n. 7 above).

54. E. Crenshaw and C. St. John, "The Organizationally Dependent Community: A Comparative Study of Neighborhood Attachment," *Urban Affairs Quarterly* 24, no. 3 (1989): 412–33.

55. Indeed, Fischer argues that several factors have contributed to a net increase in Americans'

commitments to their localities, despite the likely diminution of social ties—although here he includes not just urban dwellers but suburbanites as well. (C. S. Fischer, "Ambivalent Communities: How Americans Understand Their Localities," in *America at Century's End,* ed. A. Wolfe [Berkeley: University of California Press, 1991], pp. 79–90). In fact, the dispersal of the urban population into low-density suburbs with local governments is one major factor he cites as contributing to the overall increase in commitment. Others include the historical trend toward greater residential stability, the rise of "class-homogeneous neighborhoods," and increasing rates of home ownership.

56. R. P. Taub, *Nuance and Meaning in Community Development: Finding Community and Development* (New York: New School for Social Research, Community Development Research Center, 1990).

57. R. M. Downs and D. Stea, "Cognitive Maps and Spatial Behavior: Process and Products," in *Image and Environment,* ed. R. M. Downs and D. Stea (Chicago: Aldine, 1973), pp. 8–26; and P. Gould and R. White, *Mental Maps* (Middlesex: Penguin, 1974).

58. K. Lynch, *Image of the City* (Cambridge, Mass.: Harvard University Press, Technology Press, 1960).

59. Gould and White (n. 57 above); and Suttles, *The Social Construction of Communities* (n. 32 above).

60. A. M. Guest and B. A. Lee, "How Urbanites Define Their Neighborhoods," *Population and Environment* 7, no. 1 (1984): 32–56; S. H. Haeberle, "People or Place: Variations in Community Leaders' Subjective Definitions of Neighborhood," *Urban Affairs Quarterly* 23, no. 4 (1988): 616–34; B. A. Lee and K. E. Campbell, "Common Ground? Urban Neighborhoods as Survey Respondents See Them" (paper presented at the annual meeting of the American Sociological Association, Washington, D.C., August 1990); and Hunter, *Symbolic Communities* (n. 36 above).

61. T. Lee, "Urban Neighbourhood as a Socio-Spatial Schema," *Human Relations* 21 (1968): 241–67; Guest and Lee, "How Urbanites Define Their Neighborhoods" (n. 60 above); and Lee and Campbell, "Common Ground?" (n. 60 above).

62. Guest and Lee, "How Urbanites Define Their Neighborhoods" (n. 60 above).

63. The respondents in this study were residents of neighborhoods in Nashville, Tennessee.

However, a study of "community leaders," in this case presidents of neighborhood associations in Birmingham, Alabama, presents somewhat different results. Here, black association presidents were more likely to use physical descriptors than were whites. Gender was an even greater predictor. Women were more likely than men to use "human interactive characteristics" as opposed to physical descriptors (Haeberle [n. 60 above]).

64. Lee and Campbell, "Common Ground?" (n. 60 above), p. 8.

65. Guest and Lee, "How Urbanites Define Their Neighborhoods" (n. 60 above).

66. W. G. Haney and E. C. Knowles, "Perception of Neighborhoods by City and Suburban Residents," *Human Ecology* 6, no. 2 (1978): 201–14, quote on 207–8. It should be noted that most of the studies examining issues of neighborhood definition and resident mapping focus on a neighborhood or set of neighborhoods in one particular city and therefore call into question our ability to generalize beyond the specific context of each study to urban neighborhoods. Indeed, another study in a different city found that residents of central neighborhoods were more likely to describe larger areas than were those in peripheral neighborhoods. The difference in the history and physical layout of the cities may provide one explanation for this discrepancy in findings. In addition, resident definitions of neighborhood are highly dependent on methodological issues, such as how the question is asked. Responses concerning the areal size of one's "neighborhood," e.g., had no relation to responses concerning the areal size of the "'part' of the incorporated community" in which a respondent lived (Guest and Lee, "How Urbanites Define Their Neighborhoods" [n. 60 above]). This distinction was not examined in the Haney and Knowles study.

67. Guest and Lee, "How Urbanites Define Their Neighborhoods" (n. 60 above).

68. Identification by neighborhood or community area and consensus on neighborhood names seem tied to class. Highly educated, higher-income people are much more likely to refer to and agree on community areas and neighborhoods by name than are lower-income people (A. M. Guest and B. A. Lee, "Consensus on Locality Names within the Metropolis," *Sociology and Social Research* 67, no. 4 (1983): 375–91; and R. P. Taub, conversation with author, University of Chicago, 1993.

69. Anderson (n. 7 above).

70. F. Ladd, "A Note on 'the World Across the Street,'" *Harvard Graduate School of Education Bulletin* 12 (1967): 47–48, cited in Gould and White (n. 57 above), pp. 31–34.

71. P. Orleans, "Differential Cognition of Urban Residents: Effects of Social Scale on Mapping," in Downs and Stea, eds. (n. 57 above), pp. 115–30.

72. R. P. Taub, G. P. Surgeon, S. Lindholm, P. B. Otti, and A. Bridges, "Urban Voluntary Associations, Locality Based and Externally Induced," *American Journal of Sociology* 83, no. 2 (1977): 425–42; P. Florin and J. Walker, eds., *Nurturing the Grass Roots: Neighborhood Volunteer Organizations and America's Cities* (New York: Citizens Committee for New York City, 1989); and S. M. Combs, *From the Neighborhoods: A Sourcebook on Information and Skills Needed by Community Organizations in Chicago* (Chicago: Chicago Catholic Charities, 1984).

73. G. D. Suttles, *The Man-Made City: The Land-Use Confidence Game in Chicago* (Chicago: University of Chicago Press, 1990); and Hunter, *Symbolic Communities* (n. 36 above).

74. Taub et al. (n. 72 above).

75. Taub, Taylor, and Dunham (n. 24 above).

76. Guest and Lee, "Consensus on Locality Names" (n. 68 above).

77. Suttles, *The Social Construction of Communities* (n. 32 above), p. 45.

78. One example of the community of limited liability is the "community area" defined in Chicago (and analogous constructions in some other American cities), which was delineated in order to "define a set of subareas of the city each of which could be regarded as having a history of its own as a community, a name, an awareness on the part of its inhabitants of common interests, and a set of local businesses and organizations oriented to the local community." Chicago Fact Book Consortium, *Local Community Fact Book, Chicago Metropolitan Area, 1990* (Chicago: Chicago Fact Book Consortium, 1995), P. xvii.

79. Suttles, *The Social Construction of Communities* (n. 32 above).

80. Hunter, *Symbolic Communities* (n. 36 above); and Guest and Lee, "Consensus on Locality Names" (n. 68 above).

81. P. H. Rossi, "Community Social Indicators," in *The Human Meaning of Social Change*, ed. A. Campbell and P. E. Converse (New York: Russell Sage Foundation, 1972).

82. Warren, R. J. (n. 38 above).

83. K. E. Campbell and B. A. Lee, "Sources of Personal Neighbor Networks: Social Integration, Need or Time?" *Social Forces* 70, no. 4 (1992): 1077–1100; Lee, Campbell, and Miller (n. 31 above); and Lee and Campbell, "Neighbor Networks" (n. 31 above).

84. Lee and Campbell, "Neighbor Networks" (n. 31 above).

85. Campbell and Lee (n. 83 above); and Sampson, "Linking the Micro- and Macrolevel Dimensions" (n. 51 above).

86. Sampson, "Local Friendship Ties" (n. 7 above), and "Linking the Micro- and Macrolevel Dimensions" (n. 51 above).

87. C. J. Silverman, "Neighboring and Urbanism: Commonality versus Friendship," *Urban Affairs Quarterly* 22, no. 2 (1987): 312–28.

88. C. Keane, "Socioenvironmental Determinants of Community Formation," *Environment and Behavior* 23, no. 1 (1991): 27–46.

89. F. Furstenberg, "How Families Manage Risk and Opportunity in Dangerous Neighborhoods," in *Sociology and the Public Agenda*, ed. W. J. Wilson (Newbury Park, Calif.: Sage, 1993), pp. 231–58.

90. Ahlbrandt (n. 50 above); and Suttles, *The Social Construction of Communities* (n. 32 above).

91. M. F. Lowenthal and B. Robinson, "Social Networks and Isolation," I. Rosow, "Status and Role Change through the Life Span," and F. M. Carp, "Housing and Living Environments of Older People," all in *Handbook of Aging and the Social Sciences*, ed. R. H. Binstock and E. Shanas (New York: Van Nostrand Reinhold, 1976), pp. 432–56, 457–82, 244–73, respectively.

92. Keller (n. 3 above), p. 106.

93. Furstenberg (n. 89 above).

94. N. H. Nie, *Community Studies of the Neighborhoods of Hegewisch and South Deering* (Chicago: SPSS, 1991).

95. Ahlbrandt (n. 50 above).

96. A. M. Guest and R. S. Oropesa, "Problem-Solving Strategies of Local Areas in the Metropolis," *American Sociological Review* 49 (1984): 828–40.

97. Ahlbrandt (n. 50 above). Again, although the studies provide guidance as to how neighborhoods are defined, viewed, and used by residents and corporate actors, some caution must be raised with regard to the generalizability of their findings. In

addition to the fact that the studies are bound to context, i.e., particular neighborhoods in particular cities, the unit taken as the "neighborhood" in each case varies. In some cases, neighborhood is defined by the respondent, and likely to be affected by the manner in which the question is asked. In others, the neighborhood is defined by the analyst, using various criteria. Examples of neighborhood definition for analytic purposes include the "statistical neighborhood" or census tract (White [14 above]; and C. J. Coulton and S. Pandey, "Geographic Concentration of Poverty and Risk to Children in Urban Neighborhoods," *American Behavioral Scientist* 35, no. 3 [1992]: 238–57); the block (R. B. Taylor, S. D. Gottfredson, and S. Brower, "Block Crime and Fear: Defensible Space, Local Social Ties, and Territorial Functioning," *Journal of Research in Crime and Delinquency* 21, no. 4 [1984]: 303–31); the area within a 15-minute walk from a respondent's home (Sampson, "Local Friendship Ties" [n. 7 above]); school catchment areas and zip code areas (C. Jencks and S. Mayer, "The

Social Consequences of Growing Up in a Poor Neighborhood," in *Inner City Poverty in the United States,* ed. L. Lynn and M. McGeary [Washington, D.C.: National Academy Press, 1990], pp. 111–86); codified composites of resident definitions (R. S. Ahlbrandt, Jr., M. K. Charney, and J. V. Cunningham, "Citizen Perceptions of Their Neighborhoods," *Journal of Housing* 34, no. 7 [1977]: 338–41; and Ahlbrandt [n. 50 above]); and community areas (R. P. Taub, D. G. Taylor, and J. D. Dunham, *Paths of Neighborhood Change: Race and Crime in Urban America* [Chicago: University of Chicago Press, 1984]).

98. For a more detailed exploration of a heuristic approach to defining neighborhood, see Robert J. Chaskin, "Neighborhood as a Unit of Planning and Action: A Heuristic Approach" (University of Chicago, Chapin Hall Center for Children, Chicago, 1997), which builds on the current review and on the experience of a set of 25 neighborhood-based initiatives funded by private foundations.

4.

Alice K. Johnson

# THE REVITALIZATION OF COMMUNITY PRACTICE: CHARACTERISTICS, COMPETENCIES, AND CURRICULA FOR COMMUNITY-BASED SERVICES

## INTRODUCTION

In her "Editor's Introduction to the Journal," Marie Weil (1994) perceives that a grassroots revitalization of community practice is occurring in American society. She notes the success of social and economic development efforts with diverse populations, including inner-city populations, Native American groups, rural communities in Appalachia, and farming cooperatives in the midwest, Maine, and the deep South. In the area of social planning, new community-based initiatives have been sponsored by major philanthropic foundations. The Robert Wood Johnson Foundation and the Pew Charitable Trusts, for example, have provided funds for large-scale Health Care for the Homeless demonstration projects in 19 cities. Subsequently, this community-based approach has been adopted and widely replicated through federal legislation (cf. Johnson, 1995). In an effort to reorganize public child welfare services, The Annie E. Casey Foundation has

funded a major initiative designed to reorganize public child welfare services. One demonstration project, The Family-2-Family Initiative of the Cuyahoga Department of Children and Family Services in Cleveland, Ohio focuses on the development of clusters of neighborhood-based foster care. The project is culturally sensitive, builds on family strengths, and emphasizes a team approach which enables neighborhood residents, foster parents, churches, and schools to interact and support the family as part of the community. Through projects such as this, foundations have "predicated grants for community-based service development and system reform on intensive citizen participation and interagency collaboration" (Weil, 1994; p. xxv). In turn, these demonstration projects have influenced smaller-scale community-based efforts in social change and innovative service delivery on behalf of children and families. Behind this interest in community-based practice is the need to make direct services more effective, accessible, integrated, and comprehensive in the context of the local community where services occur. In effect, these cutting-edge foundation initiatives are pushing direct service agencies to develop a "community-based" approach to service delivery.

At the same time, changes in federal social welfare policy are shifting many federal government responsibilities to state and local levels. The signing of the Personal Responsibility and Work Opportunity Act of

Alice K. Johnson is Associate Professor at the Mandel School of Applied Social Sciences, Case Western Reserve University, 10900 Euclid Avenue, Cleveland, OH 44106-7164 (e-mail: akj3@po.ewru.edu).

The research reported in this article was carried out as part of The Human Resource Development Initiative (HRDI) for Community-Based Family Development Programs. HRDI was funded in 1994 by a grant from the W. K. Kellogg Foundation to the Mandel School of Applied Social Sciences, Case Western Reserve University, Cleveland, Ohio.

1996 has eliminated entitlement programs such as Aid to Families with Dependent Children (AFDC), Job Opportunities and Basic Skills (JOBS), and Emergency Assistance (EA) and replaced them with block grant funds allocated to the states (Freeman, 1996). As the federal government turns social program decision making over to the state and local governments, there is a new opportunity for a resurgence of community practice. In this period of fewer federal resources and more local responsibility, community practice methods "become even more important strategies to find local solutions and to strengthen local communities" (Weil, 1996, p. 490).

Although these moves toward community-based service delivery have not originated from historical community organizations models or processes, this service reorganization requires the type of skills and competencies taught in community practice. These changes represent two major concerns for social work education. On the one hand, direct service workers employed in these agencies usually have not been trained in community work. Consequently, they may not have the necessary skills to competently carry out locality-based initiatives. On the other hand, these community-based service developments may forge actual practice ahead in the field thereby outdating social work education's ability to prepare direct practice students for community-based practice.

This article begins to address these two concerns. First, the article provides a brief overview of the concept of community practice and develops a working definition of "community-based practice." Next, an extensive literature review outlines the characteristics of community-based service delivery and the competencies needed by direct practitioners working in this area. The

literature review applies key concepts gleaned from community practice literature to the concept of community-based practice. The paper also presents community practice curricula and courses that suggest ways of teaching direct practice workers the skills they need to work in the community. Finally, a conclusion section outlines future work for community practice scholars and educators in the area of community-based practice.

## LITERATURE REVIEW

### Defining Community Practice

Prior to the founding of the *Journal of Community Practice,* there was no primary place for knowledge about community practice to accumulate. With a CD-ROM search of articles published in social work journals since 1979 the author located articles on community practice. The computer searched for three sets of words appearing anywhere in the title or abstract of an article. These were "community practice," "community organization," and "community organization practice." To supplement the computer search, the author of reviewed new issues of major social work journals for relevant articles. Recent books on direct practice, macro practice, and generalist social work practice, community organization and social administration also were reviewed for content in his area.

In the literature, the term "community practice" is a generic phrase used to describe several different things. It is used to refer to various types of approaches relating to individuals, families, and groups within neighborhoods, including traditional community organization approaches, community development, social change, and advocacy. For example, "community practice" is used to describe the skills used in community organization (Drolen, 1991), the revitalization of community organization (Reisch & Wenocur, 1986), practice related to work with ethnic communities (Campfens, 1981), an empowerment-based practice model (Dodd & Gutierrez, 1990), behavioral social work practice at a community level (Mattaini, 1993), macro practice (Kurtz & Jarrett, 1985), the exposure of clinical students to community organization roles (Weil, 1982), and practices that unite community development and community psychology (Maesen, 1979). In the *Encyclopedia of Social Work,* community practice is defined as

a wide scope of practice, ranging from grassroots organization and development to human services planning and coordination. Community practice uses multiple methods of empowerment-based interventions to strengthen participation in democratic processes, assist groups and communities in advocating for their needs and organizing for social justice, and to improve the effectiveness and responsiveness of human service systems. (Weil & Gamble, 1995, p. 577)

In the *Journal of Community Practice,* Weil (1994, p. xxx-xxxi) notes that "community practice is the term that encompasses these processes of work with individuals, task groups, organizations, and communities to produce positive social outcomes in community life, human service organizations, and systems." The unifying theme in these varied uses of the term is that practice takes place in the community. Often, the phrase also suggests work with the community.

## A WORKING DEFINITION OF COMMUNITY-BASED PRACTICE

For the purpose of this article, it is useful to differentiate these broader definitions of "community practice" from "community-based" practice. The term "community-based" is used in many ways. It refers to any one of several different techniques, methods,

programmatic approaches, and/or skills related to providing direct social work services in the community. This distinction defines community-based practice as direct service delivery that uses skills traditionally associated with community social work. Encompassed in this definition is the idea that certain macro practice or "community" skills are part of what direct practitioners do in delivering services at the neighborhood or local level. Therefore, community-based practice can be defined operationally as:

a direct service strategy implemented in the context of the local community (geographic area, neighborhood, etc.). It is the integration of direct services with skills traditionally associated with community organization and community development. This integration of selected macro skills with direct practice adds the "community" component to direct practice work—hence, the name community-based practice.

By this definition, community-based practice necessitates a shift from the dichotomous separation of macro and micro orientations and toward an integration of these skills. This is not new discussion in social work (cf., Hart, 1984; Kruzich & Friesen, 1984). Porter and Peters (1981), for example, suggest an ecological framework over a generalist mode of practice for integrating macro and micro social work practice with the idea of community as the basic organizing principle. Systems theory has also been suggested, despite criticisms that it emphasizes direct social work intervention without sufficient attention to the broader contextual and social welfare issues of macro practice (Drover & Shragge, 1977).

## RESEARCH QUESTIONS AND METHODS

As noted, new developments in community-based practice are taking place. Whether driven by new funding opportunities from private foundations or the need to develop locality-based service systems in an era of decreasing federal resources, community-based services are the wave of the future. In view of these changes, what does the community practice literature suggest?

To understand the types of community skills applicable to the reorganization of social services within neighborhoods and local communities, the author computer-searched community practice articles. The search identifies approximately 75 articles published in social work journals since 1979. These articles are reviewed with two questions in mind. What are the characteristics of community-based practice? And, what kinds of knowledge and skills are needed by direct practitioners working in community-based programs? To answer these questions, content analysis is used to categorize the major findings and recommendations of each article. This review of the literature yields six characteristics of community-based service delivery: (1) neighborhood-based and family-focused; (2) strengths- and empowerment-oriented; (3) cultural sensitivity and multicultural competency; (4) comprehensive services; (5) access to integrated services and supports; and (6) teamwork and leadership skills. Relevant knowledge and recommended skills in each of these areas are summarized.

## CHARACTERISTICS OF COMMUNITY-BASED SERVICE DELIVERY

This section summarizes the findings from the literature review. In each of the six areas noted above, the characteristics of community-based service delivery are reported and relevant knowledge and skill areas for social work are provided.

## NEIGHBORHOOD-BASED AND FAMILY-FOCUSED

There is a growing grassroots movement to provide community-based services and support to high-risk young families. Three types of programs include family support programs, community-based early intervention, and clinical infant intervention. Community-based outreach is accomplished by peer-to-peer support through home visiting and building of parent support groups. These programs recognize the importance of informal support systems (kin, neighbors, friends, self-help groups) to family coping and well-being and are designed to engage natural helpers to provide emotional and instrumental help within high-risk communities. Agency barriers to implementing neighborhood-based and family-focused programs include: (1) a lack of services in some geographic areas; (2) inability of providers to bridge cultural, linguistic, and social groups; (3) limited capacity to reach out to families who are unwilling or unable to seek help; (4) non-compliance of families with guidance and referral; (5) difficulty of public services to deal with interconnected problems simultaneously such as the lack of food, poor job skills, low aspirations, and emotional issues (Halpern, 1986).

Four other articles present specific models for neighborhood-based services. Joseph and Conrad (1980) describe a model for integrated services built around the concept of the parish community. This model features natural helping networks and the use of the ecological and life model approaches to direct social work practice. Both generic and specialized service and action efforts are combined. The ecology of the natural parish setting is used to establish linkages with agencies and community organizations as a system for delivering neighborhood-based social services. Price (1987) presents the French model of the global village to restructure services in urban neighborhoods. Informal, cooperatively run, neighborhood-based services serve as alternative "institutions" to meet a variety of human needs. This neighborhood-based model uses potential human resources available in urban neighborhoods. In Canada, a comprehensive model of community-based service delivery features service integration with local public health services, access to services by locating them under one roof, the use of social and community networks, user participation in policy ind service delivery, egalitarianism in the workplace, multicultural practice, and prevention. Services are designed to serve the general population of local communities and their unique needs (Gulati & Guest, 1990). Luckey (1995) proposes an integrated community-based practice approach for HIV/AIDS prevention in African American communities. This multilevel approach is grounded in the ecosystem perspective with the community as the primary target of intervention. It is built upon the active participation in community forums by ministers, small business leaders, and others who work to support the survival of African American culture.

Other articles point out the importance of understanding different types of communities. These include the therapeutic community, geographic community, formal service providers, the intimate community of family, friends (Kruzich & Friesen, 1984), territorial communities (streets, neighborhoods, nations), and common interest communities (religious, ethnic, sporting, etc.) related to feelings of attachment and a sense of identity (Cooper, 1989).

## STRENGTHS- AND EMPOWERMENT-ORIENTED

The most serious theory-building in community practice is occurring around the topic of empowerment. Arguing that casework alienates clients and that ecological and systems approaches inadequately address issues of power, Dodd and Gutierrez (1990) propose a comprehensive model of community practice that uses empowerment as the unifying practice strategy and desired outcome. Based upon how community conditions of power and control affect both individual and community problems, the model focuses on individual growth and development and macro-system change. Interventions take place at the individual, interpersonal, organizational, and community levels and community workers must be able to bridge all three levels of intervention. The model uses three theories of empowerment: personal, interpersonal, and political. "These theories differ from traditional models of community organization practice in that the development of individuals is equally as important as the development of group action in affecting social action and social change . . . [And] the goal of a truly empowering community practice is a combination of these three elements" (p. 68–69).

Bradshaw, Soifer, and Gutierrez (1994) provide a flexible model for combining Alinsky and feminist approaches in empowering communities of color. Depending on a continual assessment of the community context, there is flexibility to alternate between these two approaches. The overall approach depends on strengths and skills within the community. Participatory, collaborative, and democratic processes are designed to identify and develop indigenous leadership. Connecting with the community, developing cultural competence in respect to age, race/ethnicity, class, and gender, and generating cohesiveness within and among communities of color are challenges to community practitioners working in this area. Rosenthal and Cairns (1994) also outline a community organizing approach that builds on the strengths rather than the weaknesses of the community. This model views the community as a co-worker in a process organized around family issues and reducing violence against children.

Another approach delineates how Freire's concepts of conscientiousness and empowerment can be applied to community practice (Reisch, Wenocur, & Sherman, 1981). Ragab, Blum, and Murphy (1981) put forth the idea of the neighborhood organization as a mediating organization whose purpose is the empowerment of the residents. Participatory action research also can be used effectively to empower poor, disadvantaged families, especially women and children (Sarri & Sarri, 1992). Karger and Reitmeir (1983) recommend a skills base relevant to community empowerment for redefining the function of community organization.

Drawing from symbolic interaction, social exchange, and conflict theory, Pecukonis and Wenocur (1994) discuss concepts of self-efficacy, perceived self-efficacy, outcome expectancy, learned helplessness and locus of control. Social learning theory and the concept of perceived self-efficacy are suggested as useful frameworks for motivating disempowered people to take action for their own lives and for the common good. Their paper discusses concepts of personal hopefulness, universal hopefulness, and the concept of collective self-efficacy in promoting social action. The authors provide ideas for working with communities "that possess the skills and resources to change the social order [but] do not necessarily do so, since they may feel helpless despite adequate resources and skill" (p. 19). Rogge (1995) synthesizes symbolic interaction, social cognition, stress and coping theory, resource mobilization, and conflict theory to develop a community practice framework for organizing communities to respond to toxic exposure and other social problems.

Behavior-analytic theory has also advanced to the point that it can apply directly to community practice (Mattaini, 1993). Behavior techniques support a strengths orientation in prompting, shaping, and reinforcing positive community empowerment. The most important competencies required of the behavioral social worker for community practice are: (1) assessment skills, (2) becoming a reinforcer, (3) group work, and (4) monitoring and evaluation skills. This article outlines different behavioral principles and provides examples of their application to community practice. The author concludes that "There is no contradiction between community empowerment and the use of behavioral technology, despite widespread misunderstanding to the contrary" (p. 425).

## CULTURAL SENSITIVITY AND MULTICULTURAL COMPETENCY

Cultural sensitivity and multicultural competency are also highly recommended as necessary skills for social workers in community practice. Gutierrez and Lewis (1994) present a community approach for working with women of color. This model modifies feminist organizing techniques so that gender and race issues can be worked on simultaneously. It builds upon the strengths and coping strategies of women of color, including participation in the labor force, strong ties with family and other women in the community, and strong connection to spirituality. Guiding principles of this model include understanding that diversity is strength, recognizing that conflict characterizes all cross-cultural work, involving women of color in leadership roles, forming small groups with women of color as group facilitators, and supporting separate programs and organizations for women of color. Practitioners who are not members of the ethnic community will have to develop knowledge, skills, and attitudes in cross-cultural practice to work with emerging ethnic communities (Daley & Wong, 1994). To become ethnically sensitive and culturally competent, Daley and Angulo (1990) recommend using ethnography and participant observation as part of an ethnically sensitive approach which respects the culture of different citizen groups.

According to Rivera and Erlich (1981), rigid cultural, social, and economic boundaries segregate many ethnic minority people (Cubans, Filipinos, Haitians, etc.) and the old mobilization style of community organizing will not work with these new minority communities. Work with these emerging minority communities requires: (1) population-based practice which engages more than one ethnic group (Daley & Angulo, 1990), (2) coalition building and collaboration among minority communities, (3) partnerships and mutual learning among professionals and citizen groups, (4) training of indigenous workers and professionals, and (5) practice based on the express needs of the minority community (Rivera & Erlich, 1984). Multicultural community organizing is proposed as a method to develop intergroup solidarity among diverse communities (Gutierrez, Alvarez, Nemon, & Lewis, 1996).

Netting, Thibault, and Ellor (1990) examine organized religion as a driving force within the social welfare state and religious organizations as human service providers. They recommend incorporating content on the activities of organized religion for special population groups into community practice curriculum. Nussbaum (1984) also touches on this theme. He proposes that Martin Luther King's concept of a "beloved community" relates to locality development and social action models of community practice. However, " . . . despite the profound impact of Dr. King and his dream upon the lives of social workers and social work educators, . . . [there is] . . . very little social work literature analyzing the relevance of his social philosophy and strategies, or applying them to either social work practice or education" (p. 155).

## COMPREHENSIVE SERVICES

The literature on community practice points out the importance of five types of services: case management, group work, networking, advocacy, and coalition-building.

## CASE MANAGEMENT

According to Roberts-DeGennaro (1987), case management combines the best ideas of direct service practice with the best ideas of community practice on behalf of a particular at-risk population. Case management integrates aspects of all three of the traditional methods of social work practice: casework, group work, and community organization. Using a systems perspective and person-in-environment approach, the case manager's role is to assist clients with problems in their social systems. Case managers provide continuity, assist in the coordination of agency contacts, and aid the client in problem solving. The case manager works with the client by linking, coordinating, negotiating, and mediating services. To successfully implement a case management practice model, substantial commitment is required from personnel at all organizational levels of social work practice. Although case management without a therapeutic component may be ineffective, direct practice workers still need training in group work and community practice to provide comprehensive case management services. Burghardt (1981) also sees casework and interviewing skills as important interpersonal components of community practice. Building upon the view that case managers engage in direct practice as well as community practice, Wolk, Sullivan, and Hartmann (1994) recommend that the management role of case managers should not be overlooked.

### GROUP WORK

Several scholars note the indispensable nature of group work. According to Bakalinsky (1984), knowledge and skill in small group dynamics is crucial in several aspects of community practice. "The practitioner may at one time or different times be engaged in forming a neighborhood group of low income residents, in staffing an agency board, or in establishing a planning group whose purpose is either the creation of a new service or coordination of existing services" (p. 87). Using literature from social psychology and community practice, Burghardt (1977) argues that a tactical understanding of group dynamics increases effectiveness. Mondros and Berman-Rossi (1991) point out the importance of small group theory in building a group and in analyzing the stages of group development.

Interpersonal skills are as important in facilitating group interaction and group processes as they are for clinical or therapeutic social work (Morton, 1981). Cnaan and Adar (1987) provide a group work model with a checklist to assist students involved in the process. The model describes the basic stages and principal content that groups cover during their progression from a collection of individuals to an active organization that solves problems. The model may be used by field workers, instructors, supervisors, and educators.

### WORKING WITH SELF-HELP GROUPS IS IMPORTANT FOR COMMUNITY WORKERS

Practitioners should know how to organize such groups, link them to resources, and coordinate their efforts with institutionalized service providers (Lauffer, 1981). Competencies are needed in organizing mutual self-help care networks in neighborhoods (Price, 1987) and in developing relationships between professionals, self-help organizations, and natural support systems of nonprofessional care-givers (Baker, 1977). According to King and Meyers (1981), self-help groups augment the effectiveness of service delivery. These authors provide a framework for understanding the characteristics of self-help groups and differentiating between two types of self-help groups-direct services and social action. Five professional roles for community practice workers with groups are described: (1) catalyst in initiating groups, (2) facilitator in on-going groups, (3) consultant to self-help groups, (4) advisory or planning board member, and (5) making referrals to the group.

*Networking, Advocacy, and Coalition-Building.* Weil (1994, p. xxvi) writes that there is a great need in community practice for networking skills so that workers "may engage effectively in coalitions and in public/private partnerships with local county, state, national and international development efforts." Karger and Reitmeir (1983) note the relevance of networking and coalition-building skills in community empowerment. Root (1981, p. 13) predicts that networks will become "increasingly important for pooling information and expertise" among advocacy groups as well as human service agencies. Recent scholarship recommends coalition-building with diverse groups, e.g., business, labor, and church leaders, around common concerns (Mary, 1994). Fabricant (1987) describes community-based practice with homeless persons and suggests that survival needs can be met most effectively through case advocacy services. His paper presents three levels of advocacy for community practice: (1) case advocacy, (2) class advocacy, and (3) organizing techniques. In working with poor and homeless persons, Johnson (1994a) proposes a model of participatory research with grassroots groups. This "scholar/advocate" approach links professionalism and community organizing, thereby providing an opportunity for social work professionals to work for social change. Weiler and Sherraden (1994) also describe a research-based advocacy project on the working poor taught as a seminar at the master's level.

## ACCESS TO INTEGRATED SERVICES AND SUPPORTS

Access to services and community supports is another aspect of community-based service delivery. A key article related to the concept of community practice in this area discusses the critical role social agencies can play in linking people to community resources. Mathews and Fawcett (1979) report on a community-based information and referral system that was developed and implemented in a mid-sized Midwestern city. The system involved used a social service directory, an interagency feedback procedure, and an information referral training manual.

Hart (1981) suggests that community practice workers also have to understand the structure and role of the public sector in service delivery. Two other competencies are the ability "to act upon the complexities of emerging public-private partnerships" and "the ability to analyze and develop policy and programmatic issues" in substantive fields such as substitute care, crisis intervention, day care, etc. (p. 49). Lauffer (1981) posits that the increasing size, complexity, and number of social services will require new competencies in program development and design, interagency coordination, resource orchestration, establishing formal links between service organizations, and skills in responding to new legislation and regulations.

## EFFECTIVE TEAMWORK AND LEADERSHIP SKILLS

Effective, responsible, and participatory teamwork includes professional and paraprofessional work within agencies as well as interdisciplinary and multi-disciplinary work. Gulati and Guest (1990) recommend the use of multi-professional as well as non-professional team members. They note, however, that the tasks carried out by paraprofessionals trained in social work at community colleges are not very different from those carried out by graduates of four-year colleges. Roberts-DeGennaro (1987) reports that para-professionals may be trained for non-therapeutic case management. Mathews and Fawcett (1979) indicate that indigenous community service workers play a critical role in linking community resources and people in need of assistance through a community-based information and referral system. Halpern (1986) reports, however, that the problems and challenges of working with para-professionals in the delivery of community-based services include " . . . infusing family support workers' interventions with 'professional' knowledge, goals, and techniques" (p. 49). He also questions " . . . the feasibility of giving an extra measure of training to lay workers in programs that work with particularly troubled young families" (p. 50).

A project that trained indigenous religious leadership (black clergy and lay leaders) as community advocates and change agents includes four phases: (1) introduction to problems/issues; (2) visits to human service institutions and an analysis of their effectiveness; (3) understanding the role of government in meeting needs; and (4) community organizations tactics and techniques, including such topics as mobilization for social action, participation in coalitions, voter registration, and strategies for social change. An evaluation showed that the participants demonstrated the use of this new knowledge and skills in their organizational activities (McKinney, 1980). Baker (1977) points out, however, a dilemma in developing relationships between professionals and self-help organizations and professionals and local nonprofessional care givers:

. . . [A]ttempts to develop programs effectively making use of the natural talents of these individuals as well as their natural linkages to particular poor minority communities have indicated that a process of professionalization has taken place . . . Changes in goals, values, and styles of living have resulted in these individuals, who were recruited partly because of their close identification with local communities,

becoming as professionalized and alienated from grassroots understanding of local problems as any other professional. (p. 142)

Organizational leadership skills are also important. Underhill (1979) describes a planned change process that emerged from an agency and its constituents. Denver Catholic Community Services developed an interdepartmental team concept of providing neighborhood-based social service centers. That paper discusses implications of the agency process and areas in which problems might occur when developing interdepartmental neighborhood services. In another setting, Weatherley (1978) reports that clinical training alone is inadequate for school social workers.

Besides direct practice skills, students must know how to work on an interdisciplinary team and to understand the administrative (management) and political dimensions of practice. Competencies of direct practitioners in school settings should include "effectiveness in consultation, advocacy, interdisciplinary team membership, and community liaison" (p. 27). Community practitioners also must use themselves as models of leadership. Modeling leadership includes self-disclosure, openness, risk, and admittance of vulnerability on part of the worker (Burghardt, 1981).

Lauffer (1981) recommends the application of new knowledge and technology from other fields and professions, including Delphi, nominal group techniques, force field analysis, and management by objectives. Understanding the use of the media is important (Brawley, 1985/86). Organizational skills in community practice also include task group leadership (Johnson, 1994b), organizational development (OD) skills (Bailey & Chatterjee, 1992; Morton, 1981; Packard, 1992), maintaining neighborhood stability through citizen participation (Blum, Burges, Davis, & Fishbein, 1979), and introducing citizen participation into human service organizations (Katan, 1981).

Inter-organizational leadership skills are important in community-based consortium development. Discussing the differences between coalition-building and consortium development, Bailey and Koney (1995) provide a four-phase framework for community-based consortium development. Community practice workers need to understand the processes and skills of effective consortium development, particularly multidisciplinary and collaborative approaches to community practice. "Many of these earlier efforts were voluntary partnerships, whereas many more recent collaborations are being mandated . . . [as] a condition for funding in today's request for proposals from both public and private institutions" (Bailey & Koney, 1996, p. 604). Weil (1994, p. xxvi) summarizes the great need in community practice for interdisciplinary and interorganizational teamwork. "Leaders, including both citizens and professionals in community practice, need high levels of skills in the basic activities of community practice: organizing and inter-group relations, inter-agency and inter-organizational planning and coordination, coalition building, technical areas of fundraising and budgeting, and increasingly, crossorganizational collaboration, planning, management, and service integration."

## INTEGRATING DIRECT PRACTICE AND COMMUNITY PRACTICE IN THE CURRICULUM

The literature search also uncovered several innovations in community practice curricula in schools of social work. This section describes frameworks for major curriculum revision as well as specific courses and innovative ways to teach community practice skills to direct practice students. This section discusses future work for scholars and educators in the area of community practice and community-based service delivery.

## Frameworks for Major Curricula Revision

A common theme in curriculum development is the need to expose direct practice social workers to community organization techniques to prepare them for community-based practice. O'Donnell (1995) suggests that community organization curriculum be redesigned with a unique curriculum that draws from both macro and micro practice. Macro practice skills include policy development and social agency administration. Micro practice skills include an understanding of human behavior and basic techniques for empowering individuals and groups through a strengths perspective. This encompasses organizing, local leadership development, and community change strategies.

Several authors describe frameworks for major curricula revision. While similar in their attempts to combine direct practice and community practice methods, they propose different organizing frameworks. These frameworks are organized around concepts of multicultural competency (Glugoski, Reisch, & Rivera, 1994), empowerment (Reisch, Wenocur, & Sherman, 1981), service delivery (Frumpkin, 1981), a continuum of practice curriculum (Gamble, Shaffer, & Weil, 1994), feminism (Brandewein, 1981), and the environment (Austin, 1986).

According to Glugoski, Reisch, and Rivera (1994), most social work curricula is organized around a dichotomy that separates social treatment (direct services) from social action (community organization). Built around the mission statement of the school of social work at San Diego State University, a multicultural framework for both micro and macro social work practice is proposed. This framework uses the concept of empowerment to integrate direct practice and social action across the three major components of education: foundation curriculum, field instruction, and research. In the foundation curriculum, social policy courses look at the effects of inequality in the distribution of power and resources to minority communities, especially in service delivery. Methods emphasize the strengths and resources of minority families and communities to determine intervention strategies. Alternative practice methods compatible with the culture of different ethnic and racial groups are presented. Human behavior courses assess the differential life chances among oppressed groups in relationship to their developmental history, the influence of group membership on individual and group behavior, and the behavioral effects of traditional cultural beliefs and indigenous practices. Third World countries often use participatory action research models to empower local communities. Within multicultural agencies, foundation field placement focuses on primary intervention and advanced placement emphasizes the organizational level.

Reisch, Wenocur, and Sherman (1981) incorporate the empowerment work of Paulo Freire in curriculum design. This framework promotes critical consciousness among students by reconceptualizing problem causation in relation to sources of social and institutional power. Faculty/student roles emphasize dialogue and students take an active part in self-directed and peer-directed approaches to problem solving. Particularly for public welfare workers, this empowerment approach "may be the key link to organizational reform and improved service delivery. It may also serve as the main link to increase the power of clients to make public organizations and institutions more responsive to their needs" (p. 111).

Since the majority of social workers provide direct services to clients, Frumpkin (1981) suggests modifying curriculum around a service delivery framework. Content on the operation of service delivery systems and viable strategies for their improved function should be offered throughout the curriculum. Gamble, Shaffer, and Weil (1994) describe a continuum of social work practice which prepares students for practice with a range of social units—individual, families, groups, organizations, and communities. This curriculum at the University of North Carolina-Chapel Hill requires both micro and macro practice experiences in course work and field work during the first year of study. Their research indicates that field work plays an important role in reinforcing macro practice activities. Brandewein (1981) also supports the blending of direct and community practice. She recommends the feminization of community practice by combining content on the women's movement with community organization practice:

The concept of wholistic social work practice calls for macro- and mezzo-practitioners who understand human behavior and small group dynamics and who can utilize interpersonal skills. It also calls for direct service micro-practitioners who understand the social structural forces affecting individual behavior and who can identify and work for the rectification of social problems on behalf of their clients. Overspecialization in one or the other track results in the lack of integration of the individual and (sic) the societal—the personal and the political. This integration is crucial to social work. (p. 188)

An environmental framework can be used in foundation curricula to identify the elements of macro practice that will enhance the implementation of clinical, or micro, practice within agencies. "In transferring the technology of macro practice to the arena of clinical practice, it is necessary to identify the contexts in which clinicians can incorporate relevant aspects of macro practice. The most logical arena for the relevance of macro skills is in the client's environment" (Austin, 1986, p. 36). Four major environmental dimensions include the agency, the functional community of the client, the service delivery network, and the social policy issues affecting the client. Depending on the environment and the reason for intervention, practice roles of organizational changer, network developer, broker, resource developer, policy advocate, and consultant emerge.

While these roles are treated as distinct entities, there is considerable overlap in practice. For example, a worker who determines that many clients coming to the agency are without adequate housing, may advocate within the agency for a new program for homeless clients to stimulate self-help activities (network/developer), write a proposal to a local foundation to get funds to set up an information transfer service (resource developer), work with local agencies to design a uniform referral method (broker), give speeches in the community on the problem of homelessness (consultant), and testify before a legislative committee to press for funds to create emergency housing facilities (policy advocate). Each of the interventions can be aimed at effecting changes in any of the four major environments. The knowledge and skills required for these interventions can be found, in large part, within the arena of macro practice (p. 37).

## Descriptions of Model Courses

The literature search on community practice identified ten articles which describe specific courses to teach community prac-

tice skills to direct practice students. These courses are similar in that they require a mix of classroom participation and social investigation in the community. Each course also requires students to work together on a group project.

Drolen (1991) describes a required undergraduate course (30 hours field education) that introduces students to the idea of community practice. As part of the course, field agencies are asked to provide students with the opportunity to work on a social or community issue that affects client functioning. A description of three student projects is provided. The author concludes that involving students in direct and deliberate macro intervention on the part of agencies is different than traditional micro practice in agencies which may consist only of inter-agency referrals, collateral visits, and patient advocacy.

Sherraden's (1993) foundation course for undergraduate students is designed to provide direct practice social workers with knowledge and skills in community practice. Her course uses a strengths perspective, empowerment, and self-determination concepts in the design of a case study of the local community. Students work in groups to complete five exercises: community observation, analysis of census materials, interviews with key informants, analysis of community history and resources, and proposals for change. Segal's (1989) course also involves practical "hands-on" experience to learn a mix of planning, policy development, social action, and administration. In this teaching model, students choose an area of social need through community analysis and proceed to develop advocacy strategies and program planning over the course of the semester. Community practitioners are an integral part of the experiential model and contribute to the students' learning.

Weil (1982) describes a master's level course designed to involve clinical students enrolled in a family and children's services concentration in macro practice. A community advisory committee and intensive faculty collaboration are integral parts of the curriculum development process. The course explores the continuum of services needed by families, gaps in services, collaborative planning and service design, and the development and coordination of resources. Teaching methods stress active learning experiences, simulations, and role development exercises. An evaluation shows the course is helpful to students in embracing community practice roles.

Action-oriented, experiential learning in the community fosters skill development in community practice. In a course designed to teach family policy, students develop group projects focusing on advocacy, policy development, planning, and social change in the community. Community practice skills include written and oral communication through public testimony and the media (Rocha & Johnson). Alcorn and Morrison (1994) report on a community planning project undertaken by a school of social work. Through this experiential learning project, students participate in organizing and implementing three town meetings.

Johnson (1994b) outlines a "policy-practice" course for teaching macro skills to direct practice social workers. An organizational model of task group development is used to form a task force within the classroom. In this example, students assume various task force member roles and investigate a social problem in the local community. The article describes the process of implementing the task force model in the classroom and describes instructor and student roles. Alexander (1994) also describes an innovative teach-

ing model applied to homelessness in a rural area. Students study research and interview service providers as a way of understanding unmet needs and existing social service interventions. Plans and strategies ranging from micro to macro practice are developed. Weiler and Sherraden (1994) describe another successful example of project-based scholarship, community work, and informational advocacy. In this graduate course, students worked with an existing advocacy organization on a research-based advocacy project on the working poor. All class members participate in data gathering, interviewing, and report writing. Findings are published and distributed by a state-wide advocacy organization.

## SUMMARY AND CONCLUSIONS

Drawing from the literature on community practice, this article has provided a working definition of community-based practice. Through an inductive approach, the characteristics and competencies recommended by scholars and educators writing in the area of community practice have been summarized. Six areas that apply to community-based practice have been outlined, including: (1) neighborhood-based and family-focused, (2) strengths- and empowerment-oriented, (3) cultural sensitivity and multicultural competency, (4) comprehensive services, (5) access to integrated services and supports, and (6) teamwork and leadership skills. This review has also summarized suggestions for major curricula revision in the area of community practice. Several authors have provided curricula designs that blend direct practice and community practice skills. These frameworks use many concepts including multicultural, empowerment, service delivery, a continuum of practice curriculum, feminism, and environmental. In addition, examples of courses that teach community practice skills to direct practice students are outlined. Typically, these courses require a mix of classroom participation and social investigation in the community and require students to work together on some kind of a group project. In summary, the amount and depth of information about community practice that has been obtained through this computerized word search is remarkable. However, to more fully understand community-based service delivery and how community practice applies to this area, much more work is needed.

First, recent changes in federal policy which shift the responsibility for entitlement programs to state and local governments require a research agenda that takes the community context into account (Coulton, 1996). As the new rules of this social contract are implemented, research on community practice is imperative. MacNair's (1996) recent article which outlines different types of research methods applicable for community practice and Brzuzy and Segal's (1996) article which proposes community-based research strategies applicable to student involvement are important and necessary markers for future research. Specifically, further work is necessary to clarify and test the working definition of community-based practice developed for the purpose of this article. Case studies and other types of research that describe and evaluate reform-oriented, direct service initiatives from a community practice point-of-view are required. This research should focus on agency-based organizations that make services more effective, accessible, integrated, and comprehensive for children, families, and vulnerable populations within local communities.

Second, in the reorganization of services toward community-based ventures, the type of competencies typically found in community practice become increasingly important. Assessing the competencies of direct practice social workers working in community-based service delivery is necessary. The use of competency-based approaches such as those developed for child welfare workers (cf., Bernotavicz, 1995; Hughes & Rycus, 1989) may provide some direction for research in this area. Knowledge of existing competencies is important for the continuing education of current workers and for developing curricula and courses that prepare students to work in community-based programs. For example, knowledge and skills in task groups, links with self-help organizations, the inclusion of paraprofessional workers, and the creation and development of community-based consortia are.just a few of the areas recommended for competent community practice. These skill areas need further attention since they probably are not covered in most macro curriculum and are taught even less often in direct practice education.

Third, this literature review can inform the development of community-based services. In addition, it can serve as a qualitative checklist for education in community practice. For example, social work educators can use the review to assess how well community practice curricula in their respective schools cover content and skills suggested by scholars who write in the area of community practice. To further assess this situation, a survey might be undertaken of the type of community practice curricula in place nationwide. Also, a survey of graduates of the type outlined by Gamble, Shaffer, and Weil (1994) might be undertaken to understand how well existing curricula at schools of social work in the United States prepare students for community practice and community-based practice roles.

Fourth, to revitalize community practice, researchers, practitioners, and educators in community practice should strive to locate their scholarship within the *Journal of Community Practice*. This will establish the journal as the repository for knowledge-building in this area. The Association for Community Organization and Social Administration (ACOSA), whose founding members initiated the *Journal of Community Practice*, might also take a leadership role in reaching out to community-based practitioners for membership. Although many of these workers were trained in direct practice, the requirements of their jobs in community-based service delivery now may well contribute to the revitalization of community practice in the next century.

## REFERENCES

Alcorn, S., & Morrison, J.D. (1994). Community Planning That Is "Caught" And "Taught": Experiential Learning From Town Meetings. *Journal of Community Practice, 1*(4), 27–43.

Alexander, G. (1994). Project Homeless: A Model For Student Involvement in Community Change. *Journal of Community Practice, 1*(3), 143–149.

Austin, M.J. (1986). Community Organization And Social Administration: Partnership Or Irrelevance? *Administration in Social Work, 10*(3), 27–39.

Bailey, D., & Chatterjee, P. (1992). Organizational Development And Community Development: True Soulmates Or Uneasy Bedfellows? *Journal of Sociology and Social Welfare, XIX*(2), 1–21.

Bailey, D., & Koney, K.M. (1995). Community-Based Consortia: One Model For Creation And Development. *Journal of Community Practice, 2*(1), 21–42.

Bailey, D., & Koney, K.M. (1996). lnterorganizational Community-Based Collaboratives:

A Strategic Response To Shape The Social Work Agenda. *Social Work, 41*(6), 602–611.

Bakalinsky, R. (1984). The Small Group In Community Organization Practice. *Social Work with Groups, 7*(2), 87–96.

Baker, F. (1977). The Interface Between Professional And Natural Support Systems. *Clinical Social Work Journal, 5*(2), 139–148.

Bernotavicz, F. (1995). A New Paradigm For Competency-Based Training. *Journal of Continuing Social Work Education, 6*(2), 3–9.

Blum, A., Burges, B., Davis, J., & Fishbein, P. (1979). Assessing Community Organizing: Issues And Approaches. *Journal of Applied Social Sciences, 3*(2), 122–148.

Bradshaw, C., Soifer, S., & Gutierrez, L. (1994). Toward A Hybrid Model For Effective Organizing In Communities Of Color. *Journal of Community Practice, l*(1), 25–41.

Brandewein, R.A. (1981). Toward The Feminization Of Community And Organization Practice. *Social Development Issues, 5*(2–3):180–199.

Brawley, E.A. (1985/86). The Mass Media: A Vital Adjunct To The New Community And Administrative Practice. *Administration in Social Work, 9*(4), 63–73.

Brzuzy, S., & Segal, E.A. (1996). Community-Based Research Strategies For Social Work Education. *Journal of Community Practice, 3*(1), 59–69.

Burghardt, S. (1977). A Community Organization Typology Of Group Development. *Journal of Sociology & Social Welfare, 4*(7), 1086–1108.

Burghardt, S. (1981). Leadership Development For The 80's: Resolving The Contradictions. *Social Development Issues, 5*(2–3):18–32.

Campfens, H. (1981). Community Practice Related to Ethnicity. *Social Development Issues, 5*(2–3):74–89.

Clapp, J.D. (1995). Organizing Inner City Neighborhoods To Reduce Alcohol And Drug Problems. *Journal of Community Practice, 2*(1), 43–60.

Cnaan, R.A., & Adar, H. (1987). An Integrative Model For Group Work In Community Organization Practice. *Social Work with Groups, 10*(3):5–24.

Cooper, J. (1989). From Casework To Community Care: 'The End Is Where We Start From' (T.S. Eliot). *British Journal of Social Work, 19*(3), 177–188.

Coulton, C.J. (1996). Poverty, Work, And Community: A Research Agenda For An Era Of Diminishing Federal Responsibility. *Social Work, 41*(5), 509–519.

Daley, J.M., & Angulo, J. (1990). People Centered Community Planning. *Journal of the Community Development Society, 21*(2), 88–103.

Daley, J.M., & Wong, P. (1994). Community Development With Emerging Ethnic Communities. *Journal of Community Practice, 1*(l), 9–24,

Dodd, P., & Gutierrez, L. (1990). Preparing Students For The Future: A Power Perspective On Community Practice. *Administration in Social Work, 14*(2), 63–78.

Drolen, C.S. (1991). Teaching Undergraduate Community Practice: An Experiential Approach. *Journal of Teaching in Social Work, 5*(l), 35–47.

Drover, G., & Shragge, E. (1977). General Systems Theory And Social Work Education: A Critique. *Canadian Journal of Social Work Education, 3*(2), 28–39.

Fabricant, M. (1987). Creating Survival Services. *Administration in Social Work, 10*(3), 71–84.

Freeman, E.M. (1996). Welfare Reforms And Services For Children And Families: Setting A New Practice, Research, And Policy Agenda. *Social Work, 41*(5), 521–532.

Frumpkin, M. (1981). Organizing Ourselves: The Role Of Community Organization In Social Work Education. *Social Development Issues, 5*(2–3): 194–199.

Gamble, D.N., Shaffer, G.L., & Weil, M.O. (1994). Assessing The Integrity Of Community Organization And Administration Content In Field Practice. *Journal of Community Practice, 1*(3), 73–92.

Glugoski, G., Reisch, M., & Rivera, F.G. (1994). A Holistic Ethno-Cultural Paradigm: A New Model For Community Organization Teaching And Practice. *Journal of Community Practice, 1*(l), 81–98.

Gulati, P., & Guest, G. (1990). The Community-Centered Model: A Garden-Variety Approach Or A Radical Transformation Of Community Practice? *Social Work, 35*(1), 63–68.

Gutierrez, L., Alvarez, A.R., Nemon, H., & Lewis, E.A. (1996). Multicultural Community Organizing: A Strategy For Change. *Social Work, 41*(5), 501–508.

Gutierrez, L.M., & Lewis, E.A. (1994). Community Organizing With Women Of Color: A Feminist Approach. *Journal of Community Practice, 1*(2), 23–44.

Halpern, R. (1986). Community-Based Support For High Risk Young Families. *Social Policy, 17*(l), 17–18, 47–50.

Hart, A.F. (1984). Clinical Social Work And Social Administration: Bridging The Culture Gap. *Administration in Social Work, 8*, 71–78.

Hart, A.F. (1981). Community Organization, Social Planning And Public Social Services. *Social Development Issues, 5*(2–3): 47–51.

Hughes, R.C., & Rycus, J.S. (1989). Target: Competent Staff, Competency-Based In-Service Training For Child Welfare. Washington, DC: Child Welfare League of America.

Johnson, A.K. (1994a). Linking Professionalism And Community Organization: A Scholar/Advocate Approach. *Journal of Community Practice, 1*(2), 65–86.

Johnson, A.K. (1994b). Teaching Students The Task Force Approach: A Policy-Practice Course. *Journal of Social Work Education, 30*(3), 336–347.

Joseph, M.V., & Conrad, A.P. (1980). A Parish Neighborhood Model For Social Work Practice. *Social Casework, 61*(7), 423–432.

Karger, H.J., & Reitmeir, M.A. (1983). Community Organization For The 1980's: Toward Developing A New Skills Base Within A Political Framework. *Social Development Issues, 7*(2), 50–62.

Katan, Y. (1981). Patterns Of Client Participation In Local Human Service Organizations: Conceptual And Operational Considerations. *Social Development Issues, 5*(2–3):134–150.

King, S.W., & Meyers, R.S. (1981). Developing Self-Help Groups: Integrating Group Work And Community Organization Strategies. *Social Development Issues, 5*(2–3): 33–45.

Kruzich, J.M., & Friesen, B.J. (1984). Blending Administrative And Community Organization Practice: The Case Of Community Residential Facilities. *Administration in Social Work, 8*(4), 55–66.

Kurtz, L.F., & Jarrett, H.H. (1985). Teaching Macro Practice And Theory In BSW Programs. *Arete, 10*(l), 33–40.

Lauffer, A. (1981). Reorganizing Community Organization: Notes On Changes In Practice

And Needed Changes In The Graduate Social Work Curriculum. *Social Development Issues, 5*(2–3):166–179.

Luckey, I. (1995). HIV/AIDS Prevention In The African American Community: An Integrated Community-Based Practice Approach. *Journal of Community Practice, 2*(4), 71–90.

MacNair, R.H. (1996). A Research Methodology For Community Practice. *Journal of Community Practice, 3*(2), 1–19.

Maesen, W.A. (1979). Community Psychology And Community Development: A Focus On Mutual Concerns. *Journal of the Community Development Society, 10*(2), 117–121.

Mary, N.L. (1994). Social Work, Economic Conversion, And Community Practice: Where Are The Social Workers? *Journal of Community Practice, 1*(4), 7–25.

Mathews, R.M., & Fawcett, S.B. (1979). A Community-Based Information And Referral System. *Journal of the Community Development Society, 10*(2), 13–25.

Mattaini, M.A. (1993). Behavior Analysis And Community Practice: A Review. *Research on Social Work Practice, 3*(4), 420–447.

McKinney, E.A. (1980). A School Of Social Work Trains Urban Indigenous Leadership In Cleveland. *Community Development Journal, 15*(3), 200–207.

Mondros, J.B., & Berman-Rossi, T. (1991). The Relevance Of Stages Of Group Development Theory To Community Organization Practice. *Social Work with Groups 14*(3/4), 203–221.

Morton, T.D. (1981). Organizational Development As A Variant Of Community Development. *Social Development Issues, 5*(2–3):90–98.

Netting, F.E., Thibault, J.M., & Ellor, J.W. (1990). Integrating Content On Organized Religion Into Macropractice Courses. *Journal of Social Work Education, 26*(1), 15–24.

Nussbaum, D. (1984). Social Work Education In The Beloved Community. *Smith College Studies in Social Work, 54*(3), 155–165.

O'Donnell, S.M. (1995). Is Community Organizing "The Greatest Job" One Could Have? Findings From A Survey Of Chicago Organizers. *Journal of Community Practice, 2*(1), 1–19.

Packard, T. (1992). Organizational Development Technologies In Community Development. *Journal of Sociology and Social Welfare, XIX*(2), 3–15.

Pecukonis, E.V., & Wenocur, S. (1994). Perceptions Of Self And Collective Efficacy In Community Organization Theory And Practice. *Journal of Community Practice, 1*(2), 5–21.

Personal Responsibility and Work Opportunity Act of 1996, Publ. L. No. 104-193.

Porter, R., & Peters, J.A. (1981). An Ecological Framework For The Integration Of Practice Methods. *Social Development Issues, 5*(2–3):157–164.

Price, L.D. (1987). Global Neighborhoods. *Social Development Issues, 11*(1), 49–55.

Ragab, I.A., Blum, A., & Murphy, M.J. (1981). Representation In Neighborhood Organizations. *Social Development Issues, 5*(2–3): 62–73.

Reisch, M., & Wenocur, S. (1986). The Future Of Community Organization in Social Work: Social Activism And The Politics Of Profession Building. *Social Service Review, 60*(1), 70–93.

Reisch, M., Wenocur, S., & Sherman, W. (1981). Empowerment, Conscientization And Animation As Core Social Work Skills. *Social Development Issues, 5*(2–3): 108–120.

Rivera, F.G., & Erlich, J.L. (1984). An Assessment Framework For Organizing In Emerging Minority Communities. In F.M. Cox, J.L. Erlich, J. Rothman, and J.E. Tropman (Eds.), *Strategies of Community Organization* (4th ed.), (pp. 3–26). Itasca, IL: F.E. Peacock.

Rivera, F.G., & Erlich, J.L. (1981). Neo-Gemeinschaft Minority Communities: Implications For Community Organization In The United States. *Community Development Journal, 16*(3), 189–200.

Roberts-DeGennaro, M. (1987). Developing Case Management As A Practice Model. *Social Casework, 68*(8), 466–470.

Rocha, C., & Johnson, A.K. (in press). Teaching Family Policy: A Policy Practice Approach. *Journal of Social Work Education.*

Rogge, M. (1995). Coordinating Theory, Evidence, And Practice: Toxic Waste Exposure In Communities. *Journal of Community Practice, 2*(2), 55–76.

Root, L.S. (1981). Theory, Practice And Curriculum: Issues Emerging From The Symposium On Community Organization For The 1980s. *Social Development Issues, 5*(2–3):10–16.

Rosenthal, S.J., & Cairns, J.M. (1994). Child Abuse Prevention: The Community As Co-Worker. *Journal of Community Practice, 1*(4), 45–61.

Sarri, R.C., & Sarri, C.M. (1992). Organizational And Community Change Through Participatory Action Research. *Administration in Social Work, 16*(3/4), 99–122.

Segal, E.A. (1989). Teaching Community Organization In The Classroom. *Arete, 14*(2), 42–47.

Sherraden, M.S. (1993). Community Studies In The Baccalaureate Social Work Curriculum. *Journal of Teaching in Social Work, 7*(1), 75–88.

Underhill, P. (1979). Organizational Change: A Return To Neighborhood Social Service Centers. *Social Thought, 5*(1), 5–18.

Weatherley, R. (1978). Educating For Survival In The School Bureaucracy. *Social Work in Education,* 19–28.

Weil, M. (1982). Community Organization Curriculum Development In Services For Families And Children: Bridging The Micro-Macro Practice Gap. *Social Development Issues, 6*(3), 40–54.

Weil, M.O. (1996). Community Building: Building Community Practice. *Social Work, 41*(5), 481–499.

Weil, M.O. (1994). Editor's Introduction To The Journal. *Journal of Community Practice, 1*(l), xxi–xxxiii.

Weil, M.O., Gamble, D.N. (1995). Community practice models (pp. 577–594). In R.L. Edwards & J.G. Hopps (Eds.), *Encyclopedia of Social Work*, 19th Edition. Washington, DC: NASW Press.

Weiler, M.T, & Sherraden, M. (1994). Classroom And Advocacy: A Project On The Working Poor In St. Louis. *Journal of Community Practice, 1*(l), 99–105.

Wolk, J.L., Sullivan, W.P., & Hartmann, D.J. (1994). The Managerial Nature Of Case Management. *Social Work, 39*(2), 152–159.

5.

Cheryl Hyde

## EXPERIENCES OF WOMEN ACTIVISTS: IMPLICATIONS FOR COMMUNITY ORGANIZING THEORY AND PRACTICE

*I long to hear that you have declared an independency—and by the way in the new Code of Laws which I suppose it will be necessary for you to make I desire you would Remember the Ladies, and be more generous and favourable to them than your ancestors....If perticuliar care and attention is not paid to the Ladies we are determined to foment a Rebelion, and will not hold ourselves bound by any Laws in which we have no voice, or Representation.*
*—Abigail Adams to John Adams*
*March 31, 1776*

The field of community organizing would be wise to heed the words of Abigail Adams to her revolutionary husband, John. Contributions of women activists have been virtually ignored by the field of social work. Consequently, social work has a diminished knowledge base and has alienated large numbers of talented women. Ironically, both the past and the future of community organizing are tied intimately with the action of women. Foremothers include Jane Addams, Dorothea Dix, and Lillian Wald. Current trends suggest that "women's issues," such as poverty, the family, and reproductive rights, will be on national, state, and local agendas for years to come. In order to prepare for the future, we need to understand the talents of the past and present.

This paper explores the experiences of women activists, primarily in the labor, peace, and feminist movements. A number of salient themes, generated in interviews with and presentations by women activists, are identified. Suggestions are made as to

how and why these themes should be integrated into community organizing practice. Given that a personal research goal of the author is to generate a community organizing theory based on the experiences of women, the discussion of themes is preceded by a newly developed analytical framework for collective practice. This project also represents a preliminary attempt to weave qualitative research methods, feminist thought, and women's experiences into an understandable and meaningful whole.

Such an approach is a departure from traditional community organizing theory and practice for a number of reasons. First, critical attention is paid to the impact of gender. Second, women's experiences are considered legitimate and credible, an important factor given that the needs, thoughts, and actions of women organizers are rarely addressed in the literature and in training. Third, the benefits of cross-fertilization are illustrated, since none of the women interviewed considered themselves "community organizers," yet their actions are quite applicable to the field. Finally, the analysis is from neither a community organizing model perspective (Rothman, 1979) nor a "how-to" approach (Alinsky, 1969,

Cheryl Hyde is a professor at the School of Social Work, Boston University.

1972; Kahn, 1982; Speeter, 1978; Staples, 1984). Rather a wholistic approach is presented that focuses on the "how" or process of organizing instead of the "what" or product of organizing. Important work along this line has been done by Brandwein (1981), Burghardt (1982), Freire (1974), Galper (1980), and Galper and Mondros (1980).

## BACKGROUND AND CONTEXT

This project reflects much of the author's thoughts and experiences as a feminist activist. This experience includes legal advocacy for women, labor education, and, currently, consciousness-raising workshops on unlearning or confronting the "Isms"—racism, sexism, heterosexism, classism, ageism, and handicapism. Much feminist analysis has been brought to bear on this project. A complete discussion on feminist scholarship, however, is beyond the scope of this paper. Nonetheless, the women's movement is a rich, yet uncultivated area for community organizing. The reference section of this paper includes a number of sources that ought to be incorporated into community organizing curricula. For the purposes of this paper, many basic tenets of feminist thought are seen in the identification of salient themes.

A nonpositivist, qualitative research approach was selected because this methodology seemed best suited for women to define their reality, rather than it being imposed upon them. The analysis is based primarily on interviews with and presentations by women activists (listed at the end of the paper). The interviews were open-ended, and much of the richness in the material results from "chasing tangents." Five issues, however, were raised in all of the interviews: (1) Reasons for becoming an activist; (2) How organizing is accomplished; (3) Structure of the organization; (4) Gender dynamics within the organization; and (5) Type of training. Additional interviews and relevant material published in a variety of social-change oriented journals supplement the analysis.

Although this paper focuses on the experiences of women activists, its application should not be limited to a female audience. The purpose of this project is defeated if the results are not considered in an integrative fashion. For a variety of reasons, including sex-role sterotyping and "either-or" analytical frameworks, there exists the temptation to dichotomize the findings. By way of a warning, two dichotomies should be mentioned: male versus female styles, and process versus product orientations. Each shall be considered briefly.

There is a growing body of literature, particularly in the area of group development, on male and female styles of leadership, power, and authority. Within this literature there is general agreement that masculine and feminine styles do exist. Furthermore, masculine styles are typified by aggressive, task-focused, and competitive traits, and feminine styles are typified by passive, interpersonal-focused, and cooperative traits (Bokemeier & Tate, 1980; Brandwein, 1981; Gilligan, 1982; Hyde, 1983; Johnson, 1976; Reed, 1981; Van Wagner & Swanson, 1979). The community organizing field needs to be attentive to these different styles, for in varying degrees they have implications for the recruitment and training of both practitioners and constituents. Reed (1981) suggests three areas in which gender differences influence the training of group leaders: assumptions about gender-related behaviors, gender composition of groups, and a group's reaction to female leaders. It is her contention, shared by others, that these issues surrounding gender need to be brought to the forefront of a training experience. Failure to acknowledge or plan for them could undermine the overall goal of the group.

The existence of masculine and feminine styles, however, does not mean that they are intrinsic traits (Brandwein, 1981:189). Many feminine traits, however, do emerge in the themes presented below. Therefore, they receive what may appear to be a lopsided emphasis, especially given that the community organizing field is seen as having a masculine orientation. This study does not conclude, however, that women are the only people capable of nurturance, emotions, and other feminine actions, nor that their behavior is limited to these traits. Such conclusions limit both women and men. As one woman involved in the peace movement states:

The notion that women are more nurturing and, therefore, should participate to save the earth is usually sexist. That's our sex role stereotype. The fact is that everyone has the capacity to nurture. That women have been socialized to do so is a reality, and it's an asset we have going for us. But at the same time we recognize it as a strength, we must deplore it as a mandate. If that's done, then I think we're talking feminism. (Popkin & Delgado, 1982:40)

Community organizing would be enhanced if a greater integration of masculine and feminine characteristics occurred. For this to happen, organizers need to be aware of these different traits, to stop dismissing feminine traits as weak and ineffective, and to encourage both men and women to acquire a more integrative style in their organizing.

A second dichotomy, often viewed as a component of the male-female split, is between process and task (or process and product). Crow (1978) and Riddle (1978) provide thoughtful discussions on the damaging impact that this dichotomization has

on organizing and social change efforts. A process orientation focuses on *how* things are accomplished and attention is paid to the development of trust, sensitivity, empathy, and support among group members. A product orientation focuses on *what* things get accomplished and attention is paid to the efficiency, action, rational order, and task completion. There are strengths and weaknesses in both approaches and a savvy organizer needs to determine a balance. There is a distinct bias, however, in this paper toward a process orientation. This is partly due to the emphasis placed on process by the women activists. It is also a reaction to the lopsided product/task orientation found within community organizing. Here again, the ideal would be an integration of process and product.

## EMERGING PARADIGM

As stated above, one goal of this project was to develop a paradigm that would prove useful for future analysis. This paradigm would emerge from and reflect the experiences of women activists, suggest a wholistic approach to community organizing, and relate all components to one another rather than force a linear or causal ordering. The result is referred to as a Wholistic Collective Practice Paradigm, illustrated in Fig. 5.1.

The four dimensions, subjective, relational, strategic, and structural, represent different concerns or levels within collective practice. Briefly, definitions for these dimensions are:

*Structural:* Focuses on the organization, its purpose, development, apparatus, and positions. Also focuses on connections between organizations.

*Strategic:* Action aspects of practice, with emphasis placed on the strategy as a

FIGURE 5.1
Wholistic Collective Practice Paradigm

Strategic

Structured

Subjective

Relational

process. Tactical steps are considered a sub-unit of this dimension.

*Relational:* Focuses on the relationships between people-people and people-organization. Stresses the collectivity, its origin, maintenance, and growth. Also focuses on the process of others engaging in strategies.

*Subjective:* Introspective or reflexive statements by the individual (such as the organizer). Captures the assessments, interpretations, and opinions of the individual. This transcends all dimensions.

Collective practice, such as mobilizing or organizing, is the process of connecting these four dimensions toward the goal of some form of intervention or social change. All of these dimensions are connected to or interdependent upon one another. No dimension is more important to the process than another, although at a given point in time one may have greater emphasis placed upon it. This paradigm can be envisioned as a mobile trying to balance its parts.

Within each of these dimensions are themes that specifically relate to the experiences of women organizers. There is considerable overlap, in that a theme is not constrained to one dimension. In fact, the power of this paradigm is that it forces us to consider that an act has implications on a variety of levels. For example, when an organizer considers a fundraising effort, she/he needs to consider the organizational structure, pre and post effort, the steps involved, the opinions, desires, and skills of

the collective and individual concerns. While the development of this paradigm is in its preliminary stage, it may provide a new frame of reference or a way of thinking about or analyzing community organizing efforts. It conveys the importance of considering a variety of dimensions simultaneously (a difficult notion to grasp, see Boulet, 1981). Furthermore, it suggests that the practitioner needs to allow the group to define its own reality, rather than imposing a predetermined, ordered plan upon it.

A number of themes appear consistently and without prompting in the descriptions of the experiences of the women interviewed. At the very least, these themes should be seriously considered in relation to current community organizing practice. A process by which these themes can be integrated into practice is important. Hopefully, these themes, and the dimensions, will serve as a foundation for the generation of a new community organizing theory.

**THEMES**

*(1) The Wholistic Organizer.* Many of the women activists stated that to be an organizer meant to involve oneself fully. One woman stated it quite eloquently: "What is my view of social change? It is a wholistic approach. It involves all, the spiritual, actions and intellect. It is engagement" (KL). This notion of total engagement or investment was echoed by others. Considerable attention was paid to personal investment and to the alienation felt when emotions were denied. Thus, an organizing effort should not focus solely on what is being done. It also needs to incorporate the intellectual and emotional needs of individuals and the collective.

The wholistic organizer should not be equated with the organizer who does everything. Alinsky believed that an organizer needs to be adept at all phases, yet this creates a power dynamic between organizer and group that many of the women felt unnecessary and detrimental. First, it places too much emphasis on the organizer as expert, a pressure that often leads to burnout and disinvestment. It also suggests that the group becomes too dependent on the organizer's expertise and will be unable to function once the organizer leaves the setting. Second, it closes a door for the organizer in terms of her or his own learning. There was overwhelming sentiment that while an organizer can offer something to the organizing effort, the effort serves as an educational experience for the organizer.

When one woman said, "...overall, the whole thing has been very enlightening" (TN), she was referring to the skills and insights she gained while being the facilitator to a self-help group. She, and others, also acknowledged that they do not know everything. Rather than limiting the group's development, this can free up the group to explore the skills and strengths of others. Thus, delegation, support, interdependence and the acknowledgment that everyone can contribute something, become focal points for the organizing process.

*(2) Fulfillment Through Organizing.* Closely tied to the wholistic organizer is the notion that organizing, aside from reaching a goal, can be a fulfilling process in and of itself. The learning and support gained while organizing became as meaningful as achieving the product. One woman described organizing as a "natural high" (KG), despite the struggles and setbacks. In fact, one way of overcoming disappointments was with support for others. The encouragement of bonding and the development of support networks were considered of primary importance by the women.

*(3) Personal as Political: The Indigenous Organizer.* A common image of a community organizer is the person who goes into the community, helps people organize around an issue, and then leaves. There is little sense as to the actual investment of the organizer into the issue. This image did not apply to these women activists. Their reasons for becoming activists varied, but the common theme was that they became involved because the problem or issue was personally exper-ienced. Reasons include:

"It started with my own health. I was misdiagnosed" (TN)

"I think I initially became involved because of self-interest. The neighborhood was going down and nobody was doing anything about it" (Hayes, p. 24).

"Whatever it (project) is, it will have a lot of personal investment. Like Braun Court, this is important. It's our home (scheduled for rezoning). I am guided by personal issues, I need that kind of investment to organize" (FS).

"Listening to the (women's) music is like being on dope without drugs. I had a lot of friends who were musicians and we would get together. It filled a need, it was something very personal. And, I can't sing or anything, but I know how to organize and thought, why not organize an event that would feature women performers" (KG).

"I feel strongly that what I'm doing is for them (her children)" (TL).

These personal reasons for being an activist stem from two main sources. One is the need to gain knowledge. Perhaps the best or, at least, most recognized example of this is the book *Our Bodies, Ourselves.* This book began with a group of women who gathered to discuss their health needs and how they were not being met by the current medical establishment. The outcome was the Boston Women's Health Collective and the publication of one of the most influential books regarding health care and self-help. Often, the need to obtain knowledge is accompanied by the need to disseminate any information so that it could help others. The women believed it was important that others have access to information and to demystify previously denied information so that it could be understood and used.

Another reason stems from a reaction to unmet needs and hostility found within male-dominated organizations. Both Freeman and Evans (1980) argue that early participants in the women's movement had endured degrading and humiliating treatment within the leftist and student movements of the 1960s. These women obtained important skills while working in the movements, yet were not given credit for their contributions and were not treated seriously. Demands for equality were scoffed at and ignored. Women caucuses began to be formed and experiences were shared, thus creating an environment that provided a springboard for the feminist movement. This analysis suggests, again, the importance of personal fulfillment and investment.

*(4) Use of Emotions.* In many of the organizing efforts, emotions provided the cornerstone. The Women's Pentagon Action (Linton & Whitham, 1982; Popkin & Delgado, 1982) was mobilized around mourning, rage, empowerment, and defiance. Every activity was tied into expressing these emotions. (In my own work, I use an equation Awareness = Pain = Healing = Growth, as a way of emotionally contextualizing an antiracism [or other ism] workshop. Exercises help participants pass through these stages.)

Women stressed the importance of bonding, of people getting to know each other so that they could work together in a way that was mutually fulfilling and rewarding. Attention to emotional or personal needs improves the overall organizing effort:

"I learned that if a person feels important, they will help and get involved" (EK). Not only does the acknowledgment of emotions and bonding help people become invested, it also serves as a source of reserve energy in the face of opposition. Knowing that others care often comforts an individual when confronted with derogatory comments, hecklers, etc. Fears and concerns can be addressed within a supportive environment. This sounds obvious, yet it is often overlooked because accomplishing the task has assumed a disproportionate emphasis, to the detriment of the group. Rather than denying emotions, they should be used as a way of building personal ties and as a context for mobilizing. When emotions are used as a focus of organizing or as a source of strength, attention must be paid to the building of support networks (they won't happen spontaneously) and to the allowance of time so that people can sufficiently express their feelings.

*(5) Attention to the Environment.* The themes identified thus far have stressed the importance of support, emotional bonding, and personal investment. Women stressed that a "safe" environment was essential to developing these interpersonal sides of organizing. A safe environment is one in which trust, respect, equality, and validation of an individual's experiences takes place. It was viewed as a high priority among most of the women: "I want a good, open working environment, where people are safe. A safe environment is definitely one of my interests and needs. It's a place where people trust one another" (FS). Most of the women said that a safe environment was all-female, although all-female environments are not necessarily safe. One woman suggested: "That with all women staffs you have differences in power and control. You don't have the male/female

battles. It is a support and sanctuary that you can invest in" (QZ).

A safe environment, however, is not an environment that is conflict free. The creation of a safe environment allows for the airing of problems, for the exchange of diverse ideas in a direct manner. In building a safe environment, attention is paid to the creation of a process through which information, grievances, and thoughts can be heard. For one woman, consensus decision making was the key. Her experience of being an organizer/participant in a local women's peace camp proved rewarding, in part because the planning group had taken considerable time in determining a consensus style that was accessible and available to all participants: "...(P)ositive stuff [was] that a lot of feelings got heard and a lot of subtle adjustments were made in the actual plan, that, because people were heard, ideas came forward and... it was very rich, very diverse...and that doesn't happen when you have an uncomfortable environment, when it's not a safe environment to talk" (MB). Taking the time to address the environment can pay off in the long run with increased commitment, greater group ownership for the project and organization, and different, creative ideas.

*(6) Gender Dynamics.* In connection with discussion on a safe environment were comments regarding gender dynamics. Most of the women saw clear differences between male and female styles of organizing that were in line with the stereotypes outlined above. These differences were particularly apparent in comments on power/control and communication:

Regarding Affinity Groups for a peace action and the lack of recognition given to a facilitator: "so they don't acknowledge what a facilitator is and it's the men that don't, I'm sure it is, that disrupt it because they don't have a sense of what collective work is and they're not

trained...but they're not comfortable with having somebody who is the person, who is trying to help everyone manage their feelings and their conflict" (MB).

"Men and women are different as organizers. One of my major complaints is with men. Organizationally, they are always dealing with power issues. Women are more trusting, more sensitive, able to communicate and relate to others....Women intuitively use group process and interpersonal skills. Where men are rational and intellectual....very un-intimate, real 'heady.' Can't listen to others." (FS)

"What I have noticed is that where men are involved, they end up being power hungry. Not cooperative." (TN)

"I was taught the Alinsky model. Charging white knight saving the day. I knew that I couldn't do that." (TL)

In order to break down the walls that exist between men and women, it is important that women's experiences and concerns are respected and treated seriously. It is also important that men become trained in other methods of decision making, leadership, and control, given the opinions against hierarchical, male-dominated, aggressive, individualistic settings.

*(7) Bridging Differences.* A common concern among these women was closing gaps that exist along racial, sexual preference, class, age and handicap lines. Consequently, confronting one's own biases, rather than ignoring them, was seen as central to individual and group development. Before, or in conjunction with an organizing effort, internal group prejudices are addressed. Rather than hide these problems so that an illusion of solidarity is created, these women stress the importance of raising these issues directly as a way of furthering growth and opportunities. Failure to do so will lead to divisiveness, anger, frustration, and, ultimately, disintegration.

*(8) Women's Culture and History.* Virtually every woman had a female role model who served as a source of inspiration and courage. These were not necessarily famous women, but they were women who helped make a struggle understandable and workable through their actions. Some of these role models were known personally as they were bosses, friends, or other activists. Others served a symbolic purpose, such as in the Women's Pentagon Action, in which women who died from the violent acts of men were remembered in ceremonies. Still others represent feminist culture (music and arts) and are viewed as a source of sustenance and connection: "I turn on 'Sweet Honey in the Rock' and understand Bernice Reagan's meanings of social actions, consciousness raising. Need this global meaning. You need emotional support" (KL).

Community organizing needs to rediscover the female organizers of its past. It should also consider the life histories of women in a variety of movements for they will suggest a different way of mobilizing.

*(9) Training.* There was no consistent view of the best training. Many of these women received their training through experience and not through any formal educational process. Some took advantage of available training opportunities presented by organizations, such as settlement houses, the Midwest Academy, and labor schools. Of concern to the field of community organizing should be the resentment felt toward the increased professionalization of the field. One woman, when asked why she went back to school, said: "It's time for the credentials" (KG); another said: "All I'm getting is a piece of paper that says I'm qualified" (FS). These women have demonstrated that grassroots experience, particularly if one is open to learning from others, is a valuable means of gaining an education of organizing.

Community organizing needs to determine ways of tapping this knowledge and creating learning situations that are meaingful to women.

## CONCLUSION

This paper has explored some common threads among women activists with the hope that these findings can be incorporated into community organizing practice. It presented an analytical paradigm that stresses a wholistic approach to collective practice. The paradigm's four dimensions—subjective, relational, strategic, and structural—comprise an integrated, interdependent whole—much like a balanced mobile. Within these dimensions are themes, nine of which were presented. Most of these themes focused on the emotional and interpersonal aspects of organizing, a view often overlooked or ignored in current community organizing theory and practice. I hope that serious consideration of these themes occurs and that community organizing, from training through the execution of efforts, changes in ways that accept and integrate the experiences of women activists. In the words of Abigail Adams, "Remember the Ladies," and the future will be stronger and more vital.

## REFERENCES

### Primary Sources

Some identifying factors have been eliminated and the initials recorded in order to ensure confidentiality.

EK. Interview, May 1984. Involvement in labor education, minority women.

FS. Interview, October 1984. Involvement in tenant rights, housing reform, youth issues, economic/poverty issues.

KG. Interview, June 1984. Involvement in consumer services, the arts, feminist networking.

KL. Presentation, October 1984. Involvement in peace work, civil rights, labor education.

LD. Presentation, October 1984. Involvement in labor organizing.

MB. Interview, May 1984. Involvement in peace work, environmental issues.

QZ. Interview, October 1984. Involvement in reproductive rights, labor organizing, neighborhood organizing.

SA. Presentation, October 1984. Involvement in desegregation, student rights, peace work.

TL. Presentation, October 1984. Involvement in women's economic rights, peace work.

TN. Interview, October 1984. Involvement in health issues.

## Secondary Sources: Interviews/Diaries

Fahey, Maureen. "Block by Block: Women in Community Organizing (an interview with Betty Deacon)," *Women: A Journal of Liberation,* 6 (1):24–28, 1978.

Hayes, Lois. "Separatism and Disobedience: The Seneca Peace Encampment," *Radical America,* 17 (4):55–64, 1983.

Linton, Rhoda, and Michele Whitham. "With Mourning, Rage, Empowerment and Defiance: The 1981 Women's Pentagon Action," *Socialist Review,* No. 63–63, 12 (3–4):11–36, May–August 1982.

Omi, Michael, and Ilene Philipson. "Misterhood Is Powerful: Interview with Ladies Against Women," *Socialist Review,* No. 68, 13 (2):9–27, March/April 1983.

Plotke, David. "Women Clerical Workers and Trade Unions: Interview with Karen Nussbaum," *Socialist Review,* No. 49, 10 (1):151–159, January–February 1980.

Popkin, Annie, and Gary Delgado. "Mobilizing Emotions: Organizing the Women's Pentagon Action, Interview with Donna Warnock," *Socialist Review,* No. 63–63, 12 (3–4):37–48, May–August 1982.

## Secondary Sources: References

Adams, Abigail. "Letter to John Adams, March 31, 1776," in *The Feminist Papers,* Alice Rossi (ed). New York: Bantam, 1973, pp. 10–11.

Alinsky, Saul D. *Reveille for Radicals,* New York: Vintage Books, 1969 (1946).

Alinsky, Saul D. *Rules for Radicals: A Pragmatic Primer for Realistic Radicals,* New York: Vintage Books, 1972.

Bokemeier, J.L., and J.L. Tate. "Women as Power Actors: A Comparative Study of Rural Communities," *Rural Sociology,* 45:238–55, Summer 1980.

Boston Women's Health Book Collective. *Our Bodies, Ourselves: A Book by and for Women,* New York: Simon and Schuster, 1973.

Boulet, Jacques. "Complementary Epistemological Foundations of Community Organization: Societal and Action Theories," *Social Development Issues,* 5 (2 & 3):121–125, Summer/Fall 1981.

Brandwein, Ruth A. "Toward the Feminization of Community and Organizational Practice," *Social Development Issues,* 5 (2 & 3):180–193, Summer/Fall 1981.

Burghardt, Steve. *The Other Side of Organizing,* Cambridge, MA: Schenkman, 1982.

Campbell, Dolores Delgado. "Shattering the Stereotypes: Chicanas as Labor Union Organizers," *Women of Color/Women Organizing,* 11:20–24, Summer 1983.

Cantarow, Ellen. *Moving the Mountain: Women Working for Social Change,* Old Westbury, NY: The Feminist Press, 1980.

Ecklein, Joan (ed). *Community Organizers,* New York: John Wiley & Sons, 1984, 2nd ed.

Cook, Blanche. "Female Support Networks and Political Activism," *Chrysalis,* 3:43–61, 1977.

Crow, Ginny. "The Process/Product Split," *Quest,* IV (4):15–23, Fall 1978.

Deckard, Barbara Sinclair. *The Women's Movement: Political, Socioeconomic and Psychological Issues,* New York: Harper & Row, 1983, 3rd ed.

Evans, Sara. *Personal Politics: The Roots of Women's Liberation in the Civil Rights Movement and the New Left,* New York: Vintage Books, 1980.

Fisher, Berenice. "Who Needs Woman Heroes?" *Heresies,* 3 (1):10–13, 1980.

Freeman, Jo. "The Origins of the Women's Liberation Movement," *American Journal of Sociology,* 78 (4):792–811.

Freire, Paulo. *Pedagogy of the Oppressed,* New York: Seabury Press, 1974.

Galper, Jeffry. *Social Work Practice: A Radical Perspective,* Englewood Cliffs, NJ: Prentice-Hall, Inc., 1980.

Galper, Jeffry, and Jacqueline Mondros. "Community Organization in Social Work in the 1980s: Fact or Fiction?" *Journal of Education for Social Work,* 16 (1):41–48, Winter 1980.

Gilligan, Carol. *In a Different Voice: Psychological Theory and Women's Development,* Cambridge, MA: Harvard University Press, 1982.

Gittell, M., and N. Naples. "Activist Women: Conflicting Ideologies," *Social Policy,* 13:25–27, Summer 1982.

Gregory, Carole E. "Black Women Activists," *Heresies,* 3 (1):14–17, 1980.

Hyde, Cheryl. "Toward a Model of Gender Sensitive Community Organizing: A Synthesis of Current Research," unpublished seminar paper, December 1983.

Johnson, A.D. "Women and Power: Toward a Theory of Effectiveness," *Journal of Social Issues,* 32 (3):99–110, 1976.

Kahn, Si. *Organizing: Guide to Grassroots Leaders,* New York: McGraw-Hill Book Company, 1982.

Lawson, Ronald, and Stephen E. Barton. "Sex Roles in Social Movements: A Case Study of the Tenant Movement in New York City," *Signs: Journal of Women in Culture and Society,* 6 (2):230–247, Winter 1980.

Masi, Dale A. *Organizing for Women: Issues Strategies, and Services,* Lexington, MA: D.C. Heath and Company, 1981.

Mayo, Marjorie (ed). *Women in the Community,* Boston: Routledge & Kegan Paul, 1977.

McAllister, Pam (ed). *Reweaving the Web of Life: Feminism and Nonviolence,* Philadelphia: New Society Publishers, 1982.

Morgan, Robin (ed). *Sisterhood Is Powerful: An Anthology of Writings from the Women's Liberation Movement,* New York: Vintage Books, 1970.

Morgan, Robin. *Going Too Far: The Personal Chronicle of a Feminist,* New York: Vintage Books, 1978.

Przestwor, Joy Chrisi. *Connecting Women in the Community: A Handbook for Programs,* Cambridge, MA: The Arthur and Elizabeth Schlesinger Library, Radcliffe College, 1984.

Reed, Beth Glover. "Gender Issues in Training Group Leaders," *Journal for Specialists in Group Work,* 161–169, August 1981.

Riddle, Dorothy. "Integrating Process and Product," *Quest,* IV (4): 23–32, Fall 1978.

Rothman, Jack. *Planning and Organizing for Social Change: Action Principles from Social Science Research,* New York: Columbia University Press, 1974.

Rothman, Jack. "Three Models of Community Organization Practice, Their Mixing and Phasing," *Strategies of Community Organization,* Fred M. Cox, John L. Erlich, Jack Rothman and John E. Tropman (eds). Itasca, IL: F.E. Peacock Publishers, Inc., 1979, 25–45.

Speeter, Greg. *Power: A Repossession Manual—Organizing Strategies for Citizens,* Amherst, MA: University of Massachusetts, Citizen Involvement Training Project, 1978.

Staples, Lee. *Roots to Power: A Manual for Grassroots Organizing,* New York: Praeger Publishers, 1984.

Steinem, Gloria. "The Politics of Talking in Groups," *MS.,* May 1981, pp. 43–45, 84–89.

Stonehall, Linda. "Cognitive Mapping: Gender Differences in the Perception of Community," *Sociological Inquiry,* 51 (2):121–128, 1981.

Van Wagner, Karen, and Cheryl Swanson. "From Machiavelli to Ms: Differences in Male-Female Power Styles," *Public Administration Review,* 39:66–72, January 1979.

West, Guida. *The National Welfare Rights Movement: The Social Protest of Poor Women,* New York: Praeger Publishers, 1981.

Women's Crisis Center, Ann Arbor. "Organizing a Women's Crisis-Service Center," *Strategies of Community Organization,* Fred M. Cox, John L. Erlich, Jack Rothman and John E. Tropman (eds). Itasca, IL: F.E. Peacock Publishers, Inc., 1979, pp. 478–483.

**6.**

**F. Ellen Netting, Peter M. Kettner, and Steven L. McMurtry**

## SELECTING APPROPRIATE TACTICS

### INTRODUCTION

…[S]trategy…refers to the development of a written plan directed at bringing about the proposed change. Deciding on a strategy can be a time-consuming and detailed process. Although many may agree that a problem exists, getting agreement on just how the situation should be changed is seldom easy. Special efforts must be concentrated on tactics designed to get the change accepted.

Tactic selection tests the professional judgment of the change agent, particularly in how to approach the target system. Certain tactics can raise ethical dilemmas. Selecting tactics calls for mature, professional judgment in community and organizational change. Social workers should be open to the possibility that practices in many of the arenas in which they operate are well entrenched and there will be a natural tendency to resist. The fact that agency missions are stated in inspiring words does not mean that all agencies carry out those missions. Practitioners must be aware that they are a part of legitimized systems that often contribute to the oppression experienced by the client group they are trying to serve. Selecting appropriate tactics requires one to think critically and to carefully analyze the target system.

---

F. Ellen Netting is a professor at Virginia Commonwealth University; Peter M. Kettner and Steven L. McMurtry are professors at Arizona State University.

### FOCUS A: SELECTING APPROPRIATE TACTICS

The choice of tactics is a critical decision point in planned change. Tactics have been defined as "any skillful method used to gain an end" (Brager et al. 1987, 288). Whereas strategy is the long-range linking of activities to achieve the desired goal, tactics are reflected in day-to-day behaviors (Brager & Holloway 1978). As the change agent engages in tactical behavior, it is important not to lose sight of the goal toward which these behaviors are directed.

Brager et al. (1987) identify four essential properties of tactics used by professional change agents: "(1) they are planned…(2) they are used to evoke specific responses…(3) they involve interaction with others…and (4) they are goal-oriented" (p. 288). In addition, it is our contention that a fifth property must be in place in professional social work change efforts: (5) the tactic will do no harm to members of the client system and, whenever possible, members of that system will be involved in tactical decision making.

Change almost always involves influencing the allocation of scarce resources—authority, status, power, goods, services, or money. Decisions about tactics, therefore, must take into consideration whether the resources are being allocated willingly or whether someone must be persuaded to make the allocation. If there is agreement on the part of the action and target systems that the proposed change is acceptable and that resources will be allocated, a collaborative approach can be adopted. If there is agreement that the proposed change is acceptable but a reluctance or refusal to allocate resources, or if there is disagreement about the need for the proposed change, then a more coercive approach may be necessary if the change effort is to proceed.

For example, a change effort may focus on the inability of physically disabled people to get around the city and travel to needed service providers. A thorough study documents the problem, and a dial-a-ride transportation service is proposed. The planning commission and city council graciously accept the report, agree on the need, and thank the Transportation for the Disabled Task Force. Three city council members favor funding, three are opposed, and one is undecided. If the undecided council member can be persuaded to favor funding, then collaborative tactics can be adopted. If, however, he or she decides to oppose funding or if a compromise would undermine the change effort, then tactics designed to coerce support must be adopted. For collaborative approaches to be adopted, there must be agreement on both the proposed change and the allocation of needed resources.

In the social work literature, tactics have been divided into three broad categories: collaboration, campaign, and contest (Brager & Holloway 1978; Brager et al. 1987). In this chapter, we use these terms to describe the relationship between the action and target systems. *Collaboration* implies a working relationship where the two systems agree that change must occur, whereas contest tactics indicate disagreement between the two systems. *Campaign* tactics are used when the target must be convinced of the importance of the change, but when communication is still possible between the two systems. The effectiveness of the "campaign" may determine whether collaboration or contest follows. *Contest* tactics are used when neither of the other two are possible any longer. Change efforts that begin with one set of tactics may progress to other sets, depending on the evolving relationship between the action and target systems. The continuum along which these tactical categories fall is as follows:

Collaboration↔Campaign↔Contest

Although we categorize these relationships, success may hinge on the change agent's ability to keep the action and target systems in a state of continual interaction. It is possible that what begins as a collaborative relationship will move to conflict when new issues arise during the change process. It is equally likely that the relationship will vascillate between various gradations of communication, with both systems uncertain about the other, even when compromise can be reached. In short, these relationships ebb and flow, sometimes unpredictably, given the political situation, and sometimes all too predictably, given the change agent's prior experience with the target system.

Our concern is that the social worker never take the relationship between the action and target system for granted. To assume that the target is immovable before communication has been attempted demonstrates poor use of professional judgment. To assume that the target will embrace the cause once the facts are known is naive. Assumptions have little place in assessing the relationship between the action and the target system. We believe that regardless of what types of tactics are used, communication should be maintained with the target system if at all possible. If communication ceases, it should be because the target system refuses to continue interaction.

Within each of the three categories are tactics that are typically used. The framework in Table 6.1 guides our discussion. Some of the following conceptualization is drawn from previous literature (Brager & Holloway 1978; Brager et al. 1987). In some areas, we offer slightly different perspectives and add new tactics. Throughout the following discussion, we attempt to provide an analytical framework to guide an action system in selecting the most appropriate mix of tactics.

## Collaboration

*Implementation.* Collaborative approaches include instances when the target and action system agree that change is needed. Under collaboration, we place (1) implementation and (2) capacity building tactics.

Implementation tactics are used when the action and target systems work together cooperatively. When these systems agree that change is needed and allocation of resources is supported by critical decision makers, the change simply needs to be implemented. Implementation will most likely involve some problem solving, but it is not expected that adversarial relationships will be a concern in these types of collaborative efforts.

*Capacity Building.* Capacity building includes the tactics of participation and empowerment. Participation refers to those activities that involve members of the client system in the change effort. Empowerment is the process of "helping a group or community to achieve political influence or relevant legal authority" (Barker 1987, p. 49).

For example, a problem may be defined as exclusion of a neighborhood from decisions that affect them. The focus of the intervention is on building a capacity for greater self-direction and self-control—that is, actually teaching people how to get involved in the decision-making processes in their communities and taking greater control over the decisions that affect their lives. This approach often emerges in situations where disenfranchised communities become targets for development, freeways, airport expansion, and other such encroachments.

Through professionally assisted change efforts, perhaps led by a neighborhood social service organization (change agent system), neighborhood resident (client system), and city council (controlling system and perhaps target system) agree that community citizens should have a greater voice in developments that affect their community. The focus of the change or intervention, however, is not on the target system (city council/planning commission) but on educating, training, and preparing community citizens for a fuller participation in decisions that affect their communities. Tactics would include education, training, and actual participation in civic organizations and activities.

Empowerment involves enabling people to become aware of their rights, and teaching them how to exercise those rights so that they become better able to take control over factors that affect their lives. Mobilizing the efforts of self-help groups and voluntary associations...as well as the client system's informal support structure may be used to assist in guiding the target system toward consensus with the change effort.

## Campaign

Campaign implies a group effort to convince target system members that a cause is just or a change is needed, and that resources should be allocated. Campaign tactics require a good deal of skill on the part of the change agent

TABLE 6.1
Tactical Behaviors

| Relationship of Action and Target Systems | Tactics |
|---|---|
| *Collaboration*<br>Target System agrees (or is easily convinced to agree) with action system that change is needed and supports allocation of resources. | 1. Implementation<br>2. Capacity building<br>   a. Participation<br>   b. Empowerment |
| *Campaign*<br>Target system is willing to communicate with action system, but there is little consensus that change is needed: or target system supports change but not allocation or resources. | 3. Education<br>4. Persuasion<br>   a. Cooptation<br>   b. Lobbying<br>5. Mass media appeal |
| *Contest*<br>Target system opposes change and/or allocation of resources and is not open to further communication about opposition. | 6. Bargaining and negotiation<br>7. Large-group or community action<br>   a. Legal (e.g., demonstrations)<br>   b. Illegal (e.g., civil disobedience)<br>8. Class action lawsuit |

and action system. Lack of consensus rules out collaboration, yet a firm disagreement has not been established. Under this heading we include the use of education, persuasion, and mass media appeals designed to influence public opinion.

*Education.* Educational tactics can be an integral part of campaigns. Therefore, we use educational tactics to describe those interactions in which the action system presents perceptions, attitudes, opinions, data, and information about the proposed change with the intent of convincing the target system to think or to act differently. The objective is to inform. The assumption is that more and better information will lead to a change in behavior. It is a difficult tactic to use because opponents of the change can also be expected to inform decision makers armed with different sets of data and information, and there is seldom an absolute "truth" in dealing with complex organizational and community problems. In many cases where education fails to produce the desired result or falls short of having the desired impact, the change agent turns to persuasion.

*Persuasion.* Persuasion refers to the art of convincing others to accept and support one's point of view or perspective on an issue. Social workers must frequently use persuasive tactics in addition to collaboration because their causes are not always embraced by decision makers, who often must be convinced through persuasion that the change is worth pursuing. This means that the change agent must understand the motives and reasoning of the target system in order to identify what incentives can be used to negotiate an agreement.

Skillful communication requires that the action system must carefully select its leadership from those persons who have the ability to persuade. Persons who are seen as nonthreatening to the target system and who can articulate the reasoning behind the planned change are particularly useful. For example, in a change effort, particular actors may be perceived as unreasonable, as troublemakers, or as chronic complainers by members of the controlling system. It is not in the best interest of the client system for those persons to be the only spokespeople for the change. Clients themselves can also be powerful spokespersons, providing information and a viewpoint that persuades people of the need for change.

Framing the problem statement to make it more palatable to target system members is a persuasive technique. This requires the ability to think as the target thinks. For example, a social worker hired as a long-term care ombudsperson was working closely with a coalition of advocates for nursing-home reform to end abuse in long-term care facilities. Nursing-home administrators were very upset over the nursing-home reform coalition and perceived them as not understanding the difficulties with which they coped on a daily basis. They sincerely wanted to provide quality care, but were frustrated by staff who were not properly trained to work with geriatric populations. By framing the problem as a training problem designed to better prepare employees and reduce turnover, the ombudsperson was able to persuade administrators to cooperate with the action system. When the ombudsperson met with the local nursing home association, she acknowledged that she was aware that the administrators wanted to operate high-quality facilities. She also noted that recent studies revealed that high staff turnover rates often contributed to lack of continuity and lower patient care, sometimes leading to abuse. She explained that she and her colleagues would be willing to develop training for nurses aides because they interacted most intimately with patients, yet were most vulnerable to high turnover. Essentially, one of the contributing factors leading to abuse was being addressed, but it was framed as reducing an administrative nightmare—high staff turnover.

Cooptation is defined as minimizing anticipated opposition by absorbing or including members of the target system in the action system. Once target system members are part of the planned changed effort, it is likely that they will assume some ownership of the change process. Persuasion is used to coopt new persons into the action system. This is valuable to the success of the change effort because it is important to include persons who are viewed as powerful by the target system. These persons may be relatively neutral and may have little interest in obstructing the change effort. However, if they can be convinced to support the change effort (or even to allow their names to be used in publicity), their participation may sway others who respect their opinions. Cooptation is most effective as a tactic when opponents or neutral parties can be helped to recognize a self-interest in the proposed change.

Cooptation can be formal or informal. Coopting individuals is called informal cooptation, whereas coopting organized groups is referred to as formal cooptation. Formal cooptation means that an entire group agrees to support a cause. Because their governing structure agrees that the change effort is worthwhile, the group may issue a statement to that effect. This formalizes the commitment, even though there are always members of any group who may, as individuals, disagree with the proposed change.

Formal cooptation of a number of groups leads to coalition building. A coalition is a loosely woven, ad hoc association of constituent groups, each of whose primary identification is outside the coalition (Haynes & Mickelson 1986). For example, the purpose of the National Health Care Campaign is to provide health care coverage to all American citizens. This change effort brings together hundreds of organizations such as the National Association of Social Workers and the American Public Health Association. On a state by state basis, health care campaign chapters are forming. Interested change agents have encouraged local groups to join in the efforts—forming a coalition dedicated to the stated goal. The diversity of the coalition contributes to a powerful alliance of individuals and groups that vascillate between collaboration and campaign tactics as they attempt to address health care needs.

Lobbying is a form of persuasion that addresses policy change under the domain of the controlling system. The action system will have to determine if it is necessary to change agency policy, to amend current legislation or to develop new legislation in order to achieve their goal. Haynes and Mickelson (1986) delineate three essential concepts for social work/lobbyists to consider. First, one should always be factual and honest. Trying to second guess or stretching the facts to support one's position is devastating to one's professional reputation as well as to the change effort's credibility. Second, any presentation should be straightforward and supported by the available data. The problem identification and analysis process...will assist the change agent in organizing the rationale for change. Third, any discussion should include the two critical concerns of decision makers—cost and social impact of what is proposed. If the cost is high, the social worker is advised to calculate the costs of allowing the identified problem to remain unresolved.

*Mass Media Appeal.* Mass media appeal refers to the development and release of newsworthy stories to the print and electronic media for the purpose of influencing public opinion. This tactic is used to pressure decision makers into a favorable resolution to the identified problem. The expectation is that if the proposed change can be presented to the public in a positive way and decision makers' refusal to support the proposed

change can be presented as obstructionist or somehow negative, then decision makers will feel pressured to change their position. Where decision makers are high-profile people like elected representatives who depend on a positive public perception, this can be an effective tactic. Use of mass media depends on news reporters' agreement that the proposed change is a newsworthy story, and assurance that one's cause will be presented accurately. Use of any media must always include consideration of clients' rights to privacy.

## Contest

Under the heading of contest we include the use of bargaining and negotiating, the use of large group or community action, or class action lawsuits. Large groups in community action can be further divided into legal and illegal tactics. Contest tactics are used in situations where: (1) the target system cannot be persuaded by the action system, (2) the target system refuses to communicate with the action system, or (3) it is perceived that only lipservice is being given to the proposed change. Contest tactics mean that the change effort becomes an open, public conflict as attempts are made to draw broad support and/or to pressure or even force the target system into supporting or at least accepting the change. Once this occurs, the action system must be prepared to face open confrontation and to escalate its coercive techniques.

Conflict is inevitable in social work practice. There will be times in the experience of every macro practitioner when incredible resistance is encountered in addressing the needs of oppressed population groups. Social work as a profession developed in response to a basic societal conflict—the persistent antagonism over individualism and the common good.

Conflicts over the rights of various population groups have spawned violent confrontations rooted in basic value systems and beliefs. We believe that physical violence and terrorism cannot be condoned in any change efforts in a civilized society. Nonviolent confrontation, however, including civil disobedience, is an option when there is a communication stalemate between the target and action systems.

Contest tactics will require widespread commitment and possible participation from members of the support system. It is critical to the success of these tactics that the support system and its subsystems—initiator, client, and change agent—are comfortable with contest tactics because there are risks that are not present when using collaboration and campaign tactics. It is likely that the time and energy necessary for effective change will increase and relationships can become disrupted. When collaborative and campaign tactics are employed, tactics can move toward contest. However, once contest tactics are employed it is not likely that one can return to collaborative or campaign tactics. Without a clear understanding of what contest tactics involve and without full commitment from the support system, contest tactics are not advised.

*Bargaining and Negotiation.* Bargaining and negotiation refer to those situations in which the action and target system confront one another with the reasons for their opposition. Bargaining and negotiation occur when there is a recognized power differential between parties and a compromise needs to be made. These tactics are more formalized than persuasion, often involving a third-party mediator. Members of the target system will typically agree to negotiate when the following factors are in place: (1) there is some understanding of the

intentions and preferred outcomes of the action system, (2) there is a degree of urgency, (3) the relative importance and scope of the proposed change is known, (4) there are resources that facilitate the exercise of power, and (5) they perceive the action system as having some legitimacy. In order to negotiate, both the action and the target systems must perceive that each has something the other wants, otherwise there is no reason to come together (Brager et al. 1987).

Bargaining and negotiation can result in a win-win situation, where both target and action systems are pleased with and fully support the outcome. The result can be a win-lose where one system is clearly the victor, or a lose-lose where both systems give something up and are disappointed in the results.

*Large Group or Community Action.* Large group or community action refers to the preparing, training, and organizing of large numbers of people who are willing to form a pressure group and advocate for change through various forms of such collective action as picketing, disruption of meetings, sit-ins, boycotting, and other pressure tactics. Peaceful demonstrations are legal activities, often used by both groups at either extreme of an issue, to express their views. Civil disobedience activities intentionally break the law. When action system members deliberately engage in illegal activities, they must be ready to accept the consequences of their actions. The change agent is responsible for making potential participants fully aware of these risks before the decision is made to proceed.

*Class Action Lawsuits.* Class action lawsuits refer to those instances where an entity is sued for a perceived violation of the law and it is expected that the finding of the court will apply to an entire class of people. These tactics are often used with highly vulnerable populations such as the chronically mentally ill, the homeless, or children, where it is unlikely that they have the capacity or the resources to protect their own rights. Public interest law organizations may be resources for the action system in developing class action tactics.

**Considerations in Selecting Tactics**

A few salient considerations need to be weighed in selecting the best tactic or mix of tactics. These considerations include:

1. What are the current *objectives* of the change effort?
2. What is the perception (by those promoting change) of the *controlling and host systems?*
3. What is the perception (by those promoting change) of the role of the *client system?*
4. What *resources* are needed and available for each tactic?
5. What are the *ethical* dilemmas inherent in the range of tactical choices?

*Objectives.* Objectives often tend to evolve as the change process moves along, and a reexamination prior to selection of tactics is in order. For example, with the problem of domestic violence, the condition may have been brought to public awareness by the perceived need for additional emergency shelter space for battered women. However, as the problem is analyzed and better understood, the objectives may shift toward consciousness raising for all women in the community who are perceived to be at risk of violence. Thus strategy and tactics would move from advocating for service provision to educating for empowerment. Since tactics

can change as objectives change, it is worthwhile to make one last check to insure that all are clear and in agreement on current objectives. The following questions can be used to guide the action system's reexamination of the change objectives.

1. What are the stated objectives of this change effort?
2. Given what has been learned in the change process thus far, do the stated objectives need to be revised?
3. Which best describes the intent of the current objectives?
   a. to solve a substantive problem or provide a needed service
   b. to increase self-direction or self-control of the client system
   c. to influence decision makers
   d. to change public opinion
   e. to shift power
   f. to mandate action
4. Do members of the action system have any concerns about the intent of the current objectives that require further discussion?

The range of objectives and likely accompanying tactics are indicated in Table 6.2.

*Controlling and Host Systems.* The controlling and host systems can be perceived in a variety of ways. If they are seen as employers or sponsors of the change, then collaboration is likely. If they are seen as supporters of, but not participants in the change, capacity building (through participation and empowerment) may be the tactic of choice. If they are seen as neutral or indifferent, a campaign strategy may be in order. If, however, they are seen as oppressive or unresponsive to their primary clientele, then some type of

TABLE 6.2
Relationship of Current Objectives to Tactics

| Current Objective | Relationship of Target and Action System | Possible Tactics |
|---|---|---|
| 1. Solving a substantive problem; providing a needed service | Collaborative | Implementation through joint action |
| 2. Self-direction; self-control | Collaborative | Capacity building through participation and empowerment |
| 3. Influencing decision makers | In disagreement but with open communication | Education, and persuasion through cooptation, lobbying, etc |
| 4. Changing public opinion | In disagreement but with open communication | Education, persuasion, mass media appeal. |
| | Adversarial | Large group or community action |
| 5. Shifting power | Adversarial | Large group or community action |
| 6. Mandating action | Adversarial | Class action lawsuit |

contest approach will likely be selected. Discussion of the following questions may assist the action system in assessing their relationship with the controlling and host system.

1. Who are the critical actors in the host and controlling system(s)?
2. What term(s) best describe(s) the action system members' perceptions of the host and controlling system actors?
   a. sponsors, supporters, co-participants, or colleagues
   b. neutral or indifferent actors
   c. uniformed barriers who are not sure about change
   d. informed barriers or opponents
   e. oppressors
   f. violators of rights
3. Are action system members' perceptions similar or dissimilar?
4. If they are dissimilar, what are the different perceptions and what are the implications of this divergence of opinion for the change effort?

Table 6.3 illustrates the various perceptions of roles that might be assigned to the controlling and host systems, and the logical tactic for each.

*Primary Client. The role of the primary client* can vary, and the way in which this role is perceived can affect selection of change tactics. Sometimes it may be difficult to determine who the primary client really is. For example, in addressing the needs of the elderly, the change agent may discover that caregivers are suffering from stress and fatigue. In this situation, one must ask if the primary beneficiaries of a change effort will be the older persons themselves or their caregivers?

If the primary client is seen as a consumer or recipient of service, then a collaborative change approach is the most likely tactic. If the primary role is as a resident of a community or potential participant in an effort to achieve self-direction and control, then a capacity building approach is, perhaps, more appropriate.

TABLE 6.3
Relationship of Controlling and Host System Roles to Tactics

| Perception of Role of Controlling and Host Systems | Relationship of Controlling, Host, and Action Systems | Possible Tactics |
|---|---|---|
| 1. Sponsors; supporters; co-participants; colleagues | Collaborative | Implementation through joint action |
| 2. Neutrality or indifference | Collaborative | Capacity building through participation and empowerment |
| 3. Uninformed barriers; not sure about change | In disagreement but with open communication | Education, and persuasion |
| 4. Informed barriers; opponents to successful change | Adversarial | Bargaining; large-group or community action |
| 5. Oppressors | Adversarial | Large group or community action |
| 6. Violators of rights | Adversarial | Class action lawsuit |

If the primary client is seen as a person who needs a service (but this need is not acknowledged by the controlling system), as a victim, or as a voter or constituent with potential power to influence decision makers, then some type of contest approach is likely to be employed. The following questions guide the action system in assessing the role of the primary client.

1. Who is defined as the primary client?
2. How do members of the action system describe the primary client?
   a. consumer or recipient of service
   b. resident of the community in need of self-direction or self-control
   c. citizen taxpayer not permitted full participation
   d. victim, underserved needy person
   e. victim, exploited person
   f. person denied civil rights
3. Do action system members agree or disagree in their descriptions of the primary client? Do clients agree or disagree?
4. What role does the primary client play within the action system?

5. How much overlap is there between the client and the action systems?
6. What mechanisms does the action system use to obtain input from the client system?

Table 6.4 displays client roles, approaches, and tactics.

*Resources.* Finally, *resources available to the action system* should be examined in relation to each of the tactics being considered. If collaboration is the tactic of choice, then several resources are needed. These include technical expertise capable of understanding whether or not the change is being properly implemented, monitored, and evaluated. In order for a capacity building tactic to be used, grass roots organizing ability, together with some teaching and training expertise, must be available to the action system. If there is conflict, either skilled persuaders, media support, large numbers of people willing to do what is necessary to bring about change, or legal expertise must be available. The following

TABLE 6.4
Relationship of Client-System Role to Tactics

| Perception of Role of Client System | Relationship Client and Target Systems | Possible Tactics |
| --- | --- | --- |
| 1. Consumer; recipient of service | Collaborative | Implementation through joint action |
| 2. Resident of the community in need of greater self-direction and self-control | Collaborative | Capacity building through participation and empowerment |
| 3. Citizen/taxpayer not permitted full participation | In disagreement but with open communication | Education and persuasion |
| 4. Victim; underserved needy person | Adversarial | Mass media appeal |
| 5. Victim; exploited person | Adversarial | Large group or community action |
| 6. Person denied civil rights | Adversarial | Class action lawsuit |

questions may assist the action system in assessing resources.

1. What tactics are being considered at this point?
2. What resources will be needed to adequately use these tactics? (e.g., expertise, training, time, funding, equipment, etc.)
3. What members of the action system have access to the needed resources?
4. If additional resources are needed, should the boundaries of the action system be expanded to include persons/groups who have access to additional resources?

Resource considerations are illustrated in Table 6.5.

*Professional Ethics.*  …Ethics are the behaviors that bring values into action. An ethical dilemma is defined as a situation in which a choice has to be made between equally important values. Tactical choices are no exception. Decisions regarding what tactics to use are based on the values held by action system members. It is often the clash of action and target system values that leads to the selection of contest tactics.

Three ethical principles [discussed in a previous chapter were] autonomy, beneficence, and justice. These principles are deeply enmeshed in macro-practice change. A clash between autonomy and beneficence occurs when the client system is not willing to risk the little they have, yet, when the action system wants to push for a quality of life change. The client system may have limited control over their lives, but their right to decide (self-determination) that they do not want to risk the little control they have must be respected by action system members if it is clear that client system opinion is being fairly represented. Alternately, the action system may be heavily composed of professionals who are acting on the principle of beneficence. They may sincerely believe that they know what is best for the client system. Rights of clients take precedence over the wishes of the action system when such a conflict emerges.

TABLE 6.5
Resources Needed by Action Systems for Each Tactic

| Tactic | Resources Needed |
| --- | --- |
| 1. Collaboration—joint action or problem solving | Technical expertise; monitoring and evaluation capability |
| 2. Capacity building | Grass roots organizing ability; teaching/training expertise; opportunities for participation; some indigenous leadership; willing participation |
| 3. Persuasion | Informed people; data/information; skilled persuaders/lobbyists |
| 4. Mass media appeal | Data/information; newsworthy issue or slant; access to news reporters; technical expertise to write news releases |
| 5. Large group or community action | Large numbers of committed people (support system); training and organizing expertise; informed leadership; bargaining and negotiating skills |
| 6. Class action lawsuits | Legal expertise; victims willing to bring action and provide information; at least enough money for court costs |

This clash was illustrated in a social work intern's first field experience. Working for a small community center in the southwest, she discovered that many of her Hispanic clients lived in a crowded apartment complex with faulty wiring and inadequate plumbing. With the backing of her agency, she began talking with clients to see if they would be willing to engage in a change process directed toward their living conditions. As she analyzed the situation, she realized that any change process would involve housing and public health personnel in the action system. Her clients begged her not to bring these concerns to the attention of local authorities. Many members of the client system were illegal aliens and they feared that their exposure to public authorities would assure their deportation. The client system was willing to accept poor housing conditions rather than risk the consequences of exposure. The client system's autonomy was in conflict with the change agent system's beneficence.

The clash between justice and autonomy is exemplified when the action system demands redistribution of resources and the target system believes that in giving up their control over valued resources they have less freedom. Macro change frequently appeals to the principle of justice, for it is usually through the redistribution of valued resources (e.g., power, money, status, etc.) that change occurs. Because justice is a basic ethical principle that raises emotions when it is violated, change agents can become so obsessed with injustice that any means is viewed as an appropriate tactic if it leads to a successful end. It is our contention that this type of thinking can lead to professional anarchy whereby tactics are perceived as weapons to punish the target system rather than as actions to enrich the client system. In these situations it may be too easy for the change to take on a life of its own and for the professional to assume a beneficent role. Righteous indignation may overtake sound judgment.

[Sometimes it is appropriate to consider] the use of covert tactics in certain situations where legitimate channels of communication have been tried and where clients agree that covert means may be their only chance for success. These considerations must be carefully weighed because the use of covert tactics usually raises ethical concerns.

To guide the action system in discussing professional ethics, we pose the following questions:

1. What are the value conflicts between the target and action systems?
2. What ethical principle(s) appear to be guiding the activities of the action system?
3. Is there the potential for a clash of ethical principles between the client and action systems?
4. If covert tactics are being considered, what conditions have led to this decision?
   a. The mission of the target agency or the community mandate is being ignored.
   b. The mission of the target agency or the community mandate is being denied for personal gain.
   c. Change efforts have been tried through legitimate channels but the target system will not listen.
   d. Client system members are fully aware of the risks involved, but are willing to take the risks.
   e. Other _____

There are very few situations where there is clearly a right or wrong tactic. Berlin (1990) explains, "we are all vulnerable to oversimplified bipolarizations. We search for order, find meaning in contrasts, and learn by maintaining an 'essential tension' between divergent experiences, events, and possibilities. It is this allowance of contrasts that differentiates either-or, narrowing and excluding bipolarizations from those that are encompassing or transforming" (p. 54).

It is common to think dichotomously (e.g., win-lose, right-wrong, good-bad, consensus-conflict). In conflict situations, dichotomous thinking may assist the radical change agent in believing that the target system represents evil, whereas the action system represents good. This fuels the fire of confrontation and is appropriate in some situations. However, we believe that the professional social worker has a responsibility to carefully analyze what is happening before making assumptions that lead directly to the use of contest tactics. This means that the majority of change efforts will utilize collaboration and campaign tactics as the action and target systems attempt to communicate with one another. Although consensus-conflict is a dichotomy, we believe that the majority of interactions happen in the various gradations in-between—where varying degrees of communication occur.

If the action system attempts to collaborate or is willing to compromise but the target system remains unmoved, then contest tactics may have to be employed. What professionals must guard against, however, is action system members making assumptions about target system members without attempting to communicate with them. In short, decisions about what tactics to use depends on the situation, the proposed change, and the relationships among actors in the action, client, and target systems.

## FOCUS B: PREPARING A WRITTEN PLAN

When all the foregoing tasks have been completed, the proposed change should be written up in the form of a short, concise plan.

This will include a few pages on the purpose, the problem, and the proposed change. A page on costs, and a few pages on expected benefits should make clear what resources will be requested, how they will be spent, and what benefits will be derived from implementation of the proposed change.

A few pages should be used to lay out the strategy and tactics, outlining roles, responsibilities and time lines in Gantt chart form. This will be helpful in insuring that the proposed strategy and tactics are well coordinated as they are implemented. Any documents from the data collection and problem analysis phases that are felt to be helpful and are clear and concise can be attached to the plan.

This brings the change effort up to the point where it is ready for action. A community or organizational problem affecting a target population has been identified and thoroughly thought out. A general approach to an intervention has been proposed, and a hypothesis developed proposing a relationship between problem, intervention, and outcomes. Alternative strategies have been carefully thought through, participants selected, issues weighed, and tactics selected.

Clearly there is more to be done prior to the full implementation of change. It is not the intent [here], however, to get into the details of project or program planning. The macro practitioner, as conceptualized here, could reasonably be expected to withdraw at the point of acceptance of the proposed change and turn responsibilities over to those who will provide leadership in implementation of the policy, program, or project experts.

## CONCLUSION

...[As with all tactics, a] proposed plan of action is sketched out, including specification of key participants, activities, and time lines.

As with all professional practice, the approach is modified by the practitioner to fit the situation. If conditions dictate immediate action, some procedures will be shortened or streamlined. If time allows and the significance of the proposed change dictates, each task will be carried out with careful attention to detail.

In any case, it is our position that some changes will always be needed in the field of human services, both in organizations and in communities. These changes, we believe, require the professional assistance and consultation of social workers knowledgeable about macro-level change. They require informed, and sometimes scholarly participation and guidance in order to insure that what is achieved is what is most needed to address the social problem in the best interest of the target population.

We believe that social workers are well qualified to lead or coordinate the planning stages of such change efforts and to bring them to the point of action, and this book is intended to assist in that process. As the change effort moves into its next stages, we would expect that the necessary expertise—legal, media, organizing, planning, designing, managing, or whatever is needed—would be sought from additional available sources and from elsewhere in the social work literature.

## REFERENCES

Barker, R. L. (1987) *The social work dictionary.* Silver Spring, MD: National Association of Social Workers.

Berlin, S. B. (1990) Dichotomous and complex thinking. *Social Service Review,* 64(1): 46–59.

Brager, G., and S. Holloway. (1978) *Changing human service organizations: Politics and practice.* New York: Free Press.

Brager, G., H. Specht, and J. L. Torczyner. (1987) *Community organizing.* New York: Columbia University Press.

Haynes, K. S., and J. S. Mickelson. (1986) *Affecting change: Social workers in the political arena.* New York: Longman.

## APPENDIX A: ACTION SYSTEM DISCUSSION IN CONSIDERATION TACTICS

### Objectives

1. What are the stated objectives of this change effort?
2. Given what has been learned in the change process thus far, do the stated objectives need to be revised?
3. Which best describes the intent of the current objectives?
   a. to solve a substantive problem or provide a needed service
   b. to increase self-direction or self-control of the client system
   c. to influence decision makers
   d. to change public opinion
   e. to shift power
   f. to mandate action
4. Do members of the action system have any concerns about the intent of the current objectives that require further discussion?

### Controlling and Host Systems

5. Who are the critical actors in the host and controlling system(s)?
6. What term(s) best describes the action system members' perceptions of the host and controlling system actors?
   a. sponsors, supporters, co-participants, or colleagues
   b. neutral or indifferent actors
   c. uninformed barriers who are not sure about change
   d. informed barriers or opponents
   e. oppressors
   f. violators of rights
7. Are action system members' perceptions similar or dissimilar?
8. If they are dissimilar, what are the different perceptions and what are the implications of this divergence of opinion for the change effort?

### Primary Client

9. Who is defined as the primary client?
10. How do members of the action system describe the primary client?
    a. consumer or recipient of service
    b. resident of the community in need of self-direction or self-control
    c. citizen taxpayer not permitted full participation
    d. victim, underserved needy person
    e. victim, exploited person
    f. person denied civil rights
11. Do action system members agree or disagree in their descriptions of the primary client?
12. What role does the primary client play within the action system?
13. How much overlap is there between the client and the action systems?
14. What mechanisms does the action system use to obtain input from the client system?

# PART TWO
# ASSESSMENT

# Introduction

Leroy ("Satchel") Paige, one of the greatest pitchers in the history of baseball, offered this assessment of the best way to promote a long healthy life:

1. Avoid fried meats, which angry up the blood.
2. If your stomach disputes you, lie down and pacify it with cool thoughts.
3. Keep the juices flowing by jangling around gently as you move.
4. Go very light on the vices, such as carrying on in society.
5. Avoid running at all times.
6. Don't look back. Something may be gaining on you.

Unfortunately, no such short, concrete, and clear list exists of guidelines for assessment in macro practice—especially not from a single, highly qualified, and experienced source. However, assessment is an essential step in helping the practitioner decide how to get from where he or she is to where he or she wants to go.

The 1939 Lane Report, in which macro practice (then "community organization") was first systematically defined, noted that a primary function was "the discovery and definition of needs" and balancing needs and resources "in order to better meet changing needs." Thus the assessment of needs was acknowledged as a central role of community practice. It also seems clear that assessment must be multidimensional if it is going to take into account the variety of factors that come into play in any given problem situation. Indeed, this ecological perspective is shared by micro practice. As Hepworth and Larson point out:

To access the problems of a client system (individual, couple, or family) thus requires extensive knowledge about that system as well as consideration of the multifarious systems (e.g., economic, legal, educational, medical, religious, social, interpersonal) that impinge upon the client system.[1]

What service needs do we want to address? In the first selection, this initial question is addressed by Siegel, Attkisson, and Carson. A strong case is made for identification and assessment of needs at the local, community, and regional level. Also stressed is a requirement for citizen and consumer participation with professional personnel in the planning process.

Thoroughly explored are key variables that merit careful consideration when an assessment of human service needs is being planned, including information, resources available, the current state of program development, and the range of community attitudes toward various approaches to assessment.

A second vital and often neglected component of assessment is the coalitions framework that becomes part of any assessment. Maria Roberts-DeGennaro uses a political-economy approach to guide practitioners in this large part of the assessment process.

Paradoxically, issues of racial and ethnic sensitivity, while part of the "politically correct" assessment process, are often reduced to a "given" that receives scant attention. Who defines these issues, based on what authority or mandate? What complexities and nuances—especially as they vary from group to group—are to be taken into account? In the third article in this section, Devore and Schlesinger address these and other dimensions that must not be discounted if practice with people of color is to be successful. Also highlighted are some of the areas where micro and macro considerations are overlapping or interwoven.

Burghardt, in the final selection, cautions practitioners to consider their personal characteristics as part of the assessment process. From an individual standpoint, this may be one of the most difficult parts of assessment for macro practice practitioners. While micro practice people are often given to introspection by the nature of much of what they do, it is often argued that the reverse is true of macro practitioners. That is, because of the level at which macro practice people operate—community, organizational, representative group, and the like—the last thing taken into account is who and what the practitioner brings to the situation. As the editors are well aware from their own experiences, this personal awareness is neglected at great peril—to both the change effort and the practitioner himself or herself.

Austin's piece on human service executives in Part Six also draws attention to self-analysis as a key component of practitioner effectiveness.

As in any ecological approach, the full range of variables must be taken into account. The cross-pressures, constraints, and limitations on current community practice suggest that adequate assessment may be absolutely vital if the majority of such efforts are not to be doomed before they ever really get started.

—John L. Erlich

---

[1]Dean H. Hepworth and JoAnn Larson, *Direct Social Work Practice,* 3rd ed. (Belmont, Calif.: Wadsworth, 1990), p. 201.

7.

Larry M. Siegel, C. Clifford Attkisson, and Linda G. Carson

# NEED IDENTIFICATION AND PROGRAM PLANNING IN THE COMMUNITY CONTEXT

Assessment of service needs is a neglected and misunderstood aspect of human service program planning. Optimally, legislative blueprints for national social and health programs should emerge from systematic, scientific need assessment efforts that are designed to identify the extent and degree of need for specific services in the general population. In practice, however, national programs emerge from a political context of confrontation between special and general interests, social service ideologies, demands for service, and the competition for access to resources. As a result, our communities are peppered with uncoordinated and loosely integrated programs that overlap and compete for sparse resources. Without adequate assessment of human service needs, this poorly monitored and uncoordinated situation will persist and worsen.

This article describes the central issues of need identification and assessment. Following the initial discussion, several basic need assessment methodologies are described and illustrated. The basic assumptions on which the article is based are that identification and assessment of service needs (a) must be undertaken at the local community and regional level in a

fashion that stimulates coordination and integration of human services at the community level; (b) must be a rationalizing force in the regional health and human service planning process; and (c) must carefully blend citizen and consumer participation with professional personnel in a planning process designed to stimulate program relevance to human service needs.

## A DEFINITION OF NEED IDENTIFICATION AND ASSESSMENT

*Need identification* describes health and social service requirements in a geographic or social area, whereas *need assessment* is aimed at estimating the relative importance of these needs. The process of need identification and assessment involves two distinct steps: (a) the application of a measuring tool or an assortment of tools to a defined social area; and, following this attempt at measurement, (b) the application of judgment to assess the significance of the information gathered in order to determine priorities for program planning and service development (Blum, 1974). Assessment is a research and planning activity that is focused on a specific social area. Within social areas, need assessment strategies are designed to provide data that will enable planners to determine the extent and kinds of needs there are in a community; to evaluate existing service resources systematically; and to provide information for planning new service programs in the

C. Clifford Attkisson is Dean of Graduate Studies and Associate Vice Chancellor for Student Academic Affairs.

light of the community's needs and human service patterns.

Basically, the various known assessment techniques produce information that describes or defines social conditions or situations. These conditions are not necessarily predetermined to be positive or negative. The interpretation of social situations depends on the values and expectations of those individuals doing the interpreting. As Blum (1974) states, "The identical situation may be seen as good by those whose value expectations are met, and as bad by those whose values are not; those whose values are unrelated, or who do not connect the condition to values, may not perceive the condition at all, or view it as a natural state of affairs [pp. 219–220]."

The same rationale may be applied when considering the term "need" in situations where assessment activities are characterized as "need identification." Need in this context might usefully be defined as the gap between what is viewed as a necessary level or condition by those responsible for this determination and what actually exists. Need is at best a relative concept and the definition of need depends primarily upon those who undertake the identification and assessment effort.

## JUSTIFICATION AND GOALS FOR NEED STUDIES

The concepts of need identification and assessment are such that there is no set of generally agreed upon steps which, when carefully followed, lead one to a comprehensive assessment of needs. The reality is that planners and program administrators must decide what information will generate the most comprehensive identification and assessment of needs in a specific geographic service area, and what proportion of program resources should reasonably be allocated for this effort. Some of the relevant variables that merit careful consideration when planning an assessment of human service needs include:

## 1. Information

What assessment data are most relevant for the local program? How easily can the desired data be obtained? What is the potential accuracy and usefulness of the data?

## 2. Resources Available

What staff and fiscal resources are available to the assessment effort? What is the cost estimate of collecting (purchasing) these data? Will the expected benefits from the data outweigh their cost? Are these resources sufficient to obtain the desired information?

## 3. State of Program Development

Is the service system new or in early program planning stages? How wide is the range of services currently available? Is there a service system organizational network?

## 4. Community Attitudes

What is the community tolerance for surveys, community forums, and other approaches to assessment?

Planning human service programs for the future will require an approach to need identification that has clear sanctions and sufficient resources. Collaborative networks must be formed to act as regional information-gathering systems. These regional systems, probably organized at the multicounty level, should perform intensive field surveys and serve as a conduit through which appropriate information will be channeled to the community level.

## CONVERGENT ANALYSIS

In a comprehensive need assessment effort *convergent analysis* may be conceptualized as the second of the two operational stages, the first one being need *identification.*

Convergent analysis is a methodological framework in which information relative to human service needs may be identified, defined, evaluated, and given priority in a progressive manner. The tasks to be completed in this final analytical stage are synthesis and integration of all collected information from a variety of data collection methods.

Convergent analysis usually begins with data internal to the service system, such as legal and fundor mandates, historical trends relevant to service delivery, and client utilization information. Other forces feeding into the initial phase of convergent analysis are the orientation, training and interests of administrators and providers, and the perspectives of advisory and policy board members. The process then integrates information assembled about a specified social area or target community via a network of techniques designed to capture a wide range of perceptions about conditions in the community.

Convergent analysis is used here in the sense that the information gathered from a range of need assessment methods, deployed both systematically and sequentially, will yield a reasonably accurate identification of community needs and an assessment of the relative priorities among the needs identified. "Convergent" in this context has several meanings. First, there is a convergence of different information coming from divergent sources (e.g., citizens, consumers, service providers, and political leaders). Second, there is a convergence of different assessment strategies, each with some overlapping, yet unique,

bits of information. Third, convergent also describes the cumulative nature of an ideal assessment procedure viewed across time. Information obtained at different (though sequential) points in time (information from a wide range of data collection method and perspectives) is convergent to the extent that it can be pooled in an ongoing fashion to yield an accurate depiction of human service needs of a particular social area. All three of the above concepts of convergence analysis imply that, with each stepwise increment of information, one more clearly approximates a valid description of the social area under study. In other words, convergent analysis provides a dynamic process for reaching a convergent and discriminant validation of the needs in a social area (Campbell & Fiske, 1959). Finally, the last meaning of convergence in our formulation is to be found in the range of organizational levels through which assessment information must be channeled. Information from both state and national perspectives "converges" on service program networks at the community level. When integrated with regionally and locally generated "need" data, this information allows for more systematic program planning and development.

## BASIC PURPOSES OF NEED IDENTIFICATION AND ASSESSMENT

Assessment provides one important informational input to a much broader *planning process* that leads to (a) the selection of and priority setting among problems and target populations to be addressed; (b) the selection and operationalization of specific community program activities; and (c) the evaluation of these program activities. Assessment information helps to assure that there will be additional inputs to prevent sole reliance on professional formulations of service needs and/or to prevent overriding influence by the most vocal or powerful community groups in program planning.

Assessment also has an important role in established community programs. In such agencies, assessment can provide a continuing examination of the relevance of existing service activities to changing human service needs and priorities.

Assessment strategies are varied, and selection of a particular strategy is dependent upon the type of information sought. Assessment efforts may study the distribution of social problems in a population and the factors that influence the distribution. In the mental health field, for example, some assessment studies attempt to relate certain social or health characteristics of a population to various rates of mental disorder; or, studies may focus upon the relation between ecological characteristics of a social area and the rates of mental disorder (Bloom, 1975). Other studies employ field survey strategies in order to identify mental health problems and service needs more specifically (Warheit, Bell, & Schwab, 1974).

Most field survey efforts are designed to assess the prevalence and incidence of those who already suffer from particular disorders and to identify those subpopulations having the highest risk of experiencing specific mental health problems within a social area. When it is possible to identify populations at risk, such findings are very important in planning for services, especially preventive ones. In addition to collecting information about the range of social and health problems in a community and specification of populations at risk, program planners must also identify cultural and linguistic barriers or other features of the service system that impede effective delivery of services—such as awareness, acceptability, accessibility, and availability of services.

Beyond describing needs, assessment is also useful in identifying those factors within the human service network which aid or impede attempts to meet those needs. First, assessment may be used to specify current and/or potential resources that can be channeled or reallocated to respond to unmet needs. Second, an assessment effort is useful in gaining an understanding of the political and social value system underlying a particular social area. These values often determine what needs are identified and also tend to determine which needs receive priority in the program planning process. Finally, analysis of assessment data may suggest new interventions and may ultimately be helpful in uncovering the etiology of certain conditions. Knowledge about social, environmental, and biologic etiology will eventually lead to more effective preventive programs (Blum, 1974; Broskowski & Baker, 1974).

## ASSESSMENT CONTRASTED WITH PROGRAM EVALUATION

Care must be taken not to confuse community need assessment with evaluation. Both program evaluation and need assessment are parts of a larger program planning–implementation–development cycle, but need assessment is an environmental monitoring system. As an environmental monitoring system, it is a conceptually separate and operationally different process when compared to and contrasted with program evaluation.

## WHEN TO DO A NEED IDENTIFICATION

Considerable attention must be given by human service programs to clarification and specification of the purposes and potential uses of a proposed assessment effort. Since the process requires a substantial expenditure of resources, it should primarily be considered when there is both an opportunity and a commitment either for planning new services or for restructuring existing ones on the basis of needs that may be identified. If there is no commitment to planning or restructuring programs in accordance with those needs identified, no useful purpose is served by an assessment effort. At best, failure to use need assessment information in planning represents a waste of resources and, at worst, certain assessment procedures (such as the "community forum") may serve to heighten community expectations that needs identified will be addressed in actual service or preventive operations.

## AN OVERVIEW OF NEED IDENTIFICATION AND ASSESSMENT METHODOLOGIES

A comprehensive, convergent analysis of human service needs requires utilization of information resources that exist in (or can be obtained from) national, regional, state, and community depositories. At the local level each human service agency has unique informational needs that logically can be identified through local effort. Beyond this, however, there is a large body of information held in common by, and/or is mutually relevant to, a number of agencies comprising the human services network within a given social area. Where informational requirements overlap, a cost-efficient and effective need assessment effort can only be undertaken and/or coordinated at the regional planning level.

The various approaches to need assessment presented in this article may be undertaken at any planning level: community, regional, state, and more rarely, national. The auspices for any particular need assessment will vary accordingly. Nevertheless, mounting effective need assessment programs will require each planning body to develop a master strategy which will coordinate assessment and dissemination of assessment information throughout an area.

A need assessment program that is organized at the regional planning level affords a number of advantages. First, a single regional assessment effort instead of numerous community efforts could guarantee a substantial conservation of financial and human resources. Tremendous duplication of effort and greatly exaggerated cost could ensue if each social agency in a given area were to undertake a unilateral assessment of community needs. Second, an ongoing regional assessment effort could also share successful models that are practical to employ on a smaller scale and that would be more appropriately undertaken at the community agency level. Third, the regional assessment activity could provide readily available, decision-relevant data to community-based programs on a regular, planned basis. And fourth, need assessment conducted under regional auspices would be less influenced by local political pressure, and in that way, could serve as a vehicle for more "objective" data than that which could be obtained at the agency level.

Without the integrative capacity, production capacity, and economic advantages of this regional approach to need assessment, it is doubtful that individual community-based programs will be able to conduct assessment programs that can adequately provide the necessary information. This state of affairs would not only be a serious blow to the development of flexible, responsive human service networks but also would seriously affect the relevance of specific agencies and services.

Several constraints limit the depth and scope of need assessment efforts undertaken by community-based agencies. First, the financial base for program planning and development may be too sparse to support an extensive assessment effort. Second, the time frame in which an assessment activity is performed may limit the scope of its findings. Many, if not most, need assessments undertaken by community-based agencies are carried out in a relatively short period of time to meet, for example, governmental grant deadlines. These efforts tend to monopolize agency assessment lines. Third, internal pressure from highly vocal consumer groups often requires that immediate action be taken on a human service problem. In such circumstances, a comprehensive, time-consuming assessment effort is neither feasible nor appropriate. In these instances, where accessibility to time and/or money is limited, need assessment plans at the agency level may still be implemented to provide useful information. Excellent examples of such an effort are provided by Beigel, Hunter, Tamerin, Chapin, and Lowery (1974) and Beigel, McCabe, Tamerin, Lowery, Chapin, and Hunter (1974).

Regardless of the level at which need assessment is undertaken (local, regional, or state) there are eight need identification and assessment approaches that can provide the basis for a convergent analysis of human service needs. Each approach can be described as serving one or more information gathering functions: (a) *compilation* of information which is available but not yet disseminated within the boundaries of the social system, (b) *development* of new information, and (c) *integration* of all relevant identification that is developed from within the system or gathered from outside the system's boundaries. One of the eight

approaches performs all three informational functions, three serve two functions, and four represent only one function. The various approaches to need assessment, where the information may be obtained, how the data are formulated, and where "need" information is best utilized in the planning and development process, are summarized in Table 7.1. Table 7.1 is developed from the perspective of the community-based human service program, and assumes that regional planning bodies will soon join the local community agency in the need assessment data collection, analysis, and dissemination process.

A need assessment approach that collects information from already existing sources and subsequently organizes it in some coherent fashion illustrates a data *compilation* function. Frequently the required information exists outside the boundaries of the community-based program, for example, the National Clearinghouses of Drug Abuse Information, Mental Health Information, and Alcohol Information. Assessment approaches may also *develop* or collect new information. Here, original information bearing on the needs of a particular community is generated. Finally, a technique is classified as an *integrator* of information when data from two or more sources are organized to effect a more valid description of human service needs than is possible when information is drawn from a single source. It is in the combination of all three informational functions (compilation, development, and integration) that a convergent analysis of human service needs is achieved.

There are several important methods that can be employed to obtain information about human service needs. This section provides an outline of the various approaches including (a) a brief definition for each strategy, (b) the time at which utilization of a particular technique is appropriate,

TABLE 7.1
Need Identification and Assessment Methods

| Methods and Method Families | Perspective Being Represented | Optimal Sponsor | Source of Information | Information Processing Function | Measurement Expertise Needed | Time and Resources Needed |
|---|---|---|---|---|---|---|
| **Indicator approaches** | | | | | | |
| 1. Social and health indicator analyses | Government and private agencies | Local, state, regional, or federal planners | Public archives, planning agencies | Compilation of existing data | Moderate to high | Moderate to extensive |
| 2. Demands for services | Service agencies and consumers | Community agencies along with above | Information systems | Compilation | Moderate | Moderate |
| **Social area survey approaches** | | | | | | |
| 3. Analysis of service providers and resources | Planners | Local and regional planners | Local records and surveys | Compilation and development of new data | Low | Moderate |
| 4. Citizen surveys | Private citizens | Regional, state, or federal planners | Face-to-face, telephone, or mailed surveys | Development of new data | High | Extensive |
| 5. Community forums | Private citizens and consumers | Community agencies | Public meetings | Integration of existing and new data | Low | Moderate |
| **Community group approaches** | | | | | | |
| 6. Nominal group techniques | Planners, service providers, citizens | All levels | Specific projects | Development of new data | Moderate | Minimal |
| 7. Delphi technique | Planners, service providers, experts | All levels | Specific projects | Development and integration | Moderate | Moderate |
| 8. Community impressions | Citizens, key informants, consumers, providers | Community agencies, regional planners | Specific projects | Development, compilation, and integration | Moderate | Minimal |

Characteristics and Technical Considerations Regarding the Use of Each Method and (c) the source(s) from which data can be obtained. Each method provides a different perspective on needs. A more lengthy discussion of each technique follows in the final major sections of this article.

## Social and Health Indicator Analysis

The social and health indicator approach to need identification consists of compiling and making inferences of need from descriptive statistics found in public records and reports. It is based on the assumption that particular descriptors, such as proximity to the urban core and socioeconomic status, are viable indicators of human service needs (Bloom, 1975; Siegel, Attkisson, & Cohn, 1977). The viability of particular indicators depends upon three factors: (a) the validity and reliability of the descriptive information, (b) the logical and statistical appropriateness of procedures used to derive the social and health indicators for the community (Schulberg & Wechsler, 1967), and (c) the subjective sense or feel for the given community which is developed through these sources of information about the community.

The Social and Health Indicator approach is invaluable as an initial descriptive approach to understanding a given social area (Sheldon & Parke, 1975). Social indicator approaches range from the very simplistic designs using one or two indicators, such as census data on income, housing or a population density index, to very complex designs that consist of many variables requiring the use of complex statistical procedures such as cluster or factor analysis (Bloom, 1975).

## Social Area Surveys

*1. Demands for Services.* This approach to need identification includes compilation of existing information and integration of those sources of information. Here the aim is to review the various human service providers' (both individual and agency) past and current services-rendered patterns and requests for service by citizens in an attempt to understand the number and types of human services demanded in a particular community. These data may be secured through structured interviews with appropriate staff and board members, extrapolations from past and current clinical records and management information systems, or analysis of agency charters, licenses, funding applications, contracts, and grants. Analysis can also identify current commitments, mandates, policies, and goal statements within the human service system. Appropriate target groups include agency management, agency staff and board members, funding organizations, and citizen advocacy groups.

*2. Analysis of Service Resources.* This need assessment device involves a descriptive enumeration of the human service agencies and individual providers within a community. It can best be classified as a compilation and integration of information that exists at the agency level. This integration may take the form of a human services directory for a particular community. Important to the process of identifying existing service resources is the assessment of whether current efforts are efficiently and effectively focused on known needs.

*3. Citizen Surveys.* Here the assessment effort is concerned with eliciting differing perspectives on the nature and magnitude of human service needs from community residents. The main function of this technique is the development of new information through stratified random sampling of the community residents. This technique is most appropriately used to supplement generalized and indirect assessments, such as social and health indicator analyses, with the more personal perspective of community residents.

## Ascertaining Community Views Through Community Group Approaches

*1. Community Forum.* This approach consists of an open meeting to which all members of a community are invited and at which all participants are urged to present their views regarding the human service needs of a particular social area. Although this information is often used to validate previously existing data, the technique itself is concerned with generating new information only; that is, obtaining community residents' input on a particular issue or issues.

*2. Nominal Group Approach.* The nominal group approach is principally a non-interactive workshop designed to maximize creativity and productivity and to minimize the argumentative style of problem-solving and competitive discussion. Within this format, a *selected group of community residents* is invited to share group subject views regarding community needs or to identify barriers to relevant, effective human service delivery in a social area. The nominal group approach is most appropriately used as a method for obtaining citizen and consumer input into the need assessment and program planning process.

*3. Delphi Approach.* This approach to need identification includes the development of a questionnaire, which is distributed to a panel of resource persons and/or a select group of community residents whose opinions on a particular issue or issues are

highly valued. From their responses, a perspective can be derived regarding human service needs. This technique is quite useful and most appropriate when respondents have a minimal amount of time available for an identification effort. The Delphi process of obtaining individual opinions on a particular issue is best classified as development of new information.

*4. Community Impressions Approach.* There are three steps to this assessment procedure. First, a small but representative group of individuals is interviewed about their views of human service needs. Second, this information is then integrated with existing data taken from public records and other assessment efforts to yield a richer understanding of the community needs. Third, the resulting community portrait is then validated and/or revised according to information gained from various groups in the community through the community forum process.

This approach serves as an information integrator and validator. It employs data from three different assessment efforts, and at the same time provides new information in the form of community impressions. The community impressions approach is an economical and necessary step on the path to a creative convergence of need assessment information gained from the various other need assessment approaches.

## SOCIAL AND HEALTH INDICATOR ANALYSIS

This approach consumes preexisting, publicly available information (census data, public health data, and criminal justice data, for example) and integrates this information in an attempt to gain a clear and parsimonious description of a social area.

It does not produce new information. Rather, it analyzes, integrates, and disseminates already existing information. Although the task sounds simple, most social and health indicator analyses are complex, expensive and time-consuming.

Social and health indicator analysis cannot be treated in a detailed and systematic manner here. For more details, see Attkisson, et al., Chapters 9 and 10.

## SOCIAL AREA SURVEY APPROACHES TO NEED IDENTIFICATION

One of the first steps in a convergent analysis of human service needs is to survey existing community service resources. Surveys of social and health agencies provide information about major problems existing in a community, about help-seeking behaviors in a community, about service resources and gaps in these resources, and about existing outreach and preventive efforts in a community.

There are three main types of information that a survey of practitioners and agencies can provide. They are (a) the analysis of *demands* for service placed upon agencies and private practitioners; (b) the specification, by type, of the various human services resources in a designated social area and their corresponding capacity to respond to human service problems; and (c) a description of the pattern and the extent of interrelationships among human service resources in the community.

In analyzing demands for service, the objective is to understand the magnitude and types of requests for human services. When assessing human service resources, however, planners are concerned with comprehending the capacity of the service systems to respond to those requests and with the quality of such responses. In delineating

the interagency relationships in a particular community, we hope to clarify the extent and kind of collaborative efforts that characterize the human service network.

## Need Identification Through Analysis of Demands for Service

This approach requires a survey of the entire human services network within a community. The typical survey seeks information not only from the primary health service agencies, for example, or institutions within a community but also from other community agencies which interface with and provide a range of supporting and interlocking services to the primary health care network. Many agencies can potentially be included: mental health clinics and centers, hospitals (including psychiatric and general hospitals), drug and alcohol treatment and related service programs, private practitioners, family service programs, public health departments, churches, probation and family courts, and other social and health organizations or service providers.

Although analysis of demand for services is an important element of a broader assessment strategy, there are a few caveats related to using this approach exclusively in assessing service needs (Feldstein, 1973; Schaefer, 1975). Even though a service is well utilized, it does not necessarily follow that this service is addressing a high-priority need in the community. A high utilization rate may possibly be due to any of the following: (a) the service is well publicized; (b) it is inexpensive; (c) it is one of the only services available in the community; (d) the various professionals in the community are unaware of alternative services; and/or (e) more pejoratively, high utilization may reflect professional preferences for particular service modalities. Reciprocally, services addressing high-priority problems may be underutilized because they are unpublicized, because client referral procedures are too cumbersome, or because they have marginal relevance to professional investments. In addition, high service utilization rates may signal the need for the development of preventive programs in a particular service area. And, finally, there are likely to be important differences between those who seek or receive care and those who do not. Many "needers" are not utilizers and some utilizers are, relatively speaking, "non-needers." These caveats should be carefully considered as indicators of the hazards involved in extrapolating from populations receiving services to the population at large.

In analyzing demands for services it may be possible to secure satisfactory response from a fairly brief, well-designed, mailed questionnaire. A followup letter or phone call to nonrespondents is usually necessary to increase the response rate. A method for substantially increasing the number of returns from mailed questionnaires has been described by Robin (1965). It involves a minimum of two and a maximum of five contacts with the potential respondent. The first contact is a prequestionnaire letter which, if possible, should be written on letterhead and cosigned by someone who represents broadly recognized authority and who is able to validate the importance of the survey and the appropriateness of the respondent's participation. Optimally, the letter must (a) request individual participation; (b) explain the assessment methodology, its importance, and possible applications; (c) inform the respondent that he or she will soon receive an assessment questionnaire; and finally (d) describe procedures for safeguarding confidentiality in handling all information. The second contact consists of a cover letter and the questionnaire. Contacts three to five

consist of a series of followup strategies, should these be necessary. The reader is referred to Robin's article for further explanation of this survey strategy (Robin, 1965).

When possible, utilization surveys should be conducted in a systematic site visit format. Personal interviews with through-the-mail followups almost always produce greater reliability and validity of survey results.

## Analysis of Existing Service Resources

Beyond assessing demands for human services it is also important for every community to identify and assess its human service resources. A count of resources by type and capacity allows human service program planners to identify gaps and duplications among existing services. This knowledge of existing resources may then be contrasted with information derived from other assessment strategies relative to estimates of met and unmet needs. Usually a single survey can produce information about both (a) demands for services in the community, and (b) existing service resources.

The specific content and format of social and health agency surveys must vary from community to community to the extent that agencies in a given social area differ in structure and service objectives. Nevertheless there are a number of general interest areas that are applicable to most agencies when conducting this type of survey:

1. Range of human services provided
2. Client entry policies, conditions of eligibility for service, including age, sex, financial criteria, geographic restrictions, and particular focal or target population groups
3. Personnel characteristics and personnel development efforts

a. Service providers by training and credentials
b. Provider training and continuing education opportunities
c. Treatment modalities provided
d. Number of individuals providing various services
e. Average client load per staff member

4. Financial characteristics
   a. Charge for services—fee schedule, eligibility for third party reimbursement, sliding scale provisions
   b. Agency support—public or private, fees and other sources of funding categorized as percentage of total support budget

5. Accessibility, availability, and awareness of services
   a. Location of facility—proximity to target populations and proximity to public transportation
   b. Intake procedure—amount of information required, publicity for the available services, hours when services are provided, comfort and acceptability of the facility to clients, and availability of child-care when necessary

6. Referrals (demand)
   a. Number within a standardized time frame
   b. Source categorized by service type or status of referring agent
   c. Reasons (symptoms, problem areas)
   d. Other characteristics such as geographic locale of referring agents, geographic origin of clients who are referred, and temporal patterns of referrals

7. Accepted for service
   a. Number over a specified time period
   b. Diagnosis or other nomenclature for designated problems

c. Sociodemographic characteristics of clients—age, race, sex, census tract, socioeconomic status
d. Those refused service and reasons for refusal

8. Waiting list
   a. Number of persons on waiting list
   b. Reasons for waiting list
   c. Symptoms or problem areas of individuals placed on waiting lists
   d. Other characteristics, such as average time on waiting list and proportion of those placed on waiting list who do not eventually receive service

9. Services provided
   a. Human service problem areas thought to be of highest priority as well as services that are in increasing demand
   b. Range of actual services provided categorized by units of service
   c. List of referral resources that interface the agency

10. Referrals initiated
    a. Frequency of referrals made (listed across the range of agencies within the social area)
    b. Problems in making referrals—including such factors as transportation, financial, language, and cultural barriers.

## Identification of Need Through Analysis of Interagency Relationships—Some Further Thoughts

An analysis of the interagency relationships including the extent of collaboration among human service resources in a community is thought to be important in a comprehensive approach to need assessment. Such exploration will (a) uncover under-utilized resources; (b) give an indication of how these resources are perceived and utilized by peer agencies; (c) determine the extent to which community exists, the degree of service duplication, and the extent to which there is inadequate integration within the human service network; and (d) identify those agencies or providers who maintain collaborative ties and who might work well in a collective effort. Suggestions for restructuring or in other ways improving services may result. This type of inquiry is probably best accomplished by site visits conducted by skilled interviewers with appropriate credentials.

The main advantages of assessing need through analysis of interagency relationships are the relatively low cost of collecting and analyzing the information and the ready availability of such information. In addition, this type of survey, which tends to increase communication between human service agencies and providers, often leads to a greater sensitivity to the needs of community residents and as a result to a more adequate integration of human services. This strategy also allows for a general inventory of community resources—information that is useful when integrating need assessment information into program planning. One particularly useful subsidiary benefit of human services resource identification is the publication and distribution of a human services information directory complete with referral procedures applicable to the network of human service providers.

The two main disadvantages to this type of need identification involve, first, the difficulty in obtaining reliable data and second, drawing conclusions about a population solely on the basis of service utilization. One must proceed with caution when attempting to estimate the needs of an entire community on the basis of information obtained from an analysis of information about a sample of persons receiving services from the community's public and private care providers. In the mental health field, for example, there is a great deal of research which suggests that there is a wide gulf between the mental health needs of a community as determined by field prevalence surveys and the number of persons receiving mental health care in the same community. Other research has shown that many residents of a community may not require new or additional mental health services, because they are receiving services from agencies or providers outside of the community. A systematic need identification and assessment program must always include data concerning (a) the extent to which identified needs are being met by resources within or outside the social area being studied, and (b) the appropriateness of reliance on external resources to meet social area needs.

## Citizen Surveys: Community Residents' Perspectives on Human Service Needs

In this section, we describe three survey techniques that allow broader citizen and community participation in the identification of needs and the establishment of service priorities than those discussed to this point. Such surveys provide citizen perspectives on the nature and magnitude of service needs in the community. Either anonymous, through-the-mail, stratified random sampling or direct interview-based methods can be employed to assemble this type of information.

Through-the-mail surveys should include a random sample of people living within a geographically defined service area. The sample may be stratified by such variables as census tract, age, race, or economic status. Almost always, respondents in such surveys are anonymous.

The following types of information that were viewed as particularly relevant to mental health planning were included by Meier (1973) in a survey of residents in Contra Costa County, California: (a) community problems in order of perceived importance; (b) sources of help perceived as available for particular problems; (c) mental health problems thought most important; (d) attitudes toward utilization of a public mental health program; (e) mental health services thought most important; (f) mental health problems experienced in their own families; (g) help received for these problems; (h) satisfaction obtained from mental health services received; and (i) nomination of providers from whom one would seek help for problems of drug abuse in children and adolescents.

In some social areas face-to-face interviews with citizens have produced a better response rate and more useful information than anonymous mailed surveys. Since most surveys of this type are not particularly complex, it may be possible, without undue difficulty, to train community volunteers as interviewers (Warheit, et al., 1974). This use of community interviewers may have several secondary benefits, which include (a) involving a cadre of community people in the actual planning phase of a program; (b) educating both the interviewers and interviewees about existing or potential services; and (c) conducting the survey in an atmosphere of familiarity, which decreases interviewee's reluctance to provide survey information. Since any survey of community residents requires considerable energy and a significant amount of financial resources, a human service program should carefully contrast the advantages and disadvantages of community surveys with those of community forums as described in this article. An approach that combines some survey features with the

methodology of a community forum will be described in a later section of this article.

Still another option worth consideration when planning a resident survey is the telephone approach, which yields a much higher rate of response than a mailed questionnaire. This may be a more viable technique for programs serving middle-income areas where more people have telephones than in low-income areas, although the bias of an increasing number of unlisted telephone numbers should not be overlooked. One study comparing advantages and disadvantages of mailing or telephoning a followup questionnaire on discharged hospital patients showed that approximately 85% of the patients and relatives completed the telephone interviews as compared with a 35% return of the mailed questionnaires. It was found that certain questions provoked markedly different responses when the type of interview was by mail rather than phone (Schwartz, 1973). We would expect that the differences in response to questions would not be as great when contrasting telephone with personal interviews as they would be when comparing telephone and mail techniques. Nevertheless, design characteristics of any type of survey determine to a great extent the response rate achieved with a survey strategy. Meier (1973), for example, employed a mailed questionnaire survey format that was unusually successful—both in terms of response rate and results.

There are three primary advantages in using the survey approach to need identification. According to Warheit et al. (1974), carefully designed and conducted surveys provide the most scientifically valid and reliable information obtainable regarding citizen views of their service needs and utilization patterns. It is also the most direct method of obtaining data about the needs of persons in a community. Finally it is very flexible and can be designed in an extremely wide variety of ways to answer questions related to human service needs. The value of selective use of surveys to assess in depth the specific needs of known high-risk populations cannot be overemphasized.

Disadvantages of the survey method of need identification include the following: In comparison to other methods, it tends to be more expensive. Some respondents are reluctant to offer information about themselves or other family members. Finally, the data obtained are based on self-report and are not independently verified in the typical case. A more thorough description of community survey methodology is presented in Attkisson et al., Chapter 10 [not reprinted here].

## ASCERTAINING COMMUNITY VIEWS THROUGH GROUP APPROACHES

In addition to surveys, there are many different ways in which citizen and consumer views of human service needs can be ascertained. In this section, we describe four methods that are useful in undertaking a relatively quick and inexpensive assessment from the perspective of the community: (a) community forums, (b) workshops using the nominal group technique, (c) the Delphi technique, and (d) the community impressions approach.

When a human services network must conduct a community assessment rapidly, any one of the community group methods may be used independently; however, they are most usefully employed in conjunction with approaches described in previous sections of this article. Once surveys have been undertaken and social and health indicator analyses have been conducted, community group methods can be used to gain an additional perspective on the reliability or the interpretation of the previously collected information. The more formal data collection procedures do not capture all relevant information and the data that are collected by formal data collection approaches may not provide an up-to-date portrait of the human service system in a community.

The community group methods can also be invaluable in determining which need areas among those detected during the formal data gathering have highest priority in the community. Because of disparate values and perspectives, different interest groups in a community will view certain conditions as more important than others: they will also hold varying notions as to the distribution of needs and the most appropriate approaches to interventions.

Linking survey with community group approaches is the only reliable mechanism for achieving a convergent analysis of needs and priorities—an analysis on which planning decisions can be based.

### Community Forums as a Means of Needs Assessment

Any person living or working in a community is potentially an information resource on the sociological and psychological aspects of that community. Community residents either directly, through personal experience, or indirectly, through observation or study, form impressions about the human service needs in a social area. The perspectives of residents concerning the accessibility, availability, acceptability, and organization of services comprise indispensable clues about the human service needs of the community as a whole. It is unlikely that any one person has a comprehensive view of human service needs or that two people have the same view. Yet, each person's view portrays some potentially important aspect of the existing reality. In the process of integrating these various viewpoints, a useful, although impressionistic, picture of the human service needs in a community begins to emerge. The community forum represents a quick and effective method of eliciting this desired information.

A community forum is an open meeting for all members of a designated community. Its purpose is to provide a setting for members of a community to express their opinions about a particular issue—in this case the human service needs of the community. Forums resemble an old fashioned "town meeting," but can be more open and flexible. Any person attending is considered an important information resource and is encouraged to express his or her views. In general, forums last 3–4 hours and may include a wide range of activities: information exchange, communication of details about new programs or projects, introduction of various community members, and more general social interaction. The major function of the forum, however, is to elicit views from as many people as possible on a single issue. Although it is possible, the forum itself rarely involves decision making on the basis of views presented. At heart it is a means of problem identification and of obtaining citizen reaction to service efforts.

For further details on planning and carrying out community forums, see Attkisson, et al. (1978), pp. 240–241 and Cox, et al. (1984).

There are four advantages in using the community forum approach. First, community forums are, without question, quite economical in relation to other methods of need assessment. Planning for the meeting, including publicity, can be accomplished in a matter of weeks, and the forum itself may only last a few hours. The costs include the publicity, the time of any paid personnel in planning and implementing the forum and in analyzing the forum results, the time of a recording secretary, the provision of necessary transportation and child-care services to facilitate attendance of certain community members, and perhaps the rental of a meeting place. Many of these tasks may be accomplished by community volunteers.

Second, forums allow a wide range of individuals from the community to express their opinions about human service needs. Since the forum is open to all members of the community, a presentation of all important views can potentially be heard. Of particular importance is the fact that the views of those individuals who fall into the underserved or nonserved category in the community can be heard.

Third, the forum may serve as a catalyst for the initiation of plans and actions about the human service needs in the community. During the forum, those who have not previously considered the question of service needs may be stimulated to do so. As a result of interest generated by the forum, one could well expect the initiation of certain activities related to meeting human service needs.

Fourth, the forum provides those responsible for the need assessment with an opportunity not only to hear from many different elements of the community about unmet needs, but also to identify those participants and agencies most interested in doing something about them. These individuals can be invaluable in the convergent analysis phase of assessment and in developing plans to meet the needs identified.

There are also four main disadvantages to community forums. First, given a sizable forum attendance, it is unlikely that everyone who wishes to speak will have a chance to do so. Thus, certain information that could be quite relevant to the assessment of needs may never be presented.

Second, not all members of the community can or will attend a forum. Certain viewpoints about unmet human service needs may not be represented at the forum. The results of the forum provide an impressionistic and probably incomplete picture of needs.

Third, although the forum does provide an opportunity for expressing many valuable perspectives, particularly concerning need identification, it is usually the case that the discussion does not go beyond this point.

Fourth, the forum may mobilize certain elements of the community, or at least heighten the awareness of existing human service needs in the community. As a result, the expectations of community members may be raised in ways that cannot or will not be met. Organizers of the forum have a responsibility to inform attendees of realistic outcomes that may be expected from the forum and to advise participants that the process of problem identification is only the first phase of a problem-solving process.

From the advantages and disadvantages of the community forum approach it can be concluded that forums are most appropriate if there is interest in (a) uncovering citizen feelings and impressions about human service needs—particularly citizens who represent those groups that are underrepresented in census data and utilization rates; and (b) identifying directly in a public arena the concerns of citizens as well as enlisting stimulating support for planning efforts directed at those needs.

## The Nominal Group Technique

A second community group approach to need identification in human services is the nominal group technique (Delbecq & Van de Ven, 1971) that is used extensively in

industrial, governmental, educational, and health organizations. The nominal group technique was developed through a series of experiments over a period of 10 years by Delbecq and his colleagues, and is a model approach to problem identification and program planning (Delbecq, Van de Ven, & Gustafson, 1975). This group process method was designed for the identification of organizational problems and formulation of appropriate and innovative tactics to solve them. Following an initial problem identification and ranking process, the nominal group is a methodology for involving critical reference groups in successive phases of program planning and development: (a) clients (consumers) and first-line staff, in the problem exploration stage; (b) external resource people and internal specialists, in solution and resource exploration; (c) key administrators and resource controllers, in priority development; (d) organizational staff in program proposal inception and development; and (e) all constituencies, in final approval and designs for evaluation.

The usefulness of the nominal group technique is based on Delbecq and Van de Ven's research, which indicated that a nominal group—one in which individuals work in the presence of one another but initially do not interact—allows production of a greater number of problem dimensions, more high-quality suggestions, and a larger number of more highly differentiated kinds of solutions than groups in which members are encouraged or allowed to interact during the generation of critical problem variables (Delbecq & Van de Ven, 1971).

The nominal group process initially involves silent, individual effort in a group setting, with working groups limited to eight to ten individuals. Basically, the process includes posing a question or a series of questions to a group and inviting each group member to list brief responses or answers to the question during a silent period of 10–15 minutes. These questions may seek possible solutions to a particular problem or may merely seek opinions about a particular human service problem in a community. When used in human service need assessment, participants may be asked to identify their own human service needs, to list the needs they perceive for other groups in the community, or to identify important factors or issues to be considered in a community program planning process. This initial silent time spent in idea generation is followed by an interval in which all ideas generated by individuals are shared with the total group. The group leader, in round-robin fashion, asks each participant to offer one idea from his or her list. Each idea is then recorded on large sheets of paper, which are then displayed for continued review by the total group. Every effort is made to record the ideas exactly as they are offered from the participants. The leader continues the round-robin until all ideas on each participant's list are exhausted. This procedure may take 1–2 hours, depending upon the type of questions posed and the number of ideas generated. During this phase, participants are asked to refrain from making comments or discussing any of the ideas, as the round-robin is for enumeration of ideas only.

Once the round-robin is completed, a discussion period follows in which participants are free to clarify, elaborate, or defend any of the ideas presented. During this discussion, participants may add new ideas to the list; they may eliminate certain ideas; they may combine ideas that seem to overlap substantially; or they may condense ideas that appear similar. One means of facilitating this process is for the leader to read one idea at a time from the list generated, to ask for discussion, comments, or

questions in reference to that idea, and then to move on to the next. Participants are not required to defend or otherwise substantiate an idea.

Once the leader feels that sufficient clarification has been achieved, each participant is then asked to select those ideas (from the total list) that are considered most important. Each person selects five or more (as desired) ideas judged personally to be most important, and ranks them accordingly. These "votes" are then tallied, and the result is the group's rank ordering of those ideas generated in order of importance. In a human services need assessment, for example, individuals may be asked to rank those identified needs which are the most critical for program planning and intervention. All selection and ranking is done individually and anonymously.

The nominal group technique allows for group decision making or idea sharing without the typical competitive problems of the interacting group. Also, each participant privately expresses his or her perception of the relative importance of the many different problem areas or need areas generated by the group as a whole. The silent period in the nominal group process is critical to the production of ideas. It allows each member time for reflection and thought. It encourages the generation of minority ideas; it avoids hidden agendas; it imposes a burden on all present to work and contribute and to have a sense of responsibility for the group's success; it facilitates creativity; it allows for the airing of personal concerns; and it is especially useful in a heterogeneous group as it does not allow any one person or point of view to dominate.

By following the silent period with round-robin sharing, all ideas are shared with the group before they are discussed and each member has assurance that all of his or her ideas will be heard. In the discussion that follows, the feedback and information-sharing benefits of the interacting group are gained. The group has a chance to question and to clarify each idea presented. Other advantages accruing to the nominal group technique include social modeling of disclosure by more secure group members, which facilitates disclosure on the part of less secure members; a setting in which the pooling of resources from a heterogeneous, potentially noncollaborative group may occur; and finally, the potential for new perspectives on or cognitive remapping of "old" or existing problems.

The main disadvantage of the nominal group technique is that it lacks precision. Votes or rankings are made without thorough or careful sorting out of all of the ideas generated into appropriate categories. Another disadvantage, and quite an important one in our experience, is that although most participants enjoy the process and feel satisfied with the results, some participants may feel manipulated because they are not used to participating in a highly structured process. These disadvantages are minor and can be handled by careful planning, preparation of participants, and followup feedback to participants.

## The Delphi Technique

An additional community groups approach to human service need identification is the Delphi technique (Dalkey, 1967; Dalkey & Helmer, 1963). The Delphi is a procedure for the systematic solicitation and collation of informed judgments on a particular topic (Delbecq et al., 1975). The Delphi is usually composed of a set of carefully designed sequential questionnaires. With each subsequent questionnaire, summarized information and opinion feedback derived from earlier questionnaires are provided. This summarized information is carefully organized to provide a common reference point against which the Delphi judges base their responses. The sequential questionnaires take the form of a structured dialogue between persons who do not meet, but whose opinions are valuable to the issue at hand.

This method for systematically eliciting and refining group judgments has three defining characteristics (Dalkey, 1969; Delbecq et al., 1975): (a) anonymous response to question or questions, (b) iteration or controlled feedback of various stages of the information collection process, and (c) statistical analysis and formulation of group responses.

First, anonymity may be ensured by the use of questionnaires or, where resources permit, on-line computer communication. Second, the Delphi exercise is conducted in a series of rounds between which a summary of the results of the previous round is distributed to each participant. Third, the form in which this controlled feedback is given is statistical, and usually consists of the group medium (Dalkey, 1967, 1969; Delbecq et al., 1975), although other less directive forms of iteration are being considered (e.g., the quantity of the individual's score).

The Delphi technique consists of five basic steps:

1. A questionnaire is developed relative to a key issue or set of issues.
2. Questionnaires are distributed to a panel of experts or key individuals. Since it is not necessary and often not desirable to have these experts meet, the questionnaire can be mailed to the participants serving on the panel.
3. When the questionnaires are returned, the results are tallied to determine areas of agreement and disagreement.

4. When disagreement occurs, a second questionnaire containing the various reasons given by the experts for their initial judgments is distributed to the panel.
5. The above steps are repeated, hopefully until an agreement can be reached.

The Delphi has typically gained widest use in areas of broad- or long-range policy formulation in, for example, the U.S. Air Force and in industry for technological forecasting and evaluation of corporate planning (Helmer, 1967). Various public agencies are beginning to use the Delphi for planning exercises related to education, health, and urban growth. Although the original experiments relating to the Delphi centered around questions having definitive factual answers, the originators believe this method is appropriate in areas of "value judgment" where preset "answers" are not available.

This method of assessment has a number of possible human service applications: to determine or develop a typology of human service needs; to explore or expose underlying assumptions or information leading to different judgments as to human service needs; to correlate informed judgments on a topic spanning a wide range of social roles and/or disciplines; and to educate the respondent group as to the diverse and interrelated aspects of human services needs (Turoff, 1971).

The Delphi involves at least two separate groups of individuals. First, the user body is composed of the individual or individuals expecting some product from the exercise which is useful to their purposes. Next there is a design and monitor team, which constructs the initial questionnaire, summarizes the returns, and designs the followup questionnaires. The final group of individuals involved in a Delphi effort are the respondents. It is important to note that this latter group of persons who are chosen to respond to the questionnaires may in some cases also be the user body.

There are four advantages to the Delphi technique. First, because participation can be anonymous, the inhibiting influences of dominant and more verbal participants are minimized. Second, due to the fact that feedback is controlled in a systematic manner, the negative influences of individual vested interests are reduced to a minimum. Third, because responses are anonymous, group pressure to conform is significantly decreased. Fourth, the Delphi is an efficient user of the respondents' time. Efficiency in the use of time allows the involvement of individuals who cannot otherwise become involved in other more time-consuming procedures.

The main disadvantage of the Delphi technique is the lack of certainty in guidelines on its use or design. For example, there are a number of important questions for which general agreement does not exist among practitioners, users, and critics: (a) Is the respondent group completely anonymous among its own members, to the design team, or to the user body? (b) Should the Delphi be used in conjunction with a committee or ongoing study effort? (c) Should the iterations (controlled feedback) be cycled to the same respondent group, or is there a series of separate respondent groups interacting independently or parallel with one another? (d) How many iterations are needed? and (e) What form should the feedback take? A further disadvantage is that extreme positions may be dropped in order to obtain agreement and consequently many divergent, yet creative ideas may be lost. This latter disadvantage is also shared by the nominal group and other similar approaches.

A use of the Delphi at the national planning level illustrates this technique (National

Institute of Drug Abuse, 1975). The Prevention Branch of the National Institute of Drug Abuse employed the Delphi process as a part of an attempt to develop "a National Strategy for Primary Drug Abuse Prevention." The project involved 420 prevention planners, administrators, and programmers from community programs, state agencies, and federal departments. The main objective was to promote the evolution of a national strategy for primary prevention that would be conceptually sound and capable of implementation. Furthermore, the effort was designed (a) to involve in the strategy development those federal, state and community-based practitioners who would be directly affected by it, and (b) to facilitate collaboration and resource sharing among the scattered advocates of primary prevention.

In order to attain these objectives, the following three tasks were proposed:

1. Development of a sound, supportable definition of primary drug abuse prevention
2. Clarification of what is being done now in prevention, as well as recommendations on the kinds of new strategies that should be implemented
3. Descriptions of the training and technical assistance resources needed at state and local levels.

The project was divided into two phases. In Phase I, a total of 70 participants were convened at three sites to address the objectives. The information generated at these sessions was then refined by 30 of the participants before and during a fourth meeting.

In Phase II, the Phase I recommendations were presented to an additional 340 prevention workers at five regional conferences. The results of the entire process were then tabulated and incorporated into a final report that included:

1. A working definition of primary drug abuse prevention
2. An exhaustive list of those activities that are now being done or should be done by preventors
3. A section devoted to training and technical assistance. This latter section describes the information and program support needs that were identified at all nine conferences.

## The Community Impressions Approach

The community impressions approach was developed by Cohn and her colleagues at the School of Public Health at the University of California, Berkeley (1972). It allows for direct focus on those groups in the population that have been identified as having the greatest human service needs and is a procedure for involving those groups in subsequent planning and evaluation activities directed at establishing programs to reduce their needs. A comprehensive view of needs combines hard data with impressions and feelings about need. In this process it is very important to identify and involve those groups with the greatest human service needs in both the assessment and subsequent planning and program development activities.

The community impressions approach integrates existing data about human service needs with community impressions about such needs. First, community impressions are obtained from key individuals living or working in the community. Then, on the basis of all available sources of data (social indicator, survey and community group data) groups identified as having the greatest human service needs are approached in order to verify findings and/or to explore human service needs further. The approach has three major steps:

*1. Key Informant Interviews.* In this approach, interviews are conducted with 10 or 15 individuals who have extensive first-hand knowledge of the community and who either live or work in the community. Interviewees are selected on the basis of the longevity of their involvement in the community and/or the nature of their involvement with the community. These informants are asked to provide their perspectives on the human service needs of different groups in the community. Thus, a public health nurse, members of any community action agencies, long-time residents, a policeman or fireman, the local health officer, and others are interviewed in order to elicit their impressions. The interviews are conducted from a list of questions about the existing human services in the community and about certain demographic characteristics of the population with the aid of a map of the community under study. Answers to questions such as "Where do the elderly live?" and "What public transportation exists between different parts of the community and the local community mental health center?" are recorded on the map. Slowly, a picture of the community, from service and demographic viewpoints, begins to emerge. Typically, the interview will result in some fairly concrete statements of need. Once 10 to 15 key community members have been interviewed, their impressions are collapsed onto one map. It is highly probable that there will be some discrepancies in both information and impressions. In analyzing the discrepancies in impressions about need, the need assessor should settle the discrepancies by erring "in favor" of identifying groups as having unmet needs (i.e., if one interviewee identified a group as having many human service problems, and another interviewee identified that same group as having few, the group should be recorded at this time as having many—this will be verified with the group under question at a later date).

*2. Integration of Existing Information.* Existing data from the widest possible range of needs assessment methods are then integrated with the community impressions. Emphasis here should be on balancing efforts to integrate as much available, existing data as possible in order to move toward a convergent analysis of needs. Once enough information has been collected to satisfy the assessor's need for factual information about the community, this "hard data" should be added to the map of impressions from interviewees, thus yielding a richer understanding of the needs of the community. This combined picture should not be taken as complete, however. It should ideally be validated with relevant groups in the community.

*3. The Community Forum.* A community forum is planned and held for each group or section of the community identified as having significant unmet human service needs (see the section on community forums). One purpose of the forum is to allow those groups identified as having unmet needs to validate or invalidate those needs. In addition to validation, however, the forum serves as an opportunity to explore in greater depth the nature and perceived etiology of these needs. Moreover, the forum serves as an opportunity to involve those persons with the greatest need in the process of defining and placing priorities on those needs. In this manner, the forum helps to complete the need assessment process while initiating the process of responding to the needs identified.

The community impressions approach has a number of advantages and disadvantages. First, it can be carried out with minimal expenditure of time and resources.

Second, it allows for consideration and convergence of a variety of informational sources, both those that represent what might be regarded as "factual clues" about human service needs and those that might be regarded as "impressionistic clues" about human service needs.

Third, it relies on more than information generated by "outsiders." Those identified as having unmet human service needs have an opportunity to determine whether or not they think and feel that they do in fact have unmet needs. Additionally, these groups have an opportunity to voice opinions about better procedures for meeting their needs and to become involved in activities that may lead to reduction of those needs.

Fourth, through the discussion and interaction that characterizes this approach, channels of communication among different human service agencies in the community may be strengthened or in some cases established. As a result, a more effective, broad-based, community approach to need assessment, to the establishment of priorities, and the allocation of resources may take place.

As fruitful as the community impressions approach may be, the results insofar as possible must be subjected to the same tests of reliability and validity that are applied to the results from the various types of need assessment surveys. Typically it is found that reasonable standards of reliability and validity cannot be confirmed, and the results must be generally considered as impressionistic. Due to this problem, there is no way to ensure that every group with human service needs will be identified or that all of the needs of those identified will have been recorded. Community impressions must be considered as one perspective about needs among many others, and divergencies in perspectives must be resolved in the subsequent program planning process.

The community impressions approach is most useful when one is interested in undertaking quickly and at little cost an assessment of the unmet human service needs in different groups within the community. The approach takes into consideration the content of data from other approaches *and* also the thoughts and feelings of various community members. The approach is particularly useful if one is committed to involving those with greatest needs in processes which will help reduce their needs.

## SUMMARY

Need identification and assessment are integral aspects of human service planning and development. *Need identification* is the process of describing the health and social service needs of a geographic area. In the *need assessment* process, planners set priorities on identified needs with reference to relative importance, available resources, and available service technology.

The area of need assessment-identification is in its nascence, and no universally accepted methodology exists that will yield a comprehensive assessment of need. Moreover, the evaluation and interpretation of human service need is influenced by (a) the vested interests and values of those formulating program goals; (b) the diffuse and interrelated nature of social and health needs; (c) the rapidly changing character of human service needs; and (d) the capabilities and interests of staff as well as the availability of appropriate service technology and adequate financing.

Within the limits of current assessment methodologies, information about needs is useful in (a) describing demands for services; (b) assessing service resources;

(c) developing detailed community descriptions; (d) delineating groups likely "to be at risk"; (e) examining the relevance of existing services; (f) clarifying those factors that influence the occurrence of social and health problems; and (g) enumerating factors that aid or impede effective service delivery.

The most comprehensive picture of human service need can be obtained through a convergent analysis of need. Convergent analysis assumes that useful information about need emerges out of a process that receives input (a) at different, although sequential points in time; (b) from a number of different organizational levels; (c) from a variety of informational sources (community members, public records, service agency data, professional staff); and (d) through a family of assessment strategies. Further assumptions basic to a convergent analysis are that no single stakeholder, no one informational source, no single organizational level, no specific technique, and no single point in time will provide a comprehensive human service need assessment. It is only through the systematic, progressive convergence of multiple perspectives filtered through multiple assessment methods that the most useful information for planning is obtained. A convergent analysis identifies the widest range of need information that is relevant for program planning and service development by assessing need at all community and organizational levels.

The variety of assessment strategies used in a convergent analysis provides three different informational functions: (a) *compiling* existing information; (b) *developing* new information; and (c) *integrating* existing and newly developed information. There are advantages and disadvantages of each need assessment strategy when viewed in isolation. However, when seen as part of a total convergence of information, deployment of a range of methods provides the basis for an integrated perspective on need.

There are three basic orientations to assessing human service need: (a) the social and health indicators approach; (b) social area surveys; and (c) the community groups approaches. The *social and health indicator approach* to need assessment compiles publicly available information, and, on the basis of these data, needs are inferred. *Social area surveys* compile and integrate information about demands for service; provide information about resources that are currently available to meet the needs of the community; and provide citizens' views about needs and need priorities. In addition, new information can be generated on a personal self-report level from community members through direct interview surveys. Finally, the community group approaches to assessment are quick and inexpensive methods to use in conjunction with other assessment techniques. The group methods provide perspectives from community members by developing new information, compiling already existing information, and integrating existing information with the perspectives of persons living in the community.

## REFERENCES

Attkisson, C. C., Hargreaves, W. A., Horowitz, M. J., & Sorenson, J. E. (Eds.). *Evaluation of human service programs.* New York: Academic Press, Inc., 1978.

Beigel, A., Hunter, E. J., Tamerin, J. S., Chapin, E. H., & Lowery, M. J. Planning for the development of comprehensive community alcoholism services: I. The prevalence survey. *American Journal of Psychiatry,* 1974, *131,* 1112–1115.

Beigel, A., McCabe, T. R., Tamerin, J. S., Lowery, M. J., Chapin, E. H., & Hunter, E. J.

Planning for the development of comprehensive community alcoholism services: II. Assessing community awareness and attitudes. *American Journal of Psychiatry,* 1974, *131,* 1116–1120.

Bloom, B. L. *Changing patterns of psychiatric care.* New York: Human Sciences Press, 1975.

Blum, H. L. *Planning for health.* New York: Human Sciences Press, 1974.

Broskowski, A., & Baker, F. Professional, organizational, and social barriers to primary prevention. *American Journal of Orthopsychiatry,* 1974, *44,* 707–719.

Campbell, D. T., & Fiske, D. W. Convergent and discriminant validation by the multitrait-multimethod matrix. *Psychological Bulletin,* 1959, *56,* 81–105.

Cohn, A. H. *Solutions to unique problems encountered in identifying the medically underserved and involving them in the planning process.* Unpublished manuscript, School of Public Health, University of California, Berkeley, California, 1972.

Cox, F. M., Erlich, J. L., Rothman, J., & Tropman, J. E. (Eds.). *Tactics and techniques of community practice.* 2nd ed. Itasca, Illinois: F. E. Peacock Publishers, Inc., 1984.

Dalkey, N. C. *Delphi.* Santa Monica, California: Rand Corporation, 1967.

Dalkey, N. C. *The Delphi method: An experimental study of group opinion.* Santa Monica, California: Rand Corporation, 1969.

Dalkey, N. C., & Helmer, O. An experimental application of the Delphi method to the use of experts. *Management Science,* 1963, *9,* 458–467.

Delbecq, A. L., & Van de Ven, A. H. A group process model for problem identification and program planning. *Journal of Applied Behavioral Science,* 1971, *7,* 466–492.

Delbecq, A. L., Van de Ven, A. H., & Gustafson, D. H. *Group techniques for program planning: A guide to nominal group and Delphi processes.* Glenview, Illinois: Scott Foresman & Company, 1975.

Demone, H. W., & Harshbarger, D. (Eds.). *A handbook of human service organizations.* New York: Behavioral Publications, 1974.

Feldstein, P. J. Research on the demand for health services. In J. B. McKinlay (Ed.), *Economic aspects of health care.* New York: Prodist, Milbank Memorial Fund, 1973.

Goldsmith, H. F., Unger, E. L., Rosen. B. M., Shambaugh, J. P., & Windle, C. D. *A typological approach to doing social area analysis.* (DHEW Publication No. ADM 76-262.) Washington, D.C.: U.S. Government Printing Office, 1975.

Helmer, O. *Analysis of the future: The Delphi method.* Santa Monica, California: Rand Corporation, 1967.

Meier, R. *Contra Costa mental health needs.* Unpublished manuscript. Contra Costa County Mental Health Services. Martinez, California, 1973.

National Institute of Drug Abuse, Prevention Branch, Division of Resource Development. *Pyramid.* 1975, *1,* 1–2. (Available from: NIDA, 1526 18th Street, N.W., Washington, D.C. 20036.)

Robin, S. A procedure for securing returns to mail questionnaires. *Sociology and Social Research,* 1965, *50,* 24–35.

Schaefer, M. E. Demand versus need for medical services in a general cost-benefit setting. *American Journal of Public Health,* 1975, *65,* 293–295.

Schulberg, H. C., & Wechsler, H. The uses and misuses of data in assessing mental health needs. *Community Mental Health Journal,* 1967, *3,* 389–395.

Schwartz, R. Follow-up by phone or by mail. *Evaluation,* 1973, *1(2),* 25–26.

Sheldon, E. B., & Parke, R. Social indicators. *Science,* 1975, *188,* 693–699.

Siegel, L. M., Attkisson, C. C., & Cohn, A. H. Mental health needs assessment: Strategies and techniques. In W. A. Hargreaves, C. C. Attkisson, & J. E. Sorensen (Eds.). *Resource materials for community mental health program evaluation* (2nd ed.). (DHEW Publication No. ADM 77-328.) Washington, D.C.: U.S. Government Printing Office, 1977.

Turoff, M. Delphi and its potential impact on information systems. *AFIPS Conference Proceedings,* 1971, *39,* 317–326.

Warheit, G. J., Bell, R. A., & Schwab, J. J. *Planning for change: Needs assessment approaches.* Rockville, Maryland: National Institute of Mental Health, 1974.

**8.**

**Maria Roberts-DeGennaro**

## CONCEPTUAL FRAMEWORK OF COALITIONS
## IN AN ORGANIZATIONAL CONTEXT

Human service organizations are struggling to survive with fewer resources. Because of the increased competition for funds, some organizations have agreed to work together in their struggle for survival by forming coalitions. These coalitions provide a convening mechanism through which a group of organizations can interact and work together around a common purpose (Roberts-DeGennaro, 1986a, 1986b, 1987, 1988). Under the "Contract With America," funds for human services are expected to be increasingly cut back due to changes in public policies, In sharing the same compelling interests to serve disadvantaged populations, it is anticipated that these organizational groups will continue to join forces and coalesce.

The author defines a coalition as an interacting group of organizational actors who (a) agree to pursue a common goal, (b) coordinate their resources in attempting to achieve this goal, and (c) adopt a common strategy in pursuing this goal. Stevenson, Pearce, and Porter (1985) defined a coalition as: "an interacting group of individuals, deliberately constructed, independent of the formal structure, lacking its own internal formal structure, consisting of mutually perceived membership, issue oriented, focused on a goal or goals external to the coalition, and requiring concerted mem-

ber action" (p. 261). For earlier definitions of coalitions, see Gamson (1961), Kelley (1968), Browne (1973), Hill (1973), Van Velzen (1973), and Boissevain (1974).

There are three major advantages for an organization to join a coalition. First, political and economic events are shaking up boundaries, structures, and assumptions related to the delivery of health and human services. In this cost-cutting environment, human service organizations are becoming increasingly motivated to coordinate their efforts and cooperate. As the need for scarce resources intensifies from further funding reductions, organizations are more likely to build coalitions in order to gain or re-gain resources. As a group of organizational actors, a coalition can exert more power and influence and mobilize more resources than a single organization.

Second, as organizational actors interact within a coalition, they are introduced to new ideas, new perspectives, and new technologies for solving problems. This helps to promote an awareness of alternative strategies that the member organizations can use in other problem situations. This interactional process strengthens the coalition's capacity to engage in cooperative problem solving. A sense of empowerment emerges as skills are sharpened in making decisions that people can agree on and enact together.

Third, a more extensive channel of internal communication can be created within

Maria Roberts-DeGennaro is Professor of Social Work at San Diego State University.

the member organizations, as a result of joining a coalition. Representatives from various programs within these organizations may be serving on committees or task forces of the coalition. This involvement serves as a source of feedback to other staff within the organization regarding the coalition's decisions and activities. This feedback loop can help to increase the staff's perspective of how problems affecting their organization also affect other organizations in the community. A "bigger" picture of the problem can then be perceived by the staff rather than maintaining a "lonely organization" perspective.

A review of the literature suggests there is a relative shortage of accepted methodologies for identifying and measuring coalitions. Typically, coalitions have been examined in three- or four-person groups (Stanton & Morris, 1987). Cobb (1991) contends that empirical studies of coalitions have produced a number of important findings, but ". . . the studies were not designed to be generally applicable to coalitions in the organization context" (p. 1058).

The purpose of this article is to present a conceptual framework of coalitions in organizational settings. The objective of the framework is to provide a conceptual context for understanding the diversity of the roles played by coalitions in changing the sociopolitical structures in which they must operate. In developing this framework, first, the political-economy perspective is used to define the nature of coalition building. This perspective represents a broad approach or strategy direction. It suggests that the human services system in which coalitions operate reflects the political processes among those groups that have control over scarce resources, namely, money and authority, and around access to these resources, as well as their allocation (Benson, 1975; Roberts, 1983; Roberts-DeGennaro, 1988).

Next, models of coalitions are used in developing this framework. Models are more specific, detailed, and coherently patterned internally than a perspective, which as previously mentioned, represents a broad approach or strategy direction (Rothman & Tropman, 1987). The author elaborates on Croan and Lees's (1979) five coalition models. In each of these models, the purpose of the coalition dictates the functions to be performed by the coalition. The author then presents case vignettes of these coalition models in order to illustrate their application to practice.

The final section of the article presents some practice considerations in building coalitions. In response to changes in the political-economic environment, coalitions are acting as a convening mechanism for sociopolitical action (Rosenthal & Mizrahi, 1994). For example, instead of waiting for federal health care reform, health care providers are joining forces and creating coalitions to reform the system on their own (Caudron, 1993). In building coalitions, Hagen and Davis (1992) believe there ". . . must be a willingness to compromise so a unified agenda and strategy can be established" (p. 500). As changes in the environment affect the availability of resources, it is suspected that those coalitions which survive will be those that are able to anticipate and adapt to these changes.

Besides using a "survival of the fittest" approach to understanding the behavior of coalitions, we need access to various perspectives and models, in order to develop theories about the practice of coalition building. In the search for a practice theory, this article aims to contribute to the knowledge base related to understanding the diverse roles that coalitions play in adapting to their political-economic environment and in shaping public policies.

## POLITICAL-ECONOMY PERSPECTIVE

According to exchange theory, coalitions form in response to the needs of their members as they seek resources from the environment (Levine & White, 1961). Organizations are then driven by resource scarcity to enter into exchanges with other organizations and so they voluntarily form coalitions. Hall, Clark, Giordano, Johnson and Van Roekel's (1977) study supported the contention that when the basis of interaction is voluntary, exchange theory can explain some aspects of a coalition's behavior.

Gillespi and Mileti (1979) argued that resource scarcity is a necessary, but not a sufficient condition for cooperative behavior among organizations in building a coalition. An organization that lacks resources for attaining a particular goal could avert the problem by designating a new goal. Therefore, exchange theory probably cannot predict when an organization might change its goals rather than interact with other organizations and join a coalition.

Benson (1975) extended the basic exchange theoretical framework. He argued, on the basis of Yuchtman and Seashore's (1967) model of acquisition of resources, that organizations seek an adequate supply of money and authority to fulfill program requirements, maintain domain, ensure their flow of resources, and extend or defend their way of doing things. Thus, scarce resources are acquired from a political-economy environment. Due to the nature of this environment, organizations can maximize their supply of money and authority by coalescing with other organizations.

The political environment, within which a coalition operates and performs, refers to the structure of authority and power, and the dominant values, goals, and ethos insti-

tutionalized within the coalition. Wamsley and Zald (1973) suggest the coalition carries out political functions in order to insure its growth and survival in this environment, including: (a) defining the mission, ethos, and priorities of the coalition; (b) developing boundary spanning units and positions to sense and adapt to environmental pressures and changes; (c) insuring the recruitment and socialization of the coalition's membership to maintain coherence and the pursuit of the coalition's goals; and (d) overseeing the internal economy and harmonizing it with shifts in goal priorities. These political functions are performed often within a rather turbulent external environment of human service cutbacks and re-organization and/or re-engineering efforts. Consequently, coalitions are continually seeking new elements of community support or potential support for human services and, in some cases, redefining tasks. As a result, they are reshaping the conditions of existence for human services. As change agents, they must know how to generate issues, mobilize constituents, and gain the support of key actors who are affected by and interested in influencing policy.

It is anticipated that political-economic forces will continue to place organizations into competitive positions with other organizations for scare resources. Who has the power in our communities to set the terms of this competition? Usually, it is the local politicians who are elected to represent the needs of citizens in their community. Coalitions are spending a considerable amount of time in preparing documentation for these politicians to demonstrate the needs of disadvantaged clients in order to justify why they need community support.

In preparing documentation on client needs, organizations are expected to develop indicators of performance and establish criteria for effectiveness. In responding to these pressures, information is needed on the outcomes of program efforts and on expected outcomes from future activities. In some coalitions, a core group of members might have the ability to provide technical assistance to other members regarding changes in the requirements for managing programs and reporting program outcomes. Members learn from each other and gain information that is useful to the organizations they represent and that can enhance services to clients (Schopler, 1994, p. 24).

In response to changes in the political-economic environment, coalitions can act as convening mechanisms for community action. Mannix and White (1992) suggest that when coalitions have been operating for a long period of time, they may be the only viable way to get anything done in some political situations. As changes in the environment affect the availability of resources, the coalitions that survive will more than likely be those that are able to anticipate and adapt to these changes.

## MODELS OF COALITIONS

In developing a conceptual framework for coalition building, a system of postulates is needed to describe ideal-types of coalitions. This system can then provide a structural design for building coalitions that implies the best possible exemplification either in reality or in conception. Croan and Lees's (1979) five coalition models are used in developing this framework: (a) information and resource-sharing; (b) technical assistance; (c) self-regulating; (d) planning and coordination of services; and (e) advocacy. These models represent a systematic arrangement of categorizing coalitions according to a purpose and a set of functions, which can be performed by the coali-

tion. In each of these models, the purpose of the coalition dictates the type of functions to be performed by the coalition. Table 8.1 depicts the purpose and functions served by these models.

In "real world" coalitions, one will find some overlap in these coalition models. A coalition may be characteristic of one or more of these models. In the first three models, the coalition works internally to improve the capacities of its member organizations. The last two models attempt to impact externally other systems rather than just their own members.

The political-economy perspective suggests there are political and economic aspects to understanding the roles played by these coalition models. Zald's (1970) analysis of the political-economy perspective defines these two aspects: (a) the political aspect suggests that organizations within a coalition have various alliances with and commitments to the other member organizations that limit and shape goals, as well as policy choices, and (b) the economic aspect suggests that the member organizations exchange goods, services, or incentives that bind the organizations to each other in the coalition.

Likewise, in each of these models, the alliances and commitments that are developed within the coalition shape the purpose and functions performed by the coalition. In addition, the exchange of goods or services within the coalition creates a bond between the member organizations, which strengthens their interest in maintaining the coalition. Through coalescing, the members anticipate that they will acquire the scarce resources needed by their respective organization.

To illustrate these models, the author has developed case vignettes. It should be noted that the case vignettes are partly fictitious and partly based on actual coalitions.

TABLE 8.1
Coalition Models

| Model | Purpose | Functions |
|-------|---------|-----------|
| Information and Resource-Sharing | Act as clearinghouse | Gather, collect, file and disseminate information; arrange forums; develop resource-sharing system; assist referral process. |
| Technical Assistance | Deliver technical services | Arrange workshops; provide grantsmanship and training services; conduct needs assessment and evaluations. |
| Self-Regulating | Set standards | Design evaluation systems; monitor members; provide certification; recommend system for allocating funds |
| Planning and Coordination of Services | Act as service coordinator | Conduct service inventory; establish master calendar; liaise with other groups; develop I & R system. |
| Advocacy | Act as change agent | Monitor legislation and policy-making bodies; organize public education workshops or campaigns; conduct lobbying efforts |

*Note.* Preparation of this table was based on material from *Building Effective Coalitions: Some Planning Considerations* by G. Croan and J. Lees, 1979, Arlington, VA: Westinghouse National Issues Center.

These vignettes are not intended to serve as case studies of these coalition models, but are presented only to briefly sketch the purpose and function of these models.

## Information and Resource-Sharing Coalition

According to Croan and Lees (1979), this model serves a definite clearinghouse function. It gathers, collates, files, and disseminates information in specific areas of interest to the coalition. The alliances within the coalition enable the member organizations to achieve objectives such as: (a) providing a means and a forum for exchanging information; (b) developing a knowledge base for organizing and plan- ning activities; (c) providing a system for using the physical facilities, staff, and/or financial resources of the member organizations; and (d) assisting the member organizations in making appropriate referrals.

An information and resource-sharing coalition could publish a newsletter which provides information about special services and events. The coalition can pool available funds in order to purchase, for example, audiovisual equipment or word processing services, that could be used by organizations in the coalition. In some cases, agency staff with special expertise may be loaned or exchanged between the member organizations. Physical facilities such as meeting rooms could be shared. Informal get-togethers can be scheduled in order to nurture the informal network within the coalition. The exchange of these goods and services binds the member organizations to each other as they seek to maximize their scarce resources.

*Case Illustration: The Women's Coalition.* This coalition was formed in response to a need expressed by numerous women's organizations to bring together the many diverse groups in a state. The common goal of these women's organizations is to collectively influence and lobby for legislation affecting women's rights and economic status. The coalition provides political information, such as action alerts on bills affecting women, in order to strengthen their local lobbying networks. Information is also provided to assist in the appointment of women from the coalition to local and state government boards and commissions.

The coalition publicizes the contributions made by these women's organizations in lobbying for proposed legislation or for changing existing laws that affect the rights of women. Coalition meetings are held throughout the state in an effort to promote communication among the various women's organizations. The coalition is successful in building the capacity of these organizations to respond to women's issues by assisting them to become more informed and knowledgeable in the political arena.

## Technical Assistance Coalition

Croan and Lees (1979) suggest this coalition model emphasizes the delivery of technical services. The alliances within the coalition enable the member organizations to receive trainings, conduct evaluations and needs assessments, and arrange other activities on a resource sharing or fee-for-service basis. This coalition model usually operates out of a central office with a coordinator who arranges for the technical assistance. An inventory of the resources, skills, and expertise available within the coalition is often conducted. Outside consultants could be hired, if additional expertise is needed in accessing the technical services.

A technical assistance coalition rarely exists only for improving the service or operating capacity of the member organizations. The technical assistance provided to the member organizations should enable them to affect other systems rather than just their own members. The opportunity to access these services through the coalition creates a bond between the member organizations to each other.

*Case Illustration: The Developmental Disabilities Coalition.* This coalition is made up of consumer advocate organizations in a state. It sponsors public forums and legislative training workshops across the state, in order to build the capacity of local and state leaders to represent the best interests of the developmentally disabled. Forums consisting of federal, state, or local leaders are coordinated for public hearing purposes. At these forums, disabled persons or their families present testimonies on the major problems and needs of the disabled population in the state.

In conjunction with these forums, legislative training workshops are coordinated for both the disabled citizens and groups working with this population. Experts provide information on the legislative process, in order to assist these groups in learning the "ins and outs" of the political system. The trainers inform the groups on how to organize effective education and communication networks to affect public policy and the decision-making process on behalf of the disabled. Through these workshops, the groups receive information and learn techniques for intervening in this process.

## Self-Regulating Coalition

Croan and Lees (1979) suggest this type of coalition assumes responsibility for setting minimum standards by which all the organizations in the coalition agree to abide. Alliances within the coalition enable the member organizations to engage in activities that shape policies. The coalition might design an evaluation system and provide certification for those member organizations that demonstrate compliance. The coalition could monitor its own organizations or even outside groups. It could also recommend to a funding agency a system for allocating funds to its member organizations.

In addition, this coalition model could encourage the upgrading of agency programs and increase standards of performance. For instance, a coalition could be formed by an association of day care centers or a network of emergency shelters to improve their standing operating procedures. Coalescing around these self-regulating activities binds the member organizations to each other. The self-regulating coalition could be formed in combination with the information and resource sharing and/or the technical assistance coalition.

*Case Illustration: Youth Shelters Coalition.* This coalition consists of several youth emergency shelters in a large metropolitan city. These shelters provide temporary housing and information and referral services for runaway youth. The shelters formed this coalition in response to criticism from local juvenile officials regarding the need to monitor shelter care services. The coalition developed a system for monitoring each of the shelters with the assistance of professional groups interested in children.

Each of the shelters receives monies from the city and the county, as well as local foundations. Representatives from the coalition are asked to recommend to these funding sources the distribution pattern for allocating funds to the shelters. If a shelter is out of compliance with the standards set by the coalition, the shelter can be blackballed by the coalition. As a result, it might not receive a recommendation from the coalition for monies until it is in compliance with the standards. Local funding sources favor the efforts of this coalition, since it provides a watchdog for ensuring quality of care to children in the community.

## Planning and Coordination of Services Coalition

According to Croan and Lees (1979), this type of coalition strives to change a situation. The alliances within the coalition provide an avenue for the member organizations to shape goals and policy choices. In order to plan and coordinate services, inventories of existing services, gaps, and duplication of services are often conducted. Other activities might include establishing a master calendar of events, developing a standard intake and referral process, or acting as a liaison with outside agencies. In some cases, experimental or pilot projects might be conducted, which, if successful, could be replicated by other organizations in the coalition.

The formation of this coalition model could be mandated by a major funding source, as a condition in order for the member organizations to receive funds. In this case, a lead organization needs to be responsible for the disbursement of funds, as well as for implementation of the overall project. Participation in the planning and service coordination activities binds the organizations to each other, as they engage in a shared decision-making process to shape goals and policy choices.

*Case Illustration: Coalition to Prevent Child Abuse.* This coalition was formed by local community-based organizations providing services to victims of child abuse. Member organizations might include parent education groups, private family and youth services organizations, the public child protective services agency, and emergency shelters for battered and neglected children. The coalition conducts an annual resource inventory so that organizations are kept up-to-date on all local resources. A grant proposal is prepared by the coalition for a community development project that would create self-help activities within the community to prevent child abuse.

The coalition makes recommendations to funding sources regarding the fiscal needs of the organizations serving this population. Even though the coalition is not mandated by the funding sources, its recommendations might be used in the allocation of fiscal resources. Therefore, the coalition acts as a liaison between the member organizations and the funding sources.

## Advocacy Coalition

Croan and Lees (1979) suggest advocacy coalitions can be formed in response to a specific crisis situation. The alliances within the coalition enable the member organizations to work toward responding to a proposed policy or legislative change, or a more generalized need, such as the lack of home health services. This coalition can also be formed to work towards improving

the power base of the organizations in the coalition. Lobbying efforts can be conducted for increasing funding allocations for health and social services, for inclusion of a community representative on a public policy-making board, or for a more equitable distribution of funds.

Organizational actors in an advocacy coalition often serve as members of policy-making boards and monitor legislation or policy decisions. They can organize public education workshops or campaigns to gain support for specific issues, such as a workshop to educate the community on the proposed allocation of federal block grant funds. Their community education work can increase public attention to an issue by the use of various forms of the mass media. This public attention can put pressure on elected decision-makers to be more responsive to the needs of their constituents. Through coalescing around these advocacy efforts, a bond is created between the member organizations, as they seek to maximize their supply of scarce resources.

*Case Illustration: Community Coalition.* This coalition was formed by a group of alternative human service organizations that were interested in pooling their efforts toward improving their power base. The coalition provides leadership in the community to persuade local government officials to allocate more funds for human services. The leadership puts pressure on local government officials to allocate funds for those human services that might suffer from the loss of funds from federal block grant legislation.

The coalition analyzes local county and city budgets in order to determine if a fair share of the funds are allocated to community-based human services. It advocates for the best use of local monies for human services when the government either contracts out for services or provides its own services. The best interests of the community are continually focused on as the coalition mobilizes its advocacy activities.

## PRACTICE CONSIDERATIONS

Regardless of the role played by a coalition in its political-economic environment, Tefft (1987) suggests a coalition faces critical challenges in at least three areas including (a) strategic effectiveness, (b) organizational maintenance, and (c) leadership. A coalition's decentralized structure can limit its strategic effectiveness if decisions are delayed in order to achieve consensus. Decision-making can also become more difficult if member interests are perceived to be jeopardized. If decisions become more controversial within a coalition or go beyond broad issues of values and strategies, the coalition may need to change its structure, including its purpose and functions.

Coalitions often rely on members to maintain the coalition, particularly if there are no paid staff. As member organizations turn over, new organizational actors might not share the same commitment to the coalition. A major challenge would be to identify incentives that will solidify their ideological commitments and integrate them into their working relationships with other members of the coalition. Incentives also need to be provided to the older organizational actors in the coalition in order to enhance their commitment. An organizing ideology needs to promote the spirit of connectedness and solidarity among members (Fisher, 1995).

Stable capable leadership is essential for a coalition's long-term effectiveness. Leadership transition is a predictable, repeated test of a coalition's viability and sense of commitment. The transition from a founding leader or leaders to whatever follows is a critical event. Frequent, unplanned leadership transitions can reduce a coalition's external orientation because of internal demands. The leadership should facilitate the process for the members to agree to some extent on the coalition's purpose, functions, and strategies (Mizrahi & Rosenthal, 1995).

Alexander (1991) suggests one of the first questions to answer in building a coalition is: "What are the precipitating problems or issues that suggest the need for a coalition?" (p. 91). The answer to this question can guide the organizational actors in determining which coalition model or combination of models would best fit their needs.

Daley and Wong (1994) believe practice models of coalition building are needed for working with emerging ethnic communities or between emerging ethnic communities and groups with similar interests. Rivera and Erlich (1984) suggest that these models should nurture and support existing social networks. Gentry (1987) states that in building coalitions an emphasis "should be on cooperation or collaboration between and among agency/organization members and not on competition" (p. 49).

Rather than attempt to establish a grand theory, the intent of this article was to present a conceptual framework that included a perspective or approach to understanding coalition building, as well as a set of ideal types or models of coalitions. Political and economic forces, structures, pressures, and constraints are the most significant motivators of change and the key factors shaping the direction of change for health and human services. Thus, the political-economy perspective should contribute to our understanding of organizational behavior in building coalitions.

# REFERENCES

Alexander, C. (1991). Creating and using coalitions. In R. Edwards & J. Yankey (Eds.), *Skills for effective human services management* (pp. 90–102). Washington, DC: NASW Press.

Benson, J. (1975). The interorganizational network as a political economy. *Administrative Science Quarterly, 20,* 229–249.

Boissevain, J. (1974). *Friend of friends: Networks, manipulators, and coalitions.* New York: St. Martin's Press.

Browne, E. (1973). *Coalition theories: A logical and empirical critique.* Beverly Hills, CA: Sage Publications.

Caudron, S. (1993). Teaming up to cut healthcare costs. *Personnel Journal, 72,* 104–118.

Cobb, A. (1991). Toward the study of organizational coalitions: Participant concerns and activities in a simulated organizational setting. *Human Relations, 44* (10), 1057–1079.

Croan, G. & Lees, J. (1979, May). *Building effective coalitions: Some planning considerations.* Prepared for the Office of Juvenile Justice and Delinquency Prevention, Law Enforcement Assistance Administration, U.S. Department of Justice. Arlington, VA: Westinghouse National Issues Center.

Daley, J. & Wong, P. (1994). Community development with emerging ethnic communities. In A. Faulkner, M. Roberts-DeGennaro & M. Weil (Eds.), *Diversity and development in community practice* (pp. 9–24). New York: The Haworth Press, Inc,

Fisher, R. (1995). Social action community organization: Proliferation, persistence, roots, and prospects. In J. Rothman, J. Erlich & J. Tropman (Eds.), *Strategies of community intervention* (pp. 327–340). Itasca, IL: F.E. Peacock Publishers.

Gamson, W. (1961). A theory of coalition formation. *American Sociological Review, 26,* 373–382.

Gentry, M. (1987). Coalition formation and processes. *Social Work with Groups, 10*(3), 39–54.

Gillespi, D. & Mileti, D. (1979). *Technostructures and interorganizational relations.* Lexington, MA: Lexington Books.

Hagen, J. & Davis, L. (1992). Working with women: Building a policy and practice agenda. *Social Work, 37*(6), 495–502.

Hall, R., Clark, J., Giodano, P., Johnson, P. & Van Roekel, M. (1977). Patterns of interorganizational relationships. *Administrative Science Quarterly, 22,* 457–474.

Hill, P. (1973). *A theory of political coalitions in simple and policy making situations.* Beverly Hills, CA: Sage Publications.

Kelley, E.W. (1968). Techniques of studying coalition formation. *Midwest Journal of Political Sciences, 12,* 62–84.

Levine, S. & White, P. (1961). Exchange as a conceptual framework for the study of interorganizational relationships. *Administrative Science Quarterly, 5,* 583–601.

Mannix, E. & White, S. (1992). The impact of distributive uncertainty on coalition formation in organizations. *Organizational Behavior and Human Decision Processes, 51*(2), 198–219.

Mizrahi, T. & Rosenthal, B. (1995). Managing dynamic tensions. In J. Tropman, J. Erlich & J. Rothman (Eds.), *Tactics and techniques of community intervention* (pp. 143–148). Itasca, IL: F.E. Peacock Publishers.

Rivera, F. & Erlich, J. (1984). An assessment framework for organizing in emerging minority communities. In F. Cox, J. Erlich, J. Rothman, & J. Tropman (Eds.), *Tactics and techniques of community practice* (pp. 98–108). Itasca, IL: F.E. Peacock Publishers.

Roberts, M. (1983). Political advocacy: An alternative strategy of administrative practice. *Social Development Issues, 7,* 22–31.

Roberts-DeGennaro, M. (1986a). Building coalitions for political advocacy efforts in the human services. *Social Work, 31,* 308–311.

Roberts-DeGennaro, M. (1986b). Factors contributing to coalition maintenance. *Journal of Sociology and Social Welfare, 13,* 248–264.

Roberts-DeGennaro, M. (1987). Patterns of exchange relationships in building a coalition. *Administration in Social Work, 11,* 59–67.

Roberts-DeGennaro, M. (1988). A study of youth services networks from a political-economy perspective. *Journal of Social Service Research, 11,* 67–73.

Rosenthal, B. & Mizrahi, T. (1994). *How to create and maintain interorganizational collaborations and coalitions.* New York: Education Center for Community Organizing at Hunter College School of Social Work.

Rothman, J. & Tropman, J. (1987). Models of community organization and macro practice perspectives: Their mixing and phasing. In F. Cox, J. Erlich, J. Rothman & J. Tropman (Eds.), *Strategies of Community Organization* (pp. 3–26). Itasca, IL: F.E. Peacock Publishers.

Schopler, J. (1994). Interorganizational groups in human services: Environmental and interpersonal relationships. *Journal of Community Practice, 1*(3), 7–27.

Stanton, W. & Morris, M. (1987). The identification of coalitions in small groups using multidimensional scaling: A methodology. *Small Group Behavior, 18,* 126–137.

Stevenson, W., Pearce, J. & Porter, L. (1985). The concept of coalition in organization theory and research. *Academy of Management Review, 10,* 256–268.

Tefft, B. (1987). Advocacy coalitions as a vehicle for mental health system reform. In E. Bennett (Ed.), *Social intervention: Theory and practice* (pp. 155–185). New York: Edwin Mellen Press.

Van Velzen, T. (1973). Coalitions and network analysis. In J. Boissevain & J. Mitchell (Eds.), *Network analysis: Studies in human interaction* (pp. 119–225). Netherlands: Mouton and Company.

Wamsley, G. & Zald, M. (1973). The political economy of public organizations. *Public Administration Review, 33,* 62–73.

Yuchtman, E. & Seashore, S. (1967). A system resource approach to organizational effectiveness. *American Sociological Review, 32,* 891–903.

Zald, M. (1970). *Organizational change: The political economy of the Y.M.C.A.* IL: University of Chicago.

## 9.

### Wynetta Devore and Elfreide Schlesinger

### ETHNIC-SENSITIVE PRACTICE WITH FAMILIES

While social work is practiced in many different settings, most practice involves work with families, whether work is carried out in the voluntary family service agency, the juvenile justice system, the schools, the health care system, and many others. Whether a marriage is tottering or a child is ill or in trouble with the law or at school, the family as a system is or should be involved. Problems are frequently traced to the family at the same time as the family is sought as source of support and solution. It is within the family that many life cycle tasks are carried out.

Understanding of family dynamics, of intergenerational struggles, and of how the ethnic reality impinges on the family's capacity to play its varying roles is crucial for the ethnic-sensitive social worker.

In this chapter, prevailing views of family functioning are reviewed. These are related to the model of ethnic-sensitive practice developed.

Case examples serve as the vehicle for illustrating how the perspectives of ethnic-sensitive practice are brought to bear on work with troubled families.

The family is a major primary group; its tasks, though universal, are interpreted in

Wynetta Devore is a professor at the School of Social Work, University of Syracuse. Elfreide Schlesinger is a professor at the School of Social Work, Rutgers.

diverse ways by each ethnic group and at each social class level.

Family functions have been and continue to be discussed in the literature. Analysts continue to concern themselves with the changes that have come about as America has moved from an agricultural to a technological society. In earlier days the family performed economic, status-giving, educational, religious, recreational, protective, and affectional functions. Other institutions such as the school and the church have assumed greater responsibility for education and religious development of family members. Much family-centered recreation has been replaced by sports events in which individuals may be participants or spectators; and by social clubs, movies, and concerts. Many activities are related to life cycle stage (Cub Scouts, Pop Warner Football, business womens' clubs, senior citizens' clubs).

The family continues to have major economic and affectional functions—generally known as the *instrumental* and *expressive* functions.

An alternative interpretation of the functions of the family has been presented by Ackerman (1958). It is a more contemporary view of the major social purposes served by the family that focuses on the development of the expressive function. Ackerman stresses (1) the provision of opportunity for "social togetherness," the matrix for the affectional bond of family relationships; (2) the opportunity to evolve a personal identity, tied to family identity; (3) the patterning of sexual roles; (4) the training for integration into social roles and the acceptance of social responsibility; as well as (5) the cultivation of learning and support for individual creativity and initiative. Ogburn's perspective (1938) in relation to the economic and affectional function and Ackerman's expansion of the

latter form a base from which to consider the family in relation to the ethnic reality.

The definitions of family are as varied as are the delineation of its functions. The one selected here is particularly useful for our purposes since it encompasses the varied family constellations which are encountered in the course of social work practice. Papajohn and Spiegel (1975) developed a framework for family analysis intended to detect family states or conditions conducive to "good" or "bad" mental health. Their framework is universal, in that it imposes no boundaries, except those determined by families themselves. Among their reference points for defining family are two that are useful for our purposes:

1. The family is a major unit of the social system. Its structural and functional characteristics extend into other subsystems such as the occupational and educational system.
2. The family is an agency for the transmission of cultural values.

In its form and function the family is connected with the values of a given ethnic group (Papajohn and Spiegel, 1975). These ethnic values are the core of ethnicity which has survived through many generations in various forms.

In presenting our model of ethnic-sensitive practice we called attention to the importance of relating the past history of ethnic groups to the contemporary situations which they confront. The exploration of that history will reveal that the values held by various groups are a product of that history, and that these cannot easily be separated from sociopolitical events. For example, the interrelatedness between the "Polish character" and its past history is clarified by this statement made by Edmund Muskie, a prominent Polish American (1966). "There is much of glory in Poland's past—glory which was the product of the love of liberty, fierce independence, intense patriotism, and courage so characteristic of the Polish people." The past to which Muskie referred included guarantees of religious freedom laid down in 1573, and the development of a constitution in 1791 which considered individual freedom as essential to the well-being of the nation. The Polish family of the present is a product of that history and may be expected to hold many of the values that Muskie identifies. Fiery independence continues to characterize many Poles. As we have noted over and over again, such values seep into the dispositions to work, to child-rearing, and to the role of women. As Polish and other ethnic families encounter mainstream America, struggles may ensue as values begin to shift or take on a different shape. Social workers must be aware of the delicate balance which sometimes ensues. The third-generation Italian father is less distrusting of the outsider than was his grandfather and may allow his daughter to date outside of the immediate ethnic circle; but at the same time he may maintain a traditional view on premarital sex (Kephart, 1977). This shift accommodates to the realities of present-day society but maintains a position in which women are held in high regard and effort is made to protect them from the outside world, which is "not to be trusted." The consequence of this evolution of values is often intergenerational conflict. Daughters in Italian families cannot appreciate the effort it may have taken for their fathers to permit them to date non-Italian men; their fathers cannot understand a changing code of sexual morality which does not condemn a bride who is not a virgin.

Each ethnic family, as a major unit of the social system, is influenced by the various aspects of the larger society. These influences serve to throw into question values which have been treasured for generations and have sustained the family for several generations in America. The resulting tension between resistance and accommodation may cause family turmoil, some of which may eventually come to the attention of a social worker.

These are but some of the kinds of family issues of which the ethnic-sensitive social worker must be particularly aware. The model for ethnic-sensitive practice presented elsewhere in this work presents a basis for attention to these aspects of family tensions.

In order to highlight how the various components of the model are brought to bear in practice, a variety of cases are presented here. Each case is distinctive in relation to the ethnic reality and how it influences the ways in which families and workers respond to the problems presented. In all cases social workers are expected to draw on the various layers of understanding and to adapt the various skills and techniques used to the ethnic reality.

To achieve the goal of ethnic-sensitive practice, social workers must be continually aware of the second layer of understanding, which relates to awareness of their own ethnicity, recognizing that such awareness is incorporated as part of the "professional self." Social workers are not immune to the feelings of ambivalence about the fact of ethnic diversity and their own location in the ethnic geography. Greeley (1974) suggests that we are all torn between pride in our heritage and resentment at being trapped in that heritage. He speculates that the ambivalence is probably the result of the immigrant experience of shame, and defensive pride in an unappreciative society. No matter what the origin or nature, social workers must be aware of their own feelings about their ethnic identity.

## The Case of Clyde Turner

When Clyde Turner saw the social worker at the Mental Health Unit of the hospital he said that he had come because he needed "a rest to get himself together." He was self-referred, but had been in mental health treatment centers before. The diagnosis made was schizophrenia. The tension and anxiety that he felt were evident in his behavior. Problems seemed to be generated by internal and external stresses.

Clyde is black; he is 20 years old and a sophomore at a university near his home. His father, Roland, is on the faculty of another university in the area; he is working on his doctoral dissertation. Eleanor, his mother, is not employed outside of their home. His sister Jeanette, age 17, is a high school student who gets excellent grades.

Clyde said that family pressure is a part of his problem. He feels that he has not had a chance to become an independent person. The family upsets him and he becomes very argumentative.

His father has urged him to take five "profitable" courses in the next semester. Clyde had planned to take three such courses and two in the humanities, which would lessen the burden of school.

In an effort to "move away" from his family Clyde joined a fraternity but when the "brothers" learned of his problems they began to ridicule him and became patronizing.

School, family, friends all became "hassles" and Clyde sought refuge in the mental health unit for a rest.

Clyde's tensions and anxieties are in the present. The diagnosis of schizophrenia is not in question. There is sufficient evidence from previous admissions to other mental health centers to confirm the schizophrenic assessment. Relief of his tension and anxiety are of primary concern.

As the model for ethnic-sensitive practice is applied, consideration must be given to the first layer of understanding, knowledge of human behavior. This knowledge provides the data that begin to explain Clyde's disease. His natural struggle for independence at the emerging adult stage is hampered by the nature of his illness. The symptoms confound him and his parents, who at middle age, have begun to look forward to a life without child care responsibilities. One of their children, however, continues to need care, which they seem unable to provide.

The Turners are a middle-class black family; that is their ethnic reality. Mr. Turner's thrust for advanced education for himself and his son are among the dispositions that often flow from that position. Unlike many black middle-class families, that status is achieved with the employment of only one adult; Mr. Turner's salary as an educator provides sufficient income to maintain their middle-class position in appropriate style.

In other ways, however, the Turners are characteristic of the black middle class as delineated by Willie (1974); (1) one family member has completed college and attends graduate school on a part-time basis after adulthood; (2) they want their children to go to college immediately after high school so that they will not need to struggle as long to attain their goals as did the parents; (3) there is little time for recreation because of intense involvement in work. Mr. Turner teaches at the college and works on his dissertation; Mrs. Turner works hard at housekeeping activities. They are socially accepted and respected in their own community. There are many adults who pursue graduate degrees in their adulthood, but for blacks there has been the continual resistance by racist institutions which were reluctant to admit them. This is part of the experience of blacks in America of which Clyde's social worker must be aware.

As Clyde and his father disagree about his selection of courses for the coming term they respond to an unconscious, unspoken, value of the black middle class. Education will enable black people to change their position in society; it will move them upward. There is no discussion about *whether* Clyde will return to school; the discussion is about *what* he will study when he returns.

In the struggle for independence Clyde sought out peers and as a result became a member of a black fraternity. It is in peer groups such as this, whose membership is comprised of one ethnic group, that one often finds comfort. These groups affirm identity through special social projects and recreational activities undertaken. For Clyde, however, they intensified stress because of their inability to respond in comforting ways to his incapacities. But, like Clyde, they too are emerging young black men seeking a place for themselves in the larger society. They may, however, be enlisted by the social worker to serve as a support group for Clyde. Efforts to provide them with a clearer picture of Clyde's difficulties may well enable them to refrain from ridicule and include Clyde more completely in the group activities.

Although there is no mention of extended family, further inquiry may uncover a kinship network that is available to give emotional support to the entire family. Although middle-class blacks may sever connection with family members as they move upward, there is significant evidence that many retain a family support system mainly because of the vulnerability of their middle-class position (McAdoo, 1978).

As a young college student Clyde is subject to the stress of academic life, even without the extreme stress of his illness. How many other students at the university suffer? What resources in counseling are available? How adequate are those that exist? How may the services of the mental health unit be expanded or adapted to meet the needs of students from any college who reside in this suburban community? How does the stress of Clyde's illness disrupt the family as they struggle to maintain middle-class status?

These are among the questions that may be raised by social workers as they work with college students of any ethnic or social class group. Attention is focused on practice which moves from dealing with individual client need to modifying those larger systems which influence, positively or negatively, the client's day-to-day activities.

It is not the intention of this discussion to suggest a specific course of action which Clyde's social worker might take—that will depend upon many aspects of this case not presented. The activity will, however, be related to the route Clyde took to the social worker. It was totally voluntary and based upon previous successful experiences in mental health settings. The mental health unit is one of the services provided in a suburban general hospital. A majority of patients, of all ethnic groups, hold middle-class status. In such a setting there is often little involvement with larger systems. Yet evidence of systematic failure as it relates to the Turner family may be seen in the pervasiveness of racism. The energy invested in overcoming the obstacles required to attain a middle-class position may have some relationship to Clyde's problems; the specifics have to be determined by the worker and family.

The ethnic-sensitive worker, having applied the perspective of the model, now has more data available that will give a wider view of the Turner family as it struggles to cope with their schizophrenic son.

### The Case of Michael Bobrowski

It was Jean Bobrowski who took her husband Michael to the Family Counseling Association. It seemed the only way to help him. Since he lost his job he sat around the house or wandered aimlessly. She was very worried and went to see Father Paul, who suggested that she take her husband to the association. The priest spoke to him also and encouraged his cooperation.

Mr. and Mrs. Bobrowski are Polish. When he was employed Mr. Bobrowski was a truck driver. His work record was poor. When he backed a truck over a gasoline pump and failed to report it to his employers, he was fired. Because he was a member of the union, Mr. Bobrowski had expected that the union would help him find other employment but this did not materialize. He is ineligible for unemployment due to the circumstances of his dismissal. Mrs. Bobrowski now takes care of other people's children; his job had been the sole source of their income. They have lost their home due to nonpayment of the mortgage.

The Bobrowskis have been married for 30 years. He is presently 55, she is 50. Their son Michael, Jr., is 28 and lives in California with his wife and young son. Debbie, their daughter, is 24, married, and lives nearby. She has two children.

Both of the Bobrowskis are members of the Polish American Home, a social club, and the American Legion. They get a great deal of pleasure from the activities of each group, but they are less active since Mr. Bobrowski lost his job.

A major problem for this family is financial; the strain is becoming evident in this couple's relationship. The lack of employment is devastating to this Polish working-class family. While difficult for most people, this particular kind of devastation is to be expected in the case of a Polish family. To the Slavic work is the reason for living; if one cannot work then one is useless.

The work of Stein (1976, 1978) suggests that this attitude cuts across all social classes. In addition, essential goals of life are to own one's own home and to amass cash wealth as a cushion for security. Mr. Bobrowski has failed in all areas. His behavior has deprived him of work and, although he wishes to work, his union has not supplied employment as he expected. He has lost his home due to his failure to pay the mortgage. There are no cash reserves set aside. His application for unemployment insurance has been denied.

The independence of character referred to by Muskie cannot be exemplified when there is no work, no home, no reserve. He is unable to protect his wife, who must now take care of other people's children in order to support the family. In their later adulthood, when there is the universal expectation of less responsibility because the children are emancipated, the Bobrowskis find themselves dependent and may need to seek resources from public agencies. The task of coping with a diminishing work role usually executed at old age must be accomplished earlier than expected. Although Mr. Bobrowski resists, it is unlikely that he will ever have steady employment again due to his poor work history.

Despite the emphasis on hard work and building up a cash reserve, the chances of attaining the security envisioned are fairly slim for Polish and other working-class families. Their income may appear to be substantial; the hard work that they do pays well. But they, as do many working-class families, have attempted to find the "good life" through the acquisition of consumer items. Many of these items are purchased "on time" and so the family income that appears to be "good" is spread out to make payments on the car, appliances, mortgage or perhaps a truck, camper, or small boat—before the purchase of food or medical care. Rubin (1976) has identified this precarious position on the edge of financial disaster as one contributor to the "worlds of pain" of the white working class.

An understanding of the realities of Michael Bobrowski's ethclass position, in which he suffers from the pain of a working-class position and failure to meet ethnic group expectation, enables the ethnic-sensitive worker to go beyond the problems of finance and depression.

An awareness of community resources will provide a direction as the worker seeks to help the family. Other resources must be enlisted by the ethnic-sensitive worker committed to simultaneous activity at micro and macro levels.

The couple is active in two secondary groups: the American Legion and the Polish American Home. Both are sources of strength in their lives. In each there is a sense of patriotism, which has been identified as a distinctive Polish characteristic. They are able to affirm their "Polishness" among other Poles at Polish American Home gatherings. Their present problems in living have caused them to become less active. They feel the stigma of unemployment and the depression which followed. Yet, this group may be able to help to diminish the sense of stigma. Mr. Bobrowski is not the only member who has problems leading to tensions and anxieties. Others may have marital conflict and problems with their children or parents. The nature of interpersonal relationships are such that similar problems may surface in many families. Is it possible for the Polish American Home to become an outreach center for the Family Counseling Association?

The Polish association could, with joint effort by the social worker and community leaders, become a part of the effort to minimize the stigma attached to mental health problems and to seeking service, which often plagues white ethnic communities (Giordano, 1973). Programs and services may be encouraged that span the life cycle, from day care services to senior citizens' activities, centered about the home and located in community-based institutions.

Mr. Bobrowski's route to the social worker was highly voluntary. He followed the suggestion of his priest, a significant person in his life. At the family association he may expect to be active in the plans for the solution of his problems. If he chooses

not to continue services, he may be encouraged to continue until the work is completed but he will not be "punished" for this decision.

As social workers consider the route to services as well as the other aspects of the model for ethnic-sensitive practice, many components of Mr. Bobrowski's life are revealed that may have been overlooked in the past.

## The Case of Bobby Ramirez

Bobby is 15 years old, the fourth of five sons in the family of Luis and Berta Ramirez. He was referred to the child welfare agency by the family court after episodes of delinquent behavior. The charges included truancy and automobile theft. On one occasion he stole a truck and demolished it. He is believed to be incorrigible at home, having little regard for the expectations set forth by his father. It is the expectation of the court that the child welfare agency will find a place for him outside the community: a foster home or, as a last resort, a residential treatment center.

The Ramirez family is Mexican American. Mr. Ramirez was born in Mexico but came to the United States as an infant; his wife Berta was born here but her parents were born in Mexico. Their eldest son, age 23, is self-supporting and lives outside of their home. The second son lives at home but is partially dependent upon his parents. The work that he finds is of an unskilled nature and does not provide him with an income essential for living. The other sons at home besides Bobby are 17 and 13; both attend school.

Mr. and Mrs. Ramirez have completed high school and are employed. Luis is a sanitation worker for the city; Berta is a domestic worker. They live with their sons in a two-bedroom house, which they rent. At one time they owned a house but lost it when they were unable to keep up the payments. There is never enough money to save for the down payment on another house, even though that is their wish.

They have barely enough money for clothing. In order to stretch the food budget, their diet often includes rice and beans prepared in the Mexican way. There is no money for recreation and so leisure time is spent with friends and family. Parties are often spontaneous. Friends, whose circumstances are similar, bring food and beer. There is dancing, drinking, eating, and a great deal of happiness in just being together.

Bobby Ramirez's route to the social worker was totally coercive; it is the decree of the court, which has also suggested a solution. In addition, he is in a state of dual marginality, that involving his ethnic minority status on the one hand and adolescence on the other (Long and Virgil, 1980): the universal tasks of coping with puberty and a growing sexual awareness, seeking for independence from parents, and developing the skills for that independence...are compounded by his ethnicity. Exposure to the Mexican American and Anglo worlds may well have produced pressures which force him to make a choice rather than make a decision; internal ambivalence develops. Garcia (1971) suggests the kinds of questions which confront Bobby and many other Mexican American youth and which may generate ambivalence: Should I reject my parents and accept the culture, ideals, and aspirations of the Anglos? If I do, will my family reject me? But, if I claim my cultural identity will I eliminate the possibility of admission to the Anglo world that offers success and escape from poverty? The temptation is to choose the Anglo way.

This beginning knowledge of Bobby's adolescent dilemma comes from the layers of understanding focused on a (1) general knowledge of human behavior and (2) an awareness of the ethnicity of others. The problem identified by the court is juvenile delinquency—a place must be found for him. As the worker begins this task, the model for ethnic-sensitive practice aids in developing insights that may make this transition less painful for all involved. Although the parents seem to concur with

the decision of the court there is pain, for Bobby has brought the honor of the family into question.

Although Bobby has ignored the authority of his father by breaking the family rules (a major transgression among Mexican Americans), Luis as the head of his household will nevertheless take part in the planning for Bobby's future. Some Mexican American fathers feel so shamed by this kind of behavior on the part of their sons that they will offer no support (Murillo, 1976). Failure in the adult policing roles does not deny him the role of representing the family in the community and in association with other systems, in this instance the child welfare department. The roles of policing and representing the family are among the activities associated with *machismo.*

In his analysis of *macho,* the masculine role, Paz (1961) sees it as one which incorporates superiority, aggressiveness, insensitivity, and invulnerability subsumed under one word—*power.* The history of this position of honor, strength, and masculinity lies in associations which lead back to a history of the "warring, sacrificing Aztecs and their medieval Spanish conquerors" (Queen and Haberstein, 1970). In the present, *machismo* calls for an aloof authoritarian head of the family who directs its activities, arbitrates disputes, polices behavior, and represents the family in the community and society.

The social worker may expect Mrs. Ramirez to be devoted to her husband and children, including the eldest son who has moved away. Children, family, and a few friends are the core of life for Mexican American women (Murillo, 1976). Even though she works as a domestic, she does not do this every day; she must leave some time for her family responsibilities.

Her employment, along with that of her husband, provides barely enough income for the family to survive. Domestics and sanitation workers clean up after others. They carry out the most menial of tasks. The completion of high school has not provided access to higher positions; racism and discrimination have limited their opportunities. Although all family members speak English fluently, their surname and physical appearance provoke attitudes which diminish them in stature and attack their self-esteem.

A smaller family would require fewer resources but a smaller family would deny a tradition which supports large families. This tradition, however, serves to diminish the opportunity to attain the ordinary material rewards of American life. Mexican Americans are much more marginal in this respect than most other populations (Moore, 1970); they have few new clothes, a limited diet, and little recreation. The ethnic reality involves a life of near poverty, but at the same time there is much pride in their ethnic heritage; this is certainly true for the adults. Support comes from ethnic associates, who in an informal way share resources. This activity is not limited to the parties mentioned earlier but may be a regular occurrence, in respect to daily needs.

The decree of the court gives the social worker and the Ramirez family little choice; Bobby must be placed outside of the home. The court, however, is representative of those macro systems which appear to be blind to the needs of those most vulnerable: the poor, ethnic minority families. To remove Bobby from the community protects automobile owners from his larceny; it does nothing to address his adolescent conflict as he is trapped between two cultures of almost equal force.

The ethnic-sensitive worker has a heightened awareness of the need to promote change in the judicial system which will recognize the larger world of Bobby Ramirez and others like him. Perhaps efforts may be made to seek out *compadres* (godparents) of offenders, as a matter of policy, to assess their ability to lend support to their godchildren and become part of the process in planning for their care. The community in which the Ramirez family lives has few recreational resources for children and teenagers, a complaint that has often been expressed by the Ramirez boys and their friends. A study of the community will determine the accuracy of their statement. If their claim is indeed true, what efforts may be made to organize the various kinship groups in the area so that together they may press for funds from the city recreation budget to provide the supervised recreation needed by all of the children in this poor ethnic neighborhood?

The model for ethnic-sensitive practice focuses the social worker's attention on how ethnicity and social class impact on the daily life of families. Bobby's acting out behavior has led him to a social worker, who with patience and greater awareness may begin to change his life and the lives of other young Mexican Americans with similar problems. In so doing the worker also takes into account the unique family dynamics involved.

## SUMMARY

Each of the families presented in this chapter (the Turners, the Bobrowskis, and the Ramirezes) is attempting to carry out the functions of family presented early in the chapter. Sometimes they succeed, sometimes they fail. The potential for success or failure is related to their social class position and their ethnicity. Willie (1974) concludes (1) that all families in America share a common value system and (2) that they adapt to the society and its values in different ways, largely because of racial discrimination. Discrimination has intensified Mr. Turner's efforts to gain more education in order to maintain and enhance his middle-class position; on the other hand, it has kept Luis Ramirez in a near poverty position, denying him power over the destiny of his family. The Bobrowskis' expectations of working-class prosperity are denied as income is used to "pay the bills" for minor luxuries.

In each family, however, there are the joys of ethnicity that come from association with others who are like them—this is a source of comfort and power of people-hood. These relationships will continue as will the family; as a collection of individuals; as a group; as a major unit of the social system; and as an agency for the transmission of cultural values (Papajohn and Spiegel, 1975). It is in the family that the stresses and strains of daily life are played out; children are born and reach adulthood; men and women love and hate; interpersonal and intrapersonal conflicts develop and subside as men, women, and children struggle with the demands of the larger society and with their own needs for sexual and emotional fulfillment. This is the base from which the ethnic-sensitive worker involved with families begins. The particular approaches to practice may vary.

Some may choose a broad-ranging psychosocial approach with the Turners, Bobrowskis, Ramirezes, and others like them. Others may find task-centered, structural approaches useful as a way of helping them to struggle with the problems presented. Others may help them to focus primarily on the external, structurally induced sources of their problems. Whichever approach they choose, ethnic-sensitive workers will be aware of how the route to the social worker constrains problem definition and work to bring those definitions into line with social work values. Essential

also is simultaneous attention to how micro and macro systems impinge on family functioning, and attention to those macro tasks which will enhance such functioning. Always crucial is awareness of the layers of understanding and a recognition that techniques and skills may need to be adapted in order to respond to the families' ethnic reality.

## REFERENCES

Ackerman, Nathan A. 1958. *The psychodynamics of family life: diagnosis and treatment of family relationships.* New York: Basic Books, Inc.

Garcia, Alejandro. 1971. "The Chicano and social work." *Social Casework, 52*(5), May.

Giordano, Joseph. 1973. *Ethnicity and mental health—research and recommendations.* New York: American Jewish Committee.

Gordon, Milton M. 1964. *Assimilation in American life: the role of race, religion and national origins.* New York: Oxford University Press.

Greeley, Andrew M. 1974. *Ethnicity in the United States: a preliminary reconnaissance.* New York: John Wiley & Sons, Inc.

Kephart, William M. 1977. *The family, society and the individual* (4th Ed.). Boston: Houghton-Mifflin Co.

Long, John M., and Virgil, Diego. 1980. "Cultural styles and adolescent sex role perceptions." In Melville, Margarita B. (Ed.). *Twice a minority: Mexican American women.* St. Louis: The C. V. Mosby Co.

McAdoo, Harriet Pipes. 1978. "Factors related to stability of upwardly mobile black families." *Journal of Marriage and Family, 40,* November.

Moore, Joan. 1970. In Queen, Stuart, A. and Haberstein, Robert W. (Eds.). *The family in various cultures.* New York: J. B. Lippincott, Co.

Murillo, Nathan. 1976. "The Mexican-American family." In Hernandez, Carrol, Haug, Marsha J., and Wagner, Nathaniel N. (Eds.). *Chicanos: social and psychological perspectives* (2nd Ed.). St. Louis: The C. V. Mosby Co.

Muskie, Edmund. 1966. "This is our heritage." In Renkiewicz, Frank (Ed.). *The Poles in American 1608–1972: a chronology and fact book.* Dobbs Ferry, N.J.: Oceana Publications, Inc.

Ogburn, William. 1938. "The changing functions of the family." In Winch, Robert F. and Goodman, Louis Wolf (Eds.). 1968. *Selected studies in marriage and the family* (3rd Ed.). New York: Holt, Rinehart and Winston, Inc.

Papajohn, John, and Spiegel, John. 1975. *Transactions in families.* San Francisco: Jossey-Bass Publishers.

Paz, Octavio. 1961. Quoted in Queen, Stuart, A. and Haberstein, Robert W. (Eds.). 1970. *The family in various cultures.* New York: J. B. Lippincott Co.

Queen, Stuart A., and Haberstein, Robert W. 1970. *The family in various cultures* (4th Ed.). New York: J.B. Lippincott Co.

Rubin, Lillian Breslow. 1976. *Worlds of pain: life in the working-class family.* New York: Basic Books, Inc.

Stein, Howard F. 1976. "A dialectical model of health and illness—attitudes and behavior among Slovac-Americans." *International Journal of Mental Health, 5*(3).

Stein, Howard F. 1978. "The Slovac-American 'swaddling ethos': homeostat for family dynamics and cultural continuity." *Family Process, 17,* March.

Willie, Charles V. 1974. "The black family and social class." *American Journal of Orthopsychiatry, 44*(1), January.

## 10.

### Stephen Burghardt

### KNOW YOURSELF: A KEY TO BETTER ORGANIZING

As organizers we often fear we will not be as good as we need to be—that in fact we are not personally able to do the work well enough (or are not knowledgeable enough) to perform well. Holding on to this fear has been the undoing of many organizers, for the simple reality of organizing life is that good organizers are *always* making mistakes and being a little less effective than they ought to be. Furthermore, our slim grass-roots resource base always makes these errors appear more glaring: You forget to find a meeting place and the leaflet cannot be done; outreach stops; plans for publicity grind to a halt. People in larger

institutions make the same errors, but no one notices as quickly, for other tasks can be carried out regardless of the occasional foul-up. Knowing this helps the grass-roots organizer a little bit, but just a little. In fact, our slim resource base necessitates some personal awareness of how we best work, the type of awareness many organizers too often would prefer ignoring.

While perhaps preferring to ignore personal issues, organizers work in situations too complex for such a unilaterally cool attitude toward personal dynamics. The following two examples give some indication of that complexity.

(1) A few years ago, a young organizer had spent the week working on a tutorial program proposal—meeting with teachers and students,

Stephen Burghardt is on the faculty of Hunter College.

getting their ideas, finding out about previous programs' successes and failures. He had been relatively efficient, and the overall report seemed a good synthesis. A meeting had been called for the potential board of directors to review progress. After a decent introduction, the organizer's response to questions grew more and more irritable. Interaction with others seemed hostile; he seemed to want to "move the agenda," even when the discussion was on the agenda. As time wore on, people were pleased with the outline of his work, but a little perplexed at his method of handling it during the meeting. Likewise, the organizer felt frustrated and drained at the end of the meeting, angry with people's "slowness" but puzzled at why he felt so "antsy" over issues he knew needed to be discussed.

(2) A number of experienced organizers were reviewing their work in the South Bronx over the previous three months. As a group of politically conscious, primarily white activists working in an all black-Latin neighborhood, they had been trying to develop a political approach to neighborhood revitalization. Some things had gone well—a few people were attending meetings and getting interested in sweat equity programs—but progress was slow. One member was singled out for particular criticism, as his functioning on the street with residents seemed awkward and defensive. The widespread opinion, including his own, was that his failure to communicate well on the street was a function of his "poor political understanding of racism." He was expected to read various books and articles and report on his progress at a later date. No attention was ever paid to the obvious fact that he was never comfortable in informal settings; all that was sufficient would be for him to learn and change. He never did. Indeed, his tendency toward withdrawn formality seemed to increase.

Both these examples illustrate some important personal questions every organizer needs to answer regarding particular personal strengths and limitations in our work. In the first instance, why was such a nuts-and-bolts meeting so difficult for the organizer to handle? What had really created the defensiveness and irritability? In the second, why did experienced people so easily ignore problems that had little to do with a person's political beliefs? Why did they seek to correct them through a "better political line"? Furthermore, what can be done for any organizer to minimize these problems?

These problems—one common to new organizers, the other to more experienced activists—speak to the heart of the personal side of organizing. Every organizer is quite good in certain areas of work, less effective in others. However, as these two examples suggest, many organizers are unwilling or unable to admit this, not for political reasons, but for personal ones. While we design strategies to be flexible and base our tactical choices on varying levels of available resources, we rarely apply the same standards to *ourselves,* inflexibly and unrealistically expecting ourselves to do whatever needs to be done, even if the results are potentially harmful to the group and, in the long run, taxing to our mental health.

There are two reasons that this happens. One is the often unconscious but nevertheless powerful acceptance of a "great man/woman theory of organizing" that expects us to be all things to all people in all kinds of organizing situations.[1] This is exemplified by Saul Alinsky's criteria for a good organizer in "The Education of An Organizer," which lists everything from political skill to good humor to high levels of intuitive insight as "musts" for your effective work.[2] Such a list is more than a little intimidating, for it leaves the new or inexperienced organizer with a sense of failure, even when her or his skills are quite adequate in many situations. Likewise, experienced organizers come to assume they *should* meet such criteria; if unable to do so, one can "correct" the problem through content-related tasks like reading and political study.

Second, these personality problems are compounded by the basic personality type of most grass-roots organizers. An informal survey of mine conducted over the years has revealed again and again that most organizers (about 70 percent) tend to be much more task- than process-oriented.[3] This means that most organizers prefer outer-directed, content-oriented issues over inner-directed, process-oriented interactions that may involve feelings, emotions, and interpersonal processes rather than mere abstract material. When this content- and outer-directed personal tendency is coupled with the above great man/woman theory of organizing, organizers often foster a blanket attempt to force ourselves through work areas of less personal effectiveness "because we should be able to do them." Indeed, for all our concern with tactics, we often give little thought to the *personal realities of tactical implementation.* "Develop your political perspective, choose your strategy and tactics, and then do it" seems to be a sufficient way to function, saving adroitness for strategic discussion and not one's actual ability to implement desired tactics.

The outcome for these twin issues, as the two painful examples underscore, is that many organizers end up being either less effective or more emotionally drained than they need to be, and thus more likely to leave organizing because of "burnout." Instead of following a few personal guidelines, these activists "push on," even when they are highly irritated with group process, disinterested in fact-finding, uncomfortable with street-smart spontaneity, or whatever. Imagine if you applied these same pressures to others. What kind of an open, democratic organizing approach would that be? It is far more freeing to respect and recognize that you begin this work with certain skills *and* limitations that are heightened or lessened in different organizing situations. You then can learn to use your abilities with greater tactical flexibility. The irony in this

kind of humbling self-respect is that it will carry over into greater respect for the people with whom we work, too—by not berating ourselves for limitations that are actually beyond our control, it is less likely we would do the same to others.

There are a number of important procedures to follow in understanding yourself in different situations that can improve tactical effectiveness. (I call this "tactical self-awareness."[4]) First, identify whether or not you are more task-oriented or process-oriented. Don't cop out by saying you are both; everyone should be both, but each of us tends to be more comfortable with one orientation than the other, especially when we are new to this work. I have spent fifteen years of learning how to deal with my task-oriented tendencies, and now can blend process and task *some* of the time, but hardly always. You won't be any different.

Second, review the organizing situations you are involved in and determine whether they emphasize process or task activities. For example, new group situations stress much discussion and group facilitation, which means a process-oriented person will be most effective here. Likewise, specific planning meetings with a high degree of content-focused work and few interpersonal demands means that the situation will be most comfortable for a task-oriented person. Apply this approach to all the activities of the week—street work, meetings, planning sessions, and so on.

Once you go through the situations for their degree of *personal fit* with your own makeup, see if it is possible for you to take greater responsibility for the ones most comfortable for you, getting others to take tasks you find more personally problematic. If this is not possible, build supports for yourself along the way. For example, at longer, process-oriented meetings, I always write a reminder in my organizing notes (or copy of the agenda notice) to "stay calm—people need to talk." This note may seem silly, but it has become a sufficient cue to remind me that the problem in the slow discussion is *with me,* not with others. Likewise, those resistant to fact-finding can allot themselves five specific days in which to do the work instead of the imagined three, allowing for the reality that their tendency to procrastinate will lengthen its completion time. You should provide similar helpful cues in situations that are troublesome for you.

You cannot run away from your limitations, of course, especially in grass-roots organizing, where resources—and personnel—are rarely to be found in abundance. However, when you take on personally more difficult tasks, try not to take on too much at once. You are not too good in informal settings but have to attend that fund-raising party? Try to tend bar or serve food, rather than serving as the official greeter. You dislike office routine but have to help maintain one? Be responsible for keeping the office clean and not keeping the books; whatever mess you make will be quickly visible and easily correctable. Over time you can note improvement and move on to more demanding tasks, but try to start with realistic, modest objectives that are attainable.

Finally, you should consistently work to undermine "great organizer" theories *by judging your progress in personal performance by relative, not absolute, standards.* The group needs to succeed, of course, but here I am talking about your own improvement in the different situations of organizing: from writing to public speaking, from being relaxed in newly formed groups to handling responsibilities for office routine. Real self-respect allows you to be less than perfect, taking pride from improvement that is real improvement for *you,* while perhaps less so for someone else. For example, I am proud that I have an almost-neat and up-to-

date filing system. I have known I should have had one for fifteen years; my present filing system has been in place for two. At the same time, I have always worked well in the formation of groups. My desk, unfortunately, is a mess, and I still need to improve daily routines. You should find yourself able to note areas of accomplishment in all parts of organizing, letting progress, however slow, be cause for quiet satisfaction.

There are other levels where tactical self-awareness is important. Perhaps the two most important relate to (1) often unconsciously derived but quite real difficulties one has with particular individuals, and (2) vestiges of racism, sexism, and class bias that are within all of us.

Tactical self-awareness deals with your awareness of how personally comfortable you are in getting certain tasks done in certain situations. Those situations almost always involve people but at times include certain individuals with whom, for some reason, you do not get along. As grass-roots organizing has few institutional barriers to help minimize interpersonal conflict, it is important to notice when these interpersonal tensions exist for no apparent reason.

For example, I knew someone who always got into arguments with a fellow steering committee member over almost every issue—until she went home to a family picnic and saw the strong physical similarity between her antagonist and a second cousin she disliked. As remarkable as this story is, we all come up against individuals who, for no discernible reason, irritate us. When this happens a little too often and you cannot identify political differences, you find that his or her work is equal to others', and so on, the chances are the problem lies within you. Try to understand its origin, looking over your personal history to identify previous events or individuals who triggered the discomfort.[5]

After you have reflected on this and are sufficiently certain that the problem has little to do with the person's actual behavior, try to get up enough courage to speak with the person about *your* problem. That person will hardly be thrilled by what you have to say (by now you may rub him or her the wrong way, too), but your honesty and willingness to share the personal issue will at least clarify the problem and might lead to a mutually rewarding discussion.

If this fails or you are just not comfortable enough to initiate such an encounter yet, plan in the future to minimize your interactions so that the work is unimpaired. If that is not possible, *work* to lessen your antagonism. For example, make certain you do not comment on their remarks or even raise your hand immediately after he or she has spoken; try not to work on the same subcommittee, especially if they call for a lot of interpersonal interaction.

The other issue, one that infiltrates all organizing, is the unresolved problem of racism, sexism, and class bias lying within us. This topic is too important to leave to the end of one chapter, ...But here it is important to look at the issue in terms of how we can begin undoing problems we want to have but nevertheless find ourselves succumbing to: the sexist joke here, the racist fear or condescending class bias there. Fight as we may to eradicate societal problems, we cannot simply eradicate these feelings by wishing them away. It is far more important—and a lot more effective—to admit they exist and work from there.

In fact, these problems are so universal, *plaguing everyone,* that some of the personal techniques used on racism, sexism, and class bias are quite similar to what has been discussed above. (This realization itself is liberating, for I believe one of the reasons people so rarely admit to these problems is the fear of being singularly identified.) To review, those techniques are:

(1) Identify which areas or issues are most problematic for you. (Don't say "all" and be too guiltily global or "none" and too politically perfect; choose fairly and realistically.)

(2) Once you know them—say, racism and sexism—do not expect to be as effective as you would be under like situations with different people. You won't be.

(3) Bring in supports and other people to make certain the tasks are done well. (I'm not talking about running away from the problem, either, but of realistically dealing with it in the context that other organizing demands need to be met. The only way to run away from these issues in grass-roots organizing is to stop being an organizer.)

(4) Measure your progress in relative, not absolute, terms.

This last is painfully hard to do, for it is hard to admit to racism, sexism, or class bias. No one *should* have any of these problems. But since we do—*and will spend a lifetime in dealing with these issues*—allow yourself to take comfort from the progress you make in confronting your bias, seeing its roots, and learning how to free yourself from that prejudice.[6] It will not be easy, but there is no alternative. Over time, as you relax and learn from others, progress can be made that opens you up to the genuine friendships, trust, and good comradeship that are so much a part of the joys of grass-roots organizing. Just allow yourself time to improve, set out and use techniques to aid in your quest, and the chances are you will achieve your goals with far deeper personal fulfillment and meaning than you ever expected.

This said, let me stress that I am *not* suggesting that relative standards of personal growth as an organizer are a substitute for meeting the absolute needs of people which are the reasons we organizers organize in the first place. At the same time, it is equally important to be less absolute about ourselves and the pace at which we ourselves can change. Indeed, if we can learn to live with and apply these standards where they need to be applied (and not reverse them) our work will undoubtedly be a much richer experience for us all.

## EXERCISES: TASK VERSUS PROCESS ORIENTATION

Before trying to determine your basic orientation, it is important to begin by identifying certain situations that are either more process- or more task-oriented in their content and demands on the activist.

### Higher process-content organizing situations:

- new group meetings
- the introductory agenda items at most meetings
- individual follow-up
- informal parties and get-togethers
- the "action" part of demonstrations, marches, and so on
- education and communication events, speak-outs, and so on

### Higher task-oriented situations:

- subcommittee meetings
- controversial, "politically loaded" agenda items
- office routine
- planning meetings
- the running of marches, demonstrations, and so on
- grant writing

### Check which of the following task-oriented skills that you are good at:

- running tight-knit meetings
- giving factual reports
- performing subcommittee tasks

- writing
- emphasizing political/economic dynamics in strategy formation
- planning
- organizational maintenance: office routines

### Check which of the following process-oriented skills that you are good at:

- running newly formed groups
- preparing social events
- facilitating discussion
- speaking informally
- emphasizing personal/subjective dynamics in strategy formation
- individual follow-up
- organizational maintenance: interpersonal relations

Once you have checked off what you do best and in which situations, look back at a recent meeting in which you were involved. Note the items on the agenda, and divide them into either task- or process-oriented sections. Which items left you feeling most comfortable and most effective? Which ones caused the most problems?

Since any one meeting has other dynamics operating that need to be considered, do this task and process itemization at a few meetings to see what orientation you are personally more comfortable with. Then, as you plan your group's actions over the next month, examine them not only for their political content and strategic considerations but for which of these two orientations seem to dominate, and which items. Try to make assignments accordingly with other members (assuming other considerations are met).

## NOTES

1. This "theory" and many of the issues discussed here are more fully developed in Steve

Burghardt, *The Other Side of Organizing* (Cambridge, Mass.: Schenkman, 1981), especially Chapters 3 and 4.

2. Saul Alinsky, "The Education of an Organizer," in *Rules for Radicals* (Boston: Beacon Press, 1967).

3. Burghardt, *Other Side,* Chapter 3.

4. See also Steve Burghardt, "Expanding the Use of Self: Steps Toward Tactical Self-Awareness," *Journal of Applied Social Science,* Summer 1981.

5. I am not advocating therapy here, unless one wants to explore these issues in greater emotional depth. One undertakes therapy only if one wants it, not as some prescription to be swallowed whole before one is ready.

6. This is especially hard for people when they first recognize how prevalent racism, sexism, or class bias is. As one organizer put it,
"It's horrible. Once I saw how racism works here on the job, I saw it *everywhere*—how people don't look blacks in the eye, their fears, my hangups, the new TV stereotypes. All I feel is this remorse and anger at myself and everyone else, and I'm feeling like I'll never get off this track—I feel obsessed." This initial "crisis of conscience" phase, if one lets oneself go through it, does pass. You can then go on to use the above techniques effectively. The reason for the first phase's apparently immobilizing power is that it is dealing with material that is objectively obvious and emotionally powerful at the same time. You suffer from "overload" in ways that *do* slow you down. However, this new integration of powerful perceptions and new material is the work to be done here. Accept this, and the process itself will become that much faster.

# PART THREE

# OPTION DEVELOPMENT
# AND DECISION MAKING

# Introduction

"Rule the Pool" announces the back of the sweatshirt worn by members of a middle-school swimming team. A quick reading of this motto might suggest that domination is the only criterion by which this team will judge how to approach its competitive endeavors. Actually, the message is probably intended much more for its effect on the opponents than as a statement of this team's philosophy. In the parlance of modern professional sports, the goal is pretty clearly intimidation.

While there is a certain appeal to the simplistic nature of a set of criteria by which one might select a single tactical option rather than another, the real world usually brings us up short. As in the example above, even if a single criterion comes easily to mind, it may well represent a misinterpretation of the facts. It would be easier if there were not such a range of possibilities open to the macro practitioner—or if the possibilities would submit themselves more rationally to a set of dimensions by which their potential effectiveness might be judged.

For most practitioners, the question is more likely, "What are the basic things that must be taken into account if a reasonable preference for one option over others is to be clarified?" Of late, it often appears that one key issue evolves around, "Is it cheap?" This may be followed by "Who is going to pay for it?" and "Who is going to take responsibility if things do not go as well as expected?"

Personalistic areas also seem more prominent than they once were. Such matters as "How am I going to look doing this," and "What's my agency going to get out of this?" seem part of the undercurrent, even if they are not expressed. Despite strong continuing rhetoric to the contrary, the needs of clients appear to have been pushed further back. From another perspective, there seems to have been a general decline in risk-taking behavior. In fact, many practitioners report that their colleagues who have taken on bureaucracies or been out front in advocating for the rights of clients have quietly been let go when cost savings have been required.

The option selection tangle has certainly been complex and fraught with peril, especially in the difficult human services environment of the 1990s. From their own experiences, the editors propose a focus on what they believe to be particularly urgent and critical issues that confront practitioners in almost all macro practice situations.

In our current era, it sometimes seems as if we are in constant battles over values—in areas ranging as widely as from pro-life and pro-choice, to giving or denying birth-control devices to teens, to providing or withholding support for endangered people across the globe. Tropman's article (Article 11) confronts the centrality of these dilemmas. Such issues as individual and family, self-reliance and interdependency, fairness, and helping those most in need are addressed. Because much of the work of planners and program developers (to say nothing of administrators and managers) impinges on matters of policy, it is frequently impossible to avoid these dilemmas. Indeed, the attempt to avoid such questions often automatically labels the practitioner as a perpetuator of the status quo—however noble the actual reason for such avoidance. To aid in the planning process as it goes forward, Tropman also offers a worksheet for taking value dilemmas directly into account.

In selection 12, Rivera and Erlich make a strong argument for key dimensions to be addressed if efforts in ethnic minority communities are to be successful. In part, option alternatives need consideration in light of the stage of development of each community. For example, newer Southeast Asian communities cannot be regarded as virtually the same as older, much more established Japanese and Chinese communities. Moreover, Rivera and Erlich propose a set of structural variables by which to judge the degree to which a target community may be more "gesellschaft" (a system in which relationships are impersonal, contractual, and utilitarian) as compared with more "gemeinschaft" (a system in which relations are personal, informal, and traditional). This appraisal, then, may be a vital guide to choosing the best possible available option in a given situation. The consequences of such a choice for community practitioners are also considered.

In selection 13, Mizrahi and Rosenthal return to the issue of "tensions" while Tropman looked at value tension, they consider operational ones. Five specific tensions—(1) cooperation/conflict, (2) mixed loyalties, (3) autonomy/accountability, (4) means/model, and (5) unity and diversity form the framework of their analysis. Decision making almost always involves community committees and community meetings. Tropman and Morningstar (Article 14) provide some specific suggestions on how practitioners can facilitate better meetings, resulting in better decisions.

While the lip-service offered in honor of all these considerations may seem both strong and clear, as a practical matter they are often caught up in the political quagmire that surrounds most substantial community practice efforts in the 21st century. The blessings of political correctness in matters as diverse as value conflicts, feminist perspectives, ethnic minority community considerations, and ethical dilemmas related to information technology are not easily come by. However, if we are to be honest with ourselves, the essential humanism of the profession demands consideration of these diverse elements of option selection.

—John L. Erlich

**11.**

**John E. Tropman**

## VALUE CONFLICTS AND DECISION MAKING: ANALYSIS AND RESOLUTION*

In complex urban society the community organizer and planner is required to make, or become involved with, complex decisions of great importance. Problems that were once considered the domain of the family—such as sex education—are more and more becoming elements of the public domain. Educational planning, health planning, social services planning, planning for children and the aged, for women going back to work and men leaving work—these and others are becoming the subject of intensive social work activity.

Essential to these planning activities is the assessment process. Many kinds of assessments, and ones we talk about in other articles, involve demographic counts, community surveys, and even personalistic assessments of the worker's own orientations and involvements. One kind of assessment that is frequently left out, however, is what might be called a values assessment. Such an assessment differs from the process of "values clarification," which often involves a recognition of the individual worker's personalistic involvements in a situation. Rather, what is important is a sense of the structure of the values involved in the different groups. Planners often have

no precedents to guide them. They frequently must rely on their subjective appraisal of the situation. Included in their appraisal are values of the community, values of the society, values of the client groups involved, and professional values, among others. This piece can provide a framework for making such an assessment, so that it is no longer necessary for the planner to "fly by the seat of her or his pants." While this piece provides no magic formula for making hard decisions, it does offer a new approach to analyzing the values involved in the planning process.

### WHAT ARE VALUES?

Values are those gut-level feelings people have about fundamental aspects of life, which give it meaning and direction. Some of the more familiar values are family values, religious values, and work values. Values are ideas to which commitments are attached. There is no rule that they must be well-ordered, complete, consistent, or unambiguous. Indeed, as planners know, the reverse is the most likely situation.

Values have many complex, changing, and often conflicting meanings. People's values vary depending on their age, race, sex, income, education, and much more. To understand our own values, as well as those of others, we must realize that values intrude in subtle and unexpected ways. Values are so much a part of us that we are often not even aware of their influence. As

*Portions of this article were supported by the American Values and the Elderly Project, sponsored by the Administration on Aging, Grant # 90-1-1325. Special thanks are given to Beverly LaLonde, Jane McClure, Sue Sweeny, and Terrence Tice for comments on an earlier draft.

John E. Tropman is a professor at the School of Social Work, The University of Michigan.

a result, we often do not have the perspective we need to make appropriate decisions or to understand the actions of others.

Planners may be in the crucial position of making precedent-setting decisions involving fundamental values. It is therefore very important that they understand the complexities of values.
Values:

- vary among different people
- shift and change
- often go unrecognized
- often conflict with one another

The purpose of this paper is to aid practitioners in exploring their own and others' values and the ways they influence many different kinds of decisions affecting the planning process.

## Value Conflicts

Our perspective on American values suggests that the values we hold often come in pairs, or sets of opposing beliefs. Part of the complex nature of values is our tendency to believe in values which compete with one another. For example, belief in family responsibility as well as individual fulfillment is one example. Americans tend to be committed to both parts of this pair of values: to the family as a central American institution, and to the importance of fulfilling our individual needs. When faced with a plan about responsibility to one's family or to one's goals, citizens are often placed in a value dilemma. Though both parts of the values pair may not carry equal weight, when we make a decision, we try to strike a balance between two desirable choices.

For example, more and more women are choosing to work while their families are growing. Though the public in general might be more accepting of this choice now than in the past, each woman still must find her own balance between independence, work, and responsibility to family. Social planners and community organizers need to be continually aware of the value tensions that are inherent in the system and make an assessment of these dilemmas and tensions a part of their ongoing "sensing" of the community or field of practice. Seven value dilemmas seem most critical.

individual——family
self-reliance——interdependency
secular——religious
equity——adequacy
struggle——entitlements
private——public
work——leisure

## VALUES DILEMMAS IN COMMUNITY PRACTICE

Social planners and community organizers are continually involved in issues of assessment. These assessments involve, typically, money and personnel, issues and answers to the problems that beset the local community, the organization, or the subgroup. Planners and organizers continually struggle with finding solutions to community problems. What is often not so clear, however, is the fact that these problems involve value conflicts characterized by high ambivalence. As suggested, values upon which decisions are based are values which all of us hold. It is not "us" versus "them" but "us" versus "us" as well.

A second point involves us and our clients. The list of value conflicts suggests that the kinds of values our profession supports, on balance, tend to be on the righthand side of the list—family, interdependency, religious, adequacy, entitlements, public, leisure—tend to be subdominant ones, not, overall, as strongly held as those values on the left—individual, self-reliance, secular, equity, struggle, private, and work values. Thus our profession, our field, and to some extent, we ourselves, are in the position of advocating subdominant values. In fact, the very concept of "community" smacks of a subdominant value, linked more to interdependency than to self-reliance. Our client groups, too, often seem more linked to subdominant values than to dominant ones. Thus, to a certain extent, as we push the more subdominant values, we threaten the major value orientations in the society, in the community, and even within ourselves.

## POLICY PLANNING AND PLANNERS

Under new guidelines, children of dependent elderly parents can be paid by the state for providing home care for their parents. Many people feel that children should do this as part of their family responsibilities without pay. Others feel that older people who need or want to work should be paid to provide home health care for other elderly people.

As a planner in the Department of Social Services, you have the option to propose payments to family members or to several elderly people who have been home care providers for many years. What do you recommend?

### Planners as Policymakers

As a practitioner, you may not consider yourself a policy maker. But you are. Policy can be defined as a decision or series of decisions that apply to a group of people or to many situations. Policy that is made in legislatures is only one level of policy. It is then up to the practitioner to interpret the laws passed in legislative bodies.

Policy is a matter of making choices. Furthermore, the most difficult policy choices involve making a decision *not*

between good and evil or right and wrong, but between two or more good choices or two or more unsatisfactory choices. Policy decisions often involve a serious conflict between two strongly held beliefs, so that it is very difficult for us to know which way to compromise.

The social planner is frequently involved in assessing situations where there is a turbulent environment, where feelings run high. Should a program be in a religious institution or a nonreligious one? Should a program be run under private auspices, or should public funds be found to support it? While the planners do not make policy, they are often involved in making the crucial recommendations that become policy.

Though these values may seem foreign and rather academic, some questions based on these values are familiar:

- How much should the government do for people?
- Does the government owe everyone an adequate income?
- Should people be allowed to work as long as they want?
- How much responsibility should the family take in caring for its older members?

These seven pairs in Table 5.1 are not the only values involved in decision making. Yet they seem to be involved again and again, whether in debate over the Social Security Act or in consulting with a client about retirement. Everyone has value orientations which influence the style and approach they take with policy issues.

For each pair of values, Table 11.1 suggests a statement that a person holding that value might agree with. The values on the left—private, equity, work, and so on—tend to favor individual efforts and rewards. Over the years public opinion

TABLE 11.1
Value Dilemmas

| 1. individual/family | suggests the need to balance between our own needs and the needs of our family. |
|---|---|
| 2. self-reliance/interdependency | emphasizes the strain between the desire to "go it alone" and the need to depend on others. |
| 3. secular/religious | suggests the tension between looking for rational explanations for life's ups and downs and turning to religious sources for support. |
| 4. equity/adequacy | refers to the conflict between fairness to all and the responsibility to help those most in need. |
| 5. struggle/entitlement | suggests the tension between the importance of working for everything we get and being entitled to certain things just because we are human beings. |
| 6. private/public | describes the conflict between use of personal or corporate means, and use of government to achieve desired social goals. |
| 7. work/leisure | confronts the issue of work and its meanings. How much work should we do, and for how long? When should work stop and leisure begin? |

has tended to support the view that the welfare of each person is an individual or private concern. Values on the other side—public, family, adequacy, for example—tend to emphasize collective well-being. Government intervention, labor unions, and other community and social organizations are supported by these values. Only recently has public opinion tended to support these values in major policy issues.

Thus, certain values tend to be balanced by an opposite value (Table 11.2). Yet, as our experience reflects, any value or set of values may conflict with any other. Depending on the issue, certain values will be viewed as more important than others. In other cases, several values pairs may seem equally relevant. Value conflicts arise because selecting one value as the basis for action automatically raises an alternative view, whether we want it to or not.

Value conflict and compromise take place on many levels ranging from the national policy-making level to the agency-practitioner level.

## PLANNER DECISIONS

You are a planner with an area agency on aging. There is a small, older area of town where a community of elderly people live, and have lived for years. The city wants the property for a new library and asks your help in developing a plan to move the people there out into institutional facilities, with their families, and so on. Two or three of the older residents come to the office and ask your help in developing a plan which will let them remain where they are.

What do you do?

Planning conflicts like this one are quite common. The issue is very complex because different legitimate views are represented. Many other examples of this kind of dilemma confront the planner, such as involvement in the merger of agencies, conflicts between city hall and other types of citizen groups, conflicts between "group home" advocates and

TABLE 11.2
Value Conflicts

| | |
|---|---|
| "It is important that I consider my needs first." | "My family's needs are of first and foremost importance." |
| "I can get along best by myself." | "People need each other to do this." |
| "Problems can best be solved by thinking them through objectively and rationally." | "Problems become smaller if we have faith in a divine force." |
| "People should be treated the same, regardless of their needs." | "People most in need should get the most help." |
| "No one should have a good standard of living without earning it." | "Everyone deserves a decent standard of living whether he/she earns it or not." |
| "People should take care of themselves." | "The government should provide for people." |
| "Work is the most meaningful thing people do." | "Other activities are at least as important as work." |

those who oppose such homes—the list goes on and on.

As a planning and community organizing professional, you must carefully think through the issue, keeping in mind the values of all concerned. Five steps will usually be involved:

1. *Defining the problem*
   What are the basic issues?
   What information is needed, overall, about them?
2. *Developing alternative strategies for action*
   Consider the options and the consequences.
   Seek to balance values conflicts.
3. *Decision*
   This is the point at which those in authority make the decision. Additional balancing of conflicts goes on at this point.
4. *Operational planning*
   Working with those involved to develop an operational plan to carry out the decision.
5. *Implementation*
   Carrying out the decision and evaluating it.

**Defining the Problem**

Which is the more important, the need of the city for the area, or the rights of the people in the area now? What alternatives are available for both groups? Is the group of older people a "community," in the sense that they share the concern of care for each other?

**Developing Alternative Strategies**

What is the range of alternatives here, including the takeover of the land and the possibility of the older people remaining in their own homes? Are there intermediate possibilities which need to be considered? What are the sets of values which need to be balanced? What may happen under these different possibilities? How can values of public and private, self-reliance and interdependence be blended?

**Decision**

Which authority, or combination of authorities, is going to make the decision? What are their values? What are the values to which they are likely to be sensitive? What

FIGURE 11.1
Worksheet for Planning Decisions

| Problem | Values Pairs | Decision Options | Compromises | Consequences |
| --- | --- | --- | --- | --- |
| _____ | _____ | _____ | _____ | _____ |
| _____ | _____ | _____ | _____ | _____ |
| _____ | _____ | _____ | _____ | _____ |
| _____ | _____ | _____ | _____ | _____ |
| _____ | _____ | _____ | _____ | _____ |

kinds of compromises could be possible? Could the community be relocated elsewhere even if the buildings cannot?

## Operational Planning

Once the decision has been made, there is an operational planning process, which can itself involve a host of additional decisions. How can the decision be carried out in the best interests of everyone? What about individual and family interests here? Can these be accommodated?

## Implementation

Putting the plan into effect requires an assessment of values, too. Equity and adequacy may be an issue in terms of what kinds of supports might be given to older people if they are forced to move. If the decision has gone the other way, then the city needs to find a new site that is adequate for its needs.

## Values in Decision Making

While practitioners are often required to go through a formal evaluation process, they are not required to go through a formal decision-making process. Sometimes this is because the situation demands immediate attention. At other times, decisions are almost instinctual or "gut-level." At still other times, agency or client pressures prevail, and you make a decision against your better judgment. Recognizing the part that values play in all decisions can give you real insight into decisions. As a result you have more control over the decisions you make and participate in.

The worksheet in Figure 11.1 is a decision-making exercise that focuses on values. It will help you deliberately weigh the values, options, and consequences involved in a decision.

## TACTICS FOR VALUES BALANCE

Given the fact that values come in opposing sets and we spend lots of our professional time trying to achieve a values balance within a situation of potential or actual conflict, what are some tactics we might use, some ideas to list in the "options" column of the chart? Following are a few suggestions, by no means an exhaustive list, but one intended to provide a guide for the practitioner.

## Averaging

Here the two value orientations are averaged. We have some public and some private, some secular and some religious, some individual and some family. This compromise idea is often useful, but it implies an equality of values, which is not always the case. Thus, there may need to be a *weighted average,* which takes account of the dominance/subdominance relationship.

## Sectoring

In sectoring, the two values are used in different topics or in different places, or for different groups. Federalism is an example of values sectoring, in which topic and place vary. Some affirmative action programs are of this kind. Here the planner seeks to prevent value conflict through actualizing the values in different sectors. Ethnic service agencies, each emphasizing the values of the particular group in question, are an example.

## Sequencing

In sequencing, the planner or organizer seeks to use time as the differentiating factor, rather than space, as in sectoring. One case might be a day program and a night program where different types of community needs are met at different times. Programs that are "improper" for schools in the day can be run at night, when the children are gone. Changing a program during the weekend because more men are likely to show up represents another approach to sequencing.

## Adjudicating

Sometimes the planner or community organizer needs an authoritative interpretation; sometimes a choice must be made. Here an appeal to authority can be helpful. Sometimes such an appeal is through the courts, usually when other authority has

failed to be convincing. Besides the courts, however, planners and community organizers can appeal to local authorities in the form of experts, political influentials, and so on.

## Power

Sometimes the "merits" of a situation are not convincing, as in adjudicating, and community organizers seek to build coalitions of leaders and influentials to force their values (or the values for which they are advocating) to become dominant in the situation. "Political" associations are often of this type.

## Decision Rule

Sometimes there are internal decision rules to which planners can appeal or organizers can use to solve a values dilemma. Sometimes these rules refer to *roles;* certain people do this, while others do that. Older and younger people may have such different roles, for example, as have men and women and parents and children. Sometimes a condition becomes the discriminating factor—in this situation, one type of behavior is all right; in that type of situation, some other type of behavior is all right.

## Pragmatism

A popular solution is the pragmatic solution. Let's be "free" of values, it is argued, and do what seems natural and "works" in the situation. Pragmatism usually is not a rule in itself but relates to having a range of means for problem solution available—averaging, sequencing, sectoring, adjudicating, decision rule, and so on. At the means level the pragmatic person is one who has a range of ways to solve a particular values conflict and does not "value" any one over another one, in general.

## CONCLUSION

Values always conflict, because there are many of them and because they tend to come in juxtaposed pairs. Much of the work a community practitioner has to do involves working through values dilemmas and providing solutions that permit the process of community development and improvement to go forward. Assessment is a key tool here. Solutions are not likely to be forthcoming if the multiple and dual aspect of the values system is not perceived by the practitioner.

A second problem of assessment lies in the different strengths of the paired values. It seems that one set of values in which we all believe is more dominant, the other more subdominant. For the values suggested here, those which fuel the social welfare enterprise in general, and community practice in particular, seem to be more on the subdominant side. If this is so, it means that progress toward achieving social work values is likely to threaten the society in general, the community in which the practitioner is working, and the practitioner. It is important to note that community practitioners, committed especially to the improvement of the condition of those who are less well represented in the system, such as minorities, the young, the old, women in broken families, are no less interested in the dominant values than others. Community practitioners must assess their own values, as well as those within the communities they serve.

If values are multiple, or in conflict, and if some values seem to be more dominant than others, how is the practitioner to resolve the inevitable differences of view within the community and within herself or himself? There are a number of techniques that can be used for this purpose, including averaging, sequencing, sectoring, and adjudicating. This suggested list mentions only some of the techniques—there are many variations that can prove very helpful, not only in assessment, but also in crafting a solution.

## BIBLIOGRAPHY

Allison, David, *The R & D Game* (Cambridge, Mass.: MIT Press, 1969).

Baier, Kurt, and Nicholas Rescher, *Values and the Future* (New York: Praeger, 1982).

Banfield, E., and J. Q. Wilson, *City Politics* (Cambridge, Mass.: Harvard University Press, 1965).

Barbour, Ian et al., *Energy and American Values* (New York: Praeger, 1982).

Bell, Daniel, *The End of Ideology: On the Exhaustion of Political Ideas in the Fifties* (Glencoe, Ill.: Free Press, 1960).

Bengston, Vern L., and Mary C. Lovejoy, "Values, Personality and Social Structure: An Intergenerational Analysis," *American Behavioral Scientist* 16, no. 6(1963): 893.

Braybrooke, David, and Charles E. Lindblom, *A Strategy of Decision: Policy Evaluation as a Social Process* (New York: Free Press, 1963).

Degler, Carl N., *Affluence and Anxiety,* 2d ed. (Glenview, Ill.: Scott, Foresman, 1975).

Dunn, William, ed., *Values, Ethics and the Practice of Policy Analysis* (Lexington, Mass.: D. C. Heath, 1983).

Ekric, Arthur A., Jr., *Ideology and Utopias* (Chicago: Quadrangle Books, 1969).

Elder, Glenn, Jr., *Children of the Great Depression* (Chicago: University of Chicago Press, 1974).

March, James, "Theories of Choice and Making Decisions," *Transaction/Society,* Vol. 20 (November/December 1982): pp. 29–39.

Marmor, Theodore, ed., *Poverty Policy* (Chicago: Aldine-Atherton, 1971).

Piven, Frances Fox, and Richard A. Cloward, *Regulating the Poor* (New York: Vintage Books, 1971).

Rokeach, Milton, ed., *Understanding Human Values: Individual and Societal* (New York: Free Press, 1979).

Tropman, John E., "The Constant Crisis: Social Welfare and the American Cultural Structure," *California Sociologist,* Vol. 1 (Winter 1978): pp. 61–87.

_____, Milan Dluhy, and Roger Lind, eds., *New Strategic Perspectives on Social Policy* (Elmsford, N.Y.: Pergamon Press, 1981).

Tropman, John E., and Jane McClure, "Policy Analysis and Older People: A Conceptual Framework," *Journal of Sociology and Social Welfare,* Vol. 5 (November 1978): pp. 822–832.

Williams, Robin, *American Society,* rev. ed. (New York: Alfred Knopf, 1961).

## 12.

## Felix G. Rivera and John L. Erlich

## AN OPTION ASSESSMENT FRAMEWORK FOR ORGANIZING IN EMERGING MINORITY COMMUNITIES

### NEO-GEMEINSCHAFT MINORITY COMMUNITIES: IMPLICATIONS FOR COMMUNITY ORGANIZATION

Social work is running scared. As the era of "slash, cut and trim" descends upon us, the fundamental weakness of the profession becomes painfully apparent. Of course, social work has been in retreat for some time. Since the early 1970s, programs directed to the needs of the minority oppressed poor have been phased out or diminished. Program controls have largely passed from the federal government and local communities to states and municipalities. From a political standpoint, it is understandable that confrontation-stimulating community organization efforts have given way faster than most other services. However, given the demographic changes and inflation of the last decade, the profession is in the position of having to respond to rapidly expanding needs with ever-declining resources. It is not a comfortable position.

One of the most pressing issues of the decade of the 1990s will be the changing nature of ethnic minority communities as it affects community organizing. The changing and emerging communities are a result of the increase in the African-American, Latino and Chicano, Asian, Pacific Islander—especially the Indochinese refugee flow—and the Native American population, and the continued oppression of these communities. Many of the gains of the last twenty years have been eroded by a society that is threatened by education and job-related affirmative action, tired of refugee programs, and alarmed by the encroachment of minorities into previously all-white communities....

The retreat from social justice has helped to set more rigid cultural, social and economic boundaries around many minority communities. Coupled with the resurgence of such racist organizations as the Ku Klux Klan and continuing racial oppressions suffered by all ethnic minorities, a unique revitalization of cultural, social and economic

Felix G. Rivera is a professor in the Department of Social Work Education, San Francisco State University; John L. Erlich is a professor of Social Work, California State University at Sacramento.

survival strategies has emerged. In part, this is a special response to the needs of new arrivals. The organization and complexity of these new communities presents a serious challenge to community organization. To meet the challenge, the profession must not only be able to support community empowerment but also join the struggle for group self-determination.

This paper addresses these issues within the context of community politics and structure. We will explore a model of the new communities that we hope will sharpen the analysis of questions about leadership, economics, power, culture, and social networks and how community organization may become an integral part of the helping process in working with them.

## THE NEW EMERGING COMMUNITIES

Ethnic minority communities are growing dramatically, and with this growth come attendant problems that are further exacerbated by different languages, cultures, and traditions. A cursory look at demographic data only begins to touch on the multi-dimensional nature of this situation.

Between 1980 and 1990, the nation's white majority decreased from 83.2 percent to 80.3 percent, while the minority population grew from 16.8 percent to 19.7 percent, or 48.8 million. All major minority groups showed a steeper rate of growth than whites, whose number increased by 6.1 percent from 188.3 million to 199.8 million, while the total population grew from 226.5 million to 248.7 million.[1] The chief of the Census Bureau's ethnic and racial division noted; "It's one of the most significant changes in the racial composition of the U.S. population in any 10-year period."[2] Any significant undercount would, of course, tend to extend these figures further in the same direction.

## Latinos and Chicanos

Among those listing themselves as "Spanish origin," there was a 50 percent increase from 1980 to 1990, from 14.6 million to 21.9 million.[3] A breakdown by subgroup was not available at the time this paper was prepared; however, there are such data for the 1990 population estimate of 48.8 million.[4] These figures break down into 13.4 million people of Mexican descent, 1,053,197 Cubans, 2.65 million Puerto Ricans, and approximately 2.4 million people from Central and South America. The Census Bureau estimates a growth rate of 50 percent from the 1980 census to 1990. Projections suggest that there will be close to 25 million Latinos and Chicanos by the year 2000 if undocumented aliens are taken into consideration.[5] With this increase in population has come a steady decline in Hispanics' relative economic position. Recent median income for Latino and Chicano families is $11,400 compared to $16,300 for the non-Latino. Puerto Ricans are the lowest on the ladder among their ethnic group with a median income of $8,000. Chicano and Latino unemployment rates hover at approximately 29 percent compared to the national average of 6 percent. Only 40 percent have completed high school compared to 46 percent for blacks and 67 percent for whites. High school dropout rates are estimated at about 85 percent for urban Latinos and Chicanos.[6] It must be pointed out that these statistics do not include the over 100,000 recently arrived refugees from Cuba nor those from El Salvador, Nicaragua, or Guatemala.

## Blacks

Blacks represented 11.7 percent of the population in 1980 and 12 percent in 1990.

Their numbers increased 12.8 percent from 26.5 million to 29.9 million.[7] The black community continues to be a horrendous showcase of racism. Unemployment rates hover at about 14 percent as an overall estimate, while black male unemployment rates stood at 42 percent as of 1992, and 37.2 percent female.[8] Among blacks 67.7 percent, compared to 81 percent of whites, completed high school; and 32.7 percent of blacks compared to 11.3 percent of whites were living in poverty.[9]

Higher socioeconomic status has not been of much help to the black community. Recent research continues to verify the trends of segregation. Blacks moving into white communities in any substantial numbers have precipitated the white withdrawal from that area with continued racial segregation being the result.[10] Furthermore, blacks living in suburbs continue to find themselves living in limited areas.[11]

### Asians and Pacific Islanders

The largest proportional increase occurred among Asians and Pacific Islanders—from 3.5 million to 7.2 million, or more than double.[12] Until recently, this has been one of the most undercounted and ignored communities in the United States. The overly simplistic lumping of all Asians into one category in the census robs the community of its variety of languages, customs, and traditions that are as varied as a black Cuban's culture compared to a white Argentinian's. The community is composed of such diverse people as Pakistanis, Koreans, East Indians, Cambodians, Chinese, Filipinos, Guamanians, Japanese, Thais, Samoans, Yaps, Laotians, Vietnamese, and Hawaiians —and the list is far from complete.

The political and economic ramifications of the census miasma have been all too real for Asians and Pacific Islanders.[13]

Some resaons given for a potentially serious undercount are language barriers, crowded housing conditions, fear of deportation, and non-Western cultural backgrounds of immigrants that worked to limit census takers' access to certain neighborhoods and discouraged community people from cooperating with the census takers.[14]

### Native Americans

Those listing themselves as "American Indian, Eskimo, or Aleut" increased 42 percent from 1.4 to 2 million.[15]... A strong resurgence of involvement in tribal activities and family customs among younger Indians is partially responsible for increased numbers and visibility.

While these demographic changes have proved disruptive to many communities ill-prepared to welcome larger numbers of Third World people, they have also contributed to a very important strengthening of ethnic community ties. For example, Filipinos, Vietnamese, Cubans, and Haitians are bringing not only their racial characteristics to the emerging communities but a revitalization of their culture to the many little Manilas, Saigons, and Havanas. This cultural infusion is helping to make many of these cultural enclaves more self-conscious and active when compared to the assimilationist orientation of most earlier refugee groups. Both their cultural uniqueness and identity as victims of a majority society force minorities to react in ways that are often similar as they cope and survive.

The political economy of minority communities is such that these communities continue to act as the mainstays of a dual labor market. And the difficulty these groups encounter in moving out of the peripheral or secondary sector makes for a continued (if forced) support of these communities that will not soon change.[16]

Another shared experience has been the persistent theorizing about patterns of assimilation becoming almost an ideology of the more and sooner the better. Research has shown this to be a flawed perspective, thus further questioning the push toward white-determined integration of ethnic minorities into the dominant society. In fact, Cubans and Mexicans researched showed an increase in consciousness about their minority positions and the conflict associated with such roles.[17]

Another study has demonstrated that young, upwardly mobile blacks have not helped in closing the racial gap because of their consciousness and, "If anything, the progressive advance up the socioeconomic ladder by both races may result in greater disparities on certain participation-related attitudes."[18]

We need to define what we mean by an ethnic minority people within the context of the demographics presented and the new communities which we define next. The unique circumstances in which minority persons find themselves lead us to define them in several ways: (a) individuals of color different from the dominant society's, (b) individuals who belong to a community in crisis with inordinately high unmet service needs, (c) individuals who are monolingual in a language other than English, (d) individuals from Third World countries coming to the United States as refugees or emigrés, and (e) individuals who are poor.

By defining them in this way, we have set conditions that must be present for an individual or group to be so identified. Thus Native Americans or blacks, even though they are citizens of the United States, are ethnic minorities because they may have high unmet human service needs and because they belong to different cultures, different races, and are poor. A black Cuban or Puerto Rican is also included in these categories because

of the language barrier—if present—and because of race and unmet service needs. An elite colonel from Cambodia or Vietnam, even while politically distant from the poor people of his country, would still come within our definition because he too has unmet service needs, is monolingual, and is racially different. The colonel's problems may be exacerbated upon entering his own ethnic community, for he may be perceived as still being the enemy. The fact is that refugees and minority citizens of the United States continue to find themselves in hostile, poor environments and that their color and culture will be used as shibboleths of exclusion rather than inclusion in the mainstream of society.

## ETHNIC MINORITY COMMUNITIES REDEFINED

In describing the current status of minority communities, the distinction made by Töennies between *gemeinschaft* and *gesellschaft* is useful. The gemeinschaft ("community") is a social system in which relationships are personal, informal, traditional, general, and sentiment-based. On the other hand, the gesellschaft ("society") is a system in which relationships are impersonal, contractual, utilitarian, specialized, and realistically based on market conditions. As Töennies noted, "In Gemeinschaft with one's family one lives from birth on, bound to it in a weal and woe.... There exists a Gemeinschaft of language, of folkways, of mores, or of beliefs."[19]

The development of minority communities with their reinvigorated support systems strongly suggests that we define them as *neo-gemeinschaft*. Our model assumes that these communities' life experiences take place within a causal, deterministic reality, based on racism and economic exploitation. We are further postulating that these systems are essentially closed once individuals enter or leave them. By closed we mean that there are definite entry and exit points in the community with definite parameters based on the respective individual cultures, sociopolitical, and economic situations.

By identifying ethnic minority communities as being *neo-gemeinschaft*, we are arguing that the primary cultural, social, political, and economic interrelationships of such communities are of fundamental importance, because these qualities are seen as major determinants of daily life in them. We also conceive of them as "new" communities because we are identifying specific groups coming together in a new country or geographical area and attempting to salvage their traditions in the face of a largely hostile existing social order. The model is based not only on empirical evidence but also on conversations with members of the various groups as well as personal experiences of the authors. *Neo-gemeinschaft* communities are an excellent example of communities becoming and evolving within an antagonistic environment. The more survival skills that are mastered by these communities, the more unique they become, thereby requiring a new and enlarged definition for their experiences.

By redefining the ethnic minority communities we get a better analytical tool for understanding how these communities are evolving. Traditional definitions of communities are like quicksilver. A summary of these definitions is presented by Effrat, who has condensed much of the literature and has arrived at three definitions: communities are categorized as institutionally distinct groups, as a solidarity of institutions, and as the arena for "primary" interaction.[20]

Cox has described communities as context, demographic characteristics, shared institutions, social system, vehicle, problems, and power relationships.[21] While the above definitions have aspects of *neo-gemeinschaft* communities, they lack the variable of race and culture within a changing context as experienced by these communities with the constant influx of new arrivals, and our additional prerequisites for being defined as a minority person. Take, for example, the immigration of more than 100,000 Cubans into the Miami area (of whom perhaps 70,000 remain). These refugees brought with them a need for redefinition of the culture beyond the established Cuban culture. Rather than putting trust in a single individual, many of these refugee groups organized along horizontal lines with no one individual recognized as the leader. Some of these communities have organized as economic collectives. Because they lack money, they employ bartering as the primary form of service sharing, putting into practice many of the craft skills learned in the home country. Indeed, many more economically secure Cubans who have been in Miami for years have partially altered their business practices to provide for barter as an alternative mode of exchange. This practice is prevalent in many minority communities.

The church has played a significant role in helping to bring groups and individuals within the community together. Churches have been required to adapt to the lifestyles of newcomers. One day they may support a fund raiser, the next they will be baptizing an infant or getting involved in organizing a housing drive. English classes and basic survival techniques (sometimes billed as "community orientations") have been offered in many churches. More established residents have been mobilized to help provide emergency food and clothing.

A more personalized church has thus been thrust upon the clergy and existing practitioners.

The physical appearance of the community is also shifting. It abounds with "mom and pop" stores, stores that often serve as centers for information exchange and informal discussions. The Latino *bodega* is one example. Billboard advertising, posters, newspapers, and magazines are in the community's native language. One telltale sign is that of cooking smells, an excellent barometer. This element of phenomenological assessment is often heralded as one of the most rewarding for obvious reasons. In coping with pressures of a dominant society, these communities are forced to turn inward for almost all needed support. One of these variables of mutual support is the social network. It is defined as:

a specific set of linkages among a defined set of persons {groups and institutions} with the...property that the characteristics of these linkages as a whole may be used to interpret the social behavior of the persons involved.[22]

The main components of social networks with which we are concerned include support, access to new and diverse information and social contacts, communication of expectations, evaluation and a shared world view, and an orientation to getting things done to improve one's lot in this country.

As Stack describes the networking process:

The most typical way people involve each other in their daily domestic lives is by entering them into an exchange relationship. Through exchange transactions, an individual personally mobilizes others as participants in his social network.[23]

The reasons for the resurgent development of these social networks are varied. One is that the transition to new communities by ethnic minorities, some of whom may have been accustomed to leadership roles in the past, throws them into a state of powerlessness when they encounter racial and ethnic segregation. This lack of social integration and acculturation (not assimilation) into the dominant society often accounts for survival-threatening poverty, delinquency, and mental health problems.[24]

Social networks function as horizontally supportive webs throughout the community, for there are few governing elites among recently arrived individuals from the home countries or other areas. Because the communities either share the stigma of forced removal from their native countries or have left their homes because they had few options for improving their quality of life due to war, political, economic, and social turmoil, the people that arrive here may find themselves lost and anomic. And although they may be citizens, they are treated as second- or third-class citizens, still experiencing the racism and economic exploitation of their ancestors. This frustrating situation stimulates mutual support networks that have little respect for old-country leadership hierarchies. Table 12.1 illustrates some of the variables unique to *neo-gemeinschaft* communities and their implications for community organization practice when compared to gesellschaft communities. The table is not meant to be exhaustive but illustrative, and serves to introduce students of community organization and community development to some of the more significant variables and their possible application to community organization strategies.

**IMPLICATIONS FOR COMMUNITY ORGANIZATION PRACTICE**

The phenomenon of new communities emerging from existing old ones is some-

TABLE 12.1
Structural Variables in Gesellschaft and Neo-Gemeinschaft Communities
and Their Implications for Community Organizing Strategies

| Variables | Gesellschaft Communities | Neo-Gemeinschaft Communities | Implications for Community Organizing Strategies |
|---|---|---|---|
| Culture (ethnicity) | The dominant society with culture and traditions not having a strong ethnic identification. English—main if only language spoken and no strong ties or identification with another country. Basically Anglo population. | Relatively homogeneous. English not spoken much, or a street variant of it. Strong tradition from the homeland making for isolated, autonomous pockets of Little Tokyos, Havanas, etc. | Knowledge of culture not enough, should be part of the culture and bilingual. Sensitive to cultural patterns and traditions. An appreciative posture a necessity. |
| Social Structure | Vertical. Limited extended family networks with no experience of oppression or racism. | Horizontal. Shared experience of racism and oppression. Many extended family networks. | Ethnic and cultural membership helps in understanding the complexities of the social structure, helps to provide access to family networks. |
| Power Structure | Mainly external elite and vertical in nature. Community gives up its power in favor of "institutional trust." | Mainly internally pluralistic, decision making usually by consensus. No trust of outside power blocks and their institutions. | Knowledge of power analysis, the formation of coalitions, "winnable" issues and knowledge of power blocks inside and outside of the community. |
| Leadership Patterns | Leadership by political culture and party system. Extended influence and authority. Charisma and person alism less important. | Charismatic leaders, *personalismo,* strong feelings of alienation and anomie. Sphere of influence limited to that community. | Knowledge and respect of the leadership patterns of the culture. An understanding of horizontal and consensual decision making, and leadership by age and wisdom. |
| Economics | All levels of economic ladder, but a strong middle class and much vertical mobility. Limited, if any, labor market segmentation. | Marginal to poor level of existence. Strong interdependence. Bartering for survival. Welfare a constant reality and reminder of their situation. Major contributors to labor market segmentation. | A thorough understanding of political economy and the need for a progressive analysis of same. The ability to identify short- and long-term issues to lessen failures. Knowledge of employment, housing, and community development strategies. |
| Physical Appearance | No unique "flavor" to the communities. A variety of housing patterns. | Strong ethnic flavor in signs, newspapers, magazines. Smells of different foods unique to the homeland. Rundown tenements and substandard housing. | Ability to understand the language and being part of the culture a necessity. |
| Social Networks | Less formal when present. Usually a "conscious" decision is made in developing them. | Strong and quite formal. Usually an integral part of the culture. | Ability to understand the language, relate to the culture, and respect network changes. |

thing community organizers have either not had to deal with or have little understood. One of the reasons is that organizers have assumed that the tenement buildings or housing projects or deteriorated neighborhoods have had some permanence, with the elements of community supports more or less in place. But this is not the case in the emerging communities, for although the buildings may be the same, the activities within present a unique challenge to organizers and other practitioners. For one thing, the literature has shown that evolving minority communities require intervention strategies that go beyond many of the traditional models of community organizing.[25] As Table 12.1 very clearly suggests, the kind of organizing we are talking about cannot be done by anyone simply with the "proper motivation." A deep and sensitive cultural awareness is required. Bilinguality is clearly preferred, although supportive roles for English-speaking monolinguals may well emerge. For certain black and Native American communities bicultural experience and deep respect may take the place of specific linguistic skills. A full appreciation of a group's culture will most often require thorough knowledge of its historical experience—including traditions, political upheavals, and folkways.

The so-called mobilization style of organizing (set up shop in relation to a particular issue, mobilize around it, win what you can, and get out) will not work. Developing the trust necessary to understand, appreciate, and gain access to social networks is going to take a lot of time and patience, much of it beyond the normal workday. Some activities border on the quasi-legal and involve economic exchanges that keep money in the community rather than flowing to outsiders. One organizing key will be to figure out ways of building up existing social networks rather than generating new structures that will undermine these networks—as some of our community action agencies did during the War on Poverty. Rather than beginning with the problems, weaknesses, and inadequacies of these communities, our analysis suggests that strengths are to be noted first and foremost, and looked upon as the basis for organization building. What survival skills work best in that community? How is this shown? The thrust of organizing should be toward empowerment, which according to Solomon:

...enables the client to perceive his or her intrinsic and extrinsic worth. It motivates the client to use every personal resource and skill, as well as

those of any other person that can be commanded, in the effort to achieve self-determined goals.[26]

The exercise of self-determination is central to the framework we have proposed. Furthermore, organizers should keep the concept of community sociotherapy in mind. Rein defines it as:

...the belief system which holds that such processes as organizing groups for self-help, protest, access to community facilities, or even revolution, can create a transformation of the individual personality. Participation in social action is viewed as a sociotherapeutic tool.[27]

This process of empowerment helps in giving people not only a sense of purpose, but a shared experience which will help in the development and nurturance of leadership, the identification of issues that are solvable and hopefully help to reduce the community's general feeling of malaise that may be hampering its development of self-determination and further animation.

## CONCLUSION

In responding to the needs of new and emerging minority communities, we have a choice. We may offer what modest services we can to these communities while focusing primarily on the trendy, fundable programs as we have in the recent past. Or we can take hold and establish a real priority for developing extensive community organization programs in the new communities. This will not be either easy or simple. The environment of self-determining communities is hazardous at best. However, if we are to believe in our own rhetoric, do we have any choice but to find ways to support *neogemeinschaft* minority communities in defining themselves, their surroundings, and their futures?

## NOTES AND REFERENCES

1. Bryce Nelson, "Percentage of Non-Whites in U.S. Rises Sharply," *Sacramento Bee,* February 24, 1981, p. A4; U.S. Census Database, 1990.
2. Ibid.
3. Ibid.
4. *Current Population Reports: Population Characteristics, Persons of Spanish Origin in the United States: March, 1978* (Washington, D.C.: U.S. Department of Commerce, Bureau of the Census, June 1979).
5. Ibid.
6. Ibid.
7. Nelson, "Percentage of Non-Whites," p. A4.
8. *Statistical Abstract of the U.S., 1993,* 113th ed. Washington, D.C.: U.S. Government Printing Office, 1994.
9. Ibid.
10. Arnold M. Denowitz, "Racial Succession in New York City, 1960–1970," *Social Forces* 59, no. 2 (December 1980): 453.
11. Wayne J. Villemez, "Race, Class and Neighborhood: Differences in the Residential Return on Individual Resources," *Social Forces* 59, no. 2 (December 1980): 428.
12. Nelson, "Percentage of Non-Whites."
13. For a detailed discussion on this issue see the papers in the "Census Issues" section of *Civil Rights of Asian and Pacific Americans: Myths and Realities* (Washington, D.C.: U.S. Commission on Civil Rights, U.S. Government Printing Office, 1980), pp. 46–49.
14. Ibid., p. 82.
15. Nelson, "Percentage of Non-Whites."
16. See, for example, R. C. Edwards, "The Social Relations of Production in the Firm and Labor Market Structure," in R. C. Edwards, M. Reich, and D. M. Gordon, eds., *Labor Market Segmentation* (Lexington, Mass.: D. C. Heath, 1975); and R. L. Bach, "Mexican Immigrants and the American State," *International Migration Review* 12 (Winter 1978): 536–558.
17. Alejandro Portes, Robert Nash Parker, and José A. Cobas, "Assimilation or Consciousness: Perceptions of U.S. Society Among Recent Latin American Immigrants to the United States," *Social Forces* 59, no. 1 (September 1980): 220–224.
18. Bruce A. Campbell, "The Interaction of Race and Socioeconomic Status in the Development of Political Attitudes," *Social Science Quarterly* 60, no. 4 (March 1980): 657.
19. Ferdinand Töennies, "Gemeinschaft and Gesellschaft," in Talcott Parsons et al., eds., *Theories of Society* (New York: Free Press, 1961) 1:191.
20. Marcia Pelly Effrat, "Approaches to Community: Conflicts and Complementaries," *Sociological Inquiry* 43, no. 3–4 (1973): 1–28.
21. Fred M. Cox, "Alternative Conceptions of Community," in Fred M. Cox, John L. Erlich, Jack Rothman, and John E. Tropman, eds., *Strategies of Community Organization,* 3d ed. (Itasca, Illinois: F. E. Peacock, Publishers, Inc., 1979), pp. 224–234.
22. J. Clyde Mitchell, ed., *Social Networks in Urban Situations* (Manchester, England: University of Manchester Press, 1969), pp. 1–50; and Roger E. Mitchell and Edison K. Trickett, "Task Force Report: Social Networks as Mediators for Social Support: Analysis of the Effects and Determinants of Social Networks," *Community Mental Health Journal,* 16, no. 1 (Spring 1980), 27–44.
23. Carol Stack, *All Our Kin: Strategies for Survival in a Black Community* (New York: Harper Colophon, 1974), p. 43. Also see Bettylou Valentine, *Hustling and Other Hard Work: Life Styles in the Ghetto* (New York: Free Press, 1978).
24. For further elaboration of this issue see Robert E. Kopsis, "Powerlessness in Racially Changing Neighborhoods," *Urban Affairs Quarterly* 14, no. 4 (June 1979): 425–442; C. S. Fischer, "On Urban Alienations and Anomie: Powerlessness and Social Isolation," *American Sociological Review,* 38, no. 3 (June 1973): 311–326, and Lee Rainwater, *Behind Ghetto Walls: Black Families in a Federal Slum* (Chicago: Aldine, 1970); and Roger E. Mitchell and Edison J. Trickett, "Task Force Report."
25. For example, see Shirley Jenkins, "The Ethnic Agency Defined," *Social Service Review,* 54 (June 1980): 250.
26. As cited in Armando Morales, "Social Work with Third World People," *Social Work* 26, 1 (January 1980): 49.
27. Martin Rein, *Social Policy: Issues of Choice and Change* (New York: Random House, 1970), p. 292.

**13.**

Terry Mizrahi and Beth Rosenthal

MANAGING DYNAMIC TENSIONS

Coalitions, as complex organizations of organizations, inherently experience dynamic tensions. Five of these tensions and their management are described below.

## 1. THE COOPERATION-CONFLICT DYNAMIC

While shared goals and a willingness to work together are the foundation of coalition functioning, in fact coalitions are characterized by conflicts as well as cooperation. Conflict inherently occurs on several levels: (1) between the coalition and the target they wish to influence, around strategies and issues such as credibility, legitimacy and power; (2) among the coalition participants around issues such as leadership, decision making and personality/ style; and (3) between the coalition and its member organizations around issues such as unshared goals, division of benefits, contributions, commitments, and representation.

Since conflict is an inevitable part of the coalition dynamic, coalition work should be approached as a conflict resolution model, where bargaining, trade-offs, negotiating, and compromise are part of all decisions, and agreements are reached by mutual consent.

## 2. MIXED LOYALTIES

Coalition members have a dual commitment—to the coalition and to their own organizations—producing a conflict between altruism and self-interest.

Coalitions that operate in the same service or issue areas as their member organizations may compete with members for resources, organizational time, and energy. There may also be confusion over which "hat" coalition members are wearing while participating in coalition business. Once a coalition is formed, this "mixed loyalties" tension affects the degree of commitment and the contributions that members are willing to make to the coalition, as well as what the coalition can expect from them.

Organizations frequently join coalitions for some protection, because they cannot or do not want to be visible on a particular issue. On the other hand, participating in a coalition means assuming a collective risk, presumably for a greater good or benefit. Once coalition members begin working together, an organization's autonomy may be compromised. Organizations may decide not to join or remain in a coalition because they want to control their own agenda, or are focused on their own survival.

Coalitions can minimize losses and risks for member organizations by using the following approaches:

(a) design collective efforts that do not threaten the turf or networks of the member organizations;

Terry Mizrahi is on the faculty of Hunter College; Beth Rosenthal is a consultant with New York City.

(b) identify and treat carefully issues or positions that could compromise members' credibility and funding;

(c) prevent direct competition between the member organizations and the coalition; and

(d) agree on actions that organizations can do in the name of the coalition versus those that they do on their own.

## 3. AUTONOMY V. ACCOUNTABILITY

A coalition must have enough autonomy to take independent action, and enough accountability to several levels within the coalition and its member organizations to retain credibility and maintain the base which is its essence. Effective coalitions decide when they can assume or need to obtain sanction from the member organizations and their constituencies.

Coalitions can balance the autonomy/accountability tension by creating a variety of ongoing communication mechanisms between the coalition and its members and their organizations. They should also clarify:

(a) how to integrate new members;

(b) who the coalition represents; and

(c) when and how different levels of participants will be involved in coalition decisions and actions.

## 4. MEANS V. MODEL

A coalition can be a means to accomplish a specific social change goal, as well as a particular model of sustained interorganizational coordination. Lack of clarity about whether the coalition is viewed primarily as a "means" or "model" can lead to differences in emphasis on process or product,

degree of commitment, visions of success and failure, willingness to compromise, and time frame for accomplishment of coalition goal.

Coalitions primarily concerned about being a *model* emphasize:

(a) a goal, structure, and operating style that reinforces internal coalition development;

(b) a commitment by member organizations to the coalition as an end in itself;

(c) suspension of action toward the social change goal if necessary to build the coalition, itself.

Some coalitions approached as a *model* later transform themselves into permanent federations or organizations.

Coalitions primarily concerned about being a *means* to accomplish a specific goal:

(a) provide "just enough" structure;

(b) avoid time-consuming process issues;

(c) promote involvement only to "produce results";

(d) either tolerate or find creative ways to work with differences.

The most effective coalitions strive for consistency in process and goal, and balance skill and leadership development with coalition efficiency.

## 5. UNITY AND DIVERSITY

Coalition members share compatible, but not identical, interests, and must both utilize diversity as a strength, and find ways to act in unison. Coalitions need enough unity to act together and enough diversity to accomplish their goal and to represent a broad base. Their functioning requires a certain degree of "syncretism"—an attempt to combine or reconcile differing beliefs in all salient areas. Coalition members must reach some amount of agreement regarding goals, strategies, domain, decision making, and evaluation.

Many coalition leaders assume that unity demands uniformity and conformity. In fact, coalitions that are too unified resemble organizations and fail to achieve the essence of the coalition—the inclusion of diversity. Moreover, excess unity can lead to competition among the groups for turf, access to resources, or visibility, and can also limit the coalition's creativity. Coalitions suffer if all their members have the same perspective, expertise, and resources.

Conversely, many coalitions pursue diversity, either strategically or indiscriminately, with an open-door membership policy. Numbers are not everything—rather, it is the specific mix of diversity needed for a "winning coalition" that is essential. Because people assume that working together will be easy, they may overlook differences that may impede coalition functioning over time. Increasing a coalition's diversity will usually slow down progress toward external goals because it takes time to evolve trust, familiarity, and comfort in working together. Coalitions can become a whole that is greater than the sum of its parts, but to realize this great potential requires making creative use of the different components.

The unity/diversity tension may manifest in eight different dimensions, as described below.

## A. Goal Differences

Goal differences affect problem definition, identification of potential coalition members and choice of social change target, strategies, and solutions.

*Managing Goal Differences.* Coalitions can utilize the following approaches to resolve or minimize goal differences:

1. Select a goal that is central to everyone's interests and is seen as something that can benefit both the diverse groups and the coalition as a whole.
2. Define a goal relevant to the members' interests, but broader than any one group could address alone.
3. Identify linkages between the issues.
4. Create a superordinate goal that transcends differences among potential coalition members, and clarify how the participants' differences support the whole.
5. Compromise on goals: Create goals where all participants can get a portion of what they really want, enough to sustain their involvement.
6. Change goals over time.
7. Show how short-term goals relate to the long-term, bigger picture.

## B. Ideological Differences

People with different political or religious ideologies approach coalition work with distinct belief systems and operating principles.

*Managing Ideological Differences.* Coalitions can use the following approaches to help member groups with different ideologies work together more effectively:

1. Address a third issue unrelated to any member organization's domain.
2. Take action only on issues on which there is total agreement and allow any group to have veto power.
3. Limit joint action strictly to goals.

4. Suspend judgment on areas of difference.
5. Compromise on public position.
6. Tone down the ideologically extreme position.

## C. Differences in Expected Outcome

Organizations may agree on a common goal, but outcome expectations may differ. This tension intensifies with a coalition's success, at which time decisions about pay-offs and rewards must be made.

*Managing Outcome Expectation Differences.* Coalitions can withstand divergence in the outcome expectations of their members by the following means:

1. Expand or redefine the pie rather than consider possible outcomes in zero sum terms.
2. Engage in issues which promise some tangible or intangible gains for each coalition member.
3. Enable each member organization to maintain the ability to act autonomously on issues that are not directly related to coalition activity, as long as they do not do so in the name of the coalition.
4. Select coalition issues that do not conflict with members' individual agendas.
5. Make explicit the trade-offs for everyone's involvement.
6. Discuss the consequences of winning or losing when there appears to be a zero sum outcome.

## D. Differences in Amount and Level of Power

Coalitions have to deal with the consequences of actual and perceived power differences among members and potential participants.

*Managing Power Differences.* To minimize power differences, coalitions can find ways to have the powerful group provide resources without dominating. When it is desirable to keep the powerful group(s) inside the coalition, the following mechanisms can be established:

1. a one group/one vote rule;
2. voting/not voting membership;
3. caucuses for smaller groups;
4. an agenda that gives less influential members the advantage.

Coalitions which exclude powerful groups from full participation can continue to draw upon their resources and support by:

1. making them affiliates or honorary members;
2. forming parallel/support coalitions;
3. providing technical/advisory status for the powerful group.

## E. Differences in Level and Intensity of Commitment

Organizations join and continue participating in coalitions for a variety of pragmatic and/or ideological reasons. Pragmatic reasons include some degree of self-interest—a quest for resources, power, or social contract; ideological motivations mean some shared value-based commitment to a cause or a concept of the "greater good."

*Managing Differences in Commitment.* To maximize commitment to the coalition effort and encourage a greater variety of organizations to participate, coalitions can:

1. Structure opportunities for multiple levels of commitment.

2. Develop membership agreements that clarify what kind and level of commitment is desirable and how it should be demonstrated.
3. Plan for fluctuations in commitment over time.
4. Provide a variety of incentives to sustain participation, addressing the actual motivations of members.
5. Assure protection to members.

## F. Differences in Type and Level of Contributions

Coalitions development requires the assessment of the amount and kinds of contributions needed, and the assignment of equivalent weights to the various contributions actually provided by members. As coalitions endure, they identify whether they have the necessary contributions required both to achieve the social change goal and to maintain the coalition.

*Managing Differences in Contributions and Rewards.* Coalitions should clarify expectations about minimum contributions, how the ratio of contributions to rewards will be determined, and how differential contributions can be made to be equivalent.

1. Balance contributions with rewards. There are several ways to do this:
   EQUITY: Organizations get out what they put in.
   EQUALITY: Regardless of what organizations put in, they get the same rewards.
   EQUIVALENCY: (Structured inequality) Some organizations get out more than they put in, while others get less.

2. Determine minimum contributions according to a coalition's priorities.

## G. Differences in Color, Gender, Sexual Preference, Nationality, and Class

Longstanding differences in experiences, priorities, and problem definitions make it difficult to develop coalitions that cross color, gender, sexual preference, nationality, and class lines.

*Managing Diversity in Color, Gender, Sexual Preference, Nationality, and Class.* Coalitions consciously pursuing diversity must factor in the time and effort to make it happen. Some useful approaches include the following:

1. Include diverse groups at the coalition's inception, rather than later, which can minimize real or perceived tokenism, paternalism, and inequality.
2. Consciously give priority to increasing diversity.
3. A majority group-initiated coalition can offer some incentives ("affirmative action") to recruit minority participants, and consciously operate in new ways to share control and build trust. True diversity requires an ongoing commitment of coalition resources to issues of importance to the minority group members.
4. A minority group-initiated coalition can present its issues within a broad framework that integrates the majority perspectives, if their involvement and support is deemed necessary.

## H. Differences in Organizational and Personal Style

Organizations and individuals bring different styles of operating and interacting to their coalition work. Some style differences evolve from color, class, and gender, and some, such as personality differences, are purely idiosyncratic.

*Managing Style Differences.* Depending on their goal and the amount of time they have to act, coalitions can either accept or attempt to minimize style differences. If there is a sense of urgency about taking coalition action, differences may be tolerated. Over the long term, coalitions committed to a model of intergroup cooperation can seek ways to minimize the negative effect on style differences. To contain differences which could become destructive, spell out common rules for interaction:

1. Create and discuss ground rules for meetings and coalition operations.
2. Develop and enforce membership criteria.
3. Structure equal time to speak.
4. Conduct criticism/self-criticism of meetings which articulates and builds a common set of expectations, values, and operating methods for coalition functioning.
5. Create a policy that allows for the exclusion of deviant or disruptive personalities or organizations, if necessary.

**14.**

## John E. Tropman and Gersh Morningstar

## THE EFFECTIVE MEETING: HOW TO ACHIEVE HIGH-QUALITY DECISIONS

### EXECUTIVE SUMMARY

Antony Jay's piece, "How to Run a Meeting That Gets Things Done," appeared in the March–April 1976 issue of *Harvard Business Review.* It was reprinted in the previous editon of *Tactics and Techniques of Community Practice.* Though the structure and dynamics of meetings have attracted much attention since the publication of that classic, meetings are still widely regarded as some sort of resented, necessary evil of organizational life. This article reviews some of the reasons why things go wrong in meetings, presents seven important principles that underly the meeting process, and proposes twelve "rules" for making meetings go right. A thorough understanding of these principles and diligent application of these rules will lead inevitably to more effective meetings with higher quality group decisions. Experience with these principles demonstrates that higher quality decisions will come even in the face of recurring problems of personality in meetings.

### INTRODUCTION

Meetings and committees are crucial to the American way of business. In spite of the

Gersh Morningstar is a consultant, editor, and writer in Florida.

fact that we have many negative attitudes and orientations toward them, meetings remain THE primary mechanism through which American business decision making is accomplished. Rarely are those decisions made in isolation. Almost always, in fact, those decisions are the direct or indirect product of some group meeting in committee.

We do love our myths about business leadership and the captains of industry. We can all recount endless apocryphal tales of the hard-headed CEO, closeted alone for days while wrestling with some potentially cataclysmic decision, emerging, finally with a directive. The fact that it seldom happens this way doesn't seem to bother us particularly.

Some business myths are not harmless. Some can lead, in fact, to real catastrophe for a company or an organization that refuses to shed them in spite of strong evidence to the contrary. Among the more dangerous are those we perpetuate about committees and the meeting process: "A committee is a group that takes minutes to waste hours"; "A camel is a horse designed by a committee"; and "If you want to be certain nothing gets done about a problem, turn it over to a committee." Reality is quite different.

Almost no important business decision is made entirely outside the meeting context, without some shaping by the meeting process, without some review by other committees. Meetings and group decisions are powerful and essential elements in any organizational enterprise. Successful business cannot function without them.

In the abstract, meetings don't deserve their bad press. Theoretically, a meeting is like an elegant, cleverly structured, intricate, action game. In our society, it is a game everyone must play at one time or another: in business, it is a game played without end. The problem is that almost everyone plays it

badly. Unlike baseball (another game the elegance of which is axiomatic), for meetings there is no organized learning system that begins in grade school, continues through high school, moves to the sand lots, then on to the minor leagues, and finally to the majors. Chris Schenkel does not broadcast the World Series of Meetings, so very few of us ever get to see the game played well. While there are a handful of meeting "major leaguers," most of us have never seen them perform. If by chance we do run across one, we view him or her as a "Natural" with inborn skills we think cannot be learned. We are, nevertheless, thrown into the game without proper training, without a knowledge of the rules, with little concept of effective game strategy and tactics, and without a clear understanding of which position (role) we are being expected to play. Our only role models for the game are poor players ourselves. So, we condemn the game when our real problem is the ineptitude of the players.

The experience of most of us with meetings leaves us wanting to get back to something that at least has the appearance of being productive. While meetings, ideally, may be places where decisions should be made, all too frequently they are exercises in inefficiency.

Cohen, March, and Olsen address this point in their famous paper, "The Garbage Can Model of Decision Making." They argue that all organizations have four forces running through them: (1) people who know the organization's problems; (2) people who know the solutions to the organization's problems but may not, themselves, know the problems; (3) people who control organizational resources; and, (4) "decision makers looking for work." Individuals representing these organizational segments need to be assembled in one place if organizational goals are to be achieved. Too frequently it doesn't happen. In some meetings people get together who know the problems but have no solutions or resources. In others, decision makers get together to take action, which may be (often is) irrelevant.

For most organizations, then, worries about the inefficiencies of group decision making are appropriate and well targeted. The solution, however—avoiding meetings, reducing their number, getting rid of committees—is the wrong approach. This solution must inevitably lessen the quality of decisions presently being made, for it truncates the base of wisdom, knowledge, and experience available for decision making.

The best solution lies in learning to play the meetings game with skill. The first step in that learning process is understanding why things go wrong.

## WHY THINGS GO WRONG

To prescribe a suitable remedy, we must first have a proper diagnosis. We begin with a series of questions: Why are meetings generally viewed with such negativity? Why don't meetings accomplish what they should accomplish? Why do so many view meetings as a waste of time? In short, why *do* things go wrong? There are many answers.

### Values

Group decision making—most group activity, in fact—runs counter to the popular view most Americans hold of themselves as fierce individualists. We believe that things run better if we do them ourselves, on our own, without having to rely on others. "I can't get any work done if I have to be in meetings all the time." The implicit assumption here is that meetings are the antithesis of work, that work is something we do alone in our offices. Not only is work viewed as best done while

alone, but credit for work is seen as an individual reward. In our arts as in our industry we glorify the individual and deprecate the group. Every day must be a replay of *High Noon*. Things go wrong in meetings because, too often, the committee room is a coliseum of conflict instead of a center of cooperation.

### Hidden Functions

Meetings and committees perform a number of hidden functions on behalf of society, which can confound and confuse decision making. Social purpose, for example, is embedded in the meeting process that is related to American traditions of representative democracy and pluralism. In our society we recognize that individuals have both a need and a right to have their say on important issues. This has extended itself into the political system of American business, where the committee has become a way in which diverse factions are allowed to argue their various points of view. It gives those who would lose out in a simple majority vote a chance to be heard.

### Lack of Training

Playing the meetings game effectively requires a certain amount of skill that can only be achieved through expert training. While we provide ample opportunities for practice (everyone participates in meetings), such practice is without guidance and focus. As important as the group decision-making process is to every aspect of business life, our society devotes little time and almost none of its resources to teaching the rules of the meetings game and training individuals in the application of those rules. Things go wrong in meetings because the participants simply have no idea how to make them go right.

## The Self-Fulfilling Prophecy

Because we have no "good meeting" referent, much of our experience with meetings is negative. Out of that experience base have come strong negative expectations about meetings and the effectiveness of the group decision-making process. We expect meetings to be time wasters, and we engage in behavior that causes them to turn out that way. Things go wrong in meetings because we expect them to go wrong.

## HOW TO MAKE THINGS GO RIGHT

### Seven General Principles of the Meetings Game

Meetings and group decision making can be improved. Learning and then applying a few simple rules (prescriptions, if you will, for curing the ailing meeting process) will quickly yield dramatic improvements in both the quality of meetings and the quality of the decisions that emerge from them. Seven broad principles form the basis for these rules, and examining those principles will help to place the twelve rules I will present in proper perspective.

An important caveat must precede that examination. Principles and rules go only part of the way toward improving business meetings and the decisions that come from them. People are people. Potential conflict between us and among us exists whenever two or more of us gather. Yet, there are places—a courtroom, a ballgame, a play, an orchestra performance—where the very existence of rules makes for better performance possibilities. Still, rules (and the principles that underlie them) do not of themselves guarantee outstanding performance in meetings. (Neither do they guarantee it in courts, ballgames, plays, and orchestra performances.) What they do

accomplish is to give groups more of a fighting chance by preventing some bad things from happening.

There are many principles involved in the meetings game. The list that follows is not exhaustive, but these seven are seen by meetings professionals as among the most important.

*1. The Role Principle.* Just as there are roles in a play that various actors fit into, there are various meeting roles; and these are as well defined as the parts in a play. At the very least these include the role of Chair and the role of Member. There is usually a Recorder role, as well, and often a Staffer role. Sometimes, too, there are specialized roles—Advisor, for example. Everyone connected with a meeting casts himself or herself (or is cast by someone else) into one of those roles. As long as each participant plays the assigned role, speaking lines and presenting behaviors appropriate to that role, meetings run as smoothly as a well-oiled machine. Problems arise when the actors attempt to expand their parts in a conscious or unconscious effort to usurp the role of someone else (usually the Chair, but all too frequently Chairs have been known to take on the Member role.)

One of the reasons most frequently reported to me for why things go wrong is "mental illness," i.e., "All the people on my committee but me are crazy." While that may be overstating the case a bit, many observers see aberrant or inappropriate behavior on the part of committee members as the root cause of some major meeting problems. These are common occurrences: a committee member voices constant anger, making other members uncomfortable, and the Chair seems incapable of firm control; one member dominates discussion to such a degree that other members get up and leave; one member gets so involved in minutia (harping on minutes, for example) that the productive work of the committee goes unaccomplished. Such disruptive behavior causes us to focus on personalities. But the real problems have very little to do with personalities. Rather, the problems arise when individuals depart from their assigned and defined roles within the meeting context.

Once we recognize that our focus should be upon the roles that participants must play in the meeting and *not* upon the personalities they bring to their parts, we move away from the negative effect that inevitably accompanies a focus on individual personalities. We can begin to consider the dynamics of the group more rationally and with more reason.

*2. The Orchestra Principle.* In considering the dynamics of the group, I have found it especially instructive to relate the meeting process to an orchestra performance. The orchestra has a score to perform (something like an agenda). There are the rehearsals before the performance (as there is some degree of preparation for any well-planned meeting.) There is a conductor to lead the orchestra through the performance (as there is a Chair to guide the meeting.) The musicians, each with his or her own contribution to make to the totality, come together as a body on a preplanned basis to make music (just as meeting participants should always be brought together on a preplanned basis to make decisions.)

We would find it surpassingly odd if we attended an orchestra concert, at the outset of which the oboe player stepped forward and played all of his notes in a Beethoven symphony and then left with the explanation, "I'm feeling a little pressed, and I've got to duck out early." That this kind of behavior happens routinely in meetings

sheds still further light on why the meeting experience is so frequently unsatisfying.

*3. The Content Principle.* This principle is closely related to the Orchestra Principle. Meetings *should* be organized by content, but they are *usually* structured by person. Individual participants are allowed (encouraged, required) to present all of the material specifically related to them, all at one time, without regard to the possibility that this material might be of many different kinds and relate to many different items with which the meeting is concerned. Thus, we have "the treasurer's report," which is generally parallel to our oboe player giving us all of his notes at once. At best, meetings organized by person result in a great deal of repetition that fosters inefficiency and lengthens meetings unnecessarily. At worst, such organization reinforces the focus on personalities and generally works to the detriment of good meetings.

*4. The Three-Character Principle.* Matters before decision groups have one of three characters: they are informational, decisional, or discussional. Each is distinctly different. In the well-played meetings game, these are separated before the meeting begins and organized together so that the group can deal with all the information items at once, all of the decision items at once, and all of the discussion items at once. This is what I mean when I say meetings should be organized by content. This kind of organization leads to dramatic increases in the efficient use of meeting time and resources and leads to better decision making by the group.

Such organization may (and usually does) require some individuals to appear more than once on the agenda. This is no more odd than our peripatetic player doing his or her thing as the score requires throughout the symphony.

*5. The No-More-Reports Principle.* Reports are a major enemy of meetings for two reasons. First, they involve one individual heavily and all the others passively, which is not the reason the group was brought together. Second, they tend to be organized by persons rather than by topics (again, the ever popular "treasurer's report" or any other "reports" where individuals get up and report on all matters pertaining to their departments, regardless of the character of the information presented.)

Reports make it difficult for groups to cope with their expected tasks because they generally require the participants to move rapidly back and forth among items of different character that have differing requisites and make differing demands. The informational content of the usual treasurer's report should, in fact, be allocated across the agenda items and presented whenever, wherever, and only to the extent that it is relevant. The information contained in any individual's "report" should emerge as a natural part of the decision or discussion processes.

*6. The No-New-Business Principle.* The introduction and discussion of new business is a meeting enemy even more formidable than reports. It achieves this status not because there is no need for new business but, rather, because introducing it at the meeting disrupts the orderly flow of the meeting process. New business is, by definition, that about which little is known. The ability of the group to process the new business is severely limited. Neither the quality of any discussion about it nor any decisions made concerning it are likely to be of high quality. Injecting new business in a meeting is roughly equivalent to a football coach introducing a new play into a critical situation of a football game, a play that not only has never been practiced but is one the players are not even familiar with. In the well-played meetings game, what might be called "new business" is introduced at the end of the meeting, without discussion and as a kind of preview of some subsequent meeting.

*7. The Proactivity Principle.* Most groups spend most of their time reacting to issues. This fosters the appearance of items on an agenda that are already at some crisis point. The reactive position is always structurally weaker than the proactive one. It is therefore in the interests of good meeting process to reach out for issues, to garner them before they require crisis management. Small problems are easier to solve than big ones. Small decisions requiring minimal discomfort are easier to make than large decisions involving great pain.

## High-Quality Decisions

The goal of the meetings game is high-quality decisions. Well-played meetings games have nothing to do with making people happier in groups (although that will happen because some of the problematic activities will have been removed or changed.) For the most part, the feelings of the players are of only minimal concern. The real focus of the game is on the output of the group over time. That output needs to be assessed on a constant basis to provide effective feedback to the players on how well they are playing the game. I am about to present twelve rules for making things go right in meetings. The last of these rules provides one possible mechanism for conducting this ongoing assessment.

## Twelve Practical Rules to Make Things Go Right

Following are twelve rules that, if applied, will help things go right in meetings. These rules focus on both the substantive and procedural structure of information. They are concerned both with meeting items and with the kinds of considerations that are desired from those items. This latter is particularly important because it is the source from which individuals come to know the kinds of things that are expected of them.

Some of these rules deal with the meeting, itself. Others deal with the preplanning and preparation that go into the meetings.

*1. The Rule of Halves.*  Identify the halfway point that lies between the end of the last meeting and the beginning of the next. During the first half of that period gather information about the kinds of items that are to be considered at the upcoming meeting.

End the item gathering at the halfway point. At that point examine all of the items that have been gathered. Remove all of those that can be handled on a one-to-one basis in people's offices. If something does not need group attention (and fully 40 percent of all items that generally come before meetings don't and should never be there), don't put it on the agenda. Removing such nongroup items permits more intensive focus upon the remaining items.

For each potential meeting item, assess what people, information, and/or resources are needed in connection with each and arrange for their presence at the upcoming session. If the appropriate information, individuals, or resources are not available, eliminate the item from the meeting. It makes very little sense to waste the group's valuable time discussing them.

Sort the candidate items into three groups: information items, decision items, and discussion items. Meeting participants not only want substantive information about what they are discussing, they want that information given to them in a procedural context. ("Are we just hearing about this? Are we deciding it? Or are we just noodling around?")

Information that once would have been presented in a single report (such as the treasurer's report) should be examined for each of its informational, decisional, and discussional components and scheduled appropriately.

*2. The Rule of Sixths.*  As the final agenda is taking form, inspect the meeting items and seek to find those that flow in about the following proportions: (1) About one sixth should be items from the past, historical items that have not yet been completed. (2) About four sixths should be, relatively speaking, here-and-now type items. (3) About one sixth should be future oriented, "blue sky" items about which the meeting participants can do some proactive, plan-ahead type thinking.

The virtue of this system is not only that good ideas are generated, but that a certain amount of affect, especially around controversial items, is allowed to be expressed in a nonthreatening situation. Individuals are allowed to express their creativity in a context in which creativity may be expected to have some impact. This becomes a "psychic income" that meeting planners can provide for the group. It is more likely to keep individuals pleased, happy, and eager to return. This is a side benefit of proactivity that reaps great rewards.

*3. The Two-Meeting Rule.*  As this system gets under way, in the meeting planning phase, look for controversial items and seek to schedule them according to the Rule of Sixths. At the very least, controversial items should be discussed at least twice, i.e., in at least two different meetings. The first discussion should be just that: a discussion. This process allows for affect to be expressed and for new ideas to be introduced about how difficult items might be approached. The next time such as issue comes up it can be for decision.

For very controversial items, two and even three iterations of discussion may be appropriate before a decision is taken. All too frequently our hesitancy to deal with controversial matters encourages us to delay them, taking them up only at the last possible moment under severe constraints of pressure and time.

*4. The Rule of Three Fourths.* By the three-fourths point in the time period between meetings, the agenda should be in its final form. Send it to the individuals attending the meeting so that they have time to review it and to read any accompanying materials. Usually the meeting packet contains three items: the agenda, minutes of the last meeting, and reports of various kinds. Each of these requires some specific attention.

*5. The Rule of the Agenda.* An agenda should look like a menu. Most agendas, unfortunately, are simply lists of topics that regularly pass up opportunities for structuring the decision-making context in a helpful fashion. With a menu-type agenda, items are segregated into their information, decision, and discussion groups. Instead of simply "the PDQ report," for example, the agenda might say something like "Information about the PDQ report" or "Decisions concerning the PDQ report" or "Discuss the PDQ report."

Below each agenda item, the "main dish" on the menu, provide a one-or two-sentence summary of the key elements of the item so that individuals scanning the agenda can have a full sense of what is involved.

As part of the item itself or in parentheses next to it use one of the three key words ("informational," "decision," or "discussion"). This allows the meeting participants to understand the context of the item.

Finally, on the right-hand side of the agenda, where price might be on a menu, put a running clock with differential amounts of time allocated to the different items. This tells the meeting participants when the meeting will start, when it will end, and how much time in the meeting is being allocated for each item.

*6. The Minutes Rule.* Provide content-focused minutes that give brief summaries of the main points of discussion. Skip a line and, in capital letters, put in the decision or action. It is here that names are mentioned, times are mentioned, and responsibilities are assigned. This cures the frequent problem of meeting attendees being unable to remember from one meeting to the next precisely what was decided. It also tends to prevent descriptions of decisions that are so vague no one later knows what they meant: "Take appropriate action."

Meeting minutes are almost always written in the wrong way—as descriptions of the meeting process, with long litanies of "he said" and "she said." Process minutes not only fail to convey fully the extent of the meeting work that went on, but they focus on individuals. Where such individuals perceive the minutes placing them in a bad light, it is not uncommon to engage in protracted discussions in order to improve their respective positions. Content minutes also tend to cure this problem.

*7. The Rule of Reports.* Use the executive summary technique and the options memo technique, as described below, for all reports to be presented at a meeting.

Most meeting planners send out too much information, sometimes so much that it becomes disinformation. Too often, a potential meeting participant will look at the huge packet of material sent to her or him as preparation for the next meeting, and put it aside "until I can really devote the appropriate amount of time to it." That time never comes, so the preparatory work becomes useless.

With the executive summary technique, all reports are reduced to no more than two pages. If an attendee wants or needs further information, it is available on request.

Options memos are designed to enhance discussion and to prevent it from becoming malfocused, one of the most common problems in groups. The technique presents all reports, written or oral, in three steps: a problem statement, a set of options that reasonable people might consider to handle the problem, and a set of recommendations for action based upon a selection from the options set.

Options memos encourage the work of the group and discourage rubber stamping of the work of a single individual or subcommittee (the "O.K., here's the problem, and here's what I think should be done about it" presentation). Options memos virtually eliminate the problem of the group focusing on whether to accept or reject a proffered solution rather than looking at the proposal, itself, as a basis for discussion and improvement.

Options memos present information that the group wants and needs. They answer latent questions and stimulate the beginning of the process of discussion. The act of discussing options often leads to the discovery of still further alternatives and may also uncover hidden difficulties. The final result is a decision on which the full force of the group has been focused. That decision is almost always an improved one with difficulties removed or diminished and positive features added.

*8. The Rule of Two Thirds.*   All meetings are divided into three parts: a "git-go" part at the beginning, a heavy work part in the middle, and a decompression part at the end. Allocate information items and simple decisions to the first third of the meeting. Process difficult items in the middle third. Deal with discussion items in the last third.

Groups need a little time to get going, so key items don't belong at the beginning of a meeting. Toward the middle of the session, maximum attendance has been achieved, and energy, both physical and psychological, is at its high point. This is the time to handle the toughest items.

The decision making that occurs in the group under this model *does* tear at the fabric of group cohesion. This cohesion needs to be rebuilt whether the group is a gathering of strangers or is made up of people who work together on a daily basis. Discussion provides a way to continue group work, on the one hand, while allowing for group rebonding on the other.

*9. The Rule of the Agenda Bell.*   Orchestrate meetings so that the emotional component follows a bell-shaped curve, as in Figure 14.1. Item 1 should always be minutes. If there are not enough people there to approve the minutes, they can be reapproved at a later point.

Item 2 is always made up of announcement items. These should take no more than about 10 percent of the total meeting time, which will prevent the meeting from becoming simply an oral newsletter.

Item 3 (a, b, c, etc.) contains decision items of only modest difficulty. Short, easy decision items allow the group to get going.

Item 4 (a, b, c, etc.) matters are the more difficult decision items.

Item 5 is always the single most difficult item on the agenda for that particular meeting. It should occupy space between the 40 percent and 60 percent points, allowing for optimum group attention and energy. Because of its difficulty, this item will almost always fol-

FIGURE 14.1
The Rule of the Agenda Bell

Remember that once you set the time frame, people adjust their internal expectations to that announcement. It's sort of an agreement.

Organize your agenda according to the agenda bell. If you cannot hand it out in advance, take a few minutes with the whole team and do it right there.

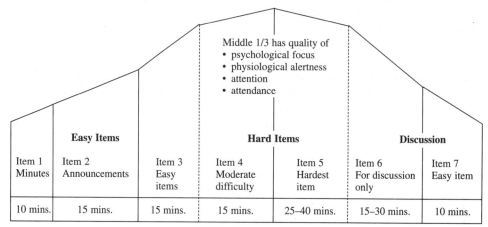

Middle 1/3 has quality of
• psychological focus
• physiological alertness
• attention
• attendance

| **Easy Items** | | | **Hard Items** | | **Discussion** | |
|---|---|---|---|---|---|---|
| Item 1<br>Minutes | Item 2<br>Announcements | Item 3<br>Easy items | Item 4<br>Moderate difficulty | Item 5<br>Hardest item | Item 6<br>For discussion only | Item 7<br>Easy item |
| 10 mins. | 15 mins. | 15 mins. | 15 mins. | 25–40 mins. | 15–30 mins. | 10 mins. |

1/3 40 mins.                    2/3 80 mins. (average)

2-hour meeting = 120 minutes

low the Two-Meeting Rule; thus, this will be at least the second time in the history of the group that this item is being considered.

By the completion of Item 5, with one minor exception, all of the decision items have been handled. Item 6 (a, b, c, etc.) is composed of discussion items. There are items where thought is needed but where final resolution is not yet appropriate or is not yet in the purview of this particular group.

Item 7 is a short, easy decision item on which all can agree. Usually this will be an item that appears to be substantially trivial in content. It is not at all trivial, however, in its importance to the meetings game. Such an item allows the meeting to end on time and on a psychological note of agreement and accomplishment. ("Well, at least we got *something* done.")

*10. The Rule of Temporal Integrity.* Start on time. End on time. Keep to the rough internal time order. Carefully planned meetings held by properly prepared meeting attendees should almost never require more than an hour and a half.

*11. The Rule of Agenda Integrity.* Deal with all of the items on the agenda. Do *not* deal with any items not on the agenda. Individuals make attendance decisions based in part upon what they are informed will be covered. They invest time in reviewing meeting materials. Maintaining the integrity of the agenda reinforces the decisions to attend and provides a substantial return on the time investment. Nothing short of an act of God justifies changing the agenda at the last moment or wandering from the agenda during the meeting.

*12. The Rule of Decision Audit and Decision Autopsy.* For important groups, go back on a year- to a year-and-a-half basis and look at some of the key decisions made by the groups. Any evaluation can be used. Here is one I have found effective.

Take a sample of past decisions. For each decision, rate it "A" if it was an all-win situation—i.e., everyone benefitted though not necessarily equally. Rate it "B" if the decision had some winners and some losers but on balance had a positive result. Give it a "C" if a decision was made but nothing happened. A "D" rating is the inverse of "B": There were both winners and losers but on balance the result was negative. An "F," also known as the "nuclear war decision," is an all-lose decision.

Calculate a grade point average for the sample and feed it back to the groups. Whatever rating mechanism is used is purely a matter of choice. What is crucial is going back and looking at decisions in an effort to assess the strengths and weaknesses in the decision-making process.

This assessment leads to the autopsy. In any such review, take the very best decisions and the very worst ones, and take them apart. Answer, to the extent possible, the questions, "What went right and why?" "What went wrong and why?" It is imperative that both good and bad decisions be lined together in the autopsy process. Using only bad decisions in the autopsy generates group defensiveness and fault-avoidance behavior.

## CONCLUSION

Meetings can be improved. Therefore, meetings should be improved. Improvement means that the output of meetings—decisions—should be of the highest possible quality. In moving toward high-quality decisions, I have presented procedures that shorten time, focus discussion, and generally make meetings less painful. However, I wish to underscore that it is *not* removing pain from the meeting that is my goal. Rather, it is making the pain pay off.

As individuals experience meetings that are productive, that invite and involve their participation, a process of reinforcement will begin that can both reverse the negative aspects of the self-fulfilling prophecy as well as use that mechanism for improvement and achievement.

## SIDEBAR

### Effective Role Playing Helps Things Go Right

In the game of football it is not enough to know the rules to play the game well. It is also important to understand what is required of each position on the team—what the quarterback does, what the center does, what the linebacker does, and so on. The same is true of the meetings game. To play it well, it is important to understand what is required of the various positions on the meeting team because, over the course of time, we will each play all of the positions.

*The Chair Role.* The Chair is one of the key roles, and most of us have never learned to chair a meeting. Often, the decision to accept the responsibilities of a meeting Chair is a fairly casual matter, made without regard to much more than whether one has the extra time available that is always assumed to go with chairing a committee. There are, however, several things that a potential Chair ought to look into.

First, does the group have enough resources to do the kinds of things that it is being asked to do? Does it have the necessary money and/or people to accomplish its task?

Second, what are the politics of the group? Are they something that can be worked with, and, if so, how? A careful political assessment done in advance can save many future problems.

Third, employ self-assessment: "What does it mean for me to be Chair of the group? What kinds of signals does my reputation in the business convey? How will others react?" It is not possible to change some of these things, of course, but knowledge allows for behavioral alterations that can lead to productive results that might never have been possible without it.

Fourth, what is the purpose of the group? If the Chair is to be the custodian of this purpose, it should be written down and provided to the other members. This is true even for "simple staff meetings" held on a frequent, regular basis. If someone else is the custodian of the mandate, then that individual should be asked for it in writing. During the crafting period, negotiations about the nature of mandate, the scope, and the resources can be undertaken.

Fifth, and most importantly, the Chair needs to inquire of himself or herself whether it is possible to move from the role of partisan to the role of statesman. Many Chairs feel that once they assume the Chair, they will be able to get their own way. Unfortunately, as Antony Jay has pointed out, self-indulgence is one of the great problems groups face. It is necessary to assume the posture of a statesman if the meeting process is to be successful, facilitating the product of the group rather than promoting ones' own wishes and desires.

The role of the Chair falls, basically, into two parts: intellectual and interpersonal. Intellectually, the Chair needs to *blend* the ideas of those in the meeting. At key points,

often after a round of discussion when everyone has had the opportunity to contribute, the Chair should summarize, suggesting to the group where it is at that moment, bracketing those areas of agreement and setting them aside, and refocusing the discussion on those items that remain. The process is really the decision process with individuals (often the Chair but not always)—summarizing, building, refocusing—until the entire decision stands before the group in a way that no individual would have anticipated.

In this process the Chair uses interrogative rather than declarative. Instead of saying, "That's a dumb idea," or "That's a terrific idea," the Chair raises questions of a "what if" nature. This is especially true of weak or bad ideas. The individual who offers a poor concept might well be the genius who provides the key to the solution of the next problem. Squelching that individual may cause him or her to retreat and contribute no further. The idea is to guide the contributing process in a way that invites the individual to confront some of the problems of the poor idea but, at the same time, receive support for the basic effort of suggesting and trying.

Jay points out that there is a sequence to the discussion process that facilitates that process if it is followed. First there is the discussion of the problem. Second, there is discussion of evidence and points of view about the problem. Third, there is an agreement about what the evidence and perspectives mean. Fourth, there is a decision. Fifth, there is action.

Insofar as possible, the Chair's job is to keep the discussion moving through these stages, seeing that each one is resolved before the next one is begun. Throughout, the Chair maintains equality for persons but equity for issues; i.e., people are all treated equally but issues are not. More attention is lavished on some issues than on others in order to achieve the appropriate and necessary group results.

With respect to interpersonal activities, the Chair must try to protect the weak participants and temper the strong in order to allow for an evenness of group participation. Those individuals who do not participate need to be invited to share their views. (They are often the ones who will protest most vocally in the restaurant after the meeting.) Feelings and affect need to be diffused. This is best accomplished by direct recognition: "Jim, you seem to feel strongly about this." We deal with the Jims directly instead of watching them glower in the corner.

The Chair supports the clash and conflict of ideas and, at the same time, seeks to find aspects of different types of suggestions that may become part of a general solution.

Throughout, the Chair has overall responsibility for the group product, not for getting her or his own way. The Chair exercises influences by asking questions and directing the discussion and by structuring and shaping the agenda and through the preparation and supervision of options memos.

The Chair's influence, then, is more indirect than direct. But this is appropriate. After all, if an issue is so clear cut that the Chair can decide it, it shouldn't be before the group in the first place.

*The Member Role.* The popular view is that the member's role is a passive one with nothing to do and nothing special to know. ("There's nothing to it. All I have to do is show up and doze off.") Like so many popular views, this one is also wrong.

To begin with, there is the matter of preparation. No procedural problems loom larger in poor meeting practice than those caused by the unprepared member. Without proper preparation, discussion becomes prattle, and the unprepared participant presents the worst of all possible role models for the other members. It is almost a truism that the unprepared members of a group will attempt to cover their lack of preparation with bluster, rancor, sarcasm, and general negativity. So, preparation is the first responsibility of the member.

Knowledge of how the meetings game is played is a second member responsibility. This means not only a thorough understanding of good meeting procedures in general (such as the meeting rules presented here), but a complete knowledge of the specific rules of the committee upon which the member sits. (While the rules of some groups are more formal than for others, all group decision-making bodies have specific rules of their own.) It is the member's responsibility throughout the life of the group to cooperate in the enforcement of committee rules. At the very least this includes such things as coming on time, coming prepared, and requiring the meeting planners to provide a straightforward agenda.

Third, the member needs constantly to monitor his or her level of participation in the meeting, contributing at a level that is appropriate for this particular group decision-making activity. Some groups are high-participation groups; others, low participation. Within either context it is the member's responsibility both to contribute at the appropriate level and to aid the Chair in seeing to it that all other members likewise contribute appropriately.

Fourth, while issue crystalization and decision focus are generally the Chair's responsibility, it does not always have to be the Chair's actions that accomplish them. The Member should be constantly alert for opportunities to provide summative reflections at various points and to assist in the crystalization of ideas.

The member should be equally alert to other members who have a tendency to dump on the group; i.e., raising problems, then sitting back with arms folded as if to defy the group to provide solutions. It is both correct and useful when one has a problem with a particular proposal or line of thinking to share that perspective, provided such sharing is accompanied by good-faith attempts to seek solutions. It is incorrect, unfair, and harmful for a member to raise an issue without making it clear to the other members what one's position is with respect to that issue. It forces the group to shift its focus away from the issue and into a mode where it must probe to see what makes the recalcitrant member happy.

Finally, members owe loyalty to the group outside the group. This means supporting group decisions that one opposed. It also means not knocking the group, its members, or its Chair in other meetings, at cocktail parties, or anywhere else.

*The Recorder Role.* The individual who is taking the meeting record (using the Rule of Minutes, of course) is in a unique position to facilitate and focus the group discussion. As the new meeting format involves not only a summarizing of discussion but also a brief statement of the actual resolution, the Recorder should use both of these to assist group functioning. As discussion is beginning to come to a close, for example, a Recorder can say something like, "Well, for the record, let me see if I understand the various points we have been discussing." A skilled Recorder can actually craft a summary on the spot and, in doing so, may uncover more or fewer areas of agreement than hitherto thought. In either case, it is to the advantage of the group. Similarly, the Recorder can shape the summative statement, itself. "As I understand it, here is what we have

concluded." This helps focus and crystalize group activity and builds support for group decisions.

*The Staffer Role.* A Staffer is an individual who is paid or assigned to assist a group in carrying out its functions. This individual is different from other participants because the Staffer is *not* a member of the group—an extremely important point. All groups know who are and who are not members, even if everyone is well acquainted with one another, as is the case for most businesses.

The Staffer performs four kinds of functions for most committees. First, the Staffer is a researcher, providing various types of information for the group (political, historical, economic, scientific, items of program history, and so on).

Second, the Staffer is a knowledge synthesizer. It is not enough simply to present a range of information to a group (though some use it as a procedure for dumping on the group). Rather, the information should be organized, synthesized, integrated. This function is an important one for the Staffer to perform. For a committee considering executive compensation, for example, the Staffer might say something like, "Here is a list of other companies and the compensation packages they provide their executives. They seem to fall into the following groups, based on what appear to me to be the following kinds of criteria, linked in the following ways to corporate income, etc."

Third, the Staffer is a writer and a documentor. The role may involve taking minutes and recording. It usually involves the preparation of reports, preparing executive summaries, and generally doing the "legwork" of the committee.

Fourth, the Staffer is an aide to the Chair. In meetings, this usually involves sitting close by the Chair in a kind of dead zone that diminishes the physical position of the

Staffer and emphasizes her or his "assisting" rather than "membering" function. The Staffer does not participate directly in discussions or decision making in the sense of giving an opinion on this matter or that.

Fifth, the Staffer is an administrator. In part, this relates to the function of aiding the Chair, and it may involve many things. The staffer may get out the minutes, may assist in preparing the agenda, may review meeting strategy with the Chair, may arrange for the meeting room, and so on. This "stage manager" activity is not especially dramatic, but it needs to be done if the setting for the meeting is to facilitate rather than hamper the meeting process.

## REFERENCES

Avery, Michael, et al., *Building United Judgment: A Handbook for Consensus Decisionmaking* (Madison, WI: The Center for Conflict Resolution, 1981).

Bell, Arthur, *Mastering the Meeting Maze* (Reading, MA: Addison-Wesley, 1990).

Clifton, Robert, and Alan Dahms, *Grassroots Administration: A Handbook for Staff and Directors of Small, Community-Based Social Service Agencies* (Prospect Heights, IL: Waveland Press, 1987).

Cohen, M., J. March, and J. Olsen, "A Garbage Can Model of Organizational Choice," *Administrative Science Quarterly* 17 (1) (March 1972): 1–25.

Frank, Milo, *How to Run a Successful Meeting in Half the Time* (New York: Simon and Schuster, 1989).

Hackman, J. Richard, *Groups That Work (And Those That Don't); Creating Conditions for Effective Teamwork* (San Francisco: Jossey-Bass, 1990).

Jay, Antony, "How to Run a Meeting That Gets Things Done," *Harvard Business Review* (March–April, 1976).

Jay, Antony, "How to Run a Meeting," in F.M. Cox, J. Erlich, J. Rothman and J.E. Tropman, *Tactics and Techniques of Community Practice,* 2nd ed. (Itasca, IL: F.E. Peacock, 1984).

Kahneman, Daniel, Paul Slovic, and Amos Tversky, *Judgment Under Uncertainty: Heuristics and Biases* (New York: Cambridge University Press, 1986).

Kieffer, George, *The Strategy of Meetings* (New York: Warner, 1988).

Kleindorfer, Paul, Howard Kunreuther, and Paul Schoemaker, *Decision Sciences* (New York: Cambridge University Press, 1993).

Mosvick, Roger, and Robert B. Nelson, *We've Got To Start Meeting Like This* (Glenview, IL: Scott, Foresman, 1987).

Schwartzman, Helen B., *The Meeting: Gatherings in Organizations and Communities* (New York: Plenum, 1989).

Thomsett, Michael C., *The Little Black Book of Business Meetings* (New York: AMACOM, 1989).

Tropman, John E., Harold Johnson, and Elmer J. Tropman, *Committee Management in the Human Services,* 2nd ed. (Chicago: Nelson-Hall, 1991).

Tropman, John E., *Meetings: How to Make Them Work For You* (New York: Van Nostrand, 1984).

# PART FOUR

# MOBILIZING, PLANNING, AND DEVELOPING

# Introduction

For planners, program developers, and organizers nothing presents more of a challenge than translating the result of assessment and option selection into action. Part of the problem revolves around what might be termed the collapse of our excessive expectations. While the resource base has continued to decline, the hopes that surrounded many macro practice endeavors of the later 1960s and early 1970s continued into the beginning of the 1990s. However, the sharp economic decline of the early part of the decade just ended has forced an almost total reevaluation of the potentials for change in social welfare.

Another dimension of the difficulty of translating agreed-upon objectives into action concerns a general decline in our civic life: Indeed, many observers suggest that there really is not much civic life left at all. A community of people generally regarded as liberals shoot down a proposal for a new emergency hospital because the sound of landing helicopters may be disturbing and lead to lower property values in the neighborhood. Providing needle exchanges for drug addicts and condoms to sexually active teenagers, despite the terrible ravages of AIDS, are both rejected on the grounds they will encourage more of the same kind of behavior that the wider community is trying to discourage. The proposal for a new homeless shelter in a new area is rejected in favor of expanding the current facilities because no one wants to accept "those kind of people" anywhere near where he or she lives.

As Kunstler notes:

Living in a cartoon landscape of junk architecture, monotonous suburbs, ravaged countryside and trashed cities, Americans sense that something is wrong. Our discontent is expressed in phrases like "the loss of community" and "no sense of place." Yet the issue of how we live is strikingly absent from the debate about national problems, especially our economic predicament.[1]

---

[1] James Kunstler, "Zoning Ourselves Out of All Sense of Community," *The Sacramento Bee,* August 11, 1993.

Despite the widely reported and heavily documented increase in societal violence, the proposals offered to combat it—typically more prisons, more police, or better policing methods—do not inspire much confidence. Where is there a shared sense of common destiny that might serve to counteract the tendency toward violence? The yuppie greed of the 1980s, transposed into "me firstism," has lost all bounds of class, race, and gender—or at least so it often appears.

Confronting the declining sense of community with tactics and techniques that require a substantial measure of cooperation, sense of shared destiny, and commitment to compromise for the larger good puts the planner, developer or organizer in a challenging position.

The first article, by Weil, offers a set of guiding frameworks in which she notes that "a feminist framework for organizing integrates methods and strategies for action with practice principles that embody feminist values and approaches." Her article encompasses the rich women's heritage of social movement leaders and community practitioners. It also incorporates a full range of feminist approaches, and explores how feminist components inform practice models, including social planning, program development, community development, and political empowerment. A series of principles by which implementation, mobilization, and development may be guided is also part of Weil's exposition.

Basing his article on more than three decades of organizing efforts, Haggstrom emphasizes what it takes to make a success of work at the grassroots. He challenges us to confront the typical top-down style of mobilizing people for action by assisting in the gathering of people from the bottom up. In a society increasingly dominated by power, influence, and money, "solutions" to human problems tend to be based on the views of elite groups—governmental bodies and large institutions. Haggstrom would have us look toward an empowering movement for change founded in neighborhoods and the people who live in them.

Religion is a vital element of the life of community members, and "faith-based" organizations have always been a key element in America's need-meeting systems. Wineburg looks at the interconnections among a range of faith-based and secular organizations in North Carolina. He finds, importantly but not surprisingly, that there is much helpful interaction—including a model for us all.

Using the hotly debated context of social welfare, Pawson and Russell explore a range of planning and development approaches. The focus is on operationalization of interventions, including community liaison, interorganizational coordination, and political empowerment.

In the final selection, Rivera and Erlich confront the prospects for organizing, planning, and development with communities of color. Detailed consideration is given to the skills and knowledge a practitioner must bring to such a community in order to be effective. The authors argue that there are important limits on what roles white practitioners ought to be playing in minority communities.

Macro-level practitioners are facing the most difficult situation to be experienced in the last 20 years. The combination of sharply declining resources coupled with a political environment hostile to the needs of poor and disadvantaged populations has not been equalled in recent memory. On the other hand, we are also in a time of change, and such times always present new creative opportunities. The challenge is to engage the full range of tactical means to achieve positive goals without being consumed in the process.

—John L. Erlich

**15.**

**Marie Weil**

## WOMEN, COMMUNITY, AND ORGANIZING

Organizing by women for social justice, equality, and human liberation is not a new phenomenon. Women have been powerful organizers in political and social action, union, civil rights, human rights, and peace movements, and in the development of social and community services, as well as in the women's movement. This chapter focuses on feminist issues in community organization and explores the role of women as organizers. Furthermore, it develops a framework for analyzing women's organizing work in general, as well as feminist community organization, articulating feminist principles for organizing.

A feminist framework for organizing integrates methods and strategies for action with practice principles that embody feminist values and approaches. For feminists, the framework's philosophical-theoretical foundation is critical because it shapes the questions that are posed, determines the problems that are identified as central, and sculpts the strategies for movement and change. While political-theoretical orientations may differ among feminists, there are strong commonalities related to the need for altering patriarchal structures and processes.

The entire history and development of feminism can be seen as a process of community organizing—from development of critical consciousness regarding the status of women and the oppression of minorities, to demystifying and reclaiming history,[1]

through the development of social and political action movements, including the creation of specialized organizations and programs to serve the needs of women.

### PRELIMINARY DEFINITIONS AND ORIENTATIONS

Before analyzing general models of community practice and specific feminist approaches, operating definitions are needed to focus discussion on the complex issues this chapter treats.

*Women* are born female; we create ourselves as women through a social process of interaction of the self with family, peers, society, and culture; and we are feminists as we commit ourselves to the equality of women, to the elimination of oppression, to the empowerment of women and minorities, and to the creation of a nonsexist society.

*Community* can refer to any of several means of identifying connections among people. It can connote (a) the relationships among residents in a specific locale, or (b) the relationships and activities of people committed to a particular interest, concern, or problem—that is, a community of interest or a functional community. Both conceptions are grounded in the idea of community as a kind of social organism. Alternatively, it can connote (c) a particular political unit or power base.[2] Common to all three types of community is an assumption of some basis of shared concern or shared perception that can draw people together.

Marie Weil is a professor at the School of Social Wrok, University of North Carolina at Chapel Hill.

*Organizing* refers to the process of pulling together to create a functional whole.[3] It may indicate the establishment of an organization dedicated to a particular purpose or may outline and orchestrate a strategy for achieving certain goals.

*Community organization* was "formally recognized as a distinct field within social work in 1962"[4] and has increasingly been included in social work curricula. The mainstream community organization literature in social work has typically followed Rothman's typology of community organization.[5] Rothman identified three models: (a) locality development—incorporating goals of "self-help," community capacity and integration (process goals)"; (b) social planning—problem solving with regard to substantive community problems (task goals)"; and (c) social action with goals related to "shifting of power relationships and resources; basic institutional change (task or process goals)."[6] As Ecklein noted, however, all social work–based community organizers are

...concerned with advancing the interests of disadvantaged groups, with improving social conditions, with the delivery of needed services, with redistribution of power and influence, with enhancement of the coping mechanisms of target populations, and with strengthening community participation and integration.7

The most recent (1985) definition of community practice, by Taylor and Roberts, is an overarching rubric encompassing practice models and theoretical orientations in the following five areas: (1) community development; (2) political action—pluralism and participation; (3) program development and coordination; (4) planning; and (5) community liaison.[8] Each of these models can, however, still embrace Rothman's earlier definition of community organization as a strategy of "purposive community change."[9] Specific goals,

strategies, target systems, and action systems will change to accord with the particular model, but all are related to process of planned change.

## WOMEN AND COMMUNITY ORGANIZATION

Many of the pioneers in social work and community organization on both local and national levels were women. Major aspects of the development of social work from the social reform movements of the late nineteenth century were led by such women as Jane Addams, Dorothea Dix, Julia Lathrop, Edith and Grace Abbott, Lillian Wald, Sophonisba Breckinridge, and Florence Kelley. Vandiver, Brandwein, and Conway documented that women played major roles in social action, as well as managing complex programs.[10]

However, the place of women within the two major traditions of community organization in social work was markedly different. Brandwein comments that men did dominate in the conservative, social maintenance tradition of the community chests and councils, which were tied to the sanctions and models of the business community. Yet women played a larger role even in this arena than they are typically credited for.[11] In contrast to the tradition of the Charity Organization Societies and councils, the social reform tradition of social work, emerging from the settlement movement, "focused on social legislation, neighborhood organizing, and advocacy for the poor and other oppressed groups"; within this tradition women were very visible and maintained many leadership positions.[12]

Social work's own drive for professionalization in the 1920s related not only to clinical aspirations but to emphasis on service and cost efficiency and adoption of business management methods. This shift brought more men into leadership positions in the planning and service coordination sector, and women in this field "tended to be confined to the smaller community councils with low budgets or in planning functions closely related to clinical services."[13] Although male administrators worked with business constituencies, women continued to lead the way in "neighborhood organizing, locality development, working with volunteers, and developing services for clients."[14] This sector of community organizing has been viewed as having less status, but it is the clear descendant of the social reform movements and can be seen to have close affinities with early and current feminist orientations.

Brandwein documented the displacement of women in community organization as beginning in the late 1950s.[15] Despite women's long history in community organization and social reform, the macro-practice field within social work has come to be dominated by men in both administrative and community practice. For a period during the late 1950s and 1960s, a fairly common point of view in social work education linked the continued life of the profession and its relative professional status to its ability to attract men into its ranks.[16] Unfortunately, the effort to develop opportunity for men coincided with the advancement of macro-practice, especially administrative and planning methods, and men quickly emerged from the ranks on a fast track to leadership in community and administrative positions considered to be more compatible with societal expectations regarding male sex-role behavior.

Another factor in this change relates to some of the patterns of male dominance that developed in the civil rights and anti-war movements of the 1960s.[17] For a variety of reasons, macro-practice came to be viewed as a male preserve in social work. Kadushin even published an article that argued for the need to maintain administration and macro-practice as a male domain so that men would not feel discomforted by their entrance into a profession preponderantly female and viewed as a "women's field."[18] The efforts to provide parity for men in professional social work education evolved into a pattern of male dominance in administration, community organization, and teaching. This pattern of male dominance has had a negative impact on the treatment of women's concerns and feminist issues in macro-practice curricula.

Feminist issues in community practice abound but have been largely ignored or underrepresented in the mainstream literature of community organization. Feminist thinking offers many positive parallels with basic social work theories of community organization, which emphasize values and methods grounded in democratic process, participatory democracy, civil and social rights, and social action. Many early leaders and workers in the development of community-based group practice and social and environmental action, as well as mental health and social justice, were women who in their lives and work embodied feminist principles. Those important women organizers and the movements with which they were involved include:

- The anti-slavery or abolitionist movement—Harriet Tubman, Sojourner Truth, Sarah and Angelina Grimké
- The mental health movement to provide care for the mentally ill—Dorothea Dix, Josephine Shaw Lowell
- The suffragist movement—Susan B. Anthony, Elizabeth Cady Stanton, Lucretia Mott, Lucy Stone
- The settlement movement—Jane Addams, Lillian Wald

- The labor reform movement—Florence Kelley and members of the National Women's Trade Union League
- The maternal and child health and child welfare movements—Lillian Wald, Julia Lathrop, Sophonisba Breckinridge
- The union movement and labor movement—Mary Van Kleeck, Emma Goldman, Rose Chernin, Frances Perkins
- Rights for blacks—National League for the Protection of Colored Women
- Legislative action and equal rights—Jane Addams, Florence Kelley, Alice Paul
- The civil rights movement and welfare rights movement—Fannie Lou Hamer, Angela Davis
- La Raza, United Farm Workers' Movement, and the Mexican American Legal Defense and Education Fund—Delores Huerta, Wilma Martinez, and Antonia Hernandez
- The older women's and men's movement—Maggie Kuhn, Gray Panthers, and OWL (Older Women's League)
- The women's movement—Theorists: Simone de Beauvoir, *The Second Sex;* Betty Friedan, *The Feminine Mystique;* Kate Millett, *Sexual Politics;* and Gloria Steinem, *Ms.* magazine. Groups: National Organization for Women, National Women's Political Caucus, Women's Action Alliance
- The peace movement—Jane Addams and Jeanette Rankin; Women Strike for Peace, Women's International League for Peace and Freedom, Women's Pentagon Action; Helen Caldicott, Physicians for Social Responsibility

Despite a rich and proud heritage of female organizers and movement leaders, the field of community organization, in both its teaching models and its major exponents, has been a male-dominated preserve, where, even though values are expressed in terms of participatory democracy, much of the focus within the dominant practice methods has been nonsupportive or antithetical to feminism. Strategies have largely been based on "macho-power" models, manipulativeness, and zero-sum gamesmanship.

This situation is reflected in the mainstream literature of community organization, where it is rare to find feminist case studies, a focus on organizing for and by women, or models employing feminist principles in organizing. Often this oversight extends even to the exclusion of the women's movement in discussions of social action. What is needed is attention to feminist ideology and action, as well as examination of how feminist practice is similar to and different from other forms of community organization. It is critical to develop and disseminate feminist models of community practice and organizing that focus on both women's issues and broader issues of social service and social justice. Continuous social action on behalf of the rights of women and other oppressed groups is needed, and feminist approaches have much to offer these efforts.

In order to develop feminist models for community organization, we need to focus on two subjects that have been largely ignored in the mainstream community organization literature: (a) women as organizers in general community practice and (b) women organizers and women's organizations focused on specific women's issues—women considered as a community of interest. The issues and problems encountered in these two practice sectors are different in several ways.

## Women and General Community Organizing

The first sector, women working as organizers in any general community organization, gives rise to a variety of issues that flow from the assumption of male dominance in political, organizational, and community structure. History indicates that even when social change is stimulated by revolution, women assume large roles in development and organizing in the early stages, but are moved back into more traditional roles as postrevolutionary society stabilizes.[19] Whether in union organizing, social agency networks, academia, or community political action, a female organizer must inevitably be conscious of the social reality pointed out by Simone de Beauvoir that she is likely to be identified as the "other."[20] She is at risk of being (a) distrusted for being female, (b) disparaged for being aggressive or not "appropriately feminine" in terms of traditional gender role expectations, or (c) treated as the token or exceptional woman—usually defined as one who looks like a woman, but thinks like a man. Any one of these positions can be damaging, not only to the organizer, but to the cause to which she is committed.

Women organizers as formal or informal leaders in a group or organization must always be conscious of and examine the reaction of others within and outside their group in terms of overt or covert sexism. They must balance attention to these issues with attention to the general strategy and social change goals.

To function effectively as a woman organizer in community practice, one needs a heightened feminist consciousness, as well as the recognition that one will continually be tested as a woman and as an organizer. When feminists are involved in general community organization or social change, they must always work to include and expand feminist agendas. They must also maintain a dual focus with regard to both process and tasks, seeking to integrate feminist goals and approaches into the general problem-solving strategy. This approach requires conscious and consistent effort to shape goals, strategies, and roles so that they approach consistency with feminist values and orientations. The woman involved in general community practice as a feminist carries the risks of the boundary spanner. She will need to maintain ties in the feminist community for support and analysis, but will need to be able to function independently in the general community practice arena, which may be either tolerant of or overtly resistant to feminist ideology.

A feminist organizing model is required, in general community issues, that acknowledges and incorporates the need to deal with sexism as well as general issues of process facilitation and task accomplishment. In addition, models or a typology of models for feminist organizing around women's issues, women's organizations, and services for women are needed.

## Women and Feminist Organizing

The central issue in feminist organizing and organizations is how to embody and carry out feminist values and principles in action strategies. The values and experiences of women form the basis for all feminist orientations and approaches to social change. Accepting that premise necessitates a heterogeneous rather than a homogeneous conception of women's realities. Differences in demographics as well as political and social points of view interact with values to shape our interpretations of social reality. Understanding differences allows for building feminist coalitions grounded in common feminist commitments, such as ending sexual harassment, rape, and physical abuse; allowing for reproductive freedom; being able to choose a partner of either sex; and having the opportunity to participate fully in public life.[21]

Feminist viewpoints extend across a continuum on which one's ideological placement is a function of one's life experiences, demographics, political involvements, and education.[22] Four theoretical models for organizing women as a community of interest are the liberal, socialist, and radical models and the feminist perspective articulated by women of color.

When feminists are engaged in organizing and in developing programs and services to meet the needs of women as a community of interest, they may operate with any (or a combination) of the orienting frameworks and action approaches grounded in a particular feminist analytical framework. These frameworks indicate the specific goals, emphases, strategies, and action systems that stem from the particular ideologies and organizing perspectives of feminists who may define themselves as liberal, socialist, radical, or women of color. Table 15.1 illustrates the particular emphases of the major feminist frameworks and lists the common components of feminist organizing that they all share. Because tolerance and the valuing of diversity are intrinsic feminist elements, each of the frameworks for organizing women leads to common feminist goals of equality and the empowerment of women.

## MAINSTREAM AND FEMINIST PRACTICE ARENAS

Feminist organizers may practice in general community settings or in specifically feminist-oriented organizations and programs. For either mainstream or feminist practice arenas, the five basic community practice models detailed by Taylor and Roberts are relevant.[23] As noted in Table 15.2, these include program development and coordination; social planning; community liaison; community development; and pluralism,

participation, and political empowerment. To utilize and participate effectively in these models, feminists must first analyze their practice environment and then incorporate feminist issues and roles into their own and the agency's work.

The feminist perspective articulated in Table 15.2 emphasizes reconceptualizing and sharing power. It furthers the democratization of macro-practice methods by emphasizing pluralism, participation, and shared decision making. In addition, the feminist perspective stresses advocacy for women and other oppressed groups and is oriented toward human liberation.

Inclusion of feminist issues and development of roles for women in these general models can assist in ensuring the following issues are addressed in community practice models: (a) empowering women and vulnerable populations; (b) demystifying the planning process; (c) diminishing power/status differentials; (d) emphasizing process; (e) clarifying the value bases of practice models and methods; (f) acting to attain the elimination of sexism, racism, and class bias; (g) questioning power structures and redefining power; and (h) establishing belief and action systems necessary for structural and institutional change.[24] A feminist perspective strengthens these models to ensure that women, minorities, and other vulnerable populations can exercise their rights as citizens and contribute to the development of society.

These generic community practice models have been adapted and implemented by feminist practitioners and organizers to develop services and programs focused on women as a specific target population and a community of interest. Feminist community practice and services may function as a specialized part of the mainstream service sector or may operate in the rapidly expanding arena of alternative services

TABLE 15.1
Women as a Community of Interest: Frameworks and Approaches

| Model Components | Frameworks and Approaches | | | |
|---|---|---|---|---|
| | Liberal | Socialist | Radical | Women of Color |
| 1. Goals and focus in organizing | Equal rights and individual liberty. Equality of opportunity, development of egalitarian gender relations. Social reform. Consciousness raising on effects of sexism. | Elimination of sexism and class oppression. | Elimination of patriarchy—meeting common human needs—creation and celebration of women's culture. Empowerment of women. | Elimination of all human oppression. Elimination of discrimination related to race, class, and gender. Solidarity within groups and among minority and other oppressed groups. |
| 2. Assumption about causation of sexism and oppression | Sex-role socialization. | Political and economic institutions of society (capitalism and patriarchy). | Patriarchy—male power and privilege. | Racism, sexism, and class discrimination as interlocking causative factors of oppression. |
| 3. Orientation to power structure | Gain power for women in institutions and develop institutions more responsive to feminist approaches. | Need for revolutionary social and political change. | Resist patriarchy and create a women's culture. Revolution as process. | Rejection of political and social oppression. Rejection of all biological determinism. Rejection of institutionalized racism and sexism. |
| 4. Emphasis on strategy for change | Reeducation of public to eliminate sex-role stereotyping. Elimination of discrimination in employment. Legislative lobbying. Local political and social organizing. Local, regional, and national political action and policy action. | Analysis and action related to economic production, sexuality, reproduction, and socialization of children. Advocacy for women. Strategies to align with and advocate for other oppressed groups. | Redefinition of social relations and creation of a woman-centered culture. Emphasis on creative dimensions of women's lives. Emphasis on process and connections. Personal growth and empowerment through personal and political action. | Articulating feminist frameworks for women of color. Connecting feminism to racial and economic oppression. Building solidarity within oppressed groups. Supporting development and advancement of minority groups. Emphasis on common humanity and needs as well as recognition and support of the uniqueness of cultures and subcultures. |
| 5. Emphasis on tactics and techniques for social change | Political and social action primarily focused within the established political and economic system. Development of broad-based coalitions and large membership. Development of local action networks connected to regional and national associations. Development of a national presence to articulate women's issues, and lobbying for equal rights. | Analysis and praxis—analysis of common grounds for oppression, and efforts to establish collective means to solve community and individual problems. | Articulating and building on women's capacities. Reclaim women's history. Analyze and validate women's experiences and perspectives. Connection of the personal to the political. Empowerment of women. Emphasis on process and consciousness raising. | Education, reeducation. Concentration on development of political and social positions that resist all forms of oppression. Building solidarity within groups. Replacing negative stereotypes of women of color and minority groups with careful analysis of capacities, strengths, and direction. Reclaiming history. Consciousness raising. Building sisterhood among women of color and other women who recognize the triple threats of racism, sexism, and poverty. |

*continued*

TABLE 15.1 (continued)
Women as a Community of Interest: Frameworks and Approaches

| Model Components | Frameworks and Approaches | | | |
|---|---|---|---|---|
| | Liberal | Socialist | Radical | Women of Color |
| 6. Major roles of change agents | Local, regional, and national level lobbying. Policy analysis and alternative policy development. Local and national political action on emerging issues. Public education and reeducation. Individual and group development through consciousness raising and mutual support. | Education, analysis, active involvement in labor activities and support of other oppressed groups. Articulation of women's issues. Development of alternative programs and services. | Analysis. Development of collectives related to services for women, support for women, women's music, arts and crafts, and literature. Definition and expansion of women's culture. | Education, analysis, consciousness raising. Redefinition of women of color. Development of political and social analysis and action frameworks. Preservation and further development of own culture. Development of groups, programs, and services to meet the needs of oppressed groups. Development of alternative programs and supports. |
| 7. Action systems— mediums of change | Local networks to respond to emerging issues. Regional and national associations to respond to issues and to support local and national action. Mutual support and consciousness-raising groups for individual and group development. | Women's study, action, and service development collectives. Alliances with other groups around common issues. | Collectives and small groups—emphasis on egalitarianism and shared power. Building enabling systems and mutual support. Building liberation through one's own actions. | Small groups or collectives focused on individual and political development of particular oppressed groups. Action within minority communities to build solidarity and promote social and economic development. Building coalitions and solidarity among oppressed groups. |

aimed specifically at women. Programs and organizations such as the Peer Consultation Project of the Southern California Rape Prevention and Study Center (SCRPSC),[25] the Family Violence Project of Jewish Family Services of Los Angeles,[26] Women Helping Women[27] in Los Angeles, the Los Angeles Commission on Assaults Against Women, the National Welfare Rights Organization, Coalition for the Medical Rights of Women, Women's Pentagon Action, National Network of Hispanic Women, and National Organization for Women all exemplify various aspects of feminist principles and commitments and community organizing.

The various roles for feminists engaged in general community practice show how women from diverse political perspectives and different ethnic and interest groups (single mothers; lesbians; older women; Asian American, black, and Hispanic women) can come together to organize around specific issues; to influence mainstream services; to develop alternative services for women; and to build unity, solidarity, and sisterhood. Unity can come from diversity when individual differences and experiences are validated and when common issues that transcend diversity can be understood in relation to shared values and articulated in unifying principles of feminist practice. The following community practice principles articulate feminist ideology and values as guides to action.

TABLE 15.2
Models of Community Organizing and Feminist Issues

| Current Community Practice Models* | Incorporation of Feminist Issues and Roles into Models |
|---|---|
| **Program Development and Coordination**<br>Incorporating mediative and political processes to bring about implementation of social program and plans, and developing program coordination. Focused on a specific target population, but primary constituency is professionals and agencies. Change focus is on full range of political and organizational interests related to a particular issue. Roles in identifying needs, designing programs, consensus building, public relations for functional communities, lobbying, and education of the public on specific issues (Kurzman, 1985). | Broadening program development foci to attend to special needs of women, particularly to the needs of women who are especially vulnerable because of health, mental health or disabling conditions, or racism or poverty.<br><br>Ensuring that women's issues are considered in the development of service networks and systems for service coordination.<br><br>Giving attention to sexism as it is experienced by professional women working in the service system and to the impact of sexism, racism, and poverty on women who are service consumers or potential consumers.<br><br>Strengthening connections and collaboration between mainstream service systems and alternative feminist and minority community programs.<br><br>Assisting in development of and advocacy for community-based and culturally sensitive services for women and minorities.<br><br>Developing women's networks and support groups for women involved in service delivery with emphasis on incorporating feminist values and principles into the operation of service systems. |
| **Social Planning**<br>Developing plans or forecasting future conditions. Research and technological focus and skills. Use of formal structure and processes to build support for outcomes intended to be logical, rational, and beneficial. Focus on application of technical skills in planning process whether role is "neutral," "transactive," or "political" in relation to sponsors' or constituencies' expectations (Rothman and Zald, 1985). | Applying technical skills and research skills in analyzing specific service needs of women, children, vulnerable populations, and oppressed populations.<br><br>Grounding planning approaches in target populations' experiences. Validating and giving credence to women's and other client groups' appraisal of need.<br><br>Working toward democratizing planning processes.<br><br>Strengthening consideration of and integrating cultural, ethnic, and sexual preference issues in service design.<br><br>Involving clients and staff in planning programs.<br><br>Recognizing that pure rationality is not a sufficient basis for planning, only, and incorporating cultural and value issues in planning processes.<br><br>Recognizing that planning is never "value-free" or "totally objective," and actively including women's values and perspectives in planning processes.<br><br>Intentionally using feminist ideology, values, and principles in planning. |

*continued*

TABLE 15.2 (continued)
Models of Community Organizing and Feminist Issues

| Current Community Practice Models* | Incorporation of Feminist Issues and Roles into Models |
|---|---|

**Community Liaison**

Holistic approach integrating social work roles in both environmental and interpersonal change processes. Specific community practice roles tied to goals and purpose of the agency for staff and administrators of direct service agencies. Administrative activities: interorganizational, boundary spanning, community relations, environmental reconnaissance, and support. Clinical staff activities: program development, needs identification, and client advocacy (Taylor, 1985).

Focusing on empowerment of and advocacy for oppressed groups—with particular attention to service needs of women, children, and minority populations.

Developing closer, functional ties to target populations; sharing information: reconceptualizing and sharing power.

Examining destructive and oppressive forces in the environment and personal and political lives of the target population.

Becoming actively involved to change oppressive and sexist forces affecting the target population.

Examining sexism and racism as they affect the community served and the agency and its staff.

Examining agency hierarchy and boundaries. Introducing feminist ideology, values, and principles in agency decision-making processes.

Working toward democratizing the work-place, and increasing clients' participation in decisions about service provision.

**Community Development**

Enabling approach—as both means to goals and a goal in itself. Dual emphasis on growth of individual and the group, neighborhood, or community. Practice roles encourage participation and social involvement for individual and group enhancement. Opportunity system for self-help. Developing local leadership and organizing structures to enable urban or rural people to improve social and economic conditions. Major strategies: building cooperation and collaboration and conflict resolution (Lappin, 1985).

Ensuring inclusion of women's issues in social and economic development.

Working to make women's culture and women's values and concerns an equal part of the development process.

Developing and supporting women's full participation in decision making and social and economic development.

Working toward empowerment of women and reconceptualization of power emphasizing inclusiveness and collective aspects.

Working toward further development of women's culture in social and economic production and in the arts.

Focusing specific attention on women's health needs, economic needs, educational interests, and opportunity structure.

Developing specific women's economic and social development projects.

Supporting self-determination of community women in developing role equity and role change.

*continued*

TABLE 15.2 (continued)
Models of Community Organizing and Feminist Issues

| Current Community Practice Models* | Incorporation of Feminist Issues and Roles into Models |
| --- | --- |
| **Pluralism, Participation, and Political Empowerment** Increasing participation and power of groups who have been excluded from decision processes in order to achieve their self-determined, desired goals. Grounded in realities of struggle, conflict, and existence of conflicting interests in any community. Roles of organizers: educator, resource developer, agitator for self-determined interests of disadvantaged groups. Individual and group growth and skill development related to central focus and goal to make democracy serve the interests of groups that have lacked power. Empowerment focus through formal citizen participation or, more important, self-generated in neighborhood and minority rights associations. Groups may develop their own alternative services or programs (Grosser and Mondros, 1985). | Maximizing the participation of women and ethnic, working class, lesbian, aged, disabled, and other relevant women's groups in social systems and institutions. Building process to strengthen morale and empower women in local groups and in representative groups. Working for inclusion of women and women's issues in social and political decision-making processes with the goal of developing collective power. Working for full representation of women in existing service, social, and political structures, and for development of separate women's organizations. Working to develop alternative women-centered programs to serve unique needs of women. Working to develop coalitions among women of diverse subgroups, to build, articulate, and enact common women's agenda. Working to increase political and service system accountability to women's concerns and the concerns of other vulnerable populations. |

*Community Practice Model descriptions are drawn from specific chapters in *Theory and Practice of Community Social Work,* Samuel H. Taylor and Robert W. Roberts, eds. (New York: Columbia University Press, 1985). See Note 23 (p. 133) for full names of authors and titles of chapters.

## Principle One—Feminist Values

Feminist organizers will act to support female values and processes. Organizers will affirm women's strengths and capacities for nurturance and caring. The values of emphasizing process, recognizing and using multidimensional thought processes, and respecting intuitive processes will be supported.

## Principle Two—Valuing Process

Feminist organizers will value and act to support both process and the products that result from process. In action, organizers will support consensus development, recognizing that diversity can be supported

and polar positions avoided. The valuing of process supports being nonjudgmental. The use of process to build connections can be an educative, democratizing, and empowering force.

## Principle Three—Consciousness Raising and Praxis

Feminist organizers will recognize and support the power and impact of consciousness-raising processes. Giving women the opportunity to reflect on, reexperience, identify, and analyze the social stereotypes and environmental forces that have impeded their development and liberation can serve as a bridge to reclaiming personal history, renaming, and reconceptualizing experiences, gaining self-confidence, and building individual as well as collective strength from action.

### Principle Four—Wholeness and Unity

Feminist organizers will work to build the sisterhood and solidarity of all women. Women face many societal forces that engender separation among them and prevent them from working together. Feminist organizers will act from a position of unity that also supports individual differences as well as intra- and intergroup diversity. Separations and dichotomies are often set up between various categories of women such as lesbians and straight women; women of color and white women; poor and middle-class women; single and married mothers; and young and old women. History attests to many attempts to place different ethnic, minority, and oppressed groups in opposition to one another. In social work, dichotomies are set up separating professional from paraprofessional women, and separating both of these groups from clients. Feminist organizers will affirm the variety and diversity of women's experience and will work to synthesize and build unity that transcends diversity.

### Principle Five— Reconceptualization of Power and Empowerment

Feminist organizers will work toward the reconceptualizing of power as "transactive," limitless, and collective, and as a process that "enables the accomplishment of aspirations."[28] Feminist organizers will work toward empowerment of women through the development of nonhierarchical and democratic structures, by the sharing

power, and by supporting self-determination and egalitarianism.

### Principle Six—Democratic Structuring

Feminist organizers will work to develop organizations, groups, and services that empower women—as members, staff, and consumers. Democratic decision-making processes will be developed and supported; and means to share information, resources, and power will be sought. Organizational tasks can be structured to clarify responsibilities and build autonomy.

### Principle Seven—The Personal Is Political

Feminist organizers will be cognizant of the ways in which systemic factors result in problematic personal conditions for women and will work to build unity among women to achieve collective solutions to oppressive situations. The interactive factors of personal growth and political-social action will be recognized and emphasized in approaches to problems and organizing strategies.

### Principle Eight—Orientation to Structural Change

Feminist organizers will recognize the need for and work toward fundamental change in organizational, institutional, and societal structures to eliminate sexism, racism, and other forms of oppression.

### FEMINIST RECONCEPTUALIZATION OF COMMUNITY PRACTICE

These principles in combination form an action framework for feminist community practice. They build on developing and converging feminist frameworks. Significantly, they also reflect basic values that are deeply rooted in American tradition; although not ascendent: "We have a long and enduring history of struggle to implement such values as egalitarianism, consensus democracy, nonexploitation, cooperation, collectivism, diversity, and nonjudgmental spirituality."[29] Feminism is clearly aligned with the two central social work value positions that support (1) the dignity and worth of each individual and (2) the responsibility of human beings for one another.[30] These two value positions undergird the feminist respect for diversity and concern for collective responsibility and action.

Feminists in community practice may be working with self-help groups, collectives, or organizations, as well as community or political and social action groups. They may take on roles as organizers, community researchers, advocate-planners, administrators, clinicians, trainers, or educators to empower citizens' groups and underserved or oppressed communities. In any of these roles, the feminist principles are applicable. Given the action framework of feminism, many women who are concerned with organizing and services will concentrate on developing programs that are gender-centered or ethnic-centered. The feminist perspective leads to commitment to work with women, children, aged people, the disabled, and other vulnerable populations.

The synthesis of roles and issues that women face in community practice, central issues in feminist frameworks and models for organizing, and feminist principles for community practice lead to a feminist reconceptualization of community practice. In this conception:

A. *Goals* will always relate to the elimination of oppression, such as sexism and racism; method will be integrated with vision.

B. *Power* will be conceptualized as facilitative, enabling, and shared within and among groups. Influence will be a means of expanding feminist approaches and achieving goals. In understanding power as "energy and initiative," feminists will challenge institutions that construe power as "domination."[31]

C. *Strategies* for change will stress the necessity for congruence of means and ends and will be grounded in egalitarianism, consensus building, cooperation, collectivism, power sharing, self-help, and mutual responsibility. Strategies will be personal, interpersonal, social, and political to achieve basic social change, building toward egalitarianism in personal interactions and social structures. Coalition building will be used to expand involvement in feminist agendas—among women and other groups.

D. *Action* will be based on the eight principles for organizing that were previously enumerated.

Within this reconceptualization of community practice (1) feminist theory is incorporated into the knowledge base for community practice; (2) feminist values are made explicit, and essential components for organizing and action are derived from feminist frameworks; (3) community practice models are adapted to be congruent with feminist goals, strategies, and values; and (4) feminist principles for community practice are articulated that build toward the empowerment of women. This construct constitutes a working model for feminist community practice focusing on the goal of empowering the disadvantaged, at the same time building power and competence for both clients and professionals.

This model can be applied in all community practice relating to clients, community groups, and organizations. The settings for feminist community practice are exciting and diverse. They range on a continuum from consciousness-raising groups, through food co-ops, women's health programs, and service programs, to the movement for world peace.

The feminist agenda for organizing, service development, and community action relates to women's needs through a variety of service approaches: (1) personal and group growth through life development, crises, and transitions; (2) problems of poverty and economic stability, and needs for food, clothing, and shelter; (3) needs for employment, job training, and elimination of discrimination and sexual harassment; (4) needs for health and mental health services; (5) needs for support and services for women who are victims of violence, or who are homeless; and (6) rehabilitative services for women who have problems of substance abuse or are in the prison-probation system. The needs for service development and political action are intertwined. Collective action is necessary to deal with these issues on two fronts: (1) pressuring and challenging existing service systems to re-form their view, treatment, and interaction with women and (2) development of alternative gender-focused and ethnic-focused programs that reflect feminist principles.

Feminists need to work toward humanizing and democratizing the general service delivery system so as to increase the input received from clients as well as workers' responsiveness to client needs. In alternative structures, feminist approaches building on mutuality, self-help, and reciprocity are hallmarks of client-worker interaction.

Action to build alternative feminist and ethnic-sensitive services and action to change the existing service system and social structure are both critical areas of feminist organizing *praxis*. As we move in these areas of action, those of us who teach must also enable and empower our students to carry forward feminist agendas.

## IMPLICATIONS FOR PROFESSIONAL EDUCATION

Feminist perspectives, community practice frameworks, and models need to be included in professional education. Dominant models of community organizing stress "macho" roles, tactics are often manipulative, power is construed as dominance, and democratic process and values may be sacrificed to achieve a desired end. Feminist students are bewildered at the contradiction they experience between their belief systems and action or organizing experiences; students who have no exposure to feminist approaches all too easily discount them or assume that power and dominance are the only game in town. Students interested in community and macro-practice need the opportunity to explore and engage with feminist theory and frameworks as well as to explore the differences in means and ends that feminist approaches embody.

Community and macro-practice courses need to connect students to the world of alternative services for women and minority communities and to explore ways to enlarge advocacy functions and develop positive connections between community-based, alternative services and mainstream services.[32] Students need exposure to feminist theory, frameworks, methods, and strategies. Student reports, role play, or other experiential exercises can be used to illustrate and engender reactions to different processes of decision making, different conceptions of power, and different models of group facilitation. Students need (1) cognitive exposure to feminist approaches; (2) experiential learning strategies in the classroom to examine issues of value clarification, role conflict, and leadership styles; and (3) practical exposure to community practice and social action through involvement in planning, organizing, and action tasks, such as service design, coalition development, and political action for social change through a community practice or political group. Participation in leading group discussions, canvassing, and lobbying are all activities that make community practice real.

Students need the opportunity to explore community practice roles, to explore feminist approaches, and to try out roles and experiment with styles. Such experiences can be designed for students specializing in macro-practice and those interested in clinical work. The community liaison role for clinicians can become the key to involving direct-service workers in community practice.[33]

Most important, students need an empowering model of professional education. Women students, especially those entering the macro-practice arena, need experience with a teaching-learning model that promotes feminist values and roles and that frees both women and men students from stereotypical sex-role behavior. Women students also need a learning model that is andragogical in its process. Andragogical models build on students' knowledge, values, sensitivities, and skills to promote self-directed learning.[34] Such learning models move students toward the realities, choices, values, and roles that shape professional practice and prepare them to take on responsibility. Such models are congruent with feminist approaches, can be used as a means of reconceptualizing power in the classroom as well as in the field, and can prepare students for the processes, decision making, and challenges of feminist community practice.

## CONCLUSION

The feminist vision in community practice is one of social, personal, and political transformation. Women have always been culture bearers. As we clarify and affirm the values of female consciousness and translate them into social action, these values to preserve, support, and humanize life become principles for commitment. These feminist principles connect to community practice. Community practice is both a direct form of service to client groups and communities and an indirect form of service carried out through interagency and professional actions. Community practice moves social work firmly into the arena of social action and social justice. As feminism unites the political and the personal, community practice is the means of moving social work from case to cause and from private troubles to public concerns. The vast range of areas of commitment in feminist community practice indicates the strength and flexibility of the approach. It is increasingly important to enact the feminist agenda for social change. In neighborhood organizing, consciousness-raising groups, collectives, organizations, political action, and the peace movement—the philosophy, perspective, and direction that feminism offers are healing, holistic, and nurturing. Feminism complements humanistic approaches. We must further develop our strategies and methods; nothing less than our survival—individual, collective, community, and global—is at stake.

## NOTES

1. Mary Bricker-Jenkins, "Of, By and For the People: Feminist Perspectives on Organizations and Leadership," paper presented at the Annual Program Meeting, Council on Social Work Education, Washington, D.C., February 1985.

2. Robert Fisher, *Let the People Decide: Neighborhood Organizing in America* (Boston: Twayne, 1984).

3. *American Heritage Dictionary of the English Language: New College Edition* (Boston: Houghton Mifflin, 1980).

4. Joan Ecklein, *Community Organizers* (2nd ed.; New York: John Wiley & Sons, 1984), p. 20.

5. Jack Rothman, "Three Models of Community Organization Practice, Their Mixing and Phrasing," in F.M. Cox, J.L. Erlich, J. Rothman, and J.E. Tropman, eds., *Strategies of Community Organization*, 3rd ed. (Itasca, Ill.: F.E. Peacock, 1979), pp. 25–45.

6. Ibid, p. 30.

7. Ecklein, *Community Organizers*, p. 4.

8. Samuel H. Taylor and Robert W. Roberts, "The Fluidity of Practice Theory: An Overview," in Taylor and Roberts, eds., *Theory and Practice of Community Social Work* (New York: Columbia University Press, 1985).

9. Rothman, "Three Models," p. 26.

10. Susan T. Vandiver, "A Herstory of Women in Social Work," in Elaine Norman and Arlene Mancuso, eds., *Women's Issues and Social Work Practice* (Itasca, Ill.: F.E. Peacock, 1980), pp. 21–38. See also Ruth A. Brandwein, "Toward Androgyny in Community and Organizational Practice," in Ann Weick and Susan T. Vandiver, eds., *Women, Power, and Change* (Washington, D.C.: National Association of Social Workers, 1981), pp. 158–170; and Jill Conway, "Women Reformers and American Culture, 1879–1930," *Journal of Social History*, 5 (Winter 1971–72), pp. 164–177.

11. Brandwein, "Toward Androgyny," pp. 159–160.

12. Ibid., p. 159.

13. Ibid., p. 160.

14. Ibid., p. 160

15. Ibid., pp. 161–162.

16. Diane Kravetz, "Sexism in a Woman's Profession," *Social Work*, 21 (November 1976), pp. 421–426.

17. Susan Evans, *Personal Politics: The Roots of Women's Liberation in the Civil Rights Movement and the New Left* (New York: Alfred A. Knopf, 1979).

18. Alfred Kadushin, "Men in a Woman's Profession," *Social Work*, 21 (November 1976), p. 444.

19. Margaret L. Anderson, *Thinking About Women: Sociological and Feminist Perspectives* (New York: Macmillan, 1983).

20. Simone de Beauvoir, *The Second Sex* (New York: Alfred A. Knopf, 1952).

21. Alison M. Jaggar and Paula S. Rothenberg, *Feminist Frameworks: Alternative Theoretical Accounts of the Relations Between Women and Men*, 2nd ed. (New York: McGraw-Hill, 1984). pp. xiv–xv.

22. Ibid.; and Anderson, *Thinking About Women*.

23. Taylor and Roberts, eds., *Theory and Practice of Community Social Work*. Chapters describing the five models of community practice adapted in this chapter are: Paul Kurzman, "Program Development and Service Coordination as Components of Community Practice"; Jack Rothman and Mayer N. Zald, "Planning Theory in Social Work Community Practice"; Taylor, "Community Work and Social Work: The Community Liaison Approach"; Ben Lappin, "Community Development: Beginnings in Social Work Enabling"; and Charles F. Grosser and Jacqueline Mondros, "Pluralism and Participation: The Political Action Approach."

24. Cheryl Ellsworth, Nancy Hooyman, Ruth Ann Ruff, Sue Bailey Stam, and Joan Hudyma Tucker, "Toward a Feminist Model for Planning For and With Women," in Weick and Vandiver, eds. *Women, Power, and Change*, pp. 146–157.

25. Vivian B. Brown, Barrie Levy, Marie Weil, and Linda Garnets, "Training Grass Roots Peer Consultants," *Consultation*, 1 (Summer 1982), pp. 23–29.

26. Interview with Carole Adkin, Betsy Giller, and Ellen Ledley, of the Family Violence Project, Jewish Family Service of Los Angeles, Calif., June 10, 1985.

27. Interview with Ilene Blaisch, LCSW, Director of Women Helping Women, a service sponsored by the Los Angeles, Calif., Section of the National Council of Jewish Women, July 29, 1985.

28. Mary Bricker-Jenkins and Nancy R. Hooyman, "Feminist Ideology Themes," discussion paper prepared for the Feminist Practice Project, National Association of Social Workers, National Committee on Women's Issues, presented at the Annual Program Meeting, Council

on Social Work Education, Detroit, Mich., March 13, 1984, p. 7. See also Bricker-Jenkins and Hooyman, "A Feminist World View: Ideological Themes from the Feminist Movement," in Bricker-Jenkins and Hooyman, eds., *Not for Women Only: Social Work Practice for a Feminist Future* (Silver Spring, Md.: National Association of Social Workers, 1986), pp. 7–22.

29. Ibid., p. 19.

30. Paula Dromi and Marie Weil, "Social Group Work Values: Their Role in a Technological Age." Paper presented at the Sixth Annual Symposium for the Advancement of Social Work with Groups, Chicago, Ill., November 1984.

31. Barbara Thorne, "Review of *Building Feminist Theory: Essays for Quest,*" *Signs,* 7, No. 3 (1982), p. 711.

32. Marie Weil, "Southeast Asians and Service Delivery—Issues in Service Provision and Institutional Racism," in *Bridging Cultures: Social Work with Southeast Asian Refugees* (Los Angeles: Asian American Health Training Center and National Institute of Mental Health Asian-Pacific Social Work Curriculum Development Project, 1981), Chap. 10.

33. Marie Weil, "Community Organization Curriculum Development in Services for Families and Children: Bridging the Micro-Macro-Practice Gap," *Social Development Issues,* 6, No. 3 (December 1982), pp. 40–54.

34. Marie Weil, "Preparing Women for Administration: A Self-Directed Learning Model," *Administration in Social Work,* 7 (Fall-Winter 1983), pp. 117–131.

## 16.

### Warren C. Haggstrom

## FOR A DEMOCRATIC REVOLUTION: THE GRASS-ROOTS PERSPECTIVE

There are two basic approaches to getting things done. The traditional way is the top-down approach: the formation of undemocratic work, military, and other organizations. In these organizations, most people who carry out the tasks of the organization don't have much say in deciding what is to be done.

The second basic approach, the grass-roots approach, is rapidly expanding, but does not yet usually involve most of the hours of the lives of those in it. When ordinary people join together on a basis of

equality to accomplish something, they are taking the grass-roots approach. Currently, in the United States, the grass-roots approach includes self-help groups (about 14 million people), neighborhood organizations (about 20 million people), and the tens of millions of people involved in grass-roots co-ops, political groupings, labor unions, religious organizations, issue movements, and other voluntary organizations—a large and growing population of Americans. The grass-roots approach not only can be more efficient than is the usual way, but it can also be more beneficial educationally and psychologically for those affected.

I anticipate that the grass-roots approach, as it becomes perfected, will gradually replace the traditional, undemocratic top-

Reproduced by permission.

The late Warren C. Haggstrom was a professor at UCLA.

down approach for getting things done. It is that replacement that I call a *democratic revolution.*

Will the democratic revolution be good or bad? The answer to that question depends on its outcomes, all things considered, for people. What is best for the people of the United States? Although the answer to this question involves economics, it also involves something broader: the entire human being.

We can begin by considering how to create social arrangements which will lead us to act in such a way that our actions have the best possible outcomes for people. That is a question of the effective *helping* of people.

Grass-roots organizing can be understood as a way to *help* people in need in our society. Helping is a *core* activity, *not* peripheral, and not necessarily involving altruism, in any complex society such as the United States. To evaluate and develop modes of helping, therefore, is to get at the very foundations of all aspects of American life.

## HELPING

Each person leads a unique life and more or less continues that life in such fashion as to realize best his or her potential for happiness or accomplishment. The extent to which a person realizes his or her positive potentialities is the extent to which she or he *flourishes*. To *help* a person is to enhance his or her level of flourishing or self-realization or to stave off threats to it.

Help may be

1. *unintended* (which would happen if, for example, the pursuit of economic self-interest within a capitalistic system were to enhance some aspects of self-realization throughout a society)

2. *intended* (which includes rushing to the aid of someone in distress)
3. *official* (that is, what is described as helping in an official report)

Official helping includes medicine, public health, social work, and so forth. The most important single characteristic of helping is the extent of *net effectiveness* of a helper.

*Definition 1: Given all the positive, negative, and other consequences of the helping activity, the net effectiveness of a helper is how many people are helped how much by the helper after subtracting the harmful consequences of his or her or its helping activity.*

Also, I propose the following:

*Postulate 1: The net effectiveness of helping is increased in direct relationship with the extent to which the helper is under the control of the person(s) helped.*

There are two main classifications of helping activity in the United States in which the helper is under the control of the person(s) being helped.

First, employees in top-down organizations help (a) those in charge of the organizations (executives, administrators, some board members), and also, but not necessarily, (b) those outside the organizations who are affected by them. For example, a worker in an automobile assembly plant helps the bosses and *may* also help those who buy the automobiles assembled by the plant. We can say that the employee as helper is controlled directly by the bosses and indirectly, just possibly, by automobile sales.

Workers also help themselves to the extent to which they define and control the work or its related benefits. They have very little control of work on an assembly line, but wages and fringe benefits help the worker outside the job itself.

Second, some enterprises, such as co-ops, are officially self-help in nature, and in these the helpers are usually *ipso facto* more nearly under the control of those helped than is the case in top-down organizations.

A third category in which helpers might appear to be controlled by those being helped consists of official helpers in private practice, for example, some physicians, clinical psychologists, clinical social workers, and so forth. However, efforts by the professions to be self-regulating and keep their practices autonomous through a variety of strategies usually has effectively removed much impact on this kind of helping by those ostensibly being helped. Actually, however, private practice in the helping professions can best be characterized as a kind of self-help activity.

In most official helping, there is not even the extremely limited impact on the helpers by those ostensibly being helped as patients and clients have on private practice. For example, social agencies are almost invulnerable to initiatives of their clients even though some of them have powerless "advisory" boards of clients whom they select. Institutions of formal education are similarly relatively invulnerable to initiatives of students except during rare times of crisis.

Postulate 1 thus applies to most official helping, making it possible for us to derive:

*Theorem 1: The net effectiveness of most official helping is far less than is that of helping in the two other main categories.*

Within the official helping process, it is crucial to consider the extent to which those officially helped actually are helped. Normally, these diverge widely.

For example, consider foreign aid by the United States to El Salvador. It may be publicized as help to the people of El Salvador by the generous people of the United States. But those actually helped may turn out to be almost entirely a tiny elite in El Salvador and a tiny elite in the United States.

It would be instructive to examine the efforts of the professional organizations of the helping professions. Do those organizations act effectively to reduce unmet need? Or do they act primarily on behalf of the self-interests of their members? Such an analysis may reveal that, contrary to their carefully cultivated public images, they are primarily self-help efforts by people not in need. In that case, we would propose:

*Postulate 2: The net effectiveness of most official helping is primarily an outcome of their self-help characteristics and is not related to the need of those being helped,* and

*Postulate 3: The net effectiveness of official helping is not closely related to the altruism of officially designated helpers.*

Let us next illustrate Theorem I and Postulates 2 and 3.

If you "think through" the following illustration, the reasons for supposing the validity of the three postulates and of Theorem I will become apparent.

## Official Helping (Poverty): An Illustration

Official helpers include physicians, psychiatrists, clinical psychologists, social workers, and members of many other recognized "helping" professions. Social work help is extended mostly through social agencies, nonprofit bureaucratic organizations often staffed in part by professional social workers. A child guidance clinic, a family service agency, and public welfare agencies all are social agencies. But this official social work approach to helping poor people is not effective for many reasons. Poverty is both economic and psychological. The economy of poverty has not been much affected in the United States for a long time. What help poor people have gotten by this means has come about through increases in general economic prosperity or through the allocation of public funds through the political process (like cash welfare payments, food stamps, rent supplements, medicare, public housing, and so forth). Neither prosperity nor legislation results from social work practice. The psychology of poverty has only worsened during recent decades—and social workers, in headlong retreat from their traditional preoccupation with poor people, have not even tried to affect it significantly.

The economy and the psychology of poverty can be positively altered only by some kind of social change. For example, so long as 6 to 8 percent unemployment is planned as normal, poverty on a large scale is also being planned as normal.

In American history, arguments about social policies designed to tackle social problems (poverty, crime, and so forth) have been based on the *stability assumption:* namely, that our society can remain pretty much the same as it mobilizes money and people (especially experts and professionals) to tackle such problems. The arguments have tended to be about money to be spent on dealing with the problem, and the nature and organization of the people to be mobilized. The grass-roots perspective arises in relation to the state of affairs resulting from the long reign of the stability assumption, a reign which has maintained, not diminished, most such problems.

Further, the creation of social situations in which poor people will tend to flourish, which will also benefit them psychologically, also requires planned social change. Given the extent to which business and political elites affect the expenditure of funds for helping purposes, social agencies cannot even try to work on any extent of social change which will make much dif-

ference without their funds being jeopardized. Social changes, then, do not and cannot help poor people very much.

Bureaucratic agencies are so structured that a key element in helping poor people remains unknown to the helpers. That element is the meaning of being poor, the collective psychology and subjectivity of poverty, as it exists within the communities of poor people. Without such understanding, it is impossible to enhance predictably the level of flourishing of poor clients.

Furthermore, the policies of social agencies are set by boards and administrators. But they are structurally removed by their positions from any direct acquaintance with the clientele of the agencies, or more seriously, those in greatest need, who may not be clients. Thus, the people in charge are the least able to make certain that help extended is appropriate for those who most need help. But even if boards and administrators had more knowledge, they do not have the right to decide for those needing help.

By working in bureaucratic agencies, social workers are led by their work situations to identify first with the agency or profession and only secondly with those needing help. The structured incentive system of agencies support agency maintenance and expansion, and there is no external force that requires attention to carrying out its intended goals. The result is that social agencies become self-absorbed narcissistic collectivities rather than instrumental to the determined perception and reduction of unmet need.

Traditional helping approaches separate helpers from those toward whom help is directed. As a result, it is in the interest of professional social workers to help themselves first. It is in the interest of professional social workers to reduce attention to people in need to, at best, a second priority. Official helpers act largely on the basis of their perceived self-interest. Impulses toward professionalization play a similar role, with similar consequences.

Most social workers haven't been selected for their interest in, or knowledge of, poor people, especially the invisible characteristics of communities of poor people. Social workers come mostly from two groups. One group, the largest, consists of people from nonpoor backgrounds, most of whom will remain ignorant of the experience of poverty and its meanings for their entire lives. The other group is made up of people trying to escape from their poverty backgrounds and from most poor people—they are those from among the poor who do not identify with, and who will never be of help to, persons with long-term low incomes. Furthermore, neither social work students nor the faculties of schools of social work have often been selected as people interested in, or educated for, social change efforts, and therefore, cannot even conceptualize what is needed if poor people are to be helped.

Because a broad public mistakenly believes that social work is dealing with the problems of poor people, the very existence of social work saps motivation and support for the implementation of alternative ways to meet needs and thereby diminishes the possibility that really effective help will eventually be extended to people who are poor.

There is little evidence of the effectiveness of social work intervention at any level. The research on the effectiveness of casework has produced results which can only be described as "profoundly discouraging" to caseworkers and their supporters. If social workers were concerned with helping people, they would be heavily involved in effectiveness research. They are not.

The knowledge base of contemporary social work appears to be weak. Although there are recipes for professional action, those recipes are often only distantly related to reasons or evidence. For that reason, it can be argued that social work is mostly superstition: a semiprofession based on a semimythology. Social work graduate students pay in money and time to acquire this dubious lore, oblivious to the comment of Socrates that "There is far greater peril in buying knowledge than in buying meat and drink." (Plato, Protogoras)

There is not, within social work, a language that promotes thinking and critical discourse. Nor are there arenas within which critical discourse can well occur. For example, such words as "empowerment," "problem solving," "help," and many others are used within social work imprecisely and in ways that violate their literal meanings. In the social work profession, matters of fact are supposed to be taken on faith. Crucial issues are thereby removed from analytic and critical discussion. Professional values thus make it impossible for the profession to advance except through the perfecting of whatever now exists.

The bureaucratic way of organizing helping leads to rule orientations and away from consequence orientations on the part of helpers. This not only ends in collective narcissism, but also leads to a disinclination to pay attention to, and relate to, unmet need.

Since the decisions of social agencies and their personnel affect actual and potential clients far more than do actual and potential client decisions affect social agencies, the agency-client relationships directly increase the dependency of those seeking help. The meaning of these dependency relationships communicates the inferiority of those needing help and therefore further harms them.

The bureaucratic organization of helping tends, because of the related self-preoccupation, to maintain the status quo regardless of external social changes which always are taking place, and also regardless of the existence of unmet need.

Unintentionally, traditional social work focuses on the inadequacies and disabilities of poor people (deficiencies which need remedying) and not on their talents, capacities, intelligence, and other strengths. This focus defines poor people by their disabilities and thereby ignores other possible definitions, which would be more helpful.

The units defined by social workers have usually ignored extended families and thereby helped to undermine mutual aid resources which traditionally have been valuable supports for them. Social agencies are defining institutions.

Are most social workers or other traditional helpers to blame for this state of affairs? I think not. It is the assumptions on the basis of which traditional helping has occurred which are responsible for the deficiencies.

In February 1917 Antonio Gramsci commented with searing love and indignation: "I hate those who are indifferent." It is true that indifference is the greatest insult which can be rendered to people in need of help. But what has caused the mass indifference, even within the helping professions, to people in great need? The motives of most of them are positive (if somewhat weak). It is rather that most traditional helpers have become entangled in evil social arrangements designed to serve political, economic, military, intellectual, and social elites, and to perpetuate and expand bureaucracies, regardless of the consequences for people. As a result, the interests of most traditional helpers have worked against their extending effective help to people in great need.

The most urgent need for help in the United States is the need of the tens of millions of poor people who not only suffer greater hardships than do affluent people (there is evidence that poverty itself shortens life expectancy in a population, increases the rates of a wide variety of diseases, and assaults the personalities of those subject to it), but who also can't afford to hire helpers for themselves.

A second problem of very great consequence is nearly universal. It is the decline during past decades of the meaningfulness of life for most people, a likely outcome of the rise of bureaucracy and consumerism and a concomitant decline in the extent to which most people take charge of and define their own lives in ways that centrally matter to them, given their life histories.

## Effective Helping

On the basis of the preceding remarks, it is clear that the net effectiveness of helping has little to do with the intentions of helpers. Further, helping is a central characteristic of any society, not something restricted to a residual category.

This discussion has stressed only the effect of placing helping in the hands of those helped. But, if one does not take a second step, the effectiveness of helping remains far below what is otherwise possible. For example, if one does no more than to place helping under the control of those being helped, then helping may tend to concentrate its benefits on small elites, and the helping may deviate from the flourishing of those helped into a pandering to their tastes, wants, pleasures, satisfactions, and prejudices, or to a small sector of their lives (as with solely economic help). Thus the net effectiveness of helping will be improved by the expansion of democracy in all facets of our society and an expansion of *thinking*. Thus, we can formulate Postulate 4 considering helping as follows:

*Other things remaining the same, the net effectiveness of helping in which the helper is under the control of the person(s) helped is increased in direct relationship with the extent to which the helping process is democratic and characterized by a thinking through of how best to proceed in helping.*

It now becomes plausible to assume that an optimal institutionalization of helping can occur through the creation of an expanding, rational, self-educative, mass social movement with enough power to effectuate its major goals.

## THE GRASS-ROOTS SOLUTION

Grass-roots organizing is a "bottom-up" process through which ordinary people join together to accomplish something. A grass-roots organizer is one who helps ordinary people to take charge of and improve their own lives through collective action directed toward accomplishing some social change. The grass-roots approach, therefore, is democratic (run by members) and is in stark contrast to the approach of accomplishing things through elites running authoritarian bureaucratic organizations (in factories, offices, social agencies, educational bureaucracies, the military, and so forth).

One basic question to ask concerning any organization called "grass roots" is "who is really in charge?" Although there are few perfect examples of a grass-roots approach, if a leader or a clique really runs things (as in political, labor union, community, or other organizations), then it is not grass roots even though it may be called "grass roots." Since words concerned with grass roots are often popular, they are frequently taken up to give a positive ring to one or another authoritarian enterprise (for example, an organization for "economic democracy," a "community development"

county department). Sophisticated and authentic grass-roots organizations typically ensure that there is much honest and open critical discussion concerning what is to be done, with the right of any person vigorously protected who wants to dissent from the rest. Some co-ops, neighborhood organizations, block clubs, political organizations, labor unions, churches, towns, and so forth are grass-roots organizations.

When grass-roots organizations join together on a democratic basis, or expand greatly without losing their democratic characteristics, in order to struggle toward securing some social change, they are trying to form a *grass-roots movement.* If they are actually to become a grass-roots movement, they must make some progress toward the change they seek. As is true of grass-root organizations, a grass-roots movement may have much or little formal structure (that is, explicit and legitimated rules to guide their internal processes).

For the first centuries of its existence, Christianity was a religious grass-roots movement. The spread of the town meetings in New England early in the history of the United States was a political grass-roots movement. The spread of co-ops in many rural localities in the midwestern and southwestern United States and in parts of Canada formed a single economic grass-roots movement, which was especially prominent in the late nineteenth and early twentieth centuries. The fast spreading ACORN (Association of Community Organizations for Reform Now), a national congery of neighborhood organizations, is a grass-roots neighborhood movement which has acquired about 34,000 dues-paying member households, mostly during the past five years.

A grass-roots movement becomes most relevant to social change by developing power. The power of such a movement usually depends upon the number of participants; the intensity of their involvement: their "staying ability"; the extent to which it is organized; the money, information, skills, and other resources available to it; its relationships to opponent vulnerabilities; and the "levels of consciousness" of its participants.

Historically, social movements have been among the most important factors in securing basic social changes. We are now seeking to combine technological innovation (another historically important source of social changes) with a scientific grass-roots movement approach with the aim of bringing about a powerful permanent process through which Americans will take charge of their society in such fashion as to flourish maximally and in so doing move toward the resolution or alleviation of all social problems, including the renewal of meaningful activity for most of the population. The progress of the grass-roots neighborhood movement during the last two decades, now involving tens of millions of people, has provided experience, sophistication, hope, and determination for the future of the grass-roots approach in our country.

## THE GENERIC GRASS-ROOTS MOVEMENT

The word "generic" refers to all aspects of people's lives: psychological, moral, social, spiritual, educational, matters of pleasure and fun, work, and so forth. The idea of the generic grass-roots movement is to create a movement that will become an effective scientific, rational, and good force for social change in our society, a movement involving most Americans that will permanently endure. We do not now know whether such a generic grass-roots movement is possible or, if it turns out to be pos-

sible, whether it can result in a major transformation of our society.

At present in our society, people with lower incomes tend to be more involved in staving off threats to their self-realization (the threat of unemployment, of being controlled by others, of being dependent, of welfare, of having to accept even worse alternative jobs, and so on), than in positive flourishing. Positive incentives are more available to those with higher incomes. It is that available incentive difference and the meanings related to it that account for much of the social class differences in vitality and activity, including intellectual activity. We may, therefore, now state:

*Postulate 5: Other things remaining the same, the grass-roots generic movement will contribute far more to the general level of personal self-realization than does the present top-down structuring of most of our society.*

## A DEMOCRATIC REVOLUTION?

Persons associated with the grass-roots movement will come to understand democratic administration (as opposed to the authoritarian approach), social change, the nature and history of social movements, power, the positives and negatives of a long-time perspective, thinking, meaning, truth, morality, relevancy, solidarity, and other topics. But, most central of all will be reality changing. Let me here briefly illustrate this essential concept. Reality consists not only of physical objects. It also consists of meanings. One meaning of a neighborhood may be that the people in it are inferior. That societally held meaning may ensure that most of the people of the neighborhood lack confidence, energy, hope, determination, much skill, and many other characteristics. That meaning of the neighborhood may have been internalized by its residents, making it difficult for them to escape it even when they leave the neighborhood.

A grass-roots organizer working in that neighborhood may begin to focus existing discontents and interests of the residents into a change process. If that organizing effort is successful, some years later the meaning of the neighborhood may become one of the adequacy, or even superiority, of its members. This new meaning, carried partly by institutionalized internal groups, will support members into greater happiness, education, constructive activity, self-esteem, a kind of self-education, and a sturdy confidence and persistence in relating to the people and institutions in the vicinity of the neighborhood. Although the physical objects (houses, streets, human bodies) of the neighborhood may have changed very little, the reality of the neighborhood would have changed a great deal. Such a process would constitute reality changing on a local scale.

The proposed generic movement can be regarded as a social invention. Like other inventions, we may know early the main outlines of what will work but still need a long struggle to perfect it, to make it practical and beneficial.

To sum up, when it comes to helping people, "realism" and careerism, given present social arrangements, are impractical and destructive even to those who engage in them. Although there is no guarantee of what will work, it is an idealism rooted in history which relates to the future through imagination, thinking, reasons, evidence, and analyses by people trying to tell the truth, which promises to work best, to be genuinely practical. But these are the qualities associated with the idealism inherent in the grass-roots perspective as it may come to be expressed in a generic grass-roots movement.

A revolution is a deliberate, basic, and sustained social transformation in a society resulting from changes in the relative power of groups within it. A revolution need not involve violence. By a "basic" transformation I mean one with substantial consequences for the general level of, and/or major varieties of, personal self-realization. We do not presuppose that a basic transformation primarily depends on something happening to the economy, the polity, the culture, technology, or any other sector or feature of society. A *democratic* revolution is one of, by, and for the people of a society. Perhaps one can now initiate in the United States a generic grass-roots movement that will eventually create an unusually desirable democratic revolution, one which will continue as a change process that will permanently work to enhance the lives of the American people.

17.

Robert J. Wineburg

# AN INVESTIGATION OF RELIGIOUS SUPPORT
# OF PUBLIC AND PRIVATE AGENCIES IN ONE COMMUNITY
# IN AN ERA OF RETRENCHMENT

Something of incredible importance happened in the 1980s that the social work literature skipped over almost completely. Religious congregations all across the United States stepped up their involvement in both providing social services from their premises, and offering a wide range of support for agencies in their communities. For those interested in social work from the community perspective, much has happened to the local service system with the involvement of these new and not so new players in the delivery of social services. This article both attempts to understand the involvement of religious congregations in one community's system of services and to view them as community-based organizations that play an important role in a community's total system of care.

## REVIEW OF THE LITERATURE

The longstanding historical link between the religious community and social services (Axin & Levin, 1982; Bremner, 1960; Coil,

1973; Johnson, 1956, 1972; Lowenberg, 1988; Lubove, 1965; Schweinitz, 1943) is more important now to scholars and practitioners in social work than in other eras of service development. The focus of domestic policy in the Reagan and Bush years, and currently in the Clinton and Gingrich era, was captured in former president Bush's now famous "Thousand Points of Light" 1988 campaign speech, which simultaneously called for decreased governmental spending and increased local and voluntary support for social welfare efforts (Karger & Stoesz, 1994). In short, there has been a steady shift toward increasing the responsibility placed on localities for developing, financing, and providing services. Agencies, often stretched to meet rising service demands with fewer resources, have turned to the religious community. There has been little in the social work or social science literature geared to understanding what this policy shift has meant to local service development.

This lack of research on such an important issue has drawn the attention of Smith (1983), Cnaan (1994), and Cormode (1994). One possible reason for the lack of research is that the social work community has often supported and advocated for the development of the social programs dismantled by the Reagan administration. Any examination of how the religious community picked up the slack caused by federal retrenchment might appear as a

Robert J. Wineburg is Associate Professor of Social Work at the University of North Carolina at Greensboro.

The author would like to acknowledge the generous support for this study from the Lilly Endowment. The author also would like to thank Professor Ellen Netting of VCU for her helpful comments and suggestions on an earlier draft of this paper.

This article is dedicated to the late Roy Lubove.

subtle promotion of policies with which the profession disagreed. Social work's hot and cold relationship with religion might also help explain the inattention to the increasing involvement of religion in social work and the nonprofit sector. Garland (1992, p. 4) characterizes social work's ambivalent relationship to religion this way:

Social Workers have viewed churches as any one or a mixture of the following: Significant community resources, dangerous organizations which foster dysfunctional coping in clients, powerful reactionary groups calling for perpetuation of a status quo that oppresses and marginalizes certain groups, voices for constructive societal action to change the status quo, an institution so irrelevant to the work of the social work profession that its role in client's lives is ignored, a profoundly significant source of informal social support and existential hope in the lives of client[s].

Throughout the 1980s and 1990s, Netting outlined many interconnections between the religious and social service communities. For example, she illustrated similarities, differences, and ambiguities between the social work and cleric roles in sectarian agencies (Netting, 1982a). She also outlined the changing funding patterns of church related agencies, informing the unsuspecting, that government support of religiously affiliated agencies has grown steadily from the 1950s to 1980 as agencies became more involved in the web of local services (Netting, 1982b). Sectarian agencies like The Salvation Army, Catholic Social Services, Jewish Family Services, and various Protestant welfare agencies are integral parts of the social service system in virtually all major communities across the country and often rely heavily on government support. In the face of the changing funding and service environment, sectarian agencies balance religious and secular concerns in the face of constant change (Netting, 1984).

Netting has also been the catalyst in connecting the fields of religion, aging, and social work (Netting, 1986; Netting & Wilson, 1987; Netting, Thibault, & Ellor, 1988). The text and subtext of her later work on these topics instructs social work educators that the religious relationship to social work can no longer be ignored (Netting, Thibault, & Ellor, 1990). When her research is viewed alongside local news accounts of congregational involvement in programs for people in need in cities like Atlanta, Washington DC, and Los Angeles (Associated Press, 1990; Cash, 1989; Green, 1989a, 1989b, 1989c; Hendrix, 1989; Hubler, 1989; Jenkins, 1990; Kurylo, 1989; Manzo, 1990; Odum, 1989; Ramos, 1989; Schwartzkopff, 1990), many levels of the interface between social work and services provided by religious organizations become clearer.

## NEW SERVICE ERA

Perhaps the diverse resources within the religious community could be viewed with the same lenses that we use to understand diverse cultural, sexual, racial ethnic, age, and gender differences—lenses of inclusion. With dwindling federal money on the horizon, and growing social problems, the best possible provision of services rests with the inclusion of the religious community into the local system of care. According to Dobkin-Hall (1990, p. 38) churches and denominationally tied institutions command nearly two-thirds of all contributions, 34% of all volunteer labor, and 10% of all wages and salaries in the nonprofit sector. Congregations comprise 30% of the total nonprofit organizations nationally (Mcliquham, 1993, p. 26). Nationally six out of ten congregations open their facilities to outside groups and 43% of volunteer time contributed by congregational members (125 million hours per month) goes to other non-religious programs and activities like education, human services and welfare activities (Hodgkinson, Weitzman, & Kirsh, 1988, p. 5; Hodgkinson, Weitzman, Kirsh, Noga, & Gorski, 1993, p. 65). Consequently, religious congregations have become central to the operation of local service networks, the domain of social work practice.

## THEORETICAL CONSIDERATIONS

Several theoretical orientations can contribute to a deeper understanding of the interplay between religious congregations and social service organizations. Two views are: (1) an historical perspective put forth by social welfare historian Roy Lubove— the continuity amidst change perspective, and (2) a social systems view of congregations as open systems as put forth by Roozen, McKinney, and Carroll (1984). The first orientation helps to clarify, from a historical perspective, why congregations leapt into service during the Reagan era, while the second helps to illuminate the sociological reasons why congregations became more involved during the Reagan years. Combined, the two views serve as a way to understand the new role of congregations and social service agencies in local service provision.

### Continuity Amidst Change

Lubove (personal communication, September 23, 1992) points out that to gain insight into how social change happens historically, it is important, if not essential, to understand how institutions often keep some continuity with the past while also changing to meet present social conditions. For example, congregations were this country's first social welfare institutions. Yet, even before nation-

hood, congregations were intertwined with public bodies to bring about community social welfare. In pre-revolutionary Virginia for example, municipal poor law officials, already serving as Anglican church officials, cared for the old, the sick, the deserted and the illegitimate children of their communities (Coll, 1973). As American society moved from a rural and agricultural economic base to an urban and industrial foundation, congregations and religious leaders were instrumental in developing voluntary organizations to meet the needs of a new urban scene. In the beginning of the 20th century when efforts to help the poor became more formal and secularized, the moral guidance approach of volunteer visitors was replaced by the new and growing profession known as social work (Lubove, 1965).

In the agricultural and industrial eras, religious organizations were intertwined with local governmental and voluntary organizations to help carry out a community's social welfare function. Religious leaders, while instrumental in developing the charity organization societies, also formed the United Way, currently the centerpiece of voluntary social welfare activities in many communities nationwide. Three of the agencies in Table 17.1 below (each of which emerged from congregational efforts and is now non-sectarian) are under the United Way umbrella locally. When the Great Depression spawned major development in the welfare state as we know it, congregations took on a subsidiary welfare function in communities. They developed their foreign missions, and denominational organizational structures (Johnson, 1956). They were no longer capable of providing the major social welfare function for their communities and the society. Congregations, however, did not stop their development nor abort their subsidiary welfare function; they just were not the main providers of local services. From

TABLE 17.1
Selection of Agencies Emerging from Congregational Initiative

| Name of Agency and Year Started | Type of Agency | Service | Religious Resources |
|---|---|---|---|
| 1) Family Life Council 1968 | Private Nonprofit-Non-Religious United Way | Family Education | Volunteer Money Space |
| 2) Pastoral Counseling Services INC 1986 | Private Nonprofit United Methodist | Counseling | Money |
| 3) Guilford Native American Association 1975 | Private Nonprofit United Way | Urban Indian Center | Volunteer Money Space |
| 4) Greensboro Youth Council 1962 | Public | Youth Leadership Training | Volunteer Space |
| 5) United Services for Older Adults 1977 | Private Nonprofit United Way | Multi-Service for Seniors | Volunteer Money Space |
| 6) Project Homestead 1991 | Private Nonprofit Independent | Com. Develop. Housing | Volunteer Space |

the continuity amidst change perspective, congregations' role in community welfare changed, but their continuous historical social welfare function remained clear and they were poised to take on new roles as the combination of the Reagan and Bush retrenchment policies and new problems like AIDS and homelessness strapped local communities.

**Congregations as Open Systems**

Roozen, McKinney, and Carroll (1984, p. 29), theorists of the public mission orientation of religious congregations, look at the role of religious congregations in public or community life from a social systems perspective. They assume that the congregation is an open system. As such, they view local congregations as community institutions having complex and changing relationships to their environment, which provide both limits and possibilities for the congregation.

Accordingly, a congregation's style of operation is profoundly influenced by its social context, especially the local community context, but a congregation, according to Roozen, McKinney, and Carroll, can transcend the determinative power of its context so that it influences its environment. The same claim is legitimate for social service agencies in local social service systems as well (Flynn, 1992). The resulting interactions between congregations and agencies, particularly during the Reagan and Bush era, changed the relationships between congregations and agencies (Wineburg, 1994).

As community social welfare institutions, congregations are agents of social control, social reform, and symbols of continuity, providing links between past and present. As community welfare institutions which shape and are shaped by their environments, there should be little wonder that they have been filling the gaps left by federal retrenchment in communities all across the country. Their proclaimed values of caring for others made them good candidates during the Reagan retrenchment, and still make them good candidates for providing assistance in the midst of hunger, homelessness, AIDS, and other concerns witnessed right at their door steps.

## PURPOSE AND BACKGROUND

One purpose of this article is to demonstrate the extent and nature that congregations are involved in charitable activities in one community with an eye toward casting them as valuable resources that could help bolster needed services in the public and private service arena. This will be accomplished by illustrating the way social service agencies in Greensboro, North Carolina use the resources of their religious community. A second purpose is to link some of the increased congregational assistance to local agencies to the change in domestic policy brought on by the Reagan and Bush policies. The third purpose is to suggest that the relationships uncovered here may represent occurrences in communities elsewhere. To strengthen that argument, reference will be made to agencies in this study that have national affiliations. Some familiar agencies nationally, that had exemplary relations with the Greensboro service system, include the Red Cross, United Cerebral Palsy, Boy and Girl Scouts, Jewish Family Services, Shepherd Center, and Lutheran Family Services—to cite several examples.

Given the historical traditions, the contributions of Netting, anecdotal data, news accounts, and a general knowledge that congregations have become more visible in service provision during that last decade, it is now appropriate to look systematically at the extent and nature of their contributions. Even if it is done on a case-by-case basis which

limits generalizability, it is an important start. The data presented here represent the third stage of a 10-year effort that first looked at 10 congregations and their relationship to a program of Greensboro Urban Ministry that provided support to women so they could work instead of be on welfare (Wineburg & Wineburg, 1986; 1987). The research next examined how 138 congregations in Greensboro provided on-site social services and helped various agencies in the community with volunteers, money, and use of their facilities (Wineburg, 1990, 1990–91, 1993). This latest effort is a 3-year study that looked at how agencies planned for, implemented, and evaluated their use of resources from the religious community.

## CURRENT STUDY

In this study, local agency directors were surveyed regarding the use of the religious community's resources in Greensboro, North Carolina. Another part of the research involved two focus groups, one with congregational volunteers and one with agency directors and clergy. The last stage was an examination of six agencies and their relationships with the religious community. To elucidate points brought out in presentation of numerical data, quotations from participants of the focus groups and case studies will be woven into the text.

### Procedure Phase I, Survey Instrument

The questionnaire for this survey was developed after extensive consultations with a local and a regional group of social service agency and congregational leaders who had been interacting prior to and throughout the Reagan and Bush era. A number of revisions resulted in a set of questions that focused on the organizational profiles of the responding agencies, and their solicitation and use of volunteers, money, facilities, and other resources from those congregations.

## Sample

The sample for the 1993 survey consisted of organizational directors from 193 public and private social agencies and self-help groups listed in the Greensboro North Carolina United Way's *Directory of Community Services.* Greensboro is a mid-sized Southern community of slightly over 190,000 people located in a metropolitan area of close to one million people. For the purpose of this study, self-help groups were included in the survey because those groups often use facilities of congregations for meetings, or they are actually started by efforts of congregants and eventually evolve into social service agencies.[1] Organizational charts were obtained from the local county Mental Health, Public Health, and Social Services Departments. Divisions of those agencies were treated like agencies, as were the social work departments of the 2 major hospitals and the social work division of the city school system. Survey instruments were sent to divisional leaders as they function somewhat like agency directors. Initially, 81 (42%) agencies responded to the survey. However, after two rounds of follow-up phone reminders, another 66 responded, increasing the total to 147 (76%). The statistical margin of error is plus or minus 3 points.

## Phase II

The second phase of this research had 3 aspects to it. First, there was a meeting with the project's local advisory group comprised of agency directors, clergy whose congregations were involved in Greensboro's social service activities, agency board members, and congregational volunteers. The meeting

was to see what members felt were the important concerns that emerged from the community survey completed the previous year. All agreed that even though the survey data yielded excellent results, before agencies could be chosen for closer case analyses, more knowledge was needed about the agency-volunteer and the agency-ministerial connection.

Second, in the winter of 1994, two focus groups were convened for the purpose of developing a strategy for categorizing questions to be used in semi-structured interviews with directors and staff in agencies chosen for case studies. One focus group was held with 8 congregational volunteers to local agencies. The other was held with 4 agency directors and two ministers. One minister was from a large White congregation and the other from a small Black congregation. The focus group sessions were transcribed and the transcripts studied by the research team members for the purpose of developing categories of inquiry used later.

Third, to get answers to the questions noted above in the Purpose section, the research team developed categories of questions to use in semi-structured interviews with selected agency directors and staff. Another meeting took place with the local advisory group who helped refine the line of inquiry and offered advice on the selection of agencies to be used in the case studies in Spring 1994. Appendix A lists the 5 general categories of our line of inquiry.

## RESULTS

### General Organizational Profile of Responding Agencies

Forty-eight (34%) of the responding agencies classified themselves as public, while 91 (66%) labeled themselves private. Twelve

(9%) of the responding agencies classified themselves as religiously affiliated, 20 (14%) claimed a United Way affiliation, 23 (20%) claimed an independent status, 24 (17%) were self-help organizations, and 50 (36%) were affiliated with national organizations. Some of the religiously affiliated agencies that are also connected to national organizations included Habitat for Humanity, Lutheran Family Services, Jewish Family Services, and the YMCA.

## Agency Development from Congregations

Twenty-six (18%) of the responding agencies in this study reported that they began their operations as a result of a congregational initiative. Shirley, the executive director of the local United Cerebral Palsy, and an affiliate of the national United Cerebral Palsy, characterized the pattern of organizational development with congregations in North Carolina this way:

We have twenty-six programs across the state and I would say probably ninety percent started in church basements. It was like a launching place for us to build a center. Sometimes we paid part of [the cost of the space]. And we got volunteers from that congregation. It [the effort] usually grew to building a children's center. We got a lot of help from volunteers to help us through the church organizations. We have volunteers from congregations coming in all the time to deal with different aspects of our centers. The volunteerism is wonderful.

Table 17.1 shows a sample of the kinds of agencies that emerged from congregational initiatives including their name, year of origin, status (public, private, denominational, United Way), contributions from congregations, and their service orientation. It is also a picture of the continuing and yet changing pattern of congregational relationships to the community system of services.

## Congregational Volunteer Support

The volunteer support noted by Shirley is by no means an anomaly in Greensboro. In fact, close to half of the agencies in the sample have used volunteers from the religious community. Over 27 different denominations contributed volunteers to agencies. When asked if volunteers at their agencies served as representatives for their congregations, 49% of the directors of responding agencies claimed that some of their volunteers served on behalf of religious congregations. Fifty-one percent did not use volunteers directly from congregations. Five of the responding public agencies indicated that they use congregational volunteers. John, a member of a Methodist congregation who participated in the focus group with congregational volunteers, characterized stepped-up congregational volunteering in the Reagan era this way when asked when his congregation became involved in supporting local agencies:

I can't pin down an exact date, but [it came], with the emerging need for volunteerism, which stemmed to some extent from the Reagan administration's decentralizing a lot of responsibility, imposing on a lot of institutions. . . . I think the Methodist church has always stressed volunteerism but with the needs increasing the way they have I think we have more volunteers at our church [in local agencies] today than we've ever had. And we need more. It all stems from recognizing a need and attempting to meet it.

Forty-two (58%) of the agencies that used congregational volunteers at the time of the study, were doing so for more than 10 years. This means that they started using congregational volunteers prior to 1982 when the effects of the Reagan policy changes started to be felt at the local level. John's comment above, regarding an "emerging need," is reflected in the fact that 29 (42%) of the responding agencies that used volunteers from congregations started doing so after the Reagan policies took effect. The breakdown is as follows: Fourteen percent had been using volunteers from 6 to 10 years (early Reagan years), while 26% had been using volunteers from 1–5 years, (later Reagan/Bush years) and 2% had been using congregational volunteers less than a year (last year of Bush administration).

**Kinds of Volunteer Use**

Using volunteers for direct services, which includes activities such as counseling, transporting or directing groups, was ranked by 42 (60%) of the agencies as being the most frequent activity performed by congregational volunteers. Twenty-one (29%) of the agencies use congregational volunteers most often for administrative purposes, which include planning, fundraising, or board member participation. The remaining 8 (11%) of the agencies use congregational volunteers most often for secretarial jobs and custodial services. In the quote below Sandy, the director of the Red Cross, characterizes how historically his agency had made sure that volunteers from the religious community played a policy and planning role in his agency. According to Sandy:

Since we're doing our [capital] campaign, I put all our old board lists together. There was not a board list that we did not have the religious community represented.

**Receiving Financial Assistance**

Not only was there extensive use of congregational volunteers by agencies, a total of 61 (52%) agencies had received money from congregations. Thirty-five (30%) were receiving financial support from congregations at the time of the survey, and 26 (22%) were not receiving money at the time

of the survey, but had received congregational finances in the past. Fifty-four (48%) of the responding agencies had never received funds from religious congregations, but 24, or just under half of those agencies were public agencies which would not be expected to receive money from congregations. Yet, it must be noted that the respondent from the Public Health department wrote a note on the questionnaire indicating that while the Public Health Department does not get funds directly from congregations, the pre-natal unit has an *Adopt a Mom* program, where a local congregation adopts a pregnant mom who cannot afford pre-natal care and "pays her pre-natal cost and transportation costs etc." The respondent also noted that she and a member of her staff brokered the relationships with the congregations.

In effect, of the 93 private agencies (excluding the 24 public agencies) responding to the question about receiving money from congregations, 61 (66%) indicated that they had received congregational money. Greensboro Urban Ministry, an interfaith agency begun in 1967, had 6 staff members in 1980 when Reagan was elected. Today they have 47 staff and a 1.3 million dollar budget. Three hundred thousand dollars of that budget comes from over 100 religious congregations in Greensboro. John, the director of Triad Health Project, an agency helping people with HIV and begun in 1987 (well into the Reagan era), outlines how his agency went through the solicitation process and how they learned from their efforts.

I would say real church outreach started with a blanket letter asking for [financial] support. We had some volunteers that went through our church list and other church lists that we got from other places, [Greensboro] Urban Ministry, Hospice, and made phone calls and said, who do we direct a letter to? The church secretary or someone would say, "Oh, you need to send it to

TABLE 17.2
Financial Contributions of Greensboro Congregations

| Pre-Reagan More Than 10 years | Post-Reagan 6–10 years | Post-Reagan 1–5 years | Post-Reagan Less than 1 year |
| --- | --- | --- | --- |
| 13 (31%) | 10 (24%) | 14 (33%) | 5 (12%) |

the minister, or you need to send it to the person who is [on the] community development committee or the social ministry committee." So really, it was the first time, two years ago that we had a decent list. I would say out of 400 churches, now we have fifty churches that send us some [money].

Table 17.2 shows the breakdown of congregational financial support for agencies, pre- and post-Reagan budget cuts. Forty-two (69%) of the agencies that received congregational finances received them after the Reagan Budget cuts took effect, and 13 (31%) had been receiving financial assistance prior to the cuts.

## Denominational Giving of Money

As John noted, his agency receives money from fifty congregations. Other agencies, to a lesser degree, receive money from multiple congregations as well. For example, fifty (79%) agencies that had received funds, received money from between one and ten different congregations. Eight (13%) of the agencies received money from up to thirty different congregations. Five (8%) of the agencies had received financial support from between thirty-eight and one hundred different congregations.

## Uses of Congregational Facilities

Table 17.3 shows that 29 (58%) of the responding agencies were using facilities prior to the effects of the Reagan retrenchment taking hold in Greensboro, while 20 (42%) agencies started using facilities dur-

ing the Reagan era. Fourteen public agencies noted that they had used congregational facilities. Two major public agencies, the Department of Social Services and the Public Health Department, indicated that they started using congregational resources in the Reagan era. Twenty-three (26%) of the agencies used the church or synagogue facilities for educational purposes, 15 (17%) used them for agency meetings or retreats, 10 (11%) used congregational facilities for community meetings, 6 (7%) used them for services for the developmentally disabled, blind or elderly and 6 (7%) used these facilities for their offices. Thirteen (15%) used the congregational facilities everyday, 10 (12%) used facilities once or twice a week, 18 (21%) used them once or twice a month and 45 (52%) used them once or twice a year. Forty-two (46%) of the responding agencies started using religious facilities during the Reagan period of retrenchment, while 49 (54%) were using facilities before the budget cuts.

## DISCUSSION

If community agencies and programs hit by the budget cuts of the 1980s are also seen as part of a larger but connected community system of local welfare institutions, then as cuts inhibited the larger system's capacity to act, congregations expanded to fulfill their own social welfare function and the broader community welfare needs of Greensboro. As noted earlier John, a congregational volunteer, emphasized that his denomination has always stressed volunteerism but his church had more volunteers than ever. The findings reported here reveal a long-term, ongoing, give and take relationship between congregations and agencies. These activities suggest that the solicitation and use of congregational resources by local agencies in Greensboro represent a very deep and intertwined embodiment and institutionalization of the community's values about philanthropy and stewardship.

Donations represent more than providing volunteers, giving money, and offering facilities to local Greensboro agencies. They represent a community ethos which has a logical structure and opens doors to even further exchanges between the religious and social service communities. The local agencies serve as conduits or mediating structures (Berger & Neuhaus, 1977) between the charitable impulses of members of religious institutions and people in need. One principle underscoring this cooperation in Greensboro is that congregations there have served as hubs for spawning new agency development and have done so continuously since the turn of the century. As Sandy, the Executive Director of the local Red Cross, noted above: " . . . there was not a board list that we did not have the religious community represented." It is logical for the Red Cross to have permanent positions for the clergy on its board. The Red Cross nationwide uses congregations for blood drives, as centers for disaster relief, and as sites to teach health education classes ranging from CPR to HIV education. The Red Cross is a United Way Agency and a local affiliate of a national organization whose interconnection to the local religious community has been carefully designed.

Shirley, the Executive Director of United Cerebral Palsy, another United Way agency and local affiliate, noted that her organization's relationship to the religious community started in church basements. It just may be that when a congregation offers its facilities to a community social agency, it actually offers a special membership into the spiritual community of that congregation, thus acknowledging its own institutional commitment to the broader community.

While clearly this is a local study, the interconnection between congregation and agency is not just a Greensboro nor a North Carolina phenomenon. In a larger discussion of the religious response to the riots that followed the Rodney King verdict, Orr, Miller, Roof, and Melton (1994, p. 16) discuss the religious social service infrastructure in Los Angeles this way:

The vastness of the social service infrastructure that has been created by the city's religious institutions rarely becomes visible. . . . The religious social service infrastructure has become vast, because the needs of the city have been vast, and because California's publicly supported infrastructure has been cut back in the face of the state's tax revolt and of its long lasting recession.

Orr, Miller, Roof and Melton, (1994, p. 20) go on to discuss the various ways that religious congregations are setting up nonprofit corporations to tap into public, corporate, and foundation support in order to deliver social services from congregations. Project Homestead listed in Table 17.1 above got its start in the same fashion.

Religious leaders are very clear that their use of non-profit corporations (which accept public funds) requires that their human service activities be guardedly secular both in design and execution. But most are aware that they are working in a gray area. The board of many of these nonprofit corporations are made up of clergy and persons associated with the churches in the areas served. Church sites are used to distribute services.

In Greensboro, like Los Angeles and presumably other cities, agencies provide the structure for congregants to display

TABLE 17.3
Use of Facilities of Greensboro Congregations by Local Agencies

| Pre-Reagan More Than 10 years | Post-Reagan 6–10 years | Post-Reagan 1–5 years | Post-Reagan Less than 1 year |
|---|---|---|---|
| 29 (58%) | 7 (14%) | 13 (26%) | 1 (2%) |

their sense of care and concern. Close to half of the agencies in Greensboro, whether they are public, private, self-help organizations, United Way or independent agencies, used congregational volunteers. Fifty-two percent have received congregational money, and over 65% have used the facilities of congregations. This base of resources and set of institutional interconnections is not unnoticed by local professional social workers who staff such agencies as Greensboro Urban Ministry, Habitat for Humanity, and Jewish Family Services. For those agencies, congregations actually serve an essential role in agency operations, providing hundreds of volunteers, money, supplies, and space.

The set of issues facing the professional social work community nationally in what appears to be a long period of retrenchment will ultimately hang on whether there are sufficient resources to accomplish the missions of the agencies and the mission of our field. While we have the obligation to develop or change policies to better serve our clients, we also have the obligation to garner all the resources necessary to serve them. The religious community is part of the local social welfare system. It would serve our field well to learn about how these organizations relate to the social welfare systems in their communities.

## CRITICAL ANALYSIS

To this point little has been said regarding what the findings here mean in terms of the latest welfare and social service reforms. Politicians, especially Republicans, are calling for more involvement from the religious community. Speaker of the House of Representatives, Newt Gingrich, impressed by the volunteer spirit he found in the home building efforts of Habitat for Humanity, supported a proposed 50 million dollar federal grant for that organization and others that build homes for the poor. Republican governor Kirk Fordice of Mississippi, proposed a program called *Faith in Families* where each of his state's five thousand religious congregations would adopt a welfare family—providing spiritual and practical support. Republican senator John Ashcroft of Missouri, proposed that states, through a block grant from the federal government, contract directly with religiously based charities for delivery of social services to the poor.

This study shows that the strength of the religious community lies in the supportive role it assumes in service delivery at the local level. I feel that there are three assumptions beneath politician's proposals for more religious involvement in service delivery that need closer scrutiny: (1) the religious community has the capacity to shift from a minor to major social service provider; (2) the religious community wants to expand its service role; and (3) the religious community will provide better services than the public sector.

*Do religious congregations and charities have the capacity to become major social service providers?* During the Reagan and Bush era, Catholic Charities alone saw a 700% increase of volunteers. According to a 1992 study by the Independent Sector, members of the nation's religious congregations provided 125 million hours a month in volunteer services to local health, welfare, and educational organizations. A third of our nation's child care is housed in religious facilities, making the religious community the single largest provider of such services in the country. If you want to give blood, attend an AA meeting, or start a scout troop, chances are good that you will wind up at a local congregation's facility not just in Greensboro, but anywhere in the country. When one stops to think that religious congregations first provide a gathering spot for communal worship, it is amazing how such organizations muster the energy and spirit to help their own members, offer their facilities to the community, support community agencies, and reach out with money and services nationally and internationally.

This study of Greensboro's public and private agencies found a huge increase in the use of congregational resources during the Reagan and Bush years. Unbelievably, 69% of the agencies receiving money from the religious community started doing so in the Reagan era. There is no doubt that the religious community can expand its service efforts. It is simply wrong to assume that it has an unlimited capacity to expand.

*Does the religious community want to increase its service efforts?* I can say with assurance, that no major religiously based service provider is pleading to take over more of the nation's social services. The calls for increased service from the religious community, and the romanticizing of its capabilities, are coming from the political arena and think tanks. Politicians who, in a subtle and patronizing way, try to co-opt the religious community into providing more services don't seem genuine. If politi-

cians dump their programs on the religious community without discussion and planning, they run the risk of being seen as co-opting those institutions, hurting people who need services, and being blamed for weakening the relationships they seemingly want to strengthen.

*Will the religious community offer better services than the public sector?* If the politicians reduce the fiscal outlay for public sector services and try to meet the same demands with just religious resources, religious social services will have to expand exponentially. Extreme pressure will be on them to contribute more volunteers, space, and money. These organizations are attractive in that they are small and less bureaucratic than government agencies and can solve problems and meet needs immediately. The spirit underscoring their effectiveness comes in part because their efforts are voluntary. Co-opting them, laying guilt trips on them, or bludgeoning them from the political bully pulpit will not create a more humane, caring, and responsive social service system. Congregations may even retreat inward offering help only to their membership. The late social welfare historian Roy Lubove used to remind his students that social welfare policy is complex despite the simple mindedness of its formulators.

## A ROLE FOR SOCIAL WORK

Some sober discussion, coupled with comprehensive community planning, and keeping in sight a clear goal for developing strong and fair partnerships among public, private, and religious organizations is the first step in reducing the complexity, and preventing simple mindedness. Social workers can lead in shaping this discussion locally, at the state level, and even nationally. With the help of local faculty, social workers could assess the level of need in their communities, the degree to which the religious community is helping, and the level to which it could expand. They can write editorials in the local paper, get on local radio and television talk shows to present a more accurate picture of the scope of the problems they face, and highlight that there is a need for resources from new sources like the religious community, and that such help can take many forms such as volunteers, money, or facility use.

At the state and national levels social workers can join forces with advocacy groups and welfare rights groups in educating legislators about the role the religious community can realistically play in a changing social service infrastructure that is becoming increasingly local in its character. They might want to emphasize to politicians that forcing voluntary action on the religious community might backfire, causing a retreat from the kind of outreach they desire by the religious community. Also on the national level we need far more research on this topic and an openness to the study of religion and social work that has been absent too long.

## CONCLUSION

The purpose of this article was to demonstrate the extent and nature that congregations are involved in charitable activities in Greensboro, North Carolina with an eye toward steering the social work community to view them as valuable resources that could help bolster needed services in the public and private service arena. While this article presents only a case study with limited generalizability, if what was uncovered here exists elsewhere, then the social work profession would be served greatly by reacquainting itself with the religious community.

## NOTE

1. This belief was somewhat confirmed with the finding that 18% of the responding agencies began as result of congregational initiatives.

## REFERENCES

Associated Press. (1990, June 30). Macon ministry helps homeless despite blaze. *Atlanta Journal*, D4.

Axinn J., & H. Levin (1982). *Social welfare a history of the American response to need.* 2nd ed. New York, NY: Harper and Row.

Berger, P., & Neuhaus, R. (1977). *To empower people*. Washington, DC: American Enterprise Institute for Public Policy Research.

Bremner, R. H. (1972). *From the depths: the discovery of poverty in the United States*. 6th ed. 1972, New York, NY: NYU Press.

Bremner, R. H. (1960). *American philanthropy*. Chicago, IL: University of Chicago Press.

Cash, S., (1990, June 28). Dekalb churches unite to help the poor. *Atlanta Constitution*, sec. XA, p. 1.

Coll, B. (1973). *Perspectives in public welfare*. Washington, DC: Department of Health Education and Welfare.

Cnaan, R. (1994). The role of congregations and religious federations in providing human services: A social work perspective. *Association of Researchers in Nonprofit Organizations and Voluntary Action, 1994 Annual Conference Proceedings* (pp. 540–544). Berkeley, CA.

Cormode, D. S. (1994). Review essay: Religion and the nonprofit sector. *Non Profit and Voluntary Sector Quarterly, 23*(2), 171–182.

Dobkin Hall, P. (1990). The history of religious philanthropy in America. In R. Winthrow & V. Hodgkinson, eds. *Faith and philanthropy in America*. San Francisco, CA: Jossey-Bass.

Flynn, J. P., (1992) *Social agency policy: analysis and presentation for community practice*. Chicago, IL: Nelson Hall.

Garland, D. R., (Ed.) (1992). *Church social work: helping the whole person in context of the church*. St. Davids, PA: North American Christians in Social Work.

Green, C. (1989, October 5). Homeless crusade catches nation's eye. *Atlanta Constitution*, sec. XJ, p. 1.

Green, C. (1989, April 21). Homeless invited to suburbia. *Atlanta Constitution*, sec. D, p. 2.

Green, C. (1989, April 2). County forms task force to combat homelessness. *Atlanta Journal*, sec, XJ, p. 1.

Hendrix, K. (1989, April 10). The cleric of Covenant House. *Los Angeles Times*, sec. V, P. 1.

Hodgkinson, V. Weitzman, M., & Kirsh, A. (1988). *From belief to commitment: The activities and finances of religious congregations in the United States: Findings from a national survey*. Washington, DC: Independent Sector.

Hodgkinson, V. Weitzman, M., Kirsh, A., Norga, S. A., & Gorski, H. A., (1993). *From belief to commitment: The activities and finances of religious congregations in the United States: Findings from a national survey*. Washington, DC: Independent Sector.

Hubler, S. (1989, December 7). Church plan for transients in Redondo Beach shelved. *Los Angeles Times*, sec. B, p. 1.

Johnson, F. E. (Ed.) (1956). *Religion and social work*. New York, NY: Institute for Religious and Social Studies.

Jenkins, M. (1990, November 26). Churches fold shelter beds, rethink homeless help. *Atlanta Journal*, sec. D, p. 1.

Kurylo, E. (1989, May 25). Service groups, churches asked to help in Census. *Atlanta Journal*, sec. C, p. 1.

Karger, H. J., & Stoesz, D. (1994). *American social welfare policy: a pluralist approach*, 2nd ed., White Plains, NY: Longman.

Lowenberg, F. M. (1988). *Religion and social work practice in contemporary American society*. New York, NY: Columbia University Press.

Lubove, R. (1965). *The professional altruist*. Cambridge, MA: Harvard University Press.

Magill, R. S. (1986). Social welfare politics in urban america. *Social Work, 31*(5), 397–400.

Manzo, K. K. (1990, March 8). Damascus church picks up, moves house to aid homeless. *Washington Post*, sec. MD, p. 10.

McLiquham, J. (1993). Survey highlights religion's role in giving. *Non Profit Times, 7*(6), 26.

Nathan, R. P., Doolittle, F. C., & Associates. (1987). *Reagan and the states*. Princeton, NJ: Princeton University Press.

Netting, F. E. (1982a). Social work and religious values in church related agencies. *Social Work and Christianity, 9*(1–2), 4–20.

Netting, F. E. (1982b). Church-related agencies and social welfare. *Social Services Review, 58*(3), 404–420.

Netting, F. E. (1984). The changing environment: Its effects on church related agencies. *Social Services Review, 2*(l), 16–30.

Netting, F. E. (1986). The religious agency: implications for social work administration. *Social Work and Christianity, 13*(2), 50–63.

Netting, F. E. & Wilson, C. C. (1987). When religion and health care meet: the church related agency. *Journal of Religion and Aging, 3*(3/4), 101–114.

Netting, F. E., Thibault, J. M., & Ellor, J. W., (1988). Spiritual integration: Gerontological interface between the religious and social service communities. *Journal of Religion and Aging, 3*(1–2), 51–60.

Netting, F. E., Thibault, J. M., & Ellor, J. W. (1990). Integrating content on organized religion into macro practice courses. *Journal of Social Work Education, 26*(1), 15–24.

Orr, J. B., Miller, D. E., Roof.,W. E., & Melton, J. G. (1994). *Politics of the spirit: Religion and multiethnicity in Los Angeles: A preliminary report of research conducted under the auspices of The Religion and Civic Order Project at UC Santa Barbara and the University of Southern California*. Los Angeles, CA: University of Southern California.

Odum, Maria. (1990, November 30). 154 Homeless who died are mourned. *Atlanta Journal*. sec. B, p. 10.

Ramos, George. (1989, August 25). Church leaders ask more pastors to house illegals. *Los Angeles Times*, sec. 11, p. 3.

Ramos, George. (1989, August 16). Pastor celebrates controversial past. *Los Angeles Times*, sec. 11, p. 3.

Roozen, D. A. McKinney, W., & Carroll, J. (1984). *Varieties of religious presence: mission in public life*. New York, NY: Pilgrim Press.

Salamon, L. M., Altschuler, D. M., & De Vita, C. J. (1985). Chicago nonprofit organizations: *The Challenge of Retrenchment*, Washington, DC: Urban Institute Research Report.

Schwartzkopff, F. (1990, August 21). Planners study homeless shelter zoning. *Atlanta Journal*, sec. XJ, p. 2.

Schweinitz, K. de (1943). *England's road to social security*. New York, NY: A. S. Barnes.

Sibley, C. (1990, October 27). Nourishing body and spirit. *Atlanta Journal*, sec. XJ, p. 13.

Smith, D. H. (1983). Churches are generally ignored in contemporary voluntary action research: Causes and consequences. *Review of Religious Research, 24*(4), 295–303.

White, G. (1990, January 20). Providing a sanctuary. *Atlanta Journal*, sec. B, p. 5.

White, G. (1989, December 13). Interfaith effort to raise funds for homeless in January drive. *Atlanta Journal*, sec. D, p. 8.

White, G. (1989, November 11). Leaving their pews to serve the public. *Atlanta Journal*, sec. D, p. 11.

White, G. (1989, June 16). Homeless issue gets attention of Methodists. *Atlanta Journal*, sec. B, p. 10.

Wineburg, R. J., & Wineburg, C. R. (1986). Localization of human services: using church volunteers to fight the feminization of poverty. *Journal of Volunteer Administration, 4*(3), 1–6.

Wineburg, C. R., & Wineburg, R. J. (1987). Local human service development: institutional utilization of volunteers to solve community problems. *Journal of Volunteer Administration, 4*(1), 9–14.

Wineburg, R. (1990). Volunteers in service to their community: congregational commitment to helping the needy. *Journal of Volunteer Administration, 9*(1), 35–47.

Wineburg, R. J. (1990–91). A community study on the ways religious congregations support individuals and human service network. *The Journal of Applied Social Sciences, 15*(l), 51–74.

Wineburg, R. (1993). Social policy, service development, and religious organizations. *Non Profit Management & Leadership, 3*(3), 283–299.

Wineburg, R. J. (1994). A longitudinal case study of religious congregations in local human services. *Non Profit and voluntary Sector Quarterly, 23*(2), 159–171.

**18.**

Geoffrey Pawson and Terry Russell

## SOCIAL PLANNING: A CHILD WELFARE EXEMPLAR

Ross suggests that the impetus for social planning is dissatisfaction within a community about a particular condition (1955:135). Gilbert and Specht (1977:1), however, contend that in most situations social plans are developed and implemented by experts who often rely on their own conception of community well-being.

In child welfare, the relationship between a child, the child's parents, and the community is a triad that requires support to maximize the potential of the relationship.

This interdependency experiences stress when the types of support that society must offer are nontraditional since parents and communities are highly protective of the sanctity of the family. Community desires to preserve the traditional meaning of family present severe barriers to legislative reform, and few politicians are willing to challenge such opinions even if they are cognizant of problems that require attention.

Hibbard (1981:557–65) argues that a new social planning paradigm rests on cultural pluralism, and although there is a range of viewpoints as to how it should be applied, the common element is the displacement of authority for planning from experts and elites to those involved in

Geoffrey Pawson is executive director of Ranch Erlo Society, Regina, Saskatchewan; Terry Russell is director of Child and Youth Services, Regina Mental Health Region, Saskatchewan.

social interactions. Social planning interventions must include the various individuals and groups that will be affected as well as the larger community that may be indirectly involved.

Boles (1980:344–59) traces the development of comprehensive day care legislation in the United States. Despite three separate bills introduced in the Congress and Senate, day care is still thought of as a program for the poor based on the assumption that it will facilitate their obtaining or maintaining employment. Boles concludes that legislation providing such care to a range of different people may be possible if programs are federally guaranteed under a specific funding formula, but the responsibility for program design and administration must rest with local providers and consumers. This allows for local differences within a pluralistic society; also, it strongly indicates that services for a range of families are likely to follow a path of incremental development.

The basic strategy of the social worker in community planning for children and families may be to support an incremental growth of services rather than fight for universal programs. As communities have opportunities to consider the benefits of programs available in other jurisdictions, citizens can be encouraged to initiate their own efforts to obtain such services. In order to minimize local resistance, practitioners should promote the establishment of quality programs that are not perceived as radical innovations. Further, efforts should be made to involve a range of potential consumer groups in planning forums that allow people involvement in designing the types of programs they are ready to utilize.

The community practitioner needs to maintain a short- and a long-term perspective in social planning. For example, new ideas in child welfare and family services can be introduced through attempts to prompt agencies and community groups to establish new programs. Although these may be rejected in the short term, the ideas that are planted may germinate later.

The potential for planned change based upon empirical data, internally consistent approaches, and trial or pilot applications is clearly evident. However, the practitioner must encourage participants to include as part of the strategy a variety of contingency plans, since what seems a logical and rational case of action to planners based upon their knowledge and perceptions may not be perceived as valuable by constituents with limited information or different needs. This suggests that community education and public relations are vital factors in the planning process. Mechanisms to educate the public can include widely circulated factual documents, public forums, conferences, community advisory groups, and other forms of constituency involvement. These mechanisms inform citizens, clarify issues, and encourage inputs that can serve to revise proposed plans in order to increase their acceptability.

Local citizen groups and their representatives should be given opportunities to exchange ideas and express their attitudes. Even planning at regional and federal levels should offer the opportunity for communities to control what happens in their jurisdiction. This does not assume that local area management is most beneficial for clients; rather, it assumes that an incremental approach based on local control is most productive in the long run, and encourages development of a variety of programs that reflect local attitudes and customs.

## COMMUNITY DEVELOPMENT

The major emphasis in community development is the process of community building where the organizer creates an identification of common interests through stimulating and facilitating community awareness and involvement and the growth of citizen leadership (Brager and Specht 1973:27). Many of these concepts have evolved in rural areas or undeveloped countries, and they have been translated, with some difficulty, to urban areas within North America (Grosser 1973:204).

An example is the case of Sandy Bay, an isolated Indian village in northern Saskatchewan, Canada. In the past thirty years, the social fabric of this community has been devastated by change due to the village's location in a resource-rich area of the province. As a result of outside intrusions, traditional patterns of mutual help through extended families and neighborhood networks began to deteriorate, and children were particularly vulnerable. Previously, children were an accepted community responsibility; if parents could not care for their children, another family provided for them.

In the early 1960's, Sandy Bay was accessible only by air or overland through the bush. Local services were provided by an outpost nurse, a policeman, and a priest, all of whom were residents in the community. When children were neglected or temporarily abandoned, a provincial child welfare worker was contacted by radiophone to come up and investigate the problem. In many cases, children were temporarily removed from the village until parents returned or family disputes were resolved. This system was extremely expensive and not particularly effective.

Because the village was identified as having some of the worst social problems in the area, a community development project was planned for Sandy Bay by the Department of Social Services. Social workers began flying into the village and

staying for several days. Initially they slept in an abandoned building because of the lack of housing, but this inconvenience was necessary in order to meet the local people and become familiar with village customs. It became clear quite early in the process that the only formal group in the community was the local chapter of Alcoholics Anonymous (AA), whose members met nightly at the recreation center. Workers joined this group every evening and noted that both children and adults came to the recreation hall to talk with this group.

Gradually, the subject of protective services was introduced by the social worker, and the group was asked to consider alternatives to the present system of care. A child care committee was formed after extensive deliberations lasting several months, during which the expectations and responsibilities of the proposed committee were examined in great detail. Finally, the committee developed both an approach to the problem that included identification of children requiring protection within the village and a resource network utilizing extended family members and neighbors (Soiseth 1970:8–9).

The Minister of Social Services for Saskatchewan formally recognized the work of the group with a plaque that was hung in the local recreation hall. Further, one member of the committee was authorized to serve as a resident child welfare worker, under the authority of existing legislation, and he was provided with an identification that indicated his status and legal authority in child welfare matters. From this small beginning, Sandy Bay residents went on meeting and set up day care services, a group home for older adolescents, foster care, and an alcohol treatment unit. The University of Regina, through its School of Social Work, was an active participator and resource for the community and made a film, *We Can,* designed to show other communities how they might proceed to resolve problems based on the Sandy Bay experience.

This example indicates the importance of developing goal congruency and consensus in a problem area. Although the community social worker, sponsor, and community were highly committed to instituting workable programs for children, it can be argued that a range of other factors helped to stimulate this interest. For the community practitioner, the existing system of care was inadequate, and there were indications that its child welfare policies and services were contributing to family breakdown rather than strengthening family life in Sandy Bay.

With the Department of Social Services serving as sponsor, both political and financial benefits were apparent. The multitude of social problems in the village were well known, and these difficulties were adding fuel to an ongoing controversy about exploitation of rural natives living in resource-rich areas of the province. If changes could be facilitated, it was anticipated that both the village and the wider community would benefit and in time there could be increased support and public responsiveness to these concerns.

In terms of the community, the villagers were most anxious to keep their children at home, but there was a sense of powerlessness. The group of AA members who formed the first child care committee were committed not only to performing designated child care functions but also to aggressively attacking the alcohol problem within the village. The skills they learned about obtaining resources and collaborating to institute programs carried over to a range of other problem areas.

Part of the strategy used by the community worker was the use of symbols. These included the plaque from the Minister and an identification card for the villager designated as a child welfare worker. The importance of these symbols is evidenced by the fact that the original plaque still hangs in the recreation hall, and when the indigenous child welfare worker lost his wallet in a canoeing accident, he immediately informed the community worker that "his card had drowned." A new one was quickly issued.

One major strength of this model rests on the community identifying common concerns. Application of this practice approach in child welfare is particularly appealing due to the high priority most people accord to serving those who require special protection. Also, this approach stimulates the transfer of power to community members, which means that they experience a sense of regaining control of decisions regarding the welfare of their children. This can be a powerful motivating force.

## COMMUNITY LIAISON

The role of working with communities through direct involvement of agency staff, usually administrators, has been identified as a legitimate community practice function. Murphy (1954:308–9) listed a variety of community interorganizational activities, while Sieder (1960) expanded on this aspect of agency operations by focusing on mobilization of support for agencies and development of community resources.

Brager and Specht (1973:223–30) indicate that an executive can offer important resources for boards such as knowledge, reports on communication with staff and other agencies, and assistance in decision-making.

Although social agencies are capable of producing positive community relationships, it is inherent in the approach that there is a need to balance the needs of clients with the needs of organizations. If the equilibrium tips in either direction, programs can be seriously affected and jeopardize the credibility of an agency or have a deleterious affect on clients.

The development and growth of a residential treatment center in Saskatchewan, Canada, reflect one aspect of the community liaison approach. In 1964, a change of provincial governments resulted in the closing of the only residential treatment center in the province due to questions about its cost effectiveness. Within two years, a large number of emotionally disturbed children were being placed in treatment centers located outside the province. A newly appointed Director of Child Welfare was most interested in reestablishing residential treatment services. When this interest became known, a professional social worker moved to mobilize professionals and citizens so that a proposal was presented that was formally accepted by the Minister of Social Welfare within two weeks.

The strategy of the social worker in developing the original proposal evolved through discussion with a variety of people who were already familiar with the attitudes of government or who had worked in the residential care field. Key variables appeared that needed to be dealt with in the proposal. First, the Minister of Social Welfare was a Mennonite farmer who highly valued rural life for raising children. The previous center had been located within a city neighborhood whose residents had opposed the program. Second, the new government was suspicious of civil service staff based on its perception that these people did not support the government and therefore should not be entrusted with developing the program. Third, although

the government was receptive to reestablishing residential treatment services, it wanted to maintain tight fiscal control in order to prevent spiraling costs. Based on this information gathered from knowledgeable people, an ad hoc group decided to locate the center in a small rural setting outside a major city. This met the requirements of the Minister while facilitating the program's ability to obtain needed professional services.

In developing community support, the community worker recruited a few respected community leaders who were well known to the government for their political support. This group also was a source for the agency's first board of directors, and their involvement alleviated the government's concern about funding a service that was in opposition to its political ideology. This type of board was not fully representative but was a rational response to the realities of the environment (Pfeffer 1972:226).

The proposed program was based on plans for a facility that would care for twelve children, and there was no attempt to conduct a survey of needs since it was already known that the demand clearly outstripped the allocated resources. By beginning small, it was hoped the program would grow over time as its worth and the need for its services were demonstrated.

Another strategy was careful timing of the project. The organizer submitted the proposal early enough to have special project money allocated by the beginning of the new budget year. Although the government agreed only to a per diem rate and monthly advance payments, this provided sufficient cash flow to arrange a mortgage on some property, refurbish the residence, and hire staff. All of this had to occur within three months, due to concern that prolonged delay or debate over the project, or other requests for programs, would jeopardize the new service.

The community worker operated as the center or linking agent of an informal system that was backed by a loosely organized board. Major interorganizational involvements focused on the public founder, and the Department of Social Welfare was kept constantly informed about developments in order to coordinate efforts.

From this small beginning, the population of the center expanded to eighty children in ten years, and a range of programs was established including group homes, specialized foster care, special education facilities, summer facilities, and wilderness programs. The first board of directors was highly committed to the program. Over time, the board became educated about the purposes of the center, and appropriate committees were appointed to set policies and oversee agency operations.

In analyzing this example within the context of the community liaison approach, the initial requirements of interorganizational involvements, mobilization of support from the community's leaders, and obtaining resources were all met. It is clear that the service was designed to suit the requirements of the government but in such a way that the integrity of the program was not violated and a needed service was initiated.

The strengths of the community liaison approach include rapid application of ideas for services based on predetermined goals. Since the goals are specific, citizen and consumer involvement can be selective, thereby creating the potential for a committed and cohesive organization. This in itself facilitates the effectiveness of the model in selected situations.

The basic weakness of this model is that it usually does not allow for a high degree of widespread community participation. By developing an organization of like-minded citizens the potential for constructive criticism may be thwarted, thereby creating the possibility that the program will not meet the needs of particular groups in the community. Further, organizational goals may become so parochial that they do not take into account other community needs or recognize the importance of collaborative action within the network of agencies. However, community liaison can produce change for community benefit as long as the weaknesses are recognized and safeguards such as advisory groups and interagency collaboration are maintained.

## PROGRAM DEVELOPMENT AND COORDINATION

Litwak and Hylton (1962:566) give three reasons for agencies to enter into formal linkages with other organizations: interdependence, information gathering, and monitoring the allocation of resources. Evan (1971:33-45) goes further, arguing that agencies use other groups as sources for new ideas, while Reid (1964:420) points out that sustained interorganizational relationships and cooperation lead to coordination.

Community practitioners can achieve coordination in a variety of ways. Two examples illustrate this point. In 1970, the Commission on Emotional and Learning Disorders in Children (CELDIC) completed a national study of Canadian children entitled *One Million Children.* Six national voluntary agencies and one international agency agreed to sponsor the study, and funding for this ambitious undertaking was provided through a combination of federal, provincial, and foundation grants, and contributions from the business community. Provincial and territorial organizations brought thousands of people together to consider the present state of children's services in Canada. Service agencies, advocacy groups, associations, and concerned citizens shared a variety of program information with each other in small gatherings that were conducted across the nation. This involvement provided a means of heightening public awareness, developing interorganizational linkages, and redefining the needs and programs required by children in various communities and regions. Also, the meetings provided a forum for informally evaluating existing service delivery systems.

From the work of CELDIC, local and national coalitions formed and pressed government for expanded resources based on their revised sense of what needs existed. This would not have occurred if there had been no opportunities to build relationships and share information. No national solutions were instituted, given the federal structure of Canada, but a variety of services strengthened, and new resources were made available through governmental and private sources. In fact, the report has provided a philosophical foundation for a decade of service development.

The second example involves the establishment of Mobile Family Services in Regina, Saskatchewan, an agency that was developed as a coordinated effort involving the city police, child welfare, family social services, and mental health agencies. The initial collaboration of these agencies was directed toward obtaining federal and provincial funding to launch innovative programs appropriate for the changing life style of youth during the 1960s. The project involved hiring young people to operate a twenty-four-hour crisis telephone program with appropriate follow-up services. Though it has been argued that the youth were co-opted, the service that resulted was beneficial to the children who were served and did help agencies to move toward more flexible modes of service and greater recog-

nition of the need to coordinate their efforts. As the youth crisis subsided and the special funding was withdrawn, the original agencies agreed to continue the project in expanded form through existing agency budgets. The expanded services included child abuse, emergency child welfare and social assistance, social service participation in emergency police calls involving suicide and domestic disputes, and emergency services. To achieve these ends, further professionalization of the service resulted, and the original emphasis on youth participation ensured the move toward quality programs and fostered the coordination of efforts among the participating agencies.

Analysis of these two examples suggests that collaboration can lead to coordination and heightened interest in particular issues that are of common concern. In these instances, collaboration stimulated and encouraged agencies to review and adapt their policies and practices in order to provide services in a more effective way. The basic strategy of the community practice involved bringing in agencies together around specific issues and arranging various community forums to encourage the design of new resources, assessment of existing services, and collaboration with integrated service delivery systems.

Use of the model assumes that there is enough goal consensus to support mutual collaboration. This is an ideal that is seldom maintained over time since disequilibrium can occur if strong agencies become sources of power unto themselves. This can lead to organizational inflexibility, which is usually the condition which prompted the original coordination effort. Also, the coordination effort can be sabotaged in the initial stage if organizational domains are threatened or agency resources are usurped. Nevertheless, this model holds considerable potential for community social workers, providing that common objectives are self-evident or can be developed.

## POLITICAL EMPOWERMENT

Generally, political empowerment occurs through some recognized authority delegating power to a particular group for specific purposes or through groups assuming power based on interest, expertise, or other resources.

In the child welfare field, the use of political empowerment as a community practice strategy has been very limited. Children and youth do not usually have an organizational base on which to build, and society does not expect the young to act as an organizational force nor does it accept them when they behave as if they are a force. Children in need of protection, often by definition, do not have parents or a concerned community who are perceived as having power. Consequently, outsiders—concerned citizens and professionals in child welfare—have unwittingly contributed to this problem through projecting a sense of powerlessness upon these children, their families, and their immediate community. As a result, political empowerment as a community social work strategy in child welfare has received only minimal emphasis to date.

Political empowerment requires commitment to a common central ideal. This is usually accomplished by adopting values that provide the ideology underlying the organizational activity (Katz and Georgopoulos 1971:356–66). In child welfare the usual ideological focus is protection of children through the provision of the best possible services. Rather than work to empower the children and families who are most centrally concerned, social workers have tended to

institutionalize programmatic solutions, and through professionalization, they lose sight of the political character of their activity (Corwin 1972: 472–75).

In children's services, the moral question is seen in the protective attitude of society toward children. Economically, child welfare services are highly dependent on public or private funding since it is not possible or socially desirable for children's programs to compete in an open-market system. Political problems are always in the background, and protective services, for example, are known to be politically volatile. Consequently, professional groups often are empowered to handle difficult child welfare matters. At no time are child welfare services autonomous from the environment in which they operate. Traditionally, the legitimacy of child welfare has been derived from the community at large that has expectations about the need to protect and care for children caught in situations that expose them to serious risks not of their own making.

Child welfare social service agencies must deal with environmental complexity, which is defined as risk, dependency, and interorganizational relationships (Osborne and Hunt 1974:231–46). In most communities attitudes toward child welfare are extremely conservative and services are dependent on public or charitable sources. Consequently, there has been extreme caution in developing approaches which are unusual or innovative. There are seldom any "risk" programs undertaken which are not first legitimized by strong endorsements from national associations. Thus, the majority of essential child welfare services are legitimized by the general community, but service providers do not often gain or even seek legitimacy from client populations or citizen groups.

Experimental programs which utilized community workers with gangs of youth have successfully transferred some power to client groups in some instances. However, this has usually been an exercise in short-term process rather than the basis of lasting change. Youth street organizations have a transitory membership which is not suited to continuing organizational responsibility or evolution. Nevertheless, the strategies of political empowerment can have an impact when they form the basis of youth work.

Probably the most significant uses of political empowerment in child welfare services to date have involved the empowerment of parents to act on behalf of their children. The parents of children with specific handicaps such as mental retardation, learning disability, and autism have become powerful forces over the last decade as child advocates, fund raisers, and service providers. Parent-dominant organizations have been especially powerful in the development of community-based alternatives to institutionalization.

These parent empowerment organizations are usually begun as parent-professional-community partnerships. The development of the political action approach usually passes through three stages. First, a group of concerned citizens take a collective action to develop an organization that will advance their interests. Second, funding problems are addressed. At this point, the political action model is often in jeopardy, since allocation of funds for specific projects often diverts the attention of the group away from more universal issues. Many groups stop at this point, and they place all of their energies into building a specific service, such as a school for retarded children. It can be argued that the provision of funds for projects is a conscious co-optation of the group by funders in order to divert the attention of the members away from more global issues.

The final phase emerges when the empowered group recognizes the range of needs that are not being met due to their involvement in providing direct services. At this point, members reassume the role of advocates. Many examples are evident, such as schools for retarded children that were operated by parents being turned over to public authorities. This frees the group to direct attention to new endeavors, often with the specific objective of starting services and then turning them over to others to operate. This form of the political empowerment model has great potential since members are usually highly committed advocates who are free to and willing to develop a strong power base.

Finally, political empowerment in child welfare is an important issue arising among certain racial and ethnic minorities, most notably blacks and the North American Indians (Cardinal 1977; Hudson and McKenzie 1981; Johnson 1981). Criticisms have been made of cross-racial adoption (Sanders 1975), the lack of appropriate foster care, and the need for provision of treatment services on reservations (Simon 1973). In Canada and the United States, ethnic and racial interest associations are extremely concerned about child welfare services which they describe as a form of cultural genocide. The disproportionate numbers of Indian children who are in the care of child welfare authorities is cause for concern (Canadian Council on Children and Youth 1978:130–5). There is little doubt that child welfare services will become an integral part of the Indian rights movement in the years to come. Community practice strategies which empower communities to care for their children will be an essential part of this movement.

**REFERENCES**

Abbott, Grace. 1938. The Child and the State, vol. 11: *The Dependent and Delinquent*

*Child, the Child of Unmarried Parents.* New York: Greenwood Press.

Axinn, June and Herman Levine. 1975. *Social Welfare: A History of the American Response to Needs.* New York: Harper and Row.

Bagnell, Kenneth. 1980. *The Little Immigrants: The Orphans Who Came to Canada.* Toronto: Macmillan of Canada.

Bartlett, Harriet M. 1958. "Toward Clarification and Improvement of Social Work Practice." *Social Work* (April), 3(2):3–9.

Betten, Neil. 1973. "American Attitudes Toward the Poor." *Current History* (July), 65(383):1–5.

Beveridge, Sir William. 1942. *Social Insurance and Allied Services.* New York: Macmillan.

Boles, Janet K. 1980. "The Politics of Child Care." *Social Service Review* (September), 54(3):344–62

Brager, George A. and Harry Specht. 1973. *Community Organizing.* New York: Columbia University Press.

Canadian Council on Children and Youth. 1978. *Admittance Restricted: The Child as Citizen in Canada.* Ottawa: M.O.M. Press.

Cardinal, Harold. 1977. *The Rebirth of Canada's Indians.* Edmonton: Hurtig.

Child Welfare League of America. 1981. *Child Welfare Planning Notes.*

————. 1982. *Urgent Bulletin* (an open letter to member agencies).

Cohen, Nathan E., ed. 1960. *The Citizen Volunteer: His Responsibility, Role, and Opportunity in Modern Society.* New York: Harper and Row.

Corwin, Ronald G. 1972. "Strategies of Organizational Survival: The Case of a National Program of Educational Reform." *Journal of Applied Behavioral Science* (July/August), 8(4):451–80.

Costin, Lela B. 1979. *Child Welfare: Policies and Practice.* New York: McGraw-Hill.

Coughlin, Bernard J. 1979. "Deinstitutionalization: A Matter of Social Order and Deviance." *Child Welfare* (May), 61(5):293–301.

Etzioni, Amitai. 1961. *Complex Organizations: A Sociological Reader.* New York: Holt, Rinehart and Winston.

Evan, William M. 1971. "The Organization-Set: Toward a Theory of Interorganizational Relations." In Mauer, ed., *Readings in Organizational Theory: Open System Approaches,* pp. 31–45.

Geismar, L.L. and Beverly Ayres. 1959. *Patterns of Change in Problem Families.* St. Paul, Minn.: Greater St. Paul Community Chest and Councils.

Gilbert, Neil and Harry Specht. 1977. *Planning for Social Welfare.* Englewood Cliffs, N.J.: Prentice Hall.

Gill, David G. 1974. "Institutions for Children." In Schorr, ed., *Children and Decent People,* pp. 53–88.

Grosser, Charles F. 1973. *New Directions in Community Organization: From Enabling to Advocacy.* New York: Praeger.

Hasenfeld, Yeheskel and Richard A. English, eds. 1975. *Human Service Organizations.* Ann Arbor, Mich.: University of Michigan Press.

Herman, Paul, ed. 1970 *Delinquency and Social Policy.* New York: Praeger.

Hibbard, Michael. 1981. "The Crisis in Social Policy Planning." *Social Service Review* (December), 55(4):557–67.

Howe, Elizabeth. 1978. "Legislative Outcomes in Human Services." *Social Service Review* (June), 52(2):173–88.

Hudson, Pete and Brad McKenzie. 1981. "Child Welfare and Native People: The Extension of Colonialism." *The Social Worker* (Summer), 49(2):63–66.

Johnson, Patrick. 1981. "Indigenous Children at Risk." *Policy Options* (November–December), 2:47–50.

Kadushin, Alfred. 1969. *Child Welfare Services.* New York: Macmillan.

Kahn, Alfred J. 1979. "Child Welfare." In *Encyclopedia of Social Work,* pp. 100–114. 17th ed. Washington, D.C.: NASW.

Katz, Daniel and Basil S. Georgopoulos. 1971. "Organizations in a Changing World." *Journal of Applied Behavioral Science* (May-June), 7(3):342–70.

Kenniston, Kenneth and the Carnegie Council on Children. 1977. *All Our Children.* New York: Harcourt Brace Jovanovich.

Kramer, Ralph M. and Harry Specht, eds. 1969. *Readings in Community Organization Practice.* Englewood Cliffs, N.J.: Prentice-Hall.

Lansburgh, Terese W. 1977. "Child Welfare: Day Care of Children." In *Encyclopedia of Social Work,* pp. 134–46. 17th ed. Washington, D.C.: NASW.

Lerman, Paul. 1970. *Community Treatment and Social Control: A Critical Analysis of Juvenile Correctional Policy.* Chicago: University of Chicago Press.

Litwak, Eugene and Lydia F. Hylton. 1962. "Interorganizational Interdependence, Intraorganizational Structure." *Administrative Science Quarterly* (March), 6:395–420. Reprinted in Hasenfeld and English, eds., *Human Services Organizations: A Book of Readings.*

Marsh, L. C. 1943. *Report on Social Security for Canada.* Ottawa: Edmund Cloutier Printer.

Mauer, John H., ed. 1971. *Readings in Organizational Theory: Open-System Approaches.* New York: Random House.

Mayer, Morris Fritz, Leon H. Richman, and Edwin A. Balcerzak. 1977. *Group Care of Children: Crossroads and Transitions.* New York: Child Welfare League of America.

Meezan, William, Stanford Katz, and Eva Monoff Russo. 1978. *Adoptions without Agencies: A Study of Independent Adoptions.* New York: Child Welfare League of America.

Murphy, Campbell G. 1954. *Community Organization Practice.* Boston: Houghton Mifflin.

Osborne, Richard N. and James G. Hunt. 1974. "Environment and Organizational Effectiveness." *Administrative Science Quarterly* (June), 19(2):231–46.

Parker, Jacqueline K. and Edward M. Carpenter. 1981. "Julia Lathrop and the Children's Bureau: The Emergence of an Institution." *Social Service Review* (March), 55(1):60–77.

Pfeffer, Jeffery. 1972c. "Size and Composition of Corporate Board of Directors: The Organization and Its Environment." *Administrative Science Quarterly* (June), 17(2):218–28.

Piper, Edward and John R. Warner, Jr. 1980–81. "Group Homes for Problem Youth: Retrospect and Prospects." *Child and Youth Services,* 3(3/4):1–11.

Platt, Anthony M. 1970. "The Rise of the Child-Saving Movement." In Herman, ed., *Delinquency and Social Policy,* pp. 15–20.

Powers, Edwin. 1970. "Crime and Punishment in Early Massachusetts, 1620–1692." In Herman, ed., *Delinquency and Social Policy,* pp. 8–12.

Pumphrey, Muriel W. and Ralph E. Pumphrey. 1973. "Private Charity in the Twentieth Century." *Current History* (July), 65(383): 29–32.

Rauch, Julia B. 1975. "Women in Social Work: Friendly Visitors in Philadelphia, 1880." *Social Service Review* (June), 49(2):241–59.

Reid, Joseph H. 1974a. "From the Executive Director." *Child Welfare League Newsletter* (Spring), 4(1):1.

_____. 1974b. "From the Executive Director." *Child Welfare League Newsletter* (Summer/Fall), 4(2):4.

Reid, William. 1964 "Interagency Coordination in Delinquency Prevention and Control." *Social Service Review* (December), 35:418–28.

Romig, Dennis A. 1978. *Justice for Our Children.* Lexington, Mass.: Lexington Books.

Rooke, Patricia T. and R. L. Schnell. 1981. "Child Welfare in English Canada, 1920–48." *Social Service Review* (September), 55(3):483–506.

Ross, Murray G. 1955. *Community Organization: Theory and Principles.* New York: Harper.

Rothman, David J. 1971. *The Discovery of the Asylum—Special Order and Disorder in the New Republic.* Boston: Little, Brown.

Ruderman, Florence A. 1968. *Child Care and Working Mothers: A Study of Arrangements for Daytime Care of Children.* New York: Child Welfare League of America.

Sanders, Douglas. 1975. "Family Law and Native People," p. 14. Unpublished background paper prepared for the Law Reform Commission of Canada.

Santiago, Letty. 1972. "From Settlement House to Antipoverty Program." *Social Work* (July), 17(4):73–78.

Schorr, Alvin L., ed. 1974. *Children and Decent People.* New York: Basic Books.

Sieder, Violet M. 1960. "The Citizen Volunteer in Historical Perspective." In Cohen, ed., *The Citizen Volunteer: His Responsibility, Role and Opportunity in Modern Society.* pp. 41–58.

Simon, Bill, Jr. 1973. "The Social Conditions of Indian Reserves in Eastern New Brunswick." Unpublished report prepared for the Union of New Brunswick Indians.

Siporin, Max. 1975, *Introduction to Social Work Practice.* New York: Macmillan.

Soiseth, Len. 1970. "A Community That Cares for Children." *Canadian Welfare* (May/June), 46(3):8–10.

Statistics Canada. 1976. *Social Security National Programs: A Review for the Period 1946 to 1975.* Ottawa: Statistics Canada.

Thompson, James D. and William J. McEwan. 1958, "Organizational Goals and Environment: Goal Setting and an Interaction Process." *American Sociological Review* (February), 23(1):23–36.

U.S. Department of Health and Human Services. 1982. *Quarterly Public Assistance Statistics: Jan.–Mar. 1981.* Washington, D.C.: U.S. GPO.

Wolins, Martin and Irving Piliavin. 1964. *Institutions or Foster Family: A Century of Debate.* New York: Child Welfare League of America.

Woodroofe, Kathleen. 1975. "The Irascible Reverend Henry Solly and His Contribution to Working Men's Clubs, Charity Organizations, and 'Industrial Villages' In Victorian England." *Social Service Review* (March), 49(1):15–32.

Young, Robert C. 1966. "Goals and Goal-Setting." *Journal of the American Institute of Planners* (March), 32(2):78–85.

Zald, Mayer N. 1963. Comparative Analysis and Measurement of Organizational Goals: The Case of Correctional Institutions for Delinquents." *Sociological Quarterly* (Summer), 4(3):206–30.

Zietz, Dorothy. 1969. *Child Welfare: Services and Perspectives.* New York: Wiley.

19.

Felix G. Rivera and John L. Erlich

## ORGANIZING WITH PEOPLE OF COLOR: A PERSPECTIVE*

*A new process of community organizing—one relying less on issue-based mobilization and more on community education, leadership development and support, and building sustainable local organizations—needs to be implemented.*
Bill Traynor, "Community Development and Community Organizing," *Shelterforce,* March–April 1993, p. 7.

### INTRODUCTION

Increasingly the anger, frustration, and pent up passions of poor people, especially poor people of color, have been directed at their own communities. Acts of many kinds of violence—from drive-by shootings to child abuse—have become such a commonplace occurrence that they generate little public reaction. The reasonable demands of neighborhood people for jobs, health care, education, decent housing, and

social services are lost in the strident distress of middle-class and lower-middle-class residents who see the quality of their lives eroding and their children's prospects declining.

Across the country, renewed efforts are underway to attack and reverse the effects of neglect, decay, and abandonment. But if the recent past is a reasonable predictor of the near future, these efforts will go largely undocumented and unrewarded.

Indeed, there is very little written material available to guide such efforts among people of color. Extensive treatments of community organizing with people of color do not seem to exist. Anecdotal and brief narrative descriptions are inadequate

---

*An earlier version of this article appeared as Chapter 1 in Felix Rivera and John L. Erlich (eds.), *Community Organizing A Diverse Society* (Boston: Allyn and Bacon, 1992).

to the task. The reasons for this deficiency are multiple, complex, and interwoven. Racism—political, economic, and social—is at the root of the problem.

At the same time, societal interest in the problems of the poor has sharply declined, especially in the 1980s. Despite all the research evidence to the contrary, the disenfranchised are again being forced to bear the major burden for their oppression. The problems of drug abuse, crime, inadequate housing, alcoholism, AIDS, teen pregnancy, and underemployment have had their most devastating impact on poor communities of color. The lack of resources to combat these problems falls most heavily on the same people. The growing national debt has served conservative forces well as an excuse for not meeting the urgent need to expand services in these areas.

As if these many problems and needs were not enough, the incredibly dramatic population increases are sobering testimony to the daunting challenges ahead for us all. Census Bureau preliminary reports show an increase in all populations of color. Out of a total of over 248 million people in the United States, almost 30 million are African American, representing 23 percent of the population and an increase of 64.6 percent over the 1980 Census figures. Native Americans, Eskimos, and Aleuts share .08 percent of the population with almost two million people, representing an increase of 33.7 percent from the last census. Asian and Pacific Islanders, over seven million strong, represent an increase of 144.9 percent from 1980, with their 2.9 percent representation; Latinos share 8.9 percent of the population with over 22 million people, an increase of 87.3 percent from the 1980 census.[7,8]

These figures are far from being fixed. A heated debate is going on about the problems of undercounting, especially in communities of color. The Census Oversight Committee claims that over two million African Americans have not been counted. They state that the undercount is between 5.5 percent and 6.5 percent, compared to an undercount of 5.2 percent in 1980. Other critics of the Census claim that the undercount is as high as nine million people. Whatever the final count will be, these statistics are a reminder of the enormous amount of work that needs to be done by agents of social work. The challenge is unparalleled in this nation's history.[2]

The government's pro-Contra and anti-Salvadorian rebel role in Central America, the invasion of Grenada and Panama, and the vast commitment to the Persian Gulf, however justified they may have been, have contributed to a decline in our commitment to racial equality. In a curious twist of logic, the withdrawal of support for communities of color at home is partly justified by resources demanded abroad because peoples of color cannot manage their own affairs.

Our priorities in foreign affairs, along with a realignment of domestic preferences, has sharply reduced not only support for community-based human services but the resources necessary to provide training for people to work in these services as well. One result is decreased interest in and demand for trailing in community organization and community development. In many cases, the rhetoric of working along multicultural lines has been a smoke screen to avoid funding programs for desperately underserved ethnic enclaves. All too many joint police and community antidrug efforts, for example, make good copy for the six o'clock news while deflecting public attention away from underlying problems of poverty and racism.

The fact that community organization has been the most resistant of the social work methods to consistent definition has further exacerbated this situation. As Erlich and Rivera have noted, community organization has evolved from being the general rubric under which all social work practice beyond the level of individual, family, and small group was subsumed—including grassroots organizing, community development, planning, administration, and policy-making—to being the smallest sub-segment of macro level practice (where it exists at all). This definitional difficulty is well-illustrated by one of the better contemporary definitions of community organization:

Community Development *refers to efforts to* mobilize people who are directly affected by a community condition (that is, the "victims," the unaffiliated, the unorganized, and the nonparticipating) into groups and organizations to enable them to take action on the social problems and issues that concern them. A typical feature of these efforts is the concern with building new organizations among people who have not been previously organized to take social action on a problem.[10,20]

However, by any definition, it was not until the 1960s that large numbers of schools of social work were willing to regard it as a legitimate concentration. Majors in community organization in graduate schools increased from 85 in 1960 to 1,125 in 1969, or from 1.5 percent to over 9 percent of full-time enrollments.[11]

By 1989, the number of students nationwide training to work as organizers had declined significantly. The Council on Social Work Education's most recent statistics demonstrate that there were 154 master's degree students (1.8%) in Community Organization and Planning, 417 (4.9%) in Administration and Management, and 101 (1.2%) in a combination of C.O. and Planning with Administration or Management. Given the fact that there are now many more schools of social work than in 1960, the trends do not augur well for community

organizing. Despite growing acceptance as a legitimate area of study in social work, urban planning, and labor studies, community organization and planning has been held hostage by the political and social vagaries of a society that has never accepted its strategies as tactics, especially if methods like public demonstrations and boycotts caused disruptive embarrassment to those in positions of political authority and power.[24]

From an educational standpoint, the result has been a diminished community organization curriculum—few field placement opportunities, few courses, and sparse literature. This is particularly surprising in light of the important, documented successes of community organization and development during the 1960s and early 1970s.[12]

Community organizing and community development by people of color have been virtually ignored. Isolated electives and rare articles in the professional journals have done little to fill this void. Work of a multicultural nature has received only slightly more attention. No book is available which addresses a broad range of the organizing efforts currently going forward in diverse minority communities. This…is a first effort to remedy that situation.

What is the status of community organization practice this…attempts to address? The civil rights gains of the 1960s in voting rights, public accommodations, and job opportunities, for example, were tempered by the belief that the African-American community had gone too far, that its gains were based on unacceptable levels of violence. Quickly forgotten by the white community was the continuing history of violence experienced by African Americans and other communities of color. "What more do they want?" was more than mere inflammatory rhetoric. These gains seemed to threaten white job security, community housing patterns, and long-cherished social interaction networks. The bitter residue of racism remains, and the resentment experienced throughout much of the United States has been part of the conservative backlash we are witnessing (as everything from Skinheads and antiminority high school violence to English-only public school curricula poignantly illustrates).

Similarly, efforts toward enfranchisement of new voters, changes in immigration laws, and women's and gay rights have also suffered from the schism between methods deemed acceptable and resulting "reasonable" benefits. As long as "someone else" did the social protesting, and as long as it was far enough away from their homes and places of work, most white people did not complain actively, or publicly resist slow, nondisruptive changes.

A concomitant shift has marked that reluctant acceptance of the "worthy" among each ethnic minority (largely dependent on whose economic interests are being threatened) while at the same time rejecting those without education, job skills, or at high risk for drug problems and sexually transmitted diseases.

Not surprisingly, with the emergence of reverse discrimination as a legitimate response to the enfranchisement of people of color, a new consciousness permeated schools of social work whose espoused philosophy was that of commitment to aiding poor and oppressed populations. It was no longer in fashion to invite a Black Panther as a speaker for a seminar on social action, or a Young Lord from New York's Puerto Rican community to discuss how they initiated the movement against lead poisoning in New York's slum tenements, or have Angela Davis address the systematic exclusion of women of color by the women's movement in key policy and strategy sessions. Instead, the invited ethnic "leaders" tended to focus on issues like creatively

funded drug education programs, multicultural day-care and pre-school efforts, and the demographics of rapidly expanding minority populations around the country.

As funding sources evaporated, people of color began being relegated to the not-so-symbolic back of the bus once again. The rapacity with which affirmative action was attacked became trendy. Ethnic studies programs were closed or cut back at alarming rates throughout the country and many community-based agencies in ethnic areas were forced to close their doors. The Supreme Court's chipping away at civil rights legislation seemed to be a culmination of much of the backlash being experienced.

## PEOPLE OF COLOR AND ORGANIZING: A TROUBLED ALLIANCE

Why has community organization not been more successful in working with people of color? What happened to some of the cross-cultural efforts that appeared to be so productive in the 1960s and early 1970s? Traditionally, much of the writing on community organization attempts to be color blind. Organizers work with specific strategies and tactics applied to different situations, but the methods that combine them rarely—if ever— change.[5,13]

Alinsky's mobilization model is a good case in point.[19] Too often the level of analysis of a community's problems has been determined by an organizing strategy that identifies a particular strata of people or social problem for intervention. By doing so, the racial and cultural uniqueness of the community is ignored. These organizers are not conservative or even liberal community organizers but well-intentioned, progressive thinkers who have been victimized by what may be termed "organizers' myopia" because of their single-minded organizing ideology or preordained methodology.[19]

One thing that becomes readily apparent...is the absence of an easily identified "radical" or "progressive" ideology along class lines. That does not mean [this piece] is apolitical; far from it. What it does point out, however, is the fact that issues surrounding race, culture, and their attendant problems are often more urgent concerns than social class that has often been historically conceptualized by white theoreticians apart from the dynamics deemed more critical to the self-determination of communities of color by communities of color. Middle-class Asians, Latinos, or African Americans are still viewed as minorities because of a most easily identifiable characteristic: skin color. Good clothes and an elegant briefcase are not much help when you need a cab in the middle of the night in Chicago or Washington, D.C.

People of color have traditionally been caught between the polarized struggles of conservative and liberal theoretical forces. Too many liberal community organizers have emphasized class issues at the expense of racism and cultural chauvinism, relegating them to "logical" extensions of the political and economic structure. Much of the neo-Marxist literature has treated race from a reductive, negative posture: "super-exploitation," and the "divide and conquer" strategies of individual capitalist employers. On the other hand, many conservative thinkers have emphasized a kind of uniqueness of each community which divides it from other communities of color, as well as separating those who can "make it" from those who cannot.[3,21,26]

These perspectives largely disregarded many questions, including the fact that racism existed long before monopoly capitalism was institutionalized. The logic fortunes of race relations are not necessarily coterminous with those of capitalism, as the persistence of racial antagonism in postcapitalist societies (like Sweden) demonstrates. The structural analysis that leads to a unified ideological interpretation of racism is thus deficient.

What too many organizers fail to consider is that there appears to be little or no history or contemporary evidence to substantiate that relations established and legitimated on the basis of race were or are identical to those established and legitimated on the basis of class. For example, the increasing violence against students of color on our college campuses cannot be explained primarily as a class phenomenon, especially when one recognizes that many of these students of color are economically similar to the white students attacking them. By continuing to look at racism as a mostly broad structural issue, organizers are underestimating the roles played by schools, churches, social welfare agencies, and other institutions in negatively influencing and changing race relations.

How might we best define the equality and liberation struggles being waged by the African-American communities? The Native-American communities? The Chinese-American and Vietnamese communities? The communities of women of color? The immediate reaction of most oppressors is based on skin color and other physical characteristics, language, culture, and lastly, class. The oversimplification of the struggles of people of color has led to unwarranted generalizations about their economic, social, political, and cultural behaviors and attitudes as groups.

Writers criticize the tendency of mainstream and radical theorists to divide society into separate domains culturally and structurally. They argue that this arbitrary bifurcation promotes tendencies toward essentialism (single-cause explanations) in contemporary thinking about race. Race and culture cannot be separated as "things in themselves."[25] They have to be linked to other social processes and dynamics operating in a society that continues oppressing communities because of skin tone. At least three dynamics—race, class, and gender—are significant in understanding oppression and the roles played by social welfare institutions in that process. None are reducible to the others, and class is not necessarily paramount.[25,18]

The phenomenological day-to-day realities of race, language, class, gender, and age help to shape ideological perspectives and give force to the hostilities with which one lives (as well as the strengths that make survival possible). The resulting process is difficult to analyze because it manifests itself differently from one community to another across the country, thereby making the task of organizing against these attacks that much more difficult a challenge. These realities do not lend themselves easily to simply categorizations by agents of social change or schools teaching community organization practice. The need for a more integrated and receptive social change paradigm in working with communities of color must be a main goal of organizers.

The conservative tradition in community organizing—especially within social work education—has also had an impact on the way organizers of color and their communities view the political implications of the social change efforts in which they have been involved. The conventional perspective that education should be ideologically value-free and politically nonpartisan has been especially evident in community organizing. Typical textbooks on organizing have avoided clear political and moral positions on issues.[9,27] These books were guided by a "professional" and largely mechanistic value base.

Fisher[11] notes:

The social work tradition views the community essentially as a social organism; it focuses on social issues such as building a sense of community, gather together social service organizations, or lobbying for and delivering social resources. It assumes that basically the community's problem is social disorganization. The organizer functions either as an "enabler" to help the community gather itself together or as an advocate to secure additional services for the community. The strategy is gradualist and consensual, which means that organizers assume a unity of interest between the power structure and the neighborhood and assume a willingness of at least some in power to meet community needs.

In contrast, Freire proposes:

...one cannot be a social worker and be like the educator who's a coldly neutral technician. To keep our options secret, to conceal them in the cobwebs of technique, or to disguise them by claiming neutrality does not constitute neutrality; quite the contrary, it helps maintain the status quo.[15]

Many professors of macro practice still resist the systematic inclusion of discussions on analyzing power and confrontational empowerment, the development of critical consciousness and racism as fundamental components of community organization. The lack of attention to critical consciousness—that is, how personal and political factors interact with each other and one's work, as well as how values, ideas, and practice skills are influenced by social forces and, in turn, influence them—is both particularly noteworthy and undermining. This neoconservative stance has had the net effect of leaving students of color (as well as white students) confused about their potential roles in their communities and how far they might go in fighting racism and social injustices.

While the rhetoric of self-determination implies that students are intended to be agents of social change, the reality clearly calls for modest improvements that do not seriously upset the status quo. The tools that might help lead to more fundamental change through a thorough questioning of what is happening and what it means to a community and a person working there are largely absent from the curriculum. Indeed, as a totality, the picture is not very promising.[14]

## A PARADIGM FOR ORGANIZING WITH PEOPLE OF COLOR

The different racial and cultural characteristics present in oppressed and disadvantaged communities represent an unprecedented challenge to organizers of the 1990s. We are defining culture as a collection of behaviors and beliefs that constitute "standards for deciding what is, standards for deciding what can be, standards for deciding how one feels about it, standards for deciding what to do about it, and standards for deciding how to go about doing it." A recent history of benign or belligerent neglect has required people of color to mobilize their skills and limited resources in creative ways that challenge prevailing community programs. Although they get little attention or help from mainstream society—indeed, in some areas, overt opposition is more typical— many of those communities are trying to tackle their problems with strategies unique to their situations.[17]

For example, the African-American community of West Oakland, California has attacked the drug problem head-on, with many community leaders making themselves visible enemies of major dealers. Also, nearby, an African-American first-grade teacher has promised to pay for the college education for her entire first-grade class if they maintain a "C" average and go on to college. The teacher annually saves $10,000 from her modest salary for this fund. In the rural mountains of Eastern Puerto Rico there is an exciting revitalization of the community through an energetic community development program. Southeast Asian communities in Boston, New York, Houston, and San Francisco have organized legal immigration and refugee task forces to help fight the arbitrary deportation of undocumented workers. Derelict neighborhoods in New York, Chicago, and Philadelphia are being revitalized through cooperatives and community development activities. Native-American tribes are attacking problems of alcoholism through indigenous healing rituals which utilize the sweat lodge ceremony as its core. Success rates are often dramatic. In the village of Akhiok, Alaska, 90 percent of its adults were chronically drunk. After Native treatments, at least 80 percent were able to sustain sobriety. The Latino community in Boston has a very successful grassroots health program called "Mujeres Latina en Action" which has successfully integrated Third World health models that include the concept of the extended family in health care delivery systems. A cultural- and gender-sensitive model of community organization is used to reach women in the barrios.

Traditionally, communities of color have not been involved in issues related to ecology and the protection of the environment. For many neighborhoods, these are among the last priorities when the many problems people face are listed. However, one example bears special attention, for it may well be a model for similar actions across the country. In California's East Los Angeles, which is predominantly Mexican American/Chicano, a group of Latina mothers was organized by a parish priest in the mid 1980s into militant urban ecologists. They call themselves Mothers of East Los Angeles. They have successfully mobilized against threats to their community, such as (1) the construction of a state prison in a residential area near neighborhood schools, (2) an above-ground oil pipeline that would have cut through their middle-to-low income barrio while avoiding much more affluent coastal towns, (3) the local use of dangerous and potentially polluting pesticides, and (4) local construction of a large incinerator. They believe in peaceful tactics and wear white kerchiefs as a symbol of their nonviolent philosophy. They are often seen pushing strollers during demonstrations, and they lobby the state capitol, engage in letter writing, and serve as pacesetters of a growing environmental movement in the Los Angeles area among people of color.

From the ethnic-sensitive practice perspective, organizing strategies in the Vietnamese or Laotian communities (and with different ethnic groups within these communities) cannot be the same as in the Puerto Rican, African-American, Native American or Japanese-American enclaves. The experience of one of the editors illustrates this point. In the early 1970s he was organizing a Mexican-American barrio. One of the outcomes of the struggle was the establishment of a storefront information and referral center. In furnishing and decorating the center, several political and cultural posters were displayed—much to the anger of the viejitos (elders) in the neighborhood. One particular poster featured Emiliano Zapata, and the staff was told in no uncertain terms that the poster had to come down because Zapata was still perceived as an enemy. Several fathers of the viejitos had fought against Zapata during the Mexican Revolution! Although the editor is a Latino, he is not of Mexican descent. However, he does know the conflicting loyalties of Mexico's revolutionary history and should have checked with the community to be sure none of the posters would be offensive. This apparently innocuous mistake set the organizing effort back many months and required

the staff to work doubly hard to regain the community's confidence.

Unfortunately, the history of organizing is replete with such examples. Certainly organizers of color must accept a share of the blame. However, the overwhelming majority of organizing writers and practitioners are white males, many of whom come from liberal or radical traditions, and who most often got their theoretical and practice feet wet in the social upheavals of the 1960s. Their apparent successes seemed destined to be color blind. From a community perspective, white radical groups were often more enamored of their political ideologies than they were committed to the needs of minority neighborhoods. The Detroit-based battles of African-Americans within the United Auto Workers is a prime example. Frequently hovering on the fringes were white radical groups looking to make the struggle their own. They were very critical of the efforts of people of color, accusing them of being culturally nationalistic and methodically not progressive enough. Too often we forget that experiencing racism, economic deprivation and social injustice are the key relevant politicizing forces in most urban areas. Indeed, it was this kind of elitist attitude that caused many minority organizers to shy away from predetermined ideological postures that seemed to define peoples *for* them. Even many liberal white groups seemed to disdain poor whites in favor of more visible organizing efforts in communities of color.

Thus, it is not sufficient to identify the three classic (and presumably "color blind") models of community practice—locality development, social planning, and social action—as being the foundation within which community organizing with people of color takes place. Factors that must be addressed are (1) the racial, ethnic, and cultural uniqueness of people of colors;

(2) the implications of these unique qualities in relation to such variables as the roles played by kinship patterns, social systems, power and leadership networks, religion, the role of language (especially among subgroups), and the economic and political configuration within each community; and (3) the process of empowerment and the development of critical consciousness. (This is in contrast to what Freire has called "naive consciousness," or a tendency to romanticize intense, satisfying past events and force the same experiences into the future without taking fully into account such multidimensional elements as those noted above.) In addition, the physical setting within which the community finds itself is an essential component for consideration as it plays a significant part in the way people view their situation. The need for a new, revised paradigm is clear and urgent.[22,15]

One of the most critical factors affecting organizing outcomes hinges on determining how strategies and tactics are played out based on the nature and intensity of contact and influence will help to determine the constraints placed on the organizers' (whether indigenous or an outsider) knowledge and identification with the community, and when and how technical skills may be brought into play. This "meta approach" will help organizers arrange their strategies and tactics within parameters that are goal, task, skill, and process specific. We suggest that the degree and nature of contacts is a three-tier process which—for the sake of simplicity—may be conceptualized as contact intensity and influence at the primary, secondary, and tertiary levels of community development (see Figure 19.1).

The primary level of involvement is most immediate and personal with the community. It is that level that requires racial, cultural, and linguistic identity. The primary level of contact intensity and influence is the most intimate level of community involvement where the only way of gaining entry into the community is to have full ethnic solidarity with the community. For example, this would not be possible for a Chinese American in a Vietnamese or African-American area.

The secondary level consists of contact and influence that is one step removed from personal identification with the community and its problems. Language—although a benefit and help—is not absolutely mandatory. Many of the functions are those of liaison with the outside community and institutions, and service as a resource with technical expertise based on the culturally unique situations experienced by the community. Examples of persons able to work at this level include a Puerto Rican in a Mexican American neighborhood or a person identified as Haitian in an African-American area.

The tertiary level is that of the outsider working for the common interests and concerns of the community. Cultural or racial similarity is not a requirement. The responsibilities of these organizers will see them involved primarily with the outside infrastructures as an advocate and broker for communities of color. However, their tasks are less that of liaison and more of a helpful technician approaching or confronting outside systems and structures. Clearly, whites and nonsimilar people of color may be particularly effective at this level.

The issue over whether or not organizers should be part of the racial and cultural group with whom they work has been given much attention within and outside communities of color. Alinsky and his Industrial Area Foundation organizers were often in the middle of this question. However, a careful review of these efforts suggests that

FIGURE 19.1
Organizer's Contact Intensity and Influence

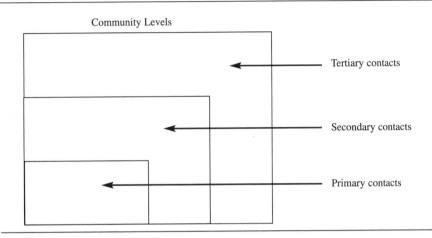

Community Levels

Tertiary contacts

Secondary contacts

Primary contacts

in most cases, indigenous organizers played key roles in the success of their organizations. Thus, it seems imperative that if communities of color are going to empower themselves by giving more than symbolic recognition to the ideal of self-determination and community control, then we must search hard for the successful roles played by people within their own communities and the lessons they can teach outside organizers. Furthermore, many emerging communities of color are underrepresented in the society's infrastructure because their languages and customs make them especially difficult to approach. In the emerging Southeast Asian communities, there are nationalities, ethnic and subethnic groups whose cultures are quite different from one another and where there exists an assortment of languages, dialects, and idioms. An outside organizer simply does not stand a chance of gaining rapid access to such unique and insular community groups. Even the Native American nations, it should be remembered, speak over 200 different languages. Clearly, special care must be taken in recruiting people to work in widely varied Indian communities—on reservations and rancherias, in both rural and urban areas.[6,10,12,19]

The knowledge necessary to understand and appreciate customs and traditions in all communities is an incredible challenge. Organizing and social strategies are complex and stress-inducing enough without further exacerbating the community's problems by having organizers who have very limited (or no) awareness of the customs, traditions, and languages of these communities. That is not to say that persons without some of this knowledge cannot fulfill certain important functions; for indeed, they have served and should continue to serve effectively in secondary and tertiary roles. But we must emphasize that the most successful organizers are those individuals who know their culture intimately: its subtleties of language, mores, and folkways. A white outsider, however sensitive and knowledgeable, simply cannot appreciate all that needs to be considered about a fundamentally different nonwhite culture or subculture. Some newly emerging communities are so well defended that there would be little chance for an outsider to gain meaningful admission to them, not to mention becoming a successful organizer. However, it must be very clear that cultural and racial similarity—by themselves—are no guarantor of organizer effectiveness or community acceptance. Indeed, an arrogant, know-it-all insider may be viewed with more suspicion than a similarly styled outsider.[16]

Despite these difficulties, there are common practice elements that may be identified as prerequisite to successful organizing. These principles are not exhaustive, but if organizers take command of these elements, they can increase the likelihood of being effective change agents in their communities. Knowing when and how to mix and phase these strategies and skill areas is critical to the successful outcome of a struggle. Organizing has to be conceptualized as a process that is educational both for the community and the organizers.

**Organizer's Profile**

What follows is a summary of those qualities—knowledge, skill, attributes, and values—that are most important in contributing to the success of organizers. It is recognized that the list is an idealized one in the sense that those few who have already fully attained the lofty heights described can probably also walk on water. Realistically, it is a set of goals to be used by organizers and communities together to help achieve desired changes. The careful reader will also note that many of these qualities are addressed by each contributor in describing a particular community...

1. Similar cultural and racial identification. The most successful organizers are those activists who can identify with their communities culturally, racially, and linguistically. There is no stronger identification with a community than truly being a part of it.

2. Familiarity with customs and traditions, social networks, and values. This dimension of organizing stresses the importance of having a thorough grounding in the customs and traditions of the community being organized. This is especially critical for those people who have cultural, racial, and linguistic identification, but who, for a variety of reasons, have been away from that community and are returning as organizers.

For example, how have the dynamics between organized religion and the community changed throughout the years? Ignored, its effect may imperil a whole organizing effort. Both the definition of the problems and the setting of goals to address them are involved. A number of Latino mental health and advocacy programs regularly consult with priests, ministers, and folk healers about the roles they all play (or might play) in advocating for mental health needs. These mental health activities are very clear about the importance of these other systems—formal and informal—in the community's spiritual life. The superstitions and religious archetypes are addressed by a variety of representatives, thereby making the advocacy work that much more relevant and effective. The Native American nations give deference to their medicine man, with no actions being taken until he has given approval. Similarly, the Vietnamese, Cambodian, and Laotian communities have strong religious leaders who help to define community commitments and directions.

All too often, there exists a cultural gap, as typified by younger, formally educated organizers working with community elders. The elders may be too conservative for the young organizers, or they disagree about tactics. Knowledge of and appreciation for the culture and traditions will help close the gap among key actors, or at least reduce the likelihood of unnecessary antagonisms.

3. An intimate knowledge of language and subgroup slang. We separate this dimension from the one just mentioned to emphasize its importance. Knowledge of a group's language style is indispensable when working with communities that are bi- or monolingual. Many embarrassing situations have arisen because of the organizer's ignorance of a community's language style. Approved idiomatic expressions in one area of the community may be totally unacceptable in another. Some expressions have sexual overtones in one community while being inoffensive to other communities. Certain expressions may denote a class bias which may be offensive to one group of people or another. The literature on sociolinguistics has done an excellent job in alerting us to the importance of language subtleties and nuances. For a discussion on the role played by the same language in culturally different populations see Harrison.[18]

4. Leadership styles and development. Organizers must be leaders and lead organizers, but they must also work with existing community leaders and help in training emerging leadership. We recognize that there are significant differences in leadership styles from one community of color to another.... Indispensable to the composition of a successful leader is the individual's personality, how the individual's roles fit within the organizing task, and how personal values help to shape a world view. However achieved, a leader should have a sense of power that may be used in a respectful manner within the community.

5. An analytical framework for political and economic analysis. This is one dimension where the understanding of the dynamics of oppression through class analysis is paramount. A sophisticated knowledge of political systems with access and leverage points is very important. It must include an appraisal of who has authority within the ethnic community as well as who in it has power (often less formally acknowledged). The sources of mediating influence between the ethnic community and wider communities also must be understood. This knowledge fulfills two needs: (1) it helps to give the organizer the necessary analytical perspective in judging where the community fits in the hierarchy of economic analysis, and (2) it serves as a tool for educating the community, thereby increasing the community's consciousness of the roles and functions of the organizer within broader economic and social systems.[23]

6. Knowledge of past organizing strategies, their strengths, and limitations. It is imperative that organizers learn how to structure their organizing activities within an historical framework. This framework helps them to look at those strategies and tactics that have succeeded and failed in each community in the past. Since so little knowledge-building is evident in the field, it is critical that organizers develop and share an historical knowledge base that helps identify the many mistakes made to finally illuminate those techniques that appeared to have recently worked best in similar situations.

7. Skills in conscientization and empowerment. A major task of the organizer in disenfranchised communities is that of empowering people through the process of developing critical consciousness. How the personal and political influence each other, and the local environment in which they are played out, is a key to this process. It is not enough to succeed in ameliorating or even solving community problems if there is little or no empowerment of the community.

At the same time, power must be understood as both a tool and part of a process by

FIGURE 19.2
Development of Critical Consciousness

Conscientization

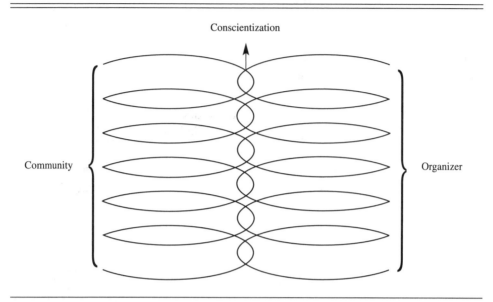

Community

Organizer

the organizer. As Rubin and Rubin write "...community organizations need not focus exclusively on campaigns to achieve specific goals; they can make building their own power a long-term effort." Power may be destructive or productive in the sense of germinating ideas and concerns, and being integrative, or community-building. Of course, power is typically experienced in poor communities as both a negative and positive. The kind of power which is based on threats is often the most common in disenfranchised areas. When Organizer A makes the Target B act in ways it does not wish to act solely because of the sanctions A can levy against B, typically this becomes an imposed "win-lose" situation. A limited special hiring program usually takes this form.[23]

Power may also be a form of exchange, when Organizer A and Target B involve themselves in a reciprocal relationship or exchange because both parties have something to win from the process. Exchange is

an integrative component of power because it involves some degree of trust, where the final outcome may be "win-win." Coalition building often takes this form. Power may also be defined as love—love for community, lifestyle, or family—which should motivate an organizer and the community.

Organizers and communities need to view each other as subjects rather than objects, as learners, and as equals. No organizer should enter a community with a sense that she or he has "the" answers for it. The development of critical consciousness through the process of conscientization may be visualized as a double spiraling helix, where both the organizer and community learn from each other the problems at hand and the strategies and tactics employed (Figure 19.2).[4]

The phenomenology of the experience is based on praxis, the melding of theory and experience, for both parties which in turn makes them stronger actors because their learning is mutual, supportive, and liberating of any preconceived notions one had about the other.

8. Skills in assessing community psychology. Organizers need to learn about the psychological makeup of their communities—free from stereotypes. Scant attention has been paid to this knowledge area by most community organizers. Methodologies without the understanding of the motivations of the communities are a risky undertaking.

Organizers also need to understand what tends to keep a community allied and synergized. What is the life cycle of the community? Is it growing, mature, or declining? Are there new arrivals? Have they been in the community for generations? Does their language work as a cohesive force, or because of the multigenerational patterns, serve as a problem in getting people together? If the community has experienced a failure recently (like the loss of a valued school), what has it done to the shared psychological identification of the community? Does it feel frustrated and powerless? Or has it served to focus anger? If the latter is the case, what strategies may be employed to mobilize the community to action?

9. Knowledge of organizational behavior and decision making. Knowledge about organizational behavior and decision making are critical to the success of an organizer. The work of Bachrach and Baratz around decisionless decisions and nondecisions as decisions has demonstrated its worth in the field. Decisionless decisions are those decision-making strategies that "just happen" and "take off on a life of their own." Nondecisions as decisions are defined as:

...a means by which demands for change in the existing allocation of benefits and privileges in the community can be suffocated before they are even voiced or kept covert; or killed before they gain access to the relevant decision-making

arena; or, fail all these things, maimed or destroyed in decisionimplementing stage of the policy process.[1]

An awareness of these dynamics is necessary both to be able to ascertain strategies being employed by the institutions targeted for change, but also, as a tactic that may also be employed by the community in its organizing.

10. Skills in evaluative and participatory research. One of the reasons communities of color have lost some of their political, economic, and legal victories is the increasing vacuum created by the lack of supportive information that has kept up with growing social problems experienced by most communities. Many communities are being victimized by data and demographics that have redefined their situations in manageable terms as far as the traditional systems are concerned. There needs to be an expanded role for organizers to include developing skills in demographic and population projections, and in social problem analysis. More organizers should develop theories about the declining social, economic, and political base of communities of color, and how people are still managing to survive in times of open hostility and encroachment on their civil rights and liberties. Crime, including drugs, is a major arena for these pressures.

Research continues to be an indispensable and very powerful tool for social change. Organizers should pay special attention to the use of participatory approaches, where both researchers and community people are involved as equal participants in securing knowledge to empower the community.*

---

*For example, an entire issue of the *Community Development Journal* was devoted to participatory research and evaluation, thus stressing its international importance in working with disenfranchised and oppressed communities (1988).

Skill in evaluation research is another indispensable tool for organizers. The editors are not just suggesting that evaluative research be used only to assess program outcomes, but more to analyze the success and value of different organizing strategies and their relevance in disparate situations.

11. Skills in program planning and development and administration management. One of the bitter lessons learned from the War on Poverty had to do with the setup for failure nature of the administrative jobs offered to many people of color. Most had little or no administrative or managerial experience. One of the editors, then little-experienced, was offered a position that required him to administer a four-county migrant education and employment training program. With crash courses on organizational behavior, information processing, and budgeting, the challenge was met, but there were many mistakes along the way. Needless to say, the mistakes were widely reported by the program's detractors and administrator's enemies.

Many administrators of color have fallen by the wayside because they had not been given the opportunity to sharpen their managerial skills, and thus, a self-fulfilling prophecy of incompetence was validated in the eyes of people who desired to see these programs fail. Organizers must be aggressive in seeking out this knowledge base and not be deterred by the institutional barriers—financial, political, or otherwise—to attaining it.

12. An awareness of self and personal strengths and limitations. Reading through the list above may raise the question, "Does such a superorganizer possessing all the enumerated skills and knowledge exist?" The answer is both yes and no.

There are people throughout the country with these skills, and many who have most of them. We ask that organizers of color

know their limitations and struggle to improve themselves. Organizers must know when to seek help, when to share responsibilities, and when to step aside to let others take over. Conversely, skilled and knowledgeable organizers must be open to sharing their expertise with communities and community leaders, especially when such sharing may mean their departure can be that much sooner.

A successful organizer is that individual who gains respect within the context of the actions being taken, not the individual who is (or appears to be) more knowledgeable than another. Honest intentions and abilities are worth more than degrees. Organizers also need to understand how to react to stresses. We all have our ways of coping with conflict. We need to know when our coping is no longer working for us, thereby jeopardizing the community. The danger of burnout is too well-documented to be ignored.

Finally, we would like to caution against "doing it for the community." Not only is this counter-productive, but also it increases the risk of feeling that one is being eaten alive by the people with whom one is working. All too often this results in another abandonment of a community whose experiences with social services have been much more of good rhetoric than serious social change.

## ENDNOTES

1. P. Bachrach and M.S. Baratz, *Power and Poverty: Theory and Practice* (New York: Oxford University Press, 1970), 42.

2. Felicity Barringer, "Two Million Blacks Not Counted Head of Census Panel Asserts," *New York Times,* March 12, 1991, p. A5–A6.

3. R. Blauner, *Racial Oppression in America* (New York: Harper & Row, 1972), 29–42.

4. Kenneth Boulding, *Three Faces of Power* (Beverly Hills: Sage Pubs., 1989), 25.

5. H. Boyte, *The Backyard Revolution: Understanding the New Citizen Movement* (Philadelphia: Temple, 1980).

6. S. Burghardt, *The Other Side of Organizing* (Cambridge, MA: Schenkman, 1982).

7. Census Bureau Press Release CB91–100, in *Census and You*. April, 1991, 3.

8. "Census Shows Profound Change in Racial Makeup of the Nation," by Felicity Barringer, *New York Times*, March 11th, 1991, A6–A9.

9. A. Dunham, *The New Community Organization* (New York: Crowell, 1970).

10. John L. Erlich and Felix G. Rivera, "Community Organization and Community Development," in N. Gilbert and H. Specht, *Handbook of the Social Services* (Englewood Cliffs, NJ: Prentice Hall, 1981), 472–489.

11. R. Fisher, "Community Organization in Historical Perspective: A Typology," *The Huston Review* (Summer 1984), 8.

12. R. Fisher, *Let the People Decide: Neighborhood Organizing in America* (Boston: Twayne, 1984).

13. G. Frederickson, *Neighborhood Control in the 1970s* (New York: Chandler, 1970).

14. P. Freire, *Education for Critical Consciousness* (New York: Seabury, 1973).

15. Paulo Freire, *The Politics of Education: Culture, Power and Liberation* (Granby, MA: Bergin & Garvey, Pubs., Inc., 1985), 29.

16. J. Gibbs, L. Huang and Associates, *Children of Color:* (San Francisco, CA: Jossey-Bass, 1989).

17. W. Goodenough, *Culture, Language, and Society* (Reading, MA: Addison-Wesley, 1971), 21–22.

18. Lawrence E. Harrison, "Underdevelopment Is a State of Mind." Cambridge: *Harvard Educational Review* (August 1988). Special Issue, "Race and Racism in American Education."

19. Sanford Horwitt, *Let Them Call Me Rebel: Saul Alinsky–His Life and Legacy* (New York: Knopf, 1989).

20. R. Kramer and H. Specht, *Readings in Community Organization Practice,* 3rd ed. (Englewood Cliffs, NJ: Prentice Hall, 1983), 15–16.

21. J. Roemer, Divide and Conquer: "Microfoundations of Marxian Theory of Wage Discrimination," *Bell Journal of Economics,* 10 (Fall, 1979), 695–705.

22. J. Rothman and J. Tropman, Models of Community Organization and Macro Practice, in F. Cox et al. (eds.), *Strategies of Community Organization,* 4th ed. (Itasca, IL: Peacock, 1987), 3–26.

23. H.J. Rubin and I. Rubin, *Community Organizing and Development* (Columbus, OH: Merrill, 1986), 234.

24. E. Spaulding, *Statistics on Social Work Education in the United States: 1989* (Alexandria, VA: Council on Social Work Education, 1990), 6.

25. E.P. Thompson, *The Making of the English Working Class* (New York: Vintage Books, 1966).

26. W. Trattner, *From Poor Law to Welfare States,* 3rd ed. (New York: Free Press, 1984).

27. R. Warren and D. Warren, *Neighborhood Organizer's Handbook* (Notre Dame, IN: Notre Dame Press, 1977).

28. Marc A. Zimmerman and Julian Rappaport, "Citizen Participation, Perceived Control, and Psychological Empowerment." *American Journal of Community Psychology* (16, 5, 1988), 725–750.

# PART FIVE
# EVALUATION AND CHANGE

# Introduction

Evaluation is perhaps that area where community practice has been most neglectful. The human services enterprise is not alone here, to be sure, and doubtless there are many reasons for our avoidance of evaluation. One, of course, is the difficulty of getting measures on some of the interventions that we seek to create. Secondly, there is every reason to believe that a considerable number of those measures don't make any difference, and the fact that negative evaluations make people feel bad often causes, or at least contributes to, avoidance. Furthermore, the fact that clients and client systems *are* our clients tends to diminish in the eyes of some the value of their feedback. Still in all, clients are customers, and we must attend to the views of those we serve more closely. Usually customers and clients will tell us if we are helping them or not, and it is important to ask.

How does one approach the whole matter of evaluation and change? There are four critical steps that should be kept in mind in designing a system of program development: monitoring, oversight, assessment, and appraisal. These four components are the necessary legs for a system of program evaluation and change; without each of them it is very difficult to be accurate, because it will turn out that key parts needed to complete the evaluation are missing.

The first step of the evaluations and change is monitoring. Monitoring is simply the data-keeping or record-keeping aspect of the program evaluation system. Without basing data on who comes to the service, how many, how often, and the like, it is very difficult to build toward the final overall appraisal. In a classroom situation, this stage would be analogous to the keeping of attendance records: A simple check whether a student was present or not provides the first step. Many organizations in the human service field (outside the human service field, too, for that matter) do not know the basic demographics of their programs and services. There is always considerable "lore" about who has been using the services, how these uses have changed, and whether anyone is being helped, and so on, but when pressed for the actual numbers, executives and program managers step away. The foundation of any system of program evaluation, then, is a basic set of numbers that outline the patterns of use.

The second step in program evaluation and change is oversight. This phase builds from phase number one, monitoring, but it is different in that it applies standards and expectations to the numbers as it looks for gaps, problems, and difficulties. Some investigations and comparisons allow for early midcourse corrections. In a classroom situation, oversight could occur when a professor applies the two-time absence rule. Thus, Jim, who is absent for three times, is invited in to discuss the issue. Alternatively a simple "pop quiz" allows the prof to have some sense of where the student is with respect to the course material. In an agency setting, an example would be the proportion of those clients who are staying longer than the twelve visits provided by policy. Oversight—which means "look over" rather than "overlook"—should be frequent, and not terribly fateful with respect to the "evaluatee"; it is that process of constant checking and comparing that allows for the correction to be made before problems in an agency or program become. too severe.

The third step of the evaluation and change system is assessment. Assessment is potentially more fateful than oversight and involves the much more occasional review and judgment about a particular person's or organization's performance. In a classroom setting, an example would be the midterm or final exam. These are more fateful, but do not totally determine. Exams allow a fair amount of information to be put together and provide an opportunity to see whether this information can indeed be pulled together by the student in question. In a business setting, a number of criteria might be applied during an assessment process, such as the quality of the product, the price of the product, the efficiency of the program, and so on. Intercomponent ratings and judgments are made at this time. In an agency, an assessment may take into account the facts that a particular program is very popular and that people do seem to be helped by the particular mode of counseling given there, but assessment is extremely expensive and only a few people are being helped at any given time. It is important to understand in the assessment process that judgments are made about the relative weights and values of these different criteria. It is also important to understand that assessments are built on monitoring and oversight.

The fourth step in the system of program evaluation and change is appraisal. Appraisal represents a final, fateful judgment on a "go" or "no go," continue or not continue, fire or retain basis, concerning that which is being evaluated. In a school setting it is analogous to the final grade—all information from the other three steps is taken into account, but finally, a judgment is made. In real estate, where the term "appraisal" has common usage, a broker will look at a house offered for sale. The broker will inspect the physical property and also records of the past sale of the house, as well as of other houses in the area, will relate those factors to the current market, and will come up with a "market value," which can then be used in setting the asking price for the house. The word appraisal, as used there, contains the twin elements of factual research and judgment; each of these elements is important. In the case of the classroom, the professor may use the final and midterm grades, any quiz grades, attendance records, and other aspects of judgment (did the student try very hard or was the student apparently lackluster?) in deciding how the grade will finally be assigned.

In program evaluation it is important to stress the systemic and step-wise nature of the approach. All too often "program evaluators" are brought into a program that is in progress and are asked to employ criteria that were never part of the original "deal" anyway. This approach naturally is troubling to those being evaluated, who rightly feel that the evaluators do not understand the complexities and difficulties that the program faced. Thus, it is absolutely imperative that program evaluation as well as personnel evaluation be an ongoing and continuous part of the activities of the agency, not an episodic, occasional element.

These four steps—monitoring, oversight, assessment, and appraisal—move evaluation to a central role in the cycle of community intervention. Evaluation, of course, as the introduction stresses is both the last and the first element in the cycle of community intervention and change. The purpose of evaluation, while retrospective in mechanism, is fundamentally forward. Evaluation's basic purpose is to make the future better, by feeding information into the assessment phase that allows for more refined diagnoses. Evaluation is both "feed-back" to participants, and "feed-forward" to the new cycle of community practitioner intervention.

This cycle is also the cycle of change. If evaluation does not help us to change, then its fundamental purpose—the feed-forward purpose—is compromised. The three problems that community practice addresses—cohesion, capability, and competence—each suggest the need for change.

The articles in this section pick up on various aspects of these concerns. Robert Washington's piece on alternative frameworks, provides different ways in which one may approach the evaluation process. William Birdsall's and Roger Manela's "The Nitty Gritty of Program Evaluation" provides some key technical tips and hints. It was prepared especially for this series, and it aims at informing the practitioner about the very basic things that are helpful in evaluating a program. Eleanor Chelimsky's piece, "The Politics of Program Evaluation," deals with one of the key aspects, the "political" or "emotional" component of program evaluation. While written some years ago, it still has an up-to-the-minute flavor, and Chelimsky places these issues in a contemporary context.

Research is an important mechanism through which evaluation occurs. In some sense, all research is a kind of "evaluation"—sometimes of programs, other times of hypotheses. Some of the tension that exists between "researchers" and "community practitioners" arises from their different approaches to methodology. Bruce Thyer looks at community practice research through the lens of single-case design, something that is exactly what community practitioners have to offer.

Another important element in evaluation is the presentation of data to various groups. As basic as such skills are, community practitioners often are less skillful than they need to be in matters of sharing quantitative information. And of course there are issues in how to use the data one does have. Douglass's piece, "How to use and Present Community Data,"addresses these issues.

One of the troubling elements to community practitioners is "statistics." Tables have measures that may not be well understood, by the practitioner and by the audience. Nothing substitutes for a course in quantitative analysis, but for a quick reference to terms and their meanings, the "Troubleshooting Guide" by Gottman and Clasen will serve admirably.

Time and time again, community practitioners ask questions about how to measure practitioners' time. Part of this question is a professional issue—how much time does the professional community practitioner judge is needed for a particular intervention? Part of the issue is organizational—how much time does the agency have available for the project? Using the professional unit method of analysis (PUMA), practitioners and bosses alike can estimate the needed time; if they cannot agree, they can at least negotiate the differences. This negotiation is aided by the Index of Dissimilarity, which provides a numerical value expressing the degree of difference that exists between two sets of allocations—whether these allocations be ideal versus real, boss versus employee, agency goals versus agency budget, or whatever. Understanding the location and magnitude of difference is a key element in beginning the change process.

Barry Checkoway addresses community change in his piece, "Core Concepts for Community Change." Checkoway not only provides an overview of selected core concepts but also challenges the reader to develop her or his own set of such concepts as an integral part of community work.

Over and over again, organizational issues and problems are at the center of resistance to change. So important are agency (organizational) issues that Part Six, coming right up, deals in depth with them. However, organizational change, as a specific form of change-in-general, can go here. We have put the article by Myers, Ufford, and Magill toward the end in this section so that it can form a kind of segue to the section on organizations themselves, their issues, and management. On-site analysis was originally developed by executives from United Way organizations in Canada—Bob Myers and Gerry McCarthy. Both of them worked as executives at the United Way of Windsor, where I came to know them because the University of Michigan School of Social Work had field placements there. I mention this background because it is important to emphasize that on-site analysis was developed by community practitioners for community practitioners. It is an outstanding process for developing organizational change.

Finally, there is the World Wide Web. The Internet has becomes a key tool for change (through information and connection) and a key force for change. Community practitioners need to exploit this resource for their own work and for community analysis, development, action and for community members as well. Nartz and Schoech use a Delphi Technique (itself a useful community practice technique) to explore many uses of the Web for community practice purposes.

—John E. Tropman

## 20.

## Robert O. Washington

## ALTERNATIVE FRAMEWORKS FOR
## PROGRAM EVALUATION

Evaluation designs are always confronted with methodological issues which call attention to the debate around the question of rigor versus relevance. On the one hand, the evaluation must be rigorous enough to stand the test of replicability and deal with the problem of attribution and rival hypotheses; on the other, it must be adaptable enough to yield decision-relevant data. The complex task of the evaluator is to strike the delicate balance between this dichotomy; this is not an easy task. Williams and Evans (1969) observed.

We have never seen a field evaluation of a social-action program that could not be faulted legitimately by good methodologists, and we may never see one. But, if we are willing to accept real-world imperfections, and to use evaluative analysis with prudence, then such analysis can provide a far better basis for decision making than we have had in the past.

If program evaluation is to inform policy formulation and program development then the minimum requisite of any efficient design is that it (1) measure change, i.e., demonstrate effect; (2) include procedures which rule out rival hypotheses which might alternatively explain the noted effect; and (3) describe how and why the change took place. On the other hand, there are factors over which the evaluator has no control which may affect a good evaluation. For example, almost all program evaluations in

the human services are conducted in a political arena. The evaluator must therefore understand how political demands for certain types of evaluative data, or how efforts to protect programs performing below standards, may influence our choice of certain evaluation designs. Moreover, the political ethos that affects the decision environment in which evaluation takes place may also require the use of analytical and statistical procedures that attempt to correct defects resulting from the use of certain designs which are less rigorous than others, although they may be the most feasible design, given the nature of the decision environment.

Since the "politics" of evaluation is a reality with which the evaluator is constantly confronted, he needs to know what his options are with respect to designs and the analytical framework which informs such designs (Washington, 1987).

There are at least four conceptual models which are generally accepted as analytical frameworks from which to select an evaluation design.

The term "conceptual model" is used here to refer to an explanatory frame of reference within which certain social and behavioral science concepts are used as tools for circumscribing evaluative behavior. This explanatory system offers the evaluator a way of thinking which defines the means to be employed as well as the ends to be served in evaluative research. The term also suggests that there are precisely

Robert O. Washington is a professor at the Graduate School, University of New Orleans.

formulated concepts drawn from business, public administration and the social sciences which provide us with clues as to what it is about human service delivery systems that should be studied and evaluated. In other words, a conceptual model provides us with a "change" or "intervention" theory which forms the analytical framework within which the evaluation will be conducted.

Since outcomes from most services imply directed social change, it is useful to have a "change" or "intervention" theory. Such a theory tends to identify what constitutes the desired change to be measured as well as to provide clues as to how the change should be measured. Usually, the change or intervention theory developed by the evaluator will be couched in a particular discipline. For example, some evaluators use organizational theory as their analytical framework. Organizational theory uses the rigorous methods of economic analysis, but also incorporates findings of behavioral science research. Using organizational theory then, the evaluator is likely to conceive a human service program as a complex social system. This framework, for example, provides the foundation for the systems model evaluation.

## THE SYSTEMS MODEL

The systems model of evaluation is based upon efficiency and relates to questions of resource allocations to produce certain outputs.

The systems model assumes that human services organizations are essentially open systems in that (1) they exist in a highly interdependent relationship of exchange with their environment—a relationship that includes the utilization of a wide variety of inputs, (2) they have the ability to make

improvements in service provision; and (3) they have the capability of modifying or changing provisions in order to adapt to client needs or demands. Although the systems model presumes an identifiable flow of interrelated events moving toward some goal, it assumes that certain resources must be devoted to essential nongoal activities as maintenance and preservation of the system. From this viewpoint, the central question in an evaluation of the effectiveness of an intervention should be: How close does the organization's allocation of resources approach an optimum distribution? Etzioni (1970), a central proponent of this model, suggests that what really is important is whether there exists a balanced distribution of resources among all organizational needs rather than the maximal satisfaction of any single organizational requirement.

The systems model of evaluation assumes that the evaluator must answer at least four questions: (1) how effective is the coordination of organizational subunits? (2) how adequate are the resources? (3) how adaptive is the organization to environment and internal demands? and (4) were the goals and subgoals met?

While the measurement of general organizational goals is central to the systems model, proponents of the systems model tend to minimize the need to measure how well a specific organizational goal is achieved. They contend that such a strategy is unproductive and often misleading since an organization constantly functions at a variety of levels with a variety of goals which are sometimes conflicting. Moreover, they contend, overattention to a specific goal will lead to underconcern for other programmatic functions. Systems protagonists also contend that allocating excessive resources (resulting in waste duplication and inefficiency) to achieve a particular goal is just as detrimental to system "steady state" as withholding such resources.

The systems model of evaluation tends to be more productive in decision making among organizations which employ program budgeting. The general idea of program budgeting is that budgetary decisions should be made by focusing upon overall goals. In other words, program budgeting is a goal-oriented program structure which presents data on all of the operations and activities of the program in categories which reflect the program's goals. Inputs, such as personnel, equipment, and maintenance, are considered only in relationship to program outcomes. Program budgeting, then, lays heavy emphasis upon relating costs to accomplishing the overall goal.

Program budgeting has two essential characteristics: (1) the budget is organized by programs rather than by objects of expenditure, and (2) the program shows not only current needs but also future needs for resources, as well as the financial implications of the programmed outputs.

From the perspective of the evaluator, program budgeting contains two important pieces of information. First is the organizational goals and objectives. The second is a statement of the financial resources required to achieve the goals and objectives.

Drawing from program budgeting procedures, the two most frequently used evaluation strategies employed in the systems model are cost-effectiveness analysis and cost-benefit analysis.

## Cost-Effectiveness Analysis

There are many and varied reasons why it may be of limited value to apply cost-benefit techniques to a particular human services program. However, such a program may be effectively evaluated with a slightly modified version of cost-benefit analysis known as cost-effectiveness analysis. Unlike cost-benefit analysis, which attempts to quantify benefits of a program in money terms, cost-effectiveness analysis utilizes output variables in nonmonetary forms to serve as indices for benefits of specific programs. The output variables are specified by various goals of a specific program, such as number of persons trained in a given skill, employment, or level of proficiency on a standardized test.

## Cost-Benefit Analysis

Cost-benefit analysis involves the use of economic theories and concepts. It is designed to tell us why a program or one of its components works in addition to how well it works. The concept of "cost-benefit" defines the relationship between the resources required (the cost) to attain certain goals and the benefits derived. One of its basic premises is that many decisions involving the location of limited resources are often made on the basis of how those resources can be most optimally used, avoiding waste, duplication, and inefficiency. Cost-benefit analysis is a tool for decision makers who need to make choices among viable competing programs designed to achieve certain goals. It is not designed to favor the "cheapest" nor the "costliest" program, but rather the optimal program in terms of the available resources and the explicit goals. Usually costs as well as benefits are given a dollar value over time, and benefit over cost ratios are computed. A ratio in excess of one indicates worthwhileness from an investment point of view. The higher the ratio, the greater the value and worth.

The cost-benefit calculus is not a wholly satisfactory tool for evaluating human services programs, because of its incapability to measure "psychic" or "social" benefits. Psychic and social benefits are defined here to refer to the state, or well-being, of the recipient or the changes that take place in attitude and behavior as outcomes. Weisbrod (1969) argues that an evaluation design built around cost-benefit analysis is likely to reach negative conclusions about the effectiveness of any human services program, since only "economic" benefits and costs are taken into account. (Remember, an evaluation design built upon the systems model is concerned primarily with "allocative efficiency.")

One of the precautions in interpreting the cost-benefit data is, while a particular human services program may be judged inefficient, it may not necessarily be considered undesirable. It may, for example, have certain favorable income redistributional consequences which are socially preferable to other benefits. As an illustration, educational programs which focus upon socialization, social competence, and good citizenship do not produce the kinds of outcomes and changes which can be measured by the "payoff-rate" concept. Thomas (1967) noted:

...the social benefits of education, whose value is almost impossible to express in quantitative terms, are a major portion of education's output. Examples of these nonquantifiable benefits are reduction of civil strife, greater social harmony between persons of diverse ethnic and social backgrounds, less capacity for the political process to be seriously influenced by extremist groups, etc. The problem for the evaluator is that such benefits, while impossible to quantify, are nonetheless of crucial importance relative to the basic justification of a particular program.

There is general agreement that the utility of a cost-benefit model as an evaluative tool lies in its emphasis on a systematic examination of alternative courses of action and their implications. But it is important to note that data from such a model should be only one piece of evidence in the appraisal process and, from the vantage point of the evaluator who is concerned more with

"social" than economic benefits, such data may not be the most significant piece of evidence. When programs have goals that go beyond simply maximizing the return on public investments irrespective of who receives the benefits, a simple cost-benefit ratio is an insufficient indicator of program effectiveness.

## THE GOAL-ATTAINMENT MODEL

Of the models to be presented, the goal-attainment model of evaluation is the most commonly used. This model, given prominence by Sherwood (1964) and expanded upon by Levinson (1966) stems from a conception of evaluation as the measurement of the degree of success or failure encountered by a program in reaching predetermined goals.

The goal-attainment model of evaluation relies heavily upon strategies which measure the degree of success in achieving specified goals. It assumes that specific goals can be assessed in isolation from other goals being sought by the program. The goal-attainment model is derived from theories and motivation (forces which energize and direct behavior) and Lewinian field theory. This model is very useful in measuring abstract goals and functions "to define the indefinable and to tangibilitate the intangible" (Mager, 1972, p. 10). A basic premise of the goal-attainment model of evaluation is that if the ultimate goal is met, then a series of prior accomplishments were fulfilled. This model emphasizes the measurement of outcomes rather than inputs, assuming that if the goal is met, then the appropriate combination of inputs was made.

The evaluator does not measure the phenomena he or she is studying directly. Rather, he or she observes and measures empirical manifestations or indices of these phenomena. It is not criteria themselves which are measured, but their equivalents-indicators. For all practical purposes, the goal-attainment model employs the ex post facto research design. Since the fundamental question asked by the model is *was the goal met?* empirical inquiry can take place only after manifestations of the independent variables have already occurred. Therefore, the focus of the model is upon the clarification of goals and program objectives, and the evaluation of their accomplishment. The evaluation of accomplishment is extended to test the hypothesis that a certain form of intervention has a beneficial outcome.

## Goal-Attainment Analysis

Analytically, measuring goal-attainment involves five steps. They are as follows:

1. *Specification of the goal to be measured.*

In using the goal-attainment model, the evaluator must make clear distinctions between goals and objectives. A goal for our purpose is a statement which represents in general terms an end to which a planned course of action is directed. A goal statement should also state, explicitly or otherwise, the outcome behavior of the consumer and/or a desired state or condition once the planned course of action is completed.

2. *Specification of the sequential set of performances that, if observed, would indicate that the goal has been achieved.*

A level of performance achieved within some temporal context which represents an approximation toward the goal is defined as an objective. An objective is operationally defined in terms of a beginning and an end point, so that either the existence or nonexistence of a desired state or the degree of achievement of that state can be estab-

lished. It may be *qualitatively* or *quantitatively* defined. A qualitatively defined objective is one that is either obtained or not in terms of empirical observation. A quantitatively defined objective is one that is obtained and can be measured in terms of degrees.

For purposes of evaluation, then, goals should as far as possible be defined operationally. That is, they should be expressed as discrete objectives. In this way, the degree of achievement of the various objectives or level of performance of the target for change can be a direct measure of goal attainment. Conceived in this way, goal attainment can be measured in terms of achieving certain objectives. Therefore, the achievement of all of the objectives should represent 100 percent goal attainment.

3. *Identification of which performances are critical to the achievement of the goal.*

An evaluation process must identify proper criteria to be used in measuring program success. In the goal-attainment model, success criteria are stated in terms of benchmarks. The use of benchmarks presumes that certain levels of performance are more critical to goal attainment than others. These are treated as criterion tasks in that they constitute specific, necessary conditions of goal attainment. Precise measures of achievement are set up, and data on them are collected systematically. Since achievement of performance is expected to occur in a time sequence, achievement of data should be expressed in terms of changes.

One of the major characteristics of the goal attainment model of evaluation is that it does not require that input factors be individually defined. For example, if one were evaluating a counseling program, one need not be concerned about the number of counseling sessions; the amount of money spent for counseling; the amount of effort the counseling staff exerts toward the achievement of counseling goals; the nature and demands of the counseling components in relationship to other program components; the characteristics inherent in staff members which affect their ability to carry out the goals or the debilitating and facilitating features of the counseling environment. As already pointed out, the basic question is: Was the goal met? Consequently, the evaluator can identify what goals were achieved, but he may or may not be able to explain why they were achieved or why others were not.

*4. Description of what is the "indicator behavior" of each performance episode.*

For the most part, indications of goal attainment will be observed as measures of changes in performance, using some normative criteria. Moreover, since achievement of objectives is defined in terms of beginning and end points, the achievement of an objective may represent the conclusion of a "performance episode." Therefore, the "indicator behavior" of a performance episode is some measurable behavior which can be observed in kind or amount within some time frame. For example, let's say that the goal is to improve morale among workers. The "indicator behavior" may be characterized as absenteeism. Measures of absenteeism are selected as *frequency* and *length*. In this case, the objective may be to reduce absenteeism each month more than it was the previous month over a six-month period. Benchmarks for measurement may be established as a reduction of at least one absence per month over the previous one.

*5. Testing collectively whether each "indicator behavior" is associated with each other.*

In most cases, the indicator behavior should be the same for each performance episode. This facilitates standardization of measurement and makes it easier for outcomes to be compared from one episode to the other. Different evaluators studying the same phenomena may report different outcomes. Without standardization, there is a problem of determining whether the differences are in fact actual differences or differences in measures. When measures are standardized, one source of the differences—the measures used—is controlled and the likelihood is then increased that the differences observed reflect differences in the phenomena.

In some situations, the nature of the change being measured will dictate different indicator behaviors from one performance episode to the other. The evaluator, therefore, must be sure that he adheres to proper research methodology to insure this; multiple measures are preferred because they yield higher validity than single measures.

Measurements of goal-attainment yield, principally, information about outcomes. For program planning, the human services worker may also need a more detailed description of the social environment that produced outcomes. More often than not program administrators need information on what were the specific levels of input, what resources they require and how these levels of input relate to outcomes. In other words, did a particular level of input make a difference?

## Strengths and Limitations of the Goal-Attainment Model

One of the major limitations of the goal-attainment model is that in an ex post facto study, the evaluator cannot always attribute goal attainment to a specific set of input variables. Also, goal attainment may be the result of environment factors over which the human services worker has no control, or there may be factors which neither the worker nor the evaluator can account for.

A third limitation of the goal-attainment model centers around the fact that evaluators often ignore the distinction between ends and means, or output and input. As Terleckyj (1970) suggests, the mere expenditure of funds for a certain goal is often equated with the intended achievement.

A fourth limitation of this model is that it may be too narrow in its evaluation methodology and too formal in its consideration of goals. Also, it may not take into account sufficiently the informal goals that emerge or the unanticipated events that produce new goals and activity.

A strength of the model is that it assumes that individual goals in a program can be evaluated in isolation from other program goals. Another strength is that the model is considered an objective and reliable analytical tool because it omits the values of the evaluator in that he is not required to make any judgments about the appropriateness of the program goals.

A third and important use of the model is its capacity to measure abstract goals by operationalizing the goal into discrete measurable objectives. Finally, perhaps, one of the major strengths of the model is that the measurement of goal attainment need not be rigidly quantitative. For example, the achievement of an objective signifies that the goal has been met to some degree in terms of some defined event. When all the objectives have been achieved, the goal is said to have been met. This argument is based upon the assumption that the goal is met if a series of prior accomplishments are fulfilled.

## When to Use Goal-Attainment Model

Evaluations may be classified in a number of ways. They may be classified by *what* is being evaluated, by *who* conducts the evaluation, by the *decision* that is to be affected by the evaluation, and by the *method* used. The appropriate classification used depends upon the purpose of the evaluation.

Evaluations may also be classified in terms of their purpose. They may be conducted in order to make decisions about resource allocation, program changes, and capacity building and for measuring accountability.

The goal-attainment model of evaluation seems to be best suited for capacity building. In other words, it serves the purpose of developing a data base, improving in-house capacity to collect and assemble relevant outcome data and measures, and provides rapid feedback on problems requiring technical assistance.

The goal-attainment model of evaluation is relatively easy to carry out but the conclusions that may be drawn are necessarily limited. Therefore, this evaluation strategy can be justified only when the relationship between inputs (as independent variables) has already been demonstrated or will be tested in subsequent studies.

## THE IMPACT MODEL

The next mode of evaluation to be discussed is the *impact* model, which involves the formulation of hypotheses that are to be tested. It employs experimental designs in which hypotheses are stated in terms of the comparative effectiveness of certain program inputs. It begins with the premise that since human services programs are designed to improve the social position of recipients, the experimental hypotheses should be stated in a manner which predicts that the intervention will be more beneficial to the recipient than the usual social practice (control condition). As implied from the foregoing, an essential difference in the application of the impact model and the goal-attainment model is in the assumptions made in the use of the impact model. One assumption is that in order for the evaluator to estimate the effects of a particular human services program, it is necessary to compare the experiences of the recipients of services with those of some reference group. Comparisons of the outcomes of the reference group represent what would have happened to the clients in the absence of the program or intervention.

A second assumption is that the impact model is predicated upon the notion of cause and effect. It consists of (1) a set of theoretical concepts or ideas which trace the dynamics of how it is expected that the program will have the desired effects, and (2) a theory which logically interrelates a set of principles and procedures, which imply that certain decisions rather than others be made with respect to day-to-day program situations.

Since most program outcomes are influenced by multiple causal factors, a search for cause-effect relationships becomes largely one of testing for associations between some arbitrarily selected causes and the hypothesized effect. The question raised by the impact model is: *"What difference does the intervention make?"* In this sense, the impact model is more rigorous than the goal-attainment model. It assumes that in order to determine what differences the intervention makes, it is necessary to measure the relationship between the program goals (the dependent variables) and a variety of independent variables, including the personal characteristics of participants, the program components, and the conditions under which the program operates. The notion that most of the dependent variables with which the evaluator deals are functions of more than one independent variable is essential to the model. Therefore, the analysis should treat simultaneously all of the independent variables which are believed to be relevant. To omit some variables in the analysis may lead to distorted conclusions due to correlation or interaction among these variables and those independent variables which are included in the analysis.

This line of reasoning calls for the use of multivariate techniques. Proponents of the impact model often complain that the weakness in the goal-attainment model is that few investigators use regression analysis, for example, as a means of controlling for the effects of population in determining differences between programs.

To maximize the use of experimental techniques, Freeman and Sherwood (1970) suggest that the impact model should incorporate three kinds of hypotheses: (1) *Causal hypothesis*—A statement concerning relationship between the input and the outcome. "A statement about the influence of one of more characteristics or processes on the condition which is the object of the program. The hypothesis assumes a causal relationship between a phenomenon and the condition or behavior in which change is sought." (2) *Intervention hypothesis*—A statement about what changes the input will produce. "A statement which specifies the relationship between the program (what is going to be done) and the phenomenon regarded, in the causal hypothesis, as associated with the behavior or condition to be ameliorated or changed." (3) *Action hypothesis*—A statement about how that change will affect the behavior or condition the worker is seeking to modify. The action hypothesis is necessary in order to assess whether the intervention, even if it results in a desired change in the causal variable, is necessarily linked to the outcome variable, that is the behavioral condition that one is actually seeking to modify. This hypothesis is also necessary because although the chain of events may be true in a real-life situation, it may not necessarily hold true when it is brought about by intervention.

Impact evaluations should provide five essential sets of information. They should provide all of the data necessary: (1) to determine if a particular program should be continued; (2) to determine which of alternative programs achieve the greatest gains for a given cost; (3) to present information on the components of each program and the mixes of components which are most effective for a given expenditure so that maximum operating efficiency can be achieved; (4) to provide relevant information for determining which programs best serve individuals with particular demographic characteristics; and (5) to suggest new program thrusts.

The impact model uses an experimental design. Therefore, it insists upon random assignment of subjects to the experimental and comparison groups. Herein lies the limitation of the model. Developing designs based upon controlled experimentation in evaluative research has always been troublesome. While it is always desirable, it is not always essential nor possible.

One of the basic principles of controlled experimentation in evaluating human services programs is that treatment and control conditions must be held constant throughout the period of intervention. Under these circumstances, experimental designs prevent rather than promote changes in the intervention, because interventions cannot be altered once the program is in process if the data about differences engendered by intervention are to be unequivocal. In this sense, the application of experimental designs to evaluation conflicts with the concept that evaluation should facilitate the continual improvement of the program. Dyer (1966) makes the following observation:

We evaluate, as best we can, each step of the program as we go along so that we can make needed changes if things are not turning out well. This view of evaluation may make some of the experimental design people uneasy because it seems to interfere with the textbook rules for running a controlled experiment. ...There is one kind of evaluation to be used when you are developing an educational procedure....I would call *concurrent* evaluation. And there is a second kind of evaluation...I would call *ex-post facto* evaluation; it is what the experimental design people are usually talking about when they use the word evaluation (p. 18).

The objective of the impact evaluations is to be able to say definitely that a particular intervention has led to a particular outcome that would not have occurred otherwise. In the absence of experimentation, this is not wholly possible. But the larger problem in conducting an experimental evaluation in the human services field is related to the ethical problem of denying services in order to have a truly experimental model.

In a true experimental design, random assignment of subjects is based upon the probability theory that each subject has an equal chance of being assigned either to the control or treatment group. In the regular course of service, clients are almost never assigned to programs on this basis.

## THE BEHAVIORAL MODEL

The behavioral model of evaluation (BME) is derived from behavioral constructs. It places a heavy emphasis upon measuring goal attainment, but regards goal statements as statements which define the dependent variable in terms of behavior(s) the client should be able to demonstrate at the end of the service intervention. It differs from the impact model in that it places little importance upon controlled experimentation on the ground that the selection of comparison groups which match up in all respects except for the intervention is rarely if ever possible.

The BME begins from the premise that the effectiveness of human services should be measured in terms of the extent to which desired changes take place in the behavior of individual clients. This model is grounded in three important behavioral science concepts which argue that: (1) the phenomenon with which the evaluator deals is behavior (dependent variable) and the independent variables which control behavior are elements of the environment (2); since behavior is a function of an environmental stimulus, then, the most effective way to change behavior is to change the environmental circumstances which influence it; and (3) since behavior is a function of the environment, the social function of human services programs is to provide the individual with the skills to cope with the environment.

The primary question raised by the behavioral model of evaluation is: *To what extent has the program intervention improved the client's ability to gain mastery over his/her environment?*

The BME conforms to what Penka and Kirk (1991) call *clinical evaluation* and often incorporates ideographic models which eschew group comparisons and experimental designs on the assumption that averages obtained from individual scores lend themselves to different interpretations from data derived from grouped means. For example, in evaluating forms of clinical practice, the basic evaluation question if often stated as: When, for whom and under what situations is the intervention most effective? Ideographic models also imply that individual-derived data differ from grouped-derived data in that, as Shontz (1976) noted, entirely different functional relations apply to group data than apply to data from individuals. He uses the following examples:

...Suppose that several members of a group perform the same task, and that the average remains stable because the performances of half the group improve from practice while the performance of the other half deteriorate from fatigue. The statement, that performance on this task remains stable and is therefore unaffected by either practice or fatigue, is clearly untrue, whether that statement is applied to the group or to the individuals who compose it.

An essential tenet of ideographic models is to use the individual or the "treatment" group as its own control by employing pre- and post-treatment measures. The assumption is that each "subject" is its own control and the behavior of the subject before treatment is a measure of the performance that would have occurred if there has been no treatment. The research design which has gained the most attention recently in ideographic outcome studies is the single organism design variously referred to as N=1, single-case design, or as Fischer refers to it, "single system design." Fischer uses the term *single system design* because it "rightly suggests that this form of research can be used with subjects other than individuals, including families, groups, organizations, and communities, all of which may be viewed as single systems for evaluation purposes." This paradigm relies heavily upon what Campbell and Stanley have called the interrupted time-series design in which two periods of observations are separated by application of the intervention. It may also be used with two equivalent samples in which treatment is used with one and is absent in the other. It may be depicted as follows:

| "One group time series": | Pre-Test | Treatment | Post-Test |
|---|---|---|---|
| | $T_1T_2T_3T_4$ | X | $T_5T_6T_7T_8T_9$ |
| "Control-group time series": | Pre-Test | Treatment | Post-Test |
| Experimental | $T_1T_2T_3T_4$ | X | $T_5T_6T_7T_8T_9$ |
| Controlled | $T_1T_2T_3T_4$ | | $T_5T_6T_7T_8T_9$ |

Wood (1978) encouraged the use of a combination of both the one-group time series and the control-group time series. In this case, one employs first the "N=1" model of an interrupted time-series in which two periods of observation are separated by application of the intervention. Then, the "N=2" paradigm, a time-lag control design, is employed, in which an intervention is applied to one subject after a base observation period but is withheld temporarily from another subject. After an experimental period, the intervention is applied to the second subject, and both subjects are monitored for a second experimental period.

As a strategy for collecting data that will lead to the discovery of individual changes in behavior, the single-organism approach has much to recommend it. Properly employed, it is at least as demanding as large sample methods, and it usually leaves less to chance.

## GOAL SPECIFICATION

Each of the four frameworks presented assume the presence of certain preconditions: (1) the program is clearly articulated; (2) the goals and/or expected effects are clearly specified; and (3) the causal assumptions linking the program to the goals and/or effects are plausible (Rutman, 1977).

Good evaluation designs also seek to determine the appropriateness of the goal and the feasibility and attaining it (Washington, 1982). The purpose of evaluation of human service programs is viewed as a system, including people and processes engaged in an interrelated flow of events and activities moving toward some goal, purpose, or end. The process of measuring the extent to which the goal has been met is not as simple as it may appear. One of the problems is that sometimes the goals of the program are not clearly defined. Goals may

either be stated poorly, or the publicly stated goals may not be the ones by which the program's activities are guided. One of the spillover effects of program evaluation, then, may be that the process of evaluation assists the administrator in sharpening a definition of the organization's mission and goals. Specifying program goals may assist the administrator in operationalizing goals structurally as part of a strategic planning process. It may also help him/her to identify indicators of success.

It is the position of this author that, when feasible, the evaluator should be hired while the program is in its early planning stage. There are indeed several advantages to this initial involvement of the evaluator. Since many agencies seldom define program goals clearly, the evaluator can not only describe accurately those goals, but can actively help the program to identify and decide upon those goals. This dual role extends to the design and description of the relationship between input variables and goals. In order to help identify goals and key variables, however, the evaluator must also have complete information about the program to be evaluated. Here again, on-the-spot involvement early in the program's planning and development stages is clearly an advantage because the evaluator can assist in setting up a data collection mechanism which collects the kind of evidence required to determine whether the goal was met.

## REFERENCES

Campbell, Donald, and Stanley, Julian, *Experimental and Quasi-Experimental Design for Research* (Chicago; Rand McNally and Company, 1963).

Dyer, Henry S., "Overview of the Evaluation Process," *On Evaluating Title I Programs* (Princeton, NJ: Educational Testing Service, 1966).

Etzioni, Amitai, "Two Approaches to Organizational Analysis: A Critique and a Suggestion," In Herbert C. Schulberg, Alan Sheldon, and Frank Baker (Eds.), *Program Evaluation in the Health Fields* (Port Washington, NY: Human Sciences Press, 1970).

Fischer, Joel, "The Social Work Revolution," *Social Work* (May 1981), pp. 199–206.

Freeman, Howard E., and Sherwood, Clarence C., *Social Research and Social Policy* (Englewood Cliffs, NJ: Prentice-Hall, 1970).

Levinson, Perry, "Evaluation of Social Welfare Program," *Welfare Review, 5* (December 1966), pp. 5–12.

Mager, Robert F., *Goal Analysis* (Belmont, CA: Fearon Publishers, 1972).

Penka, Cindy E. and Kirk, Stuart A., "Practitioner Involvement In Clinical Evaluation," *Social Work* (November 1991), pp. 513–517.

Ribich, Thomas I., *Education and Poverty* (Washington, DC: The Brookings Institution, 1968).

Rutman, Leonard, *Evaluation Research Methods: A Basic Guide* (Beverly Hills, CA: Sage Publications, 1977).

Sherwood, Clarence C., "Methodological Measurement and Social Action Considerations Related to the Assessment of Large-Scale Demonstration Programs." Paper presented at the 12th Annual Meeting of the American Statistical Association (Chicago: The Association, 1964).

Shontz, Franklin C., "Single-Organism Designs," in Peter M. Bentler, et al. (Eds.) *Data Analysis Strategies and Designs for Substance Abuse Research.* Research Issue N. 13 (Rockville, MD: National Institute on Drug Abuse, 1976), p. 29.

Terleckyj, Nestor E., "Measuring Possibilities of Social Change," *Looking Ahead, 18* (6) (August 1970).

Thomas, Alan J., "Efficiency Criteria in the Urban School System." Paper presented to the AERA, New York City, February 18, 1967. Mimeographed.

Washington, R.O., "Evaluation: Design and Method" in Thomas Meenaghan, Robert O. Washington, and Robert M. Ryan, *Macro-Practice in the Human Services* (New York: The Free Press, 1982, Chap. 4).

———, *Measuring Program Effectiveness In The Human Services* (Boston: The Social Policy Research Group, Inc., 1987).

Weisbrod, Burton A., "Benefits of Manpower Programs: Theoretical and Methodological Issues," in Somers and Wood, *Cost Benefit Analysis of Manpower Programs* (Kingston, Ontario: Queen's University, 1969).

Williams, Walter and Evans, John W., "The Policies of Evaluation: The Case of Head Start," *The Annals* (September 1969), p. 385.

Wood, Katherine, "Casework Effectiveness a New Look at the Research Evidence," *Social Work, 23* (6) (November 1978), pp. 437–458.

21.

## William C. Birdsall and Roger W. Manela

## THE NITTY GRITTY OF PROGRAM EVALUATION:
## A PRACTICAL GUIDE

### INTRODUCTION

Program evaluation carried out at the agency level must be responsive to the fact that the agency's central focus is the delivery of service. A major goal for the agency is to help its program staff and administrators improve their decisions about the operation of the agency. Some of these decisions focus on the internal operation of the agency. For example, should the agency stop an ongoing activity or start a new one? Should it hire more people, lay some people off, or reassign some of its staff? Should it try to expand its service to a new group of clients or should it narrow its focus and concentrate on a subset of the clients it now serves? Other decisions focus on external factors, such as the availability of funds or the impact of what other agencies are doing.[1]

While the issues that program evaluation addresses are important ones, the activity of program evaluation itself may be neglected or even ignored in the normal functioning of a busy agency. Unless it proves its worth, program evaluation is bound to be a low priority for an overworked agency administrator and her/his staff. Given the pressure to provide services to the agency's clients, agency staff are likely to see evaluation as justified only if it can improve the provision of service. If program evaluation is to get the attention it deserves and the resources it requires, the evaluation must become an integral part of agency operations, taking the pulse of the agency's programs and helping ensure their health. If it is seen as simply bureaucratic red tape, program evaluation will always be a low priority, guaranteed to have little impact on agency operations. But, if program evaluation is geared to inform both the long- and short-term decisions the agency must make, it is likely to flourish.

The fact that human service agencies gather and store data on the clients they serve, record the amount and type of services they provide, and keep relatively complete records on revenue by source and expenditures by type of means that, at a minimum, modern human service agencies usually have important data on how they spend their money, whom they serve, and what services they provide. Careful analysis of these data can help an agency catch administrative problems, assess the impact of its interventions on clients, and determine the costs and possibly the benefits of its activities. Such an analysis can establish the extent to which the agency's programs conform to standards of accountability and justify the current allocation of redirection of funds.

Another focus of program evaluation is on patterns of service to at-risk populations. This kind of analysis can show who is served by what activities and who gets left

William C. Birdsall is a professor at the School of Social Work, The University of Michigan; Roger W. Manela is a social worker for the Detroit Public Schools.

out. It can highlight the effects of eligibility rules and outreach programs, the ways staff interact with potential clients, and patterns of client self-selection. It can inform decisions about coordinating, consolidating or expanding a program, and it can reveal whether a program actually helps people, without causing undesirable side effects. The information from the evaluation can be used to improve current services and create new and better service programs. Over time, data collected by this kind of evaluation can be used to highlight changes in an agency's clients, the services it has provided to them, and the consequences of those services.

## EVALUATION PROCESSES

Program evaluation is a process that follows a logical sequence of steps. It begins with needs assessment and proceeds to the design or choice of an intervention. The next phase is the monitoring of the intervention process, followed by the analysis of its immediate impact on the agency's clients. The evaluation process concludes by considering the long-run consequences of the program for clients and other affected parties. Careful measurement and analysis are necessary at every stage of this process. Thorough needs assessment and careful monitoring of agency activities are essential to ensure that the program being evaluated did in fact provide appropriate interventions to the proper clients. If one does not understand or correctly identify client needs, the agency may not implement potentially effective interventions, and the services it implements may not provide what the client needs. With this kind of mismatch between client needs and agency services, an impact analysis may erroneously conclude that an intervention is ineffective when, in fact, it was inappropri-

ately applied. Without careful monitoring, an evaluator can easily draw the wrong conclusions. Good needs assessments usually are based on an understanding of what interventions are feasible, how well they are likely to work, and what consequences they are likely to produce. Proper monitoring also is grounded in an understanding of the client's perspective on her/his needs and desired outcomes. This sensitivity to the client's perspective ensures that an evaluator can have confidence that appropriate interventions have been applied to the proper persons.

## Needs Assessment

Whatever the nature of the client, be it a community, a group of people, or an individual, the client's needs must be identified and assessed before the agency can proceed. In almost all human services agencies, needs-assessment data in its most elementary form are collected on intake forms filled out for every new client. Such forms are typically used to record information on a concrete presenting problem, which could be as simple as a needed resource, an item of information, or a referral, or it could be as complex as a family collapsing in the face of long-term unemployment or parental substance abuse.

Usually the agency has some standard against which to measure need. Viewing client problems in terms of such a standard gives the agency a basis for determining who is at risk and who is not, who is eligible for service and who is not, who the program should try to reach and who it should not, who will be the clients of the program and who will not. This kind of evaluation is likely to use data from a variety of sources and develop baseline measures for the specific populations the agency serves. The focus at this stage is on identifying the populations at risk for the problems the agency addresses.

The scope of the needs assessment is important. A wider assessment can delineate the extent of a problem and help the agency mobilize support for programs that address that problem, but it is unlikely to help the agency identify specific clients. On the other hand, a needs assessment that focuses on a particular neighborhood or subpopulation will help the agency match its services with the needs of specific potential clients.

## Monitoring Ongoing Programs

Once needs have been assessed, the agency must design interventions to fit the needs, then begin to route specific clients to the appropriate intervention. If the intervention is new, it is a good idea to try the services with selected subpopulations and refine them in light of the results of these initial tests. At this stage, the goal of program evaluation is to make a fairly rapid appraisal of the agency's ability to deliver its new services. If there are any apparent problems with the new services, the evaluation should help the agency identify and correct them.

Once the agency has tested and refined its services to the point that they can be delivered on a regular basis, the focus of the evaluation should shift to monitoring whether the delivery of those services is proceeding as planned. Appropriate questions at this stage include: Are there services actually getting to the people who need them? Are there important segments of the population at risk that are not being served? How can the agency improve the ways it delivers its services?

## Impact Assessment

Monitoring how an agency delivers its services is a necessary condition for improving the way the agency operates, but it does not specifically assess the effectiveness of the services the agency provides. To do this, one must measure the direct impact of the agency's services on its clients to determine whether the clients or their situations have changed due to the agency's interventions. At this stage, the focus of program evaluation shifts to comparing the client's profile after he/she has received the agency's services with the client's profile at entry. While it is usually difficult to trace the causal linkages between the postintervention profile of the client and the particular services the agency has provided, a simple description of what has happened to the client since contacting the agency can go a long way toward helping determine whether or not the agency is accomplishing its mandate.

Ideally the evaluation should determine not just the immediate impact of a given intervention on the client, but the more ultimate outcome for the client's life. However, it is rare for an ordinary agency to have the expertise, let alone the time and resources necessary to carry out such a formal evaluation of the outcomes of its interventions. In most agencies it is a giant step just to evaluate the immediate impact of services on specific clients.

## Cost Analysis of Services

Evaluating the costs of the agency's services in order to improve those services and control their costs is another aspect of program evaluation.[2] Human service agencies keep data on their expenditures to satisfy the interests of funders and others outside of the agency. Careful analysis of the data on an agency's expenditures can help agency administrators adjust the focus of current programs as well as plan for the future. If one knows the number of clients the agency has served and the cost of serving them, one can calculate the average cost of service per client. However, this kind of gross cost data is not enough. Agencies also need to know the cost of each different intervention and which types of clients or classes of problems cost the most to serve. While such cost data do not directly imply any specific actions, they are a first step toward deciding whether some activities cost too much for the impact they produce.

## EVALUATION PRINCIPLES

The preceding section has described the stages of the evaluation process in human service agencies. The following section describes some practical principles to keep in mind when designing and carrying out program evaluation.

## 1. Perspective: Keep in Mind What Is Important

In designing and carrying out an evaluation it is essential to maintain perspective and keep the evaluation relevant to the mandate of the organization you are evaluating. To stay relevant, the evaluation should focus on analyses that the agency can use to improve its operations and the decisions it makes about its future course of action. This means that the evaluation has to focus on issues such as: (1) Who needs what services within the scope and mandate of the agency? (2) What services are being delivered, by whom, to whom? (3) Is the process of service delivery proceeding as planned, and if not, do deviations improve or hamper service delivery? (4) Are the services effective? For example, are the expected changes in clients or their situations occurring? (5) What are the short-term and long-term positive and negative consequences of

the agency's interventions on its clients, their relatives, and others in the community? (6) How efficiently are services being delivered? Are they being delivered within budget? If there are deviations from budget, are they in accord with the needs of the client and the mandate of the agency? (7) Could funds be reallocated in ways that would improve service delivery and lower cost without diminishing the effectiveness of services?

## 2. Evaluation As an Iterative Process: Return to the Important Questions

A good general pattern to follow in designing an evaluation and in analyzing data is to work back and forth across the range of questions just posed. Program evaluation is not a linear activity. It unfolds more like a spiral on which relatively narrow and focused questions are juxtaposed with larger, more general issues. One may begin by trying to focus on the analysis of a set of variables about a particular service, only to find that the analysis spirals to a larger policy issue and its implications. Analysis of the impact of the agency's programs may suggest that the needs of clients are not well addressed or even well understood. Trying to set a standard for an assessment of need may suggest a method for measuring the impact of an intervention. Monitoring an activity may raise questions about the level of understanding which personnel have of the goals of the agency. This in turn may highlight the fact that the agency's goals need clarification in all sorts of ways and for all sorts of reasons.

During the design of the intervention and again during the data analysis, one's thinking may make a number of such jumps as one's focus shifts from one level to another. This kind of serendipitous exploration of ideas and issues is inherent in the process of design and analysis, but in program evaluation it tends to be exaggerated by the range of purposes that the evaluation serves.

### 3. Readily Available Data Are Often the Best Data: Use Them

One way to simplify the design of an evaluation and reduce the effort it requires is to use available data wherever possible, such as client records or personnel records. All human service agencies routinely collect a variety of important data on clients, program activities, staff, and costs. Most of these data are gathered to satisfy demands from external sources, funders, regulators, etc., and this dictates the format of the data. Usually these data get only the most cursory analysis, and the analysis seldom relates one category of information to another, such as cost data and impact data. But, for an evaluator who can see the link between these data and analyze and present them in ways that help the agency improve its operations, they can be pure gold. For example, human service agencies routinely collect background information on their clients. If an evaluator uses these data to prepare profiles of an agency's client populations, possibly comparing the clients the agency serves with the characteristics of the broader population, these data take on new relevance for agency administrators and policy planners.

Agencies are likely to have a great deal of data on the services they provide: logs of staff activities, notes on specific interventions used with different kinds of clients, even measures of change in clients. Some of this information will be available in centralized records, but much is hidden in case reports and client files. A good program evaluator should be able to root it out and use it in an evaluation, without having to start a whole new data collection effort. Sampling extant records and analyzing

what they can tell us is an excellent beginning, and it is often sufficient in itself to provide the key to improving an agency's service delivery.

Another advantage to using available data is that intake and service delivery information is collected routinely and periodically as a normal part of agency operations. If you initiate a special data collection effort for an evaluation, you must establish special procedures, use considerable staff time or hire additional staff, and disrupt established agency routines—a good way to make evaluation unpopular. Also, by using data that the agency routinely collects, you have a built-in capability for analyzing changes over time. You can look backwards over the past, and you can build in analytic procedures that will enable the agency to continue to repeat the evaluation in the future.

### 4. Know Your Audience: Present Results for a Busy, Intelligent, Decision Maker

In so far as it is feasible, choose a simple presentation over a complex one, and use graphic instead of numeric presentations wherever possible.[3] The adage "A picture is worth a thousand words" translates in the computer age into "A graphic is worth a thousand numbers." Busy administrators and tired board members are bound to be pleased when, instead of having to struggle to understand relationships presented in tabular form, they can see those relationships at a glance when the same data are presented in simple bar or pie charts. Today there are powerful programs available on inexpensive PCs that make it easy to display statistics in a variety of graphic formats.[4] The use of such graphics not only makes it easy to interpret the data, it adds punch and professionalism to your presentations.

GRAPH 21.1
Family Situation

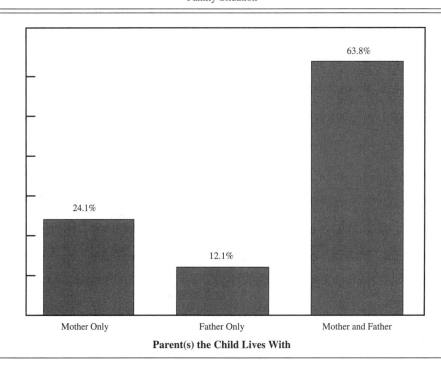

Parent(s) the Child Lives With

Combine graphic presentation with textual analysis. A graphic representation of data, no matter how clear and concise it is, cannot by itself make all the points you want to make in your analysis. It certainly cannot spell out the implications of the data. While the discovery of relationships in the data may require formal statistical analysis, pointing out those relationships to an interested audience may only require a simple explanation, such as: "Notice that referrals to our agency dropped off last winter, probably because that's when the Salvation Army began its program."

Even though a graphic is more lively than a table, it cannot make the data and the program come alive as well as anecdotes and stories about actual clients and events. This means that the data need to be complemented by text in a written report and by a script in an oral report. Until this is done, the evaluation is not complete. All too often, evaluation reports begin with a short introduction and then present nothing but statistical charts and tables, with no text to lead the reader through the analysis, point out the insights of the evaluator, and translate a sterile array of statistics into an interesting story that has a theme, presents a point of view, and draws some conclusions.

**AN EXTENDED EXAMPLE**

In the preceding sections we described program evaluation in human services agencies, presented some principles to follow when

GRAPH 21.2
Family Situation

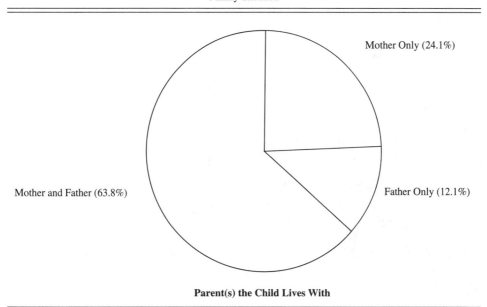

Mother Only (24.1%)

Mother and Father (63.8%)

Father Only (12.1%)

**Parent(s) the Child Lives With**

doing program evaluation, and suggested some useful techniques. In this section we give examples of how to use some of these techniques. The examples are based on the case of a small mental health program that is aimed at improving the school attendance of young children at risk of serious educational difficulties because of severe family problems. Spotty attendance in the early grades is seen as an indicator of the beginning of such difficulties. The data are based on the actual operation of the program, with some changes to prevent disclosure. Our focus is on ways to present data on client needs and client outcomes. We will comment on the strengths and limitations of these particular data for evaluation purposes, and suggest what kinds of additional information would be useful.

Virtually all human service agencies gather sufficient data to profile their clients and the problem(s) that brought them into the agency. It is important for various constituents, particularly the public and poten-

tial funders, that the agency present this information in a clear and concise form. The principle we follow in presenting such data is to use graphic presentations whenever possible. We have already noted that for persons not accustomed to analyzing data, graphs are generally much better than tables. Graphs are such a powerful presentation technique that even sophisticated audiences absorb and retain more information from a graphic presentation than from data tables.

Graph 21.1 presents the "Family Situation" of the children served by the program in the form of a bar chart. The text at the bottom and the relative size of the bars immediately tell the audience that two thirds of the children lived with both parents, about one quarter lived with their mother only and the rest lived with their father only. The percentages above the three bars serve two purposes. First, they are there for the people who want to see the actual numbers, whether for

GRAPH 21.3
Client Profile

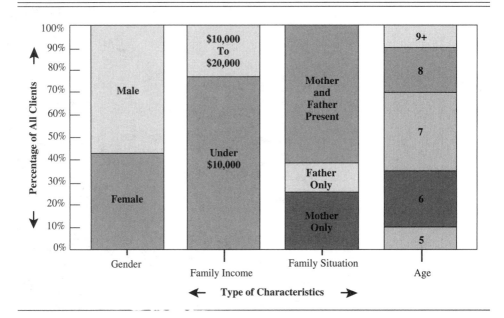

detail or for reassurance. Second, it is easy to make errors in producing a graph, and linking numbers to the bars coordinates the graphic picture with the data and its meaning.

The same information in Graph 21.1 is presented in the form of a pie chart in Graph 21.2. While bar charts are commonly used and easy to interpret, other useful graphic formats may be more appropriate for presenting certain kinds of data. For example, when the goal is to describe the composition of a group, particularly if the categories of the data are mutually exclusive, as they are in this case, a pie chart is as good or better than a bar chart.

Graph 21.3 profiles several different dimensions of the client's gender, family income, presence of parent(s), and age of children. Seeing the profile in this form, one is much more apt to remember that the children are nearly evenly divided by gender, and that the majority (nearly four-

fifths) are from families with incomes well below the poverty threshold of $13,360 for a four-person family. Higher incomes are absent because only children with a family income below $20,000 are eligible for this program. This kind of sociodemographic information, or data very similar to it, is almost always gathered on clients. Furthermore, it is relatively easy to compare these kinds of data on the program's clients over time. Such a comparison highlights changes that may occur so gradually that they would otherwise go unnoticed by those who carry out the agency's day-to-day activities. By making comparisons, over months and over years, one is able to see the extent to which an agency's clients have changed and to seek the reasons for those changes. This kind of analysis also helps one rethink the fit between the interventions the agency provides and the needs and characteristics of its clients.

GRAPH 21.4
Prevalence of Problems in the Home

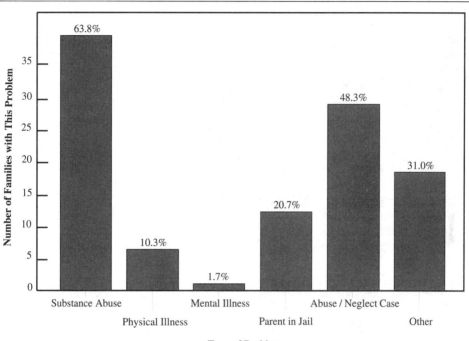

So far, we have focused on the analysis and presentation of simple demographic data on the agency's clients. A more challenging task is the analysis and presentation of information about the problems that these clients experience. Data on client problems can highlight whether the interventions the agency undertakes focus directly on client problems (e.g., protective services aiming at stopping abuse or neglect) or are incidental to them, as is true for many of the problems faced by families of the children in the program we are examining here. Establishing what clients need also is an important step toward meeting the agency's requirement for accountability, and it helps convince various persons and organizations to become stakeholders in the agency and its programs.

The problems of the children's families in the program we are examining are portrayed in Graph 21.4. (Note that any given family may have more than one type of problem. When this is the case, a pie diagram ordinarily is not appropriate.) The viewer immediately sees that substance abuse is the most prevalent problem among these families, while physical abuse and neglect also are quite prevalent.

Data such as those presented in Graph 21.4 can be very important for eliciting the support of funders, stakeholders, and the general public. The graph may tell the whole story to some viewers, but it is still important to add in either written or oral form such statements as: "Notice that nearly half of the children we serve are abused or neglected."

Virtually all agencies have records that link clients with service delivery activities, although in smaller agencies, these data may be in case files or in daily, often handwritten, time logs. It will probably require considerable effort to render these data useful. Most agencies also compile summaries of their activities with clients. These can help one assess the number and frequency of an agency's contacts with a client and what transpired during those contacts. In addition to the data presented here, the program we are considering records data on its on-going activities: the frequency of contacts with individual children, contacts with their parents, etc. For brevity, these are not portrayed, but they are crucial data for the purpose of monitoring program activities.

We turn now to data on the program's impact that help us determine the effectiveness of the program's interventions. If we find that the program has been effective, we can try to focus on how and why its effects have been achieved. If we find that the program has not been effective, we can try to identify some of the reasons and what can be done about them. The analysis and presentation of impact data is one of the more challenging aspects of program evaluation. The challenge comes from having to deal with the tentative nature of the causal connection between a program's interventions and any changes that occur in the clients or their situations. Even in the best of cases, it is difficult to conclude that any changes, positive, negative, or neutral, are "caused" by a given intervention. Probably, the best we can do is build a strong case, based on a well-reasoned argument, supported by a variety of data, that the intervention contributed to the changes. Data on impact on clients, when presented in a clear, concise manner can help agency administrators show what their programs have accomplished. Impact data also can help service delivery staff improve the effectiveness of their interventions with clients.

The goal of the program that we are considering here is to reduce attendance problems in the early grades among students who may be at risk of serious educational difficulties owing to severe family situations. (Poor attendance is an indicator of such difficulties.) The program has collected data on the absences and on the tardiness of its clients during three periods: in the semester before they entered the program, in the semester in which the program intervened to prevent absences, and in the following semester. We will focus on the data on absences and, for the sake of brevity, ignore the data on tardiness.

The distributions of absences for these three semesters are presented in Graphs 21.5, 21.6, and 21.7. We have presented these three graphs on the same page with the identical scale so that we can see precisely any shifts in the distribution of absences. By comparing the three graphs, we see that the distribution of absences shifts to the left. This indicates that absences become less frequent; there is a shift downward in the average level of absences. In fact, the average number of days absent fell from 12.7 days per term before the intervention to 11.0 days absent during the term in which the children were enrolled in this special program, to 10.0 days in the term immediately after the program. This decline in absences of 2.7 days per term that occurred between pretreatment and posttreatment is statistically significant.

The data on absences portrayed in the previous graphs are the only data available for this program that can help us determine whether it is a success or a failure.[5] But, if we were designing the evaluation from scratch, what other supporting data could

GRAPH 21.5
Preprogram Absences

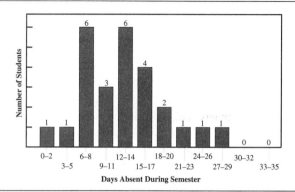

GRAPH 21.6
During-Program Absences

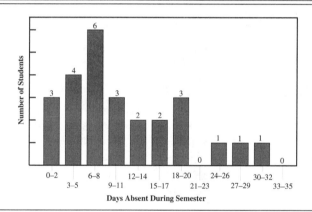

GRAPH 21.7
Postprogram Absences

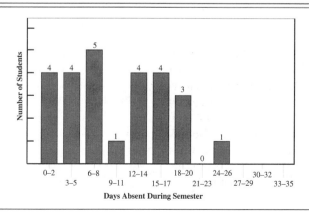

GRAPH 21.8
Absences Before and After Program

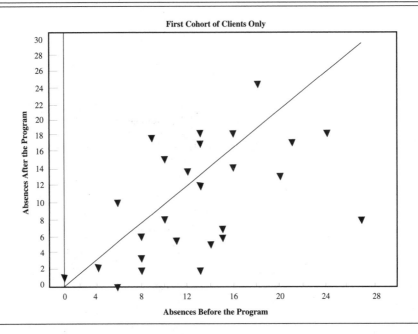

**First Cohort of Clients Only**

Absences After the Program

Absences Before the Program

we use? It would strengthen the case for the effectiveness of the program if we had supplementary data to reinforce our confidence that it is the program that is influencing the behavior of the children and their families in a way that helps improve school attendance. For example, if we knew that these students' grades improved after the intervention, it would lend considerable support to the case for the effectiveness of the program. In addition, it would help to have a record of absences and average grades of the children from the same school who were not in the program. We would expect the average absences of the children not in the program to be below 12.7 days per term (the average of our client group). After all, an important criterion for admission to the program was excessive absences. It would make a great deal of difference to our analysis if the average for the not-in-pro-

gram children is 10, in which case the clients improved to the class average. On the other hand, if the class average is 2 or 3, it means that our clients made only marginal gains, whatever the statistical significance of those gains.

The final example is Graph 21.8 which is a scatter diagram portraying the relationship between each child's level of absence before the intervention on the horizontal or x-axis and after the intervention, on the vertical or y-axis. This graph can be used to show audiences the improvement in attendance. The after-program absences of the students who are below the diagonal line (19 of the 27 students) are lower than their absences before the program; those above the diagonal have more absences; anyone on the diagonal would have an equal number of absences before and after the intervention.

## More Data That Could Help Assess Impact

Another type of data that could help establish whether the program is succeeding or not is health data on the children. Presumably, a major determinant of absences for ordinary children in the early grades is their health. These children (and at least an equivalent number of nonclient children) or their parents could be asked the frequency of visits to physicians in each of the school terms being studied. With such data, one could begin to model absences as a function of the program, taking into consideration the health of the child.

We have attempted to show that effective program evaluation need not be complicated. In fact, if there is an overriding principle in the discussion presented here, it is that keeping the evaluation simple and straightforward ensures that it will be useful to those who can benefit from it most: the agencies, their staff who deliver the services, their constituents who fund and support the delivery of those services, and ultimately the clients who receive those services.

## NOTES

1. An excellent and very practical overview of program evaluation for the potential practitioner is Posavac and Carey (1989). Another good text is Rossi and Freeman (1982). For a more detailed treatment of some topics, see Grinnell (1988). Austin et al. (1982) is a good handbook. Pietrzak et al. (1990) is a good example of the techniques applied to a particular problem—in this instance, child abuse.

2. Levin (1983) is an excellent source for all sorts of cost-based evaluation techniques. It is clear and accurate in its conceptualizations and very useful for ordinary situations. Weisbrod (1983) applies a benefit cost analysis to a mental health intervention and explains the sequence of actual decisions and judgments that must be made in a realistic context. Even if the evaluator is not intending to actually do a benefit cost analysis, Weisbrod's exposition is helpful for anyone trying to understand and apply economics to human service programs.

3. Tufte (1983) stands by itself as the source for both the principles and good practice of displaying quantitative information. Tufte (1990) builds on his earlier book, but is also an independent treatise on how we understand by seeing.

4. The graphics initially prepared for this paper were produced using Lotus 123, the most widely used spreadsheet computer program.

5. Although our data may seem limited, we have considerably more responses to the questions we are asking than many programs either collect or report.

## BIBLIOGRAPHY

Austin, M. J., Gary Cox, Naomi Gottlieb, J. David Hawkins, Jean M. Kruzich, and Ronald Rauch. (1982). *Evaluating your agency's programs.* Beverly Hills, CA: Sage Publications.

Grinnell, R. M., Jr. (Ed.). (1988). *Social work research and evaluation.* Itasca, IL: F. E. Peacock Publishers, Inc.

Levin, H. M. (1983). *Cost effectiveness: a primer.* Beverly Hills, CA: Sage Publications.

Pietrzak, J., Malia Ramler, Tanya Renner, Lucy Ford, and Neil Gilbert. (1990). Number 9 of Sage Source Books for the Human Services. *Practical program evaluation: Examples from child abuse prevention.* Beverly Hills, CA: Sage Publications.

Posavac, E. J., and Raymond G. Carey. (1989). *Program evaluation: Methods and case studies.* Englewood Cliffs, NJ: Prentice-Hall, Inc.

Rossi, P. H., and Howard E. Freeman. (1982). *Evaluation: A systematic approach.* Beverly Hills, CA: Sage Publications.

Tufte, E. R. (1983). *The visual display of quantitative information.* Cheshire, CT: Graphics Press.

Tufte, E. R. (1990). *Envisioning information.* Cheshire, CT: Graphics Press.

Weisbrod, B. A. (1983). An experiment in treating the mentally ill: A guide to benefit-cost analysis. Chapter 6 of *Economics and medical research.* Washington, DC: American Enterprise Institute.

## 22.

## Eleanor Chelimsky

## THE POLITICS OF PROGRAM EVALUATION

What do we mean when we talk about the politics of program evaluation? David Easton wrote thirty-seven years ago in *World Politics* that "the study of politics is concerned with understanding how authoritative decisions are made and executed for a society" and that "the output of a political system is a political decision or policy." Public policy, then, is the product of politics. Evaluation, with its purpose of providing high-quality information to decision makers, automatically claims a role for itself in the political process. It is based on the idea that the best information, made available to decision makers, would surely be useful to them in making and executing public policy. Unfortunately, in the very early seventies, rumors began to be heard in the land (later, alas, confirmed by studies) to the effect that evaluations were not often used in decision making.

At first we tried to come to grips with the problem by looking for ways out of the difficulty that would not require too many major changes in our paradigm or too many

Eleanor Chelimsky is director of the U.S. General Accounting Office's (GAO) Program Evaluation and Methodology Division, which conducts studies of individual government programs for Congress; the opinions expressed in this article are her own and not the policy or position of the GAO. She previously directed the MITRE Corporation's work in program evaluation, policy analysis, and research management. She has been a Fulbright scholar in Paris, president of the Evaluation Research Society, and the recipient of the 1982 Myrdal Award for Government and the GAO Distinguished and Meritorious Service Awards for 1985 and 1991. She was elected president of the American Evaluation Association, 1994–1996.

shifts in our work-style. We said that if our work was not used, this was because some evaluations simply were not good enough, forgetting—or not yet realizing—that policymakers typically use any data at hand and that some mediocre evaluation work has in fact been well used. Or we said that maybe evaluation was used, but we could not trace that use because evaluation was just one of many factors influencing decision making. We said that "use in decision making" might be too narrow a goal for evaluation, that there were many meanings—at least seven—attributable to the term "research utilization." We said that we needed to develop information supporting negotiation rather than information supporting decision making. What we were doing was turning the question of "why isn't evaluation used?" into the question "what, in fact, is reasonable use?" This in turn led to the idea that expectations for the use of evaluations were unrealistically high.

There had also been a 1973 paper in *Evaluation* by Carol Weiss, "Where Politics and Evaluation Meet," in which she made two crucial points: (1) that "as a matter of record, relatively few evaluation studies have had a noticeable effect on the making and remaking of public policy," and (2) that "only with sensitivity to the politics of evaluation research can the evaluator be as strategically useful as he should be." Thus, the lack of evaluation use was beginning to be recognized as such and to be seen not so much as a problem that could be whisked away without major changes in the evaluation paradigm, but rather as the newly perceived and difficult problem of integrating the disparate worlds of politics and evaluation research.

After the appearance of Weiss's article, and between about 1975 and 1980, a spate of articles and studies were published that sought to relate evaluations generally to the larger political and policy context within which they operate. One of the most important of these was the 1980 book by Lee Cronbach and Associates, *Toward Reform of Program Evaluation.* Looking back today at many of these studies, we can get the best sense not only of what we have learned about politics and evaluation but also how we have changed our outlook and practice.

It was typical in those studies to read statements attesting to the importance of politics to evaluation, statements such as Cronbach's: "a theory of evaluation must be as much a theory of political interaction as it is a theory of how to determine facts" or "the evaluators' professional conclusions cannot substitute for the political process." Nevertheless, there were not many cogent, action-oriented, systematic, and specific discussions of how the integration of evaluator and politics should or could take place. We did hear suggestions for the introduction of "research brokerage" or of "a bridging function," both of which sought to solve the integration problem by interposing some person or unit between the evaluation and the political user. This suggestion required a whole new breed of "interface analysis," and it never bore fruit, as James Sundquist predicted when he broached the idea in 1978 in *Knowledge and Policy: The Uncertain Connection.*

One reason that concrete suggestions were so hard to come by may have been that the political domain with which evaluation had to interact was so little understood by evaluators. In 1975, when I was

organizing the MITRE Corporation's symposium on the use of evaluation, it was considered unusual to have evaluators from many different evaluative disciplines (such as psychology, sociology, economics, political science, or operations research) and from many different substantive program areas (not only the usual health, education, and welfare; but also, for example, energy and the environment). It was a novelty for these evaluators not only to sit down together, but to sit down with their policy-making and program managing sponsors and users in different federal agencies. What came out of that symposium was a set of concrete dissatisfactions that users had with evaluation's performance, many of which were political and many of which were shocking to the evaluators present.

We heard that evaluation often cannot be used because of bureaucratic relationships and conflicts, that some program managers really prefer to be ignorant, and that evaluations will only be used if management really wants them. We heard that evaluation seemed to its users to be an ivory-tower process, and that when it emerged from that tower, it was too late to be useful, too full of jargon to be understood, too lengthy for the reading time available to users, and too likely to be answering a question quite different from the policy question originally posed. All of this was important to hear, not only because it was a kind of beginning excursion into the agency politics of evaluation, but also because the information had a chance of being assimilated or internalized by evaluators, given that most evaluations at that time had been developed for agencies of the executive branch.

When Cronbach's book on evaluation reform came out in 1980, many of the lessons of agency politics learned at the MITRE symposium had been learned by at least some evaluators. We were still far from having a political framework comprehensive enough to plan our integration work against, because, for the most part, legislative politics had remained unexamined. While Cronbach properly reproached us in 1980 for taking a too narrow view of the political arena in which agency decisions are made and evaluation use occurs, this view, in turn, seems narrow to us today because it failed to include legislative politics.

This was not just a matter of leaving something out. First, many of the points made, which are right on target about agency politics, are notably inappropriate with regard to legislative politics. For example, after considering what we have learned in six years of working with Congress, we need to rethink premises such as "a social agenda almost never calls for a choice between fixed alternatives"; or "only rarely are 'go/no go' decisions made"; or "timeliness is a much-overrated concern." Congress continually makes choices between fixed alternatives and votes on go/no go decisions; and an evaluator who did not understand the critical importance of the timing of congressional policy cycles—involving program authorization, reauthorization, appropriations, and budget—would be spinning his or her wheels and wasting a lot of money. The importance of timeliness with regard to legislative politics, at least, cannot be overstated. Second, without an understanding of legislative politics, we cannot understand—or worse, we actively misunderstand—the dynamnics of cross-branch politics; that is, the reciprocal process of legislative/executive agency interactions. I caution against overgeneralizing from agency evaluations politics to all evaluation politics.

Another result of failing to include legislative politics in our thinking is the contin-uing restriction of evaluation's application to social issues only. Over and over, we read of evaluation's preoccupation with social programs, with social reform, with social concerns; but legislative politics means that evaluation must broaden its focus to be optimally useful. Working for Congress, evaluators are expected to exercise their skills in all policy areas, social or not. Because I had included a single legislative perspective on evaluation in the MITRE symposium, I recognized the need to also include energy and the environment—two largely nonsocial, technological areas that were and are of great concern to Congress—in the 1976 symposium agenda.

To characterize the politics of evaluation today, we are dealing with a process of continuous translation for which the evaluator must assume a major share of responsibility. I represent the process as a five-part continuum, or framework, which involves, first, the development of a policy question. (I do not exclude program questions or imply that all questions for evaluation are policy questions, but, rather, I include all types of questions under this rubric insofar as they are asked by policy actors and emerge from the political process.) The policy question is then translated into an evaluation question which typically alters the policy question so that it becomes researchable. In the third part of the continuum, the evaluation question is translated into the evaluation proper: its design, its performance, and the reporting of its findings. The fourth part is the translation back into policy language of the results of the evaluation: that is, it is the policy answer to the original policy question. The fifth part entails the use of the evaluation findings somewhere in the cross-branch political process and the return, completing the continuum, to the formulation of new policy questions.

## DEVELOPING POLICY QUESTIONS

Evaluation can no longer be seen as completely a creature of the evaluator's choosing—with the evaluator being entirely free to select the program he or she wants to evaluate and to determine alone the questions to be asked about the program. Instead, insofar as we are dealing with evaluations that have been sponsored and are intended to be used in the political environment, the choice of the program to evaluate emerges in real terms from the political process. The determination of the types of policy questions to be asked are a function of the decision makers, whether legislative or executive or both. It occasionally happens that both congressional and agency policymakers are in accord about what the important questions are, as in the recent emphasis on teenage pregnancy, for example, or the earlier issue of cost containment in health care services.

My framework involves both an empowering of the decision maker with regard to the evaluation product and a shift in the role of the evaluators from the political one of seeking to reform society or, as Weiss put it, improving "the way that society copes with social problems," to the scientific one of bringing the best possible information to bear on a wide variety of policy questions. Such a change squares well with definitions of evaluation that see it as "the application of scientific research methods to the assessment of program concepts, implementation, and effectiveness" or as the provision of "careful and umbiased data" about programs, or as "a process by which society learns about itself." It does not square well with the notion that "an evaluator should not undertake to serve an agency unless he is in sympathy with its general mission," or with program advocacy or partisan definitions of evaluation in which evaluators seek to be a voice for the program, or a voice for the underdog or for some other special group. Similarly, it cannot accommodate precepts such as "it is unwise for evaluation to focus on whether a project has 'attained its goals.'" Such a precept assumes that the evaluator chooses the questions. Actually, the politics of the legislative oversight function may require that evaluators focus on the question of goal attainment.

The primary purpose of having the policy question be one that is of major concern to politicians is to maximize the use of the findings. When the user generates the questions, and when the purpose of the evaluation is to produce the highest quality information for policy or program use, this has the effect of eliminating any congressional suspicions that "the questions set for discovery (by the evaluators) have predetermined answers" or that "the assumed posture of objectivity among program evaluators masks subtle but important biases and hidden agendas."

In legislative politics, the most credible evaluations are those whose use will be maximized. This may seem paradoxical, given that high methodological quality may not ensure use, and we have seen that adversaries in the political process will often use any data that support their case. Some people believe that the best way to achieve policy use is through partisan evaluation that supports either the policymaker's ideology or the evaluator's own, but credibility involves more than methodological quality: it involves responsiveness to the specific policy question and information need. Partisan use by policymakers is not helpful for the credibility of an evaluation. On the contrary, partisanship is, at best, a short-term strategy that is not well adapted to legislative politics. In Congress, partisan work that is well received by one committee would be quickly discredited by another, and worse, the reputation for partisanship would remain with the evaluator over the longer term. Independent analysis that is strong methodologically and seeks to be as objective as humanly possible, serves a much wider legislative audience and can be the focus of cross-committee or even House- and Senate-wide debate. (We have seen this happen on three separate occasions in our work on chemical warfare.)

An evaluation that is read and whose findings are used in the policy process will have a political influence; such an influence is inherent in the fundamental interaction of evaluation with politics. Evaluation's main value to policy in the long run is not its capacity for political influence but its contribution of systematic, scholarly, independent, critical thinking to the decision making process.

Decision makers may fail to ask certain kinds of questions because either they do not want to, they do not think of them, or there is not time to get answers. In exploring some of the questions decision makers at different levels and positions in both branches of government tend to ask, I recently pointed out that there are some areas in which evaluators are not often asked questions, even though they could probably contribute powerfully to useful answers. An example of this is the rarity with which decision makers pose relevant evaluative questions prior to the introduction of a new program. As a result, there is habitually a serious dearth of evaluative information entering the area of policy formulation in time to influence the proposal.

Many of us spend much of our time doing retrospective studies: these are and will continue to be the meat and potatoes of evaluation research. Congress asks us for them and asks the executive branch to do them, and they are needed; but these studies

are not the easiest ones to insert into the political process, and they may well be the least propitious from the viewpoint of use. When we at the U.S. General Accounting Office (GAO) do one of them, we always try to focus hard on what it will be possible to accomplish uniquely through legislative means. We know how hard it will be to change much of anything in a long-established, well-entrenched agency program.

By contrast, before a program has started, evaluators can have an enormous effect in improving the reasoning behind program purposes or goals, in identifying the problems to be addressed, and in selecting the best point of intervention and the type of intervention most likely to succeed. The tempo at which new programs are sometimes introduced presents some difficulty. Recently, Senator Moynihan complained that the provisions of the Gramm-Rudman-Hollings bill were still being tinkered with while he was being asked to vote on it. The pace often becomes so frantic that the lead time necessary to gear up for evaluative work is simply impossible to obtain if results are to be ready soon enough to be useful.

At the GAO we have developed a method I call the Prospective Evaluation Synthesis which is specifically intended to be useful in the formulation of new programs. We have used this method a number of times, including a study of a proposed program focusing on teenage pregnancy. Essentially, the method seeks to gather information on what is known about past, similar programs and apply the experience to the architecture of the new one. In the case of teenage pregnancy, Senator Chafee asked us to look at the bill he was introducing; we managed to secure four good months to do the work, and it has been a major success both from the legislative point of view and our own. From a more general, political perspective, providing understanding ahead of time of how a program might work can render a valuable public service—either by helping to shore up a poorly thought-out program or by validating the basic soundness of what is to be undertaken. True, there are questions that decision makers do not pose to evaluators that could usefully be posed, which seems a priori to be a problem for the framework; however, even when evaluators have been free to choose the questions, this particular type of question has not often been asked. Also, evaluators can always influence the next round of policy questions through their products.

## TRANSLATING POLICY QUESTIONS

The second part of the continuum is the translation of the policy question into an evaluation question. We have found in working with Congress that this is one of the most sensitive and important political interactions in the entire process, and it has to be given a great deal of thought, care, and attention. This is the point at which the sponsor is going to learn if the policy question being asked is researchable. If the evaluator concludes that it is not researchable, this may be because the issue or program is immature; for example, it may be impossible to answer cause-and-effect questions if there has been little or no prior conceptual development in the field to guide the execution of such work. In this case, it would be wise to try to transform the question from the cause-and-effect type to another type that could be answered, if in fact such an answer would also be useful to the decision maker. We could move, say, from asking what the factors are that cause high quality and productivity in an organization, to asking either what is known about high

quality in an organization and how it is defined or what the characteristics are of people and work processes in a number of selected organizations whose high quality and productivity are recognized. This eminently rational process of transforming a cause-and-effect question into a descriptive question based on evidence of researchability is fraught with risks.

Sponsors do not like to have their questions modified; to them, this smacks of the researcher substituting his or her wisdom for that of the policymaker. So a change needs to be carefully and persuasively explained and negotiated. In Congress, there is often a real need for findings that are generalizable to the nation, whether or not a national study is feasible in terms of time, costs, and the type or locus of the program. In programs heavily dependent on state variation, for example, there is a continuing problem of how to obtain in-depth knowledge that can help illuminate that variation and at the same time develop more superficial but politically needed knowledge about what the situation is nationwide. The translation is not always an obvious or easy one.

In thinking of the fourth part of the framework continuum—when evaluation findings will have to be translated back into policy findings—it is critical for both the evaluator and the sponsor to remember the importance that a powerful methodology will have at that time for being persuasive if the evaluation deals with a controversial policy area. That is, it is rarely prudent to enter a burning political debate armed only with a case study, even if that case study were the most rational approach to the original policy question.

The movement from policy question to evaluation question must be carefully prepared, with a lot of thought given to the sponsor's time requirements, the cost, the relation of the type of findings expected for the particular policy need, the kind of program and its locus, the prior research done, and the likely controversiality of the issues.

The evaluator also needs to think beyond the sponsor, in this part of the continuum, to the entire federal context of the program. The question may have been raised by legislative policy actors, but in order for any evaluation recommendations to have an effect, the evaluator knows it will be necessary for executive branch policy actors to think those recommendations are right and to act on them. This entails another subcomplex of questions for the evaluator who wants the evaluation to be useful, including such issues as: "Have we got the right problem from the agency viewpoint?" If they do not think so, is that because it is unimportant or because they just do not want to think about it? Is the question symptomatic of a deeper problem that should be addressed? Who is in a position to do something about the problem? What if a power change occurred during the conduct of the evaluation—a new administration might come in or control of the Senate change hands—what effect would that have on the usefulness of the findings? The evaluators cannot necessarily do something about all of these issues, but they and others may have a great impact on the eventual use of the findings. At the minimum, legislative evaluators have a major interest in maintaining good relations with executive branch agency evaluators if those agencies must implement the recommendations and ultimately resolve the problem being treated by the evaluation.

A related consideration in conducting negotiations on the change from policy to evaluation question is that policymakers and their staffs are impatient with the typically equivocal nature of findings. For them, what is uppermost is their political

need to take unequivocal policy positions. This reemphasizes the importance for evaluators working within a policy context to be aware of the type of political debate into which their finished evaluation will likely enter, and to structure the evaluation design—once the evaluation question is settled—not so as to deal with every conceivable issue, but to produce strong, well-focused information which will be usable in that particular debate.

## DOING THE EVALUATION

The third part of the continuum involves doing the evaluation. Although the evaluator now begins a phase of the work in which he or she is in at least relative control, both the evaluation design and the writing of the report need to be understood with the political context in mind. A sixth point about the changes in evaluation practice that are brought about by the use of this framework has to do with the narrow limits of policymakers' interest in past experience. Decision makers look forward; evaluators look back. Although it is often the case that policy actors are genuinely interested in knowing what effects a program had, their interest almost never stops there. Almost invariably the evaluator will be asked to say what the evaluation findings mean in prescriptive terms: if it is a descriptive study, there will usually be a normative question posed and, nearly always, an invitation to say what the findings signify for future programs. In the GAO's Program Evaluation and Methodology Division (PEMD) we have come to understand that we must expect these kinds of questions; even in an exploratory study, if it is for Congress, we try to build in a panel of experts, carefully chosen to reflect the widest possible spectrum of political opinion as well as both substantive and methodological expertise. We bring these experts in early in the study to help us develop the criteria we know we will need to make use of in answering the normative questions that will be asked. For example, in a descriptive management study, how will we decide what degree of communication in an organization is adequate and what degree is inadequate? In a medical study, what counts as "progress" and what counts as "lack of progress" in treatment or patient management techniques? In a study of research utilization, how many omissions or distortions of the findings does it take to constitute misuse? Cronbach wrote in 1980: "An evaluation of a particular project has its greatest implications for projects that will be put in place in the future." What we have now learned is how to build features into a design that will allow us to speak a little more strongly about the significance of our findings for those future projects.

Another point of change implied by the framework for the execution of the evaluation design involves the need for a wide range of approaches and methods, often used in combination so that the strengths of one can palliate the weaknesses of another. Responsiveness to a policy question does not allow the luxury of, as Cronbach expressed it, "chapels dedicated to the glorification of particular styles." The political environment has its exigencies even here. National data are nearly always wanted. Again, there is a similar kind of mystique surrounding heavily quantitative impact evaluations; for congressional staff generally, they are the most considered studies (a 1979 survey reported by Florio, Behrmann, and Goltz in *Educational Evaluation and Policy Analysis* showed that "information on the impact of legislative policy and authorized programs is significantly greater in importance" than other types of informa-

tion, such as demographic information on populations served and affected, opinions and reactions of interested population groups, or program-descriptive information.) When the evaluation is situated within the confines of a really emotional debate, a quantitative, generalizable impact study can offer protection for the evaluator, but such a study may be neither feasible nor appropriate for the question. Even when it is the right study to do, if legislative policy staff are given a choice between timeliness and the kind of powerful methodology that could be persuasive, staff will generally choose timeliness, so great are the political pressures of deadlines on Capitol Hill. Thus, the translation from an evaluation question to a design that is appropriate (both methodologically and politically) is not always easy.

An additional point concerns getting the agreement of the sponsor on the evaluation design once it is completed. While this generally goes without saying in the executive branch, discussion of evaluation designs with legislative staff has been much less frequent. We have adopted this as a formal procedure in PEMD evaluations, using the discussions in several ways. First, the design will include some conclusions about how long the evaluation will take, what methods will be used, how likely we are to get answers to the questions posed, how unequivocal those answers are likely to be, how credible the study will be (especially if it is on a controversial subject), and what types and numbers of reports will be produced. The design meeting with the sponsor involves a staff briefing, discussion of any changes the sponsor wants, and agreement on how the evaluation will be conducted and reported. The issue of reporting relates once again to the problem of timeliness in Congress: the design will choose among various types of products—statement of fact, briefing report, testimony, full-length report—based on the sponsor's timing needs.

We have also used the design discussions to help initiate legislative staff into some technical aspects of evaluation. The necessity for this is dictated by misunderstandings that have arisen when congressional staff have not been carefully briefed on exactly what work is being pursued. The two biggest problems we have had are overly grand expectations about what can be accomplished in a short time and lack of awareness of what the immaturity of a subject area can mean for the evaluation's ability to produce strong information. In one case, we were given only twelve months to produce a study that needed twice as much time. In another, we were expected to produce a methodology in a field in which the paucity of research indicated that we could, at best, produce guidelines.

The design meeting is also useful because congressional staff will typically explain to us how they expect to use our work, and this may well lead to a modification in the design or in the planned products. It also exposes us to important cumulative insights into the legislative process and into congressional relationships with the executive branch.

It is prodigiously important for evaluation use that the overall credibility of the evaluation be assured, and that we become aware of the kinds of efforts that have to be made to achieve that credibility during the conduct of the evaluation.

The use of the framework conflicts once again with former evaluation practice. One of Cronbach's theses advised evaluators "to release findings piecemeal and informally to the audiences that need them" because "the impotence that comes with delay may be a greater risk than the possibility that early returns will be misread." A worse and much more dangerous possibility is not that those early returns will be misread but that they will be wrong—because they are early and have not been systematically checked. The rules at the GAO about indexing, referencing, and quality assurance stand us in good stead on this. Staff who have not been a part of the evaluation team are the ones who do this work, and during the sometimes incredibly detailed shakedown sessions about the support for a figure or the appropriateness of some data analysis, the cries and whimpers of maddened researchers can be heard throughout the division. Disagreeable though the quality control process usually is, nearly everyone is glad we have it. We tend not to release information until we are sure it has satisfied the quality control process because we have learned that a loss of credibility takes a long time to recover from and can in fact prove fatal. While we recognize the extreme importance of early information on Capitol Hill, credibility is even more important: it is the critical prerequisite for use over the long term. Whether the issue is fairness, balance, methodological quality, or just plain old accuracy, no effort to establish credibility is ever wasted.

## ANSWERING POLICY QUESTIONS

In the fourth part of the continuum, the evaluation results are translated into policy answers to the original policy question. Here we are trying to communicate evaluation findings to a political audience in such a way that the findings will be both well understood and persuasive. This implies changes to typical evaluation practice. Another point speaks to the difficulty of establishing priorities among the findings. In politics, priorities are the heart of the matter—not ideology, not even consistency or persistency, but putting first things first at the right time. In evaluation, on the other hand, this is not only one of the most difficult things to achieve, it is rarely thought about at all. We evaluators have the habit of laying out all our results in the same careful, neutral phrases, leaving it to the scientifically trained audience to perceive the areas of success, of promise, of no result, of failure. We document everything, usually in the same neutral tone, with what has been described by Cronbach as "self-defeating thoroughness." The problem is that all of the evaluation's findings seem important to its author. It is painfully difficult to order them in a policy context, to trim surgically what is not relevant, to condense, to rank, to decide not only which finding is the most important but which is the most important that policy can do something about.

Once again we hear the cries and laments of unhappy evaluators. From the viewpoint of use, it is crucial to discriminate in communicating results between what is important and what is not and to be clear about how the findings should or could be acted on. Some findings are difficult to be clear about, except to say bluntly that they are not clear. In other cases, we simply do not know the answer to the policy question. It is important, from a political viewpoint, for us to become comfortable with the idea of saying that a conclusive answer is not available when in fact it is not. In our work, we have found that the knowledge that no knowledge exists is important policy information that decision makers do not necessarily have. In many cases, for example, Congress will be told by an executive agency that there is no evidence of certain unfavorable results in some program. What that often means is that the agency has not looked for such evidence. This is different from being able to say, "We have looked seriously and systematically, and there is no evidence one way or the other." If there is no evidence and this can be shown, then the way is cleared to get support for research that will, if possible, develop the needed information.

In trying to make findings clear, useful, and effectively available to policymakers, communication techniques need to be developed that may depart greatly from typical evaluation practice. A first effort has to do with banishing evaluation jargon. This is important not just because policymakers do not understand it but because it seems to them to hint at some private club, some special understanding, some incomprehensible ritual from which they are excluded. This gives rise not just to impatience but to irritation with the evaluator which carries over to the evaluation. It is the kind of irritation that H. L. Mencken expressed when he said a metaphysician was one who, when you remark that twice two makes four, demands to know what you mean by twice, what by two, what by makes, and what by four. The intelligibility of an evaluation report is critical for the use of its findings.

A second effort has to do with varying the written products so that the information can be presented briefly and succinctly but is backed up with all the supporting data needed by a variety of audiences. A third effort involves paralleling the delivery of reports with as much oral communication as possible. This is the style of reporting that is most natural to policymakers, especially those on Capitol Hill. Congressional staff and members of Congress are used to listening to constituents and lobbyists; they gather ideas and form judgments not only by reading but especially by talking with staff and colleagues, by holding committee hearings, by interacting personally with a wide variety of people. In this environment, oral briefings are crucial; testimony can be more useful than a major report. We now see video apparatus being pressed into service to help reconcile the tension between the need to document and the need for easy expression and understanding.

In general, when we think about the entire process, starting with the original policy question, of doing evaluation, we see that we have moved purposefully away from the anecdote or war story as a credible answer to a policy question. As evaluators, we are typically trying to get a sense of the size of a problem, of its range, its frequency, its direction, its average characteristics. After having determined the evaluation results, when we must move back into the political forum the policy question emerged from originally, we find that one of the most effective ways to present findings is to rediscover the anecdote, to illustrate the general findings via specific cases and analogies that graphically focus attention on and explain the larger points. When used in this manner, anecdotes are not expected to stand alone as answers to policy questions; instead, they are used as representative of the broader evaluative evidence—to explain the findings, to increase the political understanding and comfort level, and, above all, to improve the likelihood that the evaluation findings will be used.

## USING THE FINDINGS/GENERATING NEW QUESTIONS

The fifth and last part of the continuum involves use and the generation of new questions. In traditional agency focused evaluation practice, it has often been difficult to trace the use of evaluation findings. This is less true with legislative evaluation, where use can be measured in a number of ways. We have seen our own evaluations figure in program reauthorization. One example is our

assessment of homeless and runaway youth centers which was a major factor in the doubling of the centers' reauthorization funds; another example is the change in the law—based on our findings about the situation of working mothers in the Aid to Families with Dependent Children (AFDC) program—that was enacted to allow a prolonged period of health insurance for earner families. Hearings are often organized around our findings. Examples are recent hearings on such issues as the Medicare Prospective Payment System, the defense industrial base, student aid, educational research, hazardous waste, poverty indicators, drinking age laws, and many others. Our findings and recommendations are incorporated in legislative direction to the executive branch. An example is our finding in the science and math teachers' study of the need for evaluation in the National Science Foundation (NSF) teacher-training programs, which NSF was then directed to perform by the Senate Appropriations Committee. We can measure the use of our findings in legislative debates that directly affect up-or-down congressional votes. Here I would cite our work on chemical warfare which, year after year, figured notably in the national argument about whether or not to produce binary chemical weapons. In legislative evaluation, use occurs—indeed, use is the rule, not the exception—and it is measurable.

We achieve a further use of evaluation findings through the synthesis method we have developed which brings together previous evaluations in a topic area, analyzes and compares them—reuses them—with the intent of developing a general finding about knowledge in that area. We engage in the same process of reuse in conducting the prospective evaluation synthesis.

The evaluator has the ability to influence successive rounds of policy questions that need to be asked but that, for one reason or another, may not be generated by policy actors. I see two types of questions that we must try to influence. The first type is descriptive: It is truly amazing how difficult it is to persuade policymakers of the importance of descriptive information. Our work on hazardous waste found that we simply do not know how many million metric tons of it are being generated every year in this country. Questions asking what is the size of a problem, how many people are involved in a program, what characteristics they have, what services they receive and how they feel about them, or, in a technological communications program, say, how many messages are sent, who sends them, and who receives them—these types of questions do not get asked in some agencies. As a result, more sophisticated questions about program benefits or effects cannot be adequately answered when Congress needs those answers.

A political factor contributing to the lack of strong program description is that, as Ernest W. Stromsdorfer noted, "the more political support there is for a program, the more limited will be the available systematic information on that program." Defense programs are a good example of this, and the fact that much of the information involved is classified, nonpublic information does not help. Rarely is there archiving of test and evaluation findings, even on a need-to-know basis; every effort to evaluate every weapon system has to start from scratch. Congress is beginning to look a little more carefully at the evaluative basis for moving into production with some weapon systems, so this may change.

On the other hand, relatively unpopular programs tend to produce more information and to be evaluated more often. Herman Leonard, in *Checks Unbalanced: The Quiet Side of Public Spending,* looks at some popular and unpopular programs and their ability to spend money without drawing attention to themselves. He points out, among other things, that social security has been able to commit over $100 billion annually for the last forty years without much discussion, while political controversy surrounds AFDC's budget of $10 billion or so. A large amount of systematic descriptive information is available on AFDC while a host of other more popular programs (such as defense and social security) have been largely able to avoid much public scrutiny.

The second type of question that is not asked much in executive agencies (it most definitely is asked in Congress) is the question of impact. Here the impediment remains twofold: the threat to decision makers and the paucity of incentives for accountability. Whereas, over the years, we have seen quite a few of these studies done in the executive branch despite the threat they unquestionably pose, over the past five years we have seen a marked reduction in results-oriented evaluations. Sometimes, the only way for these evaluations to be done in the executive branch is to have Congress mandate them, as has often happened in the past.

While it is true we have given up, for policy studies, some of our traditional freedom to choose programs and questions, leaving these now to emerge from the political arena, it is not clear that we would have been successful in any case in getting agency policymakers to ask many impact or descriptive questions. Where sponsored policy studies are concerned, the evaluator's freedom to ask certain questions may have always been more nominal than real. On the other hand, by noting the absence of answers to these questions in our findings and by recommending to Congress that these questions be asked, it is possible that we can get more attention paid to their importance the second time around.

## WHAT HAVE WE LEARNED?

What have we learned about the politics of program evaluation? I can point to a number of lessons. First, we have learned that, to be successful, we must be useful to others, not ourselves. That means understanding the political system in which evaluation operates and understanding the information needs of those policy actors who are the users of evaluations.

We have also learned to conceptualize the political system a little more broadly, to include all sectors that make the kinds of policy decisions into which evaluation feeds—that is, not just executive but also legislative branch policymaking. Indeed, if the judicial branch continues to increase its use of cost-benefit and risk analysis, we will need to study and include the judiciary as well. Such study would certainly include evaluative ramifications on the kinds of evidence that need to be produced, and political ramifications of judicial use on decision making in the executive and legislative branches. This is important because evaluation's interactions with legislative and executive branch policy actors can be profoundly modified by the inclusion of a new set of policy actors from a different branch of government. Policy is never made in isolation: Legislative policy affects executive branch policy integrally, and the converse is equally true. Evaluators need to understand political interactions—no matter which branch they are working for.

We have learned that evaluators working for the legislative branch will be pressed to go beyond earlier horizons of social programs. The congressional functions require evaluative skills in such areas as defense; the environment; energy and natural resources; as well as, for example, in health, education, and welfare.

Planning for use involves understanding the political conditions under which evalu-ation findings will be used. We have learned that two of these conditions are that (1) the policy question posed must be of fundamental interest to the intended user, and (2) the eventual evaluation findings must answer that question. Both of these conditions empower the decision maker at the expense of a certain amount of the evaluators' discretion.

We have learned that a third political condition for use is credibility. If the evaluation is assailable on grounds of poor methodological quality or on grounds of partisanship, this will reduce the use made of its findings in Congress. The high quality and acknowledged objectivity of a study cannot ensure use if the policy question is not of interest; but poor quality and subjectivity will weaken use, no matter what the question is.

A fourth condition for use is timeliness. Evaluators working for the legislative branch must be concerned about the timing of the final product and how it dovetails with congressional policy cycles and plans for use. We have learned that what is most important sometimes is not having the best design, but having an adequate design that will bring the findings in at the time they were promised.

Overall, we have learned that there is no perfect evaluation design but that, rather, evaluators must try to achieve a balance involving timing, methodological strength, and cost. Often it is a matter of degree: A methodology that doubles the time necessary for performing an evaluation will be unacceptable no matter what its advantages. One which moderately increases the time while strengthening the conclusiveness of the information to be obtained may be enthusiastically accepted under some political circumstances.

Planning for use always incorporates the question, "who will implement the study recommendations?" We have learned that good relations with the implementing executive agency may be the sine qua non of that ultimate use.

Evaluators have not conducted many prospective studies. But we have learned that one of the most felicitous times for the introduction of evaluative thinking into the policy forum is before a new bill is proposed. New techniques need to be developed to enable the doing of this work on a very short time schedule.

Panels of experts can serve an important legitimizing function. We have learned that carefully chosen panels are a powerful aid in strengthening the political credibility of an evaluation's findings, especially when the study is of a controversial subject.

It is important for an evaluator to have mastered a wide variety of evaluation approaches. No single design or method can be counted on to address the diversity of policy questions that political debates engender.

The transition from policy question to evaluative question to evaluation design is not a straightforward process, and it usually involves several iterations. We have learned that, no matter how many negotiations there have been, it is wise to be sure the user agrees with the finished design and understands both how the study will be conducted and what kind of information will be available at its conclusion.

We have learned that indexing, referencing, and general checking of draft reports are activities that are worth their weight in gold: Although time is important, and all this checking does have to be planned for, there is enormous risk attached to any weakening of credibility.

Prioritization of the evaluation findings is also a condition for use. We have learned that telling all is tantamount to telling nothing. The important thing is to answer the policy question as clearly and simply as possible, to emphasize a few critical and striking numbers, and to do all that in such a way as to highlight those findings that give rise to policy action. Much time needs to be devoted to thinking out how we will present our findings so that they can be intelligible to our several audiences.

In the legislative branch, the use of evaluation findings is the rule, not the exception. In the past six years of working with Congress, we have learned that evaluations are a demonstrably important adjunct of policymaking, that they do figure in go/no go decisions, and that they often set the agenda for national debates.

A further use of evaluations can be achieved via studies employing metaanalysis or evaluation synthesis. Such secondary evaluation is a major tool in helping decision makers to make sense out of conflicting findings and to improve the quality of information available to them.

Descriptive questions are not typically raised by policymakers, which means that systematic information about some programs is often missing. We have learned that emphasizing in an evaluation report that such information is both missing and needed can help to get it provided at a later date.

Questions of impact seem to be asked less and less by executive branch agencies, more and more by legislative policymakers. We have learned that a legislative user can have strong leverage on programs, through the authorization and appropriations process or through oversight.

Finally, the fact of taking political processes into account when doing an evaluation transforms the way in which time is allocated. We have learned to devote much more time than we used to to negotiation, discussion, briefing, checking accuracy, prioritizing, and presentation.

I sum up all of these political lessons by saying that things have changed with respect to evaluation use. Beyond any doubt, the use in policymaking by Congress that we are seeing now is real, measurable, and growing dramatically. But if we are making progress, we owe a large debt of gratitude to those who cried failure in the past. They focused our attention on the political environment in which we expected our work to be useful but about which we knew little. This was important because use does not happen by itself. It requires some major modifications of traditional evaluation practice.

This is not to say that it is time to cry victory. We cannot do that until executive agencies realize there is growing risk in failing to evaluate their programs: If they do not, legislative agencies will. On the other hand, we have dispelled the notion that evaluation is not useful in policymaking. There is every reason to be hopeful about the future of evaluation research and practice, given the important role it is playing in improving the quality of information available to decision makers.

## 23.

**Bruce A. Thyer**

## PROMOTING RESEARCH ON COMMUNITY PRACTICE: USING SINGLE-SYSTEM DESIGNS

During the past two decades, one of the most significant methodological advances within social work research has involved the incorporation of single-system research designs (SSRDs) as a technique to monitor practice outcomes (Task Force, 1991; Thyer & Thyer, 1992; Thyer, 1993). Although SSRDs have been primarily advocated as tools to evaluate clinical social work, they have also been widely utilized in the conduct of organizational and community-based practice (see Greene, Winett, Von Houten, Geller, and

Bruce A. Thyer is Research Professor in the School of Social Work, University of Georgia, Athens, GA 30602.

Iwata, 1987). Just as conventional group research tools, such as the group pretest-posttest design or the Student *t* test, can be applied to virtually all areas of practice research, so too can SSRDs be useful in examining the outcomes of intervention with systems of differing levels, from the micro to the macro.

This paper presents an overview of the fundamental requirements needed to conduct SSRDs, focusing on organizational and community research conducted by social workers and other human service professionals. This paper will first describe the differing research designs and then provide several examples of the real application of SSRDs in community practice.

TABLE 23.1
Prerequisites for Conducting Single-System Research in Organizations.

1. Select a practical and valid outcome measure which can be repeatedly assessed over time.

2. Assess this outcome measure over time.

3. Display the results on a graph, with time on the horizontal axis, and the outcome measure on the vertical axis.

4. Visually inspect the line depicted by joining the data points.

5. Make any inferences which are reasonable (e.g., Are the data clearly *improving*? Are the data clearly *deteriorating*? Do the data clearly depict *no change*? Are the data *unclear*?). Seek concurrence from your colleagues.

## BASIC PRINCIPLES OF SINGLE-SYSTEM RESEARCH DESIGNS

SSRDs present the social worker with only two prerequisites. The first is the need to develop a reliable, repeatable, and valid measure of community or organizational functioning (see Fellin, Rothman, & Meyer, 1967). The second is to actually assess this measure over time. This allows the social worker to empirically answer the evaluative question "Did organizational or community functioning change (improve) over time?" When administrative and organizational resources allow more sophisticated designs, it also may be possible to answer the more complex, experimental question "Did social work intervention actually *cause* the observed improvements?" These prerequisites are summarized in Table 23.1.

The distinction between the so-called evaluative and experimental questions is important. Too often, conducting social work research is presented as an idealized activity that translates poorly to real-life investigations conducted in actual agency or community-based settings. Social work texts often gloss over the difficulties of implementing 'pure' research designs in community and organizational practice. Thus, when the nascent researcher encounters these practical difficulties and is unprepared to deal with them, the researcher often abandons evaluation research as an intrinsic part of social work practice.

For example, basic science is primarily concerned with the development of theory and the testing of hypotheses, with the aim of producing generalizable knowledge. Evaluation research is more practical, not necessarily concerned with promulgating generalizable knowledge but often with discovering specific knowledge valid only for the particular agency, organization, or community being studied. Social worker practitioners are more concerned with empirically ascertaining what has actually happened in our specific practice setting, not necessarily with demonstrating propositions valid across all similar settings. It is important to see if one's organization or community has changed. It is also important (albeit more difficult) to demonstrate that such changes resulted from one's social work intervention.

Once social workers have gathered data over time, they depict them on a simple line graph. Usually time (e.g., days, weeks, months, years) is presented on the bottom, horizontal axis, and the outcome measure is presented on the left, vertical, axis. Usually social workers use visual inspection alone to make inferences regarding changes. Each weekday the business sections of local newspapers depict line graphs constructed as above, portraying the Dow-Jones stock averages for the past few days, weeks, months, or years. It is easy to determine if a trend has been in the direction of growth, stability, decline, or wildly erratic, all without recourse to complex statistics. Similarly, during the 1996 presidential campaign, monthly and weekly graphs portrayed the numbers of voters who supported various candidates. It is usually easy to make accurate inferences regarding significant change (assuming that the outcome measure is a reliable and valid one) by visual inspection alone. Single-system research designs use the same logic, whether the unit of analysis is the daily weight of an obese client (clinical social work), ratings of group atmosphere (group work), employee absenteeism (organizational practice), or weekly crime statistics for a given neighborhood (community practice).

Sometimes social work research textbooks advocate using inferential statistics to make inferences from SSRD data. I do not recommend this for several reasons. The added dimension of using inferential statistics, if seen as essential to analyze SSRD data, will deter those who are unfamiliar with specialized statistical knowledge from attempting evaluation research. A second reason is that many of the recommended statistical tests are based upon the usual assumptions of parametric analysis (equality of variances, a normal distribution, and independence of the data). Using SSRDS, often the data points, which determine the degrees of freedom for parametric statistics, are small in number, particularly if the design has different phases (see below). The small number of data points (i.e., degrees of freedom) makes statistical inference problematic because the data points have low sensitivity (low power) to detect differences. A third reason is that SSRDs by their very nature contradict the most important assumption of parametric tests, the independence of the data. For example, in a group design that examines sense of empowerment in two different community groups, the data are truly independent. The data from one group are in no reasonable way connected with or influenced by the data from the other group. Single-system research designs only have data from one system (group, organization, community), assessed repeatedly. Therefore the data are not 'independent' in a statistical sense, and may be serially dependent (or autocorrelated). If significant autocorrelation exists in data, parametric tests are invalid.

A fourth reason to rely solely upon visual inspection of data is that it reduces the likelihood that small but reliable differences will be detected. This is called a Type 2 error, missing a 'true' difference when one exists. The opposite is a Type 1 error, claiming that a difference exists, when it really doesn't. In practice research evaluating social work interventions, researchers are not usually interested in statistically reliable changes which are practically unimportant. Researchers want to find interventions that make a major, practical difference. Visual inspection alone increases Type 2 errors, missing some valid, but small, differences, and decreases Type I errors, making exaggerated claims. In essence, using visual inspection alone results in a conservative analysis of one's data. This is good, and partially corrects for the tendency in social work research to over-emphasize statistically significant but practically unimportant changes in the data.

There are some specialized methods of statistical inference that may be validly applied to SSRD data, such as the Box-Jenkins time series analysis. This has the drawback of requiring a minimum of 50 data-points, and a computer program to run the test. Few, community researchers will conduct SSRD studies with this number of data points, or have the necessary computer resources to use such tests. On balance, I advise the beginning community or organizational practitioner undertaking evaluation research with SSRDs to use only visual inspection of the data to make inferences about change.

## VARIETIES OF SINGLE-SYSTEM RESEARCH DESIGNS

Single-system research designs can be grouped roughly into two categories: those suitable for simple evaluations of outcomes, and those labeled as experimental designs, given their potential to isolate causation.

### The Evaluative Designs

Perhaps the most practical evaluative SSRD is the A-B design. Researchers repeatedly gather data prior to social work intervention (called the A phase, or baseline), and then continue to collect data after intervention begins. This second period is called the B or intervention phase. On line graphs the A and B phases usually are separated by a dashed vertical line to distinguish the two time periods. Sometimes, if the data in the baseline are gathered over a sufficiently long time, and are fairly stable (i.e., reflecting a clear trend upward, downward, or as not changing appreciably), and if the data in the B phase have clearly changed from those in the A phase, it may be quite visually compelling to conclude that the intervention caused these observed changes.

Such causal inferences need to be made quite cautiously however, given the numerous rival hypotheses which could explain differences in the two phases. The problem may have improved spontaneously, or it may be cyclic (and the baseline was not long enough to detect this). Data-collection procedures should not differ between the two phases. And most importantly, the data may have changed coincidentally with introducing the intervention because of an extraneous factor unrelated to treatment (e.g., a concurrent historical event within the community). Because the A-B design is usually inadequate to rule out these rival explanations, it is useful to evaluate or document changes, not to prove that an intervention caused them.

### The Experimental SSRDs

To rule out alternative explanations for positive change observed in an SSRD, researchers must use more complex designs. Most commonly these involve the intentional or accidental removal of an intervention, one or more times, while continuing to monitor the outcome measures. Such designs can take various forms, like the A-B-A, which reflects the researcher's taking a baseline followed by intervention period, followed by removing the intervention (which may be interpreted as restoring baseline conditions). The A-B-A-B design is formatted similarly, except that the second baseline is followed by reinstating the same intervention.

The experimental logic of these designs can be called relying on unlikely successive coincidences. In an A-B design, it may be argued plausibly that a clear change in the data between the two phases could be due to 'chance' factors. In the A-B-A design, with marked improvements during the B phase, followed by a return to baseline functioning during the second A phase, the skeptic is forced to argue that some 'coincidental' effect unrelated to intervention was observed not just once, but twice in a row. In the A-B-A-B design, our skeptical colleague must argue that this coincidence happened three successive times in a row. In essence the principle makes use of the experimental technique called replication to rule out rival causal influences. The A-B design permits one demonstration of a possible effect. The A-B-A demonstrates it once, then replicates it. The A-B-A-B replicates an effect twice following the initial demonstration. Repeated replication weakens the plausibility of alternative explanations.

The intentional removal of an apparently effective social work intervention may pose ethical or professional problems. However, the researcher can use the unintentional removal of treatments (e.g., the community practitioner takes a vacation, or is hospitalized) to retrospectively construct an A-B-A or A-B-A-B design. In many cases, community programs or public policies change or end, and researchers can format the data as an SSRD using removal phases as described in this section. Social worker Gerald Hannah wrote about an example of community-based research that used an A-B-A-B design to demonstrate the value of an intervention intended to help poor clients meet their financial obligations (Hannah and Risley, 1981).

An experimental SSRD that does not rely on removing social work intervention is called a multiple-baseline (MBL) design. This involves, for example, taking data in two or more communities with similar problems. Researchers measure the problem repeatedly across the two communities over time. This constitutes taking a baseline, the A phase. Next, researchers introduce a social work intervention into only one community, and continue to record data for both of them, the one receiving an intervention, and the other still "being baselined." After some time, researchers introduce the same intervention into the second community, continuing to take data for both over time.

The logic of the MBL also relies on replication and on the principle of unlikely successive coincidences. If introducing intervention to the first community yields an obvious improvement, and the second community's data remain unchanged, and if the second community displays a similar improvement when the intervention is introduced later, then researchers come closer to eliminating rival explanations for positive change, apart from the social work intervention. If the MBL design is conducted in two communities with results as described above, then it possesses the same experimental rigor as the A-B-A design, that is, one demonstration followed by one replication. If the MBL is conducted in three communities, then it is analogous in internal validity to the A-B-A-B design (one demonstration, and two replications).

Again, researchers do not usually use inferential statistics to interpret MBL designs. By limiting analysis to visual inspection, researchers may not learn about the trivial impact of social work interventions. Visual inspection of the data is a conservative way to ensure that the visually significant results have a powerful effect.

Next, this paper examines how others have actually used SSRDs to evaluate community and organizational practice.

## SOME EXAMPLES OF USING SSRDs IN COMMUNITY PRACTICE

### An A-B-A-B Design

Promoting community-based self-help groups is a laudable goal for social workers engaged in empowerment practice. Helping poor and historically oppressed groups to organize themselves sufficiently to generate a self-sustaining community group is often the beginning of assistance aimed at the ultimate goal of self-empowerment. In a study by Miller and Miller (1970), a wel-

FIGURE 23.1
Number of Welfare Recipients Attending Each of the First 26 Meetings of the Self-Help Groups

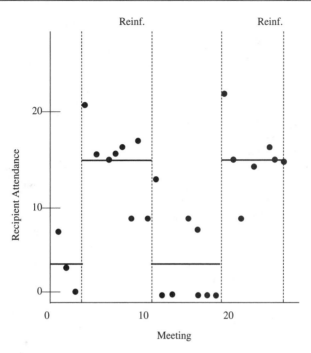

Figure 23.1 from: Miller, L. K., & Miller, O. L. (1970). Reinforcing self-help group activities of welfare recipients. *Journal of Applied Behavior Analysis, 3,* 57–64. Used by permission.

fare counselor was charged with helping AFDC recipients start such a self-help group. In this report, the outcome measure was the numbers of AFDC clients attending each group meeting. During the first three meetings (the first A phase, or baseline condition), about 100 potential group members (AFDC clients) were informed of the forthcoming meeting and urged to attend. The self-help group's President (a client receiving AFDC) conducted the meetings. In meetings, members discussed problems and explored potential solutions, and the counselor provided information about potential resources to solve problems. The meetings focussed on two problems, problems specific to AFDC matters (e.g., delayed checks, amount of money authorized, medical authorizations, etc.) and to the community as a whole (e.g., urban renewal, police, school board, city government, etc.).

Attendance was fairly low, ranging from a high of 8 to a low of zero clients by the third meeting. In the face of this low attendance, which precluded development of an effective community organization, the welfare worker undertook the following intervention. Prior to the fourth meeting, the welfare worker mailed the usual invitation to participate, but also informed potential clients that if they attended, they could select two Christmas toys for each child in their family. At subsequent meetings, attendees could choose from a variety of goods (toys, appliances, rugs, kitchen utensils), services (extra assistance in finding a house, help in processing an AFDC grievance, negotiating with the landlord over needed home improvements), or information (birth control, additional social service resources) at the end of each meeting, These reinforcers were all donated items, or otherwise made available by the welfare counselor through efforts beyond her regular duties.

The counselor provided external incentives contingent upon self-help group attendance for eight consecutive meetings (the first intervention, or B phase). Attendance during the B phase ranged from 9–21 participants, with an average of 15 per group meeting.

Unexpectedly the welfare counselor required major surgery, and during the next eight meetings there were no reinforcers for group attendance. This inadvertent removal of the contingency program comprised the second A or baseline phase. During these eight meetings, group attendance ranged from zero to 12, with an average of three clients participating. When the worker returned and restored the reinforcement program for attendance (and thus the second B or intervention phase), the number attending averaged 16, ranging from 8–22 clients per meeting. Figure 23.1 shows these data.

The clear shift in attendance, detectable solely by visual inspection of the data, demonstrates that the worker's reinforcement program was responsible (in a causal sense) for promoting the attendance of AFDC clients at community-based self-help meetings. Supplemental data revealed that the contingency program encouraged the same people to return to the meetings, and that without extrinsic reinforcement, group members increased their participation in related groups, such as a Model Cities Advisory Board, a Citizen's Advisory Board, City Council, School Board, and related

groups. This suggests (but does not prove) that after ensuring sufficient exposure to the self-help group experience using external incentives, that the naturally occurring reinforcers encountered through such participation take over to promote further community involvement.

## A Multiple-Baseline Design

Briscoe, Hoffman, and Bailey (1975) present a fine example of using a multiple-baseline design. The study focused on teaching effective problem-solving skills to nine African-American, low SES, board members of a community-based self-help project. At board meetings, members spoke at the same time, did not listen to each other, and jumped from topic to topic without resolving issues. The researchers defined what constituted effective problem-solving behaviors (e.g., identifying problems, presenting possible solutions, deciding on actions to be taken), and recorded reliable baseline measures of these skills from videotapes of the community board meetings. Researchers took separate measures of how often board members engaged in three discrete behavioral skills: (1) clearly identified a problem, (2) suggested a solution, and (3) agreed upon some specific actions to be taken to work towards solving a problem.

The counselor trained group members to improve each of these skills in a staggered sequence. All three skills were baselined over the meetings, and after five community board meetings, the counselor trained members only in identifying problems. After three more meetings, the counselor trained members only in suggesting solutions. Two meetings later, the counselor trained members only in developing specific actions to help resolve problems. Figure 23.2 shows the data.

FIGURE 23.2
Number of Problem-Solving Statements, Solution Statements, and Action Statements Made During the
Board Meetings by All Nine Board Members

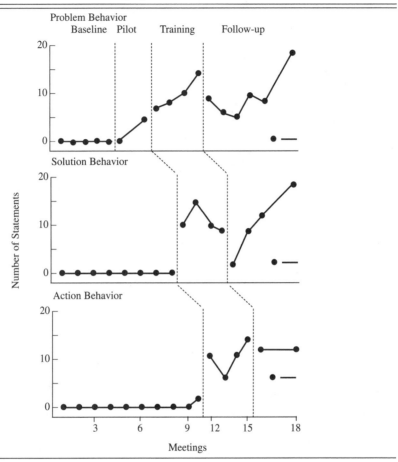

It is clear that during the baseline phases the three targeted skills were not improving. When training was provided to identify problems, this skill occurred much more frequently during subsequent board meetings, but the other skills did not improve. Only when training in the other two problem-solving skills was provided did they too sequentially improve.

The replicated sequence of no improvements followed by improvements only after specific training strongly suggests that the skills training was causally responsible for the observed changes in the community board members' behavior. The original report provides data for the individual board members. In addition, two university professors who taught courses in group problem solving, and two community leaders active on local policy boards, blindly reviewed the videotapes, and were asked to judge in which ones was there greater evidence of problem-solving skills. They judged that the post-training tapes represented significantly

FIGURE 23.3

Incidence of DUI Arrests Occurring on All Sundays, Mondays, etc.,
Between January Through June, 1987, in Athens, Georgia

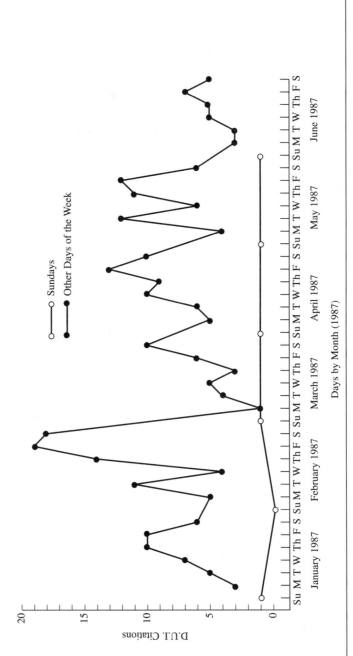

Figure 23.3 from: Briscoe, R. V., Hoffman, D. B., & Bailey, J. S. (1975). Behavioral community psychology: Training a community board to problem solve. *Journal of Applied Behavior Analysis, 8,* 157–168. Used by permission.

better problem-solving skills for two of the three skills which were trained. These qualitative data corroborate the contention that the problem-solving training protocol the researchers developed was effective in teaching these community board members useful group skills.

## Design Variations

The application of the basic principles of SSRDs is only limited by the creativity of the practitioner or by the practical constraints of existing data. One example making use of retrospectively gathered data to evaluate a public policy was reported by Ligon and Thyer (1993). Many cities/counties continue to enforce Blue Laws, that is, legislation that prohibits the sale of alcohol during certain times of the day, or days of the week. The city of Athens, Georgia, had one such law which prohibited the sale of liquor on Sundays. Ligon and Thyer obtained data on the numbers of citations for driving under the influence (DUIs) issued by Athens police over two years. They compared the citations issued on Sundays versus the other days of the week. Figure 23.3 shows the data. One line connects the Sunday data points, and the data points from the remaining days of the week are connected with a separate line. These results are clearly consistent with the hypothesis that banning alcohol sales on a given day reduces the numbers of drunk drivers, although a causal link cannot be inferred due to the numerous other explanations for these data that could not be excluded.

## Some Hypothetical Examples

The potential for SSRDs to be applied to the evaluation of community-based interventions is far greater than their applica-

tions to date. This may be attributable in part to the pervasive lack of empirically-based appraisals of community practice in general using group or SSRDs. Here are a few hypothetical examples to which these designs could be applied.

Many communities organize neighborhood watch campaigns; they post signs notifying potential criminals that neighbors will report suspicious persons to the police. In some instances, communities organize patrols of local unarmed citizens to survey the neighborhood and report crimes. How well do these programs work? To find out, the researchers could track the numbers of reported crimes, perhaps by type (burglary, rape, assault, etc.) by week or month for some time prior to establishing a neighborhood watch program (this would constitute a baseline, or 'A' phase). Then they continue data gathering and depict it graphically during and/or after the new program is implemented (this would be the intervention, or 'B' phase). Most citizens, police officials, and policy makers would be favorably impressed if crime statistics declined appreciably after a neighborhood watch program was established. Data, formatted as an A-B SSRD, could encourage citizen participation in such programs and support funding for their maintenance.

In another example, union officials sometimes enter local communities and attempt to enroll workers in a union. For these labor organizers, the number of new workers enrolled each week or month is a highly useful outcome measure of the success of their efforts. Researchers can track and graph these numbers, forming a baseline of the success of standard recruitment tactics. If the union introduces new recruiting methods (like a free newsletter describing unsafe working conditions, discriminatory hiring practices, and/or unfair management at the local factory, or sponsoring recruitment picnics with free food, drinks, and speakers), an A-B design can estimate their success.

In a recent study, McConnell, Dwyer, and Leeming (1996) reported that a free fire safety training program provided for the residents of public housing in Memphis, Tennessee, aimed to reduce the incidence of fires. If training resources mandated that the fire-safety training be provided sequentially, that is first to Building #1 residents, then Building #2, then #3, and so forth, a multiple-baseline design may emerge. In this case the outcome measures could be the incidence of fires in the months before and after the training, and/or the incidence of code violations found by fire safety inspectors. Imagine a graph similar to Figure 23.2, where the top A-B design depicts Building #I, the middle A-B design Building #2, etc. If safety officials trained residents of Building #1 first, and code violations diminished there, but remained high in the other apartment buildings, and then declined there after training, this might compel a researcher to conclude that the fire safety program was causally responsible for safety improvements.

John Wodarski and his colleagues (Slavin, Wodarski, & Blackburn, 1981) used a multiple-baseline design this way to evaluate an electricity conservation program among the elderly residents of three Baltimore apartment buildings. The researchers monitored the electricity use for weeks prior to the conservation program. They first introduced the conservation program to Tower #1, but not to #2 and #3. After a few weeks they introduced it to #2 but not #3, and then finally in Tower #3. Each apartment complex saw significant savings in energy use, but only *after* the conservation program was introduced sequentially.

## CONCLUSION

There are many examples of researchers using SSRDs to evaluate psychosocial interventions at the level of community practice. To date however, community psychologists primarily use this methodology, rather than social workers (see Greene et al., 1987). The same is true in evaluative work of organizations (see Daniels, 1989). The methodological prerequisites to conduct an evaluation study using an SSRD are not onerous, and are simply consistent with good community and administrative practice. These prerequisites are: developing clear measures of a situation, and gathering reliable, valid data on these measures over time.

Admittedly, the findings may not be generalizable, since they may be derived from a single community or organization, as opposed to the randomly selected sample of clients favored by clinical researchers. But researchers using group designs rarely obtain truly random samples and the results of group research designs often suffer from a corresponding lack of external validity (generalizability), similar to SSRD-derived results.

The design and conduct of SSRDs often can make use of already existing data available through various community resources or agency files. Professionals can grasp the concept of SSRDS, and the lack of complex inferential statistics to interpret results recommends them over group design studies.

The growing chorus of voices asking for empirical data to buttress social work claims of effectiveness can now be heard throughout the spectrum of human services, micro through macro. Community and organizationally based practitioners as well as their direct practice counterparts, are being urged to provide evidence that the constituents they are serving are indeed benefiting. The research tools known as single-system research designs are one useful strategy for providing such evidence.

## REFERENCES

Briscoe, R. V., Hoffman, D. B., & Bailey, J. S. (1975). Behavioral community psychology: Training a community board to problem solve. *Journal of Applied Analysis, 8,* 157–168.

Daniels, A. C. (1989). *Performance management: Improving quality productivity through positive reinforcement.* Tucker, GA: Performance Management Publications.

Fellin, P., Rothman, J., & Meyer, H. (1967). Implications of the socio-behavioral approach for community organization practice. In E. J. Thomas (Eds.). *The socio-behavioral approach and applications to social work* (pp. 73–86). New York: Council on Social Work Education.

Greene, B. F., Winett, R. A., Van Houten, R., Geller, E. S., & Iwata, B. A. (1987). *Behavior analysis in the community.* Lawrence, KS: Society for the Experimental Analysis of Behavior.

Hannah, G. T. & Risley, T R. (1981). Experiments in a community mental health center: Increasing client payments for outpatient services. *Journal of Applied Behavior Analysis, 14,* 141–157.

Ligon, J., & Thyer, B. A. (1993). The effects of a Sunday liquor sales ban on DUI arrests. *Journal of Alcohol and Drug Education, 38*(2), 33–40.

McConnell, C. F., Dwyer, W. O., & Leeming, F. C. (1996). A behavioral approach to reducing fires in public housing. *Journal of Community Psychology, 24,* 201–212.

Miller, L. K., & Miller, 0. L. (1970). Reinforcing self-help group activities of welfare recipients. *Journal of Applied Behavior Analysis, 3,* 57–64.

Slavin, R. E., Wodarski, J. S., & Blackburn, B. L. (1981). A group contingency for electricity conservation in master-metered apartments. *Journal of Applied Behavior Analysis, 14,* 357–363.

Task Force on Social Work Research (1991). *Building social work knowledge for effective services and policies.* Austin, TX: School of Social Work, The University of Texas.

Thyer, B. A. (1993). Single-system research designs. In R. M. Grinnell, Jr. (Ed.), *Social work research and evaluation* (4th edition, pp. 94–117). Itasca, IL: F. E. Peacock.

Thyer, B. A., & Thyer, K. B. (1992). Single-system research designs in social work practice: A bibliography from 1965–1990. *Research on Social Work Practice, 2,* 99–116.

**24.**

## Richard L. Douglass

## HOW TO USE AND PRESENT COMMUNITY DATA

The demand for quantitative demonstrations of service needs, measurements of change in target populations, effectiveness of programs, and other aspects of accountability for health and human services increases constantly. All levels of government private foundations and organizations that reimburse service providers expect clear and reliable estimates of service demand, as well as justification for program

Richard L. Douglass is a professor in the Program in Health Administration, Eastern Michigan University.

activities and outcomes. Health and human service workers and administrators must accommodate this emphasis on data-based planning and evaluation and learn to do it well as a regular aspect of professional life. The future will be more quantitatively oriented as our ability to deal with data accompanies the ubiquitous computer terminals on most professional desks.

## REASONS FOR INCREASING EMPHASIS ON QUANTIFICATION

The reasons for increasing emphasis on detailed data analysis in planning and evaluation are related to the ability and interest of service providers to find out more precisely what services should be offered and the extent to which services are effective. At the administrative level, the relative effectiveness of different approaches to similar problems can be determined only with sufficient and appropriate data.

For almost twenty years, health and human services financing has been in direct competition with other national priorities and political philosophies, forcing service providers to become more precise in terms of resource allocation and accountability. Sponsors of services use data to determine priority services and target populations. Routine outcome and process data are also used to select recipients of competitive grant support for continuation of programs and the initiation of new projects. Regulatory and accreditation obligations are similarly focused on quantification of all aspects of service delivery and management.

An immediate by-product of the increased expectation for quantification of service needs, activities, and outcomes is that successful administrators have discovered that improved information helps them to plan and provide better programs. Thus

the external demand for increased quantification has generated a demand within the service delivery system itself for more precise and adequate measurement.

The remarkable evolution of new technologies to supply inexpensive measurement, data storage, and sophisticated analysis has accelerated the ability of services to provide meaningful data and to respond to both internal and external data analysis expectations. Community data sources, like state, county, and national statistical information are more accurate, current, and available for utilization than ever before. Professional boundaries are becoming ambiguous, with integrated service systems and interdisciplinary approaches to community problems. Social services and mental health and public health professionals now recognize the interactive nature of their activities and that economic problems—housing and transportation, for instance—have fundamentally important implications for services that have been offered only within strict departmental boundaries in the past. Dealing with complicated human problems is difficult without meaningful data to identify priorities, change, and resource needs.

To summarize, the competition among human services for scarce resources, the demand for accountability, professional recognition of the value of accurate measurement for planning and administering services, and an influx of quantitatively skilled personnel and technologies have interacted to produce an emphasis on quantification in the human services. This trend has been long in coming. Most other fields have developed quantitative methods earlier. However, many human service professionals have misgivings about translating the human condition into numerical abstractions and often are quite threatened by the trend toward quantification. Hopefully the information presented here will serve to reduce the anxiety.

## WHAT ARE COMMUNITY DATA?

Practitioners in health and human services frequently are unaware of many useful data sources bearing on community dynamics, population movements and changes, economic conditions, housing characteristics, etc. Such collections of community data are not often recognized because of a hesitation to use them and, in some cases, a reluctance to make them available.

Community data are compilations of periodic measures of the status of the community, activities of specific organizations and services, and other descriptive information including health, vital statistics, housing, and economic conditions. Community data consist of records, often collected routinely for purposes of documentation for regulatory accounting purposes.

Any specific analysis of such information with the intent of identifying changes or trends, or of making inferences about social conditions, is secondary to the purposes for which the data are collected. Thus, they are called "secondary data." In contrast, measurements specifically intended to be used for a particular analysis are referred to as "primary data." The utility of primary and secondary data for the community practitioner is largely determined by their characteristics. These will be discussed below.

## PRIMARY AND SECONDARY DATA

As indicated above, primary data are those sets of measurements collected by investigators for a specific purpose. Primary data include specially designed surveys of community residents, organization representa-

tives, or service recipients. Primary data can take the form of special data collected during intake, termination, or follow-up interviews with the clients of social services. However, the overriding distinction between primary and secondary data is that primary data are collected only for a specific analytic purpose at hand, while secondary data are routinely collected for various purposes including documentation and subsequent use by others.[1]

Primary data, unlike case records, are not prepared routinely by community service organizations. Special-purpose measurements, however, frequently are routinized.

The difference between routine and routinized is subtle, but significant. Routinely collected data, such as client records, often are characterized by considerable missing information, less than optimum quality controls, and little or no understanding on the part of personnel recording the measurements of why the data are being collected. Frequently, there is no perceived need for the data, and the recording process is a burden to staff members.

Routinized data collection procedures are most common to primary data. The value and immediate utility of the measurements are usually well understood by the personnel involved in data collection. For these reasons, primary data tend to be specific and precise. Secondary data collection can be well supervised and the recording process routinized with adequate quality control. However, with the exception of secondary data generally collected by the Bureau of the Census and other highly skilled organizations, it would be folly to assume that secondary data generally approach the level of standardization and accuracy achieved with primary data collection.

Operational consistency of the data is the primary issue raised in routinizing or changing data collection methods. Operational consistency is defined as the comparability of measurements of a variable between groups or jurisdictions, or for single groups or jurisdictions over a period of time. Data collection is often poorly controlled. Routine data frequently have errors of recording, missing measurements, inconsistently defined meanings, and other shortcomings. Such negative characteristics reduce their utility for human service professionals. With the exceptions noted, primary data are more likely to be operationally consistent than are secondary data.

However, primary data are expensive to gather. Because the measurements are uniquely defined, designed, and collected, primary data collection requires the allocation of new resources that can substantially exceed the budget allocation for expected planning and evaluation activities. In addition to being expensive, primary data cannot be collected to measure events or characteristics from the past. Furthermore, the collection of primary data may present problems of confidentiality and practicality.

Thus, secondary data are often the only realistic source of community information. The likelihood of errors and operational inconsistencies in secondary data must be identified and understood clearly before a reasoned analysis can be made. Secondary data are available to community services from a variety of sources, discussed below. These and other sources of secondary data contain a wealth of information that is potentially useful for those who plan, manage, offer services, and evaluate community programs.

Major uses of secondary data in human service programs are: (1) to describe a community statistically; (2) to identify human service needs in the community; (3) to test hypotheses of change in a social condition after a change in services or the introduction of a new program; and (4) to anticipate changes in the profiles of need, service delivery, and program priorities in the future.

Accurate and useful description of change depends upon the operational consistency (or reliability) and the correspondence of the measurement used to the concept or idea being measured (or validity). While primary data often are more valid and reliable, secondary data may well be the only practical source of data because of constraints on staff, time, and budget. Fortunately, a careful search for secondary data often results in data that are adequate for the needs of the investigator at a minimal cost.

## SOURCES OF COMMUNITY DATA

A practitioner should undertake a thorough search to identify sources of information available locally and their usefulness before considering the collection of primary data. Because special-purpose investigations are often costly, there is a considerable payoff if existing data are uncovered. Possible sources of information include:

1. Federal and state government agencies, e.g., the Departments of Labor, Commerce and its Bureau of the Census, Housing and Urban Development, Health and Human Services, and Education, as well as comparable state agencies;
2. City and county planning departments and regional councils of governments;
3. State and local health departments and specialized units such as the Public Health Service Center for Disease Control and the National Center for Health Statistics;
4. Federations of social, health, and recreation agencies such as community welfare councils and united community services;
5. Comprehensive regional health-planning councils;

6. Medical health associations and community mental health agencies;
7. Funding agencies, both public (see 1 and 3 above) and private, such as the United Way, religious charities, and community chests;
8. Clearinghouses in many problem areas; for instance the Alcohol, Drug Abuse, and Mental Health Administration maintains clearinghouses that administer data banks and publish summary data on drug abuse, alcohol abuse, and mental health; its Biometry Branch publishes a useful "Statistical Note" series;
9. Universities, including departments, schools, libraries, research institutes, and individual faculty members with relevant research interests;
10. Libraries and local newspaper archives;
11. Annual reports and documents provided by hospitals and third-party payors for medical, mental health, and health care services and resource allocations.

## PRESENTATION OF COMMUNITY DATA

The statistical analysis of community data is beyond the scope of this article. However, the utilization of data eventually depends upon the clarity and accuracy of printed presentation. By this I mean the tables, charts, graphs, and other displays of numerical information that any data analysis ultimately requires. This section will describe the construction and variety of ways that numerical information can be presented.

### Tables: Numbers, Titles, Columns, Rows, and Cells

A table is an orderly arrangement of numerical information in columns and rows. There are few hard and fast rules for table construction. Perhaps the wisest are those given by a former director of the Bureau of the Census who wrote in the foreword of a manual on tabular presentation.

In the final analysis, there are only two rules in tabular presentation that should be applied rigidly: first, the use of common sense when planning a table, and second, the viewing of the proposed table from the standpoint of the user. The details of mechanical arrangement must be governed by a single objective; that is, to make the statistical table as easy to read and to understand as the nature of the material will permit.[2]

*Numbers.* If more than one table is used in a report, each table should be numbered to indicate its place in the series. It is also easier to refer in the text to a specific table by use of its number.

*Titles.* Each table should have a title to indicate the *what, where,* and *when* of the contents of the table. Table 24.1 is used to illustrate these points. *What* the table contains indicates whether absolute numbers, computed numbers, or both are used; the title indicates how the contents of the table have been defined. For example, the title for Table 24.1 states that homeless black men are described by demographic characteristics. The *where* indicates the geographic area to which the information applies, as signified by "Dade County, Florida." The *when* is the time for which the data apply, August 1991.

The title should be as brief as possible; however, the content of the table should be absolutely clear from reading it. Titles of more than two lines are usually avoided. Further information needed for the understanding of the contents of the table can be placed in a headnote. The headnote follows the title and may be printed in smaller type and enclosed in brackets or parentheses. The information in the headnote should apply to many if not all items in the table.

TABLE 24.1
Demographic Characteristics of Homeless Black Men*
(Community Homeless Assistance Plan, Dade County, Florida, August 1991)

| Characteristic | No. | (%) |
|---|---|---|
| Age | | |
| 18–24 | 10 | ( 9) |
| 25–34 | 47 | (42) |
| 35–44 | 45 | (40) |
| ≥45 | 11 | (10) |
| Marital Status | | |
| Never married | 62 | (55) |
| Married | 3 | ( 3) |
| Common-law spouse | 4 | ( 4) |
| Separated | 27 | (24) |
| Divorced | 15 | (13) |
| Other | 2 | ( 2) |
| Education | | |
| Less than high school diploma | 39 | (35) |
| High school diploma/General educational development certificate | 43 | (38) |
| Some college/Technical school | 26 | (23) |
| College degree | 5 | ( 4) |

*Sample size = 113.
SOURCE: Centers for Disease Control, Morbidity and Mortality Report, December 20, 1992.[3]

Such information may also be given in a note to the table.

In Table 24.1 the headnote indicates that the homeless men included in that table are those occurring within Dade County, Florida, and do not refer to homeless black men elsewhere. It also indicates that the data refer only to men who participated in the homeless assistance program.

*Columns.* Each column has a heading to state what is referred to in that column. In Table 24.2, one heading is "Institutional Category." The other headings refer to racial categories and total percentages.

In column headings, capitalization is headline style—important words are capitalized. (In published tables, this often depends on the style of the publisher.) In order to save space, there is a temptation to use abbreviations. These should be avoided unless the abbreviations will be readily understood, as those for the names of states, or days of the week. (In published tables, vertical rules dividing columns are usually omitted in the interest of economy.

*Rows.* The left-hand column of the table is called the stub; it contains row headings, which serve the same purpose as column headings, indicating what is contained in a particular row. The stub indicates the variable that is classified in the row headings, as shown in Table 24.2.

If data are stratified by more than one variable, for example, by age and sex, ethnicity, or cause of death, the variable that is stratified, or classified, in the stub is mentioned first in the title of the table. In Table 24.2, the stub column contains the various strata of institutional category, so institutional classifications are mentioned. Unlike column headings, only the initial words and proper nouns are capitalized in the row headings (or stubs), and abbreviations are used only when they are readily understood.

TABLE 24.2
Prior Institutionalization of Elderly Homeless Persons in Detroit, Percentage Estimates by Race, Population
Estimate of Homeless Persons over Age 59, Detroit, Michigan, July 1989

| Institutional Category | White n(est)% | | Black n(est)% | | Total n(est)% | |
|---|---|---|---|---|---|---|
| Alcohol or drug abuse inpatient treatment | 149 | 9% | 281 | 71% | 430 | 26% |
| Mental hospital impatient | 373 | 23% | 132 | 8% | 505 | 31% |
| State or federal prison | 118 | 7% | 362 | 22% | 480 | 29% |
| Total by race | 640 White Estimates | 86% | 695 Black Estimates | 77% | 1415 Total Estimates | 86% |

SOURCE: Detroit Area Agency on Aging, Detroit, Michigan, 1992.[4]

If stratification of items in a table is by two variables, as in Table 24.1, common sense suggests that the one having the greater number of categories will appear in the stub column. If classification is by age and sex or age and ethnicity, there will be more age groups than categories for sex and ethnicity, so the age groups will appear as row headings in the stub column. If deaths are stratified by age and by all causes of death (as in a table appearing in an annual report of a health department), there would be many more causes of death than age groups, so the causes of death would appear as row headings in the stub column while the age groups would be used for column captions.

The order in which row headings or column headings are arranged depends largely on whether or not there is progression. In a table presenting an age distribution, the youngest age group would appear as the first row followed by the other age groups in ascending order of magnitude. If the information in the table represents a time series, that is, information for different years, months, or days, the proper chronological order would be followed in the stub column or in the column headings.

If there is no progression from one group or another, as is usually the case with quali-

tative information, the order in presentation of row headings (or column headings) is determined by the size of the frequencies to which they apply. The category with the largest numbers should appear first, followed by other categories in descending order of magnitude of their frequencies.

*Cells.* Below the column headings, to the right of the row headings in the stub column, is the so-called "field" of the table, made up of cells. A cell is a space representing an interaction of a column and a row and containing a number or a symbol. The number may be an absolute number (as the number of homeless white former prisoners) or it may be relative number (a percentage of all former prisoners who are elderly, homeless persons in Table 24.2).

If the table contains computed values, such as percentages or rates, they should be expressed with the same number of decimal places. One would not record such values as:

| | | |
|---|---|---|
| 25.485 | but as | 25.5 |
| 12 | | 12.0 |
| 3.61 | | 3.6 |
| .7149 | | 0.7 |
| 11.6 | | 11.6 |

Percentages and rates are usually expressed with one decimal place to show that they are computed values, not absolute numbers. If rounding to the nearest tenth gives a whole number, this is written with a zero in the tenths position, as the 12.0 above. If the value is less than 1, this is written with a zero in the units position, as 0.7.

If computed values are included in the table, the reader should be informed as to what they represent. If they are rates, are they rates per 100, per 1,000, or per 100,000? If the computed values are rates per 1,000 this information may sometimes be included in the title, in a headnote, in a column caption, or in a spanner caption. Occasionally, the information may be given in a footnote.

In some tables both column and row totals will be given, while in others only one set of totals will be given. Occasionally, no totals will be given in a table, as in one that might give the number of births and deaths in Michigan for each year from 1900 to 1986. In such a table, neither row nor column totals would have any meaning.

If the totals are considered to be important, of more importance than individual items in the table, column totals will appear at the top of the columns and row totals will appear on the left, in the first column following the stub column. If the totals are of less importance than other items in the table, however, the column totals will appear at the bottom of the columns and the row totals in the column on the extreme right.

## Graphs: Bar Chart, Histogram, Frequency Polygon, Time-Series

A graph presents numerical information in pictorial, visual form. The graph does not present the information more accurately than does a table, but presents it in such a form so that contrasts and comparisons are more readily seen than in a table. Graphs are most meaningfully used in combination with tabular presentations of the same information.

*Bar Chart.* Such a chart or graph consists of a series of rectangles, equal in width, equally spaced, but varying in length, the length of each rectangle or bar being dependent upon the amount that it represents.

Bar charts are usually used with qualitative variables or categorical measures (such as type of housing, type of treatment) when measurements have been grouped into categories (such as age groups divided into under 15 years, 15–64 years, and 65 years and over), or an unlimited array of other stratifications (race, geography, economic status, disease categories, etc.). Bar charts are also useful for chronological data when there is a wide gap between years, such as 1920, 1960, 1970, and 1990.

The bars may be horizontal or they may be vertical. While it is by no means a rule, there is a tendency to use vertical rather than horizontal bars when the information is for time periods.

To construct a bar chart, a scale is first drawn or computed. If bars are to be horizontal, the scale appears at the top of the graph; if vertical bars are to be used, the scale will appear at the left. The scale must start at zero and extend to some value beyond the highest amount represented by any of the bars. The scale is divided into equal intervals, with the intervals usually being 2, 5, 10, 20, 25, 100, etc., depending upon the quantities represented by the bars. If the scale is to be a part of the completed graph, the scale should have a caption indicating what the numbers represent—population in thousands, rate per 100,000 population, etc. If the scale is eliminated in the final graph, this information must be conveyed to the reader in the title or in a footnote, as illustrated in Figure 24.1.

FIGURE 24.1
Percentage of Drug Use Among Homeless Black Men*
(Community Homeless Assistance Plan, Dade County, Florida, August 1991)

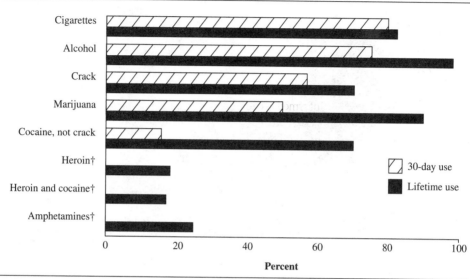

*Sample size = 113.

†No use was reported during the 30 days preceding the interview.

SOURCE: Centers for Disease Control, Morbidity and Mortality Report, December 20, 1991.

All bars are equal in thickness and equally spaced, the space between bars usually being approximately one-half the thickness of the bars and the first bar being placed this same distance from the scales. The length of each bar is determined by the scale, although it is often necessary to approximate its length.

If there is progression, bars would be arranged in order of that progression. In Figure 24.1, each category of drug abuse appears in order, regardless of the bar lengths. However, with most qualitative variables there is no such progression, and bars are arranged in order of length, with the longest horizontal bar appearing at the top or, if vertical bars are used, at the left.

Each bar should be labeled to indicate what and how much it represents. If all bars are quite long and if the labels are short the information may appear on the bar itself. It is also possible to label the bars on the right, but a better practice is to put the part of the label indicating what the bar represents on the left, the amount on the bar itself.

In order to show more contrast the bars should be colored or crosshatched. Generally, the same color or the same crosshatching pattern will be used rather than using a different color or a different pattern for each bar.

Like a table, a graph should have a title telling the *what, where,* and *when* of the information portrayed. If the graph is for display purposes only, the title may appear at either the top of the graph or below it. For graphs included in reports or publications, it is common to find the title below the graph. If more than one graph appears in the series, they are numbered and are referred to as "Figure 24.1," "Figure 24.2," and so on.

FIGURE 24.2
Age Distribution of Prisoners Aged 60 and Older in the
Custody of the Michigan Department of Corrections, July 1991*

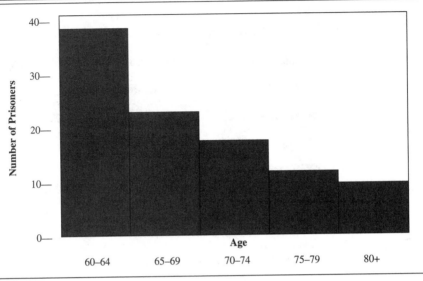

*20% Probability sample.
SOURCE: Michigan Department of Corrections, Lansing, Michigan, 1991.[5]

*Histogram.*  This form of graph is used to show a frequency distribution, preferably a distribution with groups of equal intervals. A histogram has two scales, one on the vertical axis, and one on the horizontal axis. The vertical scale usually presents the frequency (size) of the concept or variable. The horizontal scale is used for some set of characteristics of the population or subject of the graph. This is the principal difference between a bar chart and a histogram. The horizontal axis of a histogram is always an ordinal or interval measure, progressing from left to right. These conventions are illustrated in Figure 24.2.

The scale on the vertical axis should start at 0, as the picture will be distorted if the scale starts at some value other than 0. (If there is another logical starting point—Zero should be represented, as in Figure 24.2.) The scale on the vertical axis would be divided into equal intervals, the intervals being 2, 5, 10, 20, 25, 100, or even higher values, depending upon the highest frequency in the distribution. If the highest frequency were 79 the scale would be set up in intervals of 10, going up to 80; if the highest frequency were 790 the scale would be set up in intervals of 100, going up to 800. For Figure 24.2 the maximum frequency is 41.

The horizontal scale starts at the lower boundary of the lowest measurement group. For example, in Figure 24.2 the first age category is 60–64. The scale proceeds to 65–69, 70–74, 75–79 and 80 plus.

Each scale should have an identification indicating what the measurement is (on the horizontal scale) and what the frequency represents (on the vertical scale). When very large frequencies are involved, the scale on the vertical axis might have a cap-

FIGURE 24.3
Percentage of General Assistance Recipients Who Were Also Homeless, Including the Initial Six Months
Subsequent to Elimination of the General Assistance Program in 1992, by Year, Wayne County, Michigan, 1985–91

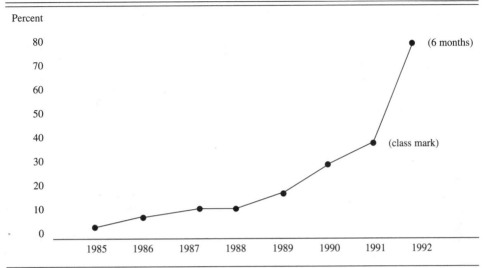

SOURCE: Wayne County Board of Commissioners, Detroit, Michigan, 1992.

tion "Number in thousands" or "Number in millions," thus reducing the number of figures used on the scale itself.

In Figure 24.2, for the first measurement group, prisoners aged 60–64, a line is drawn parallel to the horizontal axis from the lower boundary to the upper boundary at a height determined by the number of prisoners included in that age group. Vertical lines then connect this line to the horizontal axis forming a rectangle. The procedure is repeated for each measurement group so that the resulting graph consists of a series of rectangles, similar in appearance to the bar chart in Figure 24.1, but differing from it in that there is *no space between the rectangles.* A histogram's horizontal axis is always a continuous dimension.

*Frequency Polygon.* The same type of information that was used for the histogram could also have been used for making one form of line graph known as the frequency

polygon (Figure 24.3). The scales on the horizontal and vertical axes would be set up in the same way as for the histogram.

Instead of drawing a line between the upper and lower boundaries of a measurement group, a point is plotted at the height determined by the frequency of the group, at the midpoint class mark or median of the measurement group. The class mark is the average frequency for the group, as defined by units of the horizontal axis. When the frequencies for each measurement group have been plotted, the points are joined by straight lines. The frequency polygon has an advantage over the histogram in that more than one frequency distribution can be shown on the same graph. A special-purpose frequency polygon is a time-series.

*Time-Series.* If a graph is to illustrate a time-series, points are plotted at a height, according to the scale on the vertical axis, corresponding to the amount that is represented. If the quantity to be plotted is an average, the point is plotted midway between two points on the scale on the horizontal (time) axis. In a time-series graph, the horizontal (time) axis is always presented with equal units of time.

With respect to changes taking place over time, there are two techniques to be considered related to the amount of change that has taken place and the rate at which change has taken place. For example, we might wish to draw a graph to show the changes in the new-home purchase rate from 1960 to 1990. If we were interested in the amount of change, the graph would be drawn with the scale on the vertical axis being an arithmetic scale; if we were concerned with the rate of change, then the scale on the vertical axis would be a logarithmic one (both are shown below).

Note that in the scale on the left, equal distances on the scale represent the same amount of increase, in this instance, an increase of 2. On the scale on the right, equal distances do not represent the same amount of increase but they do indicate the same rate of increase, with each increment representing an increase of 100 percent or doubling of the value.

Most graphs used to show the rate of change will be made on a semilogarithmic grid; that is, one on which one scale (the scale on the horizontal axis) will be divided arithmetically, equal lengths of the scale representing the same number of years, while the vertical scale, against which the frequencies are to be plotted, will be scaled logarithmically.

## SUMMING UP

This brief introduction to the area of data utilization should complement the realization that in a more competitive world, health and human service delivery systems will be obligated to become highly quantitative for the justification, planning, and evaluation of services. Those who would administer and manage such services will recognize that accreditation, licensure, certification for reimbursement, and acquisition of new resources cannot proceed without a basic sophistication concerning data collection, analysis, and presentation. We can expect that improved and more universal quantification of services will stimulate comparative assessment and the design of improved services with greater levels of efficiency—objectives that should be agreeable to all of us who recognize that the problems we confront usually exceed our capacity to respond.

| 10 | 32 |
|----|----|
| 8  | 16 |
| 6  | 8  |
| 4  | 4  |
| 2  | 2  |
| 0  | 0  |
| Arithmetic | Logarithmic |

## NOTES

1. It should be noted that data collected for a specific purpose may subsequently be used for other purposes, taking on the character of "secondary data." The principal examples are survey data collected by universities and private polling organizations which are stored in libraries and made available to investigators for purposes other than those for which they were originally collected.

2. U.S. Bureau of the Census. *Bureau of the Census Manual of Tabular Presentation,* by Bruce L. Jenkinson (Washington, DC: U.S. Government Printing Office, 1949), p. iii.

3. Centers for Disease Control, USDHHS PHS. *Morbidity and Mortality Weekly Report,* 40 (50), December 20, 1992, pp. 866–867.

4. Douglass, R. L., et al. *Aging, Adrift, and Alone: Detroit's Elderly Homeless* (Detroit: Detroit Area Agency on Aging, 1988).

5. Douglass, R. L. *Oldtimers: Michigan's Elderly Prisoners* (Lansing, MI: Michigan Department of Corrections, 1991).

## 25.

### John Gottman and Robert Clasen

### TROUBLESHOOTING GUIDE FOR RESEARCH AND EVALUATION

## WHY A TROUBLESHOOTING GUIDE?

The idea of this guide is to give you an intuitive feel for what kinds of techniques are available for research and evaluation so that you can be an intelligent seeker of these tools.

## I. DESCRIPTIVE STATISTICS

### Purpose:

To describe a population from a variable by describing the distribution of that variable in the population.

### Example:

Distribution of Income per Month in the Pokohaches Swamp School District. It presents a table of incomes and the percent of the population earning that income.

### Useful Concepts:

The *Mean* is a measure of central tendency of the distribution (the arithmetic average).

The *Standard Deviation* is a measure of the amount of variability of a given variable around the average. If most people have values of the variable close to the average, the standard deviation will be small.

*Probability* is the likelihood of an event's occurrence, or the relative frequency of a value or set of values of the variable. For example if 80% of the people earn between 4 and 6 thousand dollars a year, the probability if 0.80 that an individual chosen at random from the population will earn between 4 and 6 thousand.

## II. INFERENTIAL STATISTICS

### Purpose:

To make inferences about a population from knowledge about a random sample or random samples from that population.
*Example:*
Gallup Poll of opinions.

### Useful Concepts:

*Random Sampling* is a procedure for selecting a group to study which insures that each member of the population will have an equal chance of being selected to be in the sample.

The *Central Limit Theorem* establishes the importance of the normal distribution because the distribution of all sample means of a certain size is normally distributed regardless of the original distribution's shape.

*Statistical Significance* gives the maximum risk of generalizing from a sample to the population. Risk is the probability of error. "Statistically significant at $p$ 0.05" means that there is less than a 5% risk in generalizing from sample to population.

The *Null Hypothesis* is a hypothesis that the population mean equals a fixed constant $= _0$, or that two samples come from the same population $_1 = _2$.

A *Statistically Significant Result at the 0.05 level* means that there is less than a 5% risk in rejecting the null hypothesis that $= _0$ (or that $_1 = _2$).

The *Variance Accounted For* is an index of correlation between two variables. If you account for variance in weight by the variable height, it means that height and weight are correlated. (The square root of the variance accounted for is the correlation coefficient, e.g., 49% variance accounted for is equivalent to a correlation coefficient of 0.70.)

*t-Tests* are tests for comparing the means of two samples to test the hypothesis that they really came from the same population and the observed difference is not larger than sampling error.

The *Chi-Square Test* is a test for comparing two samples when the measurement operation is counting. This test compares observed to expected frequencies. In the table below, we can see that in the sample in question, the males were predominantly brown-eyed and the females blue-eyed whereas we would have expected the color of eyes not to be sexlinked.

|  | Males | Females |
|---|---|---|
| Brown Eyes | 15 | 6 |
| Blue Eyes | 7 | 16 |

## III. EXPERIMENTAL DESIGN

### Purpose:

To eliminate plausible rival hypotheses that account for observed differences.

### Example:

We know that the tested reading comprehension of girls is better than that of boys. One hypothesis is that the observed difference is due to the interest of the material read in school. A "design" is the detailing of the strategy to be employed in eliminating the rival hypotheses. Designs depend upon many factors including sample size, observation intervals, number of variables, and kind of data.

|  | Fashion Story | Baseball Story | Total |
|---|---|---|---|
| Boys | 25 | 43 | 68 |
| Girls | 55 | 20 | 75 |
| Totals | 80 | 63 | |

Note that the number in the top, left-hand box is the average score of boys on the fashion story (25). Here we can see that overall girls read better (75 as opposed to 68) but that boys do better on the baseball story than girls.

Someone suggests a plausible rival hypothesis: "How do you know boys don't do better on the baseball story just because they have previous knowledge on the subject and the girls don't? It may not be interest at all." We would then have to control for that variable in our design.

**Useful Concepts:**

*Dependent Variable*—This is the variable we are studying. For our example, it's reading comprehension.

*Independent Variable*—This is the variable we're trying to use to explain the observed variation in the dependent variable. For example, we might hope to explain differences in reading comprehension by the variable of the masculinity or femininity of the story.

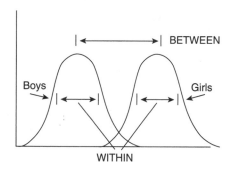

Total Variance in Reading Comprehension = Variance due to Sex Differences + Variance due to Interest Differences in Story Material + An Interaction of Sex and Material + Sampling Error.

*F-Test*—This test may be used to compare variances after the total variance is partitioned. For example, does the variance due to sex seem large in relation to sampling error?

The *F*-Test is mainly a ratio of between-cell variance to within-cell variance. In the curves in the figure on the top, the within cell variance is large compared to the between cell variance. In the figure on the bottom, the within-cell variance is small compared to the between-cell variance.

*Partitioning Variance*—The central idea of this procedure is to partition the total variance into independent parts, each of which represents a different variable's effect.

*Interaction*—In the design given in the example above, we can plot the cell means.

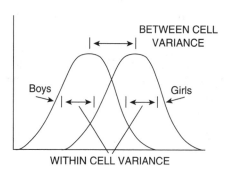

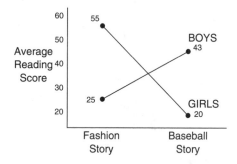

This is an example of interaction. Interaction is zero if the lines are parallel. In this case an interaction of zero would mean that boys (or girls) read better on all stories.

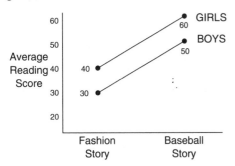

|  |  | Fashion Story | Baseball Story |
|---|---|---|---|
| B O Y S | High Socioeconomic Status | | |
| | Low Socioeconomic Status | | |
| G I R L S | High Socioeconomic Status | | |
| | Low Socioeconomic Status | | |

Interactions can cross (be "transverse") or just diverge (be "divergent").

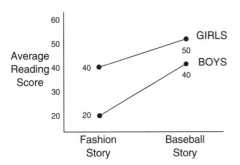

In this case, while girls are still reading better than boys, the difference is reduced in the baseball story.

*Analysis of Variance*—The analysis of variance is an experimental design for studying differences between cell means or combinations of cell means. The means are compared with respect to a common variance unit.

*Blocking*—Sometimes we want to split our design by blocking on a variable. For example, we may want to look at that reading data for high and low socioeconomic status children. Then our design would be:

We do this hoping to reduce the within-cell variability by introducing a new variable. We also may wish to contend with the plausible rival hypothesis that we have not accounted for socioeconomic status and

that perhaps that variable would explain our results.

*Analysis of Covariance* is a way of trying to control statistically for a variable which we are not able to control experimentally.

For example, two groups may differ in IQ. We could block by IQ, or we could use an analysis of covariance.

Here's how an analysis of covariance works. The dependent variable is related to a *covariate*. (Reading is related to IQ.) We use this relationship to try to predict reading score from IQ. Then we subtract the predicted score from the actual score and analyze the residual. We still hope to reduce the within-cell variability.

[Generally analysis of covariance is inferior to blocking unless the correlation between dependent variable and covariate is greater than 0.60 (Myers, 1966).]

*Internal and External Validity*—Campbell and Stanley (1963) list sources of plausible rival hypotheses which may jeopardize the conclusions of any experimental design. Please read their excellent article for an elaboration of these and examples of commonly used designs compared on these factors.

*Internal Validity*—factors representing extraneous variables which will confound the experimental variable if not controlled.

1. *History*—specific events occurring between the first and second measurement in addition to the experimental variable.

2. *Maturation*—processes within the subjects operating as a function of the passage of time, per se (growing older, hungrier, fatigued, or less attentive).
3. *Testing*—the effects of testing upon the scores of a subsequent testing.
4. *Instrumentation*—changes in obtained measurement due to changes in instrument calibration or changes in the observers or judges.
5. *Statistical Regression*—a phenomenon occurring when groups have been selected on the basis of extreme scores.
6. *Selection*—biases resulting from the differential selection of subjects for the comparison groups.
7. *Experimental Mortality*—the differential loss of subjects from the comparison groups.
8. *Selection-Maturation Interaction, etc.*—interaction effects between the aforementioned variables which can be mistaken for the effects of the experimental variable.

*External Validity*—factors which jeopardize the representativeness or one's ability to generalize.

1. *Interaction Effects*—effects of selection biases and the experimental variable.
2. *Reactive or Interaction Effect of Pretesting*—The pretesting modifies the subject in such a way that he responds to the experimental treatment differently than will unpretested persons in the same population.
3. *Reactive Effects of Experimental Procedures*—effects arising from the experimental setting which will not occur in nonexperimental settings.
4. *Multiple-Treatment Interference*—effects due to multiple treatments applied to the same subjects where prior treatments influence subsequent treatments in the series because their effects are not erasable.

## Samples of Common Designs

1. One-Shot Case Study
   (lousy design)

| X | $T_2$ |
|---|---|

Intervention          Posttest

2. One-Group Pretest-Posttest

| $T_1$ | X | $T_2$ |
|---|---|---|

Pretest     Int.     Posttest

3. Randomized Control Group

| | | | |
|---|---|---|---|
| Group 1 (R) | $T_1$ | X | $T_2$ |
| Group 2 (R) | $T_1$ | | $T_2$ |

       Pretest    Int.    Posttest

(R) = Subjects are randomly assigned to groups. Group 2 gets everything but the intervention, X.

4. Posttest-Only Design

| | | |
|---|---|---|
| Group 1 (R) | X | $T_2$ |
| Group 2 (R) | | $T_2$ |

           Int.    Posttest

Group 2 gets the posttest only.

5. Solomon Four-Group Design

| | | | |
|---|---|---|---|
| Group 1 (R) | $T_1$ | X | $T_2$ |
| Group 2 (R) | $T_1$ | | $T_2$ |
| Group 3 (R) | | X | $T_2$ |
| Group 4 (R) | | | $T_2$ |

       Pretest    Int.    Posttest

This design is equivalent to a two-by-two $(2 \times 2)$ *factorial design.*

| | | |
|---|---|---|
| Intervention | Group 1 | Group 3 |
| No Intervention | Group 2 | Group 4 |

(Every group gets
a posttest)

This design is recommended as a good experimental design by Campbell and Stanley (1963).

6. Interrupted Time-Series Design

$$\boxed{T_1\, T_2 \qquad T_N \, x \, T_{N+1}\, T_{N+2} \qquad\qquad T_{N+M}}$$

7. Time-Lagged Time-Series Design

Group 1 $\boxed{\begin{array}{l} T_1 T_2\ T_N x T_{N+1} T_{N+2}\ T_{N+M}\ T_{N+M+1} \\ T_1 T_2\ T_N\ T_{N+1} T_{N+2}\ T_{N+M} x T_{N+M+1} \end{array}}$
Group 2

8. Time-Series Flip-Flop Design

Group 1 $\boxed{\begin{array}{l} T_1 T_2\ T_N X_Z T_{N+1}\ T_{N+M} S_B T_{N+M+1} \\ T_1 T_2\ T_N X_B T_{N+1}\ T_{N+M} X_A T_{N+M+1} \end{array}}$
Group 2

The time-series designs are recommended...as excellent quasiexperimental designs. They can also be used to monitor and assess change in one person (doesn't have to be groups).

## IV. MEASUREMENT

### Purpose:

We often wish to make the assumption that we are measuring one variable on one continuum. Some techniques in measurement design allow us to test these assumptions.

### Example:

Designing an opinionnaire to measure students' attitudes toward school, peers, teachers, studies, and teaching methods. A student is asked to register the extent of his agreement with statements such as

Disagree Neutral Agree

School is fun    1   2   3   4   5   6   7

by circling the number which best represents his opinion. Certain items are clustered as belonging to one scale or another.

### Useful Concepts:

*Reliability*—the extent to which the measurement procedure gives similar results under similar conditions. Methods of assessing:

1. *Stability (test-retest)* correlation between two successive measurements with the same test or inventory must assume times of testing are "similar conditions."
2. *Alternate forms*—two forms are constructed by randomly sampling items from a domain and a correlation is computed between "equivalent forms."
3. *Split-half*—a procedure used in place of alternate forms by dividing the items in half, hopefully into "equivalent halves."
4. *KR-20 and KR-21* are formulas used to assess an alternate form reliability. Formula 21 is given here (less accurate than formula 20, but easier to compute) where the items are scored 1 if "right," 0 if "wrong," K is number of items, S is standard deviation, and M is the mean of the scale.

$$r = \frac{K}{K-1}\left(1 - \frac{M\,(K{-}M)}{KS^2}\right)$$

*Validity* is the extent to which a measurement procedure measures what it claims to measure. Methods of assessing:

1. *Content Validity* (snapshot). How well does the individual's performance in this situation correlate with his performance in other similar situations?
2. *Criterion-Related Validity* (motion picture). How well does this individual's performance on this measurement predict his performance in future related

situations (how well do achievement test scores predict grades in college?)?

3. *Construct Validity.* Does the measurement procedure make sense as measuring what it claims to? Do the items which are supposed to be on one scale "hang together"? This can be assessed empirically by relating the extent to which presumably related constructs explain variation on the instrument in question. Here is an example where this kind of validity is crucial. Suppose you show that 92% of all high school seniors cannot read election ballots with comprehension. The instrument is *face valid.* It has construct validity and you don't need to show content or criterion validity.

*Convergent Operations.* Different measurement procedures have different weaknesses. More confidence is obtained in a result when several different measurement procedures point to (or converge to) the same result.

*Scales* are attempts at quantifying a construct and converting it into a continuum.

1. *Likert Scale.* A scale composed of items each of which the subject rates on a scale. Examples:

a. School is fun. *SA A N D SD* (*SA* = strongly agree, *A* = agree, *N* = Neutral, *D* = disagree, *SD* = strongly disagree)
b. School is (check the blank):
   Fun: – : – : – : – : – : – : – : Dull

Item *b* is sometimes called a *semantic differential* item. In this kind of item we can put any two words on either side of the line, for example,

   Strong: – : – : – : – : – : – : – : Weak

2. *Thurstone type* or *equal-appearing interval* scales. These scales scale the items

themselves. Items are first sorted by judges into three categories, then each category is broken down into three others along a continuum (hostility, favorableness, disruptiveness, assertiveness). Items are eliminated if there is large disagreement between judges. Items are selected to have mean values (across judges) spread across the continuum from 1 to 9, preferably equally spaced. The individual taking the inventory checks those times with which he agrees (or finds hostile or disruptive). He is given the score which is the sum of the mean judges' ratings for items checked. We might scale situations for the degree of assertiveness required and ask the subject to check the situations which are problems for him. The items not checked could be used to give an assertiveness score for him by adding the average of judged ratings. This places the individual along an assertiveness continuum.

3. *Guttman-Type* scales have items which vary along an attribute. Items can be ordered in difficulty, complexity, or value-loading so that answers to the last item will imply success or approval to all those preceding. Examples:

*Difficulty:*
  I can add two numbers.
  I can multiply two numbers.
  I can divide two numbers.
  I can compute a mean.
  I can compute the standard deviation.
*Favorableness:*
1. Would you object to a retarded person living in your community?
2. Would you object to a retarded person working where you work?
3. Would you object to having lunch with a retarded person at work?
4. Would you object to a retarded person coming to your home for dinner?
5. Would you object to a retarded person marrying a member of your family?

*Item Analysis* is a procedure for selecting only items which discriminate in the same way the overall instrument is intended to discriminate.

A correlation is computed between each item and the total score on the instrument. For *dichotomous items* (yes, no; pass, fail) a two-by-two chi-square table is constructed.

For a multiple-choice test we wish there to be a strong relationship between choosing the correct alternative and high total score; also we want there to be a weak relationship between choosing distractors and high total score.

*Factor Analysis in Measurement Design* is a method for analyzing the extent to which items cluster by studying their intercorrelations. We have confidence in the conclusion that our test has four independent scales if the items within scales correlate highly but items across scales do not correlate very highly (see analysis of data).

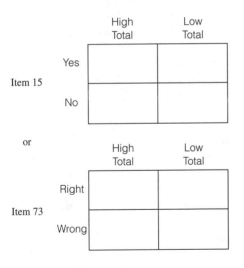

|  | High Total | Low Total |
|---|---|---|
| **Item 15** — Yes | | |
| No | | |

or

|  | High Total | Low Total |
|---|---|---|
| **Item 73** — Right | | |
| Wrong | | |

## V. ANALYSIS OF DATA

### Purpose:

To study the nature of relationships between variables.

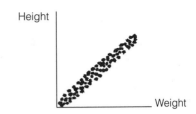

Strong *positive correlation.*

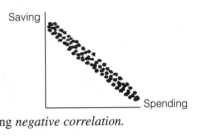

Strong *negative correlation.*

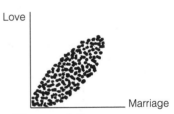

Weak *positive correlation.*

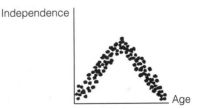

Curvilinear correlation (*positive sometimes, negative others*)

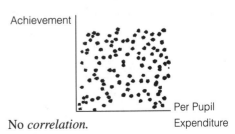

No *correlation.*

## Example:

We wish to determine which variables will predict whether a citizen will vote Republican (or Democratic) in the forthcoming election.

## Useful Concepts:

*Correlation* measures the degree of relationship between two variables. Usually a scatter diagram will provide an index for the eyeball.

The *Correlation Coefficient* gives an index of the degree of association (linear). 0 is no correlation, -1 is strongest negative, 1 is strongest positive correlation.

*Partial Correlations* involve calculating the correlation coefficient between two variables while statistically holding another variable constant. For example, ice cream sales may correlate with crime rates but not if the average daily temperature were controlled. Since we cannot control average daily temperature experimentally, we do it statistically. The correlation between ice cream sales and crime rate may be high but the partial correlation, controlling average daily temperature, may be quite low. Blaylock (1961) uses this technique to argue from correlation to causation.

*Regression* is a statistical procedure which is like a recipe for converting from one variable to another using the best (least-squares) equation.

*Multiple Regression* is a statistical procedure like a recipe relating one variable to a set of other variables. For example, if we relate high school dropout rates to school expenditures, teacher experience, and the average number of library books in the classroom, we will have a recipe that says, "our best guess from the multiple regression is that if we spend $3 more per pupil, dropout rates may decline by 2%. We could spend $1 per pupil by buying some books, and the other $2 by hiring more experienced teachers."

The multiple regression gives you a mathematical equation of the relationships between one variable and a set of variables.

It's like a recipe in the sense that how good a cake turns out is related to a host of variables (how much sugar, salt, flour, etc., you add). It differs from a recipe in that you can improve the product by adding more of anything, except that some variables are more important than others.

*Factor Analysis* is a technique for data reduction. It analyzes the statistical dependencies between a set of variables by looking at the way variables correlate. For example, it may reduce a set of 50 variables into 3 basic variables. Each of the three will be statistically independent (zero correlation if the variables are normally distributed) of the other two. Each of the three will be linear combinations of the original set of fifty. Some of the fifty will "load" more highly on one factor, others will load on other factors. Each factor is a weighted sum of the original fifty.

The three factors should try to account for as much of the variance in the original fifty as possible.

The problem comes in *naming* the factors, i.e., giving them some physical interpretation in the real world. This is where the procedure becomes subjective.

No one has really derived the sampling distributions of factor loading coefficients, so it's not clear how *stable* factors are. (See Principal Components Analysis.)

*Principal Components Analysis* tries to reduce data by a geometrical transformation of the original variables. An example is a scatterplot in three dimensions which gives a swarm of points in the shape of a football.

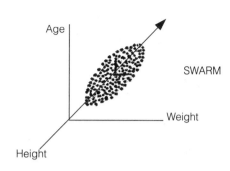

The new axes are those emanating from the swarm. The principal component is the main axis of the football. If most variance in the swarm is along one principal component (which will be a combination of the first three variables), we have reduced our data from three variables (which were correlated) to one variable. In general, we will reduce a large set of variables into a smaller set. Each variable in the smaller set is a linear combination (a weighted sum) of the original variables, and the new smaller set of variables are independent of one another.

The problem comes with interpretations—it's usually worse with principal components than factor analysis although the geometrical meaning is clearer.

*Canonical Correlations* are a procedure for factor analyzing two batteries of tests simultaneously to extract factors which are uncorrelated within their batteries but which provide high correlation of pairs of factors across batteries. For example, a researcher may have one battery of interest measures and another battery of skill or ability measures and he wants to know the overlap in measurement variance between the two systems of measures.

*Multiple Correlation* finds the optimal weighting to maximize the correlation between several variables (predictors) and another variable (the criterion).

*Multivariate Analysis of Variance* is a generalization of the analysis of variance to the situation where several variables are measured and these variables are statistically related.

The research issue behind the generalized tests is whether two or more sample groups should be thought of as arising from a single multivariate population or from two or more multivariate populations.

*Discriminant Function Analysis* is a procedure for predicting group membership of an individual on the basis of a set of other variables.

For example, if we can take medical measurements of various kinds, can we find the best way to combine these (weight them) to predict whether or not a person has cancer?

*Discriminant Function Analysis* is used extensively in theory construction finding *which* variables in *what* combination predict political party membership or any other group membership.

*Time-Series Analysis* is a procedure for analyzing observations over time for predicting trends, understanding the basis for fluctuations, and assessing the effects of interventions.

## REFERENCES

Blaylock, H. M. *Evaluating State and Local Programs at the State and Local Level*. Kalamazoo, MI: W. E. Upjohn, 1990.

Dowdy, G., & S. Wearden. *Statistics for Research* (2nd ed.). New York: Wiley Interscience, 1991.

Rutter, Michael. *Studies of Psychosocial Risk: The Power of Longitudinal Data*. New York: Cambridge University Press, 1988.

True, June A. *Finding Out: Conducting and Evaluating Social Research*. Belmont, CA: Wadsworth, 1989.

**26.**

## John E. Tropman and Elmer J. Tropman

## INDEX OF DISSIMILARITY AND THE PROFESSIONAL
## UNIT METHOD OF ANALYSIS

### INTRODUCTION

Community organizers, planners, administrators, and policy professionals often seek easy ways to understand themselves and the processes in which they are engaged— and to find ways to communicate these processes to others. Two techniques—the Index of Dissimilarity (ID) and the Professional Unit Method of Analysis (PUMA)—can help accomplish these goals.

ID is a method for making ideal/real comparisons: What does the organizer want to do compared with what the agency wants to do? What does the strategic plan propose compared with what is actually being done on a day-to-day basis?

PUMA allows a quick and easy conversion of organizational human resources (employees doing work) into financial resources (dollars) and back again. This method is excellent in the office, and works well with boards when applying for grants and contracts. For best results, ID and PUMA can be used together.

### THE INDEX OF DISSIMILARITY

The Index of Dissimilarity is useful in making ideal–actual assessments. It provides a numerical value that differentiates the orga-

nizer's or agency's actual activities from desires activities. ID is a relatively quick, yet sophisticated, measure that provides lots of information for minimum effort. It works in the following way:

Construct a small, simple questionnaire. It is simply a list of the major organizational activities or programs, plus some empty lines.

| Program Area | Should Be [A] | Actually Is [B] |
|---|---|---|
| Goal/Activity 1 | ____ | ____ |
| Goal/Activity 2 | ____ | ____ |
| Goal/Activity 3 | ____ | ____ |
| Goal/Activity 4 | ____ | ____ |
| Innovation | 15% | ____ |
| Goal/Activity *i* (*individual item*) | ____ | ____ |
| *Total* | *100%* | *100%* |

Organizers are asked to allocate the percentage of organizational time they feel *should* go to each activity, across from the activity (see above). In order for the index to work, calculations must not exceed 100%! Since workers may wish to propose allocating time to activities that are not currently undertaken for the organization, they can do so by filling in the name of the activity in the Goal/Activity *i* line (in the above chart). Note that we have added an item for

The late Elmer J. Tropman was director of the Forbes Fund of the Pittsburgh Foundation, Pittsburgh, PA.

"innovation"—doing new things, and undertaking new tasks. We have set this proportion at 15% in terms of ideal. "Real" is often 0%!

In the next column, the worker places the percentage of time that he or she feels *is* spent in the same activities. (In most instances, there are important ideal/real differences.) Then do up the worksheet.

Column C is the subtraction of column B from column A. Then the percentage differences in column C are summed, disregarding sign, and divided by two. The resulting number is called the Index of Dissimilarity, and it shows how different the organization's current activity is from that which it wants to be doing. This kind of information is excellent material that the worker can then use to refocus, redirect, and reinspirit himself or herself or the organization.

The important thing about the use of percentage allocations is that they clarify the choice process. Often, workers and agencies do not really know where their energies are going, but they do know that they are rushed in some areas, and things are not being done in others. By forcing the choice through the use of the 100% mechanism, differences in approach and emphasis are pinpointed.

Executives, for example, may wish to review with the staff whether their sense of agency effort—measured in worker weeks divided by program—makes sense in term of the priorities and values of the agency. It is common in human service agencies to experience organizational "drift" in which agency allocation, personnel and resources, moves slowly away from desired goals and objectives to other ones.

## Index of Dissimilarity Worksheet

|  | (A)<br>"Should" % | (B)<br>Actual % | (C)<br>A-B% (ignore sign) |
|---|---|---|---|
| 1. Goal 1 | — | — | — |
| 2. Goal 2 | — | — | — |
| 3. Goal 3 | — | — | — |
| 4. Goal 4 | — | — | — |
| 5. Innovation | 15% | — | — |
| 6. Individual Items | — | — | — |
| 7. Individual Items | — | — | — |
|  | 100% | 100% | $\Sigma\left(\frac{|A-B|}{2}\right)$ |

Index of Dissimilarity $\Sigma\left(\frac{|A-B|}{2}\right)$

A variety of informal and historical mechanisms cause this process to occur, and it is frequently unnoticed. Actually, it is the rule rather than the exception that this process occurs. A strategic assessment would note such a reallocation, at which time corrective or redirective activities could begin. It may also be the case that the agency is doing exactly what it is supposed to be doing in terms of its goals and objectives. But upon review, it turns out that the agency's goals and objectives should change. There again, the Professional Unit System will allow the overall allocation of effort to be seen more clearly, both in terms of personnel on the one hand, and in terms of dollars on the other.

One point should be stressed. The fact that there are differences does not make next steps immediately clear. Sometimes there needs to be a revision of activities to bring them more in line with goals. Sometimes more realistic goals need to be established. But the fact that one is analyzing the process will make the difference.

The Index of Dissimilarity is extremely flexible. Community organizers may want to use it to look at themselves, as well as their own allocation of time during the day or week in relationship to their own career and professional development interests.[1] Agency executives may wish to use it with staff, comparing the executives' assignment of workload and the staff's own percentage allocations. The fact that there are differences only points out what has already been known. What the index begins to show is the amount and scope of these differences and their location. As the beginning of a

strategic process, either at the board level or within the organization, this technique provides a good start. Executives may also want to use it with community groups, or with the board of directors. The point is that there can be a broad range of applications. These uses are strengthened when they are combined, at the organizational level, with the Professional Unit Method of Analysis (PUMA).

## PROFESSIONAL UNIT METHOD OF ANALYSIS: PUMA

One key question posed by workers and agency directors relates to establishing a common, easy-to-understand basis for assessing exactly the extent of resources, in terms of personnel/money, available to do all organizational tasks. With that as a base, it is possible to begin looking at how those resources are allocated.

The first step is developing a professional unit that is simple enough to allow workers and directors to have an intuitive understanding of the process. However, this "unit" must be complete enough to be useful. Such a system is the Professional Unit Method of Analysis. When developed, it will work well for the worker, agency, board, and strategic planning effort. It will also work well for the executive, in terms of developing material and assignments with staff. Here's how to do it:

1. The worker (or executive director, or perhaps a small committee staff) calculates the number of direct service workers available to the agency. In this case, consider only individuals who perform the actual work of the agency, not those who do administration, supervision, janitorial work, secretarial work, and so on. In a community organization agency, it would be the

---

[1]One important application involves looking at four "life sectors" (time on self, time on job, time on family, time on civic involvement) with the ID. Ideal/real comparisons often reveal lots of time spent on the job, and little time on self and family and civic activities.

number of organizers (FTE, or Full Time Equivalent workers); in a clinical agency, it would be the number of clinicians, up to and including fractional amounts. In a planning agency, it would be the number of junior and senior planners, and so on. These are called direct service workers; the other workers are "support staff" for purposes here. Even the executive, unless she or he happens to see a client or spend some time actually reviewing some particular planning reports or policy documents, would be considered support staff. Let's assume it is known for purposes of these examples that an agency has ten direct service staff.

2. The next step is to calculate the number of weeks of work that are available to the direct service staff to do the agency work. In calculations that we have done in a number of trials, the approximate number turns out to be around 45 or 46 weeks out of the total 52 in a year. (Individuals have time off for vacation, sick leave, and things of that kind). But for purposes of ease of multiplication in this example, let us assume that the agency executive and board have 50 weeks of staff time per worker available for assignment to whatever tasks the agency chooses to undertake. This number is very important; it represents the total resource of the agency to actually do agency tasks, whether these tasks are community organization, clinical work, planning, or whatever.

3. The third step is to multiply the total number of workers by the total number of weeks available for work. In the example selected, there are a total of 500 worker weeks available for all agency programs and activities.

4. Divide the number of worker weeks into the total budget of the agency. This calculation gives the total dollar amount per worker week. In the example selected, let us further assume that the agency's budget is $500,000. What this would mean is that the total amount of money per worker week is equal to $1,000.

What the executive can now begin to do with this material is to engage in a process of analysis. PUMA fuses dollars and people into a single, easily comprehensible unit. Much of our planning and decision making is often done in terms of money (or disembodies monetary units), which removes it from the reality of human service organization activity. Therefore, the PUMA allows a crisper, cleaner approach to strategic thinking. After all, once organizational objectives have been determined, one has to begin to allocate staff and budget to them, along with ample support staff. PUMA provides the kind of overall broad picture and factual basis that allows organizations to look at both what they are doing and what they might be doing, and to try to see whether or not the actual activities correspond with the desired ones.

Once the number of PUMA units have been established, it is possible to translate them into the index of dissimilarity. In all cases, the total number of PUMA units equals 100%, and the resulting fractions can be used to look at organizational allocation overall (total number of PUMA units) or fractions of efforts with one's employees (her or his PUMA units).

## CONCLUSION

Community organization workers are also in need of tips and hints that will help make their job easier. Especially in the rough and tumble world of human service, the problem of strategic analysis of resources is often overlooked. These two techniques can be most helpful.

27.

**Barry Checkoway**

## CORE CONCEPTS FOR COMMUNITY CHANGE

Core concepts are abstract ideas generalized from particular situations. They reduce such situations to their fundamentals, expressing their basic elements in a few summary words. When used in reference to fields like community change, they take on some of the qualities of "praxis principles" with potential to integrate information about "thought" and "action" in a new combination.

Core concepts can serve positive purposes for community change. First they can form the basis for decisions about actions to take in the community. When people are faced with a decision among various possibilities, for example, core concepts can provide a reminder of purpose or an expression of vision that helps clarify the choice.

Second, they can cause an awakening that is truly transformational. Amidst the routine confusion of everyday events, people suddenly put the pieces together and make sense of their situation in a new way. When people "see" an underlying concept that sheds new light on their lives, it can "change their world" and motivate them to pursue new forms of social action. In some cases, this awakening can be revolutionary (Fanon, 1968; Freire, 1970; Gatt-Fly, 1983).

Where do core concepts come from? Ideally, people establish their own principles through a process in which they themselves participate. Instead, however, many

principles come as traditions from the past, tenets from ideological movements, or commands from beneficent or repressive regimes. Such concepts may have power behind them, but their authority is always arguable when they do not derive from the people themselves.

Educators and trainers often communicate core concepts as a form of "do this!" knowledge with or without having a scientific basis for their statements. Some people are eager to have this type of expert information, but the potential for empowerment is greater when people think for themselves rather than depend upon professionals. This contrasts with the pattern in which professionals expropriate knowledge and treat people like passive recipients of services rather than as active participants in the process. When practice wisdom derives from collective reflection, it reappropriates knowledge and promotes participation in the community (Brown, 1993; Gaventa, 1988).

This article is intended for people who have potential to create community change, and for those who might help others learn more about the process. It assumes that these people are limitless in numbers and boundless in opportunities—including ordinary citizens and local leaders, professional practitioners and change-agents, and teachers and trainers in schools and communities. It recognizes that people will differ in their roles, but that all will benefit from reflecting upon experience and learning lessons for future action. It offers some core concepts based on research and prac-

Barry Checkoway is Professor of Social Work and Urban Planning at the University of Michigan.

tice, but does not prescribe them as the only ones, and challenges you to formulate your own.

Following are some core concepts for community change. They are based on my knowledge of practice theory and process models in social work, urban planning, and related fields; on empirical research on practice initiatives in community organization, social planning, and neighborhood development; and on practice in rural and urban communities in industrial countries and developing areas worldwide. My knowledge base has led me to these particular concepts, but different ways of knowing should surely produce different areas. If you question these concepts, and substitute your own, my purpose will be served.

It would be possible for some people to search for and find an overall pattern or model in this presentation of concepts. For example, some concepts focus on community and organization as forms of intervention, others on the types of people and strategies involved in the process, and others on believing in change and its cultural context. I appreciate the need to find an overall pattern, but do not want to suggest that there is single sequencing of elements to be followed. On the contrary, I believe that there is no single model that fits all approaches to practice, and, again, that the key is to formulate your own concepts and to create a framework that fits your particular situation.

## STRENGTHENING COMMUNITY

Community is a process of people acting collectively with others who share some common concern. This is not the only meaning of the term, which also refers to a place where people live, or a group of people with similar interests, or relationships which have social cohesion or continuity in time. These other meanings may find expression in the process, but they are not the process itself (Checkoway 1991; Suttles, 1972).

Strengthening community can take various forms, such as organizing a group for social action, planning a local program, or developing a neighborhood service. As long as people are acting collectively, then the process is taking place. Used this way, community is more than a noun or adjective, but also a verb that refers to the process as well as its product. Perhaps a better term for the process is not community, but "community-building."

Community is one of several levels of intervention in society. For example, there are personal or interpersonal interventions with individuals and families; organizational approaches to leadership and management of institutions; and macroscale efforts to influence public policy in the larger society. Community interventions are the ones that take collective action and mediate between the individual and the society. Community is an important level of intervention, but it is not the only one.

Community-building is facilitated or limited by the unit that is selected for change (Eng, 1988). Emphasis is often placed on the community as a spatial unit or physical place—such as a village or a neighborhood—whose boundaries facilitate or limit the organizing process (Unger & Wandersman, 1985). Some analysts argue that place is being replaced by "community without propinquity," facilitated by transportation or telecommunications technology enabling some people to join together in nonspatial ways (Catalfo, 1993; Webber, 1963). Nonspatial community is contingent upon access to technology, whereas place remains important to those whose resources are limited.

Some people care about the "general welfare" of the "community as a whole." Looking down from the municipal building, for example, they identify issues whose resolution will presumably benefit the whole community. However, most communities are not monolithic; they include various groups whose differences call for more multicultural forms of intervention. People who care about the whole community often care about no one community and benefit some segments more than others (Rivera & Erlich, 1992; Heskin & Heffner, 1987).

Community-building also has limitations as a form of intervention. First, there are personal crises that require immediate action by an experienced professional. It is as inappropriate for individuals to take some of their personal troubles to a community meeting, as it is for community groups to seek solace for neighborhood problems in the office of a psychotherapist. Second, communities vary in their levels of readiness for change. Some "healthy" or "competent" communities create change with fervor, whereas others lack resources or are unsure how to proceed (Cottrell, 1983; Iscoe, 1974; Lackey, 1987). Third, even the healthiest communities may have difficulties influencing the larger society in which they operate. Local communities should not be expected to solve problems whose causes lie elsewhere, or whose solutions are beyond their reach.

However, the forces which limit community-building do not diminish its significance as a "unit of solution" in the world (Steuart, 1993). Indeed, obstacles are a normal part of the change process, and successful efforts to overcome them amplify the potential of community-building as a form of intervention. What is *your* community? What is your *unit* of solution?

## JOINING TOGETHER, IN SOLIDARITY

Imagine a series of "stick figure" drawings moving across a piece of paper. First there is a person standing alone, then the person is talking with two others, and then the three are bringing a group together in front of a hut in the village. Suddenly the whole group comes to life. They are alive with emotion, everyone wanting to speak in animated fashion. There is energy that could lead to a new level of collective action. It is like a fire whose combined ingredients give light and warmth; the fire starts with a single match, and burns because the twigs catch alight and the logs fuel the flame (Hope & Timmel, 1984).

The concept is that a number of people joining together in solidarity can accomplish more than one person acting alone. It is the notion of "collective action," "strength in unity," or the Swahili term *Harambee*, "joining together."

Joining together helps people to realize that their individual problems have social causes and collective solutions. As individuals unite in solidarity, they reduce their isolation and interact with others in ways that have psychosocial benefits and contribute to their perceived and real power (Bandura, 1982; Checkoway, Freeman, & Hovaguimian, 1988). This does not devalue the importance of individual initiative, but instead recognizes the strength that comes from joining together.

Solidarity can build upon common concerns that arise from a place in which people live or work, or from preexisting social or cultural characteristics such as race or gender. These characteristics have potential for solidarity, but are insufficient to build community in the absence of joining together. People who share common concerns still need some sort of process to make them salient for the purpose of community-building.

## GETTING ORGANIZED

Community change can start with unplanned actions or random events, but it is only when people get organized that lasting chance takes place.

"Getting organized" is the process by which people develop some sort of structure for joining together over time. It takes its most basic expression when individuals form into a coherent unity and establish a mechanism for systematic planning and limited effort. This "organizing moment" is a key dynamic in the process of community change (Biddle & Biddle, 1965).

"Organizing" is the process by which individuals work together to accomplish more than any one of them acting alone (Kahn, 1991; Kendall, 1991; Rubin & Rubin, 1992; Staples, 1984). It is illustrated by an image of individuals isolated together in a row of small cramped cells, then pushing against the walls that separate them, then breaking through the walls and touching others, and finally standing strong with their arms linked together in a single unit (Speeter, 1978). This process transcends time and place, and finds its expression in sayings worldwide, such as in Mauritania: "Two eyes see better than one" or Madagascar: "Cross the river in a crowd, and the crocodile won't eat you" or Ethiopia: "When spider webs unite, they can tie up the lion" (Hope & Timmel, 1984).

Organizing is an empowering process that enhances psychosocial well-being. It enables individuals to increase their individual coping capacity, personal confidence, and feelings of control. Its therapeutic effects are especially important for individuals whose alienation keeps them from organizing on their own behalf, or whose displacement causes them to "blame themselves" for the forces acting upon them (Minkler, 1990; Rappaport, 1981, Ryun, 1976; Zimmerman, 1992).

Organizing builds collective capacity and a "sense of community." Strategy can include stages in which people form groups to win victories on initial issues that enable them to strengthen their structural organization and to take on more major issues. In one community people organize to halt an expressway from encroaching on their area, form an areawide coalition of organizations, and plan programs of their own. In another community, they organize to protest slum landlords, rehabilitate abandoned housing, and develop services responsive to local needs. Sense of community is a catalyst for participation (Chavis & Wandersman, 1990; McMillan & Chavis, 1986).

"Organization" is the structure established for organizing over the long haul. It may include forms of problem-solving and program-planning, goal-setting and decision-making, role-definition and team-building administrative structuring and organizational development. It may be informal or formal, collectivist or bureaucratic, and horizontal or vertical, depending upon the situation.

What is the appropriate organizational form for community change? Will it differ among rich and poor, Black and White, men and women? There is no single answer to these questions, except that good practice fits the appropriate form to the particular situation.

## STARTING WITH PEOPLE

A central tenet of community change is that it should start with people who have concerns and who know what they want to accomplish. The premise is that people are the best judge of their own situation, and that the process should originate in the experience of the people themselves (Tweeten & Brinkman, 1976).

As part of their training, professionals learn how to assess the needs of their clients. For example, social workers take courses that teach techniques in how to approach their target populations, conduct interviews and ask questions about their lives, and gather information for diagnosis and intervention. The belief is that accurate information on client needs will make professionals more responsive to the people they serve.

However, needs assessment by providers for the purpose of service delivery is different from participatory assessment for the purpose of community change. Many methods of assessment are available, only some of which actively involve the community in the process. These methods take time and lack the status of those that treat respondents like human subjects—but they do start with the people themselves (Eng & Blanchard, 1991; Marti-Costa & Serrano-Garcia, 1987).

Also, the usual focus on the needs of people carries the risk of ignoring their substantial strengths, and making them dependent upon the professionals who assess and define their capacity. Endless emphasis on the deficits of people may result in losses of self-esteem or "learned helplessness" in which individuals feel unable to do things that otherwise are within their grasp (Garber & Seligman, 1980). It is especially important to appreciate the strengths of communities whose overemphasis on their disadvantages can cause them to lose confidence in themselves (McKnight & Kretzman, n.d.).

*Are* people the best judge of their own situation? Werner and Bower (1983) draw two pictures, one of an expert standing over a respondent and asking preconceived questions listed on a clipboard, the other of villagers sitting together and discussing their common interests with the help of an indigenous facilitator from the village. The caption reads: "For local health workers and their communities, the need is not to gather information. . . . but to gather everyone together and look at what they already know" (p. 6).

*Do* people know what they want and what is best for themselves, including their actual needs and potential strengths? Democratic ideology says that the people are sovereign in this type of knowledge. But if consciousness is a social construction that results from the form of a given society—and if people's expressed beliefs are not always of their own making—then what? Or if people have consciousness that may be viewed as harmful to them—such as the villagers who believe that their children's worms are caused by angry gods rather than by bacteria in the water, or the residents who attribute neighborhood decline to their own cultural flaws rather than to disinvestment by the banks—then what?

## DEVELOPING LEADERSHIP

Who *are* the people? Are they the ordinary citizens, as in the Aristotelian sense that "the people at large should be sovereign rather than the few best"? This view gives primacy to the role of the average person, assumes that they are—or are becoming more—equal in their participation, and looks to the grassroots as the foundation for change (Kasperson & Breitbart 1974).

Or are they the community leaders, such as the elected members of the town council or the officers of the neighborhood association? The politics of leadership is an admission of inequality rather than a reaffirmation of full participation, but it recognizes the role of representation, and is the prevalent form of democracy in the world today. Real leaders are indigenous and accountable representatives of the people whom they serve rather than the ones who are assigned to them from the outside (Pitkin, 1969).

Where are the leaders of the community? They are found by their formal positions in established institutions, although formal leaders are not always the real ones; by their reputations in getting things done, although perceptions of leadership are subject to change; by their influence in important decisions, although each decision may have its own patterns of influence; or by the scope of their participation, although the extent of participation is not necessarily a measure of its impact. It is possible to find them among the poorest people in the world, although this infrastructure is not readily accessible to outsiders (Tait & Bokenheimer, n.d.; Werner, 1993; Werner & Bower, 1983).

Which types of leaders are best? Should the leader be "authoritarian" by making a decision and announcing it to the community; or "consultative" by identifying the alternatives and asking the community for its input; or "enabling" by helping the community to identify its issues and facilitating its decisions? Again, the answers will vary with the situation (Hope & Timmel, 1984).

How can a community develop new leaders? This question is so fundamental that most communities tend to ignore it. Instead, they tend to appropriate leadership by promoting people who already hold positions in established institutions and who, as a result, are either unrepresentative of the community or unable to invest time for the job. However, community change offers opportunities to develop new leaders rather than to appropriate old ones—to identify people with potential and encourage them to lead (Checkoway, 1981).

## AGENTS OF CHANGE

Community change has a history of voluntary action that arises from "the hearts and minds of the people," including indigenous individuals who emerge spontaneously and facilitate the process through their commitment to social values rather than through the promise of remuneration. Most of the world's great change-agents—such as Jesus Christ or Mahatma Gandhi—have been volunteers.

Recent years have witnessed an increase in the number of people with professional careers as agents of community change. This role is emerging in different ways in different areas—for example, promotura de salud, community organizer, adult educator, cultural worker, social animator—that together recognize some of the professional expertise and technical skills that are needed. In one or another area these individuals can create community change. They can enter a community, bring people together, and build a powerful organization. They can formulate an action strategy, build support for implementation, and generate one project from another.

There also are support networks that strengthen the work of change-agents. These networks include institutions with funding for proposals, communications vehicles to facilitate information exchange, interorganizational coalitions to develop alliances, and training programs to build community capacity. These networks are instrumental in the "resource mobilization" of some agents of change (Berger & Neuhaus, 1977; McCarthy & Zald, 1973).

One legacy of Saul Alinsky (1969, 1971) was to promote the role of the community organizer as a professional worker. According to Alinsky, community organization took trained workers with technical expertise and special skills. He distinguished among the "organizer," "leader," and "people," and sought to strengthen their collaboration. Professional expertise is no substitute for voluntary action, to be sure, but change-agents can contribute to the process (Horwitt, 1989; Reitzes & Reitzes, 1980).

## SEVERAL STRATEGIES

There are several strategies, skills, and styles of community change. "Strategies" include approaches to mobilize individuals around issues through highly visible demonstrations, or to organize grassroots groups for social action. They can involve people in policy planning through committees and meetings of government agencies, or advocate for groups by representing them in legislative or other established institutional arenas. They can raise critical consciousness through small group discussions, or develop neighborhood services of their own. These strategies are separable, each with its own empirical basis and practice pattern, but also with mixing and phasing among them (Checkoway, 1991; Rothman & Tropman, 1987).

"Skills" include practical tools to enter the community, assess local conditions, and formulate plans for program implementation. They include efforts to make contact with people, bring them together, and form and build organizations. They include efforts to identify and negotiate with decision-makers, relate to other groups in the community, and develop the confidence and competence needed to keep the process going. There are various process models in community work which describe types of basic skills (Henderson & Thomas, 1987).

"Styles" affect the manner in which strategies and skills will be received or supported by the community. Conflict style assumes that power is scarce and that confrontation may be necessary for its redistribution; campaign style assumes that it is possible to persuade people to see things in a particular way; and consensus style assumes that power is abundant and that people are in relative agreement on how to share it (Warren, 1972). The selection of a style that fits in the community is sometimes more important than the issues themselves. People who are conflictual or consensual may avoid taking action on an important issue if the tactics are inappropriate to their style.

Strategic choice is a key diagnostic step in various fields of practice. For example, a teacher listens to the classroom discussion and asks an awakening question; a chess player conceptualizes the board and makes a move; and an athlete senses the action on the playing field and finds an opening. Just as these people diagnose their situation and take appropriate action, so too does an agent of community change. And some do it with more or less skill than others (Schon, 1983).

Like other fields, community change also has people who misdiagnose their situation and prescribe inappropriate action. For example, they are the ones who convince villagers to pray for forgiveness from the gods when the real cause of problems is the urbanization of the society; or who convince residents of their responsibility to sweep the streets when the real cause of litter is neglect by the sanitation department. Misdiagnosis can have harmful effects in any practice field.

Selecting an appropriate strategy, skill, or style is central to community change. Some people do it naturally, others learn by trial and error, and others ignore it altogether, although these last are ignorant indeed.

## BELIEVING IN CHANGE

Basic to the process of creating change is a belief in its possibility. This belief is instrumental to the process, and also is an end in itself.

Believing in change has an uneven distribution, which Werner and Bower (1983) view as levels on a continuum. At one level are people who strongly believe that change is possible. They perceive that community problems have solutions over which they have control, they show confidence in their own ability, and they take decisive actions that produce results. These people are relatively few in number and tend to have disproportionate power.

At another level are people who are weaker in their orientation to change. They are aware of community problems, but only periodically try to do something about them. They participate in the community to a limited extent, but this is only occasional in occurrence. They are many in number and sometimes susceptible to mobilization. When this happens, it can be revolutionary, but it does not happen very often.

At another level are people who do not believe that change is possible. They face problems in their personal lives, but generally do not view them as issues around which to organize. They have informal support from family and friends, but often feel alienated from formal participation in the community. They appear to lack the consciousness needed to create change, although appearances can be deceiving and awakenings can occur when conditions are right.

What explains the differences in beliefs among people? Some analysts attribute them to characteristics of the people themselves, praising or blaming them for their own orientation. Others attribute them to the uneven distribution of resources that permits some people to organize more powerfully than others. Yet others attribute them to institutional patterns of privilege and oppression that discriminate among groups and shape their consciousness, which is not independent but instead results from these patterns. It is tragic when institutions rob people of their spirit and cause them to blame themselves for situations which are not of their making, but this "false consciousness" is a powerful force in the world (Hyde, 1994).

How can people help others to strengthen their own belief in the possibility of change? Freire (1970) describes a pedagogy in which individuals discuss the root causes of problems and strengthen their capacity for concerted action; Werner and Bower (1983) describe a process in which the facilitator asks "but why?" questions about the chain of causes and about the specific steps needed to alter the situation; and Horton (1990) discusses a school whose workshops draw people together to identify individual problems and develop collective solutions. For them, community change is an awakening process that motivates people for action (Hope & Timmel, 1984).

## AN EMPOWERING PROCESS

Empowerment is a multilevel process by which people perceive that they have control over their situation. It can refer to an individual who feels a sense of personal control over his or her life; an organization that engages its members and influences the community of which it is a part; or a community in which individuals and organizations work together to solve problems and create change (Rappaport, 1987; Sarason, 1984; Schulz, Israel, Zimmerman, & Checkoway, 1995, 1993; Zimmerman, forthcoming).

Some people experience personal transformations as a result of community change. Charles Kieffer (1984) describes several such people and finds that first they feel powerless and alienated from the world ("You feel powerless, you feel helpless"); then an immediate threat or violation of their integrity has sufficient force to spark their initial participation ("No! I'm going to stay here and fight . . . !"); then they develop supportive relationships with an outside organizer or community counterparts in a collective structure that contributes to a more critical understanding of social and political relations ("It was so important that someone cared enough to be there encouraging me, pushing me . . . no matter how afraid I was"); then they sharpen their skills and strengthen their sense of themselves in the political process ("All of a sudden I grew up . . . "); and then finally they view themselves as leaders and search for personally meaningful ways of applying their new abilities and helping others in the community ("It's changed my whole life—personal, professional, everything. My values have changed. Everything has changed").

Empowerment is commonly viewed as a process that operates on a single level of practice. Thus some social workers claim that if a person feels empowered, then empowerment has taken place even if the person has no actual influence in the community. However, there is an emerging notion of empowerment as a process with multiple levels. For example, Gutierrez (1990) reviews the social work literature on empowerment and finds that the goal of empowerment is most often expressed as an increase in personal power, that it tends not to distinguish the individual perception and actual increase in personal power, and that it tends not to reconcile personal and political power. She suggests that the goal of empowerment is not

individual but multilevel and concludes: "It is not sufficient to focus only on developing a sense of personal power or working toward social change, but efforts to change should encompass individual, interpersonal, and institutional levels of practice" (p. 152).

Empowerment thus can be viewed as a multilevel process that includes individual involvement, organizational development, and community change. Any one of these elements has potential to serve positive functions. At its best, however, empowerment includes all three of these levels.

## MULTICULTURAL, NOT MONOCULTURAL

Community change builds on the notion of community as a form of intervention, but what happens when the community is viewed as multicultural?

In a society in which people seem similar in their social or cultural characteristics, or in which a majority group has dominance over minorities, it is possible to understand the existence of "monocultural" institutions that emphasize assimilation, ignore diversity, or permit powerholders from the dominant coalition to promote the status quo (Crowfoot & Chesler, n.d.; Jackson & Holvino, 1988). As society becomes more socially diverse in the number of "other" groups, however, these changes challenge institutions to recognize differences and reformulate their practice (Daley & Wong, 1994).

Multicultural community change is a process that recognizes the differences between groups while also increasing interaction and cooperation among them. It assumes that there are intrapersonal and interpersonal differences among individuals, intracommunity and intercommunity differences among groups, and opportunities for conflict or collaboration among them.

Multicultural community change is neither "culturally-sensitive" practice that makes change more responsive of particular groups (Gutierrez & Lewis, 1992) nor "anti-oppressive" organizing that mobilizes people to deal with their enemies (Crowfoot & Chesler, n.d.), but rather a new form that recognizes differences and builds bridges at the community level (Bradshaw, Soifer, & Gutierrez, 1994).

When the community is viewed as multicultural, it raises questions about each element of the change process. Does the organization represent the social diversity of the community? Do the leaders show commitment to the multicultural mission? Do meetings facilitate the verbal and non-verbal communications differences among groups? These are the types of questions whose answers require new forms of intervention in most communities.

Multiculturalism is neither "normal" nor "politically correct" in societies where prejudice and discrimination prevail, or where people from the majority coalition use their power to prevent their displacement by the growing number of others. It is problematic when the concept of community does not keep up with changes in society.

## WHAT ABOUT YOU?

These core concepts provide perspectives on community change as a process of joining together, in solidarity. It includes efforts at starting where people are, awakening the need for action, and developing a structure for change. It views the community as a unit of solution, and community change as an awakening process based upon several strategies and skills.

These concepts are based on a belief that creating community change is an empowering process. It assumes that power is a present or potential resource in every person or community. There is always another community that can become empowered. The key is for people to recognize and act upon the power or potential that they already have.

Core concepts integrate thought and action in a new combination that contributes to the change process. This may seem simplistic, but many people are quick to react to a crisis rather than to reflect upon their principles first. "Take care of the crisis first" is a common notion in professional practice, but it would be as mistaken to act without thought as it is to reflect without taking action.

People would benefit from developing their own core concepts for community change. The concepts expressed here are one version, and cannot substitute for your own formulation. If you question these concepts—which I sincerely hope you will—or substitute your own, my purpose will be served. What are *your* core concepts for community change?

## REFERENCES

Alinsky, S. (1969). *Reveille for radicals*. New York: Vintage Books.

Alinsky, S. (1971). *Rules for radicals: A practical primer for realistic radicals*. New York: Vintage.

Bandura, A. (1982). Self-efficacy mechanism in human agency. *American Psychologist, 37*: 122–47.

Berger, P. J., & J. Neuhaus. (1977). *To empower people: The role of mediating structures in public policy*. Washington: American Enterprise Institute for Public Policy Research.

Biddle, W. W., & L. J. Biddle. (1965). *The community development process: The rediscovery of local initiative*. New York: Holt, Rinehart and Winston.

Bradshaw, C., Soifer, S., & Gutierrez, L. (1994). Toward a hybrid model for effective organizing in communities of color. *Journal of Community Practice, 1*(1), 25–42.

Brown, L. D. (1993). Social change through collective reflection with Asian non-governmental development orgzanizations. *Human Relations, 46*, 249–245.

Catalfo, P. (1993). America online. In S. Walker (Ed.), *Changing community*. St. Paul: Graywolf Press.

Chavis, D. M., & Wandersman, A. (1990). Sense of community in the urban environment: A catalyst for participation and community development. *American Journal of Community Psychology, 18*: 55–81.

Checkoway, B. (1991). *Six strategies of community change*. Jerusalem: The Hebrew University.

Checkoway, B. (Ed.) (1981). *Citizens and health care: Participation and planning for social change*. New York: Pergamon Press.

Checkoway, B., Freeman, H., & Hovaguimian, T. (Eds.) (1988). Community-based initiatives to reduce social isolation and to improve health of the elderly. *Danish Medical Bulletin, 6*: Special Supplement.

Cottrell, L. S. (1993). The competent community. In R. Warren & L. Lyons (Eds.), *New perspectives on the American community*. Homewood: Dorsey Press.

Crowfoot, J., & Chesler, M. (n.d.). *The concept of the enemy: Reflections on the strategic use of language*. Ann Arbor: School of Education.

Daley, J. M., & Wong, P. (1994). Community development with emerging ethnic communities. *Journal of Community Practice, 1*(1), 9–24.

Eng, E. (1988). Extending the unit of practice from the individual to the community. *Danish Medical Bulletin, 6*, 45–52.

Eng, E., & Blanchard, L. (1991). Action-oriented community diagnosis. *International Quarterly of Community Health Education, 11*, 93–110.

Fanon, F. (1968). *The wretched of the earth*. New York: Grove Press.

Freire, P. (1970). *Pedagogy of the oppressed*. New York: Seabury Press.

Garber, J., & Seligman, M. (Eds.), (1980). *Human helplessness: Theory and applications*. New York: Academic Press.

Gatt-Fly, (1983). *AH-HAH! A new approach to popular education*. Toronto: Between the Lines.

Gaventa, J. (1988). Participatory research in America. *Convergence, 21*, 19–27.

Gutierrez, L. M. (1990). Working with women of color: An empowerment perspective. *Social Work, 35*, 149–52.

Gutierrez, L. M., & Lewis, E. A. (1994). Community organizing with women of color: A feminist approach. *Journal of Community Practice, 1*(2), 23–44.

Henderson, P., & Thomas, D. N. (1987). *Skills in neighbourhood work*. London: George Allen and Unwin.

Heskin, A. D., & Heffner, R. A. (1987). Learning about bilingual, multicultural organizing. *The Journal of Applied Behavioral Science, 23*: 525–41.

Hope, A., & Timmel, S. (1984). *Training for transformation: A handbook for community workers*. Gweru, Zimbabwe: Mambo Press.

Horton, M. (1990). *The long haul: An autobiography*. New York: Doubleday.

Horwitt, S. D. (1989). *Let them call me rebel: Saul Alinsky, his life and legacy*. New York: Random House.

Hyde, C. (1994). Commitment to social change: Voices from the feminist movement. *Journal of Community Practice, 1*(2), 45–64.

Iscoe, I. (1974). Community psychology and the competent community. *American Psychologist, 29*, 607–13.

Jackson, B., & Holvina, E. (1988). *Multicultural organization development*. Ann Arbor: Program on Conflict Management Alternatives.

Kahn, S. (1991). *Organizing: A guide for grassroots leaders*. Silver Spring: National Association of Social Workers.

Kasperson, R. E., &. Brietbart, M. (1974). *Participation, decentralization, and advocacy planning*. Washington: Association of American Geographers.

Kendall, J. (1991). *Organizing for social change: A manual for activism in the 1990s*. Washington: Seven Locks Press.

Kieffer, C. (1984). Citizen empowerment: A developmental perspective. *Prevention in Human Services, 3*, 9–36.

Lackey, A. S. (1987). Healthy communities: The goal of community development. *Journal of the Community Development Society, 18*, 1–17.

Marti-Costa, S., & Serrano-Garcia, I. (1987). Needs assessment and community development. In F. M. Cox, J. L. Erlich, J. Rothman, & J. E. Tropman, (Eds.), *Strategies of community organization* (pp. 362–72). Itasca: F. E. Peacock.

McCarthy, J., & Zald, M. (1973). *The trend of social movements in America: professionalization and resource mobilization*. Morristown: General Learning Corporation.

McKnight, J. L., & J. Kretzman. (n. d.). *Mapping community capacity*. Evanston: Center for Urban Affairs and Policy Research.

McMillan, D. W., & Chavis, D. M. (1986). Sense of community: A definition and theory. *Journal of Community Psychology, 14*, 6–23.

Minkler, M. (1990). Improving health through community organization. In K. Glanz, F. M. Lewis, & B. K. Rimen (Eds.). *Health behavior and health education* (pp. 257–87). San Francisco: Jossey-Bass.

Pitkin, H. F. (1969). *Representation*. New York: Atherton Press.

Rappaport, J. (1981). In praise of paradox: A social policy of empowerment over prevention. *American Journal of Community Psychology, 9*, 1–25.

Rappaport, J. (1987). Terms of empowerment/exemplars of prevention: Toward a theory for community psychology. *American Journal of Community Psychology, 15*, 121–44.

Reitzes, D. C., & Reitzes, D. C. (1980). Saul D. Alinsky's contribution to community development. *Journal of the Community Development Society, 11*, 39–5.

Rivera, F. G., & Erlich, J. L. (Eds.), (1992). *Community organizing in a diverse society*. Boston: Allyn and Bacon.

Rothman, J., with J. E. Tropman. (1987). Models of community organization and macro practice perspectives: Their mixing and phasing. In F. M. Cox, J. L. Erlich, J. Rothman & J. E. Tropman (Eds.), *Strategies of community organization* (pp. 3–25). Itasca: F. E. Peacock.

Rubin, H. J., & Rubin, I. S. (1992). *Community organizing and development*. New York: Macmillan.

Ryun, W. (1976). *Blaming the victim*. New York: Vintage Books.

Sarason, S. B. (1984). *The psychological sense of community: Prospects for a community psychology*. San Francisco: Jossey-Bass.

Schon, D. (1983). *The reflective practitioner: How professionals think in action*. New York: Basic Books.

Schulz, A., Israel, B. A., Zimmerman, M. A., & Checkoway, B. N. (1995). Empowerment as a multi-level construct: Perceived control at the individual, organizational and community levels. *Health Education Research, 10*, 309–27.

Speeter, G. (1978). *Power: A repossession manual-organizing strategies for citizens*. Amherst: Citizen Involvement Training Project.

Staples, L. (1984). *Roots to power: A manual for grassroots organizing*. New York: Praeger.

Steuart, G. W. (1993). Social and cultural perspectives: Community intervention and mental health. *Health Education Quarterly, Supplement 1*: S99–12.

Suttles, G. D. (1972). *The social construction of communities*. Chicago: University of Chicago Press.

Tait, J. L. & Bokenheimer, H. (n.d.). *Identifying the community power actors: A guide for change agents*. Ames: Cooperative Extension Service.

Tweeten, L., & Brinkman, G. L. (1976). *Micropolitan development*. Ames: Iowa State University Press.

Unger, D. G., & Wandersman, A. (1985). The importance of neighborhoods: The social, cognitive, and affective components of neighboring. *American Journal of Community Psychology, 13*, 139–70.

Warren, R. L. (1972). *The community in America*. Chicago: Rand McNally.

Webber, M. (1963). Order in diversity: Community without propinquity. In L. Wingo (Ed.), *Cities and space: The future use of urban level*. Baltimore: Johns Hopkins Press.

Werner, D. (1993). *Where there is no doctor*. Palo Alto: The Hesperian Foundation.

Werner, D., & Bower, B. (1983). *Helping health workers learn*. Palo Alto: The Hesperian Foundation.

Zimmerman, M. A. (forthcoming). Empowerment theory: Psychological, organizational and community levels of analysis. In J. Rappaport and E. Seidman (Eds.), *Handbook of community psychology*. New York: Plenum Press.

Zimmerman, M. A. et al. (1992). Further explorations in empowerment theory: An empirical analysis of psychological empowerment. *American Journal of Community Psychology, 20*: 707–727.

**28.**

## Robert J. Myers, Peter Ufford, and Mary-Scot Magill

## ON-SITE ANALYSIS: A PRACTICAL APPROACH
## TO ORGANIZATIONAL CHANGE

On-site analysis has now been used successfully to help people in organizations in a number of settings in Canada, Australia, and the United States. Host organizations of "on-sites" and "on-site follow-ups" have included voluntary agencies, private enterprise, educational institutions, international agencies, and a variety of government and nongovernment organizations.

### WHAT IS "ON-SITE ANALYSIS"?

On-site analysis is an organizational problem-solving and staff development process. It is also an intensive and challenging group evaluation and problem-solving process. People doing similar work in other organizations join with the staff of an organization to help them analyze their operations at the workplace, or "on-site." The process is facilitated by a leader who is trained and experienced in its specific analysis and problem-solving techniques. The entire analysis, including the writing and presentation of a final

From *On-Site Analysis: A Practical Approach to Organizational Change* by Robert J. Myers, Peter Ufford, and Mary-Scot Magill. OSCA Publishing, 94 Markland Dr., Etobicoke, ON M9C1N8.

Robert J. Myers is chairman, Greenshield of Canada, and president, On-Site Analysis; Peter Ufford is consultant to the president of External Affairs, University of British Columbia; Mary-Scot Magill is a consultant in Toronto.

report, is completed in no longer than five and no fewer than three full days.

**On-site analysis helps an organization by using methods that will enhance not only its operations but also its staff's development and capacities.** Together the group of "visiting" and "host" participants assess organizational strengths and weaknesses, identify and prioritize problems, and develop practical recommendations (action plans) to solve them. On-site analysis is a participative yet structured group process. The people working in the organization are involved in every step of the group assessment and problem-solving process guided by the on-site leader.

### FACT-BASED GROUP
### PROBLEM-SOLVING

On-site analysis follows a prescribed methodology which includes a trained team leader who facilitates and manages the entire process, ensuring that everything is "up for question and review." An on-site analysis, or "on-site," as it is commonly referred to, is not an "audit" performed by an "external" group. Nor is it an "external review" whereby problems are identified and solved "for" an organization by "outside experts."

Throughout the on-site process, current organizational realities and trends (often including environmental factors) are identified and taken into account by all participants. The goals of on-site analysis include identifying strengths and weaknesses, protecting and enhancing selected strengths, selecting problems to be solved, generating alternative solutions to them, and developing practical recommendations for change— *including practical first steps that can be acted on immediately.*

After dealing with perceptions, organizational strengths and weaknesses are identified from *facts* obtained through the questioning and probing that are part of every on-site analysis. The problems revealed by the analysis of facts, rather than those which may have been *perceived* to be most critical by members of the host organization at the outset, become the focus of the remaining analysis and group problem-solving steps. In some cases, the problems revealed through analysis are the same (or similar to) those already perceived by *some* members of the organization. Surprisingly often, they are different.

## THE REPORT

The results of on-site analysis are prepared in a report that is written and finalized by all participants in the on-site (not just the visiting team) as part of the three-to-five day process itself. The report is never written or finalized by the "outsiders" to be sent back to the organization afterwards, as is often the case with other types of consultation. Its drafting and final production by the group is an integral part of the on-site analysis.

The content of the report includes summaries of the analysis, observations, conclusions, and concrete recommendations (action plans) developed by the group throughout the week. It is both a record of the most important discoveries of the group and a blueprint for action following the on-site if recommendations are accepted.

The report is *presented* to an appropriate group, such as the board of directors, on the final day of the on-site. In the case of an organization choosing on-site analysis as a practical staff development or training exercise only, this presentation may be made only to other staff—but such is rarely the case.

We would like to emphasize that although on-site analysis formally closes with the presentation of the report written and revised by all members of the group as part of the on-site, the report itself is not the "product." *The learning for participants* and *the change that results in the organization* are the products of the on-site process.

## THE GOALS AND METHODS OF ON-SITE ANALYSIS

The primary goal of on-site analysis is to bring about an environment in which change to improve organizational performance and effectiveness can occur. This includes an analysis of strengths and problems, and steps to enhance the strengths and solve the problems. It results in a staff team who clearly understand the current situation and are committed to do something to improve it. In many cases, it actually starts change to occur.

**These primary goals are achieved through a group problem-solving process which includes a rigorous, fact-based assessment of exactly what the organization is doing at the time of the analysis and what it has been doing over the previous three-to-five years.** Areas of greatest potential for improvement are identified by the group, and those agreed to be most important become the focus for the remaining steps of the process.

On-site analysis is specifically designed to ensure that facts about what is and has been happening in the organization are scrutinized and worked with by the group as a group. One result of this is the emergence of a common perception of organizational strengths and weaknesses—an understanding of the organization's performance now and over the past five years that is shared by all participants.

On-site analysis provides a unique organizational problem-solving opportunity that includes identifying strengths and problems (based on facts vs. perceptions) and reaching agreement about the problems and their solutions. It also contributes to staff development.

On-site analysis is designed to build *consensus* about both the strengths of the organization that need to be protected and might be further strengthened and the weaknesses that most need to be addressed. It is designed to produce *clarity* (about the facts), *consensus* (about what the facts reveal), and *commitment* (to action, that is, to what must be done to improve operations)—to use the "three C's" popularized by Warren Bennis years ago.

**The important secondary goal of on-site analysis is to encourage practical learning for all participants.** This includes the demonstration or modelling and experience of effective group analysis and problem-solving techniques that can be applied to many other situations and the conceptual and technical learning which often take place for both visiting and host participants as well as what is learned about the host organization itself.

### THE RESULTS OF OUR EXPERIENCE TO DATE

Since the beginning of the program, more than 500 "on-sites" and "on-site follow-ups" have been conducted in Canada and elsewhere. Over 250 of these have been

part of United Way/Centraide Canada's service to its members. According to the staff and volunteers involved, these have been invaluable in helping communities improve local operations. The program has benefitted the national organization and individuals working with it in a number of other ways as well. Responses from other participating organizations, including those outside the voluntary sector, have been equally positive.

Regardless of the type of organization or enterprise, the majority of major on-site recommendations have been implemented and positive results evident within a year following completion of the analyses. The on-site process has therefore been successful to date in terms of resulting in implementation of major recommendations for change. This is the only "yardstick" which we feel adequately measures the impact and usefulness of on-site analysis.

We believe that the successful results of on-site analysis to date stem from both the assumptions about people and problem-solving on which the process is based and a methodology which applies proven theories about how people learn and when they institute change—both in themselves and in their organizations.

### COMMON ASSUMPTIONS—AND DIFFICULTIES—IN CONSULTATION OR MANAGEMENT

On-site analysis is designed to break through many of the barriers to effective help (help that does result in organizational change) that so easily arise from some of the more traditional assumptions about the role of consultants (or managers) and the appropriate involvement of members of the host organization (or of one's own staff) in evaluation and problem-solving.

## What We Don't Believe...

In many aspects of their lives, most people hold certain beliefs which influence their expectations, and their expectations, in turn, often influence their choices and behavior—their actions. This is also true of people either working in or trying to help organizations. While it is perhaps unintentional and would often be denied, we have observed that the traditional role of the consultant (and often of managers) is frequently consistent with at least some of the following assumptions:

- that people working in an organization (or "under" a manager) are by and large incapable of solving their own problems
- that the consultant or manager is the one who can or must come up with solutions (i.e., is expected to be the "expert")
- that "involving the staff" usually means "obtaining information from" them, either written or by interview, usually one at a time as opposed to any group discussion
- that it is the proper role of the consultant or manager to write reports, which may or may not include suggestions and ideas of some members of the staff
- that the people in the host organization whom it is most important to involve are those who will be evaluating the results
- that the evaluation of the consultant may be largely or even entirely based on the originality of the proposed solutions (content) and not on whether they are implemented; the same may occasionally be true of managers considered to be "ineffective, but brilliant nonetheless!"
- that it is not necessarily the responsibility of consultants to outline the practical "first steps" that must be taken immediately in order to implement the solution(s) they propose.

Many similar assumptions would be held by some managers, and would necessarily influence both the way they work and the way they feel they are *expected* to work with their colleagues.

## THE ON-SITE APPROACH (WHAT WE DO BELIEVE)

On-site analysis is based on very different assumptions about organizational problems and the role of the consultant or manager. These include different assumptions about people's capabilities, the impact of perceptions, and the value of "number crunching" and open group processes in effecting change. We believe that:

- People working in organizations are usually capable of solving their own problems; most often the help that they need is with problem-solving methodology.
- People doing similar work in different organizations can offer invaluable (and seldom tapped) help to one another, especially when offered in a situation that does not require them to give "expert advice" or to "sell" solutions.
- For all of us, "facts" are not always what they appear to be; individual perceptions of facts and their significance are often based on individual history, attitudes, assumptions, and values; these can be natural barriers to effective organizational problem-solving.
- Because of the effect of varying perceptions, addressing only presented or perceived problems will not necessarily solve the most pressing problems, achieve consensus, or initiate change in an organization.
- Identifying problems accurately takes time; doing so as a group requires even more time, involving people in ways often entirely new to them, and in a more "open" process than many are accustomed to.

The process of "global analysis," a major step of the on-site process, helps find the facts that, with a trained leader skilled in group problem-solving, lead the group to identifying and agreeing on *what needs to be done to improve the situation(s) causing problems.* This then becomes the shared agenda for group problem-solving.

We also believe that:

- Separating the problem-solving process from any group (or staff) negatively affects their "ownership" of solutions; without involvement, people are less likely to be committed to implementing resulting recommendations for change.
- The host and visiting team members should write the report *together* as part of the problem-solving process for both the learning and additional ownership of results which this can and does create.

Perhaps most importantly, we feel strongly that:

- Evaluation of the problem-solving process should be based not on the ideas which are presented, but on *whether or not change occurs in the organization as a result*, and that
- Recommendations must begin with what can be done in the short run, including a number of obvious, practical steps that can be taken immediately. Only then can attention and planning be effectively focussed on longer term results.

## ON-SITE METHODOLOGY AND EXPERIENTIAL LEARNING

The methods of on-site analysis are based on the above assumptions and on well-researched and documented observations about the effectiveness of experiential learning compared with other methods. These include those which indicate that *people learn best by:*

- being involved in the (educational) process
- being challenged to think and to contribute
- having to share, interpret, generalize and summarize what they are learning as they learn it
- working in intensive, focussed groups—hand in hand with individual assignments
- learning by doing, and having to apply what is learned as it is learned
- working in settings which "deemphasize" status (levelling or "equalizing" processes can encourage participation)
- being involved in setting objectives
- having action plans and clear roles in those plans for meeting objectives they have been involved in setting
- having the opportunity to carry out plans and assume new roles
- pursuing any personal or professional goals that may be part of their motivation to learn.

On-site analysis is specifically designed to encourage and afford considerable learning for both visiting and host participants.

## CRITICAL TO METHODOLOGY: FULL PARTICIPATION

Almost all of us (consultants, managers, teachers, leaders of any sort) enjoy being considered experts at least some of the time. However, in on-site analysis it is the composition of the team (visiting and host) which ensures that most of the needed expertise (skills, knowledge, and abilities) is available in the group.

**In on-site analysis, the leader's role in bringing about participation and contributions from the entire group is as important as his or her own expertise, analytical skill, and problem-solving ability.** An on-site analysis is completed in an intensive, focussed, and thorough review in which everything is questioned. Follow-up on-site assistance or other on-sites are similarly intensive and focussed.

**The on-site leader must assume the role of challenger: He or she must use *challenging techniques* as well as the usual facilitation skills.** The participation of the host and visiting team members through being challenged to think and to contribute to finding facts and making observations from them helps to build clarity and consensus about organizational strengths and weaknesses. It also helps establish group commitment to the resulting recommendations.

Experiential learning and full participation contribute to creating the "climate" that will be needed to implement recommended changes—and strengthen participants' commitment to doing so. Writing and presenting the report as a group becomes yet another vehicle of learning that can help to bring about change or the environment that is needed for change to occur.

## ORGANIZATIONAL GOALS: CLARITY AND NEW (OR RENEWED) COMMITMENT

Though we admit it may not be true of everyone, we have observed that many people want to do a better job, and want to achieve positive results for their organizations. Many also want to learn through new experiences, and are motivated by opportunities to develop new skills and competencies.

A process which gives birth to new ideas, new perceptions, new objectives, and plans of action can be stimulating and exciting for people who want to learn. On-site analysis is frequently such a process.

On-site analysis can result in a number of positive "by-products" for individuals working in an organization, such as clarification of (and new or renewed commitment to) organizational goals. While such benefits cannot be guaranteed for every participant, they can and often do result from on-site analysis.

Through consensus about the organization's current state, about the problems that most need to be solved, and about the solutions most likely to solve them, on-site analysis fosters *commitment to change* and is *specific and definite about how to begin to make that change happen.*

The clarity of the shared (and often new) perceptions of what the facts reveal about the organization which emerges through the analysis leads eventually to consensus about and ownership of identified strengths and problems, and to a shared commitment to finding solutions. Our experience has shown all three (clarity, consensus, and commitment) to be essential if consultation is to be effective in bringing about change in organizations.

. . .

## WHAT HAPPENS DURING ON-SITE ANALYSIS?

At first glance some elements of the on-site process may appear to be similar to those of other consultative techniques. Consider headings #1, 3, and 5 below for example. However, each step of on-site analysis serves a purpose often different from the traditional purpose of similar activities, and each is carried out in ways that differ considerably from more traditional approaches, as explained in the text below each heading. In on-site analysis:

1. **Facts are obtained and analyzed (clarity)** but only after *perceptions* have been identified and assessed. Usually wide-ranging perceptions of "the facts" are identified, some of which become the basis of the review. In on-site analysis this preliminary stage is followed by a *deliberate switch of focus from perception* to facts. After facts (numerical data only) have been thoroughly analyzed by the group as a group, the subsequent assessment of organizational strengths and weaknesses is often different from perceptions initially held about the organization—including some thought to be based on facts.

2. **Strengths are identified and protected or enhanced.** After strengths and weaknesses have been identified, the first task of on-site analysis is to concentrate on protecting and enhancing strengths. In our experience, strengths are often taken for granted and are therefore not protected; also, because they are seen as strengths, they are seldom scrutinized for ways they can be improved to become even greater assets to the organization.

3. **Weaknesses (problems) are identified** from observations and conclusions *based only on the examined facts*. Again, the problems identified through the group's analysis are often quite different from those initially known or perceived to be problems.

Because it is a group process based on facts obtained by and displayed before the entire group, "global analysis" (analysis of facts about the organization as a whole) results in *a shared perception of, and agreement about, the problems that most need to be solved*.

Even where analysis reveals that strengths and weaknesses had already been accurately

**Basic Elements: Steps in the On-Site Process**

While various adaptations of on-site analysis afford experienced leaders greater flexibility in using the process to help people identify and do what needs to be done to improve performance, a standard on-site analysis follows a prescribed format of thirteen basic steps:

Step 1 Preparing for the On-Site—Including the Background Questionnaire

2 Leader's Meeting with Visiting Team

3 On-Site Reception

4 On-Site Interviews

5 Opening Session and Report Back on Interviews

6 Perceptual Snapshot

7 Global Analysis

8 Group Identification of Strengths and Weaknesses, Problem Identification, and Next-Level Analysis

9 Problem Selection and Group Problem-Solving, including Enhancing Strengths and Solving Problems

10 Writing the On-Site Report

11 The Essential "Dry Run" Presentation

12 Presentation of the On-Site Report

13 The On-Site Follow-Up

identified, the process of global analysis ensures that they are clearly understood and agreed to be so by *all* members of the group. All too often, only one or two members will have seen the problems clearly but have been unable to obtain general agreement about their analysis and therefore about the proposed solutions. Global analysis directly addresses this common difficulty.

The clarity and commitment for members of the organization that result from going through global analysis together can have tremendous benefits for the team's future effectiveness.

The consensus which results from global analysis can also be invaluable in creating enthusiasm and a willingness to "get on with" solving problems for all members of a group who now clearly understand the situation, and can communicate with one another from a common, factual basis rather than varying individual perceptions and opinions.

4. **Solutions are developed and selected** using specific *group* problem-solving techniques which often result in solutions that may have been "unthinkable" or not thought of at all prior to the on-site. We have found that solutions generated and selected by the group are seldom those perceived to be "obvious" ones beforehand; still, selected solutions often do seem obvious (even simple) by the time the group has developed and selected them as part of the on-site process.

5. **Recommendations are made.** In on-site analysis, final recommendations are made and agreed on *by the full group*. Most recommendations also include *practical first steps* that can be acted on immediately to initiate change in desired directions.

6. **On-site follow-up.** We recommend that all on-sites should be "followed up" at a mutually agreed upon time 3–8 months later. The usual follow-up is a day and a half long and repeats the basic on-site group process, i.e., analysis, identification of strengths and weaknesses, development and selection of solutions, etc. The follow-up on-site is not a review of the on-site report, but rather a fresh look at the situation a few months later.

## WHAT IS IT LIKE FOR PARTICIPANTS?

The on-site process is intensive and challenging. It is *intensive* because of the singular focus and need to work as a group for several long, consecutive days in ways that many people may not be accustomed to, even those used to "working in groups." It is *challenging* because it requires people to examine (and sometimes discard) their perceptions to make observations from facts, to develop conclusions, to identify problems, and to look beyond their "first answers" again and again for other possibly better ones.

Participating in on-site analysis can nonetheless be a very positive experience. It can be positive because of the sense of liberation (sometimes exhilaration!) that can come from finding *new ways of seeing and dealing with challenges*. This sense of positive excitement is often heightened because it is shared; these "breakthroughs" or "insights" are usually arrived at as a group.

On the other hand, people should be forewarned that the discomfort of participating in on-site analysis can also be heightened because:

(a) people do work together as a group through long, intensive days, and

(b) they are guided by a leader whose role is to maintain the challenging, probing, "never-say-die" atmosphere in search of "another and another" (possibly better) idea or answer.

. . .

## CHANGE IS THE BOTTOM LINE

Good ideas are seldom in short supply, but people in organizations are often without the means to implement them.

With help from the on-site process, ideas are developed and solutions selected on the basis of newly generated common perceptions of the organization's current achievement and areas of greatest potential for improvement. There is *a clear and common view of both the strengths that need to be enhanced or protected and the problems that need to be solved.* Finally, there is a common (and, in the end, public) commitment to plans of action most likely to protect identified strengths and solve identified problems.

We usually remind people at the opening reception of any on-site analysis that what the on-site will produce are some ideas and recommendations that will be developed by the host and visiting participants working together as a team throughout the next few days.

*What happens to those recommendations will be up to the organization to decide.* If nothing better than what they are already doing results from the process, they can always return to doing what they were doing before the on-site began. (As far as we know, *no one* has yet selected that option!)

A new way of looking at an organization's activity that is shared by the entire staff and includes a set of practical recommendations that everyone agrees are based on facts about the organization's current situation can be a potent incentive to begin to make things happen.

On-site analysis creates *the opportunity to arrive at that "new way of looking," and to do so as a group.* It is different—but (so far!) it *does* work—both for organizations and for the people working in them.

. . .

**29.**

**Matthew Nartz and Dick Schoech**

**USE OF THE INTERNET FOR COMMUNITY PRACTICE:**

**A DELPHI STUDY**

## INTRODUCTION

The growth of the Internet and its applications has expanded the human potential for
interaction and information exchange. To
avoid going blindly into this new frontier, we
need experts familiar with the current situation to look into the future to determine our
next step. Community practitioners need to
be made aware of the usefulness of the
Internet for the growth and development of
their practice. Most specifically, community
practitioners need to see the current and
future potential of Internet tools for evolving
and enhancing their work. The goal of this
research was to use the Delphi Technique to
elicit the opinion of Internet community
practice experts about the effectiveness of
current and future Internet tools for the most
predominant Internet community practice
models and to identify barriers to the effectiveness of Internet community practice

## LITERATURE AND INTERNET REVIEW

This section reviews the literature and several community practice Internet sites. It

Matthew Nartz, MSSW, is a recent graduate of the
University of Texas at Arlington School of Social
Work. He is currently the Southeast and South
American Cost Analyst for Delta Air Lines Cargo
Operations.

Dick Schoech, Ph.D., is a Professor at the
University of Texas at Arlington School of Social
Work. He teaches administration, community practice,
and computer applications.

develops a conceptual framework for the
research and presents the research questions.

## Community Practice on the Internet

"Before the Internet took center stage, the
term 'community network' was a sociological concept that described the pattern of
communications and relationships in a
community" (Schuler, 1996, p. 25). This
"low tech" web of community was composed of the face-to-face interaction of the
community members.

The beginnings of computer-based community practice can be traced to computer professionals in the early 1970s. Community
Memory in Berkley, California, was an
early effort to facilitate the free exchange of
information for communities around the
world. Community Memory provided users
access to ideas and information from other
users and organizations in their community.
"From a variety of public locations including community centers, the Public Library,
and Milt's Laundromat, participants could
read forums for free, contribute their
thoughts for a quarter, or start a new forum
for a dollar" (Schuler, 1995, p. 1). The
objectives were broad and varied, but they
primarily advanced the social goals of
"building community awareness, encouraging involvement in local decision-making,
or developing economic opportunities in
disadvantaged communities" (Schuler,
1996, p. 25). The Computer Memory phenomenon was repeated all over the world

by community activists, often in conjunction with other local institutions (Rheingold, 1993; Doheny-Farina, 1996). These early efforts were characterized by three overlapping objectives—information dissemination, connecting individuals with a common interest or common physical location, and advancing social goals.

In his book titled *Community Computer Networks: Building Electronic Greenbelts*, Cisler detailed aspects of community networks. These "electronic greenbelts" were defined as "one or more computers providing services to people using computers and terminals to gain access to those services and to each other" (Cisler, 1993, p. 1). These networks formed a bond between geographically separated people who shared a common interest or profession. The network could also serve a geographical area such as a municipality, county, or region. The population that comprises a "greenbelt" was not as important as the information contained and the relationships formed within such networks.

Cisler (1992) invited a group of 53 people to explore and examine a variety of subjects directly related to Internet community practice. The subjects included various computer network projects, newly enhanced democratic participation, and new technology innovations (primarily multimedia) that could promote the growth of this field. These discussion groups were led and attended by experts who brought up many perceived problems in today's society that may be resolved using these new technological innovations. This good news was tempered with the caution that, without equitable access, getting people involved in the political process may give some groups familiar with the use of technology an unrepresentative amount of power.

Community practitioners were slower than other professions to use computer and networking technology due to its cost and limited availability. Cordero (1991) found that New York community organizers used computer technology for mailing lists, newsletters, and databases on issues such as tenant harassment, building repossession, and crime. Computers allowed smaller agencies to carry out functions that were previously limited to larger organizations and to provide more and better services to their communities. Problems included training and obtaining the staff resources to construct the databases and enter the large amount of data. Cordero did not find agencies using telecommunications for networking.

One of the first efforts to build a human service community using electronic communications was the Computer Use in Social Services Network (CUSSN, http://www.uta.edu/cussn/). CUSSN went on-line in 1986 with CUSSNet, a free, distributed, personal computer– and telephone-based network built on FidoNet. The goal of CUSSNet was the linking of people, resources, and ideas. Within a year, CUSSNet nodes in 17 U.S. cities and three foreign countries exchanged messages, distributed software, and operated many group discussion areas (Schoech, 1986). Many client self-help communities were also built on the FidoNet infrastructure—for example, Alcoholics Anonymous bulletin boards.

Other studies support the value of networking for community practice (Stoecker & Stuber, 1997). One well-researched effort was CHESS (Comprehensive Health Enhancement Support System). CHESS was an integrated set of computer services that allows people with difficult health issues, such as breast cancer or AIDS/HIV, to form support communities (Gustafson et al., 1993). CHESS used personal computers that were placed in users' homes and linked together via modem through a central computer. CHESS services include information, referrals, decision support, and social support. CHESS goals were to improve the emotional health status of users, increase the cost-effective use of health and human services, and reduce the incidence of risk-taking behaviors that can lead to injury or illness. CHESS users reported improved cognitive functioning, more social support, more active participation in their health care, a more active lifestyle, and fewer negative emotions compared to control subjects, who reported that they remained the same or got worse on these variables (Boberg et al., 1995).

By the early 1990s, the foundation work for community practice use of computer and telecommunications had been done, but few efforts existed due to cost and technological complexity. The introduction of the Internet in the mid 1990s changed community practice and technology use, providing a low-cost network with multiple tools and worldwide standards. With networking available to almost anyone for roughly the cost of a computer, telephone line, and small access fee, community practitioners quickly began to use the Internet.

Chow & Coulton (1996) realized that community-based practice called "for intervention strategies that are based on careful planning and thorough assessment of the ecological conditions in today's urban neighborhoods" (p. 1). They stressed that the most important tool available for community practitioners is access to accurate and updated community data. They developed an Internet gopher site that provided neighborhood groups with substantial information on their communities. While gopher Internet technology provided users with text menus, it was later World Wide Web Internet technology that offered a graphical, point and click Internet interface through an easy-to-use browser. Today,

most Internet sites use Web technology.

A study by Guard et al. (1997) shows the Web as the perfect solution for disseminating health care information, but cites such impediments as the lack of organization of large amounts of information as well as the inability to serve those who do not have access to computers and communication technology. The authors set up a community health network that was easy to use and accessible through terminals at locations such as public libraries and hospital waiting rooms.

Nicotera (1997) found listservs and newsgroups to be a valuable resource for information dissemination and exchange. Listservs provide a more personalized form of information dissemination, but newsgroups allow an expanded form of interaction between users. Although they differ on methods of access, both tools provide users the capability to spread ideas and information. The findings on newsgroups were supported by information found on the Internet by Kelley (1998).

Brogden & Williams (1995) describe BARBARA (Broad Range of Community Based Telecommunications Application in Rural Areas), a project founded on the perceived inequity of service delivery between urban and rural areas. The higher level of service that was available was causing a large population movement into the urban areas. In order to ease this flow, the project designers used telecommunications and multimedia in four different countries to bring the services out into rural areas using computer telecommunications.

Finn (1998) surveyed 209 human service agencies that solicit volunteers over the Web and found that agencies varied considerably in their Web site goals, development and maintenance costs, number of hits, and their success in soliciting volunteers, goods, and services. Web site goals included community information, information and referral, volunteer recruitment, special events publicity, fundraising, receiving community feedback, advocacy, and soliciting goods and services. Finn found Web site goal achievement to be "modest," that is, accounting for less than 10 percent of agency volunteers, goods, and services. Agencies were generally satisfied with their Web activities but frustrated with the time and resources required to manage the sites.

## Community Practice Web Sites

A review of several of the most progressive community practice Web sites was conducted to develop the framework for this study.

**Boulder Community Network (http://bcn.boulder.co.us/):** Since 1994, the Boulder Community Network has provided information on subjects such as current events, education, employment, government, community, environment, health, and housing. This site, maintained mostly by volunteers, allows human service and other nonprofit organizations the ability to publish their information on the Web. The Boulder Community Network provides these organizations no-cost Web space, resources, and the assistance to allow the organizations to join the Internet community and to receive the benefits that it provides.

**Ozarks Regional Information Online Network (http://www.orion.org/):** The Ozarks Regional Information Online Network (ORION) was started as a local network in 1993 and became a Web site in April 1994. Using Internet technology, such as free e-mail accounts, chat rooms, and newsgroups, the community members discuss relevant topics and assist each other. The helping process strengthens the bond between members as they interact in finding information, identifying Web sites, or

answering questions on how to best use Web resources. The site also features the option that the user is allowed to see who else is logged onto the site. Users may seek out recognized experts on a certain subject or refer others to them if they know they are on-line. The free e-mail feature is not to be understated, as many connect through public terminals in libraries. The services of the library, local government, and community interests are the most used.

**Access Minnesota (http://www.extension.umn.edu/Accessmn/):** The University of Minnesota set up the Access Minnesota Web site in the spring of 1995. Working in conjunction with government, public radio, and television entities, Access Minnesota provides citizens direct access, via private and public computer terminals, to information located on the Internet. On this Web site, users can find resources such as education, government, library, and Internet links.

**Neighborhood Knowledge Los Angeles (http://nkla.sppsr.ucla.edu/):** The Community Building Institute has operated the Neighborhood Knowledge L.A. site since 1997. This site takes a proactive stance on the continual decline of Los Angeles neighborhoods. It provides residents with information such as building code violation, property tax delinquency, and residential building permit records in order to raise both their awareness and their potential to act on problems. The building code violation records are the most frequently used database, receiving about 400 hits a month. Property tax delinquency records run a close second, with about 350 hits per month (D. Krouk, personal communication, October 22, 1997). These sources link to other relevant databases, such as recent sales by zip code, which allow the user convenient, updated information that would be impossible for residents to obtain. The site also provides bulletin boards to help raise awareness and build coalitions. L.A. Pages is another database where organizations such as the L.A. Housing Corporation, A Community of Friends, and the East L.A. Community Corporation provide residents with housing opportunities.

**City of Phoenix (http://www.ci.-phoenix.az.us/):** Since June 1995, the City of Phoenix Web site has provided e-mail, surveys, and information on a variety of topics relevant to the daily life of citizens. Subjects include election results, calendar of community events, community involvement, volunteer programs, neighborhood improvement, planning, and zoning. Links allow users to connect to a variety of agencies that, hopefully, will address their needs. One of the most outstanding features is updates on Arizona state legislation that affects community life. Users see not only upcoming changes in state policy, but also addresses, locations, protocols, and key contact people in order to get in touch with their legislators and become involved in the legislative process. A neighborhood legislative liaison enhances the average citizens' effect on the legislative process by teaching users the intricacies of the legislative process using on-line workshops.

### Conceptual Framework for This Study

The literature and Web site review revealed four primary, though overlapping, models of Internet community practice. These models are information dissemination, community building, mobilization, and community planning (Figure 29.1). These models use six primary Internet tools:

1. E-mail: Allows users to compose messages and transmit them in seconds to one or more recipients anywhere in the world.

2. Text: Allows users to read printed matter on pages of a Web site and to navigate the sites and the Web via clickable links.
3. Search Engines: Help a user find desired information or resources by searching for key words that the user specifies.
4. Listservs: Allow users to receive and post messages on topics, after which each message is sent to all subscribers to the list.
5. Newsgroups: Allow users to go to one place on the Internet and view previous messages on topics and add new messages.
6. Chat: Allows a group of users connected at the same time to send messages to each other in real time.

### Research Questions

Four research questions were developed from the review of the literature and community practice Web sites:

1. What are the current and future demographics of Internet community practice Web sites?
2. Which current and future Internet tools are most useful for the four identified models of Internet community practice?
3. Which new Internet community practice models and Internet tools have the most potential?
4. What barriers exist to Internet community practice?

### METHODS

### Data-Gathering Technique

The Delphi Technique is a method of eliciting and refining the judgments of experts. This is accomplished by extracting and cultivating responses using a sequence of ques-

FIGURE 29.1
Community Practice Models Found on the Internet

| Model | Definition | Purpose | Example |
|---|---|---|---|
| Information dissemination | Informational one-way roads with little or no interaction or exchange between the user and the provider | Educating and raising awareness | An agency Web site providing information on such issues as welfare reform , e. g., the Boulder Community Network |
| Community building | Sites for building geographic or interest-based communities | Bringing people together, sharing resources, social involvement, and expansion of individual interactions | Community networks that serve the purpose of linking people and human service agencies together, such as the Ozarks Regional Information Online Network |
| Mobilization | Sites for fighting a battle of us versus them, as opposed to only building an us | Increase interaction among users in order to further a cause | Political activism and advocacy sites are good examples of this model, e.g., City of Phoenix |
| Community planning | Site for allowing the interaction necessary for rational and planned construction of a better service delivery system | Tying various stakeholders (citizens, government, and agencies) together | City or some United Way Web sites that provide solution-based bulletin boards, chat, forums, and virtual meetings, e.g., the City of Phoenix Web site |

tionnaires given to a select group of individuals recognized as experts in the area being studied. The replies are anonymously gathered, summarized, and revised until an agreement of thought is established (Linstone & Turoff, 1975). The Delphi technique involves anonymity of responses, feedback to the group as a whole or to individuals, and the opportunity for any respondent to modify an earlier judgment. The model followed in this study is the Policy Delphi, wherein the objective is to expose the strongest viewpoints concerning a particular issue rather than to construct a consensus (Turoff & Hiltz, 1995).

**Description of the Instruments**

This study used three instruments, a demographic questionnaire, an initial Delphi questionnaire, and a final Delphi questionnaire. The instruments were pretested using five graduate-level students who possessed a working knowledge of community practice and the Internet.

The demographic questionnaire gathered identifying information on the participants and their Web sites. This questionnaire includes variables such as participant name, title, Web site beginning date, the number of visits or hits the Web site received per month, Web site features, and user demographics.

The first Delphi questionnaire provided questions on the most useful current and future Internet models and tools. The questionnaire also covered current and predicted barriers to community practice on the Internet and perceived changes in the users' demographics. Respondents were asked to rate models and tools on a Likert scale and to give the rationale for their answers. The Likert scale used was 4=very useful, 3=useful, 2=slightly useful, and 1=least/not useful for community practice.

The second Delphi questionnaire contained the results of the first Delphi questionnaire, along with questions to indicate if respondents agreed or disagreed with the results and to request the rationale for their responses.

## Sample

A purposive sample of 21 Web sites was selected from the population of community practice Web sites found on the Internet. Care was taken to ensure that the sample included diversity of geographical zones, diversity of community practice models, and good Web site design. The sites selected were thought to represent the "best and brightest" of the Internet community practice Web sites, and thus were able to offer the most productive input for the study.

## Procedures

The person identified as the developer/operator of the 21 sites selected was sent an introductory e-mail outlining the purpose of the study and requesting his or her participation. The 13 positive responses were sent the demographic questionnaire requesting information about their Web site. The 10 respondents who returned the demographic questionnaire were then sent the first Delphi questionnaire. The eight who returned the first Delphi questionnaire were e-mailed the second Delphi questionnaire, which five participants returned.

## FINDINGS AND DISCUSSION

### Current and Future Sites Demographics

*Respondents.* The respondents were all highly involved in the creation and development of their site. All held high-ranking positions in their organization, such as coordinators, directors, and technology specialists. A lack of time was the primary reason given for the inability to participate in the study.

*Site Data.* The oldest site has been on-line since November of 1993, while the newest Web site has been in existence for only seven months. Although three of the 10 respondents could not determine how many visitors or hits they received, an examination of the questionnaires from the other five respondents revealed that these sites have received a great amount of use in the short time that they have been on-line.

The mean number of hits reported was 370,744 per month and the median was 350,000. The most used sites received about 680,000 hits per month, while the least used site received 2,500 hits. It is important to point out that the most used Web site is one of the most established, having been on-line for about two and a half years. Time has allowed the Web site not only to establish a large, strong user base, but also to grow with user needs. This long period has also allowed this Web site to form connections with many other organizations, to incorporate these organizations into its Web site, and to expand the number of services available. The idea that time on-line leads to a higher user rate is further supported by the fact that the site that reported the least amount of use had been on-line for the least amount of time. Of the eight respondents, two indicated that they served a community of interest, two indicated they served a geographical community, and the four reported they served both. While the major function of these Web sites is to provide service to their immediate geographical areas, those who also linked a community of interest found the Internet community to be the primary users.

Overall, the respondents indicated a theme of extended use of the Internet.

FIGURE 29.2
Relevance of Internet Tools for Current Community Practice

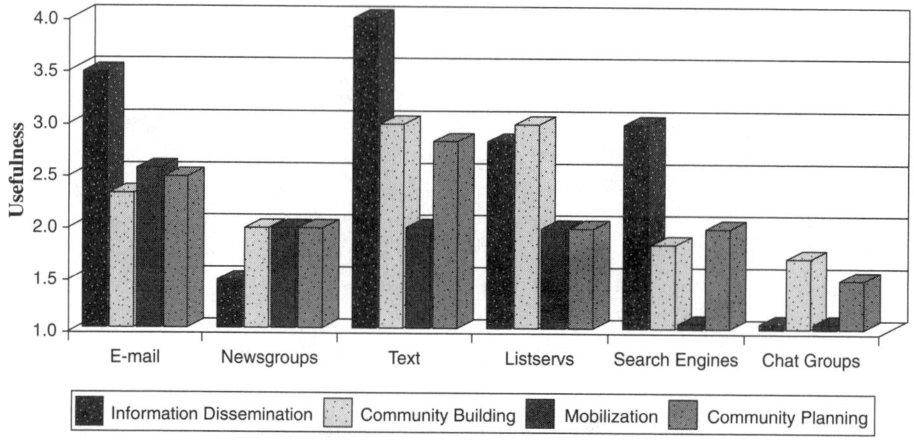

Scale: 4=very useful, 3=useful, 2=slightly useful, 1=least/not useful.

Respondents predicted the site to grow in all demographic categories, but particularly among the young and old—the young because they would most likely be taking on leadership roles and developing the new models for the future, the old because they are a user group with high human service needs and the free time necessary for extended Internet use. Respondents predicted overall growth that will incorporate Internet use into the daily lives of the entire population of this country. Community practitioners need to realize this growth and adapt their services to take advantage of on-line service delivery mechanisms.

*Features of Sites.* The features of the Web sites varied from site to site to include e-mail, listserv, chat, information directories, and links to other sites. The sites used these features primarily to provide and disseminate information, to increase interaction between community members, and to offer training.

## Usefulness of Internet Tools for Community Practice

Figure 29.2 graphically depicts the current usefulness and Figure 29.3 depicts the future usefulness of each Internet tool for the four models of Internet community practice found on the Internet. Figure 29.4 presents current and future scores and averages. The results will be discussed by model of Internet community practice.

*Information Dissemination.* The four respondents whose Web site used the information dissemination model of community practice indicated that text was the most useful Internet tool (4.0). E-mail came in second in importance, with a mean rating of 3.5. Search engines received a mean rating of 3.0. Listservs received a mean rating of 2.85. Newsgroups received a mean rating of 1.5. Chat was determined to be the least useful of the tools, receiving a mean rating of 1.0.

FIGURE 29.3
Relevance of Internet Tools for Future Community Practice

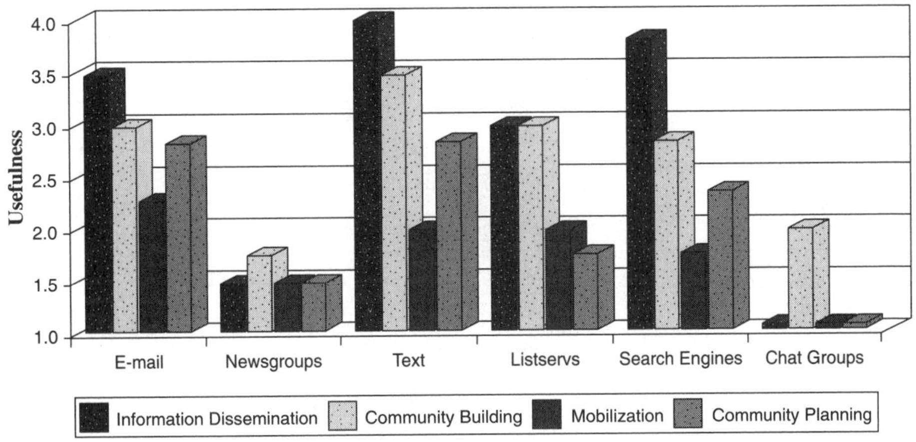

Scale: 4=very useful, 3=useful, 2=slightly useful, 1=least/not useful.

Future usefulness of Internet tools for information dissemination was predicted to be almost identical to current usefulness, with the exception of search engines, which changed from a current mean of 3 to a future mean of 3.85.

*Community Building.* The four respondents whose Web site used the community building model indicated that text and listservs were equally useful (mean 3.0). Text allows organizations and groups to form a presence on the Internet and easily disseminate information to allow users to form an affiliation with the organization. The listservs tool provides a medium for the discussion of a variety of topics, and thus allows a community of interests to form. E-mail was also indicated to be useful, receiving a mean rating of 2.33. Search engines received a mean rating of 1.85. Newsgroups were indicated to be only slightly useful, with a mean rating of 2.0. Chat was found the least useful tool, receiving a mean rating of 1.66.

Future usefulness of Internet tools for community building was similar to current usefulness, with search engines seen as much more useful in the future (mean 1.85 to 2.85). E-mail, text, and chat were seen as having slightly higher future usefulness, listservs the same, and newsgroups slightly lower future usefulness.

*Mobilization.* The four respondents using the mobilization model found e-mail to be the most useful tool of the Internet (mean 2.25). E-mail allows the mobilizing organization to disseminate information quickly in order to fight a common cause. Text and listservs were second in usefulness with a 2.0 mean rating. Search engines and chat came in last with a 1.0 (least/not useful) mean rating.

Future usefulness of Internet tools for mobilization was identical to current usefulness for text, listservs, and chat. Future usefulness was slightly lower for e-mail and newsgroups and higher for search engines.

FIGURE 29.4
Mean Scores for All Community Practice Models, Current and Future

| Community Practice Models | E-mail | Current usefulness (mean scores) Newsgroups | Text | Listservs | Search Engines | Chat Groups |
|---|---|---|---|---|---|---|
| Information dissemination | 3.5 | 1.5 | 4 | 2.85 | 3 | 1 |
| Community building | 2.33 | 2 | 3 | 3 | 1.85 | 1.66 |
| Mobilization | 2.55 | 2 | 2 | 2 | 1 | 1 |
| Community planning | 2.5 | 2 | 2.85 | 2 | 2 | 1.5 |
| Total average | 2.72 | 1.875 | 2.9625 | 2.4625 | 1.9625 | 1.29 |
| | | Future usefulness (mean scores) | | | | |
| Information dissemination | 3.5 | 1.5 | 4 | 3 | 3.85 | 1 |
| Community building | 3 | 1.66 | 3.5 | 3 | 2.85 | 2 |
| Mobilization | 2.25 | 1.5 | 2 | 2 | 1.66 | 1 |
| Community planning | 2.85 | 1.5 | 2.85 | 1.66 | 2.33 | 1 |
| Total average | 2.9 | 1.54 | 3.0875 | 2.415 | 2.6725 | 1.25 |

*Community Planning.* The four respondents whose Web site used the community planning model indicated that text was the most useful Internet tool (mean 2.85). Electronic mail was second with a mean rating of 2.5. Text and e-mail were used primarily to accomplish the first step in the community planning process—that is, to educate and raise awareness about the situation or need. Once this is done, the community planning process can continue on the Web site using other tools such as newsgroups. Newsgroups, search engines, and listservs were perceived as only slightly useful, receiving a mean rating of 2.0. Chat was shown the least useful tool, receiving a mean rating of 1.5. This low score for chat indicates that on-line meetings are not currently being held in chat rooms.

Future usefulness of Internet tools for community planning was identical to current usefulness for text, lower for listservs, newsgroups, and chat, and higher for e-mail and search engines. This low ranking for chat and listservs indicates that on-line committee work was not envisioned in the future.

*All Models.* When current scores for all models were combined (Figure 29.4), text is clearly the most useful Internet tool, followed by e-mail. Listservs received a neutral rating. Newsgroups and chat were found the least useful. Future perceived usefulness was very similar. However, search engines switched places with listservs to become slightly above neutral in usefulness. It is interesting that respondents in all community practice models rated only search engines as having more future usefulness. This is consistent with the high rating given to text. As a site adds more text, a search engine becomes a more useful tool. The future usefulness of newsgroups was seen as lower or the same as current usefulness for all models.

## New Internet Tools and Internet Community Practice Models

Respondents identified no future Internet community practice models. One respondent stated that his organization desired to implement all of its currently offered "real world" services on the Internet, but offered no new models. One respondent stated "we are not likely to change the focus of our site a lot in the future." Respondents identified only one new Internet tool with potential in future service delivery—Web conferencing. Web conferencing can be differentiated from a standard chat group in its set structure of time, audience, and moderator. Where a chat group has a constant flow of people in and out, a Web conference has a selected audience, set agenda, and moderator to lead the discussion. One respondent stated, "I think that web and other conferencing will improve the interactivity of the Internet, which will enhance its usefulness as a community building tool beyond listservs."

### Respondent's Rationales and Discussion

*Current use.* Respondents made several important points in the rationale for their answers. Speed and ease of use affect the importance placed upon Internet tools. For example, one respondent stated, "from a technology point of view, our features represent the 'low hanging fruit,' the things we do easily are perceived of greatest value to the departments." Chat is a relatively new concept in Internet community practice, and once it becomes more familiar and integrated into practice, the rating may grow. For example, one respondent stated "chat may have ranked higher had it been in place earlier in our operation." The developers prefer lower-end technology in order to serve more users. Web tools primarily reflect the amount of utilization of the tools rather than effectiveness of the tool. This focus on quantity versus quality reflects the use of hits as one of the primary criteria for evaluating the success of a Web site. Clearly, additional success criteria are needed, such as goal achievement as described by Finn (1998).

*Future Use.* Since most respondents had no Web site changes planned, responses about

the future were very similar to responses for current use. One respondent indicated that the organization had just received a grant for the development of a chat group tool and saw chat growing in importance. In the second Delphi questionnaire, another respondent disagreed with this prediction, stating that little importance was put in chat and "the time chat was placed in operation does not matter." Newsgroups and chat are useful, but often they are used only by small groups of regular users. Search engines are seen as useful for those already exploring a given topic, but are generally not useful for initiating new members into current community activities.

### Barriers to Effective Internet Community Practice

Respondents to the first Delphi questionnaire listed nine barriers to Internet community practice. Respondents to the second Delphi questionnaire agreed with all of the listed barriers.

One group of barriers concerned the agency. Time to properly operate the Web site was seen as a major barrier. This was especially true for organizations that provide their services in the real world as well. One respondent summed this up by simply stating, "so much to do, so little time." Two respondents saw staffing as a barrier. With this new and rapidly developing field, a solid talent base is extremely hard to find, especially in the areas of data communications and databases. Three respondents mentioned that the difficulty of maintaining the quality and currency of information was a barrier. In addition, users must be educated to identify the reliability of sources of information on the Internet. Three respondents indicated that the lack of competent marketing could be a barrier to Internet community practice.

One respondent stated that "there is so much information out there, it is difficult for us to get ours in front of people." The problem of receiving outside support was also identified. Developers often cite the difficulties involved in raising funds for their operations. One respondent noted, "people do not seem to want to pay for Internet services for the public good." One respondent even went so far as to say that, without sponsorship in place, he did not advise even starting a Web site.

Another group of barriers concerned technology. Browser consistency was mentioned, because developers must make sure that all of their features and services are compatible with all Web browsers. Two respondents saw bandwidth, or the speed of data transfer, as a barrier because users are often using slow modems and outdated technology to access sites. Web site designers need to keep in mind that their primary purpose is to provide their services effectively, and not to win design innovation awards. Two respondents stated that the rapid change of technology was a barrier to effective service delivery. One respondent noted that a large number of people involved in this practice—either government or nonprofit organizations—do not fully grasp the nature and significance of computer-related changes that are presently occurring. These changes are affecting work structure as well as service delivery. With the rapid changes in technology taking place, a concerted effort was required to stay current.

A final group of barriers concerned the user. Four respondents indicated that the lack of Internet access would continue to be a barrier to Internet community practice. Several significant initiatives are underway to address access problems. Access is the focus of the community networks movement that has established Free-Nets in many parts of the U.S. (Chapman & Rhodes, 1997). Access has been a key theme of proposals funded by the approximately $100 million awarded annually by the Telecommunications and Information Infrastructure Assistance Program (TIIAP) of the Department of Commerce. Many community networking projects are described on the TIIAP Web site (http://www.ntia.doc.gov/otiahome/tiiap/).

Access was seen as a difficult barrier to solve, especially for low-income populations and people with disabilities. Special techniques are needed to improve access for people with sight or hearing problems or other special needs. The Bobby Web site (http://www.cast.org/bobby/) will automatically check out any site and provide advice on making it more barrier free. Two respondents saw user skills as a barrier. Web site developers must concentrate on providing service to those with very little skills, yet be flexible enough to grow and develop with their users as they grow.

A common theme was that all barriers would continue into the future. One respondent commented that most of the barriers, except for the speed of data flow, would grow even more significant as time passes.

## DISCUSSION

Use of Internet community practice Web sites was found to be quite high, and growing every day. The experts concluded that we are most likely seeing only the beginning of growth in this field. The longer these Web sites are on-line, the more use they receive. Web site operators/designers should realize that their relationship with their users is dynamic rather than passive. The Web sites need to interact with their users in a symbiotic process that aids in the growth of the community as a whole.

The respondents valued certain Internet features over others regardless of the Internet community practice model used. There are slight variations from model to model, but the common theme was that text and e-mail are the most useful Internet tools, while newsgroups and chat were the least useful. However, respondents assumed an active Web site development effort. Text must continually be kept current, and staff need to "routinely log in and look at messages daily" (Di Ponio, 1996, p. 88). The respondents did not view the Internet tool of listservs highly. This contradicts the study by Nicotera (1997) and the advice given by Kelley (1998).

These findings on the usefulness of Internet tools have several explanations. The first is that Internet community practice, no matter what model, primarily concerns disseminating information in a general manner such as on a Web site, or in a personal manner, such as in email. Other community practice techniques and tools are secondary. Another explanation is that the Internet is so new that the distinct models of community practice are not yet fully developed. Supporting this explanation is the low use of chat, even by the community planning Web sites. As human service clients become connected to the Internet and agency webmasters become more skilled, we expect the value of many tools to increase for certain models—for example, chat for developing community issues. Another explanation is that current respondents are so busy that they found it difficult to distinguish the present from the future. Supporting this explanation were two respondents who indicated that they did not view leading edge technology as important. They saw that their primary role was to provide information to the lowest common denominator, and they, therefore, spent their time looking at the current situation with little thought to future technological developments.

## IMPLICATIONS FOR PRACTICE

The purpose of Internet use and the needs of the community should dictate the specific tools that a Web site offers. Figures 29.2 and 29.3 illustrate the Internet tools that will best serve different goals. Community practice agencies wanting to use the Internet would be wise to develop their initial Web sites for information dissemination and begin email communications with agencies, clients, and the public. They should establish a listserv if the goals for being on the Web involve information dissemination and community building. As the site grows, a search engine tool should be added. Newsgroups and chat should be added only after careful consideration and evidence from some of the more mature sites that illustrate that these tools are valuable. The sophistication of the Web site should not outgrow the sophistication of the users.

The barriers that this study identified are numerous, but they may be overcome with an adequate amount of effort and diligence. One such barrier is the skill level of the users, which can be overcome if one of the goals of the Web site is user education. Web site developers may dedicate a section of their Web sites to educate users on various Internet techniques and provide numerous links to sites with tutorials. Other barriers point to the need for restructuring an agency to help deal with the demands of Internet community practice, which requires resource development and marketing (both internal and external) to reach its potential. Do not expect the barriers to be resolved anytime soon, but the process can be sped up with effort and forethought.

This study found that the current participating agencies are so consumed by maintaining their Web sites that they had difficulty envisioning future models of Internet-
based community practice. For example,
none mentioned multiagency coordination,
for which the Internet is beginning to play a
role. None mentioned intranets and extra-
nets, which are becoming popular in the corporate world. Perhaps some new models
must be developed in academic institutions
where funded research allows for experimentation. It should also be noted that only
one site in the sample was based in an academic institution and supported by a university. University research ties may be
necessary for the field of Internet-based
community practice to progress more rapidly. One question needing research is how
citizens are using these Internet community
practice Web sites. An examination of the
processes that a user goes through in the use
of a Web site could identify problems and
lead to advances in Web site design.

This study also pointed to the usefulness
of using the Internet to conduct research
and the usefulness of adopting research
techniques, such as a Delphi study, for the
Internet. The authors recommend the use of
a Web site to present the Delphi questionnaires and a moderated listserv to carry out
the Delphi discussion. These tools would
overcome the formatting problems of email
with attached files that were found. Internet
tools may allow the Delphi process to
progress more quickly, maintain momentum and interest, and prevent the dropout
rate associated with this study. For an additional study of computer-based Delphi
processes, see Turoff and Hiltz (1995). It is
also recommended that, due to the high
dropout rate that this study experienced,
future researchers start with larger samples

and devise new methods to attract and
maintain the interest of the subjects.

The participants of this study stated that
this exercise was beneficial, because they
learned new ideas from examining others'
responses. What seems to be lacking between
the community networks is, strangely
enough, networking. The ties between the
various Internet community practice Web
sites projects are either very weak or nonexistent. "In general, community network
developers have not explored just what the
nature of a stronger or closer relationship
between them would mean" (Schuler, 1996,
p. 26). This may be because these organizations just do not have the resources available
to put forth the effort to provide assistance to
other networks. The pressures upon these
organizations are many (funding, low
staffing, and public interest), and these organizations receive very little support from
their communities (Schuler, 1996). They
must spend most of their available resources
serving their primary agency goals and
objectives by providing services to their target populations (Stoecker and Stuber, 1997).
In fact, the issue of steady funding is a serious problem for even with the most popular
and successful sites (Cisler, 1993). The lack
of an outward vision of support and interaction with other community practice Web sites
is an issue that needs to be dealt with if these
networks are to be able to realize their potential. One small but meaningful effort is the
HSWEB listserv, where human service Web
developers share information.

## CONCLUSION

Community practitioners need to embrace
the new frontier of the Internet. Internet users
are predicted to grow in all demographic cat-

egories and to impact the daily lives of the entire population of this country. Community practitioners need to realize this growth and use Internet tools to adapt their services to serve this on-line population. The most useful tools vary by the models of community practice an agency uses. The tools and models used in Internet community practice appear to fit with the methods, values, and models in standard community practice, but with more benefits. These benefits include increased interaction, greater availability of resources, larger client base, and more efficient service delivery.

## REFERENCES

Boberg, E. W., Gustafson, D. H., Hawkins, R. P., Chan, C. L., Bicker, E., Suzanne, P., & Berhe, H. (1995). Development, acceptance, and use patterns of a computer-based education and social support system for people living with AIDS/HIV infection. *Computers in Human Behavior, 11*(2), 289–311.

Brogden, J., & Williams, C. (1995). Using advanced communications and multimedia applications to provide real life benefits to remote rural areas: BARBARA. *Computers in Human Services, 12*(1/2): 141–150.

Chapman, G., & L. Rhodes (1997). Nurturing neighborhood nets. Retrieved August 7, 1998, from the World Wide Web: http://web.mit.edu/techreview/www/articles/oct97/chapman.html.

Chow, J., & Coulton, C. (1996). Strategic use of community database for planning and practice. *Computers in Human Services, 13*(3): 57–72.

Cisler, S. (1992). Building local civic nets. *Computer professionals for social responsibility* [On-line], 5 pages. Retrieved August 17, 1997, from the World Wide Web: http://www.cpsr.org/dox/program/community-nets/report_building_local_civic_net.html.

Cisler, S. (1993). *Community computer networks: building electronic greenbelts. Computer Professionals for Social Responsibility.* Retrieved

August 17, 1997, from the World Wide Web: http://www.cpsr.org/program/communitynets/building_electronic_greenbelts.html.

Cordero, A. (1991). Computers and community organizing: Issues and examples from New York City. *Computers for Social Change and Community Organizing, 13*(2): 89–103.

Di Ponio, S. (1996). Community care computing in a metropolitan borough council: The perspectives of clients, practitioners and managers. In F. E. Yates (Ed.), *Creative Computing in Health and Social Care.* New York: John Wiley & Sons

Doheny-Farina, S. (1996). *The wired neighborhood,* New Haven, CT: Yale University Press.

Finn, J. (1998). Seeking volunteers and contributions: An exploratory study of nonprofit agencies on the Internet. *Computers in Human Services, 15*(4), 39–56.

Guard, J., Morris, T., Schick, L., Marine, S., Kaya, B., Haag, D., Shoemaker, S., & Tsipis, G. (1997). A community approach to serving health information needs: The Ohio valley community health information network. *Health Care on the Internet, 1*(1): 73 –82.

Gustafson, D., Wise, M., McTavish, F., Taylor, J. O., Wolberg, W., Stewart, J., Smalley, R. V., and K. Bosworth. (1993). Development and pilot evaluation of a computer-based support system for women with breast cancer. *Journal of Psychosocial Oncology, 11*(4) 96 –93.

Kelley, M. (1998). How to use the Internet for organizing. Retrieved August 7, 1998, from the World Wide Web: http://www.nonviolence.org/support/.

Linstone, H., & Turoff, M. (1975). *The Delphi method: Techniques and applications.* New York: Addison Wesley.

Nicotera, C. L. (1997). An overview of newsgroups and mailing lists. *Health Care on the Internet, 1*(1): 43–58.

Rheingold, H. (1993). *The virtual community.* Reading, MA: Addison-Wesley.

Schoech, D. (1986, Summer). Announcing CUSSnet. *CUSSN Newsletter, 6*(2), Arlington: University of Texas at Arlington, Box 19129, Arlington, TX 76019.

Schuler, D. (1995). Creating public space in cyberspace: The rise of the new community networks. Computer Professionals for

Social Responsibility. Retrieved August 7, 1998, from the World Wide Web: http://www.vcn.bc.ca/sig/comm-nets/schuler.html.

Schuler, D. (1996). *New community networks: Wired for change.* New York: Addison-Wesley.

Stoecker, R., & Stuber, A. C. S. (1997). Limited access: The information superhighway and Ohio's neighborhood-based organizations— the Urban University and Neighborhood Network. *Computers in Human Services, 14*(3), 39–57.

Turoff, M., & Hiltz, R. (1995). Computer based Delphi processes. In M. Adler & E. Ziglio (Eds.), *Gazing into the oracle : The Delphi Method and its application to social policy and public health.* London: Jessica Kingsley Publishers.

# PART SIX
# ADMINISTRATION AND MANAGEMENT

# Introduction

The human service field is made up of hundreds of thousands of organizations, big and little, in a not-for-profit sector. Additionally, much of government (for example, the departments of social services and health) and significant portions of the commercial sector (the human resources departments) are human service enterprises. The administration and management of these programs is the highest concern. Without effective and efficient management and administration, not only will the programs themselves falter, causing pain and disruption to clients and staff, but also, at another level, this same bumbling will erode confidence in the ability of the social service sector to deliver social service programs.

Historically the social service sector has been instructed by boards and the community at large "to become more businesslike." Our management practices of emphasizing greater degrees of concern for and involvement of the staff were labeled "bleeding heartism" and "silly" approaches to dealing with "the hard facts of administration." It is perhaps a sad comfort for us now to observe that many of the very businesses whose practices we were supposed to emulate have failed spectacularly. Indeed, the decline of American business has become a publicly accepted fact. The techniques that business had used in the past proved incapable of producing the quality and quantity of goods required for global competition. Perhaps even worse, a subset of those failures involved ethically questionable and possibly criminal behavior—the billions of dollars lost in the "thrift scandal," the organizations that bribe foreign governments, and so on. Suffice it to say that there is no magic management solution. Furthermore, the very practices that we were faulted for are now gaining favor, as the importance of employees as people is being recognized.

Thus, American professional practices have new prominence, but there are new responsibilities as well. Part Six will focus on several critical issues.

The Executive Director (ED), Chief Professional Officer (CPO) or Chief

Executive Officer (CEO) is a crucial element into the functioning of any agency. David Austin, in "The Human Service Executive," provides an outstanding discussion of the issues facing the person in this position, and of the different styles he or she might adopt, and pays special attention to issues of gender and minority status in the executive role. (More on Austin's approach can be found in a book by Robert Quinn, *Beyond Rational Management* [San Francisco: Jossey-Bass, 1989].) While this article is especially helpful for executives, it is helpful to all community practitioners who work for executives, or who have executives as targets of change.

Part of the executive's job is "policy"—its development, its implementation, change. The article on policy management provides some tips for doing the policy job, useful not only to executives but to all community practitioners. One place where policy, executive interest, and community interest often end up is at board meetings. Agency boards have the responsibility not only to respond to community interests, but to lead community innovation. "The Role of the Board in the Planning Process" addresses crucial board issues and makes suggestions about how to deal with them.

Gender issues are among the more sensitive ones in community practice agencies, especially because the "styles" that women and men use may have some difference foci. "Women's Ways and Effective Management" explores these differences.

Working in agencies carries burdens enough just because of the complexities of the job. As Austin has already pointed out, however, gender and minority status can only add complexities to a complex job for agency administrators. Winn's work on "Black Public Administrators" and the expectations that swirl around them explores these thorny issues. Havassy's "Effective Second-Story Bureaucrats" looks in detail at the "middle manager" in the human service agency

A classic question in "community practice" deals with the degree to which "freedom" in communities can be brought about by organizations—which stress "control" inside. The famous political analyst Robert Michels raised this question about socialist parties in his work on political parties (*Political Parties: A Sociological Study of the Oligarchical Tendencies of Modern Democracy.* New York; Hearst's International Library, 1915) Michels found that organizations tend, over time, to be run by the few—the iron law of oligarchy. This trend is especially problematic in community practice agencies, which are trying to bring about greater involvement and participation among excluded members of various communities. In "Transforming Human Service Organizations Through Empowerment of Staff," Cohen and Austin take community practice "inside" and explore ways to empower staff within the agency.

Gilson looks at a "case"—in this case the YWCA. How organizations change, what besets them as they do, and how they can (if they can) harmonize the past with the present are all issues that confront community practitioners on a daily basis. And Westley looks at the issues of change in organizations, change in collections of organizations, and change in organizational ecosystems.

—John E. Tropman

30.

## David M. Austin

## THE HUMAN SERVICE EXECUTIVE

Little systematic attention is given to the role of the executive in human service organizations in contemporary social work literature. When it does deal with the executive, the literature reflects a number of traditional attitudes. One is the suspicion held by practitioners in human service professions towards administrators in general as the source of fiscal constraints and intrusive rules and regulations. Another is the suspicion that social movement activists hold towards persons in positions of public authority, the "bosses," holding them personally accountable for the continued existence of social problems. Still another perspective regards with great suspicion the continued male domination of executive positions in service organizations largely staffed by women (Kravetz & Austin, 1984).

Current textbooks in social work administration focus on "management" as a generic process, or on "entry level" or "mid-management" positions. This analysis, however, deals specifically with the position of senior administrator, or chief executive officer, in human service organizations.

There are two highly visible and distinctive models of the organizational executive in the society-at-large. The most widely recognized model is that of the Chief Executive Officer (CEO) of the for-profit corporate firm. The corporate executive role combines policymaking—as a

David M. Austin is a Bert Kruger Smith Centennial professor at the School of Social Work, The University of Texas at Austin.

member of the corporation board of directors—and implementation—as the senior administrator. Conceptually, this is the simplest version of the chief executive officer role. There is ultimately a single yardstick to measure the effectiveness of executive performance—financial returns to the shareholders.

The second widely recognized executive model is that of the generalist public administrator, the federal department executive, the state agency administrator, the city manager (Gortner, Mahler & Nicholson, 1987). According to long-established principles of public administration (Wilson, 1978) the public administrator is responsible for policy implementation but is not a policymaker—elected legislative bodies make policy. This is, in fact, a more complex version of the CEO role. There are several different yardsticks to measure the effectiveness of public administrator performance: consistency of implementation with legislative intent; continuity of the governmental organization; and break-even financial management, that is, operating within the limits of available financial resources. In the instance of both the corporate CEO and the public administrator, however, the quality of the products actually produced by the organization, while important, is not the most critical yardstick for judging executive performance.

Analyses of the CEO role in voluntary nonprofit and governmental human service organizations often attempt to fit the characteristics of that position into one of these two widely recognized models. However, the role of the executive in human service organizations is, in many ways, a distinctive, and even more complicated, role (Austin, 1983). The characteristics of the position of human service executive are shaped not only by the organizational characteristics which voluntary nonprofit and governmental human service organizations share with other types of formal organizations, but also by the distinctive characteristics of human service organizations (Austin, 1988).

Similar to corporate executives, human service executives, particularly those who are also experienced professional specialists, are usually active participants in policy formation, as well as in implementation, even if the executive position is formally defined as not being a policymaking position. In fact, most policy issues come to the policy board as a recommendation of the executive. Similar to the public administrator, the human service executive is concerned with the congruence of implementation to policy, with organizational continuity, and with "break-even" financial performance. And, similar to the public administrator, the human service executive has no direct personal economic stake in the financial performance of the organization. Specifically, the executive salary does not increase in proportion to the size of the organizational budget.

But the role of human service executive is also distinctly different from either the corporate executive or the public administrator. One of the critical differences is that the most important yardstick for judging executive performance in a human service organization is the quality of the services actually produced by the organization (Patti, 1987). In turn, one of the important and distinctive characteristics of the position of human service executive is that it involves dealing with the interface between two distinctive social structures—the service production organization and the organized human service profession.

## THE EXECUTIVE POSITION

The characteristics of the executive position have been analyzed in a variety of ways. The approach used in this analysis is based on the concept that the executive position, and the preferred style of executive performance, involves an interactive, adaptive "contingency" process between an individual and a structural context. That process is shaped, in turn, by both the operational characteristics of a particular organization, and the situation of that organization in its environment.

The same organization may require different executive performance styles at different stages in the development of the organization. Human service organizations producing similar products, but in different environments, may require a different mix of elements in the executive position. Different individuals may shape the specific elements in the executive position in different ways. Moreover, effective executive performance may require that a particular individual uses different executive styles at different times during an executive career. There is no single universal definition of the characteristics of the executive role, or of the "best" style of executive performance. The following discussion examines an inclusive model which may be useful, however, in analyzing the mix of elements in the executive position in a given organization at a particular time.

### The "Competing Values" Model of Executive Functions

One inclusive framework for the analysis of the functions of service production organizations is the competing values approach presented by Robert E. Quinn in *Beyond Rational Management: Mastering the Paradoxes and Competing Demands*

FIGURE 30.1
Competing Values Framework: Effectiveness

**Human Relations Model**       **Open Systems Model**

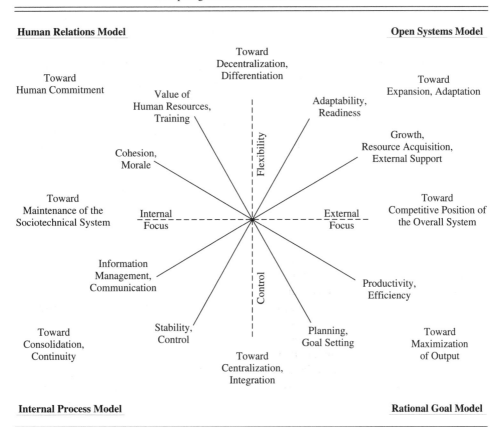

Toward Human Commitment

Toward Decentralization, Differentiation

Toward Expansion, Adaptation

Value of Human Resources, Training

Adaptability, Readiness

Cohesion, Morale

Growth, Resource Acquisition, External Support

Flexibility

Toward Maintenance of the Sociotechnical System

Internal Focus

External Focus

Toward Competitive Position of the Overall System

Information Management, Communication

Control

Productivity, Efficiency

Toward Consolidation, Continuity

Stability, Control

Planning, Goal Setting

Toward Maximization of Output

Toward Centralization, Integration

**Internal Process Model**       **Rational Goal Model**

From: R.E. Quinn (1988) *Beyond Rational Management: Mastering the Paradoxes and Competing Demands of High Performance*, used with permission from Jossey-Bass Publishers, San Francisco.

*of High Performance* (1988). (See Figure 30.1.) This analytic framework is built around two dimensions, representing competing orientations, or "values" in the organizational context—centralization-decentralization and internal-external.

The combination of these two dimensions distinguishes four sectors of organizational activity with very different and often antagonistic functional requirements: (1) human resources mobilization and motivation; (2) organization and control of production processes; (3) resource acquisition and

adaptation to the task environment; and (4) goal-oriented strategic management. This competing-values analysis of organizational functions has been applied by Edwards, Faerman and McGrath (1986) to the assessment of performance effectiveness of human service organizations.

However, this analytic framework can also be used for examining the component elements of the executive position in human service organizations on the premise that the chief executive officer is ultimately responsible for all aspects of organizational performance. In combination these four sectors deal with the two major criteria for assessing organizational outcomes—quality of services produced and continuity of the organization.

No single executive position involves equal emphasis on all four of these sectors. In any given organization the senior administrator may be primarily involved in some sectors while other persons who are part of the executive component may carry major responsibilities for activities in other sectors. Yet, the chief executive officer is ultimately responsible for the effectiveness or organizational performance in all four sectors. The following material summarizes some of the key concepts associated with each sector of organizational performance, including relevant executive roles. (See Figure 30.2.)

*1. Mobilization and Motivation of Human Resources.* One of the major sectors of executive responsibility involves the mobilization and motivation of the personnel who constitute the human resources of the organization. This sector is particularly critical in human service organizations, which are "labor-intensive," and in which most of the services are produced and delivered through person-to-person interactions. In the competing values model this sector is defined by the concepts of "internal" and "decentralized." The focus is on the role of the executive in dealing with those individuals who are "internal" to the organization, and who, as autonomous individuals with the skill competencies required in service production, represent decentralized centers of authority and influence which cannot be directly controlled by the executive. Quinn (1988) identifies two specific executive roles in this sector: *mentor* and *group facilitator.*

In many human service organizations the employed staff includes members of one or more professional disciplines, an important factor in the decentralized pattern of interpersonal relationships which must be dealt with. The human resources of human service organizations also often include a wide variety of volunteer personnel, including both service volunteers and policymaking volunteers. Moreover, given the role of co-production in the service technologies of human service organizations, service users may be a critical element in human resource mobilization and motivation. Symbols and traditions, the use of special events, and the definition of organizational values are all elements of "organizational culture" which may be significant in motivation.

The processes of human resources mobilization and motivation are often identified, as they are in the Quinn framework, with a "human relations model" and "commitment," or with an emphasis on "cohesion/morale" as in the Blake and Mouton Managerial Grid (1964). The "human relations" model for human resource mobilization and motivation, emphasizing group processes, team-building and participatory decision making, has often been advocated as being particularly congruent with, and supportive of, the "humanistic" and "service" orientation of human service practitioners. The strong emphasis on the importance of morale, or "commitment," in such organizations may also be associated, in part, with the fact that few human service organizations are able, either for structural reasons or financial reasons, to use financial rewards, or rapid career advancement, as major methods of individual motivation.

Under the participatory "human relations" model the primary role of the executive may be viewed as being the ultimate "team leader." However, it is not clear that the "human relations" model, developed by management personnel primarily around

FIGURE 30.2
Competing Values Framework of Leadership Roles

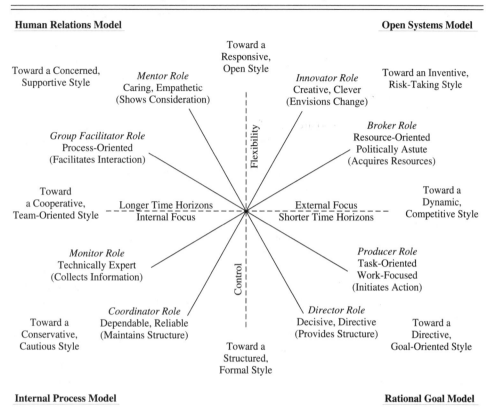

From: R.E. Quinn (1988) *Beyond Rational Management: Mastering the Paradoxes and Competing Demands of High Performance,* used with permission from Jossey-Bass Publishers, San Francisco.

efforts to improve work group performance in industrial production, using "T-groups," "management by objectives," "parallel organizations," and "quality circles," is the only relevant model for the mobilization and motivation of personnel in human service organizations. In the human service organization the quality of service often depends primarily on the competence and commitment of individual staff personnel interacting with individual service users in a co-production process, rather than on the work group. Indeed, decentralized individual responsibility, or "professional autonomy," may be more important in motivation than elaborate group participation processes in an organization in which ultimate authority is, in realty, highly centralized.

Moreover, to the extent that a model of internal participatory decision making, primarily involving employed personnel, becomes the controlling framework for decision making in all aspects of the organization, the interests of other stakeholders may be undervalued. Critical as it is, the mobilization and motivation of organizational human resources is only one of four functional sectors of executive performance.

*2. Internal Organization of Production Processes.* Given the labor-intensive, individualized nature of most human service production activities, the systematic organization of personnel activities and the monitoring of service production activities are also major elements in the executive position. In the competing values model this sector is defined by the concepts of "internal" and "centralization." It involves the technical areas commonly dealt with in discussions of management tasks (the organizing, staffing, directing, coordinating, reporting and budgeting functions of the "classical" model of public administration) —budgeting and fiscal controls, time control and scheduling procedures, information and communication systems, personnel administration systems, the structure of formal authority, reporting systems, technical training programs, evaluation and quality control, technical equipment and management of facilities. Quinn (1988) identifies two executive roles in this sector: *monitor* and *coordinator.*

In a small organization the chief executive officer may carry out many of these tasks directly. However, these are also the executive tasks which, in larger organizations, are most likely to involve technical staff specialists, and sometimes very large staff components, for example in financial management, or personnel administration. This is also an area in which "rational" and "systematic" procedures often have their widest application, and, indeed, "scientific management" focuses almost entirely on technologies applicable to this sector.

In the past decade, computerization has been a major feature in all of these technical areas, illustrating the fact that they, in many instances, involve structured decision-making choices among known alternatives—the available combinations of direct salary and fringe benefits for staff compensation, the possible variations in employee work schedules and user demand schedules which can be fitted together, using queuing theory, to design the most efficient work-load schedule for direct service personnel, the choice of a communication system or of computer software programs, the design of organizational facilities, the procedures for handling organizational funds.

There are also the areas in which consistent decisions, centrally controlled, appear to have a direct connection with efficiency, and effectiveness, and in which "command and control" techniques developed in goods production industries have most frequently been applied. However, the effectiveness of such approaches must also be judged by their impact on the equally important processes of motivation and commitment among the people involved in the organization. The development of the concept of "sociotechnical design" represents one effort to combine the objectives of efficiency and personnel motivation (Barko & Pasmore, 1986).

In human service organizations, in particular, this sector involves complex decisions about program organization, or the structure of production roles involving professional specialists, and professional technology. These program structure and technology issues include decisions about the most effective and efficient way for specialized professional personnel to participate in the implementation of "intensive" technology (Thompson, 1967), as well as decisions about the role of less specialized "generalists," and "paraprofessionals," clerical staff, volunteers, and service users.

Given the complexities and uncertainties of professional production activities, executive performance in this sector may be viewed as being based primarily on the experience of the executive with the "core" production technologies of the organization, rather than on knowledge of the more general management technologies. Executives in human service organizations are often selected primarily on the basis of professional education and previous professional experience. However, the quality of actual executive performance is often shaped by the requirements of the other three sectors in which the professional executive may have had limited experience.

*3. Resource Mobilization and Organizational Adaptation in the Task Environment.* Given the degree to which human service organizations, both voluntary nonprofit and governmental, are environmentally dependent, the executive is constantly involved in activities which cross the formal boundaries of the organization. These include, among others, financial resource procurement, personnel recruitment, the establishment and maintenance of organizational legitimation, making adaptations in organizational programs in response to environmental changes, managing external requirements for reporting and accountability, negotiation of informal and formal interorganizational agreements on user referral, cost-sharing in joint projects, and participation in action coalitions. In the competing values model this sector is defined by the concepts of "decentralization" and "external." That is, it involves dealing with individuals, and organizations, that are not under the direct control of the executive, and that are external to the formal boundaries of the organization. Quinn (1988) identifies two executive roles relevant to this sector: *innovator* and *broker.*

This sector involves, in particular, the political or "open systems" dimension of executive performance least subject to technical rationalization or computerization. The quality of executive performance may be viewed as involving "political" or "negotiating" skills, and an understanding of the nature of power relationships in the task environment. It is also the sector in which individual short-term "contingency" decision making by the executive may frequently be required, in contrast to the systematic and long-term participatory internal decision making processes which may be important in human resource mobilization and motivation. It is, perhaps, the sector of activity least likely to be fully delegated to other members of an executive component. However, it may also be the sector which policy makers, both volunteer and legislative, define as their particular area of activity, with explicit limits being placed on the scope of activities of the executive.

The effectiveness of the process of "contingency decision making," or "strategic adaptation," whether carried out by "policy makers," or the executive, or both, may be severely constrained by considerations involving other performance sectors. For example, successful "opportunity seizing" initiatives involving responses to short-term funding opportunities may be inconsistent with overall organizational goals, may require substantial expenditures for the development of new technical production procedures, and may disrupt the cohesiveness and morale of organizational participants.

*4. Strategic Management for Goal Accomplishment.* The fourth sector of executive performance is the goal-oriented process of improving both effectiveness and efficiency, and enhancing the relative position of the organization in its environment. In the competing values framework this sector is defined by the concepts of "centralization" and "external." This sector encompasses organization-centered activities identified as productivity improvement and goal setting in which the executive plays a central role. Again Quinn

(1988) identifies two executive roles in this sector: *producer* and *director.*

Since human service organizations are established as "goal-achievement" organizations, that is, to accomplish particular societal objectives, goal definition is particularly important. For "externally dependent" human service organizations this involves efforts to estimate developments in the environment, including the user environment, as well as developments potentially affecting the availability of financial and personnel resources, technological developments, political and legislative developments. Moreover, in nonprofit and governmental human service organizations, organizational continuity takes on a high value, since the "sunk costs" involved in the original effort to create the organization, and the "good will" represented in the community legitimation of the organization, cannot be converted to a set of financial resources to be used for another purpose.

The range of task responsibilities of the executive in these four functional sectors thus includes the interpersonal processes of personnel motivation, the technical competencies involved in organizing and monitoring production, the political processes involved in dealing with the task environment, and the analytic and conceptual processes involved in productivity improvement and goal accomplishment. As Quinn emphasizes, these involve "competing values" and paradoxes, since the conceptual orientation and skills most needed in one sector may be the exact opposite of those required in another sector.

The distribution of time and energy among these four task sectors will vary from time to time within any one organization, and will vary among different organizations in different environments. Responsibilities may be divided up differently among the individuals who are part of what often must be a multi-person executive component. Indi-

viduals who are part of such a multi-persons executive component will bring different mixtures of skills. Fundamentally, however, it is the responsibility of the chief executive officer in the human service organization to have an overview of the pattern of activities in all four sectors and to determine the extent to which the requirements of effective performance are being met in all four sectors.

## EXECUTIVE STYLE

Many textbooks on administration deal with administrative style through a description of two traditional theories identified as "scientific management," that is, the executive as a rational analyst and believer in "command and control," and "human relations management," the executive functioning primarily as an interactive process leader within a structure of participatory decision making groups. Both of these theories are rooted, fundamentally, in a United States model of industrial production in which there is an assumption of an almost total separation in the relationships between "management" and "workers." This separation involves not only differences in roles and responsibilities, but, in general, involved differences in socio-economic background, and often differences in ethnic/cultural background between the two groups of organizational participants. This pattern of separation is reinforced by a general lack of career mobility opportunities between industrial production roles and management roles with industrial managers being recruited largely from among college and university graduates without production experience (Reich, 1983).

Consistent with this model is the assumption of a fundamental conflict of interests between "workers" and "bosses" which must be systematically "managed" by executives in order to achieve efficiency and effectiveness in production. Scientific management (Theory X), and various forms of human relations management (Theory Y and Theory Z), are alternative approaches, designed by management, to deal with the "alienation" which develops out of this separation of interests.

"Successful" application of either of these management approaches in the industrial context means increased production of "goods" with increased efficiency. Both scientific management and human relations management have been promoted as "the solution" to issues of effective executive performance in human service organizations. Indeed, a great deal of attention has been devoted in the 1970s and 1980s to the executive application of the principles of "scientific management," often with a substantial sacrifice of motivation and commitment among staff personnel. Alternatively, application of "human relations" methods has been advocated as the solution to problems of motivation. However, both of these traditional models of administrative style have limited applicability to human service organizations because several of the underlying assumptions do not apply.

The basic assumption of a fundamental structural conflict of interests between administrators and direct service personnel does not apply (although the actual situation in some individual organizations may appear to support such an assumption). In most human service organizations executives and direct service personnel share some form of common professional identity. Executives, and other administrative personnel, in general, are recruited from among persons with at least some direct service, "front-line" experience. Systematic socio-economic and ethnic/cultural distinctions between administrators and direct service workers are less likely to be a major factor, although there are often very obvious gender differences between the majority of front-line workers and the majority of administrators (Alexander & Kerson, 1980).

The "intensive" or individualized nature of service production technology, whether it involves the handling of an individual child abuse family situation, teaching a classroom of elementary students, or providing nursing care for a terminally ill AIDS patient, works against the model of increasing efficiency solely through the application of standardized, scientifically tested production techniques. On the other hand, the motivations which support "committed" participation of both employed personnel and volunteers in service production activities are as likely to be individualistic as they are to be based on membership in a cohesive "work group."

Indeed, the level of "commitment" among both employed staff and volunteers, which is a major factor in the effectiveness (and efficiency) of human service production, is more likely to be connected with organizational goals and with personal concerns about the needs of service users than with other members of a "production work group." While "participatory" process among organizational members, including union organization, can be valuable for a number of reasons, any consistent connection between the intensity of such processes as a regular ongoing part of organizational life and increased service productivity or improved service effectiveness is difficult to establish.

Given the differences between large-scale industrial firms and human service organizations, models of executive style other than "scientific management" and "human relations" are essential for understanding the characteristics of effective executive performance in human service organizations.

*The Managerial Grid* by Blake and Mouton (1964) is one of the more widely recognized behavioral models of executive style which attempts to overcome the dichotomy between task-oriented scientific management and motivation-oriented human relations. The Grid combines two dimensions, one dealing with productivity/ efficiency and the second dealing with morale/cohesion, in effect combining the scientific management emphasis on technology and the human relations emphasis on interpersonal processes and motivation. The preferred "9,9" executive maximizes both dimensions.

These two dimensions, however, deal only with the competencies required in the internal quadrants of the Quinn model, "internal processes" and "human relations." That is, they focus primarily on executive competencies and behavioral styles involved in *intra*organizational processes. The Grid does not deal directly with the behavioral styles which are effective in the external processes involved in maintaining the resource flow from the task environment, and in goal-oriented planning and development for the organization.

The resource dependency of human service organizations, both voluntary nonprofit and governmental, points to the importance of the "political" skills required for building and maintaining effective linkages with external sources of legitimation and funding. Similarly, the role of external factors in shaping the goal-oriented development of the organization highlight the importance of the cognitive skills involved in analyzing information about the environment which may guide the pattern of future development of the organization.

## Interactive Leadership as an Executive Style

The relevant behavioral model for the human service executive is that of *inter-active leadership*. Leadership is a widely used but seldom defined concept. Indeed, most textbooks dealing with administrative theory tend to ignore the concept of executive leadership. A full discussion of interactive leadership as an executive style is beyond the scope of this article. But two key elements can be emphasized. One is the pattern of active, personal involvement of the executive in a continuous process of interaction with other organizational participants, both individually and in groups. The second is the inclusive focus of attention by the executive on the total organization and its context, that is, a "systems management" approach. Such an approach involves a balance between attention to effectiveness of service production, and attention to the continuity and development of the organization over time.

The model of an interactive style of executive leadership has been described in the writings of Sayles (1979) and Peters and Waterman (1982) among others. The emphasis is on the pattern of personal interaction between the executive and other people throughout the organization including service users. This includes interaction with individuals as well as being part of a variety of group processes.

It would appear that both to learn about social systems and to cope with them, the appropriate working level is the process level. This means that managers and researchers alike need to concentrate on the behavioral interaction that underpins organizational life (Sayles, 1979, p. 8).

Sayles suggests that the central concept of executive behavior is "action in time," that is, a never-ending series of contacts with other people which have as their focus two elements of systems management: *contingency responses* and *reduction of uncertainty* (1979). Peters and Waterman (1982) describe the core focus of executive activity as "managing ambiguity and paradox," while Quinn (1988) focuses on "managing the contradictions of organizational life." All three of these authors are critical of the rational "scientific management" model for executive behavior, focusing instead on an evolving, interactive, problem-solving approach, which includes the use of participatory groups but also includes a high level of individual one-to-one activity on the part of the executive.

A particularly critical element in the interactive pattern of leadership in human service organizations involves the relationship of the executive to professional specialists. Most textbooks on administration ignore the distinctive role of professional specialists as self-directed service producers. Indeed, some of the literature on administration in human service organizations argues for a "deprofessionalized" model of staffing (Epstein & Conrad, 1978). However, as in most human service organizations, when the executive comes from a professional background, the relationship between the executive role and the professional role can become particularly complex. In some settings the executive as professional may function as the senior practitioner, ultimate professional supervisor, and professional consultant (and even as part-time practitioner). However, a pattern of monopolizing both the role of senior administrator and senior professional may seriously limit the ability of other professional practitioners in the organization to function independently. Moreover, a preoccupation by executives with maintaining or enhancing their personal professional identity may mean that inadequate attention is given to organizational members who are not part of the same profession.

Other executives who are professionals may suppress their personal professional identity, and avoid personal relationships

with professional practitioners in the organization, in favor of a technically oriented identity as an administrator, and a "command and control" approach to the organization of professional activities. Neither of these two models, the executive as professional practitioner, or as the "pure" administrator, is really consistent with the model of interactive executive leadership. The interactive human services executive who is also a professional can maintain a professional identity while allowing other members of the professional staff to carry major responsibility for professional leadership. Moreover, interactions with other professional staff members should be balanced by interactions with other organizational members.

A second element of the interactive executive leadership style is an inclusive focus on the full range of organizational functions as described earlier in the competing-values framework (Quinn, 1988). This involves the management of a complex process of interpersonal communication which emphasizes the unity of the organization within a decentralized structure in the face of the organizational forces which tend to fragment and divide. Sayles (1979) describes it as the "recombination of elements separated by the division of labor" (p. 26). This includes an emphasis on the purpose of the organization as a whole, including attention to the symbols and traditions which embody the social values and social goals which underlie the existence of the organization.

Particularly important for the interactive executive is an understanding of the tensions that can exist, for example, between maximizing participatory processes in order to reinforce motivation and commitment among staff personnel and being personally involved in the systematic analysis of financial, social and political forces which may shape the goals of the organization in ways that are not consistent with staff preferences (Quinn, 1988). Similar tensions exist between the carefully controlled application of technical knowledge about the most effective, and most efficient, production methodologies, and the highly interactive, and unpredictable, "political" support-building processes which go on with critical external constituencies (Quinn, 1988).

It is a critical function of interactive executive leadership to pay attention to the "whole" of the organization, as well as to the balance among the "parts." This includes attention to the future, as well as to the present, to organizational maintenance as well as to organizational effectiveness. While the production of effective and useful services for individuals in need of those services is the primary objective of organizational activity, the organization itself is a major tool for that production. It embodies past investments not only in facilities and equipment but also in the efforts involved in creating and maintaining the organization to the present. It is a critical resource for service production in the future in response to the "needs" of future service users. Executive attention to maintenance and development of the organization as a community resource is, therefore, of equal importance as a leadership function as the attention which is given to current production activities.

## MEMBERS OF ETHNIC MINORITY GROUPS AND WOMEN IN EXECUTIVE POSITIONS

Any analysis of the position of the human service chief executive officer needs to give specific attention to the dynamics affecting members of ethnic minority groups and women in such positions. In most human service industries, women are the largest group of organizational employees, and are often the largest group of service users. Similarly, members of ethnic minority groups are represented among both employees and service users in nonprofit and governmental human service organizations in larger proportions than in most other sectors of society. The number of women in general, and of men and women from ethnic minority backgrounds who are seeking executive positions, is steadily increasing. This means that during the rest of this century and into the 21st century there will be a steady, and probably turbulent, process of change in the ethnic and gender pattern of executives in human service organizations (Alexander & Kerson, 1980).

Currently, however, executive positions in human service organizations, as well as in much of the rest of society, are perceived as being embedded in a white, male culture (Chernesky, 1983). Ethnic minorities and women in executive positions are under pressure to adapt, in varying ways and to varying degrees, to the characteristics of this culture (Arguello, 1984).

There is an increasing body of journal literature which deals with particular aspects of the pressures facing women, both in gaining access to executive positions in human services and in functioning effectively in those positions. There is a much more limited body of published material dealing specifically with the experience of persons from ethnic minority backgrounds (Arguello, 1984). Again, however, it is striking that textbooks on administration give relatively little attention to these specific issues. Among all of the issues potentially involved in such situations two are touched on briefly here. One issue is that of the relationship of persons of ethnic minority background to the white male executive culture, and the personal problem of "marginality." The other issue involves the role of persons of ethnic minority background who are in executive positions in bringing about changes in their organizations, in particular, in implementing affirmative action employment objectives.

In the case of individuals of ethnic minority background there are many pressures to conform to the informal expectations of the white male executive culture, and to suppress culturally rooted patterns of personal behavior which are not viewed as consistent with that culture. One of the alternatives is to attempt to become wholly accepted within the dominant white male culture and to adopt the symbols, and values, of that culture, while curtailing any involvement in, or identification with, their own distinctive cultural background. While this may be viewed as the best option for personal career success, it may also have very high personal costs. It is, in general, never possible for individuals who are not inherently part of that culture to become a total participant in the informal aspects of that culture, regardless of the quality of individual performance in an executive position.

There is, therefore, always the potential risk of cultural "marginality," that is, of becoming an individual without a real personal definition of cultural identity. Marginality can also be intensified by the pressures of functioning constantly in a situation in which a different cultural group is dominant even if there are no overt expressions of discrimination or antagonism. In situations of serious organizational conflict "marginal" individuals may find themselves isolated without any systematic source of support, either personal or political. One of the factors in the resistance of many white/Anglo males, who are otherwise reasonable individuals, to the changes which are not taking place is anxiety over the possibility of having to function in organizational settings in which it is not taken for granted that the white male culture is dominant at the executive level.

One of the alternatives in handling the potential stresses of "marginality" may be the maintenance of a personalized support system, that is, being part of a group, or network, in which one is not a "marginal" person, but a support system which also does not make extensive demands on the time or resources of the individual, or embody values which are significantly in conflict with the executive culture.

Another alternative for executives of ethnic minority background, and women executives, is to make an explicit decision to maintain dual cultural identities, that is, to establish a place for oneself in the dominant white male executive culture by giving serious attention to the informal expectations within that culture, as well as to the formal requirements of role performance, while also investing substantial time and effort in maintaining an identity which is rooted in the culture of origin. Such a decision involves extra costs in time and money. Moreover, while this may provide an alternative base of personal identification, special psychological costs are involved when there are situations in which the cultural expectations or values of different groups are in direct conflict.

These issues of cultural identity and cultural linkages can be particularly acute when policy and/or administrative decisions represent conflicts between important values, for example, between individualized responses to individual service situations and consistency with established rules and procedures. When the participants in the white male executive culture identify with the concept of absolute choices between "right" and "wrong," that is, with clear-cut definitions of rules and regulations, support by executives of ethnic minority background of decisions affecting individual service users which conflict with those principles may be criticized as "biased," or "special-interest pleading," particularly when persons of ethnic minority background are those involved as service users. Support of across-the-board enforcement of rules, however, may be viewed by others as denial of one's own culture background, and a refusal to recognize the real problems of real people.

A second potential source of stress involves the relation of executives who are from ethnic minority backgrounds, as well as women executives in general, to processes of change going on within human service professions, such as the use of affirmative action initiatives to increase the number of women or of persons of ethnic minority background in administrative positions. Norms of administrative impartiality may argue against explicit support for efforts to bring such changes within the organization, while personal commitments to principles of social justice, together with the requirements of affirmative action policies, may argue for active executive support of such change efforts.

But such proactive action often involves extra personal costs, and may involve risks to the extent that affirmative action efforts conflict with the preferences of other persons in executive and policy-making positions. Again, such efforts may be attacked as "special interest" advocacy. However, the failure of persons with executive authority to play an active role in bringing about change may well be viewed by other persons from ethnic minority backgrounds as clear evidence of "institutional racism."

Leadership expectations, and stresses, for persons from ethnic minority backgrounds in executive positions, as well as for women, are likely to be more complicated and more intense than those for persons who are part of the dominant white male executive culture during the changes which may characterize the next twenty-five to fifty years in the United States.

This requires simultaneous attention to structural sources of extra stress and to the development of personal supports that may help in coping with such stresses.

## SUMMARY

The position of chief executive officer in human service organizations is critically important for the development of effective services in education, health care, and social services. Within social work the particular requirements of this position have received little attention. The human service executive position involves comprehensive responsibility for systems management, that is, for dealing with the interrelated elements of personnel motivation, production technology, resource mobilization, and goal-oriented planning and organizational development. Models of scientific management and human relations management developed in for-profit industrial firms have been introduced with very little examination of their applicability to human service programs. A critical element in human service administration is the interaction between executive management and professional specialists. A model of interactive executive leadership is the most relevant to the requirements of human service organizations. However, any serious examination of the position of the executive in human service organizations must also give specific attention to the conditions facing individuals from ethnic minority backgrounds and women in such positions.

## REFERENCES

Alexander, L. B. & Kerson, T. S. Room at the top: Women in social administration. In F. Perlmutter & S. Slavin (Eds.), *Leadership in social administration.* Philadelphia: Temple University Press, 1980.

Arguello, D.F. Minorities in administration: A review of ethnicity's influence in management. *Administration in Social Work*, 1984, *8*(3), 17–28.

Austin, D. M. Administrative practice in human services: Future directions for curriculum development. *Journal of Applied Behavioral Science*, 1983, *19*(2), 141–151.

Austin, D. M. *The political economy of human service programs.* Greenwich, CT: JAI Press, 1988.

Barko, W. & Pasmore, W. Sociotechnical systems: Innovations in designing high-performing systems. *Journal of Applied Behavioral Science*, 1986, *22*(3).

Blake, R. R. & Mouton, J. S. *The managerial grid.* Houston: Gulf Publishing, 1964.

Chernesky, R.H. The sex dimension of organizational processes: Its impact on women managers. *Administration in Social Work*, 1983, *7*(3/4), 133–141.

Edwards, R. L., Faerman, S.R. & McGrath, M. R. The competing values approach to organizational effectiveness: A tool for agency administrators. *Administration in Social Work*, 1986, *10*(4), 1–14.

Epstein, J. & Conrad, K. The empirical limits of social work professionalization. In R. Sarri & Y. Hasenfeld (Eds), *The management of human services.* New York: Columbia University Press, 1978.

Gortner, H. F., Mahler, J. & Nicholson, J. B. *Organization theory: A public perspective.* Chicago: Dorsey Press, 1987.

Kravetz, D. & Austin, C. D. Women's issues in social service administration: The views and experiences of women administrators. *Administration in Social Work*, 1984, *8*(4), 25–37.

Patti, R. J. Managing for service effectiveness in social welfare: Toward a performance model. *Administration in Social Work*, 1987, *11*(3/4), 7–22.

Patti, R. J. *Social welfare administration: Managing social programs in a developmental context.* Englewood Cliffs, NJ: Prentice-Hall, Inc., 1983.

Peters, T. J. & Waterman, R. H. *In search of excellence.* New York: Warner Books, 1982.

Quinn, R. E. *Beyond rational management: Mastering the paradoxes and competing demands of high performance.* San Francisco: Jossey-Bass, 1988.

Reich, R. B. *The next American frontier.* New York: Times Books, 1983.

Sayles, L. E. *Leadership.* New York: McGraw-Hill, 1979.

Thompson, J. D. *Organizations in action.* New York: McGraw-Hill, 1967.

Wilson, W. The study of administration. In J. M. Shafritz & A. C. Hyde (Eds.), *Classics of public administration.* Oak Park, IL: Moore Publishing Co., 1978.

**31.**

**John E. Tropman**

**POLICY MANAGEMENT IN THE SOCIAL AGENCY**

## INTRODUCTION

In this brief article we will focus on key elements of policy, from a methods perspective. In social work, the concept of "policy" is used in two senses—social policy and policy management.

Social policy focuses on the substance of policy, and is interested, through analysis and proposal, in advancing more humane, just, and inclusive laws, rules, and guidelines. Policy management refers to the central skills needed to bring these kinds of changes about. It is a social work method, like administration and community organization, and shares much with them. To make a distinction among them, one might say that policy managers mobilize and direct ideas, while administration mobilizes and directs workers, and community organization mobilizes and directs communities.

## THREE RESOURCES FOR AGENCIES

Basically, organizations are run on three kinds of resources—money, people, and ideas.

*Money* is the agency's financial resource; it buys the staff and equipment needed to develop and deliver programs. *People* are the human energy of the agency. As workers, they deliver the programs and make them work. *Ideas* provide the agency's conceptual energy—what to do, who to involve, how to influence. Ideas provide the vision and set the purpose for the organization. Ideas—as innovations—

become the new programs of the organization. Ideas of justice, inclusion, and diversity become new social policies and then social programs.

In most organizations we spend a lot of time on the money resource; less, and often considerably less, on the people resource; and almost none on the idea resource. Many organizations have adequate money and adequate staff, but no ideas about how, really, to apply them efficiently and effectively.

## A DEFINITION OF POLICY

Ideas are the start of policy, and any discussion of policy needs to begin here. **Policy is an idea, which is a guide to action, is written, and has the approval of legitimate authority.**

Policy begins with an idea. That thought is then transformed into action guidelines. Those action guidelines are then written down, reviewed, discussed, changed, and finally approved by legitimate authority. The form of a policy can be a law, new governmental regulations, or personnel policy passed by the agency board of directors.

## THE WORK OF POLICY MANAGEMENT

Policy work involves paying some attention to each of the policy elements. The first task of the policy manager is to ensure that there is a **constant supply of new ideas** into the agency. In this sense, ideas are resources just like money and people. And, like money and people, they need to be organized, shaped, and applied to organization goals if they are to be of any use. Hence the policy manager—or worker playing the policy manager role—is continually seeking new ideas from staff, from other agencies, from the media, from anywhere, and circulating them around to see if there is anything there worth following up on. Seeking new ideas is a major task.

**Turning ideas into guidelines for action** is the second major policy management task. Ideas from elsewhere need to be tailored to the agency. Policy managers will involve others in this process—workers, community people, administrators, and so on. It is essential that appropriate, realistic applications of new ideas be developed. It is also essential that someone have the responsibility for orchestrating this process. We use the word "orchestrating" to indicate that the policy manager is not the person who "does it all." Rather, the policy manager is one who sees that it gets done, in a process that may involve many others.

**Writing it down** is the third major responsibility. Usually there are many, many drafts. Indeed, it is through the writing process that the guidelines for action are developed. Someone once said that "Writing is God's way of letting us know how sloppy our thinking really is!" An idea is suggested, and everyone agrees "it" would be good, but there is often much unclarity about what "it" actually is. Writing the guidelines down allows those involved to actually envision the steps of action. Many problems often surface at this phase, and consequently new drafts are´ written to take those concerns into account. Obviously, this often is a time-consuming process.

**Approval by legitimate authority** is the final step in the policy management

process. Approval involves taking the proposal to some authoritative group—the agency's board, a city council, or a state legislature. Getting approval is a complex process in and of itself, often involving more modifications of the draft policy in question. But it is a crucial step in the policy management process, and requires much attention to exactly what happens during that process, who the influential persons might be, how they can be influenced, and so on.

## POLICY SKILLS

There are numerous specific policy skills which, for purposes here, can be grouped into two general areas—intellectual, referring to managing ideas, and interpersonal, referring to managing people.

**Intellectual skills** refer to abilities like writing, seeking, storing, and organizing new ideas for future use. They involve the ability to be critical of suggestions while not being hostile, to see both the "forest and the trees," to manage decision-making settings (see Article 14 on running effective meetings), as well as blending ideas from different sources. Intellectual skills also include a large element of the practical, which makes the policy manager different from the thinker. The policy manager's goal is to help ideas become practical. In some contexts, this part of the policy manager role is called the "policy technician" or "policy analyst."

**Interpersonal skills,** on the other hand, focus on working with people. Skills here involve persuading, listening, reinterpreting and rephrasing, brokering, and negotiating. The individual is the crucial component, and seeking to understand what the person really wants, and working to meet those needs through appropriate modifications in the policy proposal is an important part of the interpersonal skill repertoire. In addition, the interpersonal side of the policy manager is similar to aspects of the community organizer. In each role, there are building of networks and development of relationships with opinion leaders, as well as elements of "pressing the flesh" or "working the room," which are so necessary to building both the general and specific interpersonal relations required for success in policy development and enactment.

## THE STAGES OF POLICY

The policy process has well-recognized stages. At each, both intellectual and interpersonal skills are needed to accomplish the tasks and to progress to the next phase.

The **problem** phase involves developing ideas about what is wrong, and what different thinkers and interests judge the problem to be. Often, the policy manager will do research here to determine the scientific thinking on the subject, as well as to talk with any individuals affected by "the problem."

After the problem has been defined, developing policy **options**—different approaches to corrective action—must be considered. Frequently the policy manager will find out what other communities, agencies, and firms have done about a similar problem. The various solutions are organized into several options for consideration.

From this list of options, authoritative bodies select one (or several) **decisions,** which is hard, because it allocates goods

and values in the system, and defines "winners and losers." Nonetheless, as the well-known saying goes, "not to decide is to decide." Policy managers must help decision groups come to closure.

**Planning** is the next step. It involves developing the more specific operating guidelines that will make the policy decision workable.

Running the **program** is next. Here, the policy is actually put into practice, and information from what happens is placed in the **feedback loop,** which is the process of evaluation. There is a continual monitoring—of the program and efforts made—to see what modifications must occur in the policy process. As the diagram suggests, modifications can take place throughout the process, and at any point during it. In its most extended form, the feedback loop reaches all the way back to the problem, so that the problem is redefined and the policy process once again is activated.

## POLICY, PRACTICE, AND THE POLICY/PRACTICE GAP

Sometimes, people think that policy is "the way we do things around here." That is practice. Almost all policies (and the plans and programs attached to them) have some variation in actual practice. In general, as long as such variation is small, it is fine. Variation often represents a way in which the actual situation is dealt with while respecting the essential sense of the policy. However, if the policy/practice gap begins to increase, it is time for a closer look. In most cases of this sort, the feedback loop has become inoperative, and there seems to be no way that policy can be changed. All too often, in situations like this, the policy is left alone, and the practice is changed! However, it is much better to keep any policy up-to-date, and monitoring the policy/practice gap is a good place to begin.

## VISION AND STRATEGIC POLICY MANAGEMENT

One of the most important policies for an agency is its strategic direction. Regretfully, many agencies have neither a strategic direction nor a strategic plan. The policy manager, or person designated to play policy-management functions, can help the agency in developing strategic planning.

One begins with a **SWOT** analysis as part of the problem definition phase. SWOT stands for strengths, weaknesses, opportunities, and threats. Teams are assigned to develop reports in each area, with respect to the agency. What are its strengths? What are its weaknesses? What opportunities are available for exploitation? What threats face it? Policy managers are useful in helping each of the groups work out their information and reports.

When data have been collected on these points, a conference is held to process the information. At this conference, a **vision** for and of the agency is developed (or redeveloped, improved, or reaffirmed) that provides direction, invokes opportunities, neutralizes threats, builds on strengths, and corrects weaknesses.

From this step—visioning—a strategic plan emerges. (Here, again, the policy manager might be a key draftsperson.) This plan lists several specific goals that will make the vision come to life. Then, operational goals are developed from the strategic plan, with timelines and responsible persons defined.

## CONCLUSION

This brief discussion of policy management provides an introduction to the policy-management process, and to some of the skills and actions it requires. It is intended as a first step in the development of policy competency and, through that, improving the documents that guide and direct our social agencies.

## REFERENCES

Tropman, John E. (1986). *Policy management in the human services.* New York: Columbia.
Tropman, John E. (1987). Policy analysis. In A. Minahan (Ed.), *The encyclopedia of social work.* Silver Spring, MD: NASW.

## 32.

### John E. Tropman

### THE ROLE OF THE BOARD IN THE PLANNING PROCESS

The planning process in community organization has historically involved citizens in decisions that affected them. Yet, we have not seriously attended to the problems of collective decision making inherent in this involvement. Sometimes the problems resulting from this neglect catch up with us. Those instances in which human service organizations have been faulted for spending inordinate amounts of money on fund raising and fund procurement represent one example. Another is lack of proper and vigorous attention on the part of the organization's board of directors to take regular responsibility for policy decisions and direction. Alternatively, one is reminded—and injunctions for maximum feasible participation of the poor are one example—of the fact that board memberships have all too frequently tilted in the direction of the corporate benefactor rather than the beneficiaries. Such a tilt was inappropriate even in the days of charitable institutions, but now, since many clients (through insurance programs indirectly) are paying part of the freight for their own service, their representation on boards becomes even more imperative.

### THREE ROLES FOR THE POLICY BOARD

Inherent in this planning process is decision making. And in human service organiza-

tions the boards represent the organization's policy center, or that place where decisions are made. A lot of organizational lore suggests that it is the executive and her or his cadre of associates who are really the "powers behind the throne" and the boards are "rubber stamps" bouncing, as it were, from issue to issue with no substantive input. Where this is the case, it represents a failure of both legal responsibility under most state charters, and of trusteeship responsibility in terms of the civic purpose that boards are charged to accomplish. Legally, for example, "directors of New York State not-for-profit corporations are required by statute to discharge their duties in good faith and with that degree of diligence, care and skill which ordinarily prudent men would exercise under similar circumstances in a like position" (Weber, 1975, p. 7). That standard of care which must be taken by the directors in the exercise of their duty means that many could be liable for various kinds of legal action if it can be shown that they were too cavalier in their attitudes. The area of legal responsibilities is too complex to detail here, but all community organizers should familiarize themselves with the state codes governing not-for-profit corporations in their state and locality.

More complex is the board's responsibility in the planning process for civic purpose. Most boards get together because, ostensibly, they are interested in improving the civic climate in the area in which they live. The individual directors (board members) share in this wish. Yet, all too

Special thanks to Kathryn Walter, who materially assisted in the preparation of a longer version of this piece, and to Nancy Smith, of Aurora Associates, Washington, D.C., for her helpful comments.

often, boards fail to accomplish the very civic purpose for which they are set up. Part of the reason lies in poor organization and poor decision-making styles. These difficulties are not unique to boards by any means, but relate to all kinds of decision-making groups. The piece later in this volume on effective meetings provides some suggestions for *meeting* structure that will be helpful in the board context as well as the planning committee context. However, there are a number of issues that deal with the board itself that need to be considered. The purpose of this paper is to suggest three of these issues in particular: the board as a decision maker and a decision overseer with some suggestions about ways in which the board can better handle those responsibilities; board responsibility for role appropriateness and internal and external functions, in particular; and the board as a trainer and developer of members and of the agency itself.

By way of introducing these topics, I suggest that the common term "board members" be changed to "director." In the corporate world people who serve on boards are called directors of the corporation. The word suggests greater power and vigor than does the more passive-sounding term "member." Under not-for-profit corporation laws, the term "directors" is used. They work jointly with the executive director to accomplish the organizational purpose from its definition to its implementation. Perhaps this change can move the perspective of many "members" from a more reactive posture to a proactive one.

The role of boards in the overall planning process is to make decisions and to see to it that those decisions are carried through. To do this, of course, boards work with the executive director and they share with the executive co-responsibility for the integrity of the organization's mission and

role. The accomplishment of these purposes requires thought, organization, and structure. And to this end the remaining sections of this paper are devoted.

The target being addressed here is the formal board, one with bylaws, legal responsibilities, and a professional staff. The target is not the grass-roots association, or even some policy professional groups (local chapters of the National Association of Social Workers, for example). Those kinds of groups tend to be less formal and structured than the processes contemplated here. However, there are many times when less formal processes are appropriate and useful. Neighborhood groups may wish to use an approach that mixes task and process goals. One danger with using less formal approaches and procedures is the possible failure to accomplish the tasks through inadequate attention to the set of procedures and programs with which the group is charged. Overformalization is less likely to occur, but it also presents dangers. The key is balance.

All boards and directors groups *plan*, and to that extent they can use the suggestions outlined in this paper. They will need other procedures to meet other goals and should be aware that multiple functions require multiple procedures, not the use of one set to the exclusion of others.

## BOARDS AS DECISION MAKERS AND DECISION OVERSEERS

### Policy and Administration

The role of the board extends beyond policy making to the overseeing of policy implementation as well. The line dividing "policy" functions from "administrative" functions is always unclear. I prefer the notion of intersecting sets as described in Figure 32.1.

Industrial consultants suggest, and my own information confirms the idea, that approximately one-half of board time is wasted in unnecessary agenda items, items for which there is insufficient information and so on. Therefore, board organization represents one of the most important elements of decision quality. Referring to Figure 32.1, the entire board meets on policy matters. Subcommittees, the nature of which I will suggest in a moment, meet with the executive and staff in the policy-administration intersect area, and the executive handles the administrative matters. Obviously, there is no rule for neatly allocating one item or another into the various categories, but generally speaking, the broader the scope in terms of the organization, the larger the number of people a particular proposal affects, the more a particular proposal or organizational action will cost, or the more an organization is committed based on a particular action, the more such an action is likely to be policy and to require board approval. Thus, the board itself makes decisions. The subcommittee structure both oversees decisions and develops proposals for board action. Without an appropriate subcommittee structure it is very difficult to carry out the decision-making and oversight role. I have identified nine subcommittees that are important on an ongoing basis:

1. The Executive Committee
2. The Budget and Finance Committee
3. The Resource Development Committee
4. The Personnel Committee
5. The Program Committee
6. The Public Relations Committee
7. The Community Relations Committee
8. The Nominating Committee
9. The Recruitment and Training Committee

FIGURE 32.1
Functions of Boards of Directors

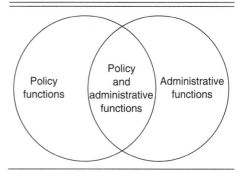

*The Executive Committee.* The executive committee is composed of the president, officers, the executive director, and committee chairs from the board. It usually can take action in emergency situations when the board cannot meet, and it is often involved in sorting out those activities and proposals that need board approval. It coordinates the work of the other subcommittees and takes overall responsibility for the operation of the board itself.

*The Budget and Finance Committee.* The budget and finance committee deals with matters of budget generation and financial oversight, reviewing financial trajectories on a monthly basis at least and sometimes on a weekly basis. It is involved with the chief budget officer of the organization in preparing budgets and making proposals for new expenditures, handling emergencies, and so on. It is best to involve people from the financial community here so that access to banks and other kinds of financing can be facilitated when necessary. The budget and finance committee reports both overall budgetary strategy and specific budget proposals to the board.

*The Resource Development Committee.* This committee seeks to develop financial resources for the agency or organization. Its activity may involve seeking funds through public contributions, planning fund-raising events, securing grants, developing donations of property, and so on. It is important that all board members have an opportunity to serve on this committee, because raising resources is a difficult task and people "burn out." Also, the need to raise funds, as well as spend them, introduces a note of realism into the allocations process.

*The Personnel Committee.* The personnel committee develops the personnel practices guide for the organization, staying in tough with staff and their concerns, on the one hand, as well as the broader personnel community on the other. Issues involved can refer to compensation, burnout, holidays, and so on. It also typically handles grievances and selection of top agency staff.

*The Program Committee.* The program committee provides structure and purpose for the organized mission and role of the agency itself. Usually agencies have somewhat general missions and roles, which need to be given concrete programmatic manifestations. This or that activity needs to be undertaken while some other activity needs to be stopped; all activities need to be monitored and evaluated. The program committee, often composed of professionals in the area of concern, makes programmatic recommendations to the board. It generally works more closely with staff than other committees.

*The Public Relations Committee.* The public relations committee enhances and improves the agency's image with the general public. It prepares annual reports, news releases, and other pieces of public information. It seeks favorable publicity about the agency. Sometimes this committee is merged with the community relations committee, but its function tends to be focused more on

media. Interviews with staff, preparing newsletters, and press releases are all tasks of the public relations committee.

*The Community Relations Committee.* The community relations committee focuses on the personal aspects of community involvement, for example, organizing tours of the agency, providing speakers for public functions, and interpreting the agency's mission and role to key people in the community. While the public relations committee tends to concentrate on involving the media, the community relations committee focuses on involving people. Often community relations links to political figures at local, state, and national levels.

*The Nominations Committee.* The nominations committee usually meets on a yearly basis, sometimes intensively for a period of time, to develop a slate of officers. At times it also reviews the appointments of top staff. It may also be merged with the recruitment and training committee, although it is preferable to keep these functions separate. While the nominations committee moves people who have already participated in organizational life into officership, the recruitment and training committee works to secure people from the outside and to bring them into the organization.

*The Recruitment and Training Committee.* The recruitment and training committee seeks to interest previously uninvolved individuals in the organization and its mission and role. This committee may develop a list of potential members in advance of any specific vacancy. In the recruitment phase, its members meet with individuals, interpret the kind of job the agency is doing, and seek to promote involvement. Its training responsibilities include preparing the board members' manual, conducting annual training sessions for the entire board, and providing additional training for individual board members if they so desire. It is important that each board member of a human service organization have one personal improvement opportunity a year made available through board membership. The reimbursement policy for this effort should be part of the recruitment and training committee task.

### How Big a Board

In general, the minimum number of members per subcommittee should be three. Thus, if three people were assigned to each of these committees, there would be a minimum board size of twenty-seven. There are usually at least three extra members for ad hoc assignments, resulting in a board of thirty. A rule of thumb for board size is the number of subcommittees plus one (for ad hoc assignments) times three.

### Subcommittee Structure

The subcommittee structure just discussed may appear to some to violate the notions of openness, spontaneity, and freedom, which should characterize the human service board. I believe just the contrary. Most boards deal with technical legal issues of great importance involving quite a bit of money. These issues cannot be approached casually or in an offhand manner; rather, they must be given sustained thought. My view is that a board operates more effectively when working from a subcommittee's recommendation. Therefore, with rare exceptions, I recommend that boards assign upcoming tasks to subcommittees, requesting that the subcommittees study the matter with appropriate staff and other members of the organization and the community to develop a proposal for

action with alternative considerations and present the proposal to the board. When this groundwork is laid, the board can deal with the matter much more effectively and efficiently than it can if it is trying both to make the decision and to acquire relevant information at the same time.

### Subcommittee Functions

Basically, subcommittees have five major functions. The first is to generate decision options, the point I just made. Second, once a decision has been made in an area germane to the functioning of the subcommittee, it is the subcommittee's task to oversee the implementation of that decision. Oversight here does not mean scrutiny on a daily basis; rather it means that the subcommittee receives periodic reports on how things are going, raises questions, and gets to the executive, president, and full board if necessary. Third, subcommittees evaluate and pass recommendations to the board on activities in their area of concern and responsibility. Fourth, subcommittees become the center of the trusteeship-generating function because they seek to foresee problems. The finance committee that does not foresee difficulties is the finance committee that may find itself liable for civil action. The job and responsibility of subcommittees is to be proactive, to take leadership roles and to present suggestions based on these two orientations to the board itself. Fifth, through carrying out these four functions, the subcommittee educates the whole board and thus provides for board growth in its respective area of concern.

### From Administrative Board to Policy Board—The Problem of Transition

One particular problem that boards in the human services field have is to accomplish the transition from "administrative board" to policy board. This transition occurs in the following way. Often a human service organization has been founded by a group of interested citizens who initially get together and *are* the agency. As time passes, federal or state monies may be acquired. As more stable funding becomes available, an executive director and perhaps a secretary are hired, and the organization is beginning to move from a very informal, nonbureaucratic, personal organization to one that is more formal and bureaucratic, and includes a board of directors legally chartered under the laws of the state. This transition often leaves the agency founders feeling left out, in second place, and needing to move on. And, indeed, some organizational analysts indicate that the kinds of people who are organizational founders are very different from those who are organizational maintainers. One cannot prescribe a solution to these problems any more than one can prescribe for a safe adolescence. One can only point out the kinds of problems and difficulties that are likely to occur, to alert people to expect them, and to be sensitive to them. One such problem stems from the need for founding directors to adjust their behavior to more of a policy role and to become less involved with the actual day-to-day operation of the agency. If the member desires such day-to-day interaction, it would be better to volunteer at another agency rather than to seek to maintain old relationships and patterns in the agency that member founded. A new member, brought in to join a board which was founded in this fashion, is likely to feel irritation and then resign. One has to understand the difference between involvement of founding members as opposed to maintaining members. While this does not mean that license should be given to founding members, an understanding of their perspective often helps to locate their interests and wishes more accurately.

## Decision Accountability

One of the most important initial steps in evaluating decisions and being accountable for them is to make them in the first place. All too often when a problematic decision comes up, people ask, "When did we make that decision?" And, indeed, upon scrutiny of the records it becomes very unclear because the decision was not made at one point, but evolved at several points. The subcommittee system permits the specific identification of areas of responsibility and the development of decisional formats in those areas of responsibility. These decision proposals then go to the full board where they are acted upon and recorded in the minutes. At the end of the year or whatever time is appropriate, one can go back and ask the question, "What decisions did we make during the particular year?" and review the collective impact on the structure and quality of those decisions overall. Because it is often difficult to assess a decision's impact immediately after it has been made, such retrospective assessment is essential to accountability. Sometimes the wisdom or foolishness of a decision emerges only after time has passed. Such accountability review also takes into consideration the extent to which the information available at the time was sufficient and accurate. If an organization continually makes decisions that, as it later turns out, were ill informed, then the process of information generation needs to be studied.

The other aspect of accountability, of course, is implementation. Here the performance audit is useful. The performance audit means taking a specific look at some areas of organizational activity, assessing the speed, quality, integrity, and intelligence with which a decision was implemented. A board is not only responsible for making a decision: it is responsible for seeing to it that the decision is efficiently carried out. Generally, this responsibility falls to the executive director, and it is usually in concert with the executive that the board exercises implementive oversight and control.

## BOARD'S RESPONSIBILITY FOR ROLE APPROPRIATENESS

Board members and the board itself are responsible for acting appropriately within the context of their role. We have discussed the individual requisites of that role, particularly as they regard legal responsibilities and the avoidance of acting in self-aggrandizing and self-profiting ways. More importantly, we have mentioned the positive aspects of one's personal role, that is, acting as a trustee of civic purpose and taking a proactive, accomplishment-oriented posture.

As a means to accomplishing these ends, there are particulars of role performance that are appropriate in carrying out one's organizational responsibilities. For example, there are appropriate ways for a chair to behave and there are appropriate things for a chair to do, which a chair *must* do if organizational purposes are to be achieved. Similarly, there are appropriate member, staff and executives roles. These will not be detailed here; they are discussed at length elsewhere (Tropman, 1980). Suffice to say that there *are* role requisites for chair, member, staffer, and executive. In addition, one can violate, through inappropriate personal behavior, these requisites. I use the phrase *appropriate* to indicate the convention as social rather than legal, but it has force nonetheless.

## The Role of the Board: Internal Functions

In this section, I will discuss the role of the board itself, rather than the roles of the individual members. The board as an entity is responsible for acting appropriately. But what is "appropriate"? There appears to be a great deal of role confusion. I suggest seven functions that a board may perform and discuss them in terms of the different role behaviors that might be required when these different functions are being performed. Just as individuals may well be different at various points during the working day, depending upon the tasks they need to accomplish, so boards need to think about changing their own behavior as a group entity when tasks are different. The seven functions can be divided into two parts: internal functions and external functions. Internal functions relate to deciding policy, overseeing policy, and administering policy. External functions focus upon the interorganizational system.

*Policy Decision Functions.* These typically relate to the board as a whole and refer to those aspects of its role that involve formal legal authority as specified under articles of incorporation and under statutes of the state. Decisions made here are typically referred to as "policy decisions" although other types of decisions may have policy impact as well. Crucial to the policy-deciding function is adequate information, adequate time for review, adequate feedback from appropriate parties, and reasonably prompt action consistent with the available information. What needs to be avoided here is decisional pre- and postmaturity. Prematurity occurs when an item is brought to a policy-deciding meeting in advance of adequate available information. Typically, a great deal of time is spent on such an issue, and then it is postponed. Decisional prematurity is one of the most significant causes of decisional postmaturity. A decision delayed is, all too often, a decision denied. It is legitimate for a director to accuse a board of undue delay. The problem of what is "undue" is difficult. There is no issue on which more information cannot be garnered and on which additional perspectives would not be useful. However, there are often a series of external constraints such as grant deadlines, fiscal year deadlines, and so on, which make the very best informed decision useless if it comes too late. Therefore, within the policy-deciding function, boards need to achieve a balance between information on the one hand, and decisional needs and pressures on the other.

*Policy-Overseeing Functions.* Policy-overseeing functions—seeing that decisions are implemented—are typically accomplished through the subcommittee structure. They involve policy-generating and review components, as well as assessment and program audit elements. Policy oversight occurs once a formal decision is made by the board of directors, and not before. However, the concept of policy oversight involves a certain amount of policy proactivity—that is, the anticipation of upcoming events and the proposed adjustment of existent policies to take those new events into account. Members of policy-overseeing groups must be clear about the scope and extent of the particular policy that is being monitored and should neither overextend their role to encompass areas tangential to it nor ignore or minimize the responsibilities that they do have.

*Policy-Administering Committee.* During unique organizational situations, a policy-administering committee is set up by a board of directors. For example, in an agency crisis, power may be delegated to a small group along with appropriate financial resources, and secretarial and other logistical support to handle a particular situation. Most typically, fast-breaking type situations require the development of such a task force; the task force dissolves when those situations have been resolved.

A second situation in which the administering committee appears is during the initiation stage of an organization. That is, a group of people get together to do a task, make the decisions as they go along, and get enjoyment and gratification from accomplishment of the task itself. Soon they "turn into" an "agency." They then must begin to play more of a "director's" role.

## The Role of the Board: External Functions

Boards of directors of human service agencies play four external roles that are quite different in nature and quality from the internal roles. As agencies move into the interorganizational environment, they no longer have the imperative control given them by their charter and articles of incorporation. Rather, they move from a position based on authority to a stance based on cooperation. There are four external roles that boards may play (and sometimes they may create other community committees that play these roles, too): policy sharing, policy advisory, policy coordinating, and policy implementing.

*Policy Sharing.* Policy sharing is a role in which the board agrees to cooperate with other similar agencies, to acquaint them, and be acquainted with ongoing programs. It does not imply any adjustment in program, nor does it imply that any particular program is right, wrong, appropriate, or inappropriate. It simply reflects an agreement to get together and "show and tell" one's program. This reflects a cooperative posture only.

*The Policy-Coordinating Functions.* Sometimes policy sharing leads to a policy-coordinating function. For example, a board will be asked to perform roles with respect to other organizations in terms of program adjustment. "We'll handle young kids and you handle older kids," it might be suggested. Or "We'll handle boys and you handle girls." These types of adjustments require either prior agreement from the board or actual board agreement once the proposal is made. I suggest that policy coordination without board approval be permitted on a case basis only. Agency or organizational coordination requires conjoint planning and conjoint agreement.

*Policy Implementing.* Sometimes, within the interorganizational system, the board of directors becomes part of a team asked to implement a particular community-wide decision. Again, we are speaking of delegated functions and functions that require constant board oversight and approval. A board member joining a community-wide group for coordinating and implementing purposes does not mean that that individual carries any kind of board approval unless that approval has been specifically given. This is an important function for the board to play, and I strongly encourage boards to participate in policy-sharing, policy-coordinating, and policy-implementing activities at the community level. In such a situation, however, a special subcommittee might well be developed to handle the relationship of the particular organization to the constellation of organizations which are seeking to accomplish even larger social tasks.

*Policy Advisory.* Sometimes a board is asked for a collective opinion on a matter of community concern. The mayor, for example, may call and ask what your agency thinks about an issue. It is not sufficient to simply chew the matter around and then let the executive write up some kind of recommendation. Rather, the matter must be discussed and language must be prepared to reflect the board's perspective. It must be approved by the board and entered into the minutes. A "decision" is actually made during the policy advisory process, but the decision is a piece of advice!

There are certainly many other roles that boards as boards may play. However, these seven, divided between internal and external roles, represent the beginning of a perspective suggesting some of the differences that might be involved. I think that boards need to pay more attention to the external system than they have in the past—particularly in the human service community. Boards, as I have experienced them, tend to be more inwardly focused, playing roles as corporate citizens in the collective community less and less frequently. While it is appropriate that a balance be struck, the emphasis on the word *balance* suggests that some time, and I think more time, needs to be spent in collaborative, coordinating, implementive, and sharing types of roles. Decision-making boards often find it difficult to play these external roles because they relinquish the authority they are used to having when they deal with internal matters. This shift from authoritative posture to cooperative posture is difficult, but it must be carried out in any case.

## THE BOARD AS A TRAINER AND DEVELOPER

Boards have a responsibility for training new members and for developing ongoing members. Nowhere has this need been more seriously recognized than during the efforts to provide "maximum feasible participation of the poor" during the 1960s in the United States. During that time many individuals lacking board experience were brought on to the governing body of nonprofit charitable organizations. Rarely were they provided with any kind of orientation. Joseph Weber and Nellie Hartogs (1974) found that executives rated orientation among the lowest of priorities, while finance and personnel were among the highest. Given the perspectives in this paper, orientation becomes an absolute necessity for new members, and ongoing training is even more a requisite for all directors because they are unlikely to know what to do. Beyond the members, there needs to be some assessment of the growth of the board itself. I will consider the last point first and then suggest ways in which members can improve themselves.

## Board Growth and Development

How do we gauge whether the board is growing and moving in a more sophisticated direction and improving the quality of decisions? There is no one way, but many boards are moving to an annual program evaluation and assessment system. There are two categories of assessment generally used. One concerns itself with member meeting satisfaction, and the second is concerned with assessment of decision quality.

*Meeting Satisfaction.* To measure member meeting satisfaction, the board itself should develop an instrument to assess how well the members felt the meetings had gone during the year. There are a number of categories, such as length of time, pleasantness, adequacy of information, and so on. By developing its own instrument, the board has a greater investment and thus, it

is much more likely to follow through on using it and be identified with its results. The training and recruitment committee (one of the board's subcommittees) can be asked to take some responsibility here. It is important to keep in mind, however, that satisfaction with the meetings does not necessarily mean that good decisions were made, although dissatisfaction with the meetings is more likely an indicator that poor decisions were made.

*Decision Quality.* Implicit here, of course, and an assumption of any decision quality assessment, is that the minutes are so written and the board processes so structured, that it is possible to pull from the minutes a list of decisions made by the board. These must be listed in terms of their substantive content and orientation, not simply listed as "approval of the budget," but rather sentences and phrases which indicate the nature of and the direction of budgetary thrust for the year. These should be listed on a sheet and reviewed during an assessment session. People are now asked what they think of these decisions. Has any information come up that suggests that they were ill considered? The board rates its decisions on a scale of 1 to 10, A to Z, or any other appropriate scale. The very act of sitting down and reviewing decisions is, in itself, a positive process.

*Review and Refurbishment.* In addition to reviewing decisions, there is the policy review and refurbishment function. I feel that every seven years boards need to take an in-depth look at their mission, role, and articles of incorporation to ascertain whether any adjustments are necessary. During each year of the six intermediate years, one specific area of agency board relationships is selected for review and refurbished and improved, if needed. Personnel policy might be scrutinized one year, financial policies in another year, and so on. Thus, at the end of the seventh year, all of the subparts of the organization will have been reviewed. Meeting satisfaction and decision quality assessments, when combined with policy review and refurbishment and supplemented with information from the program audits, provide a useful overview of the organizational activity. These reviews could be accomplished during a yearly one to two-day retreat, or at a special meeting in which people can look at the organization, and in doing so, reconsider their own role in it.

*Assessment of the Member.* Assessment of the member is considerably more difficult because of its personal nature. It is best, therefore, to begin on a positive side. I think that each member should have the opportunity for at least one personal growth experience per year. Typically this means attendance at a professional meeting or workshop paid for by the organization. I feel very strongly that this type of compensation (if indeed it is compensation) should represent a priority activity for agencies. Many agencies are very scrupulous about seeking staff development but completely indifferent to board development. In any event, one should assess with members whether there has been the opportunity for personal growth experience and whether that has added to the overall functioning of the board.

In addition, development programs should be run by the organization for board members (and possibly staff) once or twice a year. There are numerous training films available for board members, an outside expert could be invited to speak on board problems and activities, or a relevant article could be distributed and a board discussion organized. It is important that individual members be given the opportunity, within the context of their board membership, to think about their role. That thinking and self-reflection will undoubtedly be positively applied to the specific board in question. There are a number of personal assessment instruments available (see Figure 32.2).

Using these assessments should permit individuals to think through their own roles in a challenging but nonthreatening situation.

## Board Training

Every organized board should have a manual for directors. Again, I stress the use of the word "directors," not members, to emphasize the more vigorous and active director role.

The board manual should begin with a statement of mission, the purpose of the organization, and a brief history and "raison d'etre" of the organization. The legal responsibilities of the organization should then be detailed and should refer the reader to the articles of incorporation listed in the appendix. Following this opening section, there should be a statement of the expected responsibilities of membership, which outlines the role of the director and details the subcommittees and their functions and purposes. A third section, which can be replaced regularly, should deal with the current operating structure of the organization: names, addresses, and telephone numbers of directors; past directors; advisory committees; training program plans; retreat dates; meeting schedules—all of the specific paraphernalia of directorship. It is useful to have the names and addresses of staff on a separate sheet, which can be updated as frequently as necessary. Another section should contain a compilation of annual reports. This gives each member an opportunity to see what the

FIGURE 32.2
Exercise: Am I a Good Board Member?

Is it possible to identify the attributes of the perfect volunteer board member? The question is academic because all human beings are a combination of strengths and of weaknesses. A good board, therefore, blends imperfect human beings into an effective working team.

There are certain attributes which help to make good board members. Some of these are listed here.

0 = No ......... 10 = Yes

Good Board Members:                                              I Am        Others Are

1. Are dedicated to helping others and modest in the light of their responsibilities as board members.
2. Approach their responsibilities in the spirit of a trustee on behalf of contributors, their intended beneficiaries, and the public at large.
3. Stand up for their convictions, even at the cost of misunderstanding or disapproval in business or social life.
4. Back up other board members and staff, rising to their defense when they are unjustly criticized or attacked.
5. Treat staff as a partner in a high calling, maintaining overall supervision and control, but not interfering with day-to-day administration.
6. Avoid being overawed by others on the board, whether they be executive staff, tycoons of business, labor or society; professionals in social work, education, medicine, etc.
7. Welcome information and the best available advice but reserve the right to arrive at decisions on the basis of their own judgment.
8. Respect the right of other board members and of staff to disagree with them and to have a fair hearing of their points of view.
9. Accept as routine that decisions must be made by majority vote and will at times go against one or more members.
10. Criticize when necessary, in a constructive way, if possible suggesting an alternative course.
11. Recognize that time and energy are limited and that overcommitment may prove self-defeating.
12. Endeavor to keep disagreements and controversies impersonal, and to promote unity.
13. Maintain loyalty to their agency, within a higher loyalty to the welfare of the community and humanity as a whole.

SOURCE: "Volunteer Board Member in Philanthropy," National Information Bureau, 419 South Park Avenue, New York, New York 10016. (Reprinted with permission.)

agency has done over time and consider what it is likely to do in the future. Future or projected plans can also be listed here. In addition, it is useful to have a single summary sheet giving historical demographic facts about the agency, such as its annual budget, per capita expenditure on children, and the like.

Finally, if the board feels that there is any pertinent reading material essential to the board member, it can be included as well. This is only a skeletal suggestion for a board manual. Some are more simple and direct; others are more complicated and intricate. What is important is that the board develops its own manual. Following well-accepted practices of community organization, the involvement of the board in developing its own guidelines should be an important guiding principle.

## New Director Training Session

One of the most important types of board training activities is the new director training session. If the suggestion made earlier in this document is followed and the two-tier involvement process used, the new director will not begin from zero. This is too often the case, however, and it frequently takes six months to a year for the new director to become a useful participating member. In either case, whether the new director has participated in ancillary groups or is an inexperienced person in this area, there should be an orientation process. It need not be long, but it should include certain basic matters. First, the substantive thrust, purpose, mission, and commitments of the organization should be explained. While the new director may feel that his/her motives for membership are being changed or detracted by this kind of orientation, substantive contributions will come later; the board members need to know what he or she is getting into first.

A second aspect of the training should deal with the principles of good group decision making. Often this section of the new-member training program can be linked to a training program offered to other individuals on the board. Mutual education involving discussion, participation, and the acquisition of new knowledge is one very good way to establish the new member–old member bonding required for effective and efficient decision making.

## CONCLUSION

This paper has presented some systematic concerns and perspectives on the modern board. It is a much more complex, intricate, and involved process than anyone previously considered. The model board represents one of the essential vehicles through which the pluralism of American values is expressed and through which the historic striving for democratic involvement and participation for decisions which affect individual lives can be orchestrated. And yet, despite these important large-scale social functions, as well as the crucial day-to-day decision functions, board membership is casually, if not shabbily, treated. This casualness and shabbiness is a conspiracy of everyone—members who accept directorships without proper scrutiny and review, those of us who extend invitations to directorship in a thoughtless and off-hand manner, executives who put board training at the bottom of the list of priority activities, and society itself, which tends to undervalue, if not devalue, group activities. Human service organizations, whether they be philanthropic or nonprofit, must receive leadership, stewardship, and trusteeship from their boards of directors if they are to survive for the future. No area of the modernization process has been as ignored as the boards of directors in terms of research, training, or suggestion. Those who are seeking to learn more about this area and improve it, hone it, and fine-tune it, are to be commended. It is not a job full of praise and thanks. Rather, one is likely to be greeted with some indifference, ambivalence, and lack of concern. It reminds one of the story of the board training session in which a man said ignorance and apathy are the two major enemies of board activities. A listening board member looked at another and said, "Do you think that is right?" The other board member replied, "I don't know and I don't care." That's the problem as it lies before us. This paper represents a small attempt to move things in the other direction, to reduce apathy and ignorance.

## REFERENCES

Tropman, John E. *Effective Meetings* (Beverly Hills, Calif.: Sage, 1980).

Weber, Joseph. *Managing Boards of Directors* (New York: The Greater New York Fund, 1975).

_____ and Nellie Hartogs. *Boards of Directors* (New York: Oceana Publications, 1974).

## BIBLIOGRAPHY

Bennis, Warren G., "RX for Corporate Boards," *Technology Review* (December/January 1979).

_____, "The Crisis of Corporate Boards," *Technology Review* (November 1978).

Bridges, Edwin M., Wayne J. Doyle, and David J. Mahand, "Effects of Hierarchical Differentiation on Group Productivity, Efficiency and Risk Taking," *Administrative Science Quarterly* 13 (1968).

Conrad, William R. Jr., and William E. Glenn, "The Effective Voluntary Board of Directors" (Athens, Ohio: Swallow Press Books, 1983).

Glover, E. Elizabeth, *Guide for Board Organization and Administrative Structure* (New York: Child Welfare League of America, 1972).

Greenleaf, Robert K., "1. The Servant as Leader," "2. Trustees as Servants," "3. The Institution as Servant," and "4. The Servant: Retrospect and Prospect," *The Servant Series* (Peterborough, N.H.: Windy Row Press, 43 Grove St., Peterborough, N.H. 03455, 1973).

Griggsby, C., "Separable Liabilities in Directory Trusts," *California Law Review* 60, no. 4 (1972).

Hawkins, A.J., "The Personal Liability of Charity Trustees," *The Law Quarterly Review* 95 (January 1979): 99–116.

Hone, Michael C., "Responsibilities of the Directors of Non-Profit Corporations Under the Proposed Revision of the Model Non-Profit Corporation Act." Paper presented at the American Bar Association Annual Meeting, August 1981 (unpublished paper, School of Law, University of San Francisco).

Houle, Cyril O., "Governing Boards" (San Francisco: Jossey-Bass, 1989).

Levy, Leslie, "Reforming Board Reform," *Harvard Business Review* 59 (January/February 1981): 166–172.

Mueller, Robert Kirk, "The Incomplete Board: the Unfolding of Corporate Governance." (Lexington, Mass.: D.C. Heath and Company, 1981).

National Information Bureau, "The Volunteer Board Member in Philanthropy," (New York: National Information Bureau, 1979).

Oleck, Howard L., *Non-Profit Corporations, Organizations and Associates* (Englewood Cliffs, N.J.: Prentice-Hall, 1980).

Ott, J. Steven, and Joy M. Shafritz, "The Facts on File Dictionary of Nonprofit Organization Management" (New York: Facts on File Publications, 1986).

Palmerie, Victor H., "Corporate Responsibility and the Competent Board," *Harvard Business Review* 57 (May/June 1979): 46–48.

Pascarella, Perry, "The CEO of the 80's," *Industry Week* (January 7, 1980).

Perham, John C., "Non-Profit Boards Under Fire," *Dun's Review* 114, no. 4 (October 1979): 108–113.

Prybil, Lawrence D., "Accountability Invested Trust," *Hospitals* 50 (April 1, 1976): 48–50.

Solomon, Louis D., "Restructuring the Corporate Board of Directors: Fond Hope— Faint Promise?" *Michigan Law Review* 76, no. 4 (March 1978).

Topinka, James E., Barbara H. Shilling, and Carolyn Mar, *A Guide to the California Non-Profit Public Benefit Corporation Law* (San Francisco: The Management Center, 150 Post St., Suite 640, San Francisco, CA 94108).

Trecker, Harley, "Boards Can Be Better: The Productive Board Meeting" (Hartford, Conn.: Community Council of Greater Hartford, April 1980).

_____, "Boards Can Be Better: Board and Staff, The Leadership Team" (Hartford, Conn.: Community Council of Greater Hartford, May 1980).

_____, "Boards Can Be Better: Overview" (Hartford, Conn.: Community Council of Greater Hartford, February 1980).

_____, "Boards Can Be Better: An Annual Check-up for Boards" (Hartford, Conn.: Community Council of Greater Hartford, June 1980).

Tropman, John E., "A Comparative Analysis of Community Organization Agencies," in I. Speigal, ed. *Community Organization: Studies in Constraint* (Beverly Hills, Calif.: Sage, 1972).

_____, *Effective Meetings* (Beverly Hills, Calif.: Sage, 1980).

_____, Harold R. Johnson, and Elmer J. Tropman, *The Essentials of Committee Management* (Chicago: Nelson-Hall, 1979).

Waldo, Charles N., "Boards of Directors: Their Changing Roles, Structures, and Information Needs" (Westport, Conn.: Quorum Books, 1985).

_____, "A Working Guide for Directors of Not-For-Profit Organizations" (Westport, Conn.: Quorum Books, 1986).

Weber, Joseph, *Managing Boards of Directors* (New York: The Greater New York Fund, 1975).

_____, and Nellie Hartogs, *Boards of Directors* (New York: Oceana Publications, 1974).

Weihe, Vernon, "Are Your Board Members Dressed for Their Role?" *Canadian Welfare* 52 (1976).

_____, "Keeping Board Members Informed," unpublished paper, School of Social Professions, University of Kentucky, 1979.

Williams, Harold M., "Corporate Accountability," *Vital Speeches* 44, no. 15 (May 15, 1978): 558–563.

Zelman, William, "Liability for Social Agency Boards," *Social Work* 22, 4 (July 1977): 270–274.

## 33.

### Roslyn H. Chernesky and Marcia J. Bombyk

### WOMEN'S WAYS AND EFFECTIVE MANAGEMENT

It is no longer unusual to suggest that the managerial style of women may differ from that of men, that the qualities women bring to organizations may be strengths rather than weaknesses, or that today's organizations are in need of what women have to offer in order to thrive and be effective. As the debate in the recent *Harvard Business Review* reflects (Debate, 1991), these ideas are not universally accepted

The authors would like to thank the editor of AFFILIA and SAGE Publications, Inc., for permission to reprint this study originally published in Chernesky, R.H., & Bombyk, M.J. (1988, Spring), Women's Ways and Effective Management, *AFFILIA* 3(1), 48-61, © 1988 Women and Social Work, Inc.

Roslyn H. Chernesky and Marcia J. Bombyk are professors at the Graduate School of Social Services, Fordham University.

and are frequently regarded with skepticism; however, their possibility is at least being discussed and studied.

This article presents an overview of the qualities associated with women and links these qualities to the ways women manage. The authors describe their study of women managers and how they perceive of gender differences in their approach to management (Chernesky & Bombyk, 1988). The data offer empirical support for the idea that women bring a unique view and understanding of their experience of caring to their administrative positions. The study complements the growing literature in which selected women describe their gender-based management style (Cantor & Bernay, 1992; Hegelsen, 1991; Loden, 1985; Rosener, 1990). The article concludes with a discussion of the implications of women's unique management style as well as some of the risks inherent in conceiving of gender-based management styles.

When it was suggested more than ten years ago that women manage differently than men (Baird & Bradley, 1979; Hooyman, 1978; Rosener & Schwartz, 1980), such a possibility was largely ignored and denied. In a period of rapid increase in the number of women in executive, managerial, and administrative jobs, great strides had been made in convincing those who hire administrators that women were no different than men in the way they managed. The Women's Bureau (1985) reported that women holding managerial positions rose from 22 percent in 1975 to almost 40 percent in 1985. Between 1977 and 1985 the number of women managers increased by 102 percent, while the number of male managers increased only 4 percent (Women's Bureau, U.S. Department of Labor, 1985). Women learned how to be accepted and acquire the look of successful managers, especially by dressing "like one of the boys." They took seriously the warnings that to act "like women" would only confirm that they were unsuitable for executive leadership. The message was clear: Behavior associated with women, and especially behavior that was stereotypical of women, was undesirable, and a sign of weakness.

Not surprisingly, a number of studies during this period, from the mid-1970s to the mid-1980s, demonstrated that the way women and men managed was more similar than different (Chapman, 1975; Donnell & Hall, 1980; Harlan & Weiss, 1982). A more definitive analysis meta-analyzed seventeen studies of gender differences in leadership, concluding that it was not possible to claim that gender influenced leadership behavior in nonlaboratory settings (Dobbins & Platz, 1986). Determining that women and men managers do not differ bolstered the popular thesis during this period that management and leadership behaviors were gender-neutral.

## INTEREST IN NEW LEADERSHIP

Despite the effort of demonstrating that women managers were the same as men, the possibility that women's management style was different from that of men remained intriguing. It captured the imagination of many who saw a need for fundamental changes in American industry, corporations, and service organizations and those who looked toward Japanese management, Theory Z, quality circles, and total quality management. The lack of effective management was increasingly considered the major reason why American business was neither competitive nor productive.

The traditional style of management was rapidly losing favor. There was increasing evidence that workers preferred managers who supported worker participation and showed a high concern for interpersonal relationships (Hornstein, Heilman, Mone, Tartell, 1987). Controlling, autocratic leadership, and preoccupation with tasks and productivity at the expense of relationships were seen as less effective leadership approaches. A consensus was emerging that this style of management, which Rosener (1990) refers to as the command-and-control approach, was outdated and inappropriate for today's organizations (Bradford, 1991; Cohen, 1991).

The times were calling for a new kind of leadership and new kinds of organizations. Zaleznik (1989) claimed "business in America has lost its way, adrift in a sea of managerial mediocrity desperately needing leadership..." (p.11). He described how the overconcentration of the "dominating managerial mystique" guides today's managers who impose structure and process to establish control, preserve order, and prevent chaos. Burns (1979) referred to the new management style as "transforming leadership" in which the leader "taps the needs and raises the aspirations and helps shape the values—and hence mobilizes the potential followers." Kanter (1983) identified "change master" skills needed for today's organizations, which include kaleidoscope thinking, the ability to articulate and communicate visions, the ability to build coalitions and teams to carry out ideas, and the sharing of credit so that everyone who works is rewarded.

The preferred leadership style became relationship-oriented, supportive, democratic, and participative. The most appropriate leader today is one who can "lead others to lead themselves" (Manz & Sims, 1991, p. 18). Referred to as an "interactive style" (Rosener, 1990), or "coaching" (Evered & Selman, 1989), the new style disdains beliefs about being in charge, controlling and commanding others, prescribing behaviors, and maintaining order and replaces them with beliefs about empowering people to contribute more fully and productively (Block, 1987). Effective managers build trust and commitment without relying on their hierarchical position, bring out the best thinking in work groups, help integrate different points of view, and encourage consensus problem solving and decision making.

## WOMEN'S WAYS

The connection between the newest kind of leadership desired in managers today and the qualities women are said to bring to management has become increasingly apparent. Rosener and Schwartz (1980)

suggested that women's approach was based on synthesizing, intuition, and qualitative thinking. Loden (1985) noted that concern for people, interpersonal skills, intuitive management, and creative problem solving were qualities that women were encouraged to develop and rely on, and therefore bring to management.

Drawing upon psychological theories, Grant (1988) identified qualities unique to women. She suggests that women engage in cooperative communication, seeking a means of conciliation with others instead of getting involved in competition or confrontation. Women strongly value interpersonal ties, show concern for others and give importance to attachment and connectedness. They view power as a transforming force from within, equated with giving, caring, nurturance, and strength. Women's capacity for empathy with others and seeing themselves as connected to others leads them to value closeness and nurture intimacy. Thus, women are more able to express different emotions and feelings of vulnerability. Finally, women's biology, related to pregnancy and childbirth, grounds them in an earthly practicality and concreteness regarding day-to-day realities.

Women's management style therefore reflects their experience of caring, cooperating, and connectedness. Women bring to their positions sensitivity and empathy toward others, enabling them to foster a sense of belonging among workers, which in turn breeds loyalty and encourages people to do their best (Hughey & Gelman, 1986). Women dislike hierarchical structures that place the leader at the top of the ladder, alone and isolated. They prefer to be in the center of things so they can be "connected to all those around them as if by invisible strands or threads constructed around the central point" (Helgesen, 1990). Women encourage participation, share power and information, enhance other people's self-worth, and get others excited about their work (Rosener, 1990).

## WOMEN'S WAYS OF MANAGING

The study presented here is a first step toward understanding how women administrators actually implement their managerial responsibilities in ways that reflect and stem from their being women. Data were collected using a questionnaire mailed to all 381 women affiliated with the Executive Women in Human Services, a network of women in management positions in New York City that was founded in 1979. Of the 381, 92 responded, for a response rate of 24 percent.

The respondents ranged in age from 32 to 74, and the mean age was 47 years. They were all experienced administrators (the mean years of administrative experience were 12, and none had been administrators for fewer than 2 years). Furthermore, they were generally highly educated; two-thirds had master's degrees, and 45 percent held master's degrees in social work, and there were as many holders of doctorates as of bachelor's degrees (15 percent each). (Only 4 percent had only a high school diploma.) The majority (64 percent) had obtained some formal training in administration, irrespective of their terminal degree or discipline.

More than half the respondents (63 percent) held top-level executive positions, and 37 percent were in middle management. The majority of agencies in which they were employed, which varied widely in size, provided direct services. Twenty-nine percent of the respondents managed fewer than 10 staff members; 42 percent, 20–60 staff members; 28 percent, more than 60 staff members; and 16 percent, over 100 staff members. Forty-three percent were responsible for budgets of under $1 million; 39 percent, for budgets of $1–$5 million; 18 percent, for budgets of over $5 million, and 9 percent, for budgets of over $15 million.

## FINDINGS

The respondents overwhelmingly thought (78 percent) that they brought qualities, values, or perspectives to their administrative positions that were different from those of men. All those who believed in their unique qualities cited examples; the 178 examples that were given could be placed in nine relatively discrete categories, as shown in Table 33.1. Only a small proportion (8 percent) did not fit into the categories.

The nine categories are closely related to the areas that are considered characteristic of a woman's approach to administration, according to feminist theory. For example, the respondents stressed their sense of caring and their concern for people as well as the quality of the environment, sensitivity to the needs of women workers, investment in workers, a cooperative orientation, openness in communication, a global perspective, recognition of inequities, and intuition.

Nearly two-thirds (62 percent) of the respondents believed they were doing something that a typical male administrator in their position would probably not do. Only 15 percent thought they were not doing anything that was different, and 22 percent were not sure. The respondents cited eighty-nine examples to illustrate what they thought they were doing differently. Using content analysis, the authors determined that just over half were examples that demonstrated the respondents' sensitivity to

TABLE 33.1
Qualities That Women State They Bring to Administration That Are Different from Those of Men

| Quality | Percentage Cited (N = 77) |
|---|---|
| Concern for people; sensitivity, empathy, and compassion; a tendency to nurture or mother | 60 |
| Investment in workers, support of workers, attempt to give workers responsibilities, help workers get promoted, serve as mentors | 32 |
| Appreciate of dual roles and responsibilities of women workers in relation to family and career and of the skills as well as the problems they bring, given their socialization and experiences | 26 |
| Commitment to staff participation in decision making, to cooperation and collaboration among workers as opposed to hierarchical and competitive structures, and to process rather than product | 26 |
| Patience, intuition, concern with details, and a broader and more global perspective of life and the world | 21 |
| Communication that is open and honest, a willingness to admit doubt or error, comfort with giving compliments and with just listening | 18 |
| Recognition of sexism, discrimination, and inequities in the workplace; commitment to affirmative action | 13 |
| Sensitivity to programming for and the service needs of women and children | 9 |
| Concern with the quality of the work environment and improving the physical work conditions | 8 |

workers and their problems. These women executives believed that they listened more to their workers' concerns, became more involved in their workers' lives, and did more to help their workers cope with the stress they faced than would male executives. They cited their use of such administrative prerogatives as establishing flextime, extending maternity leave, and allowing staff members to bring their children to work on days when school is closed.

How women administrators are more visible and available to workers was the second most frequently cited example of differences by 18 percent. Many stressed their efforts to keep communication open and to keep staff informed about what was going on, especially with the board of directors. Illustrations included pitching in to get done on time, remembering the birthdays of workers with a token celebration, and helping out by handling clients when staff members were unavailable. The most frequently mentioned action was that of fixing up offices to make them more pleasant for working.

The respondents' identification of the kinds of tasks one would expect to be influenced by being a woman and their illustrations were consistent with the authors' expectations. Their comments on "handling conflict among workers," for example, emphasized the desire to resolve the conflict as quickly as possible through a process that brings the parties together. Their illustrations of "leadership style" emphasized cooperation, participation, and a nonhierarchical approach that includes, rather than excludes, as many people as possible. "Developing staff" reflected a transforming relationship style in which the respondents' concern for the growth and learning of staff were paramount. "Maintaining job satisfaction" and "motivating workers" also emphasized their concern for others and their attempts to make life easier for their workers. The examples they gave included altering work schedules and hours to accommodate workers, involving workers in decision making, and paying particular attention to opportunities to provide positive feedback, support, and appreciation.

In summary, the study demonstrated that women do believe that they bring special qualities, values, and perspectives to their administrative positions because they are women and that they believe that they act on their uniqueness, doing things and carrying out their administrative tasks differently from their male counterparts. How the respondents claimed they are different and what they claimed they are doing differently conformed to the authors' expectations about gender differences. The results thus provide strong support for the notion that women administrators bring to their positions women's experience of caring. Women anticipate, interpret, and respond to the needs of others and thereby are sensitive and empathic toward others as well as nurturing and cooperative.

**IMPLICATIONS FOR PRACTICE**

While the debate continues as to whether men and women have different management styles and if any differences are indeed significant, several important issues have emerged and will influence management thinking for some time. First, it is no longer possible to believe that management or leadership styles are gender neutral. Second, there has been a clear shift in the preferred style from what had been the more traditional command-and-control approach to the heretofore less favored care-and-empower style. Third, women managers are likely to benefit most from this shift since women seem to be more comfortable with the requirements of the new leadership style than men.

In a climate that sought tough leaders and extolled the "leader as a striking figure on a rearing white horse, crying 'Follow me!'" (Manz & Sims, 1991), in which administrative man (Denhardt & Perkins, 1976) was taken at face value, women (as well as some men) were disadvantaged. Aware that their behavioral styles did not fit the ideal management model, women had three alternatives. They could accept that they were failures who could not prove themselves to be effective managers, no matter how hard they tried. Or, they could learn how to conform to the dominant style, thereby rejecting a more comfortable style, which may have come to them more naturally. Others could be among those who Gordon (1991) claims choose to abandon careers as managers, seeing that as the only alternative.

For years women managers experienced the kinds of frustration and rejection that outsiders, in general, experience. Not surprisingly, these incidents affected their performance and behavior (Chernesky, 1986), invariably confirming that they did not understand or appreciate the rules of the game and did not warrant being players. While the adjustment and coping patterns required of individual women managers interfered with their ease in managing, organizations were simultaneously denied the unique contributions women could more easily make. Similarly, male managers were often constrained to use a traditional leadership style that was expected of them when they, too, may have preferred an alternative approach.

The current debate allows women managers a greater opportunity to use a style that they may prefer, one that is just as likely to be gender-related as the supposedly gender-neutral traditional style.

Women managers will now be able to hold on to and be proud of their leadership style, and not feel defensive about it nor necessarily feel the need to adapt to the style their male colleagues choose. Men managers should be equally comforted in the knowledge that they, too, can make use of leadership styles that were previously considered signs of weakness.

## CAUTIONARY NOTE

Although we are excited about the growing support for this new leadership style as well as the current interest in gender-related management styles, we are reminded how easily such thinking reflects a backlash against women (Faludi, 1991). For example, this line of thinking supports the sex-stereotyping of women that has already worked to channel women into jobs and positions for which their qualities and skills were considered most suitable. We are likely to see women continue to predominate in positions where human relations or interpersonal skills are highly valued. These have traditionally been lower-level management jobs, such as supervision, where people skills are viewed as more essential than technical or conceptual skills (Katz, 1986).

If an organization's need for caring, participation, and empowerment is left to women and is not developed by men managers, neither men nor women will be fulfilling their managerial potential and performing optimally for the organization. A healthy organization, according to Sargent (1981), is an androgynous organization, one in which both masculine and feminine behaviors are valued and incorporated. Such an organization would free all individuals to behave in ways that can benefit them both personally and professionally.

## CONCLUSION

The pressure to conform to an ideal style will continue despite a shift in the image of the ideal. It is the very notion that there is a "best" leadership style that has dominated the history of management thinking and has created tensions, denied opportunities to differ, and cast some individuals as more desirable and valuable to an organization than others. We are concerned about this tendency.

There is sufficient data on leadership and effectiveness to remind us that just because a style is natural or comfortable does not mean that it is the best or even the correct style to use under the circumstances. Flexibility and adaptability are important indicators of effective leadership. Reliance on any one style is bound to be detrimental. Excessive emphasis on a care-and-empower style can create a variation on the management mystique that will result in its being as ineffective as the traditional approach. Perhaps future thinking about the elements of effective management will be directed at the balance and synthesis of these currently polarized approaches.

## REFERENCES

Baird, J. E., & Bradley, P. H. (1979). Styles of management and communication: A comparative study of men and women. *Communication Monographs, 46*, 101–111.

Block, P. (1987). *The empowered manager*. San Francisco: Jossey-Bass.

Bradford, D. L. (1991). Debate: Ways men and women lead. *Harvard Business Review, 69*, 158–159.

Burns, J. M. (1979). *Leadership*. New York: Harper and Row.

Cantor, D. W., & Bernay, T. (1992). *Women in power: The secrets of leadership*. New York: Houghton Mifflin Co.

Chapman, J. B. (1975). Comparison of male and female leadership styles. *Academy of Management Journal, 18*, 645–650.

Chernesky, R. H. (1986). A new model of supervision. In N. Van Den Bergh & L. B. Cooper (Eds.), *Feminist visions for social work* (pp. 163–186). Silver Spring, MD: National Association of Social Workers.

Chernesky, R. H., & Bombyk, M. J. (1988). Women's ways and effective management. *AFFILIA: Journal of Women and Social Work, 3*(1), 48–60.

Cohen, A.R. (1991). Debate: Ways men and women lead. *Harvard Business Review*, 69, 159.

Debate: Ways men and women lead (1991). *Harvard Business Review*, 69, 150–160.

Denhardt, R. H., and Perkins, J. (1976). The coming death of administrative man. *Public Administrative Review, 38,* 379–384.

Dobbins, G. H., & Platz, S. (1986). Sex differences in leadership: How real are they? *Academy of Management Review, 29,* 118–125.

Donnell, S. M., & Hall, J. (1980). Men and women managers: A significant case of no significant difference. *Organizational Dynamics, 8,* 60–77.

Evered, R. D., & Selman, J. C. (1989 August). Coaching and the art of management. *Organizational Dynamics, 18*(2), 16–32.

Faludi, S. (1991). *Backlash: The Undeclared War Against American Women.* New York: Crown.

Gordon, S. (1991). *Prisoners of Men's Dreams.* Boston: Little Brown & Co.

Grant, J. (1988). Women as managers: What they can offer to organizations. *Organizational Dynamics, 16*(3), 56–63.

Harlan, A., & Weiss, C. L. (1982). Sex differences in factors affecting managerial career advancement. In P. A. Wallace (ed.), *Women in the Workplace* (pp. 59–100). Boston: Auburn House.

Helgesen, S. (1990). *The Female Advantage: Women's Ways of Leadership.* New York: Doubleday.

Hooyman, N. (1976). Roots of administrative styles: Modes and models. In E. Wattenberg (Ed.), *Room at the Top* (pp. 15–19). Minneapolis: University of Minnesota Press.

Hornstein, H. A., Heilman, M.E., Mone, E., & Tartell, R. (1987). Responding to contingent leadership behavior. *Organizational Dynamics, 15*(4), 56–65.

Hughey, A. & Gelman, E. (1986, March 17). Managing the women's way. *Newsweek,* pp. 46–47.

Kanter, R. M. (1983). *The Change Masters.* New York: Simon & Schuster.

Katz, R. L. (1986). Skills of an effective administrator. *Harvard Business Review*, 52, 91–102.

Loden, M. (1985). *Feminine Leadership or How to Succeed Without Being One of the Boys.* New York: Times Books.

Manz, C. C., & Sims, H. P. (1991). Superledership: Beyond the myth of heroic leadership. *Organizational Dynamics, 19*(4), 18–35.

Rosener, J. B. (1990). Ways women lead. *Harvard Business Review, 68,* 119–125.

Rosener, L., & Schwartz, P. (1980). Women, leadership and the 1980s: What kind of leaders do we need? *New Leadership in the Public Interest.* New York: NOW Legal Defense & Education Fund, 25–36.

Sargent, A. G. (1981). *The Androgynous Manager.* New York: AMACON.

Women's Bureau. (1985 July). *Facts on U.S. Working Women.* Washington, DC: U.S. Department of Labor.

Zaleznik, A. (1989). *The Managerial Mystique: Restoring Leadership in Business.* New York: Harper & Row.

34.

Mylon Winn

# BLACK PUBLIC ADMINISTRATORS
# AND OPPOSING EXPECTATIONS

## INTRODUCTION

A law student once stated that most of the significant issues in civil rights had been resolved by the courts. This conclusion may be correct if it means there is a legal basis for addressing various civil rights issues, but the same conclusion cannot be made about the experiences of black public administrators in the administrative arm of government. Lawrence Howard suggests that black administrators are expected to buffer white-controlled organizations against demands from the black community.[1]* Whether one agrees or disagrees with Howard, he implies that black administrators find themselves in a difficult position. Many would agree that most black administrators make significant contributions to organizations, that is, that they do more than serve as buffers. However, the administrative experiences of blacks do include having to deal with different expectations from members of the organization and the black community.[2]

Frederick Mosher believes that resolving different expectations is the most difficult moral problem faced by public administrators.[3] This situation is further complicated

when one group pursuing their interest needs government services to help alleviate the effects of racial discrimination.

This chapter will focus on how black public administrators can address the different expectations they may encounter by discussing the bases of expectations from blacks and from members of the organization. The chapter will then suggest that by minimizing different expectations black public administrators can concentrate on responding to the public need for government service through policy-making and program management.

## THE BASIS OF BLACK EXPECTATIONS FOR THE PUBLIC SECTOR

One objective of black politics is to influence political decisions about the delivery of public benefits. Charles Hamilton points out that because black influence is limited it is necessary to resort to "demand making tactics" in order to eliminate barriers caused by a lack of political power.[4] Limited success, according to Hamilton, has led blacks to redefine the criteria for participation in the political process. Redefining the criteria for participation is important because it means (1) that blacks can claim a share of public benefits without posing a threat to other groups feeding at the public trough and (2) that blacks can alter their ability to influence government and increase their numbers in decision-making positions. The outcome is

Mylon Winn is an associate professor at the School of Public and Environmental Affairs, Indiana University–Purdue at Indianapolis.

*The "black community" is defined as blacks who live in a specific area in the community as well as blacks who are employed by an agency.

that government benefits are increased and the status of blacks is improved. Altering the relationship between blacks and the political system has one other important benefit, which Milton Morris points out in his discussion of the influence of blacks on public policy. Morris believes that blacks occupy the "untenable position of being almost entirely dependent on the beneficence of a political system that has been so clearly unsympathetic over time."[5] Changing their untenable position is a goal that seemed to have been a possibility during the 1960s and 1970s. The possibility that surfaced during those decades can be linked to several developments. Jewel Prestage points out that since 1900 blacks have been in an "uphill battle to achieve full participation in the political process."[6] Significant legal victories, such as the outlawing of white primaries in 1944 and the passage of the civil rights acts in 1957, 1960 and 1964, the anti-poll tax amendment in 1963 and the federal Voting Rights Act of 1965 are all a part of the uphill battle. This progress was accomplished through government and therefore enhances the importance of public institutions in the fight against racial discrimination. Success encourages hope that government will deliver, which is translated into expectations for public administrators who are charged with implementing as well as enforcing antidiscrimination laws.

During the 1960s and 1970s the preference for controlling institutions within the black community meant that self-government was viewed as a means of limiting, if not eliminating, the effects of racial discrimination. Even in this instance the need is for sympathetic public administrators who are supportive of the goals of black self-government. Perhaps more important than sympathetic administrators is having black public administrators who have experienced the negativeness of racism. The

point is that while sympathetic white administrators can be helpful, having experienced racism provides an insight that makes the black public administrator more understanding, perceptive and willing to oppose racism.

The belief that black public administrators will be more responsive becomes the basis of accountability. When black public administrators fail to satisfy the standards of accountability, they may be reprimanded, for instance, by being accused of selling out their brothers and sisters. Such pressure can be a heavy burden for the black person who is sensitive to this kind of accusation. Adam Herbert believes that the ability of nonwhite administrators to fulfill their responsibilities will become increasingly difficult if there is a "collective perception" that minority administrators have exclusive understanding of the problems faced by people experiencing the effects of discrimination.[7]

## JUDGING TACTICS USED BY BLACKS: A CULTURAL FACTOR

Michael Lipsky observes that powerless groups must operate in the political arena with little to use for bargaining.[8] Because they do not have conventional political resources, they must rely on unconventional methods when dealing with organizations. Blacks may use tactics they consider legitimate which are inconsistent with ideas of professionalism favored by public administrators. Tactics such as office demonstrations, verbal outbursts during meetings and nonverbal behavior used to intimidate administrators are viewed as "disruptive behavior characteristic of a lower-class cultural way of life."[9] Judgment of this kind suggests that different cultural values are being used to reject the validity of tactics used by blacks.

The judgmental values being used can be traced to Woodrow Wilson, who advised that European public administrators should be Americanized in language, thought, principles and objectives.[10] This means simply that public administration should be compatible with American cultural values.

Individualism is an important value in American culture which has been translated into organizational responses. Deryl Hunt argues that "conventional public administration tends to execute public policies as if the clientele were composed of discrete individuals."[11] This approach contributes to an orderly process of administration which provides a basis for administrative control. Subculture values that challenge the preference for orderliness and control are judged rigidly and, if perceived as a threat, rejected.

The different perceptions about the legitimacy of tactics used by blacks brings to mind Edward Hall's conclusion that culture determines what makes sense and depends on the context where the evaluation is made. The result, according to Hall, is that "people in culture-contact situations frequently fail to really understand each other."[12] The lack of understanding may be called racism, but the labeling does not get at the purpose of this kind of behavior. To the extent that public administration reflects the dominant culture (which is significant), the purpose is to support and maintain the belief that will ensure the survival of dominant culture and professional values.

Blacks educated in public administration programs or who progressed through the ranks are familiar with professional values that may influence their organizational roles. Herbert discusses several role determinants which he believes influence minority administrators' perception of their responsibility to their employing agency and their community. Two of Herbert's role determinants most relevant to the discus-

sion here are system demands and colleague pressure. System demands refer to organizational performance expectations that are manipulated through various rewards and sanctions. The objective is to get administrators to follow orders without questioning their validity and to conform to organizational standards of acceptable behavior. Herbert suggests that there is a pronounced effort to find suitable minorities. However, prospective candidates are subject to being weeded out if they are judged to be non-team players.

Colleague pressure involves judging whether a worker's job performance is acceptable to his or her colleagues. Herbert gives several examples of the extremes some minorities will go to in order to be accepted by their peers. For instance, minority police officers may be more forceful in order to gain the attention of their peers and get promoted; minority welfare workers will apply the rules rigidly to clients in order to be perceived as competent; and minority teachers will blame the students rather than the quality of the academic experience in order to be accepted by colleagues.[13] These examples demonstrate that blacks are subject to pressures to assume traditional roles that are compatible with dominant group organizational behavior. Resisting the pressures to conform means not responding to the dominant culture values that are the bases of organizational practices and behaviors. Carried a step further, practices and behaviors become professional standards that administrators are expected to incorporate into their value systems.

The discussion thus far has argued that black administrators may experience pressures from their colleagues and the employing organization. The pressure is to choose one or the other, which the black administrator may be unable to do without being labeled a "sellout" by blacks and a "non-team player" by the organization. This dilemma is an example of expectations that create an ethical problem for black public administrators. There is an option available which can help minimize, if not eliminate, the dilemma.

## ETHICS: A DEFINITION WITH EXPLANATION

One problem in discussing ethics is first to find a suitable definition. The definition of ethics used here borrows heavily from the work of Jeremy Plant. According to Plant, ethics is "'right conduct,' which is appropriate to particular situations."[14] It is difficult to argue against situational ethics as long as the administrator making ethical decisions realizes that ethical relativism cannot be extended into the realm of the unreasonable. Frederick Mosher's argument that "standards of ethical behavior that are applicable and sufficient to a private citizen in his private social relationships are not in themselves adequate for the public decisions of an administrator" suggests that, regardless of the situation, what is reasonable for public administrators should exceed ethical standards for private citizens.[15]

## ETHICS: AN APPROACH TO RESOLVING OPPOSITE EXPECTATIONS

Resolving opposite expectations should be based on standards reflecting ethical values. Stephen Bailey's memorial essay to Paul Appleby is a starting point for a partial discussion of ethical standards. Bailey's essentials of moral behavior—mental attitudes and moral qualities—are prerequisites for ethical conduct as well as necessary qualities

for all public administrators. According to Bailey, mental attitudes involve an awareness on the part of public servants of the problems caused by personal and private goals versus the public interest; of the morally ambivalent effect of public policies; of the shifting of context and values priorities, which create administrative dilemmas; of the increasing difficulty of making ethical choices as administrators progress upward in an organization's hierarchy; of the need for flexibility in resolving administrative uncertainties that involve moral choices; and of the effect of using procedure, rules and standards nonproductively and the advantages of using them to promote fair and open administration. Bailey views these qualities as part of the essentials and turns his discussion to the moral qualities needed to practice ethical public administration.[16]

The essential moral qualities are optimism, courage and fairness, tempered by charity. Optimism is the ability to face uncertain and contradictory situations without becoming dysfunctional. Optimism is the basis for creativity in response to political conflicts that require risky solutions. Courage involves not retreating from unpopular, contradictory, and unclear situations when withdrawing is an easy solution. Administrators must not be afraid to make decisions and avoid passing the buck. Fairness tempered by charity means relying on standards of justice which encourage the exercising of power fairly and compassionately. Charity is the good quality that compensates for limited information and helps restrain the inclination for personal gain in favor of the public interest.[17] Bailey's essentials cannot be ignored, because they emphasize moral ambiguities as well as propose prerequisites for ethical conduct. However, Bailey does ignore what he calls the obvious virtues—honesty, patience, sensitivity, etc.—and concentrates on his essentials. In a culture-contact situation, administrators cannot ignore the obvious, because by doing so they will find themselves between groups with opposing perspectives that may seem unresolvable.

## ETHICS AS OBVIOUS VIRTUES AND THE BLACK ADMINISTRATOR

The obvious virtues that black administrators can rely on are responsiveness and administrative integrity. To be responsive, black administrators must be accessible, able to communicate and, within reason, willing to share information. Responsiveness is accomplished through formal and informal interaction with members of the black community and white collegues. For instance, through responsiveness black administrators are able to share information with members of the black community. In situations where a policy is being made, black administrators can help members of the black community understand issues and their effects. This information can be used to formulate a response. The implication here is that when members of the black community fail to act, black administrators can argue that they have been supportive and thus have lived up to their responsibility.

Responsiveness to white colleagues includes being a competent administrator who does not resort to excessive actions in order to gain a colleague's acceptance. Administrative competence is a factor that lends itself to the accomplishing side of the obvious virtues. While being an ethical person is essential, an initial requirement for being competent is that black administrators must have the knowledge and the managerial skills as well as the ability to practice these skills successfully.

Among reasonable people, administrative competence should be viewed as a basis for limiting doubts about the ability of black administrators to perform their job responsibilities. It is more important, however, that competent black administrators be perceived as having some commitment to professional standards that many administrators find acceptable. Yet black administrators must keep in mind that, while professionalism is a desirable quality, responsiveness through professionalism may adversely affect problem identification, limits decision-making and policy-making and inhibits their ability to deal with routine and nonroutine situations creatively.[18]

In situations where black administrators find they are between their colleagues and the black community, they can turn to the obvious virtue—responsiveness. Equal responsiveness to colleagues and the black community can help minimize differences. Further, being equally responsive communicates a sense of fairness, which means that one of Bailey's essential moral qualities is to be utilized. Responsiveness is an important avenue for dealing with both the black community and colleagues, but it must be accompanied by administrative integrity. Administrative integrity includes honesty, being trusted and having moral convictions. In practice, administrative integrity involves black administrators' being honest in their dealings with colleagues and members of the black community. Honesty is the basis for developing trust, which is necessary if pressure on black administrators is to be minimized.

When people experience moral conflict because they disagree with an organizational policy or practice, they must be prepared to take an ethically based position opposing the policy or practice. In order to take an ethical position, individuals must "know they possess the moral beliefs and integrity of conviction to endure and fight for their position."[19] Where black public administrators are concerned, they must have ethical convictions that are applied fairly and consistently when dealing with colleagues and the black community. This is difficult, but blacks, as well as all other public administrators, do not have the luxury of being selectively ethical.[20] Honesty, trust, and moral convictions are worthwhile qualities that black public administrators must use, qualities that provide a basis for interacting with all others. Through interaction, black public administrators can identify a basis that can be used to eliminate cultural differences that serve as barriers. By eliminating barriers, black administrators can remove the need to serve as mediators and avoid being accused of serving as buffers to protect white administrators from demands of the black community.

## CONCLUSION AND IMPLICATIONS FOR POLICY-MAKING

It can be argued that all administrators experience the push and pull of interest groups and professional standards. This is true, but the race element is an additional factor that affects black administrators uniquely. The effect, as previously argued, is that black administrators find themselves having to respond to demands from white colleagues and from the black community. To respond to these demands, black administrators must become mediators.

Black administrators must realize that mediation involves devising alternatives to perceptions that their white colleagues and members of the black community have about how they should conduct themselves as administrators. It is argued that their conduct should be based on ethical administration, which means practicing the obvious virtues discussed previously. Black admin-

istrators should realize that mediation involves devising proposals that exceed the constraints imposed by demands made by members of the black community and organizational colleagues. Proposals should introduce conditions that both sides can accept and use as a basis for additional discussion. The effect is that instead of being in the middle, black administrators can assume an active role in shifting, to some degree, the focus of their activities from responding to interest-based demands to administration and policy-making. To shift from interest-based demands, black administrators must have credibility with colleagues and with members of the black community. Credibility is based on responsiveness to issues and concerns held by each side. It is the basis for each side's inclination to accept proposals as well as their willingness to engage in discussions intended to develop ideas that both groups can accept. In this sense the limitation of cultural logic is transcended and the focus can shift to problem resolution, decision-making and policy development.

In conclusion, the discussion of ethical administration—the obvious virtues—is intended to introduce a degree of consistency that protects an administrator's credibility. Ethical administration is no panacea for the conflict that can emerge in situations where there is culture based on conflict, but it does offer a dimension that is consistent with the legacy left by Martin Luther King, Jr.[21] Adam Herbert believes that minority administrators have "life experiences which give them an appreciation for certain social, economic, and political realities which they can often articulate more effectively than others."[22] Thus, if black administrators are not hampered by limitations imposed by their colleagues and the black community, they can focus on articulating these experiences in the policy process.

## NOTES

I am indebted to Nancy J. Winn, John Hodges and T. McN. Simpson for their helpful and insightful comments on an earlier draft of this chapter.

1. Lawrence C. Howard, "Black Praxis of Governance: Toward an Alternative Paradigm for Public Administration," *Journal of Afro-American Issues* 3 (Spring 1975): 145.

2. On this point, see Adam W. Herbert, "The Minority Public Administrator: Problems, Prospects and Challenges." *Public Administration Review* 34 (November/December 1974): 556–563.

3. Frederick C. Mosher, *Democracy and the Public Service,* 2d ed. (New York: Oxford University Press, 1982), p. 230.

4. Charles V. Hamilton, "Racial, Ethnic and Social Class Politics and Administration," *Public Administration Review* 32 (October 1972): 638–645.

5. Milton D. Morris, *The Politics of Black America* (New York: Harper & Row, 1975), p. 281.

6. See Jewel L. Prestage, "Black Political Participation," in Bryan T. Downes (ed.), *Cities and Suburbs* (Belmont, Calif.: Wadsworth, 1971), p. 195.

7. Herbert, "The Minority Public Administrator," p. 559.

8. Michael Lipsky, "Protest as a Political Resource," in Downes, *Cities and Suburbs.*

9. For a more detailed discussion on this point, see Hamilton, "Racial, Ethnic and Social Class Politics and Administration," p. 646.

10. Woodrow Wilson, "The Study of Administration," *Political Science Quarterly* 2 (June 1887): 197–222.

11. Deryl G. Hunt, "The Black Perspective on Management," *Public Administration Review* 34 (November/December 1974): 521.

12. Edward T. Hall, *Beyond Culture* (Garden City, N.Y.: Anchor, 1976), p. 188.

13. Herbert, "The Minority Public Administrator," pp. 560–561.

14. Jeremy F. Plant, "Ethics and Public Personnel Administration," In Steven W. Hays and Richard C. Kearney (eds.), *Public Personnel Administration* (Englewood Cliffs, N.J.: Prentice-Hall, 1983), pp. 290–296.

15. Mosher, *Democracy and the Public Service,* p. 230.

16. Stephen K. Bailey, "Ethics and the Public Service," in Roscoe C. Martin (ed.), *Public Administration and Democracy* (Syracuse, N.Y.: Syracuse University Press, 1965), p. 292.

17. Ibid., pp. 293–297.

18. Mosher, *Democracy and the Public Service,* chap. 5.

19. J. Patrick Dobel, "Doing Good by Staying In," *Public Personnel Management* 2 (Summer 1982): 126–139.

20. For further discussion on this point, see Melbourne S. Cumming, "Andrew Young: A Profile in Politico-Religious Activism," *Western Journal of Black Studies* 3 (Winter 1979): 228–232.

21. Peter A. French, *Ethics in Government* (Englewood Cliffs, N.J.: Prentice-Hall, 1983), p. 10.

22. Adam W. Herbert, "The Evolving Challenges of Black Urban Administration," *Journal of Afro-American Issues* 3 (Spring 1975): 177.

35.

Henry M. Havassy

## EFFECTIVE SECOND-STORY BUREAUCRATS: MASTERING THE PARADOX OF DIVERSITY

Middle managers in human services are often seen as caught in the middle between the conflicting expectations and demands of superiors and subordinates (Feldman, 1980; Holloway, 1980; Perlmutter, 1983). In addition to conflicts within the organizational hierarchy, other sets of conflicting expectations and demands make the middle manager's challenge even more complex (Kahn, Wolfe, Quinn, Snoek, & Rosenthal, 1964; Mills, 1976, 1980; Whetten, 1978). Conventional wisdom tends to view middle managers as powerless and frustrated. However, research and experience show that their position can be one of critical importance and significant influence and that some individuals are exceptionally effective in this role (Kanter, 1982; Keller, Szylagyi, & Holland, 1976; Schuler, 1977; Whetten, 1978). Much can be learned from the way successful managers view and carry out their roles.

This article addresses three interrelated issues: (1) the multiple-role conflicts inherent in the position of middle managers, (2) empirical findings on how effective middle managers in human service organizations deal with these conflicts, and (3) practice implications for middle managers and organizations.

## MANAGERS IN THE MIDDLE

In this study, middle managers were defined by three conditions: (1) they report to organizational superiors who have little or no direct contact with the actual service-delivery context; (2) they manage line supervisors or direct-service providers who have contact with the client community but little or no direct contact with the higher levels of the vertical organization; and (3) their work site is located in the service-delivery community. Lipsky (1980) called direct-service providers "street-level bureaucrats"; thus, middle managers can be seen as "second-story bureaucrats." Although this term may seem pejorative, the opposite is intended. Second-story bureaucrats, although operating at neither the upper level nor the street level, make daily decisions that make the bureaucracy work and that strongly influence the quality of service provided. As such, they are key people whose potential and importance are often underestimated. Some examples of second-story bureaucrats include the director of a local welfare office, a family service agency, a neighborhood mental health clinic, or a community center; a hospital unit director; a school principal; and a head nurse.

Henry M. Havassy is a lecturer at the School of Social Work, Haifa University, Mt. Carmel, Haifa, 31999 Israel. This article is based on a paper presented at the Annual Conference of the National Association of Social Workers, New Orleans, September 1987. The author is grateful to Irit Erera, Zvi Eisikovits, the anonymous reviewers, and the editorial staff for most helpful comments on an earlier draft, and to Robert Biller, Terry Cooper, Samuel Taylor, and Francine Rabinovitz for their help in developing this research.

Second-story bureaucrats are in a unique position linking social resources and human needs, that is, linking human-service intentions and delivery. They are at the nexus of many different groups and social systems—at the nerve center where those groups and systems connect and interact (Figure 35.1). Each group or system is a role-set for the middle manager, that is, a source of expectations and demands (Gross, Mason, & McEachern, 1958; Katz & Kahn, 1966; Merton, 1957). These multiple role-sets are often at odds with one another, causing intersender conflict and role overload: "Pressures from one role sender oppose pressures from one or more other senders... [and] various senders' expectations...[are] impossible to complete" (Kahn et al., 1964, p. 20; also see Kahn & Quinn, 1970; Merton, 1957). Organizationally, upper management expects middle managers to obtain worker compliance and implement policy; subordinates expect middle managers to represent their interests and accommodate their needs (Dalton, 1959; Holloway, 1980; Likert, 1961; Perlmutter, 1983). Similarly, middle managers work at the nexus between the norms and expectations of society in general and those of the local community, which includes clients, community organizations, local leaders, and other services. The expectations of the general society and those of the local community may conflict over basic values and specific issues related to the delivery of human services. Finally, the middle manager must respond to both the norms of the profession and the day-to-day reality of service delivery. Professional norms and standards reflect performance expectations that may conflict with day-to-day pressures of service delivery in specific cases.

Each of these constituencies has resources needed for, and plays a part in, effective service delivery. However, each constituency has a different perspective on its needs, the services to be provided, and the appropriate process of doing so. The diversity of perspectives is paradoxical: Different perspectives may conflict sharply with one another, yet *each is valid within its own framework of values and concepts.* Each captures a part of reality. Therefore, a critical role of the second-story bureaucrat is bridging the different perspectives to integrate the resources needed for effective service delivery (Abramszbk, 1980; Mintzberg, 1973; Pettes, 1979; Wexley & Yukl, 1977), Weick (1979) claimed that organizing is the negotiation of the meaning of situations. In these terms, the middle manager's role is to negotiate, among actors with different perspectives or constituencies, both a workable level of common meaning about the nature of a given situation, and a subsequent course of action acceptable to all parties.

## STUDY OF EFFECTIVE MIDDLE MANAGERS

The current study was conducted to explicate the role of second-story bureaucrats and the factors that contribute to effective performance of this role. Effective second-story bureaucrats were interviewed in depth to learn how they bridge the various vertical and horizontal systems. Management studies based on interviews of successful practitioners have been used often in recent years (Bennis & Nanus, 1985; Kanter, 1983; Klauss et al., 1981; Peters & Waterman, 1982). In-depth interviews enable access to managers' perceptions of the multiple meanings of situations and behavior, and can be used to explore the interplay between these varied interpretations in ways much more sensitive than are possible with a standardized questionnaire.

FIGURE 35.1
Position of Second-Story Bureaucrat Between Systems

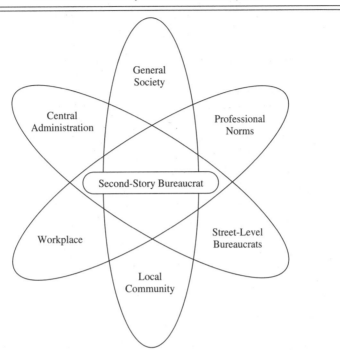

## Research Sample

Expert second-story bureaucrats were identified with the help of academics, senior executives, and middle managers in city and county bureaucracies and nonprofit organizations. The second-story bureaucrats (*n* = 23) worked in diverse organizational settings and human-service fields. Nominators were asked to identify individuals who were exceptionally effective in the second-story bureaucrat role. The nominations were then validated by a questionnaire sent to the subject's immediate supervisor, a subordinate, a peer, and (when possible) a respondent from the community. Although there are no generally

accepted criteria for professional effectiveness and different respondents surely used different criteria, there was almost complete consensus regarding the excellence of the managers in the sample (compare Kanter, 1983, p. 373).

A limitation of this design is that the second-story bureaucrats were interviewed, and three who had been interviewed previously were reinterviewed. The purpose of this round was to further test the model developed in the first two rounds and to clarify the interpretation of the data. This round was followed by a final group session that focused on the explanatory model rather than on the details of the data.

## MODEL OF EFFECTIVE SECOND-STORY BUREAUCRAT BEHAVIOR

The study showed that although these 23 effective managers experienced all the conflicts and contradictions typical of middle management, they were able to master them. The interviews produced inventories of management behaviors and techniques commonly used by these individuals. These behaviors and techniques are generally recognized skills of good management and thus by themselves are not sufficient to explain why these managers are particularly effective. The explanation is to be found in qualitative differences in using the techniques. Effective second-story bureaucrats seem more like master artisans than superior technicians.

A good technician has the skills and knowledge to efficiently produce standardized, interchangeable products or outcomes. Only when the circumstances or needs tend to be uniform are the technician's products predictably effective. On the other hand, an artisan is sensitive to emerging needs and requirements and can apply requisite skill and knowledge contextually in situations that require idiosyncratic responses. The products of the artisan are individualized and unique (Bensman & Lilienfeld, 1973; Eisikovits & Beker, 1983).

The iterative interviewing and data synthesis process produced a model to explain the artisanship of these second-story bureaucrats. This composite model reflects the management behavior of the interviewees as a group but does not describe any one of them exactly. Through systematic interviewing and intersubject validation, the practice wisdom of these expert informants was captured, reconceptualized, and used as the basis for the model (Figure 35.2) (Argyris & Schon, 1974; Glaser & Strauss, 1967; Schon, 1983).

The composite model includes four elements: (1) the ability to engage diversity, (2) an orientation toward emergent social systems, (3) the commitment to efficacy, and (4) a mission-and-value orientation. The remainder of this article will elaborate the first element, the ability to engage diversity. (The entire model is elaborated in Havassy, 1986).

## ABILITY TO ENGAGE DIVERSITY

The model shows that effective second-story bureaucrats are able to deal with their multiple role-sets by virtue of their ability to engage diversity and to learn from the richness of different and even conflicting perceptions within a given situation. "Engaging diversity" is a complex process that includes interacting and meshing with different perspectives, accepting and dealing with the differences rather than trying to unify or gloss over them. It entails a commitment to maintain, master, and use the diversity of perspectives. Three interdependent factors jointly produce the ability to engage diversity: (1) considerable tolerance for ambiguity, (2) maintenance of multiple loyalties, and (3) cross-system translation.

### Tolerance for Ambiguity

The capacity to simultaneously grasp the different and seemingly contradictory aspects of a situation at the nexus of multiple systems is at the core of the second-story bureaucrat's effectiveness. Rather than being paralyzed by diversity and apparent conflicts or inconsistencies, effective middle managers can see or create an underlying interconnectedness. As one manager said, "You need to see everything from six points of view simultaneously!" In

FIGURE 35.2
Model of Effective Second-Story Bureaucrat Behavior

**Effective
Second-Story
Bureaucrat
Behavior**

General
Society

Workplace

Engaging
Diversity

Emergent Systems
Orientation

Central
Administration

**Second-Story
Bureaucrat**

Street-Level
Bureaucrats

Commitment to
Efficacy

Mission & Values
Orientation

Professional
Norms

Local
Community

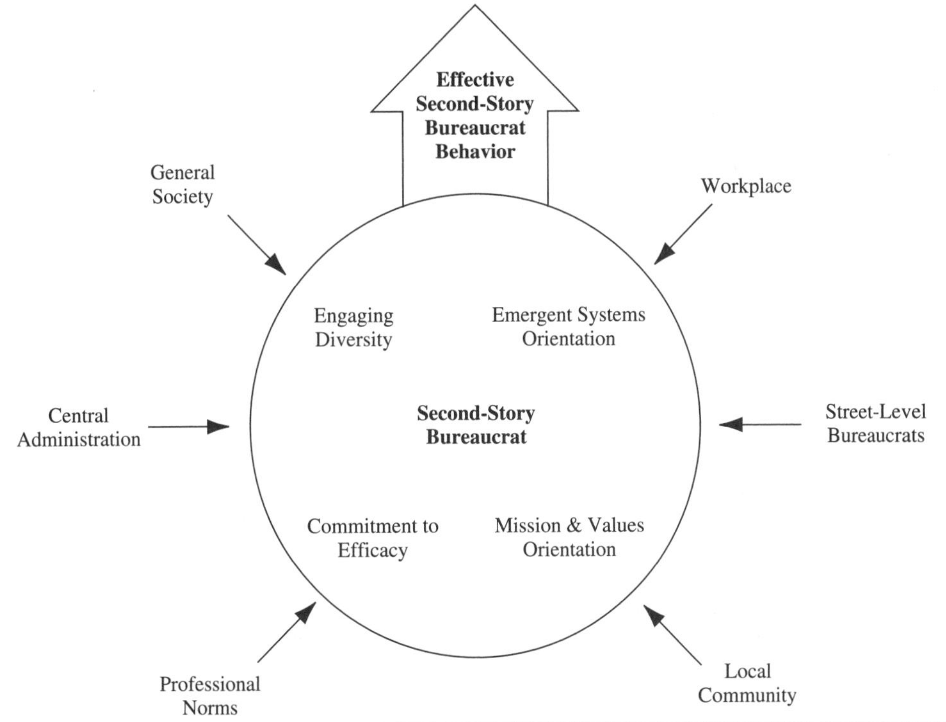

accepting this diversity, they are able to develop a much richer understanding of a situation and its potentiality than would be possible by espousing one perspective at the expense of the others.

The managers did not like to view seemingly conflicting viewpoints as opposites. In their thinking, these managers naturally went to a level of analysis where the "opposites" were interrelated. One interviewee said, "I see a real polarization when I see opposites. It's either this or that, and I don't see [how you can then put them together]. When you say differences or divergent opinions, I can see ownership of that." Here is a wonderful example of perception creating reality. Conventional definitions of a situation may lead others to become immo-

bilized or to access the potential of only one of several facets of a situation. The way that effective second-story bureaucrats define their situation provides a rich understanding and facilitates action that is flexible and appropriate to the context.

## Multiple Loyalties

The second-story bureaucrat is a boundary agent between various constituencies that present different demands and expectations, including that of loyalty to each. Boundary agents, by importing to their organization the views of its environment, are liable to have their own loyalty questioned (Adams, 1980; Mills, 1980; Mintzberg, 1973). When outside their organizations, boundary agents may be suspect because of assumed loyalty to their own organization. Second-story bureaucrats are able to effectively span the boundaries between various systems by maintaining loyalty to multiple groups. This maintenance of multiple loyalties is based on their ability to see beyond temporary or issue-specific contradictions and conflicts. In the words of one interviewee, "It's keeping a balance between the needs expressed from above…and what people bring to me as their problems and needs. Unless I feel there's a balance…I will not be satisfied with my work."

These multiple loyalties come together into a systemic loyalty, geared to general service values and goals rather than to a simple organizational or parochial loyalty. Second-story bureaucrats actively avoid creating or reinforcing a we-they view of the relations between different groups; they emphasize the underlying unity and try to help each party understand the larger picture that encompasses the needs and concerns of the different sides. Another interviewee said, "…we have to see that we [branch and central units] are one agency. It's not us versus them.…"

The second-story bureaucrats in this study stressed that integrity is intertwined and strongly interdependent with the ability to maintain multiple loyalties. They repeatedly stated their belief that "you really can't trick people for very long. They find you out and then the trust, which is so important, is gone." Their credibility derives in large measure from their ability to internally maintain and externally display these loyalties.

### Transcending Diversity: Cross-System Translation

Effective action requires the second-story bureaucrat to mobilize and use resources from horizontal and vertical systems and to influence others to take action leading to desirable results. A key to the effectiveness of the managers interviewed is their ability to put their grasp of diversity and their multiple loyalties into action through cross-system translation.

"Cross-system translation" is expressing needs, expectations, and demands of one system in the terms and concepts of another system. The effective manager is able to share in the view of each group without being limited to it. He or she is thus able to translate or interpret the situation into each system's terms and concepts in a way that enables each group to act in a way that is appropriate and meaningful for that group. For example, in the hands of an effective second-story bureaucrat, "head office" reporting forms required of a caseworker may take on meaning as a professional review and evaluation tool.

At its best, this translation can go a step further and enable the different parties to interact directly, without the ongoing mediation of the manager in the middle. The process of cross-system translation does not necessarily bring the different parties to share the same view of the situation, nor should it. Instead, the process develops compatible views that enable the different parties to interact directly and constructively, enriching one another's understanding of the situation. A challenge of the role is to know when to translate and when to get out of the middle and enable direct communication. It can be as difficult to step out of the situation as it is to bring people together. Yet, if the second-story bureaucrat does not do so, she or he can become an impediment to communication:

You've got to…go beyond just communicating in different ways [with different groups]. You need to come up with a common language and a common goal that's acceptable to the whole, to the two [so-called] opposites…The different groups do not need to share the same view, but [they need] to be able to communicate.

## Engaging Diversity in Practice

*Identifying with Diverse Constituencies.* When dealing with different constituencies, effective second-story bureaucrats can identify with each point of view and see it as containing a valid understanding of the situation, without necessarily agreeing with everything. For example, a community mental health clinic was called upon to run an extended-hours program. Even before this demand, the staff had been feeling overworked. The director fought to avoid the extended-hours program, but his superior insisted that the program was needed and that it was equitable, in the division of labor within the region, for this clinic to take on the program. The second-story bureaucrat was able to understand and accept the positions of both his superior and his staff. How did he reconcile the two?

I came back to staff, and as enthusiastic as I can be, said, "Look, we have to do this extended-hours program, so let's do the best program that we can and be creative." As a middle manager, it was my job, once I lost that battle, to really make it an exciting, meaningful program. It did turn out to be a dynamite program. We did outreach and let the various agencies that open on the weekend know that we too were open.…It turned out to be the model weekend program in the region.…

If I had told my staff. "We're ordered to do this thing. Let's do the minimum," people would drag in there and hate what they're doing. Morale problems would escalate.…They would feel like they're spinning their wheels and getting no satisfaction out of it. In this case, not only did I abide by the regional decision, but in the interest of my own organization's health I had to make this as meaningful as possible for staff as well as for the people we serve.

The demand for extended hours came from higher levels of management in response to perceived political and service needs. However, in presenting the demand to his staff, the second-story bureaucrat translated it into terms of professional values and responsibility and of local-unit identity and pride. Thus, although the demand came down through the vertical system, the actual program was defined within the horizontal system. The result fully satisfied the superiors, provided much intrinsic satisfaction for the staff, and gave clients dedicated service at convenient hours.

*Creating Win–Win Situations.* In situations of conflict like the case above, effective second-story bureaucrats can see and absorb the perspectives of the different groups involved. They are not limited to taking one side or another or taking no side and seeking compromise through mutual concession. They fully engage conflicts, take both sides, and seek satisfaction of the real issues and demands of all parties (Follett, 1973). This method helps reframe the conflict situation for one or all sides in a way that enables satisfactory action and offers the possibility of creating win–win situations. Cross-system translation enriches the effective manager's understanding of the situation, and the interaction between perspectives creates action choices that could not come from within any one perspective. Interacting with the various parties in this positive way makes it possible to access more resources from the different systems and parties.

Obviously these managers are not always successful in resolving conflicts in this manner. But they perform at their best in conflict situations when they absorb and maintain diverse viewpoints and maintain multiple loyalties to create situations that are satisfactory for all. This process can be seen in the case of the extended-hours program and in the following case:

Upper management issued a directive on how [preparation of child welfare court reports] was to be done. I read it and said it would not work. I feel that my job is to make things work. I knew that the goal was to get the kind of controls and supports workers needed so that the reports got to court on time. That was a given. I let upper management know that the directive was not workable, and why. I developed an alternative with my staff...and later it became a model for replication. I'm never one to say, "OK, you say implement, we implement." I just don't feel that's right. That's not fair to the clients, not fair to administration....But I analyze where and why it doesn't work and where there might be a better way. I try to get input from my staff, and see where they're at and what can be done and what can't be done....I'm not trying to be a maverick, just trying to be responsible and make things work.

*Embracing Independence and Conformity.* Understanding the paradox of diversity leads to an ability to think independently—to question what makes sense, what is right, and whether there is another way of thinking or acting.

It's the ability to perceive and to know that things can be different and then to ask the right questions....My gift, if you want to call it that, is the ability to walk out and just ask questions of the organization, of how we handle clients, how staff does things, the whole process. What are we about? What can we do better?

Because second-story bureaucrats have contact with different groups and their perspectives, they are able both to conform to, and to see the limitations of, any one perspective. It would be easier to simplify such a situation by choosing one group and conforming to its expectations. However, these managers tend to take the more difficult but more rewarding route of embracing multiple perspectives, and with them, both conformity and independence.

Many of these observations may seem to be commonplace and even obvious. But we only need ask how many managers we know who exhibit the capacity to embrace

multiple perspectives and to translate values and viewpoints from one system to another. Further, by rediscovering the obvious we highlight it and enhance our awareness of its relative significance.

## IMPLICATIONS

### Organizations and Managers

Middle managers can play an important role in bridging systems and groups in and around the organization. As organizations come to recognize this role, they can learn to take maximum advantage of it. Organizational structures and procedures can be developed to use second-story bureaucrats as translators, interpreters, and facilitators to communication across system boundaries, rather than as neutral conduits of information and instructions. An organizational climate of open communication and decentralized decision making helps to legitimize and facilitate the second-story bureaucrat's bridging of diversity. In addition to the organizational benefit of richer and more productive communication, the legitimation and appreciation of this role can ease some of the stress commonly associated with the middle manager position.

Individual second-story bureaucrats can evaluate their own ability to engage diversity. Some will find strengths in this area that they had taken for granted and, by "rediscovering" them, can make better use of themselves and their ability. Others will find that they need to improve their ability to embrace and mediate diversity. Understanding that this ability is composed of accepting the paradox of diversity, maintaining multiple loyalties, and translating across systems can focus such efforts.

## Selection and Training

The ability to engage diversity does not appear to be an ability that a person either has fully or does not have at all; rather, the ability seems to be present in degrees that differ from person to person. Accordingly, there are implications for both selecting and training second-story bureaucrats.

An important consideration in selecting candidates for second-story bureaucrat roles should be their ability to engage diversity. Using this criterion requires the development of appropriate assessment tools, such as role play and problem-solving simulations that reveal action choices in situations of conflicting demands and expectations.

Although it is unlikely that managerial training programs can radically change a person's ability to engage diversity, they may be able to effect significant improvement. Such training can be divided into conceptualization and skill-development components.

Training can help managers conceptualize the processes of linking various groups and social systems. It can sensitize individuals to the diversity of perspectives and to alternative approaches to dealing with a given situation; it can help them to understand, legitimize, and value different perspectives and approaches. This enhanced conceptualization can help in-service trainees to understand and interpret their experiences—both successes and failures—and to identify new action choices. It can help prepare preservice trainees for the diversity and complexity that await them and can provide a conceptual base to help them maximize their individual abilities to engage diversity.

Training can improve skills in translating situations, ideas, and needs into the perspectives of different groups; facilitating effective direct communication between such groups; moving fluently among various roles; and defining and expressing loyalties to different constituencies. The metaphor of the artisan suggests an important training consideration: Artisans learn by doing and modeling, by going through stages of apprenticeship. Likewise, second-story bureaucrats might profit most from experiential learning and mentorship to achieve the sensitivity and flexibility required for the contextual use of standard skills.

## Research

The value of expert informants has been recognized and demonstrated in other qualitative studies. However, further research comparing more and less effective second-story bureaucrats is likely to further clarify and elaborate the model, sharpening the identification of the characteristics of effective practitioners. Whereas this study used reputation as a criterion for effectiveness, other studies could use other criteria, such as normative performance expectations, and compare the modi operandi of more and less effective managers.

Another limitation of the study design is that it is based on a partial set of observations. The interviewees reported their interactions with other organizational actors, but the study did not have access to the observations of these others about the same events and behaviors. Studies encompassing other relevant actors in the role-sets could enhance understanding of effective second-story bureaucrat behavior and strengthen the findings of this study.

Qualitative methodologies such as the one used in this study have the advantage of both collecting in-depth information about the experience of organizational actors and giving such actors the opportunity and skills to practice reflectively. For instance, if second-story bureaucrats were taught to be participant observers of their own practice, they could simultaneously develop valuable knowledge and enhance their own performance. The "reflective practitioner" model developed by Schon (1983) comes closest to what is suggested here.

Whether a manager is caught between different systems or bridges them can be the difference between effectiveness and mediocrity for the services and between efficacy and powerlessness for the manager. The ability to engage diversity is a key element in the effective manager's success in bridging and linking. Understanding this key can help second-story bureaucrats take maximum advantage of their abilities, and it can help organizations to select and train those individuals best suited for such a role and to take maximum advantage of the contribution that middle managers can make to effective human services.

**REFERENCES**

Abramszbk, L. W. (1980). The new M.S.W. supervisor: Problems of role transition. *Social Casework, 61,* 83–87.

Adams, J. S. (1980). Interorganizational processes and organization boundary activities. In B. Staw & L. L. Cummings (Eds.), *Research in organizational behavior* (Vol. 2, pp. 321–355). Greenwich, CT: JAI Press.

Argyris, C., & Schon, D. (1974). *Theory in practice.* San Francisco: Jossey-Bass.

Bennis, W., & Nanus, B. (1985). *Leaders: The strategies for taking charge.* New York: Harper & Row.

Bensman, J., & Lilienfeld, R. (1973). *Craft consciousness.* New York: John Wiley & Sons.

Dalton, M. (1959). *Men who manage: Fusions of feeling and theory in administration.* New York: John Wiley & Sons.

Eisikovits, Z., & Beker, J. (1983). Beyond professionalism: The child and youth care worker as craftsman. *Child Care Quarterly, 12*(2), 93–112.

Feldman, S. (1980, Spring). The middle management muddle. *Administration in Mental Health, 8,* 3–11.

Follett, M. P. (1973). Constructive conflict. In E. M. Fox & L. Urwick (Eds.), *Dynamic administration: The collected papers of Mary Parker Follett.* New York: Hippocrene Books.

Glaser, B., & Strauss, R. (1967). *The discovery of grounded theory.* Chicago: Aldine.

Gross, N., Mason, W. L., & McEachern, A. W. (1958). *Explorations in role analysis.* New York: John Wiley & Sons.

Havassy, H. M. (1986). *Second-story bureaucrats in human services: Middle managers as a critical link in effective policy formation and implementation.* Unpublished doctoral dissertation, University of Southern California, Los Angeles.

Helmer, O., & Rescher, N. (1960). *On the epistemology of the inexact sciences.* Santa Monica, CA: Rand Corporation.

Holloway, S. (1980, Winter). Up the hierarchy: From clinician to administration. *Administration in Social Work, 4,* 1–14.

Kahn, R., & Quinn, R. (1970). Role stress: A framework for analysis. In A. McLean (Ed.), *Mental health and work organizations.* Chicago: Rand McNally.

Kahn, R., Wolfe, D., Quinn, R., Snoek, D., & Rosenthal, R. (1964). *Organizational stress: Studies in role conflict and ambiguity.* New York: John Wiley & Sons.

Kanter, R. M. (1982, July–August). The middle manager as innovator. *Harvard Business Review, 60,* 95–105.

Kanter, R. M. (1983). *The change masters: Innovation and entrepreneurship in the American corporation.* New York: Simon & Schuster.

Katz, D., & Kahn, R. (1966). *The social psychology of organizations.* New York: John Wiley & Sons.

Keller, R. T., Szylagyi, A. D., & Holland, W. D. (1976). Boundary spanning activity and employee relations: An empirical study. *Human Relations, 29,* 699–710.

Klauss, R., Fisher, D., Flanders, L., Carlson, L., Griffith, M., & Hoyer, M. (1981). *Senior executive service competencies: A superior managers' model.* Washington, DC: U.S. Office of Personnel Management.

Likert, R. (1961). *New patterns of management.* New York: McGraw-Hill.

Lipsky, M. (1980). *Street-level bureaucracy.* New York: Russell Sage Foundation.

Merton, R. (1957). *Social theory and social structure.* Glencoe, IL: Free Press.

Mills, R. H. (1976). Role requirements as sources of organizational stress. *Journal of Applied Psychology, 61,* 171–179.

Mills, R. H. (1980). Organization boundary roles. In C. L. Cooper & R. Payne (Eds.), *Current concerns in occupational stress.* New York: John Wiley & Sons.

Mintzberg, H. (1973). *The nature of managerial work.* New York: Harper & Row.

Perlmutter, F.D. (1983, Fall/Winter). Caught in between: The middle management bind. *Administration in Social Work, 7,* 147–169.

Peters, T. J., & Waterman, R. H., Jr. (1982). *In search of excellence: Lessons from America's best run companies.* New York: Harper & Row.

Pettes, D. E. (1979). *Staff and student supervision.* London: George Allen & Unwin.

Schon, D. A. (1983). *The reflective practitioner: How professionals think in action.* New York: Basic Books.

Schuler, R. S. (1977). Role conflict and ambiguity as a function of the task-structure-technology interaction. *Organizational Behavior and Human Performance, 20,* 66–74.

Strauss, A. A. (1987). *Qualitative analysis for social scientists.* Cambridge: Cambridge University Press.

Weick, K. (1979). *The social psychology of organizing* (2nd ed.). Reading, MA: Addison-Wesley.

Wexley, K. N., & Yukl, G. A. (1977). *Organizational behavior and personnel psychology.* Homewood, IL: Richard D. Irwin.

Whetten, D. A. (1978). Coping with incompatible expectations: An integrated view of role conflict. *Administrative Science Quarterly, 23,* 254–280.

36.

**Burton J. Cohen and Michael J. Austin**

# TRANSFORMING HUMAN SERVICES ORGANIZATIONS THROUGH EMPOWERMENT OF STAFF

## INTRODUCTION

The concept of empowerment within the field of social work has become what Donald Schon (1971) calls an "idea in good currency." It is widely espoused and has the capacity to attract both attention and resources. Some would argue that it has even become an intrinsic part of the mission

Burton J. Cohen is Adjunct Associate Professor in the School of Social Work, University of Pennsylvania.

Michael J. Austin is Professor in the School of Social Welfare, University of California at Berkeley.

and practice of social work (Hartman, 1993). Despite its widespread acceptance, the concept of empowerment has been applied almost exclusively to the relationship between professional social workers and their clients. Social workers are educated to acquire the practice skills needed to effectively empower those whom they serve—the poor, the mentally ill, the elderly, racial and ethnic minorities, etc.

Given this practice, it is surprising, and even ironic, that little attention has been paid to the issue of empowering the workers themselves. In fact, there is evidence that social workers do feel powerless in the organizational settings in which they work. A study of social workers in the state of Massachusetts concludes that bureaucratization, centralization, and controls imposed by funding sources have produced feelings of isolation, lack of autonomy, and burnout (Arches, 1991). Another study that explored child welfare as a "world of work" found that child welfare workers are "fundamentally powerless to change systems that need to be changed, alienated from co-workers who could offer much needed support, laden with responsibilities for which they carry little or no authority, and generally functioning without necessary resources" (Esposito and Fine, 1985; p. 735).

Empowerment is the process through which an individual or group develops the capacity to define and attain its own goals. Staff empowerment, therefore, is the process through which the staff in a social work agency develop the capacity to make decisions that affect their work lives and how they do their jobs. It is accompanied by both an acknowledgement on the part of the agency and a self-awareness on the part of the workers themselves.

The social work profession can no longer avoid this critical issue for several reasons. First, many social service organizations are faced with "reinventing" the way they deliver services. This challenge may be driven by cutbacks in funding, by the appearance of new insurance and reimbursement systems, or by the need to become more effective and competitive in today's markets. An organization's success will largely depend on its ability to use the knowledge and experience of its own workers, many of whom see themselves as powerless and have little faith that their ideas will be seriously considered.

Second, the recruitment and retention of social work staff has become a major concern in many areas of social work (Pecora, Briar,

and Zlotnik, 1989). While economic concerns (pay and benefits) clearly contribute to this problem, frustration and cynicism about the work environment is also a significant factor in workers' decisions about employment (Vinokur-Kaplan, 1991). To recruit and retain workers, human services organizations must become more desirable places to work, and staff empowerment is one of the key components of this effort (Cohen, 1992).

Finally, and perhaps most significantly, it is unrealistic to expect social workers to be successful in empowering their clients if they themselves feel powerless in the contexts of their agencies. As Freire (1983) has stated, those who are powerless and "who have adapted to the structure of domination in which they are immersed, and have become resigned to it, are inhibited from waging the struggle for freedom" (p. 32). Powerlessness and oppression are "domesticating" and "act to submerge people's consciousness." In order for social workers to empower their clients, they themselves must no longer be prey to "the force of oppression." As Freire says, they "must emerge from it and turn upon it. This can be done only by means of praxis: reflection and action upon the world in order to transform it" (p. 36).

This paper examines the prevailing model of staff empowerment and involvement in organizational change. It identifies and challenges several of the basic assumptions of this approach and proposes a new model. Finally, it presents two examples of how the model might operate in an actual agency setting, and discusses how the model can be related to social work education and research.

## THE PREVAILING MODEL
## OF STAFF EMPOWERMENT

A few researchers have suggested the connection between client empowerment and the empowerment of social work staff. Pinderhughes (1983) noted that by being aware of "the ways in which we have experienced powerlessness and defended against it, we are better prepared to empower our clients" (p. 338). Hegar and Hunzeker (1988) found that "the public child welfare agency is a disempowering force in the lives of those who must deal with it, child welfare workers as well as clients" (p. 500). They suggest that workers can overcome their feelings of powerlessness by learning how power operates in human systems, creating mutual support groups, developing an entrepreneurial spirit, engaging in political advocacy, and using the principles of adult learning. Labonte (1990) suggests that the criteria for empowerment need to exist for professionals as well as for those whom they serve. The criteria he identifies are: (1) the ability to make choices; (2) the ability to reflect critically and solve problems; (3) increased access to resources; (4) increased collective bargaining power; and (5) improved status, self-esteem, and cultural identity.

By far, the most popular view of social work staff involvement and empowerment today is articulated in two frequently cited books. The first, *Changing Human Services Organizations* (Brager and Holloway, 1978), is concerned with "change from below" or change efforts "initiated by staff at lower or middle levels of the hierarchy of the organizations they wish to alter" (p. 1). The authors provide a prescriptive model for workers who are willing to take the initiative to work for change in discrete problem areas. The proposed model consists of a four-step sequential process of (1) initial assessment, (2) pre-initiation, (3) implementation, and (4) institutionalization.

The second book, *Change from Within: Humanizing Social Welfare Organizations* (Resnick and Patti, 1980), is a collection of articles addressed to the "practitioner-change agent" (an individual, ad hoc group, or formal sub-unit) who seeks to produce change in the organization of which it is a part. The authors also emphasize change from below, as compared to planned change initiated by administrators or organization development consultants. The intervention model proposed consists of seven interrelated activities: (1) problem analysis, (2) goal formulation and analysis of resistance, (3) action system development and maintenance, (4) formulation of a plan of action, (5) implementation of the plan, (6) assessment of decision implementation, and (7) retrieval and transmission of learning.

These books have provided the foundation for most of our current thinking about how social workers can become involved in changing their workplace and improving conditions for themselves and their clients. Together, they led to a new area of formal practice that Holloway (1987) refers to as "staff-initiated organizational change" (SIOC). Although they do not specifically use the term "empowerment," the processes they describe are comparable and directed towards the same desired result. Today, however, there is a critical need to reexamine this model and to go beyond it in light of changes in how we view the organizational change process, how we conceptualize the role of the professional social worker in a bureaucratic setting, and new ideas about organizational learning.

The SIOC model rests on three basic assumptions:

1. There is no organizational sanction for worker participation in decision-making.
2. Social workers in human services organizations should be able to function as autonomous professionals.
3. Organizational change is an orderly sequential process with learning occurring at the end.

Although these assumptions may still represent the prevailing view and reality in most human services organizations, each of them should be challenged. Let us examine each.

1. *There is no organizational sanction for worker participation in decision-making.* This is stated explicitly in the prevailing model. Holloway (1987) states that "whereas it is the legitimate prerogative of the executive to initiate organizational innovation, no comparable organizational authority exists to sanction the efforts of the line worker who contemplates reform" (p. 730). Resnick and Patti (1980) state that "the practitioner-change agent has little official vested legitimacy as a change agent." Whatever legitimacy the workers have "derives largely from the internalized professional norms and values that may or may not be recognized as legitimate by the organization" (p. 20). This assumption tends to cloak much of SIOC under a mantle of "covert activity." The organizational climate is assumed to be antagonistic and inhospitable. The individual worker is presented with an untenable situation. S/he has an "ethical obligation to place professional values above organizational allegiance" (Resnick and Patti, 1980, p. 217). Such covert or "unobtrusive" activity may be necessary under certain conditions, but in general is likely to lead to unsuccessful and frustrating efforts, leaving the workers feeling as powerless as when they began.

2. *Social workers in human services organizations should be able to function as autonomous professionals.* "Staff-initiated organizational change" is presented as a necessary intrusion on professional practice in order to combat the inherent tendencies of bureaucratic organizations, and their administrators, to compromise the delivery of services to clients. Rather than a function that should be built into the social worker's job, or designed into the structure of the organization, SIOC is seen as a necessary evil. Resnick and Patti (1980) state that "it is comforting to think of a delivery system in which workers can function as autonomous professionals, unfettered by bureaucratic constraints." They view SIOC as a viable alternative that can be pursued "until that occurs" (p. 228). Brager and Holloway (1978) view the seeking of professional autonomy as the "commonly preferred" approach for professionals seeking to "reduce the uncertainty in organizational life" (p. 83). They view the press for autonomy and control as "a rational response to unpredictable or limiting circumstances" (p. 85).

3. *Organizational change is an orderly sequential process with learning occurring at the end.* SIOC views organizational change as proceeding through sequential phases from problem identification through implementation and institutionalization. Holloway (1987) suggests that "distinct functions and tasks must be accomplished in each phase if the process is to succeed" (p. 732). Resnick and Patti (1980) suggest a seven-phase linear model where "in practice, the components are highly interdependent" (p. 12). The final step involves "conceptualizing and communicating what they [the action systems] have learned from this experience" (p. 11). This suggests an orderly process of directed diffusion in which successful change efforts are communicated through centralized channels, training sessions and formal guidelines. This model of diffusion of innovation has been challenged in recent years because of its failure to explain how large organizations successfully manage fundamental change.

## A NEW MODEL OF EMPOWERING SOCIAL WORK STAFF

While the SIOC model has been an important contribution and the predominant approach to empowering social work staff in an organizational setting, we believe it has serious shortcomings. The practitioner-change agent, without any formal sanction, and in a culture that values professional autonomy and minimizes teamwork, is expected to proceed through an orderly sequential process where one step follows the other in a predictable and linear fashion. It is unrealistic to expect this process to succeed very often in the turbulent settings that characterize most human services organizations today. The process is unlikely to produce satisfying results for the practitioner-change, and it is unlikely to lead to the fundamental changes that are required today in human services organizations. It takes into account neither the growing acceptance in our society of employee involvement efforts that are formally sanctioned nor the growing presence of labor unions in human services settings, especially in the public sector.

The model that we propose is not in common practice today. However, we believe it represents the directions in which human services organizations ought to move if we truly wish to empower staff and create more responsive and effective service delivery systems. Our model challenges each of the three previously stated assumptions of SIOC. It reframes them as a new set of design principles that together comprise a new model of empowerment-based practice as follows:

1. *Worker participation in organizational improvement efforts should be designed into the organizational structure and formally sanctioned.* Recent thinking about organizational change acknowledges that top-down administrative change simply does not work. This has been accepted in major corporations (Kantor, 1987), public school systems, and non-profit organizations. One study of organizational change in six large corporations found that many change efforts failed because they relied too heavily on the promulgation of company-wide programs, and because they believed that employee behavior could be changed by altering a company's formal structure and systems (Beer, Eisenstat and Spector, 1990, p. 158). In these settings, successful organizational change is typically seen as occurring first at the periphery of the organization, with high staff involvement and empowered general managers of smaller units. A good example can be found in some public school systems, where tightly controlled, centrally administered bureaucracies are giving way to decentralized systems where principals and teachers have much more control over what happens in their schools. School-based management and shared decision-making are powerful ideas that are taking hold.

Human services bureaucracies could be decentralized and managed through shared decision-making in the same way. It is no longer acceptable that worker involvement in organizational improvement and change is not formally sanctioned. Worker participation needs to be formally sanctioned by top management, labor unions, and public officials. For top management, this means learning to demonstrate support for worker involvement and then giving workers and middle managers the space to explore innovative solutions. For labor leaders (as well as management leaders), this means learning to explore methods of collaboration and joint decision-making (Herrick, 1990). It also requires designing a planned approach to staff empowerment. Staff involvement must be structured into the organization's "way of doing business" in order for it to be successful and lasting.

2. *Participation in organizational improvement should be built into the professional social worker's role and should be seen as part of the job.* The image of the autonomous professional social worker is unrealistic in the typical human services agency. It can also be dysfunctional. The various tasks and roles are too interrelated; the level of uncertainty is too great. By redesigning job descriptions and expectations, the social worker can work collaboratively with other professionals to improve the agency's capacity to serve clients.

Professional autonomy is often seen as a rational way "to reduce uncertainty in organizational life" (Brager and Holloway, 1978, p. 83). However, professional autonomy can lead to fragmented service, intra-agency infighting, and a failure to anticipate the consequences of one's actions. Rather than seeking to *reduce* uncertainty, professional social workers should consider ways to *acknowledge* and *manage* it more effectively. This will entail becoming less autonomous and more collaborative. Workers should be expected to spend part of their time meeting with colleagues from their own work unit and from other parts of their agency to identify and solve problems, and to suggest better ways to provide service. This should not be seen as superfluous, but as a recognized part of the job, for which social workers are rewarded along with meeting their direct service requirements. They should also receive training in areas such as group problem solving, meeting facilitation, and negotiation skills.

3. *Opportunities for individual and organizational learning should be designed and encouraged throughout the change process.* The capacity to engage in continuous learning has become the primary survival strategy for organizations in the 1990s (Senge, 1990; Cohen and Austin, 1994; Kochan and Useem, 1992). Learning occurs as organizations struggle to redesign themselves by challenging assumptions, building a shared vision of the future, and experimenting with new approaches. It requires individuals to seriously reconsider the results of their actions and to explore new responsibilities and joint problem solving that may be unfamiliar and even uncomfortable.

Organizational learning is essential if a human services organization is to transform itself to meet its highest potential. It is not an orderly process, but as with participation, organizational learning must be designed into the structure and ongoing behavior of an organization if it is to be taken seriously. There are at least four strategies for incorporating organizational learning into human services organizations. The first is to encourage dialogue across hierarchical levels, across agency divisions, and within work units. Dialogue provides opportunities to reconsider assumptions and stereotypes, and to engage in joint problem solving instead of blaming. The second strategy is to provide more intense opportunities for reflection, "taking stock," and redesign through off-site retreats or similar events that allow workers to step back, see the larger picture, and imagine alternative futures. The third strategy is to encourage "looking at the data." Total Quality Management (Deming, 1982) and other recent approaches to organizational improvement are based largely on techniques for line workers to collect data as part of the work process and then use the data for making decisions. The fourth strategy is to adopt an "action research mentality." This means that every member of the organization becomes a researcher (Trist, 1976), that experimentation can take place throughout the organization, and that all are empowered to produce experience-based knowledge.

## EXAMPLES OF STAFF EMPOWERMENT

We know of no human services settings where the model we have proposed is totally in operation. However, there are settings with at least some of the features proposed and where experiments are taking place to improve the quality of working life through staff empowerment.

### 1. *Philadelphia Department of Human Services*

The Children and Youth Division of the Department of Human Services provides public child welfare services for the City of Philadelphia. The agency has been plagued for years with insufficient resources to deal with a rising incidence of child abuse and neglect, frequent media attacks, low staff morale, and infighting throughout the organization. Various studies and investigative reports outlining the problems of the agency have had little effect. Training efforts aimed at upgrading the skills of individuals had little success because they ignored the systemic nature of many of the problems and the complex web of interrelationships that prevented individuals from addressing the problems in isolation. Eventually, the top administrators and outside consultants agreed on a new strategy. Rather than trying to change the whole agency at once, developmental efforts would be focused on individual Sections (each containing five units and 30 staff members) that were willing to view themselves as experimental. Opportunities for a high degree of worker involvement and participation would be created. The role of the Section Administrator would be redesigned from that of "quality control agent" to the leader of a work system that would be responsible for finding ways to improve its performance and the job satisfaction of its workers.

The first experimental Section was one of five Intake Sections, whose workers investigate reported incidents of abuse or neglect and determine whether a case should be accepted for ongoing services. In addition, there are now three experimental Sections out of the 10 Sections that provide ongoing services. Three other sections that provide specialized services (e.g., adoptions, court services, prevention, agency administered foster care) are also involved, but to a lesser degree. Of the first four, three Sections have organized a steering committee composed of workers, supervisors, a union steward, and the Administrator that meets regularly to coordinate various initiatives and respond to problems that arise. The fourth uses the Section as a whole as the coordinating body. Each Section has committees working on specific issues. Examples include staff development for the Section, improving relationships with other parts of the agency, reviewing cases, improving relationships with the courts and legal system. Some of the ideas that are proposed can simply be implemented by a Section with no higher approval needed. Some require that formal proposals be written and submitted to top management for approval. Each of the four Sections has also held an all-day off-site retreat to strengthen their identity as a Section, to talk about what they want the Section to become, and to identify issues they want to address.

In one of the more significant initiatives to date, the Intake Section and one of the ongoing services Sections got together and proposed that they work on the same set of cases, i.e., all cases coming into the ongoing services Section will come from the experimental intake Section. This runs counter to the normal practice in the agency, whereby cases move randomly from an intake Section to any one of 10 identical ongoing services Sections, providing little opportunity for ongoing communication and few opportunities for learning and adjustment. A one-year experiment was designed and proposed, aimed at improving continuity and coordination and improving working relationships between the two Sections. The experiment was approved by top management and after the first year, the results were promising and both Sections wished to continue the arrangement. Recently, several other Administrators have expressed an interest in creating similar linkages for their Sections, and this is now being actively explored.

### 2. *A Grant Program for Line Staff in Social Service and Mental Health Agencies*

Successful grant programs can bring thousands of new dollars into a human services organization, but the initiative and program ideas typically come from top management. The process of developing proposals is usually several steps removed from the line staff who interact directly with clients, and may not address new ideas that could make a significant impact at the line-staff level with relatively little expense. In 1992, the Zellerbach Family Fund in California began an experiment to see whether a mini-grant program would empower line workers and lead to innovations in public mental health and social services agencies at the county level. The program set out to provide a limited number of small grants (up to $5000) to fund service improvements proposed by line staff in four counties.

The program was supported by agency directors in all four counties, who agreed to announce the program to their staffs and to give those who won grants paid work time to implement their ideas, if necessary. The program was only open to line workers; management and supervisory personnel could not submit proposals. Applicants were required to submit a brief description of their idea and to tell how it was expected to improve the quality of their work or services.

The results have been encouraging. In the four counties, 125 staff members were involved in the submission of proposals. Proposals were evaluated by a review committee using eight specific criteria, including creativity and originality, potential influence on clients' lives, feasibility of implementing the idea, and possible replication of the idea in other sites.

Altogether, eight grants were awarded—four to social services agencies and four to mental health agencies. Grant amounts ranged from $2000 to $5000. Examples of the winning ideas in social services agencies were:

- Personal safety training and crisis debriefing for child welfare workers to help in overcoming traumatic experiences.
- A Black Parenting Program for African-American parents of children in the child protective services system.

Winning ideas in the mental health agencies included:

- Establishment of a loan fund for clients participating in housing programs funded through the agency.

- Training mental health and school staff to provide school-based group sessions for children traumatized by violence.

There is some evidence that the program has had an impact even beyond the specific ideas that were selected. The program generated many new ideas for relatively inexpensive improvements in services. In some cases, ideas that were not selected through the Foundation project were funded directly through their agency's budget. In a few other cases, the Foundation later decided to fund "runner-up" proposals from separate grant funds.

This program has demonstrated that line staff are capable of generating many low-cost ideas that can improve service delivery and their work environment. Often this potential is overlooked or underused in traditional grant processes. The project also helped Foundation staff and agency directors to become more aware of the concerns and working environment of public human services employees.

The Philadelphia and California examples both contain, to some degree, elements of the empowerment model described in the previous section. In each case, worker participation was formally sanctioned and designed into the organization. In the first case, this was through worker involvement in committees that made decisions concerning their work unit, or Section. In the second case, it was through a structured proposal and review process. In each case, the activities were seen as part of the professional social worker's job and as something that would improve service delivery, even though participation was voluntary. Both projects encouraged collaboration and working in teams. Finally, in each case learning has occurred throughout the process and in ways that may not have been originally intended. In the first case, the spread of new ideas has not followed an orderly, sequential diffusion process, but has been more ad hoc and serendipitous. In the second case, many ideas that were not originally selected influenced agency and foundation decision-making.

## TRANSLATING THE MODEL INTO SOCIAL WORK EDUCATION AND RESEARCH

This paper has focused on the need for a new framework for thinking about social work practice in human services organizations, based on the empowerment of social work staff and their involvement in organizational improvement. If the social work profession truly wants to empower social workers in their professional practice, we also have to be concerned with the application of this framework to social work education and research. All three of these arenas are interdependent and we can't change one without affecting the others.

Students, themselves, are often a disempowered group with too little control over what they learn and how they learn it. The educational experience for social work students should model the involvement and responsibility that we want them to have as staff in social work organizations. The application of our model would lead to educational programs with several significant features, First, schools of social work should provide an environment and structure in which students can be primarily responsible for their own learning. This implies rethinking how courses are constructed and the roles of students and teachers. Second, field placements should provide students with opportunities to understand and engage in organizational problem solving. This should be a component of the field experience whether the students are primarily interested in direct practice or macro-practice. Third, the stu-

dent experience should include opportunities to participate in classroom and school-wide decisions.

Another way to help empower social work staff is to actively engage them in research on their own practice. Social work research can often be disempowering for practitioners as well as for clients. Research is often viewed as an intrusion and an activity unconnected from the problems confronting those engaged in practice. Social work staff and clients are typically the "objects" of research, rather than partners.

Social work research can be reframed as an interactive process that can lead to individual and organizational learning. Engaging in research can be empowering if it gives staff the opportunity to identify and explore problems that are of concern to them and leads to staff involvement in interventions that address these problems. This is compatible with the "action research" approach (Rappoport, 1970; Trist, 1978), which views researchers as collaborators with those in an action setting, and which is directed towards producing change as well as producing scientific knowledge.

## CONCLUSION: HOW STAFF EMPOWERMENT CAN TRANSFORM HUMAN SERVICES ORGANIZATIONS

Empowerment has become a popular concept in the field of social work, primarily as a feature of the practice relationship between social workers and their clients. Equally important is the need for empowerment of social workers themselves within the organizational settings in which they work, an aspect of empowerment that has received much less attention. Creating workplaces that empower staff raises major challenges for the social work profession, and for social work staff at all levels.

The prevailing perspective on staff empowerment and involvement is known as "staff-initiated organizational change." The SIOC model is a "bottom-up" approach that starts with line social workers who have no official sanction for getting involved in organizational decisions that affect their work. This approach accepts the notion that changes will be modest. Brager and Holloway (1978) state that "accomplishing discrete and limited organizational change is the best workers can do from within the agencies that employ them" (p. 17). We need to build on and move beyond this approach by making staff empowerment a critical process formally sanctioned by the organization.

Clearly, social workers need more than discrete and limited change in many of our human services organizations today. Significant transformations are needed in our systems for providing child welfare services, mental health services, services for senior citizens, and other human services. However, the challenge of bringing about significant transformation in large, complex human services organizations is unresolved. Top-down administrative change programs often fail to produce change in human services organizations. Relying on legislative or judicial interventions to transform human services systems has also been disappointing.

We need an integrated approach to learning and change that is an alternative to either a "top-down" or a "bottom-up" approach. Organizational leaders who are committed to major reform and to empowering workers are presented with an especially difficult challenge and a paradox: "directing a 'non-directive' change process" (Beer, Eisenstat, and Spector, 1990, p. 159). They have to provide leadership and direction to the change process without mandating specific solutions. This can be especially difficult for top managers who have risen to their positions in bureaucratic command and control organizations, and in organizational environments that are often highly regulated and rule-driven.

Our model of staff empowerment supports organizational transformation from within by engaging both the top and the bottom. It focuses on the staff's ability to manage its own work and work environment, but with the support of top management. Staff empowerment can lead to revitalization, a type of organizational transformation characterized by a change in how the organization defines its style of operations (Kimberly and Quinn, 1984). While the process may appear to be too incremental and the results limited, a series of "small wins" can add up and set larger forces in motion (Weick, 1984). Ultimately, the momentum can build and the learning processes that are unleashed can lead to fundamental change. For this to happen though, staff empowerment needs to be framed differently than in the past. Staff involvement in organizational change should be formally sanctioned and designed into the organizational work system. Participation in these efforts needs to be built into the professional role and viewed as part of the social worker's job. Finally, opportunities for reflection and learning combined with action, need to be encouraged and promoted throughout the organizational change process.

## REFERENCES

Arches, J. (1991). Social structure, burnout, and job satisfaction. *Social Work, 36*(3), 202–206.

Beer, M., Eisenstat, R., & Spector, B. (1990). Why change programs don't produce change. *Harvard Business Review, 68*(6), 158–166.

Brager, G. & Holloway, S. (1978). *Changing human service organizations: politics and practice.* New York: The Free Press.

Cohen, B. & Austin, M. (1994). Organizational learning and change in a public child welfare agency. *Administration in Social Work, 18*(1), 1–19.

Cohen, B. (1992, December). *Making human services organizations good places to work.* Paper presented at the NAPCWA National Meeting, San Diego, CA.

Deming, W. E. (1982). *Out of the crisis.* Cambridge: Massachusetts Institute of Technology.

Esposito, G. & Fine, M. (1985). The field of child welfare as a world of work. In J. Laird & A. Hartman (Eds.), *A handbook of child welfare.* New York: The Free Press.

Freire, P. (1970). *Pedagogy of the oppressed.* New York: Continuum Publishing Corp.

Hartman, A. (1993). The professional is political. *Social Work, 38*(4) 365–366, 504.

Hegar, R. & Hunzeker, J. (1988). Moving toward empowerment-based practice in public child welfare. *Social Work, 33*(6), 499–502.

Herrick, N. (1990). *Joint management and employee participation.* San Francisco: Jossey-Bass Publishers.

Holloway, S. (1987). Staff initiated organizational change. In A. Minihan (Ed.), *Encyclopedia of social work*, 18th Edition, Vol. 2. Silver Spring, MD: National Association of Social Workers.

Kantor, R. (1989). *When giants learn to dance.* New York: Simon and Schuster Inc.

Kimberly, J. & Quinn, R. (1984). *Managing organizational transitions.* Homewood, IL: Richard D. Irwin.

Kochan, T. & Useem, M. (1992). *Transforming organizations.* New York: Oxford University Press.

Labonte, R. (1990). Empowerment: notes on professional and community dimensions. *Canadian Review of Social Policy, (26),* 1–12.

Pecora, P., Briar, K., & Zlotnick, J. (1989). *Addressing the program and personnel crisis in child welfare.* Silver Spring, MD: National Association of Social Workers.

Pinderhughes, E. (1983). Empowerment for our clients and for ourselves. *Social Casework, (64),* 331–338.

Rapoport, R. (1970). Three dilemmas in action research. *Human Relations, 23*(6), 499–513.

Resnick, H. & Patti, R. (1980). *Change from within: humanizing social welfare organizations.* Philadelphia: Temple University Press.

Schon, D. (1971). *Beyond the stable state.* New York: W. W. Norton & Co.

Senge, P. (1990). *The fifth discipline: the art & practice of the learning organization.* New York: Doubleday.

Trist, E. (1976). Action research and adaptive planning. In A. Clark (Ed.), *Experimenting with organizational life: the action research approach.* (pp. 223–236). New York: Plenum Press.

Vinokur-Kaplan, D. (1991). Job satisfaction among social workers in public and voluntary child welfare agencies. *Child Welfare 70*(1), 81–91.

Weick, K, (1984). Small wins: redefining the scale of social problems. *American Psychologist, 39*(1), 40–49.

37.

Stephen French Gilson

## THE YWCA WOMEN'S ADVOCACY PROGRAM:
## A CASE STUDY OF DOMESTIC VIOLENCE
## AND SEXUAL ASSAULT SERVICES

### INTRODUCTION

Anti-violence organizations have been founded through a broad array of circumstances and strategies, ranging from local grassroots collectives through "within-system" service organizations (Ferree and Martin, 1995a; Matthews, 1994). Feminist organizations, many with an anti-violence focus, cannot be categorized as either bureaucratic or collectivist; rather, the organizational qualities involve multiple dimensions, such as "feminist ideology, feminist values, feminist goals, feminist outcomes (for members and society), founding circumstances, structures, practice, members and membership, scope and scale, and external relations" (Martin, 1990, p. 182; see also Arnold, 1995; Ferree and Martin, 1995b; Fried, 1994). Domestic violence and anti-rape services are also influenced by issues of race, class, disability, and the ideological views of the women establishing the anti-violence organizations and activities, the coalitions that develop in response to addressing the multiple needs of battered and sexually assaulted women, the women seeking services, and the communities in which the services are located (Arnold, 1995; Matthews, 1994; Murray, 1988). Women develop anti-violence

responses through the lens of such complexity and organizational diversity.

Within this broad orientation, alternative service organizations, many with a feminist focus, emerged (Perlmutter, 1988; Schwartz, Gottesman and Perlmutter, 1988). Alternative service organizations are created to fill a perceived void left by traditional human service organizations. Their founders seek to address needs not met, to be innovative in structure and practice, and to work for social change. The founders' commitment to the principles of social change is reflected in their desire to provide services to individuals and communities with specific needs and/or challenges to which traditional human service organizations fail to respond. Commonly, alternative service organizations have determined that the service mandates of traditional agencies are slow to develop, slow to change, and do not readily respond to emerging service participant groups. Generally, these alternative service organizations "tend to be small, be resource poor, be staffed by the nonprofessional but ideologically committed, use staff who are members of the group being served, and engage in participatory government" (Inglehart and Becerra, 1995, p. 167). In addition to battered women's shelters and sexual assault services, other examples of alternative service organizations are shelters for runaway youth, crisis centers, and self-help or peer support centers (Inglehart and Becerra, 1995).

The first shelters for assaulted and bat-

Stephen French Gilson is Assistant Professor at the School of Social Work, Virginia Commonwealth University.

tered women were established during the 1970s (Murray, 1988; Srinivasan and Davis, 1991; see also Martin, 1981). Concurrently, the anti-rape movement emerged, with increasing recognition that the traditional human service systems had at best been unresponsive, and more often were supporting and perpetuating abusive behaviors (Perlmutter, 1988; Schwartz, Gottesman and Perlmutter, 1988; Wilkerson, 1988). For some, the initial phase of the shelter movement and the anti-rape movement was characterized by mobilization activities (Tice, 1990) and tactics that are required during the early phase of social movements (Morris and Mueller, 1992). Early efforts commonly focused on organizing, building, and establishing support for the opening of shelters. Shelters, developed through grassroots efforts, were generally organized around the principles of consensual decision-making, with a focus on the political aspects of the personal experience. Through this approach, organizations emphasizing empowerment and self-determination sought to decrease the power relationships between the women living in the shelter and the staff. Structural change, not just provision of counseling and other direct services, is critical in political change and struggle (Arnold, 1995; Gottlieb, 1992; Hyde, 1992; Wood and Middleman, 1992). The establishment of shelters and services across different settings was followed by shifts toward maintenance efforts and organizational survival, efforts to maintain a social critique perspective, and efforts "to ensure longevity and produce specific policy outcomes" (Tice, 1990, p. 88).

The shift away from social change and toward maintenance was coincident with the bureaucratization of the women's shelter movement. For some of the shelters, which began as grassroots and alternative services oriented toward providing protection, empowerment, and advocacy, there has been an unanticipated shift from an essential collectivist structure toward an environment inculcated with bureaucratic practices (Srinivasan and Davis, 1991; Tice, 1990). Some domestic violence organizations and shelters are changing from interpreting and responding to violence against women through social advocacy and self-help to "a more narrow individualized analysis of the causes of violence and a 'professional' practice" (Murray, 1988, p. 77; see also Arnold, 1995).

The anti-rape movement, nationally, grew out of "collectivist feminist organizing" that often was "critical and suspicious of the state" (Matthews, 1995, p. 293). Rape crisis centers adopted varying tactics in conflicts with public funding agencies. These tactics included "overt opposition, apparent accommodation, and active engagement," depending upon "general ideological histories" (p. 296) and "depend[ing] on the environment, local and extra-local, immediate, and historical" circumstance of each center and conflict (Matthews, 1995, p. 304).

The transformation from a principally collectivist structure toward a bureaucratic practice does not automatically indicate a move away from an alternative service organization administrative arrangement and accompanying organizational principles (Inglehart and Becerra, 1995; Schwartz, Gottesman, and Perlmutter, 1988; Srinivasan and Davis, 1991). Rather, a complement of collectivist and bureaucratic approaches effectively responds to changing internal and external dynamics (Martin, 1990).

Within many of the early shelters, staff and service participants have informal and egalitarian relationships that are oriented toward empowerment of staff as well as service participants. In these shelters, staff members and service participants jointly developed policies and program-operating procedures. Using a self-help model, staff encouraged service participants to return as volunteers and workers (Murray, 1988; Matthews, 1994; Srinivasan and Davis, 1991; Wilkerson 1988). As social service workers increasingly recognized that the needs of women and children are complex and multifaceted, we have identified a role for professionals within battered women's services (Wood and Middleman, 1992). This introduction of professionalism, however, risks re-victimizing women based on a therapeutic ideology wherein women who have been battered and/or assaulted are given diagnoses. Giving women who have been assaulted psychiatric diagnoses risks identifying domestic violence as a mental health issue rather than interpreting it as a social and political problem. Once women are given diagnoses, they become clients who may be identified as good, bad, or difficult dependent upon their willingness to engage in and follow treatment plans (Ferraro as cited in Srinivasan and Davis, 1991; see also Murray, 1988). The best defense against creating a structure that re-victimizes service participants is to maintain an alternative social organization and a feminist administrative focus (Ferree and Martin, 1995a; Fried, 1994; Hyde, 1992; Inglehart and Becerra, 1995; Martin, 1990; Matthews, 1994; Murray, 1988; Schwartz, Gottesman, and Perlmutter, 1988; Srinivasan and Davis, 1991).[1] To prevent a return to patriarchal structures and practices, feminist practitioners[2] (Nes and Iadicola, 1989; Wood and Middleman, 1992) must conduct an evaluation of the current organizational environment (Srinivasan and Davis, 1991).

The current study opens discussion of the relationship of specialized feminist services or programs within a feminist host organization that has a multifaceted service commitment. Central to the discussion are two principal issues. First, this principally grassroots collectivism of anti-violence services has transformed itself into an organization that has developed ties to an institutional environment without forfeiting its commitment to feminist practice and the social movement organization. The suggestion that feminist organizational qualities include much more than simply the issue of collectivism versus bureaucracy will serve as a background for the current analysis. The second issue is organizational transformation. This case study provides an avenue to discuss some of the emerging dynamics of a host organization and program relationship.

The intent of the program evaluation was not to examine either the issue of host transformation or of host program relationships. Rather, those issues emerged following completion of the evaluation, and as a consequence of continuing discussions regarding feminist organizations and social movement (for a more complete elaboration of these issues, please see: Ferree and Martin, 1995b; Hyde, 1992; Martin, 1990; Matthews, 1994).

## CASE STUDY OF A WOMEN'S SERVICE FOR SURVIVORS OF DOMESTIC VIOLENCE AND SEXUAL ASSAULT AND RAPE

### Purpose of the Evaluation

The Executive Director of the YWCA of Richmond, Board of Directors, Women's Advocacy Program (WAP) administrators and staff undertook an evaluation of the WAP to provide feedback and program review. When used in combination with quality assurance and funding agent program review reports, the qualitative evaluation was intended to provide a more complete statement of the needs of the women and their families in the greater metropolitan Richmond, Virginia area, as well as to examine the response style and capabilities of the WAP. As such, the evaluator designed the review to identify the strengths and challenges of the current program and guide future program planning. The agency director initiated this program evaluation and assured that the service system would take responsibility for the environment where staff and service participants work together. At a minimum, this evaluation enacted the WAP's commitment to examine the services provided and their delivery.

The Executive Director of the YWCA of Richmond requested the study as a planned, normative program evaluation and critique. The program evaluation was conducted by the author under the auspices of the Community Services Associates Program of Virginia Commonwealth University. The format and process of the evaluation developed as a result of discussions held between the Executive Director of the YWCA and the Program Evaluator. The Program Evaluator was aware of but had not had prior direct contact with the YWCA nor the WAP.

The Program Evaluator was male, creating a potential confound that was raised for discussion by the Evaluator at all meetings and interviews. Given the nature of the services provided through the WAP, the history of oppression of women by men, and the personal experiences of some of the participants, the Evaluator felt that this issue should be raised and discussed. In an effort to compensate for sex biases, the Program Evaluator asked a female consultant to review the overall approach, the interview processes, data units and categories for data reduction, and data analysis for content validity. Despite assurances to the contrary from all stakeholders and participants involved in this process,

the evaluator believes that it is impossible to underestimate the impact of having women-focused services evaluated by a male.

**Overview of the Program Evaluated**

In addition to WAP services, the YWCA of Richmond also provides child care and health and fitness services. The WAP operates under the auspices of the Board of Directors of the YWCA and is administratively directed by the Executive Director. The current program evaluation was limited to a review of the WAP, which has been in operation since 1979. The evaluator reviewed the following program elements: the two shelters for women and their children who are survivors of domestic violence; the non-shelter domestic violence program; and the women's sexual assault program. Services provided by the WAP include domestic violence and sexual assault outreach services, 24-hour hotlines, counseling for walk-ins, and ongoing community-based services.

The WAP, established initially as the Women's Victim Advocacy Program, grew out of a Task Force on Battered Women that was formed in 1977 by the Richmond Chapter of the National Organization for Women. The Task Force, which is described as a "grassroots" community organization, began with two primary goals: (a) to determine what type of emergency housing services existed and what agency(ies) would be willing to establish such services; and (b) to survey public and private agencies to identify "the types of services available to abused wives in Richmond and . . . to document the incidence of battered wives in the Richmond Community" (YWCA of Richmond, n.d.a, p. 3). In response to a recognition that "battered women were seen as part of a greater problem known as family/domestic violence" (p. 3), the Task Force changed its name in

TABLE 37.1
Race/Ethnicity of Staff, Board of Directors, and Service Participants

| | Staff | Board of Directors | (Service Participants) | | |
| --- | --- | --- | --- | --- | --- |
| | | | Shelter DV Svcs*† | Non-Shelter DV Svcs* Services | Sexual Assault |
| Black | 64 | 50 | 50.0 | 24.9 | 46.6 |
| White | 34 | 50 | 41.3 | 42.6 | 50.2 |
| Hispanic | 0 | 0 | 2.8 | .1 | 0 |
| Asian | 2 | 0 | 1.0 | .9 | .35 |
| Native American | 0 | 0 | .2 | .1 | .35 |
| Other/ Unknown | 0 | 0 | 4.7 | 31.4 | 2.5 |

NOTE. Numbers of percentage of total
*For Fiscal Year 1993/1994
†Includes adults and children
DV = domestic violence

1977 to the Richmond Domestic Violence Project (YWCA of Richmond, n.d.a). Since 1979, the WAP has provided a variety of services including "a 24-hour hot line, information and referral, individual and group counseling, emergency shelter, and public education" (YWCA of Richmond, n.d.a, p. 4). Until the first shelter building was purchased in 1981 by the YWCA, the program provided shelter at "safe homes" owned by volunteers but operated by the YWCA (YWCA of Richmond, n.d.a). The Rape Crisis Out reach Program was established in 1979 as a component of the WAP. A committee of the YWCA, the Young Women Committed to Action, began to focus increasingly on the issue of rape. It adopted the name ROAR (Richmond Organized Against Rape) in 1974. The work of ROAR was initially focused on public education and referring survivors of rape to other agencies and organizations for counseling, In 1977, the group established the Richmond Hotline as a volunteer hotline that provided "crisis counseling for rape survivors . . . and train[ed] volunteers to do crisis counseling in hospitals

and homes" (YWCA of Richmond, n.d.c, p. vi). In 1979, the Richmond Hotline was integrated into the Rape Crisis Outreach Program. The Rape Crisis Outreach Program provides a range of services including two 24-hour hotlines, individual crisis counseling for rape survivors, companion support/ accompaniment, advocacy, technical assistance, information and referral, and training for professionals and volunteers (YWCA of Richmond, n.d.c).

The Richmond YWCA is a 501(c)3 private nonprofit agency affiliated with the YWCA of the U.S.A. It defines itself as a women's membership movement" as reflected in the agency mission statement (YWCA of Richmond, 1994b, Section IV, p. 1). Funding sources include the United Way, state and local government grants, membership/program fees, contributions, investments, rental income, and special events. The YWCA gives nearly 50 percent of its income to the WAP (YWCA of Richmond, 1994a).

The YWCA strives to have its staff and Board of Directors reflect the racial and ethnic composition of the local community (see Table 37.1). It employs both females and males; however, the Board of Directors By-Laws limit its membership to women. Within the WAP, all direct employees and volunteers are women, except for one contract employee hired to co-lead a support group for male survivors of childhood sexual assault.

The purpose of the WAP, as reflected in the following statement of purpose, is to combine direct services and community advocacy.

The Women's Advocacy Program is committed to the empowerment of women to exercise the right to self-determination and responsibility for choices. As a program we abhor the use of violence as an instrument of power and control with the family as well as in society. We are committed to the elimination of societal attitudes, practices, and policies—including sexism, racism, and classism—that allow and perpetuate violence. (YWCA of Richmond, n.d.b, p. 1)

## METHODS

The program evaluation process consisted of three elements determined during a series of three meetings with the Executive Director, the Associate Director of Operations, and the Associate Director of Programs. We determined that the program evaluation would include: (a) review of written materials, including, but not limited to brochures, annual plans and reports, program policy statements, personnel policies, client intake forms, sample daily logs, and program files; (b) site reviews, which included informal consultation with Association staff and visits to both Domestic Violence Shelters (Richmond City and Chesterfield County), the Non-Shelter Domestic Violence Services sites, and the Women's Sexual Assault Services site; and (c) formal guided interviews, each lasting between 45 and 90 minutes with

representatives of stakeholder groups.

This was a modified participant-driven process, wherein we identified stakeholders and encouraged them to participate in designing the protocol (Greene, 1994; Rodwell and Woody, 1994). We identified the following primary stakeholder groups: the Board of Directors; funding sources; referral sources; YWCA staff, current service participants; and former service participants. In the YWCA staff category, participants included administrative staff and services staff. The Service Participant stakeholder group included service participants who had received services through at least one of the three WAP service components. I interviewed representatives from each stakeholder group. Three members of the Board of Directors; two representatives of funding sources; two representatives of referral sources; three members of the YWCA staff; three current service participants; and two former service participants completed the formal interviewing.[3]

The site review, led by agency staff, consisted of a guided "walk through" and an orientation to the physical setting, documentation used, and operation procedures. To maintain confidentiality of site location, the Executive Director transported the author to the Domestic Violence Shelter sites. During each site visit, I conducted informal interviews with service staff. Out of respect for confidentiality and privacy, I did not interview service participants.

As a result of the data gathered during the meetings with the Executive and Associate Directors, review of written documents, and site visits (including informal interviews), I developed seven guided interview questions, including one that sought comments and responses not addressed by the other questions (see Appendix). These questions served as the basis for the formal interviews with all of the stakeholders. The questions focused on the strengths and challenges of the programs, the definition of goals, interaction of the programs internally and externally, definition of the primary service needs of the women who seek services, and recommendations to address the needs of the women served. I selected interview participants based upon willingness and availability, and conducted all interviews one-on-one at the central program location. I provided participants with an oral description of the rationale, nature, and intent of the interview, and assured them that their individual responses would remain confidential. I explained that I would present their collective responses to the Executive Director, the WAP staff, and the Board of Directors. The participants did not receive any compensation for their participation. All interview participants were women. I conducted one interview by telephone due to scheduling conflicts. I recorded all responses and the participants verified my notations.

I categorized all data into Strengths, Challenges, and Recommendations, and later into more specific subdivisions. The analysis of this case study provides the basis for a theoretical assessment of the provision of alternative feminist-focused services within a larger, more conventional administrative structure.

## RESULTS

It is important to consider the impact internally and externally of the development of complementary collectivist and bureaucratic structures within the same organization. This study highlights the struggle to address the complex and multiple needs of the women who have been assaulted. It is particularly critical to use the knowledge and skills acquired through professional education and practice without re-victimizing women as traditional social service systems commonly do.

## Strengths

WAP stakeholders viewed basic safety and security from victimization and assault as the essential foundation for virtually all services or programs, as they explain:

The WAP is a place where you can get away to be safe from the abuser. (Service Participant)

The WAP provides the opportunity for women to get out of dangerous or harmful situations, it provides support, housing, and counseling. (Community Representative)

Survey participants across stakeholder groups asserted a defined need for programs that provided physical and emotional sanctuary. Service participants noted the staff's commitment to assisting women in crisis and they appreciated the staff's compassion. Participants felt that staff provided services in a considerate, humane, and thoughtful manner. Women who sought services often perceived themselves to be vulnerable, physically, socially, and emotionally; therefore, staff accessibility is crucial to the provision of a safe and predictable environment. Consistent with the observations made by Wood and Middleman (1992) regarding the role, value, and function of self-help groups, women identify that the services provide a sense of personal strength by enabling them to associate with others who share their experiences, feelings, and struggles:

A strength of the program is the women themselves; [there is] a sense of someone knowing what is happening in your life, 'instant acceptance,' being a part of the experience [as] both facilitators and members. (Service Participant)

The main strength is that they help you to get well, not like a ladies quilting party; here we are dealing with very real problems. (Service Participant)

The individual treatment because sometimes you do not want to say some things in a group; the group because it helps you know that you are not alone, that others have and have had similar experiences and feelings. (Service Participant)

WAP's services are designed to address the individual needs of service participants. WAP's service components encompass a variety of supports:

They provide food if you do not have the resources right away; you can get donated clothes for you and your children. (Service Participant)

There are unique activities for women who are drug addicted, support groups for men who are survivors of childhood sexual abuse, and groups for teens, such as the date rape group. (Community Representative)

Recognizing that battering and rape occur across social, economic, racial, and ethnic lines, and across political affiliation, residence, and employment location, the WAP offers services in a variety of locations, both within the city of Richmond and surrounding counties. Although the WAP does not collect data on the economic status of the women who seek domestic violence services, some stakeholders suggested that poor women, including a disproportionate number of racial and/or ethnic minorities, seek services through shelters while middle- and upper-class women have access to alternative housing. This experience is consistent with observations made by Matthews (1994) in her work on the anti-rape movement and in Murray's (1988) study of a battered women's shelter. In the current study, one Service Participant noted that in the WAP's domestic violence services:

There is a lack of women from different walks of life and different experiences in many of the programs.

Another Service Participant noted that:

A lot of people think that it [domestic violence and sexual assault] occurs in lower socio-economic status black communities. When it happens in middle- and upper-class white communities, it is hidden; it is embarrassing. People do not want anyone to find out, so they cover it up.

While there is a stated connection in the mission statements of the YWCA and the WAP among the issues of violence, sexism, classism, and racism, the YWCA needs to more vigorously address these connections. Establishing connections between anti-racism and anti-violence provides the YWCA and the WAP with rare opportunities and challenges. The inequalities of segregation, and discrimination of race (Hagan, 1994) are often parallel to the experiences of women. The experience of unequal access to economic benefits and the disproportionate exposure to violence that racial and ethnic minorities (Hagan, 1994) and women experience, are also similar. Given the anti-violence advocacy and service orientation of the YWCA and the WAP, they are reasonable candidates to encourage discussion of the connection between the violent crime and low-income women and minority communities experience.

The difficulties of providing services in non-urban as well as urban/suburban areas (Tice, 1990), and the multiple kinds of assistance that battered women often need (Arnold, 1995) affect the service delivery of the WAP as a whole. The variety of referral options, lack of transportation access, potential lack of anonymity, and organizational politics related to feminist activism all complicate the provision of domestic violence and rape crisis services (Arnold, 1995; Tice, 1990). The existence of these complicating factors has forced the WAP to develop creative solutions and responses, which in turn has led to the YWCA being recognized as experienced in tackling challenging issues. Although the WAP has won public acceptance of its mission and is recognized as a vital part of the Richmond area community, the capacity of any alternative service organization to remain viable is, in part, dependent upon its connections to similar organizations. Agencies must maximize use of community resources to meet the wide range of needs of the women and children served. To this end, collaboration is key. For example, rather than expend the resources needed to acquire expertise to serve children with emotional problems in the shelter programs, the WAP could establish collaborative agreements with public and private service providers. The WAP would do well to establish a network of support services with other alternative service organizations within the greater Richmond area. Examples of these alternative service organizations are the Fan Free Clinic, the Friends Association For Childcare, and health services that are identified as women's services. Use of community resources to address ancillary service needs, which would subsequently permit a more directed focus on domestic violence and rape crisis services, would lessen the potential for internal conflict over goals, ideologies, and tactics. It is critical that the WAP attend to the ideology(ies) of the organizations with which it develops even loose alliances. The key to WAP's success in maintaining its autonomy and program direction will be its recognition of the consequences of collaboration as well as any perceived benefits (e.g., funding and ancillary services).

The strengths of the WAP indicate that it is possible to respond to a changing internal and external social, political, and economic climate without forsaking the essential ideology, practice, and administrative perspective of a feminist-oriented, alternative women's services program. This is not to suggest that fundamental

dilemmas and risks are not present in any collaboration with the public or other nonfeminist community agencies. In order to successfully form such collaborations, the WAP must maintain its autonomy (Matthews, 1995), and vision of the work to be done and methods for doing it. As Matthews (1995) has noted, among these tactical choices are "overt opposition, apparent accommodation, and active engagement" (p. 296). WAP's choices should be influenced by its origination as a grass roots liberal/cultural feminist organization and the support that emerges from its relationship to its host agency, the YWCA of Richmond (Hyde, 1992; 1995).

The program as a whole has gone through overturns, strife, and inner conflict, but still as a whole the Women's Advocacy Program has been able to survive and get things accomplished. (Program Representative)

Given the social, political, and economic changes that are forecast nationally as well as within the state, vigilance is essential for the WAP's survival. The greatest threat to the WAP may well be the emergence of the conservative New Right (Hyde, 1995), not the internal struggles that accompany organizational transformation and adaptation (Arnold, 1995; Mueller, 1995).

### Challenges and Recommendations

*Defining Services.* The fact that the mission of the YWCA is broader than provision of shelter services diverts the attention of the conventional host organization away from domestic violence and sexual assault services. The mission of the YWCA includes a focus on "the elimination of racism wherever it exists and by any means necessary" (YWCA of Richmond, 1994b, Section IV, p. 1). However, it was suggested by one Program Representative that:

Being a part of an established national organization puts limits on what we do.

In the current case study, while efforts of working toward the elimination of racism and the provision of domestic violence and rape crisis services may be quite compatible, they are not synonymous; and while the theories that support such activities may be complementary, the agenda and strategies may be quite different (Please see: Adam, 1989; Davis, 1994; Nes and Iadicola, 1989; Omi and Winant, 1994; Takaki, 1993; West, 1993).

*Availability of Resources.* Many programs have limited financial, staff, and space resources to support domestic violence and rape crisis services (Davis and Hagen, 1988; Rodriguez, 1988; Tice, 1990). One WAP Program Representative noted that:

There is a problem of a lack of match between resources and expectations.

Domestic violence and rape crisis programs must carefully identity what services they can provide with available resources so as to not overextend or dilute service quality. The needs of the women and children who seek services may include economic support, alcohol and other drug use services, medical care, mental health services, day care, and immediate maternal needs.

*Staff Turnover.* WAP experiences a high level of staff turnover, even for a social service agency. On the YWCA's Management Team, between August 1992 and August 1993, one employee out of the seven left the program. Within the WAP staff, ten out of 15, or 67.0%, of the employees left. There was a slight reduction in turnover rate (40.0%) with the WAP staff between August 1993 and August 1994, but the rate is still of concern (C. Pond, personal com-

munication, August, 1995). There are a number of reasons for this: low pay due to budget constraints (Rodriguez, 1988), staff experience of secondary trauma and fear (Stout and Thomas, 1991), tensions associated with balancing collectivism and bureaucratization (Inglehart and Beccerra, 1995; Srinivasan and Davis, 1991), and the shift toward professionalization of service delivery (Tice, 1990). As Program Representatives explain:

Women's Advocacy Program staff are expected to do big things, serve a high volume of clients. Despite having the largest number of staff [within the YWCA], the Women's Advocacy Program staff are not being given adequate resources; for example, staff training, cost reimbursement for expenses, availability of time off.

Quick turnover has put limitations on what we have been able to accomplish.

The nature of what we do and the type of populations that we serve create stresses.

A high rate of staff turnover at the direct care level interrupts the continuity of service delivery. In addition, it means the WAP must devote much of its time, energy, and attention toward hiring and re-training rather than enhancing services and service delivery.

*Training.* Some women served through the WAP have other needs such as alcohol and or other drug abuse, mental health conditions, and untreated medical problems. Others may need educational and vocational services. While their children may not have been physically abused or battered, they have likely experienced other challenges such as withdrawal from school due to frequent moves, periods of dramatic insecurity, or a lack of consistent empathic attention. All of these factors contribute to problems in social relationships. To provide responsive services to this wide range of needs, the WAP must make a commitment to "ongoing in-service training and support" for staff (Weil, 1988, p. 80). For professionals who are trained in educational settings that often reflect conservative approaches to administration and practice, this may mean unlearning as well as learning (Perlmutter, 1988):

We need to have sufficient staff that are qualified to assume their position. I am not talking about degrees or certificates, but rather a person that can relate to or has gone through some of the things that I have gone through. (Service Participant)

The direct practitioner, whether professional or volunteer, requires information regarding approaches to assessment and/or intervention techniques, as well as in-service training to examine the assumptions implicit in their practice (Nes and Iadicola, 1989) and evaluate the social arrangements of the community (Wood and Middleman, 1992). This information may help administrators and direct service providers determine how best to maintain a commitment to social change and provide women-centered services within an alternative service program (Hyde, 1992).

*Communication.* In the effort to define the "potential complementarity" of bureaucratic and collectivist structures (Tice, 1990, p. 88), the lines and patterns of horizontal communication are at risk of becoming unclear. This is apparent at the WAP, where information is not consistently communicated among administration, supervisors, and direct staff.

In an emergency situation when I needed to see my therapist, [and she was not in her office] there was a lack of information in the reception area about availability of the therapist or how to access the therapist during an emergency. (Service Participant)

We need openness and sharing of information so that everyone in the WAP, administration-level individuals from the YWCA, other advocacy groups, and other social service groups communicate. (Program Representative)

Programs within the WAP organization do not always share information with each other. For example, shelter residents are not aware of the full range of group and individual counseling services available. Additionally, when critical incidents occur within shelters, they are not consistently or regularly reported to either the Executive or Associate Directors.

*Service Issues.* Domestic violence and rape crisis services are highly specialized. A practice perspective supports complete evaluation of the full range of individual needs of women and children, including medical and psychological issues. It appreciates that women may react idiosyncratically to their individual problems (Gottlieb, 1992). Service providers should always anticipate that some service participants' needs will exceed the capabilities of the organization.

Being a part of an established national organization puts limits on what we do . . . There needs to be more effort to interface with other agencies to better access what women need . . . We need to ask how the public views programming; are we maximizing use of facilities; are we cross-utilizing facilities and information resources; are we putting staff in 'their' best positions; are we providing adequate services? (Program Representative)

Consider the provision of educational and mental health services to children. In this study, the downtown site children's services are strong, but are less available at the two shelter sites. A practical and cost-effective response to this situation would be to contract, or develop cooperative agreements with other community services, to address these needs. Lack of adequate transportation, common to many non-urban and rural settings, is another challenge the WAP faces (Tice, 1990). Solutions to such circumstances may require development of formal agreements with transportation or social service agencies; these agreements must appreciate the ideological and philosophical perspective of feminist practices and alternative service administrative structures.

Once a woman and her children have received shelter services for an established period of time (for example 30 days at the WAP), there may be no transitional housing services to move to, due to limited funding. Shelter service programs can help ease this transition by formally linking these women with non-shelter service programs. Agencies must establish a formal procedure to follow up with women who have received domestic violence and rape crisis services in order to: (a) help better assure the safety of former service participants; (b) maintain outreach to women as their needs change; and (c) monitor the effectiveness of the services received. Shelter agencies should also seek working agreements among specific community programs to provide "case management" and domestic violence or rape crisis services. Such agreements can help women as their needs evolve over time.

## IMPLICATIONS

Creating an alternative program specifically for women within the structure of a larger, more conventional organization allows that program to extend the dialogue of the "political analysis of personal problems and empowerment of women" (Gottlieb, 1992, p. 302) to the larger organization (Weil, 1988). However, it is critical for the integrity of both the alternative program and the larger organization to identify

areas of ideological and service overlap as well as boundaries. This allows focus on a feminist perspective of empowerment and advocacy, and supports the efficacy and effectiveness of domestic violence and rape crisis services (Wood and Middleman, 1992; Srinivasan and Davis, 1991).

Taking a democratic-collectivist (Rothschild-Whitt, 1979) approach to determining which services fall within the purview of the domestic violence and rape crisis program requires ongoing internal dialogue and consensual decision-making. Staff, administration, Board of Directors, and service participants should together examine the relevancy of the mission statement(s) of the program(s) to create a statement, whether extant or new, that accurately reflects the program's intent and focus. Careful definition of what services can and should be provided allows focused hiring, training, and support of staff while also increasing the quality of the services provided. This dialogue will help maintain the "commitment to a social change-critique model" (Tice, 1990, p. 86) that supports feminist practice and alternative service organizational structures.

While attending to supportive features of collectivist structure (e.g., ad hoc decision-making, consensus building, a decreased reliance on strict rules) (Rothschild-Whitt, 1979; Srinivasan and Davis, 1991), it is critical to attend to the potential for miscommunication, excessive individual discretion, and lack of service consistency. While agencies must avoid development of negative bureaucratic and hierarchical structures that interfere with responsivity and creativity (Gottlieb, 1992), they may benefit from formal procedures that create a consistent and accurate communication network between administration and staff, and among all of its programs. This would address the problems that occur when staff in one department do not have the same information as staff in another department. A formal communication network, when consistently used in alternative service organizations, would help staff feel as if they are a part of the decisions being made and in turn enhance collectivity (Rothschild-Whitt, 1979).

As the service needs of women and children change, and as service providers develop increasingly sophisticated service delivery to survivors of violence, trauma, and aggression, a program must examine its service practices. It is critical that

the problem of women battering is seen to be rooted in the power differential between men and women in this society. It follows that the battered woman's plight is not viewed as a function of her pathology. Rather, it is seen to be largely the result of this gender-based inequality, and all women are at risk. . . . [Further, we must avoid] victim blaming and psychological diagnoses, such as dependence, codependence, low self-esteem, and learned helplessness—a view that leads social workers to try to change the women instead of the situations in which the women are trapped. (Wood and Middleman, 1992, p. 86)

**CONCLUSIONS**

The examination of what services are to be provided, by whom, and where requires consideration of the ideology, philosophy, and theory of feminist practice. A fundamental struggle for the alternative programs is to avoid the practices, "patriarchal structures" (Srinivasan and Davis, 1991, p. 38), and "coercive tactics" (Wood and Middleman, 1992, p. 82) that oppress women. If alternative service organizations are to avoid such regressive practices, they must incorporate inclusion, reflective self-examination, critique, and program evaluation into their ongoing operation. During the early period of the establishment of domestic violence and sexual assault services, organizations

structured from a bureaucratic framework were considered counter-democratic and repressive. As evidenced by the current case study, bureaucracy practiced from an alternative service organizational framework may encourage and ensure creativity, program critique, and evolution, and support a reaffirmation of the founding program ideology. The transformation from mobilization to program maintenance can be formulated around feminist practices that are supportive of women who are, or have been, survivors of domestic violence and sexual assault.

The emergence of complementary collectivist and bureaucratic structures also appears to be essential as alternative service organizations are required to compete with mainstream organizations for public financial support and private foundation grants. As such, the viability of women's services such as shelters may need to be able to provide services and care in environments that are evaluated by mainstream social service and health departments, For such services to respond to the demands of external funding sources and regulatory agents, their administration and staff must engage in collective problemsolving.

It is also quite clear that it is possible to create and maintain an alternative service organization with a feminist focus within a larger, more conventional organization. Essential to this process is retention of a clear alternative service vision. This ability demands skill and strength among administrators and staff alike. Administrators must hold a clear appreciation and commitment to alternative services within a work environment where collective political action, empowerment, and self-determination are considered essential. Staff must be willing to engage in self-critique and evaluate the beliefs, values, and assumptions that guide their work. Only through a shared vision can agencies develop and maintain emancipatory and self-determined services that address the needs of women and support social change.

## NOTES

1. Feminist administration and feminist organizations do not exist as singular dimensions. Martin (1990) has identified 10 dimensions that provide a framework for "comparing feminist and nonfeminist organizations or for deriving types of feminist organizations and analyzing them" (p. 182). Ferree and Martin (1995a) both discuss and provide discussions of the need to examine contemporary feminist organizations along dimensions that include examination of the mix of both collectivist and bureaucratic "structures, practices, and goals as they work to survive and to transform society" (p. 6). Hyde (1992) provides an insightful articulation of the functioning of a social movement organization within a human service (host) agency. Further feminist service movement organizations should be analyzed in terms of ideology and environmental relations that appreciates that "little common ground exists between feminism and the New Right" (Hyde, 1995, p, 307), and that "many right wing groups are women serving women" (Hyde, personal correspondence).

2. The author recognizes that a definition of feminist practice is quite broad and as discussed by Nes and Iadicola (1989) incorporates several models that include but are not limited to liberal, radical, and socialist models. As noted by Nes and Iadicola, what these models do hold in common is a focus on the need to examine human nature in terms of sex roles, evaluate the social order, discuss sex-based issues of inequality and the factors that maintain and support that inequality, evaluate social structures, consider the political aspects of personal experiences, identify strategies of social and structural change, and consider strategies for sex-role changes (please see Gottlieb, 1992 and Wood and Middleman, 1992).

3. To better insure confidentiality of Board members and members of the YWCA staff, they are referred to as "Program Representatives." Representatives of funding sources and referral sources are referred to as "Community Representatives." Current and former service participants are referred to as "Service Participants."

## REFERENCES

Adam, B. (1989). Feminist social theory needs time. Reflections on the relation between feminist thought, social theory and time as an important parameter in social analysis. *The Sociological Review, 37,* 458–473.

Arnold, G. (1995). Dilemmas of feminist coalitions: Collective identity and strategic effectiveness in the battered women's movement. In M. M. Ferree & P. Y. Martin (Eds.), *Feminist organizations: Harvest of the new women's movement* (pp. 276–290). Philadelphia: Temple University Press.

Davis, L. V. (1994). *Building on women's strengths: A social work agenda for the twenty-first century.* Binghamton, NY: The Haworth Press, Inc.

Davis, L. V., & Hagen J. L. (1988). Services for battered women: The public policy response. *Social Service Review, 62,* 649–667.

Ferree, M. M., & Martin, P. Y. (1995a). Doing the work of the movement: Feminist Organizations. In M. M. Ferree & P. Y. Martin (Eds.), *Feminist organizations: Harvest of the new women's movement. (pp. 3–2).* Philadelphia: Temple University Press.

Ferree, M. M., & Martin, P. Y. (Eds.). (1995b). *Feminist organizations: Harvest of the new women's movement.* Philadelphia: Temple University Press.

Fried, A. (1994). "It's hard to change what we want to change": Rape crisis centers as organizations. *Gender and Society, 8,* 562–583.

Gottlieb, N. (1992). Empowerment, political analyses, and services for women. In Y. Hasenfeld (Ed.), *Human services as complex organizations* (pp. 301–319). Newbury Park, CA: Sage.

Greene, J. C. (1994). Qualitative program evaluation: Practice and promise. In N. D. Denzin & Y. S. Lincoln (Eds.), *Handbook of qualitative research* (pp. 530–544). Thousand Oaks, CA: Sage.

Hagan, J. (1994). *Crime and disrepute.* Thousand Oaks, CA: Pine Forge Press.

Hyde, C. (1995). Feminist social movement organizations survive the new right. In M. M. Ferree & P. Y. Martin (Eds.), *Feminist organizations: Harvest of the new women's movement* (pp. 306–322). Philadelphia: Temple University Press.

Hyde, C. (1992). The ideational system of social movement agencies: An examination of feminist health centers. In Y. Hasenfeld (Ed.), *Human services as complex organizations* (pp. 121–144). Newbury Park, CA: Sage.

Inglehart, A. P., & Becerra, R. M. (1995). *Social services and the ethnic community*. Boston: Allyn and Bacon.

Martin, D. (1981). *Battered wives*. (Rev. ed., updated). San Francisco: Volcano Press.

Martin, P. Y. (1990). Rethinking feminist organizations. *Gender and Society, 4*, 182–206.

Matthews, N. (1995). Feminist clashes with the state: Tactical choices by state-funded rape crisis centers. In M. M. Ferree & P. Y. Martin (Eds.), *Feminist organizations: Harvest of the new women's movement* (pp. 291–305). Philadelphia: Temple University Press.

Matthews, N. A. (1994). *Confronting rape: The feminist anti-rape movement and the state*. London: Routledge.

Morris, A. D., & Mueller, C. M. (Eds.). (1992). *Frontiers in social movement theory*. New Haven: Yale University.

Mueller, C. (1995). The organizational basis of conflict in contemporary feminism. In M. M. Ferree & P. Y. Martin (Eds.), *Feminist organizations: Harvest of the new women's movement*. (pp. 263–275). Philadelphia: Temple University Press.

Murray, S. B. (1988). The unhappy marriage of theory and practice: An analysis of a battered women's shelter. *NWSA Journal, 1*, 75–92.

Nes, J. A., & Iadicola, P. (1989). Toward a definition of feminist social work: A comparison of liberal, radical, and socialist models. *Social Work, 34*, 12–21.

Omi, M., & Winant, H. (1994). *Racial formation in the United States: From the 1960s to the 1990s* (2nd ed.). New York: Routledge.

Perlmutter, F. D. (1988). Administering alternative social agencies: Educational Implications. *Administration in Social Work, 12*(2), 109–118.

Rodriguez, N. M. (1988). Transcending bureaucracy: Feminist politics at a shelter for battered women. *Gender and Society, 2*, 214–227.

Rodwell, M. K, & Woody III, D. (1994). Constructivist evaluation: The policy/practice context. In E. Sherman & W. J. Reid (Eds.), *Qualitative research in social work* (pp. 315–327). New York: Columbia University.

Rothschild-Whitt, J. (1979). The collectivist organization: An alternative to rational-bureaucratic models. *American Sociological Review, 44*, 509–527.

Schwartz, A. Y., Gottesman, E. W., & Perlmutter, F. D. (1988). Blackwell: A case study in feminist administration. *Administration in Social Work, 12*(2), 5–15.

Srinivasan, M., & Davis, L. V. (1991). A shelter: An organization like any other? *Affilia, 6*(1), 38–57.

Stout, K. D., & Thomas, S. (1991). Fear and dangerousness in shelter work with battered women. *Affilia, 6*(2), 74–86.

Takaki, R. (1993). *A different mirror: A history of multicultural America*. Boston: Little, Brown.

Tice, K. W. (1990). A case study of battered women's shelters in Appalachia. *Affilia 5*(3), 83–100.

Weil, M. (1988). Creating an alternative work culture in a public service setting. *Administration in Social Work, 12*(2), 69–82.

West, C. (1993). *Race matters*. Boston: Beacon.

Wilkerson, A. E. (1988). Epilogue. *Administration in Social Work, 12*(2), 119–128.

Wood, G. G., & Middleman, R. R. (1992). Groups to empower battered women. *Affilia, 7*(4), 82–95.

YWCA of Richmond. (n.d.a). *A history of WAP's domestic violence program*. Richmond, VA: Author.

YWCA of Richmond. (1994a). *Annual report*. Richmond, VA: Author.

YWCA of Richmond. (1994b). *Board manual*. Richmond, VA: Author.

YWCA of Richmond. (n.d.b). *Mission statement of the Women's Advocacy Program*. Richmond, VA: Author.

YWCA of Richmond. (n.d.c). *The history of the Rape Crisis Outreach Program*. Richmond, VA: Author.

**38.**

**Frances Westley**

## GOVERNING DESIGN: THE MANAGEMENT OF SOCIAL SYSTEMS AND ECOSYSTEMS MANAGEMENT

*What had that flower to do with being white,*
*The wayside blue and innocent heal-all?*
*What brought the kindred spider to that height,*
*Then steered the white moth thither in the night?*
*What but design of darkness to appall?*
*If design govern in a thing so small*
　　　　　　　　　　　　—Robert Frost
　　　　　　　　　　　　from "Design"

The preceding lines were penned by the poet Robert Frost, surely the greatest spokesman in the artistic world for the strange and haunting similarities between the processes of nature and the symbolic constructions of man. These lines were inspired by the discovery by the poet, in an early morning walk, of a white spider poised on a white albino flower, holding up the wings of a dead, white moth—elements in nature of death and life, camouflage and discovery. For Frost the whiteness also symbolized good against evil, light against dark. And so, in a typical Frostian twist, he sees "design," an order that joins man and nature, defying the forces of disorder and darkness and then almost self-mockingly questions his own perception: Does design operate in things so small?

This rich book of essays is about this question in its most profound sense. Is there a design that cuts across the workings of nature and the workings of humans? Can we grasp its outlines through the careful obser-

vation of detail? Can we learn wisdom from the patterns of change and stability that we observe over time in the intertwining of ecological and social systems? In his conception of "creative destruction" Holling (chapter 1) proposes a model that he argues convincingly is a powerful explanation of processes observed across a variety of ecosystems; the material in these cases pertaining to human system suggests similar forces may be at work there. In employing this model and gathering together these case studies, this book is exemplary in its ambition to marry macrolevel theory to a level of detail, as rich as that which Frost observed. But unlike Frost, this book not only contemplates the possibility of design, but seeks to offer a ground for practical action, a stimulus for pro-active change on the part of scientists and managers responsible for the future of fragile ecosystems.

As a social scientist and researcher in the area of management of contemporary organizations, I come to this ambitious project from the opposite direction of most of the case writers. However, my aim is the same, to contribute to helping to build the bridge between the biological and social sciences in an effort to understand and perhaps better

From *Barriers and Bridges to the Renewal of Ecosystems and Institutions,* Gunderson, L. H., Holling, C. S., and Light, S. L. (Eds.). New York: Columbia University Press, 1995.

manage this interface. More specifically, I will set out in this chapter to address three themes raised across these cases, the theme of the relation between research, policy, and effective action; the theme of collaboration/consensus building; and the theme of system change and learning. My objective is to explore each of these issues from the point of view of current theory and practice in management.

Management itself is a discipline born from the coming together of old knowledge, from diverse sources, into new perspectives. It is related to and fuelled by many of the disciplines in the social sciences, but it differs from the social sciences in its overarching drive toward practice and its concern with technical knowledge in the widest sense of that word (technology as a set of knowledge and beliefs on causal relations; a logic that is complete when the system is closed [Thompson 1967]). Hence it is a discipline that, at its best, offers practical guidance as well as theoretical reflection about the challenges raised in these cases.

This chapter will begin with an exploration of the nature of planning, the ways in which conventional planning can be an impediment to organizational responsiveness, and the means researchers and practitioners have evolved to circumvent these difficulties. In particular, in this section I will deal with the following subpoints: (1) the role of planning as an intervening variable between knowledge and action, (2) under what circumstances planning is receptive to scientific knowledge, (3) why action is so seldom an outcome of planning, (4) how vision acts as an action generator, and (5) how learning may be an effective bridge between knowledge and action.

Second, I will look at the literature in management on interorganizational collaboration and networks. As all the cases in this volume have underlined the importance of consensus building and collaboration in solving problems, it is useful to reflect on what social scientists have learned about which kind of dynamics result in successful collaborations, how interorganizational networks originate and what are the effects of these different origins, and what are the limits of consensus building and collaboration (e.g., the point at which networks of human organizations, like populations of other organisms, become overconnnected and hence vulnerable).

In the third and last section, I will look at the recent literature on managing organizational change, as it pertains to organizational revitalization. If organizations and social systems go through the same cycles of creative destruction that Holling and his associates have discovered in ecosystems, is there any way to short-circuit the process, to avoid or at least shorten the periods when the system is rigid and unresponsive, maximize the periods in which the system is tuned to its environment and responding creatively? As Holling (this volume) has pointed out in his essay, the ideal may be the social equivalent of the endotherm: some exchange of loss of internal variability (as long as it is associated with specific kinds of regulation), for heightened ability to explore, sense, and respond to a variety of external environments. How would these principles translate into management of change?

We shall therefore begin this chapter with a description of how responsive action is created in individual organizations, continue with how collaborations emerge, and conclude with a discussion of how a continual change in organizations as well as ecosystems can be managed. In other words, does the field of management offer any clues as to whether creative destruction of social systems as well as ecosystems can be managed, and if so, how?

## STRATEGIES FOR RESPONSIVE ACTION: MANAGING SMALL DETAILS

One of the rewarding aspects of reading the cases and essays in this book is that they are integrated around several simple, elegant models or images. The first of course is the four-box model of creative destruction that offers an integrated explanation of the dynamics of social and ecological systems. The other is a model of adaptive management and the image of organization/environment relationships implied by that model. As I read it, adaptive management is a way of managing in order to ensure that the organizations responsible for ecosystems are responsive to the variations, rhythms, and cycles of change natural in that system and are able to react quickly with appropriate management techniques. The image suggests that certain guidelines, based on a scientific understanding of that ecosystem and a related definition of ecosystem health, act as umbrella principles to integrate action.

It is a compelling image, with an appeal that transcends the management of ecosystems. In the past decade—in response to radical shifts in world economics, resource bases, population dynamics, and competitive structures—private- and public-sector organizations in all domains have wrestled with similar challenges. The field of studies in strategic management has struggled with the problem of how to position an organization, in an ever-changing environment, to ensure system health and survival. As in many of the government organizations described in the cases, the dominant focus for many years has been on control. The organization has been viewed as "a lone gunman in the wild west . . . at war with its environment. Its tools were analysis and planning . . . careful evaluation of the opportunities and threats, strengths and weaknesses . . . In an attempt to forecast the future, master and tame the environment, and use it for organizational ends" (Astley 1984). The process was viewed as deliberate: "most strategists (strategic management researchers) adhere strongly to a belief in systematic, denable strategy procedures and structures that can be measured, analyzed and compared" (Daft and Buenger 1990). The effective organization was viewed as a machine; strategic planning was the engine that ran it, rational, mechanical, analytic, and programmatic (Bowman 1990).

Recently, however, there is evidence that this paradigm is eroding in favor of an image of organizations that are much more "embedded" in their environments (Granovettor 1985) and strategy as a more natural, emergent process, the end result of the creation of meaning within the system and of ongoing learning linked to these meanings.

This fundamental shift in paradigm has been led as much by experience of practitioners as by theory in management science. North American companies have become disenchanted with strategic planning in recent years because of the low success rate in implementing them (a review of implementation rates of major corporations, conducted by the leading business publication in the United States in the late 1980s, suggested that only about 3% of strategic plans were actually implemented), and the relatively poor showing of North American companies in a variety of industries, when compared with their counterparts in Europe and Japan (who had never practiced strategic planning with the same fervor) (Hayes, 1985). Disillusioned, American corporations have abandoned their "love affair with corporate grand strategy" (Pascale 1987).

The implications of this paradigm shift are far-reaching for both theory and practice in management. The shift of focus from control to responsiveness has meant a reevaluation of the function of planning and a search for alternate processes better at generating learning and meaning (all considered key criteria of responsive action). In this section, therefore, I will begin by exploring in greater depth the problems with planning in relation to responsive action. I will continue by examining processes that (1) contribute to the generation of meaning and (2) contribute to the generation of learning. I will conclude with some thoughts of the practical applications of these processes.

### Planning as Intervening Variable: The Knowledge/Planning/Action Connection

When one thinks of adaptive management, one thinks of responsive action, action that is triggered by change in the environment. The smaller or more subtle the trigger, the more "responsive" the action. But the link between stimulus and response at the level of the organization is less direct than that in single organisms (and it is far from direct even there). For in organizations, numerous actors must be coordinated to interpret the stimuli and to integrate their response. Enter the need for planning.

Modern theorists in social science argue that for conditions for social action to be optimal, three aspects of social structure must reinforce each other (Giddens 1984; Collins 1981). These three are "structures of signification" (the interpretive schemas that give meaning to our activities, sometimes identified as the myths, paradigms, mind-sets, or ideologies that: "frame" our activities), "structures of legitimation" (the rules and norms that organize our activity, and that govern the routines that make up our daily life) and "structures of domination" (the allocation of resources and decision-making

power that governs our ability to take effective action).

Planning, in all its forms, is a structure of signification, functioning primarily as a means of organizational sense-making. Ideally, the planning process reduces equivocality of information so that choice is possible. Planning is not in itself a paradigm. But as a technology for sense-making and choice generation, its form is fundamentally determined by the myths or paradigms that dominate a given organization, determining the perceptions of the environment and of the organization's role in that environment. So planning acts as an intervening variable between knowledge and action in large, complex systems. But under which circumstances is it a barrier and under which is it a bridge?

*When Is Planning Receptive to Scientific Knowledge?* One of the issues raised in these cases is under what circumstances is policy-making receptive to knowledge generated in scientific studies. Integrating such knowledge into the planning process is only the first step in creating responsive action, but it is an important one. The answer, from both the literature on planning and that on evidence in these cases, is that utilization depends on (1) the *form* of the scientific knowledge and (2) the strength and dominance of the organization paradigm informing the planning process.

Formal planning processes, as we have noted earlier, are based on myths of the relationship between organization and environment as one of "instrumental rationality." Such exercises are highly linear processes, involving a series of preformulated steps and systematic scanning processes. Scientific information can be useful, but only if it is packaged in such a way that it is easy to plug into such formulas. It cannot be ambiguous, excessively complex, or subject to multiple interpretations. It must fit with the "mental maps" (models of reality based on past experience, assumptions, industry recipes that inform the planning processes); otherwise the information will be filtered out as not being pertinent (Aguilar 1967; Spender 1989).

This may explain the fact (mentioned in the Great Lakes case in chapter 6) that when the government commissions specific studies, it is more likely to incorporate the findings in planning processes, as these are likely structured in ways that fit with those processes. Indeed, under such circumstances, the knowledge/planning link becomes so well established as to be well worn, almost routinized. Francis and Regier (chapter 6) point out that in the Great Lakes case "governments commissioned the IJC to organize increasingly convoluted, drawn-out studies (almost continuously over the last 25 years)." However, new theories of science, based on a view of natural systems as "emergent, evolutionary, and open" represent too great a challenge to the assumptions underlying formal planning processes to be easily entertained by these processes.

So formal planning processes are able to incorporate stimuli from the environment, in the form of scientific information, as long as that information does not challenge the paradigms upon which the planning processes are based. The stronger (strength = closed, focused, monolithic, and orthodox) that paradigm, the more unreceptive to stimuli the organization becomes. Studies of highly successful firms that create intensive focus and unified cultures indicate they do so at the expense of responsiveness. The singlemindedness that initially gives them an edge over competition and results in success, over time reduces internal diversity. Certain functions are cut, as they are not seen as core or central; disconfirming information is neither sought nor fully entertained. Deviants are expelled as extraneous, and successful routines are rigidly maintained (Miller 1992). The result is that the highly focused organization over time ceases to pick up stimuli signaling fundamental changes in the environment and gradually reduces internal diversity until it is insufficient to respond to new demands from the environment.

Fortunately for the link between knowledge and planning, the large bureaucracies, such as governments, most likely to engage in formal planning processes are also least likely to have strong and unified ideologies (Gouldner 1976). Unfortunately for responsive action, however, that same absence of strong, overt ideologies represents a positive barrier to action.

*The Failure of Planning to Produce Action.* Studies in strategy process have indicated that action is a fundamentally irrational process. Action is made up of two components, the motivation to act and the availability of resources to support action. The first, motivation, is grounded in emotion, as it is through emotion, not logic, that energy is mobilized (Hochschild 1983). Availability of resources depends on how physical and human resources (money, time, space, technology, authority) have been organized. Resources do not flow equally to all parts of an organization, but tend to lump in certain functional and hierarchical pockets, according to the ability of groups within the organization to claim and control the distribution of resources (Ransom, Hinings, and Greenwood 1980). The link between the two is the degree of authority of dominant paradigms or structures of signification.

Contemporary literature on organizations uses such terms as *organizational cultures* (Schein 1985), *ideologies* (Brunsson 1985), or *myths* (Jonsson and Lundin 1977) to refer to these interpretative schemas that provide a unified conceptual field and a shortcut to action. Common interpretative schemas "substitute for decisions. Many organizational actions arise without decision making, because the actors perceive situations similarly and share expectations and general values" (Brunsson 1982). When all organizational actors share the same paradigm and it is strong and overt, the problem of *what* to do (choice) is greatly diminished. For example, a university department with a strong emphasis on research and a belief that certain methodological approaches are superior to others in the execution of research will find considerably fewer candidates to choose between, and the choice will be simpler. The emphasis can therefore be in "creating expectations, motivations, and commitment"—energizing organizational actors to engage in activities that will secure the chosen candidate (Brunsson 1985). Such organizational contexts are often described as strong cultures and are excellent action generators (Miller 1992; Peters and Waterman 1982).

If, however, there is much dispute among department members as to what kind of colleague is best, then the ideology is "nonconclusive," and considerable effort has to be expended on making the choice. Formal planning procedures as rationalistic decision modes are good tools for choice. Planning, as noted earlier, is a linear, rational process. At its best it scrupulously avoids the irrationalities that make for strong commitments, the synthesis that motivates social action (Brunsson 1985). The logics of choice and action are fundamentally different.

This may explain why in the Great Lakes case scientific study seemed to be carried on *in lieu of action*. Although in this case inaction was probably beneficial, since action might have resulted in the kind of

engineering projects that caused problems in the Florida Everglades, the pattern of scientific study as alternative to action is similar to that which Jansson and Velner found in the Baltic Sea and Baskerville found in the forestry case. In such cases, the planning process has taken on a magical, tension-reducing function, much like witchcraft in traditional societies (Gimpl and Dakin 1984). It cycles repeatedly between information and choice; action is almost irrelevant.

Organizations that engage in formal planning processes and rely on these, implicitly or explicitly, split themselves into formulators (thinkers) and implementers (doers). However, they assume that their strategies in themselves will act as a motivator for the doers. This does not generally prove to be true; instead the recipients of the strategic plans, from middle management down, often find the plans bewildering, demotivating, and alienating (Westley 1990). Evidence suggests that formal planning processes are already devoid of the richness of information necessary to generate meaning. In addition, as plans filter down through hierarchical levels they lose more nuance and the process rarely allows for face-to-face communication complex enough to generate understanding at lower levels (Daft and Lengel 1984). Unless the poverty of understanding inherent in the planning process is compensated for by clear values and ideologies, middle managers are poorly motivated to act. Powerless and alienated, they are likely to engage either in increased political activity or in increasingly bureaucratic behavior (Izreali 1975).

*The Role of Vision in Generating Action.* In sharp contrast to the formal planning process described earlier is the kind of sense-making generated by visionary leaders. Whereas planning is a technology for institutionalizing vision, visionary leaders shape and reshape the myths themselves. These are sense-making processes akin to second-order learning.

Studies of visionary leaders indicates a strong facility with creating and manipulating emotionally evocative symbols (Weber 1922; Conger 1989; Westley 1991, 1992). Again, symbolic language is qualitatively different from the language of science and planning. It is colorful, emotional, heavily dependent on literary devices that build a bridge between the communicator and the audience (Burke 1950). It is inspired, however, by the material at hand: The followers "lead" the visionary as much as they are led by him/her (Westley and Mintzberg 1989). Visionary leaders throughout history are brilliant *bricoleurs*; they fabricate new and vital meanings out of the fragments available (Wallace 1961). In so doing, they overcome contradictions and create new synthesis. Myths are powerful devices for reconciling seemingly paradoxical elements in cultures, for making sense of the nonsensical (Levi-Strauss 1955; Leach 1964). In addition, visionary leaders rely heavily on face-to-face exchanges and on generating intensive communication exchanges within their organizations. They appeal directly to the middle and lower "action" levels of organizations alienated by planning processes (Mintzberg and Westley 1992; Vredenburg and Westley 1993). In visionary models of strategy the system remains flexible and responsive not because of a nested system of decision rules, but because of nested authority and meanings. Those closest to the action are empowered to act, and they do so in the interests of a common purpose and mission.

Visionary leaders play a key role in all the cases in this volume. Whether it is an Art Marshall in the Everglades or an Odén in Sweden, they have proved critical to the evolution of the social system and its relationship to the natural system. They have appeared at times of crisis, to forge new alliances between knowledge and action when the paradigms that forged old bridges had proved bankrupt as a platform for effective management of ecosystems. With time, though, these intense visionary perspectives must be routinized into less focused structures if the organization is to remain adaptive and responsive to stimuli from the environment.

In sum, then, responsiveness, if defined as the organization's ability to detect and understand changes in stimuli coming from the environment, is helped by nonconclusive ideologies and rational choice processes, such as planning. On the other hand, responsive action, defined as the organization's ability to translate the perception of changed stimuli into appropriate action, is inhibited by nonconclusive ideologies and rational-choice processes. Or put another way, strong ideologies, myths, and paradigms are important to action but potentially detrimental to interpreting and incorporating new information about the environment. It may be assumed (although we do not have enough detail to be sure) that some instances of the failure to use scientific information (Baskerville 1995, chapter 2) were due to the presence of strong ideologies and action tendencies in the government at the time. Conversely, the failure to act in the "Turning Green Lines into Red" era (Light, Gunderson, & Holling 1995, chapter 3), despite outcry from scientists and "landmark legislation," signifies the absence of a strong ideology (perhaps due to Bill Storch's death) and a tendency for the government to engage in rational choice processes as opposed to action.

This discontinuity between knowledge and action and the role played by structures of signification presents an important challenge for those wishing to make management of ecosystems truly adaptive. It is clear that for adaptive management to succeed, organizations must find sense-making processes that *simultaneously* open the organization to new stimuli and provide strong action generation.

*How Can Learning Be an Effective Bridge Between Knowledge and Action?* One of the reasons that dominant ideologies or paradigms are so resistant to change is that the dominance is taken for granted by organizational members. Normally, in most large organizations, a variety of different myths/paradigms and ideologies abound (Jonsson and Lundin 1977), each representing the viewpoint of different groups or "communities of practice" within the organization (Brown and Duguid 1991). When a single paradigm dominates an organization, this is generally because a powerful visionary or coalition has also dominated, controlling the flow of information and resources in a way that is unquestioned and unchallenged by others (Ransom, Hinings, and Greenwood 1980). Securing access to strategic conversations in order to influence interpretive schemas or to secure resources in order to fund divergent action is rarely even attempted (Westley 1990).

The organization so dominated does, as I have noted, become increasingly resistant to new sources of information, either that coming in from the environment or that coming from inside the organization. The result, as illustrated by examples, particularly from the Florida Everglades case, is management systems disconnected from the environment they seek to manage. Crisis is needed to shake such conclusive ideologies, and organizations in this state are prone either to crisis or to demise.

However, it is possible to design "changeful" organizations (as opposed to the "change-prone" organizations described earlier) (Brunsson 1985). Studies of highly adaptive systems suggest that the design need only provide mechanisms that facilitate the learning processes inherent in all human activity and that ensure the dissemination of that learning throughout the organization. Learning provides an alternative to crisis, as it introduces redundancies and inconsistencies into the structures of organizations that may serve to modify the conclusive nature of existing ideologies. Like planning processes, learning designs ensure greater receptivity to environmental stimuli. The same processes, happily, also seem to act as a functional equivalent of ideologies in generating action.

Learning and innovation as mental processes are "an almost instinctive propensity of the human organism, activated under the merest provocation of desire for a richer or more orderly experience" (Wallace 1961). The challenge is not, therefore, so much to structure organizations to learn as to structure them to take advantage of and incorporate the ongoing learning that is occurring, what is called the "tacit" knowledge of all organizations.

Several years ago Xerox vice-president John Seely Brown commissioned a qualitative study of how "learning" occurred at Xerox. An anthropologist was hired to follow around technicians as they made service calls and product development people as they worked on new products and product modifications. What the study revealed was that (1) formal routines and procedures were used not so much to guide action but to compare end states (i.e., as justification), (2) learning was socially constructed through exchange of stories ("war stories") based on improvisations in a problem-solving context, and (3) innovators let the world do some of the work (i.e., they took their solutions from those suggested/provided by the environment, not from analytic or abstract reasoning processes) (Brown and Duguid 1991).

What these findings suggest is that at the grass-roots or "local" level, individuals in organizations constantly respond to subtle changes in their environments and that these responses represent sources of innovation and learning. Second, they suggest that informal, face-to-face conversations are the best way to transmit learning. Finally, they suggest that the rules, procedures, and routines in most organizations act as barriers to learning unless they are treated as purely heuristic. The study concluded that much innovation directly contradicts the officially sanctioned formal operating procedures of organizations, as well as the rational decision rules. Learning, like action, is an irrational, highly social activity more connected to the construction of meaning (structures of signification) than to rules or authority (Weick 1991). If organizations, particularly large bureaucratic organizations, wish to increase responsiveness and adaptability, they must harness the instinctive learning of the front lines, as opposed to actively inhibiting it (Hamel and Prahalad 1989).

Practically, implementing the preceding conclusions involves providing opportunity for face-to-face exchanges horizontally, between functions. Such horizontal, cross-functional contacts provide synergy—integration without loss of individuality. Unlike conclusive ideologies that act as "restricted codes" to limit what data are made available for interpretation, cross-functional discussions provide a forum for "elaborate codes"-discourse linked to problem solving (Bernstein, 1971). Such exchanges put learnings generated at the functional and technical level into the context of the whole organization, a context in which strategic implications are clearly rec-

ognizable (Collins 1981; Westley 1990). Such exchanges have been correlated with organizations capable of ongoing innovative action in response to their environments (Kanter 1983; Quinn 1985; Mintzberg and McHugh 1985).

Second, implementing learning systems involves structuring a vertical flow of strategic information. In an interesting study of Honda's entry into the North American motorcycle market, Pascale (1984) showed that the insight that led to the introduction of the small motorbikes that revolutionized the motor cycle industry came without any planning at all. Honda had *planned* to introduce its large machines and had sent over two salesmen to North America to set up distribution channels. After months of discouragement and on the brink of abandoning the project, one of the salesmen observed that many people had been stopping him on the street to inquire about where he got the small motorcycle he was riding (which he had brought for his own transportation). The salesmen thought that because of this expressed interest, there might be a market for the small motorbikes. On the strength of that hunch the top management of Honda decided to radically switch their "strategy" of entering the North American market. Small motorbikes were a huge success, and the motorcycle market was revolutionized.

What is useful here for the management of ecosystems is the recognition not only that the strategic innovation emerged from the lower levels of the organization (where stimulus response times are generally and necessarily shorter than those at higher levels of the organization), but that the strategic apex was so responsive to the hunches of two people close to the market but far from the top of the organization. In terms of ecosystem management, the equivalent might be the readiness of policy makers to be responsive to the input and recommendations of practitioners in the field (such is field biologists and wildlife managers) as well as to those of scientists and policy specialists.

The ability to integrate the highest and lowest levels of the organization is critical in a political system where, as is pointed out in numerous cases, the policy level is often very removed physically, conceptually, and technically from those individuals at lower levels in the system who are in touch in an immediate, day-to-day way with the environment and are hence in a position to detect changes most easily in that environment. Unfortunately, such managers are often low in status in the overall system and are disregarded as poorly trained "scientifically." Similarly, in the North American corporation there has been a tendency to ignore "intelligence" collected by those in the front lines (Albaum 1964) not only because strategy is viewed as the purview of the strategic apex but because reliance on statistical analysis of market surveys, for example, is seen as more valuable intelligence than the "hunches" or insights of those on the front lines. Many middle- and lower-level managers are deliberately excluded from the rich, face-to-face discussions that forge the backdrop, the meanings, and the frames for policy decisions. Participation in such activity is emblematic of elite status. Instead they are presented with formal policies, sets of statistics and planning documents stripped of the context and divorced from the stimuli that occasioned them (Westley 1990).

So why was top management at Honda prepared to listen and to entertain the hunches of their salesmen? Pascale indicates two important structuring devices that the company uses to make the communication flow from the bottom up as smooth and effective in terms of action as that flowing from the top down. The first is the fact that Honda does not isolate top managers from other levels of the organization. Top managers are not even assigned offices. Instead they are given desks in the corner of workstations. Their time is seen as valuably involved in staying in touch with the ongoing activities of their workers. Second, there is a careful effort to create a balance of elites in the organization, so that no single function becomes the star function in terms of power and influence over the strategy-making process. Again in many North American corporations, as well as government organizations, finance holds sway as the important function and most decisions are made with the bottom line in view. Such dominance breeds conclusive ideologies. It also blocks learning emerging from other functional areas that have strategic significance for the organization as a whole (Kanter 1983). Finally, it prevents the cross-functional integration vital for generating innovation.

In addition to cross—functional discussions and involved top management, studies of large organizations suggest that the role of middle-level management may be crucial in ensuring responsive action (Burgelman 1983a,b,c; Nonaka 1988). Middle managers are in critical positions to act as information brokers and shock absorbers between the strategic apex and the technical core. If they are allowed to question the strategic apex about the rationale behind strategic decisions, they can understand the significance of particular innovations for overall strategic directions and can act as interpreters of strategic directions to the technical core and champions of innovations and intelligence emerging from that group. This can be facilitated if managers are better trained in symbolic as well as rational forms of discourse, a practice common in classical training of leaders (Burke 1950) but no longer followed in modern, technologically driven organizations (Gouldner 1976).

However, no matter how skillful middle managers are as change agents, their role is restricted by the rules and norms that govern the organization. The day-to-day interactions of superior and subordinates must be structured so that the subordinate is allowed to challenge decisions made by the superior without necessarily dominating the outcome and, equally important, be respected for the concerns and innovative capacity that such a challenge implies. Superiors who allow such challenges are more likely to have more innovative and responsive subordinates. Such conversations act to "nest" not only decision rules but meaning and authority structures (Westley 1990). Although the accusation is often made that managers and policy makers focus on the short term and therefore fall short of a vision of a management system that could encompass the scale of changes such as those in ecosystems, in fact humans tend to focus on the mesoscale, thinking in terms of structures and organizational systems. They fail equally in focusing on the microdynamics of interaction, the level at which these structural elements are produced and reproduced and where change, if it is to occur, must begin and end (Giddens 1984; Collins 1981).

Of course, in more decentralized, less hierarchical organizations such as those Mintzberg described as "adhocracies," the learning model of strategy is epitomized. Here, as in many Japanese and European organizations, strategy is never formally announced; it emerges and evolves from the collective activity. As such, it is only partially under the control of conscious thought and formulation, and implementations are virtually indistinguishable. Thus, it is the ultimately adaptive form (Mintzberg and McHugh 1985), but very remote from the bureaucratic systems that govern the management of many ecosystems. In the latter systems, discontinuities between knowledge and planning or between planning and action can best be bridged by a "learning" design-one that encourages strategic conversations across functions and levels, simultaneously regenerating meanings and transmitting learnings.

## Summary

In the preceding discussion I have reviewed five themes that have implications for the cases in this book as well as for our purposes of finding practical perspectives on the challenges involved in ecosystem management. Our discussion so far has stayed at the level of single organizations and the issue of how to link knowledge to policy and policy to action. I have suggested that for successful social action rules, resources and meanings need not only to be nested at each hierarchical level, but also to be integrated across functions with each other. In practical terms it suggests that managers wishing to ensure a more adaptive management system should be sensitive to the following process issues:

1. For management systems to be adaptive to ecosystem dynamics, formal planning procedures should be minimized, or at least treated experimentally.
2. Strong ideologies should also be treated with caution. Although forging meanings, which are nested and coupled with a more even distribution of authority across the organization, is necessary for action, these meanings should not be maintained at the expense of diversity.
3. Middle managers should be encouraged to develop symbolic skills and to act as integrators between the strategic apex and the operating core. Mechanisms

should be designed to ensure strategic conversations across functions and between levels. The more the strategies of the top can be influenced by the learning of the bottom, the more responsive the organization is likely to become.

I shall now turn to the second major theme of this chapter, that of the conditions facilitating and limiting interorganizational collaboration.

## INTERORGANIZATIONAL COLLABORATION AND CONSENSUS: WEAVING WEBS

Throughout these cases the need for interorganizational collaboration is stressed again and again. This is not surprising considering the complexity of organizations and jurisdictions represented by most of these cases. We rarely find human management systems patterned in terms of an ecosystem. Instead we find a number of "stakeholders" who have a vested interest in the ecosystem (Vredenburg and Westley 1993). In the cases in this book these range from government organizations to university consortiums, international commissions, citizen organizations, public and private companies, and native peoples. Some of these stakeholders have a central concern with managing the ecosystem (such as the Corps of Engineers in the Everglades). Others are concerned with the ecosystem as a source of raw materials (as in the New Brunswick Forestry) or as a disposal site for waste (as in the Chesapeake Bay), a recreation site, or a primary dwelling place (as in the Columbia River). Overall stakeholders represent a highly fragmented group whose interests concerning the ecosystem are very diverse and differ in intensity. It is not surprising therefore

that the result, as described in these cases, is one of disconnected initiatives, sometimes conflictual, rarely cooperative, that bear little resemblance to a managed entity.

Yet the need to forge collaboration and consensus is a critical one. For one thing, no one organization, even in the case of the least complex (jurisdictionally) ecosystem, can solve the problems of ecosystem management unilaterally. These are metaproblems, or problem domains that demand "cultivation of domain-based, interorganizational competence" (Trist 1983). Yet society in general is weak in these capabilities.

Although the cases here describe numerous unsuccessful collaborations and some few successful ones, little attention is given to the microdynamics of what makes a successful collaboration. We are aware, on reading the cases, that the collaborations differ in kind, particularly that some were government initiatives and others (the "shadow networks") stemmed from efforts of citizen groups or university-based scientists, but there is little discussion of how these collaborations originated or of whether these differences in origin are related to the success/failure of the collaboration. Finally, there is a general recognition that collaboration is necessary there and an implicit assumption more collaboration/consensus will make the successful implementation of adaptive management more likely. But is there a limit to collaboration? Can there be too much consensus at the interorganizational level? These are questions prompted by the descriptions of collaboration in the cases, for which research in management has potential answers. I will deal with each in turn.

### What Makes a Successful Collaboration?

Considerable work on the dynamics of interorganizational collaborations has established a number of features that make for successful collaborations between organizations. In the early stages the need to define the problem is paramount (Gray 1989). Therefore the extent to which all stakeholders can be brought to the table simultaneously will impact on whatever the problem is defined with a sufficient degree of complexity. The process is iterative. Problem definitions will result in more stakeholders surfacing, who will then enrich the problem definition further (Westley and Vredenburg 1991; Gray 1985). If major stakeholders are left out at the problem definition stage, however, the chances of successful problem definition are reduced (Gray and Hay 1986).

Willingness to come to the table may also be an issue, affected by such things as mutual recognition of the need for collaboration, perception of legitimacy of all involved stakeholders, and the presence of a legitimate convener (Gray 1985).

Once they are brought to the table, stakeholders will attempt to set the direction for collaboration. Whether they are successful or not will be determined by such factors as the coincidence of values and the dispersal of power. The representatives of the stakeholder organizations who come to the table are limited by such factors as the level of commitment of their home organizations, the amount of resources at their disposal with which to negotiate, and their own conflicting loyalties (Kanter 1989). Inequalities in any of these areas, a common occurrence in complex collaborations, will weaken the collaboration, signaling to the collaborators that they are not equally needy and therefore will not benefit equally from the collaboration. For example, in describing the collaborations between business leaders, government, and environmental groups on Canada's National Roundtable, one observer described said,

It is a strange sensation. You have the provincial treasurer sitting there with his flunkies behind him, the environmental minister sitting there with his people behind him, the man from the premier's office with his people behind him, and the chairman of this or that large company with his resources all lined up on one side, and cowering at the other end of the table are the few lone environmentalists with their bits of paper. This forces the environmentalists into strange stances. They either drive toward a purely ideological stance or begin to get coopted. They tend either to get extremely obstreperous or to say, "I can't argue with this; I'll give in" or to just walk away from the table.

From the preceding it is evident that it is not only shared understandings, myths, paradigms, and values that make for successful collaborations. Power is a central and underaddressed issue in these cases. Much of the aggravation attributed to the special interest groups in the New Brunswick Forestry case, who used the media as a tool to gain access to the public arena and lobby for single-issue reforms, is characteristic of a situation in which there is a perceived power imbalance. In such cases appeals to the media can be an effective means of righting such imbalances. However, once a problem needing collaboration moves into the public arena, stakeholders tend to become frozen in polarized positions, and any real negotiation becomes difficult (Hilgartner and Bosk 1988).

If the public arena is to be avoided, however, great sensitivity about redistribution of power on the part of those with the most resources is critical, but not easily accomplished. The tendency is toward strong demands for equality from those less powerful and little concern for equality on the part of the powerful. Members of one public service organization that I recently advised were quick to point out that other service organizations got special treatment from the municipal government because their results were easier to measure. They felt this should be changed. They greeted with alarm, however, the idea that they should take care to give credit to these same service organizations for their less visible part in emergency rescue operations. They were used to receiving the lion's share of media and public attention and were reluctant to share it. Both inequalities (distribution of government resources and distribution of media attention) were detrimental to building the on-going collaborative structures necessary for dealing with the increasingly large scale of public disasters with which all had to contend. But most organizations hoard power.

If the organizations are successful in setting directions, there remains the task of maintaining ongoing relationships, dependent on achieving a balance of power among participants and voluntary alignment of directions (Trist 1983). In this stage problems often result from the inability of the collaborators to maintain commitment "back home." This may be particularly true of organizations in pivotal positions of bridging two previously polarized camps. Such bridging attempts are inherently fragile because the bridging organization will have more invested than other organizations and must struggle with the same need to secure the commitment of their home constituencies (Westley and Vredenburg 1991a).

In sum, most individuals socialized in hierarchical organizations are not prepared for the kind of adaptive, interactive negotiation under relatively unstructured conditions (in terms of clear authority, rules, and meanings) of the successful collaboration (Kantor 1989). Individuals who work in adhocracies (and here I would include many research institutes and university settings) are used to a freer, more egalitarian setting and have less need to "represent" their organizations when they engage in collaborations outside their "home" institutions. This may account for the vitality and resiliency of the "shadow networks" described, particularly in the Everglades and Great Lakes cases. This resiliency may also be due, however, to the way in which these shadow networks originated, as compared to those collaborations initiated or mandated by the government. It would appear that the origin of the collaboration does have an impact on its trajectory.

*The Origins of Interorganizing.* In these cases three types of collaborations may be distinguished: those that originated by the organizing and inspirational leadership of a visionary, those that originated by being mandated by government, and those that seemed to spring up spontaneously, such as citizens movements and interuniversity networks. This is consistent with the pattern of interorganizing that we have discovered in a variety of collaborative domains. In line with the models of strategy making within organizations discussed earlier, we have termed these three, respectively, "vision-led," "planning-led," and "learning-led" forms of organizing (Westley and Vredenburg 1991b).

Each of these three forms, it would appear, has particular strengths and vulnerabilities, in addition to those described earlier, that are evident across all forms of collaboration. These become apparent when the forms are compared on the basis of the fundamental tasks that need to be accomplished for ongoing collaboration. Much has been written about the early stages of collaboration, the need for issue definition, stakeholder convening, and direction setting. However, consistent with what we know about strategic action within an organization, it is evident that in addition to the necessary structures of signification, realized collaborations must also create structures of domination (e.g., a mobilization of resources and empowerment for action) and structures of legitimization (e.g., institutionalization of the collaboration, development of norms for interaction, terminology for expectations, rules for balanced and productive participation).

The three forms of interorganizing may be said to vary in their ability to complete these four tasks (issue definition, resource mobilization, action mobilization, and institutionalization; Table 38.1). The planning mode—exemplified in this case by the various joint commissions, government tasks forces, and think tanks mandated by government—helps in the mobilization of resources and structuring; it is weaker at issue definition and action mobilization.

Issue definition and action mobilization are hampered in the planning mode by the fact that it is difficult and rare for politicians to operate out of the public arena. As noted earlier, however, decision making and negotiation in the public arena are often constrained by media coverage, which has a tendency to distort and polarize issues, and by the pressure from the public and back-home organizations of the collaborators to become paranoid about whether or not their issues are being adequately defended. Hence the issue definition may be prematurely closed to avoid undue controversy, losing in the process sufficient complexity to represent all stakeholders adequately on an ongoing basis. This has a disempowering impact. Stakeholders may withdraw and feel slighted. Also, as action mobilization is dependent not only on the representatives but also on the willingness of back-home constituencies to commit energy to the ongoing collaboration, the public arena model may severely hamper implementation of decisions arrived at by the collaborators.

On the other hand, planning-led collaborations are particularly strong at resource mobilization, for government agencies can mandate the resources necessary for setting up the collaboration, and often do so before the issue definition stage begins. As far as institutionalizing is concerned, planning-mandated collaborations often use procedures set up by the government for its ongoing operations. The institutionalized collaboration is then subsumed into the bureaucracy of government, which may help perpetuate it but does not strengthen its action-generating capabilities.

In contrast, the vision-led collaborations are often strong at issue definition and action mobilization and are creative at resource mobilization. As noted earlier, visionaries excel at using symbols to capture the complex and various interests that must be integrated and forging them into a compelling scenario. Their use of symbols and emotionally evocative language and the intensity of their personal commitment create a "hunger for enactment," a powerful motivation to action, in those whom they reach (Westley 1992).

Visionaries are often also adept at creative resource mobilization. Many visionaries operating at the interorganizational level avoid more conventional channels of resource mobilization, such as government grants, out of fear of the restrictions that may accompany them (Westley and Vredenburg 1992). Instead they often mobilize sufficient commitment on the part of followers so that they are willing to divert personal and "home organizational" resources to making the vision real. This may have the negative side effect of network burnout as network participants become exhausted by the extra demands for resources that the leader inspires (Westley 1992).

On the other hand, visionaries are notoriously bad at the institutionalization tasks necessary for ongoing collaboration. As visionaries tend to resist structuring

TABLE 38.1
Issue Definition, Mobilization of Actions and Resources by Mode of Organizational Change

|  | Issue Definition | Action Mobilization | Resource Mobilization | Structuring |
|---|---|---|---|---|
| Planning Mode | "Public arena" dynamics may force early closure of issue definition without sufficient data | "Public area" dynamics immobilize stakeholders, making coalition cooperation difficult | Resource channels secured often in advance of issue definition | Procedures/normal task allocations often limited to preexisting structures |
| Learning Mode | Incremental issue definition through individual initiative or negotiations | Commitment in advance of issue definition | Need to "piggy-back" on other institutions to mobilize. Resources may be coopted in process | Lack of resources may make structuring difficult |
| Vision Mode | Visionary particularly skilled in issue definition process | Link between affect and action fully utilized | Creative resource mobilization | Overdependence on visionary leader. Failure to institutionalize process or assure resource flow |

and place a high value on creativity, "routinization" processes often do not begin until after the visionary leaves the domain, that is, if the collaboration survives his or her departure. The death of Bill Storch in the No Easy Answers period of the Everglades left a void that was only filled by another visionary, Art Marshall, Marshall "carried the mantle of high priest of the environmental community in Florida," and after 10 years his vision was incorporated into public policy. It would be interesting to know, however, to what extent it was Marshall himself who was responsible for the institutionalization or whether others handled the structuring issues, as is often the case with visionaries (Westley 1992). Key to the continuity over time of vision-led collaborations is the development of a stable team, capable of turning visions into structures.

Perhaps the most interesting of the three modes of interorganizing are the learning-led collaborations, partly because their origins are harder to grasp from a research point of view. Learning-led collaborations seem to emerge from a groundswell of concern, the composite of experiences, and reactions of many individuals simultaneously to certain stimuli. Under certain conditions, concern, usually stimulated by the media or by a visible crisis, will snowball into action. Clearly, the action is triggered by individuals, but they are not necessarily visionaries, and they do not use symbols to motivate action. Rather, like setting a match to dry kindling, a small initiative will result in a conflagration of like initiatives, and a direction will emerge without ever having been planned. (See Mintzberg and McHugh [1985] for an excellent case description of such emergent strategies.)

Clearly, in learning-led strategies there is no difficulty in issue definition, for by the time the issue emerges, consensus (achieved through much discussion) has already been reached. This may be helped by the fact that participants in such collaborations often consider themselves to be representing only themselves. Hence a shadow network of interested scientists does not necessarily mean that a network has been forged between institutions (X, Y, and Z university, for example). It is individuals who, as professionals, consider themselves independent agents with regard to their activity in the problem domain who unite to collaborate. The challenge of having to "sell" the collaborations to back-home organizations is therefore minimized.

On the other hand, when the coalition starts to enter into negotiations with other organizations, it may be at a disadvantage because it will be relatively resource poor. Learning-led networks or coalitions are often "thinly institutionalized" (Zald and McCarthy 1987), which means that they do not have a rich resource base, a foundation of action routines, or established structures of significance on which to draw. This ,means that they may be at a disadvantage when attempting to collaborate with more established organizations. Sometimes this disparity can be outweighed by such factors as the scientific reputation of members, but with citizen groups such as those described in the New Brunswick Forestry case and the Great Lakes case, even this resource may be unavailable.

Therefore although action mobilization may precede issue definition (as emergent strategy is action followed by justification), learning-led coalitions often founder on the lack of availability of resources to fund their activities. They are forced to "piggyback" on larger institutions (e.g., the media, the church, private-sector organizations) in order to distribute their message or underwrite their activities. In attempts to enter larger collaborations, such as those surrounding management of an ecosystem, they may find their position distorted by their associations. For example, an NGO with a government grant may lose some independence of position, for using the media as an outlet means taking on whatever distortions the media introduce. Without such associations the power imbalances described in the roundtable example earlier may result. Scarcity of resources may also hamper the development of an infrastructure to sustain the collaboration. Hence many learning-led collaborations are temporary coalitions that enter into negotiations within the problem domain for a period of time and then disappear.

In summary, then, the three different kinds of collaborations that are found throughout these cases may be characterized as planning led, vision led, and learning led. Planning-led collaborations tend to be long on resources and structuring potential; vision-led collaborations are powerful instruments for issue definition, action mobilization, and creative resource mobilization; and learning-led collaborations are strong at issue definition and action mobilization. As an actor in any one of the three types of collaborations it is helpful to recognize both these strengths and the vulnerabilities. All three types have their successes, but collaborations that are planning led must be particularly careful at the issue definition stage, those that are learning led must be careful in mobilizing resources, and ones that are vision led must be careful in institutionalizing processes.

But these cases, with their sweeping overview, offer food for thought at another level of analysis. If attempts at managing ecosystems such as these exhibit such a rich array of different forms of collaboration, all existing at the same time, what is the relationship among the social forms? Should one form supersede all others? Should there be a kind of rationalization process in the domain, with these apparently "redundant" collaborative forms merging into one central referent organization, as has been suggested by some domain theorists (Trist 1983)? How much organization is good for a problem domain, in terms of the ultimate goal of problem resolution (or adaptive ecosystem management, as is the case in this book)?

*The Limits to Interorganizing.* One fascinating fact about the multiple collaborations that seem to occur around attempts to manage ecosystems has to do with the relationship among the different collaborations. Is the presence of numerous networks, coalitions, and task forces at the interorganizational level a positive or a negative factor?

In the New Brunswick Forestry case it would seem evident that the presence of citizen's lobby groups was counterproductive in terms of the government's efforts to solve the problem in a sustainable manner. In fact, Baskerville states baldly, "In general, special interest groups stop things" (Baskerville 1995, chapter 2). In his view the presence of multiple groups with multiple viewpoints heightens conflict. On the other hand, certainly the most "successful" case of ecosystem management would appear to be the Chesapeake Bay study, which also demonstrated the most unified action among the groups, and the highest intergroup consensus around issue definition. In fact, Constanza and Greer (chapter 4) isolate this creation of broad consensus as the primary factor in the effective action that occurred in the problem domain.

Scholars in the area of collaborative theory have long viewed networks in particular

as an inherently unstable form, a stage in the development from an underorganized to an organized domain. Although such networks serve to link organizations, theorists such as Trist (1983) and Gray (1989) have argued that an attribute of successful collaborations is the establishment of more permanent, less fluid, and more centralized organizations. Ideally, such "referent" organizations are democratic, are nonhierarchical, and do not constrain members of collaborations, but they help to focus all activity on a unitary purpose: to achieve effective action within the problem domain. Networks, unless they become "centered" in such a referent organization, are "not in themselves purposeful" (Trist 1983).

Hence theory would argue with the evidence in New Brunswick (Baskerville 1995, chapter 2) and the Chesapeake (Costanza & Greer 1995, chapter 4) cases: a redundancy of collaborations—planning led, vision led, learning led—merely introduce conflict and confusion into the management of ecosystems. What is needed for effective action is greater organization among such collaborations, to avoid redundancies and create a more ordered focus.

Yet such a conclusion sets off alarm bells. For what then do we make of the Great Lakes case, where a multitude of different types of collaboration coexisted over time, often at cross purposes and with little consensus, and yet appeared to offer a rich field for action? Although the redundancy might seem dysfunctional from a system perspective, it appeared that individuals used it for their own ends. If they were blocked in one interorganizational forum, they would try another avenue. For example, individuals from the IJC who had been instrumental in innovative policies in this planning-led context, then used a coalition of senior officials of fisheries industries to introduce a similar ecosystem approach to the fisheries, Some of these same individuals also participated in the university-initiated networks, making recommendations to the GLFC (Great Lakes Fisheries Commission).

As Regier noted (personal conversation), individuals who have made their career in attempting to save and manage the Great Lakes ecosystem, might, over 20 years, move through a variety of positions in different kinds of networks, carrying with them concepts and creating delicate linkages between different types of collaborations. Activists in environmental lobby groups who propose changes go on to be the commissioners who implement those changes 20 years later. A number of the case writers in this book have themselves played different roles in initiating, supporting, and using a variety of collaborative contexts to realize their aim. In the opening paragraphs of his text, Baskerville (chapter 2) admits to being student, researcher, professor of ecology, assistant deputy minister, policy consultant to the provincial government, and chairman of the board that heard disputes with respect to Crown forest management. Cutting across the seemingly redundant collaborative initiatives are the traces of individual career paths; people use the redundancy to achieve purposes that might not be achieved in simpler, more centralized structures.

From the perspective, therefore, of the individual, redundancy and variety in types and forms of collaborative initiatives within a problem domain may provide room to maneuver. Human beings find considerable freedom in the ability to change roles and move from one context to another (Rubenstein and Woodman 1984). Such freedom is also associated with the creation of energy, energy that can be contributed to problem resolution (Marks 1977). At the micro level of human days and ways, therefore, redundancy may be important for the creativity and energy required to solve metaproblems.

At the microlevel, on the other hand, one is tempted to extend Holling's endotherm analogy (chapter 1) to the interorganizational domain. The larger social system represented by all the stakeholders within the domain may be more resilient if, in fact, there is a redundancy of mechanisms for sensing and responding to change. To the degree that these become rationalized and focused, the system may seem more efficient in the short run, but it may actually become more vulnerable.

Another way of looking at it is to think of the stakeholder organizations as patches in a metapopulation. Metapopulation theory suggests that it is not the survival of single patches that is important. Rather, it is the nature of the linkages between the patches that determines the survival of the metapopulation. If the contact is too restricted, the isolated patch may be short-lived; but if the contact is too dense, the metapopulation is also at risk (Shaffer 1985; Oliveri et al. 1990).

In short, there may be limits to the amount and kind of consensus and focused collaboration that is desirable. It is preferable to have redundancy if that allows creative individuals multiple avenues to reach their ends and increases the amount of energy in the system. It is better to have imperfect consensus, even conflict, if that maintains a situation of some diversity of approach and hence flexibility in the system to explore radical options. As in the case of the excellent organization that fails by the same means that it succeeded (Miller 1992), an overly organized problem domain with a high level of consensus may be less responsive to ongoing change than one that is less organized.

This leads us to consider the interorganizational domain as a system in its own right and to wonder about long-term system dynamics in terms of Holling's four-box model. Perhaps at their optimum level, many learning-led networks, such as informal collegia of scientists, act as a resource and a fertile redundancy, "advancing fundamental reframing and innovation" (Everglades case). Systems in which the variety of coalitions and collaborative forums offer this stimulating and healthy kind of exchange may well be in the box 4 "reconfiguration" phase.

However, as such groups continue to proliferate, as the domain becomes more organized, issues become more clearly defined and viewpoints become more entrenched (Westley and Vredenburg 1991). As in the exploitation stage (box 1), either the appearance of a visionary provides a centralizing and integrating momentum (as was the case with an Art Marshall), a strong, planning-led initiative demands integration across initiatives, or groups themselves will begin to act competitively and opportunistically to secure resources (niches), with manifest conflict (as in the Forestry case). Ultimately, there will be a shakeout, as the stronger coalitions survive and the weaker ones are eliminated.

If the first or second form of exploitation occurs, the result may be highly productive consolidation (box 2), of the kind seen in the Chesapeake Bay case. However, the dynamics of Holling's model would suggest that this consolidation, although seemingly effective, may not in fact be as resilient as the system in a box 4 or in box 1. As Baskerville notes the chapter 2:

Attention to structures that facilitate all party learning is urgent. There is a need to learn how to embrace error and to break from the "priesthood" approach where only a single group or agency holds wisdom. Clearly the forest will continue to change *whatever policy is in place*, and industry will change in response to the forest and in response to international market pressures, as well as in response to public policy.

The key issue will be the degree to which these policy and forest management changes are reasoned (adaptive).

It is probable that a consensus of all parties around an adaptive management approach is likely to be more resilient than a consensus among all stakeholders around, say, a control and harvest approach, as the former puts emphasis on scanning, testing, and responding to changes in the ecosystem and the latter is concerned with controlling the variability within the ecosystem to ensure a steady supply for human consumption. However, it is important to realize that consensus on *any* policy if it includes the whole interorganizational domain represents a state of consolidation and conservation and will tend to become increasingly centralized, routinized, fixed in single-loop learning, and committed to fixed allocation of authority and resources. In short, consensus and consolidation go hand in hand. And as we discussed earlier, such systems, be they single organizations or interorganizational systems spanning problem domains, are more vulnerable to crisis. A boundary created around an interorganizational system, by the simple mechanism of strong ties within the system (ties of meaning, resource exchange, or norms of action) is still a boundary. The bounded system is vulnerable to crisis coming from outside its boundaries.

In a landmark study Granovettor (1973) compared two communities in the Boston area, both threatened with urban renewal plans that would destroy their integrity. One was a close-knit ethnic community with many bonds of kinship, shared culture, and clear social norms. The other was a middle-class "bedroom" community with very little internal organization. Although the shared value systems and tight organization of the ethnic communities would suggest that they would be better able to mobilize to react to the crisis, it was the middle-class community that survived. Granovettor attributes this to the "looser ties" that connected the middle-class residents not only to others within the community *but also to those outside the community*, whose influence and resources they were able to tap to stop the project. There seems to be an inverse correlation between how dense the ties or connections are within a bounded system and how many "loose" ties exist between members of that system and others outside it. If change therefore is coming from outside the social system (influences from other social systems, for example) or crisis to the natural system originating outside the ecosystem, the interorganizational domain in a box 2 "consolidation" state will be more vulnerable than those in a box 4 or box 1. Redundancies, as long as they represent multiple sensitivities and the ability to explore other "environments" for opportunities, may be as important for social systems as for organisms. Disorder in problem domains may be as valuable as order, diversity as important as consensus.

## Summary

In this section I have again explored a literature that has developed separately but in parallel with the work on adaptive management: that concerning the microdynamics of successful collaboration, the origins and types of collaborations, and the relationship between the pattern of collaborations and system health. These cases offer a rich description of the multitude of collaborative initiatives, networks, and coalitions that spring up in attempting to negotiate problem domains as complicated as the management of ecosystems. The following are some practical lessons that can be drawn from analyzing the social system dynamics from a management point of view:

1. Although consensus building is clearly a critical issue in the management of successful collaboration, power dispersal is equally important. Actors involved in collaborative efforts must ensure that some equal access to resources is provided, even if this involves designing processes that give a higher profile to stakeholders who are weak but important to problem resolution or sensitizing powerful stakeholders to the need to share resources.

2. A variety of different kinds of interorganizational collaborations can be recognized in these cases. We have identified three generic types: *planning-led collaborations*, which tend to take the shape of task forces, roundtables, committees; *vision-led networks*, associated with the activities of single visionaries and their supporters; and *learning-led networks*, which take the form of social movements, scientific consortia, community forums. Over time all three, if successful, have a tendency to crystallize into formal organizations. However, each of the three has different vulnerabilities. Actors involved in planning-led initiatives should be aware that such initiatives need careful attention to issue definition, to avoid premature closure and alienation of important stakeholders. Those involved in vision-led initiatives should be aware that the demands for resources of time and money may exhaust network members. Burn-out is common, and the visionary is unlikely to be concerned with evolving institutional structures to support his or her ideas. Finally, those involved in learning-led initiatives must recognize that the crucial challenge is to secure enough resources to survive; "piggy-back" arrangements may be necessary and should be pursued as far as possible without compromising the issue at hand.

3. Looked at from the macroperspective, the interorganizational domain is a larger

social system and therefore may be affected by the same system dynamics that affect single organisms or ecosystems. Although consensus and organization at the domain level are clearly desirable, too much consensus and organization may make the interorganizational system vulnerable. For the actor in such systems, therefore, it is important to resist too much organization and centralization. Shadow networks should perhaps resist being turned into task forces; task forces should perhaps resist being turned into intergovernmental committees. Although the idea that policy should be treated as experiment is a brilliant one, it is difficult to achieve. Scientists should continue to be wary of politicians prepared to turn theory into policy. A healthy tension between the two, a redundancy of efforts and activities may offer the most fertile ground for individuals to manage the process of change.

But how manageable is this process? In this final section I shall address my third and last theme: Can (and should) human systems be managed to avoid the cycles of creative destruction?

## MANAGING CYCLES OF CHANGE: THE GRAND DESIGN

Anthropologists, economists, and sociologists interested in change at the macrolevel have long recognized cycles of change similar to those that Hollings model captures at the ecosystem level. In addition to Schumpeter (1934), scholars such as Weber (1922) and Wallace (1966) have postulated that social systems go through a round involving (1) the creation of a new social order, often associated with a visionary leader, that is then encoded and institutionalized, a pattern Weber refers to as the "rou-

tinization of charisma." Eventually, it becomes (2) consolidated into an organized set of structures containing action routines, taken-for-granted assumptions about the meaning of such routines, and patterned flows of resources and authority. Such highly structured systems are not devised for learning; rather, they are devised for efficiency and routine (Weick 1991). It seems that as the consolidation progresses, adaptability decreases. However, change continues outside the system, and if the organization fails to adapt, it will become increasingly cut off or closed and subject to entropy. Eventually, (3) a crisis is produced both at the individual and at the organizational level. At the level of the organization this is often experienced as a sudden dropoff in performance and accounted for by such phrases as "the market suddenly dried up" or "the market moved out from under us." At the level of the individual, this is often experienced as a crisis of meaning. Rituals and routines that sustained daily life and guided daily contact seem suddenly meaningless or to break down altogether, occasioning acute psychological distress (Geertz 1976). In some cases the organization or social system goes into slow or rapid decline. In others, however, a period of (4) revitalization or reorganization occurs. This is characterized by highly individualistic, apparently chaotic behavior. A plethora of new ideas, initiatives (say, in the area of start-up ventures), and myths seem to circulate, some of which are imported from other systems and others of which are forged by individual actors within the system. Many of these initiatives seem contradictory. The possibility of conflict and generalized disorder is high, and there is an absence of overall direction in the system. Despite the learning going on, for new order to emerge, these learnings must be reintegrated into a new vision or myth and encoded in a new organizational structure.

FIGURE 38.1
Cycle of revitalization (Wallace 1966).

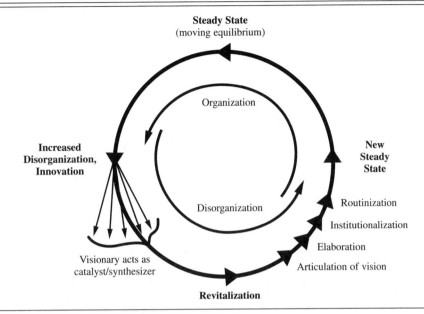

This often occurs because of the intervention of a visionary, and the cycle starts again (Figure 38.1).

It is easy enough to overlay this cycle of social change onto the four-box model of ecosystem change. It has in it the same sense of inevitability, of natural rhythm that the ecosystem cycles contain. But from the point of view of the actor, of the manager existing within a system and attempting to solve such problems as how to manage an ecosystem adoptively, this similarity is not comforting. For we seek from our social systems the same overall stability that natural resource managers have sought for in ecosystems: change, yes; growth, yes; learning, yes—but against a stable backdrop, a structured order.

Perhaps this is a mistake. Perhaps the crisis and renewals that occurred in the Florida Everglades management systems are as natural and as *healthy* as those occurring in the Florida Everglades. Perhaps, as we have suggested earlier, no one-policy approach, even an adaptive one, should dominate for too long a time. Maybe *should* is irrelevant because the cycles are inevitable.

On the other hand, longitudinal studies of organizations have suggested that those that survive over long periods of time *do* find ways of managing (rather than avoiding) such cycles. The key seems to be in avoiding the extremes of order and structuring, on the one hand, and of disorder and confusion, on the other.

Earlier in this paper we noted that strategy within organizations can be characterized as vision, learning, and planning. These three tendencies can also be recognized at the interorganizational level. Overlaying these tendencies on the cycle of change we can see that the stage of reorganization is dominated by learning processes; that of

FIGURE 38.2
Sequences of the means of change (Mintzberg and Westley 1992).

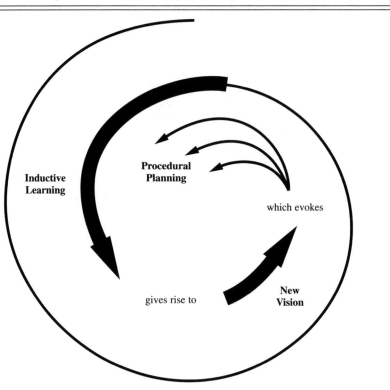

consolidation, by planing processes; and that of renewal/exploitation, by visionary processes (Figure 38.2). Clearly, each process has a role in the overall cycle. If the organization is to survive, however, the planning stage can never become so rigid as to prevent adaption completely, and the learning stage can never dominate so completely that coordinated social action becomes impossible.

A series of longitudinal studies of strategy as a pattern in a stream of activity carried out at McGill University suggests a number of different configurations equated with survival. Three of these concern us here: the pattern of periodic bumps, the pattern of oscillating shifts, and the pattern of regular progress (Mintzberg and Westley 1992; Figure 38.3).

In the pattern of *periodic bumps*, organizations go through long periods of stability and then experience a quantum shift, a sudden reorganization. Such organizations do not adapt easily. Change and adjustment are avoided in favor of routine and stability until, no longer avoidable, comprehensive change of the nature of a turnaround, or revolution is effected (Mintzberg 1978; Mintzberg and Waters 1982; Miller and Friesen 1984 for case descriptions of this kind of change). When viewed closely, however, it appears that when such sudden

FIGURE 38.3
Patterns of organizational change (Mintzberg and Westley 1992).

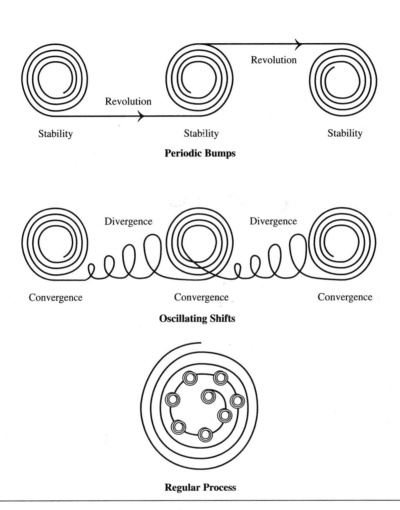

**Periodic Bumps**

**Oscillating Shifts**

**Regular Process**

shifts occur, incremental adjustments through grass-roots learning have undoubtedly been going on for some time. As in the case of individual conversion, months of internal reorientation lead to a moment of gestalt shift, experienced as a sudden and dramatic change (Westley 1977; Gerlach and Hines 1970). Like the carapace of the spider, however, which falls off in an instant, a new one hidden under the old is ready to take its place. Before a radical change new myths abound in organizations, each one a candidate for dominance (Jonsson and Lundin 1977). When crisis occurs, and the old myth disintegrates, another is ready to take its place. Still, when looked at over time, such periodic bumps appear as long periods of stability followed by sudden shifts. The moment of shift is perilous. Those organizations that survive are often dependent on leadership with the vision to make new sense out of the diversity.

The pattern of *oscillating shifts* represents a less radical or extreme form of change. An example of an organization that has demonstrated this pattern is the National Film Board of Canada. A publicly owned documentary film company, the film board is organized in terms of studios, each of which provides a basis for independent film makers. The film makers have complete latitude as to the films they make. Tile result of all this independent activity, however, when viewed over time, is a pattern of startlingly regular cycles with convergence around a particular theme occurring for about 6 years followed by 6 years of divergence and experimentation. None of the convergence was leader led. Rather, it happened spontaneously because of the tendency for film makers to interact and learn from each other (Mintzberg and McHugh 1985). The particular structure of the film board (an adhocracy) was loose enough to allow for divergence without falling apart, tight enough in terms of structures of signification, interactive norms to stimulate repeated convergence. The pattern was learning led, therefore, but with enough planning on the part of management to ensure the maintenance of a stable resource base to support the experimentation.

The last pattern, one of *regular progress*, is one of continual and regular revitalization. One good example of such an organization is the Catholic church, which has survived for centuries, partly because of the (intermittent) ability of the popes to manage innovation in an enlightened way. At several important junctures, notably during the early thirteenth century and in the twentieth century, the church was headed by excellent administrators who carefully monitored new (poten-

tially heretical) initiatives within the church and, instead of ignoring or expelling such movements, found a way to incorporate the new initiatives into the existing structures of the church, infusing the latter with new energy (Mintzberg and Westley 1992).

Another example is provided by McGill University, in which the activities at the grass roots are allowed to shape the direction of the university and the planners work not to control but to nourish and shape that activity. Such organizations change continually inside without changing position in a radical sense. Adjustment is continuous. The adaptation of the organization is led by the adaptation of responsive individuals connected to the environment (social) through a variety of professional networks (Mintzberg and Rose, in progress),

In each of these different patterns the balance between change and continuity is achieved in a different way, through gradual, hidden diversity and sudden shifts, through a rhythm of convergence and divergence resulting from patterns of interaction and patterns of creativity, through planned cultivation of creativity. In all three, however, there is exhibited a continual tolerance for diversity coupled with a positive response to orchestration. As Clark said of ecosystems, so one could say of social systems: The metaphor of the garden seems to work best. Resilient social systems, like resilient ecosystems, seem to be managed by people who ask, "What kinds of gardens do we want, and what kind can we get?"

It appears, then, that despite the fact that social systems, like ecosystems, evolve through a four-box cycle of creative destruction and that these are to some extent inevitable, it is possible for actors within these systems to manage in such a way that the crises are minimally destructive and the rigidity is not excessive, while the regenerative learning and sense of direction remain strong. Finding the balance point is a continual process of adjustment; however, the job is never finished.

And now I have come full circle in my discussion as well. For the key lies in the way in which process is designed in such organizations, Some organizations are more highly structured and hierarchical: For them the challenge is to create and maintain mechanisms for influence and communication from those levels where change and adjustment are a part of everyday life. Other organizations, such as adhocracies, seem to create themselves new everyday. For such organizations the challenge lies in creating enough structures so that convergence and direction are possible. The same processes that will allow the social system to remain resilient will also allow it to respond to the ecosystems it seeks to manage: tolerance for diversity, openness to new ideas and information, balance between efficiency and redundancy, willingness to move in new directions while maintaining internal stability. As one commentator on business and the environment noted:

Companies that take the environment seriously change not only their processes and products, but also the way they run themselves. Often these changes go hand in hand with improvement in the general quality of management. Badly managed companies are rarely kind to the environment; conversely, companies that try the hardest to reduce the damage they do to the environment usually manage well. Why the link? . . . (such) goals demand a tolerance for ambiguity that irritates most managers . . . state-of-the-art management tools to handle complexity . . . the skills to deal with multiple stakeholders and to think in networks, not hierarchies [Cairncross 1992].

It would appear that not only do dynamics in social systems create crisis in ecosystems and vice versa but also that the same means must be employed to create organizations capable of managing ecosystem resiliency and organizations

capable of resiliency in their own right. Barren, overly structured organizations create barren, brittle ecosystems. Green, growing organizations may be able to manage green, living ecosystems. The clue to understanding this similarity lies in the construction of models, such as those in this volume, which charts this parallel on a grand scale. The key to managing this similarity lies in the design of the details within organizations and networks, where the grand order is founded in small processes.

## REFERENCES

Aguilar, J. (1967). *Scanning the Business Environment*. New York: Macmillan.

Albaum, G. (1964). Horizontal information flow: An exploratory study. *Academy of Management* (March): 21–33.

Baskerville, G. L. (1995). The forestry problem. Adaptive lurches of renewal. Pp. 37–102 in L.H. Gunderson, C. S. Holling, and S. S. Light, ed., *Barriers and Bridges to the Renewal of Ecosystems and Institutions*. New York: Columbia University Press.

Brown, J. S., & Duguid, P. (1991). Organizational learning and communities of practice. *Organizational Science* 2(1):40–52.

Brunsson, N. (1985). *The Irrational Organization*. New York: John Wiley.

Burgelman, R. (1983a). A model of interaction, strategic behavior, corporate context and the concept of strategy. *Academy of Management Review* 8(1):61–90.

Burgelman, R. (1983b). A process model of internal corporate venturing in a diversified major firm. *Administrative Science Quarterly* 28:223–244.

Burgelman, R. (1983c). Corporate entrepreneurship and strategic management: Insights from a process study. *Management Science* 29(3):1349–1364).

Burke, K. (1950). *A Rhetoric of Motives*. Englewood Cliffs, NJ: Prentice-Hall.

Cairncross, F. (1992). *Costing the Earth*. Boston: Harvard Business School Press.

Collins, R. (1981). On the microfoundations of macrosociology. *American Journal of Sociology* 86(5):984–1013.

Conger, J. (1989). *The Charismatic Leader*. San Francisco: Jossey-Bass.

Costanza, R., & Greer, J. (1995). The Chesapeake Bay and its watershed: A model for sustainable ecosystem management? Pp. 169–213 in L. H. Gunderson, C. S. Holling, & S. S. Light, ed., *Barriers and Bridges to the Renewal of Ecosystems and Institutions*. New York: Columbia University Press.

Daft, R., & Buenger, V. (1990). Hitching a ride on a fast train to no where: The past and future of strategic management research. Pp. 81–103 in J. W. Fredrickson, ed., *Perspectives on Strategic Management*. New York: Harper & Row.

Daft, R., & Lengel, R. (1984). Information richness. Pp. 191–233 in B. Straw, ed., *Research in organizational Behavior*, vol. 6. Greenwich, CT: JAI Press.

Francis, G. R., & Regier, H. A. (1995). Barriers and bridges to the restoration of the Great Lakes Basin ecosystem. Pp. 238–291 in L. H. Gunderson, C. S. Holling, and S. S. Light, ed., *Barriers and Bridges to the Renewal of Ecosystems and Institutions*. New York: Columbia University Press.

Geertz, C. (1976). Funeral rites in Java. In W. A. Lessa and E. Z. Vogt, eds., *Reader in Comparative Religions*. New York: Harper & Row.

Gerlach, L. P., & Hines, V. (1970). *People, Power, Change*. New York: Bobbs-Merrill.

Giddens, W. (1984). *The Construction of Society: Outline of the Theory of Structuration*. Oxford: Policy Press.

Gimpl, M. L., & Dakin, S. R. (1984). *Opening Pandora's Box: A Sociological Analysis of Scientists' Discourse*. New York: Cambridge University Press.

Gouldner, A. (1976). *Dialectic of Ideology and Technology*. London: Macmillan.

Granovettor, M. (1973). The strengths of weak ties. *American Journal of Sociology* 78(6): 1360–1380.

Granovettor, M. (1985). Economic action and social structure: The problem of embeddedness. *American Journal of Sociology* 91(3):481–510.

Gray, B. (1985). Conditions facilitating interorganizational collaboration. *Human Relations* 38:911–936.

Gray, B. (1989). *Collaborating: Finding Common Ground for Multiparty Problems*. San Francisco: Jossey-Bass.

Gray, B., & Hay, T. (1986). Political limits to interorganizational consensus and change. *Journal of Applied Behavioral Science* 22:95–112.

Hamel, G., & Prahalad, C. K. (1989). Strategic intent. *Harvard Business Review* 67:63–76.

Hayes, R. H. (1985). Strategic planning: Forward in reverse? *Harvard Business Review* 63 (Nov/Dec): 111–119.

Hilgartner, S., & Bosk, C. L. (1988). The rise and fall of social problems: A public arenas model. *American Journal of Sociology* 94:53–78.

Hochschild, A. R. (1983). *The Managed Heart*. Berkley: University of California Press.

Holling, C. S. (1995). What barriers? What bridges. Pp. 3–34 in L. H. Gunderson, C. S. Holling, S. S. Light, ed., *Barriers and Bridges to the Renewal of Ecosystems and Institutions*. New York: Columbia University Press.

lzreali, D. N. (1975). The middle manager and the tactics of power expansion. *Sloan Management Review* 17(Winter): 57–70.

Jonsson, S. A, & Lundin, R. A. (1977). Myths and wishful thinking as management tools. In P. C. Nystrom and W. H. Starbuck, eds., *Prescriptive Models of Organizations*. Amsterdam: North Holland.

Kanter, R. M. (1983). *The Change Master*. New York: Simon and Schuster.

Kanter, R. M. (1989). Becoming PALs: Pooling, allying and linking across companies. *Academy of Management Executive* 33:183–193.

Leach, E. (1964). Anthropological aspects of language: Animal categories and verbal abuse. In E. H. Lenneberg, ed., *New Directions in the Study of Language*. Pp. 23–63. Boston: M.I.T. Press.

Levi-Strauss, C. (1955). The structural study of myth. *Journal of American Folklore* 67:428–444.

Light, S. S., Gunderson, L. H., & Holling C. S. (1995). The Everglades: Evolution of management in a turbulent ecosystem. Pp. 103–168 in L. H. Gunderson, C. S. Holling, & S. S. Light, ed., *Barriers and Bridges to the Renewal of Ecosystems and Institutions*. New York: Columbia University Press.

Marks, S. R. (1977). Multiple roles and role strain: Some notes on human energy, time and commitment. *American Sociological Review* 42:921–926.

Miller, D. (1992). The Icarus paradox: How exceptional companies bring their own downfall. *Business Horizons* January/February:24–35.

Miller, D., & Friesen, C. P. H. (1984). *Organizations: A Quantum View*. Englewood Cliffs, NJ: Prentice-Hall.

Mintzberg, H. (1978). Patterns in strategy formation. *Management Science* 24(9):934–948.

Mintzberg, H., & Waters, J. (1982). Tracking strategy in an entrepreneurial firm. *Academy of Management Journal* 25:465–499.

Mintzberg, H., & McHugh, A. (1985). Strategy Formation in adhocracy. *Administrative Science Quarterly* 30(2):160–197.

Mintzberg, H., & Waters, J. A. (1985). Of strategies, deliberate and emergent. *Strategic Management Journal* 6(3):257–272.

Mintzberg, H., & Westley, F. (1992). Cycles of organizational change. *Strategic Management Journal* 13:39–59.

Mintzberg, H., & Rose, J. (1990). Strategic management upside down: A study of McGill University from 1829 to 1980. Montreal: McGill University.

Nonaka, I. (1988). Creating organizational order out of chaos. *California Management Review* 30(3):57–73.

Oliveri, I., Couvet, D., & Gouyon, P. H. (1990). The genetics of transient populations: Research at the metapopulation level. *Tree* 5(7):207–210.

Pascale, R. (1984). Perspectives on strategy: The real story behind Honda's success. *California Management Review* 26(3):47–72.

Peters, T. J, & Waterman, R. H. (1982). *In Search of Excellence*. New York: Harper & Row.

Quinn, J. B. (1985). Managing innovation: Controlled chaos. *Harvard Business Review* 63 (March/June): 73–84.

Ransom, S. S., Hinings, S., & Greenwood, R. (1980). The structure of organizational Structures. *Administrative Science Quarterly* 25:117.

Rubenstein, D., & Woodman, R. W. (1984). Spiderman and the Burma Raiders: Collateral organizational theory in action. *Journal of Applied Behavioral Science* 20(1):1–21.

Schein, E. (1985). (2nd ed. 1992). *Organizational Culture and Leadership: A Dynamic View*. San Francisco: Jossey-Bass.

Schumpeter, J. A. (1934). *The Theory of Economic Development*. Cambridge, MA: Harvard University Press.

Shaffer, M. L. (1985). The metapopulation and species conservation: The special case of the northern spotted owl. In R. J. Guitierrez and A. B. Carey, eds., *Ecology and Management of the Spotted Owl*. General Technical Report, USDA Forest Service, Pacific Northwest Forest and Range Equipment Station, Portland.

Spender, J. C. (1989). *Industrial Recipes: The Nature and Sources of Managerial Judgment*. Oxford, England: Basil Blackwell.

Trist, E. (1983). Referent organizations and the development of interorganizational domains. *Human Relations* 36:269–284.

Wallace, A. (1961). *Culture and Personality*. New York: Random House.

Wallace, A. (1966). *Religion: An Anthropological View*. New York: Macmillan.

Weber, M. (1922). *Economy and Society*. Berkeley: University of California Press.

Weick, K. (1991). The nontraditional quality of organizational learning. *Organization Science* 2(1):116–124.

Westley, F. (1977). Searching for surrender. *American Behavioral Science* 20(6): 925–940.

Westley, F. (1990). Middle managers and strategy: Microdynamics of inclusion. *Strategic Management Journal* 11:337–352.

Westley, F. (1991). Bob Geldof and Live Aid: The effective side of global social Innovation. *Human Relations* 44(10):1011–1036.

Westley, F. (1992). Vision worlds. Strategic vision as social interaction. *Advances in Strategic Management* 8:271–305.

Westley, F., & Mintzberg, H. (1989) Strategic management and visionary leadership. *Strategic Management Journal* 10:17–32.

Westley, F., & Vredenburg, H. (1990a). Strategic bridging: The alliances of business and environmentalists. *Journal of Applied Behavioral Science* 27(1):65–90.

Westley, F., & Vredenburg, H. (1990b). Three models of interorganizing. Paper presented at the Society for Strategic Management, Toronto, October.

Westley, F., and Vredenburg, H. (1992). Managing the Ark: Interorganizational collaboration and the preservation of biodiversity. McGill Working Paper No. 92-11-16. Montreal: McGill University.

Zaid, M., & McCarthy, J. D. (1987). *Social Movements in an Organizational Society*. New Brunswick, NJ: Transaction Books.

# Appendix:
# Internet Resources

In the world of today, community practice as well as community practitoners need to take advantage of Internet resources. Whether one is thinking of strategy, or tactics, or some mixing and phasing, there is much that can be done with the web.

One type of use is in obtaining simple information. It is now so easy to get all kinds of data that might have been unavailable or fugitive previously.

Second, one can access the information much more quickly than was true in the past. Not only is such speed satisfying, but it gives workers and agencies more time for the actual tasks of organizing.

Third, the web provides a chance to actually *do* some of the organizing and mobilizing of people around issues. Through connecting to organizations and individuals, organizers can enhance social networking—between worker and citizen, and between and among citizens and citizen groups. De Tocqueville never thought that "associations" might be electronic ones!

Fourth, of course, is that the web is a way to store information economically.

No doubt there are additional uses for the web. What follows is a preliminary list of websites, developed by Aaron Goldsmith, MSW, to help you on your way. As you know, sites change; some of the addresses might be different by the time you go there. But this is a start. Good organizing!

—John Tropman

## INTERNET RESOURCES—NONPROFIT

### MACRO SITES—CAREER ORIENTED

| | |
|---|---|
| http://www.nonprofitcareer.com/ | Nonprofit Career Network |
| http://www.execsearches.com/exec/ | Headhunter for nonprofit, public sector, and socially conscious organizations |
| http://www.philanthropy.com/jobs.dir/jobsmain.htm | The Chronicle of Philanthropy—Job openings |

### NATIONAL ASSOCIATIONS AND BOARDS

| | |
|---|---|
| http://www.naco.org/ | National Association of Counties |
| http://www.asaenet.org/main/ | American Society for Association Executives |
| http://www.ncna.org/ | The National Council of Nonprofit Associations |
| http://www.ncppp.org/ | The National Council for Public-Private Partnerships |
| http://www.ncnb.org/main.htm | National Center for Nonprofit Boards |

### NONPROFIT RESOURCES—META SITES

| | |
|---|---|
| http://www.nonprofits.org/ | Internet Nonprofit Center |
| http://www.granted.org/ | Community Resource Institute |
| http://comnet.org/index.html | Michigan Comnet |
| http://www.nonline.com/ | Nonline Nonprofit Network |
| http://www.clark.net/pub/pwalker/ General_Nonprofit_Resources/ | Nonprofit Resources Catalogue |

### STATE AND FEDERAL GOVERNMENT—NONPROFIT LINKS

| | |
|---|---|
| http://www.nonprofit.gov/ | Nonprofit gateway to federal government information and services |
| http://www.sbaonline.sba.gov/nonprofit/ | Small Business Administration's nonprofit site |
| http://www.irs.gov/bus_info/eo/eo-types.html | IRS: Types of tax-exempt organizations |
| http://www.irs.gov/bus_info/eo/eo-tkit.html | IRS: Tax-exempt organizations tax kit |

### NONPROFIT MANAGEMENT

| | |
|---|---|
| http://www.nptimes.com/ | Nonprofit Times—The leading business publication for nonprofit management |
| http://www.pfdf.org/ | The Peter F. Drucker Foundation for Nonprofit Management |

### NONPROFITS AND TECHNOLOGY

| | |
|---|---|
| http://conference.pj.org/ | Philanthropy News Network: Nonprofits and technology conferences |
| http://www.wecaretoo.coM | WeCareToo: Offers free website service and site management to nonprofits |
| http://www.icomm.ca/ | An Internet service provider helping nonprofit organizations |
| http://ombwatch.org/npt/ | Nonprofits' policy and technology project— U.S. Office of Management and Budget |

### NONPROFIT FOUNDATIONS AND THINK TANKS

| | |
|---|---|
| http://fdncenter.org/ | The Foundation Center |
| http://www.indepsec.org/ | Independent sector |
| http://www.nira.go.jp/ice/tt-info/nwdtt99/index.html | A World Directory of Think Tanks (circa: 1999) |

### SOCIAL WORK LINKS

| | |
|---|---|
| http://www.abecsw.org/ | American Board of Examiners in Clinical Social Work |
| http://www.socialworkonline.com/resource.htm | Internet Resources for Social Workers—Meta site |
| http://www.naswdc.org/ | National Association of Social Workers |
| http://www.cswf.org/ | Clinical Social Work Federation |

# Name Index

# Subject Index

TACTICS AND TECHNIQUES OF COMMUNITY INTERVENTION
Fourth Edition
Edited by John Beasley
Production supervision by Kim Vander Steen
Cover design by Cynthia Crampton Design, Park Ridge, Illinois
Composition by Point West, Inc., Carol Stream, Illinois
Typeface, Times Roman
Paper, Finch Opaque
Printed and bound by Victor Graphics, Baltimore, Maryland